WORKSHOPS IN COMPUTING
Series edited by C. J. van Rijsbergen

Also in this series

Algebraic Methodology and Software Technology (AMAST'93)
Proceedings of the Third International Conference on Algebraic Methodology and Software Technology, University of Twente, Enschede, The Netherlands, 21–25 June 1993
M. Nivat, C. Rattray, T. Rus and G. Scollo (Eds)

Logic Program Synthesis and Transformation
Proceedings of LOPSTR 93, International Workshop on Logic Program Synthesis and Transformation, Louvain-la-Neuve, Belgium, 7–9 July 1993
Yves Deville (Ed.)

Database Programming Languages (DBPL-4)
Proceedings of the Fourth International Workshop on Database Programming Languages – Object Models and Languages, Manhattan, New York City, USA, 30 August–1 September 1993
Catriel Beeri, Atsushi Ohori and Dennis E. Shasha (Eds)

Music Education: An Artificial Intelligence Approach, Proceedings of a Workshop held as part of AI-ED 93, World Conference on Artificial Intelligence in Education, Edinburgh, Scotland, 25 August 1993
Matt Smith, Alan Smaill and Geraint A. Wiggins (Eds)

Rules in Database Systems
Proceedings of the 1st International Workshop on Rules in Database Systems, Edinburgh, Scotland, 30 August–1 September 1993
Norman W. Paton and M. Howard Williams (Eds)

Semantics of Specification Languages (SoSL)
Proceedings of the International Workshop on Semantics of Specification Languages, Utrecht, The Netherlands, 25–27 October 1993
D.J. Andrews, J.F. Groote and C.A. Middelburg (Eds)

Security for Object-Oriented Systems
Proceedings of the OOPSLA-93 Conference Workshop on Security for Object-Oriented Systems, Washington DC, USA, 26 September 1993
B. Thuraisingham, R. Sandhu and T.C. Ting (Eds)

Functional Programming, Glasgow 1993
Proceedings of the 1993 Glasgow Workshop on Functional Programming, Ayr, Scotland, 5–7 July 1993
John T. O'Donnell and Kevin Hammond (Eds)

Z User Workshop, Cambridge 1994
Proceedings of the Eighth Z User Meeting, Cambridge, 29–30 June 1994
J.P. Bowen and J.A. Hall (Eds)

6th Refinement Workshop
Proceedings of the 6th Refinement Workshop, organised by BCS-FACS, London, 5–7 January 1994
David Till (Ed.)

Incompleteness and Uncertainty in Information Systems
Proceedings of the SOFTEKS Workshop on Incompleteness and Uncertainty in Information Systems, Concordia University, Montreal, Canada, 8–9 October 1993
V.S. Alagar, S. Bergler and F.Q. Dong (Eds)

Rough Sets, Fuzzy Sets and Knowledge Discovery
Proceedings of the International Workshop on Rough Sets and Knowledge Discovery (RSKD'93), Banff, Alberta, Canada, 12–15 October 1993
Wojciech P. Ziarko (Ed.)

Algebra of Communicating Processes
Proceeedings of ACP94, the First Workshop on the Algebra of Communicating Processes, Utrecht, The Netherlands, 16–17 May 1994
A. Ponse, C. Verhoef and S.F.M. van Vlijmen (Eds)

Interfaces to Database Systems (IDS94)
Proceedings of the Second International Workshop on Interfaces to Database Systems, Lancaster University, 13–15 July 1994
Pete Sawyer (Ed.)

Persistent Object Systems
Proceedings of the Sixth International Workshop on Persistent Object Systems, Tarascon, Provence, France, 5–9 September 1994
Malcolm Atkinson, David Maier and Véronique Benzaken (Eds)

Functional Programming, Glasgow 1994
Proceedings of the 1994 Glasgow Workshop on Functional Programming, Ayr, Scotland, 12–14 September 1994
Kevin Hammond, David N. Turner and Patrick M. Sansom (Eds)

continued on back page...

J. Eder and L.A. Kalinichenko (Eds)

East/West Database Workshop

Proceedings of the Second International East/West Database Workshop, Klagenfurt, Austria, 25–28 September 1994

Published in collaboration with the
British Computer Society

 Springer

London Berlin Heidelberg New York
Paris Tokyo Hong Kong
Barcelona Budapest

Johann Eder
Institut für Informatik, Universität Klagenfurt,
Universitätsstrasse 65, A-9020 Klagenfurt, Austria

Leonid A. Kalinichenko
Institute for Problems of Informatics, Russian Academy of Sciences,
Vavilov Street, 30/6 117900, Moscow, V-334 Russian Federation

ISBN 3-540-19946-2 Springer-Verlag Berlin Heidelberg New York

British Library Cataloguing in Publication Data
East/West Database Workshop: Proceedings of the Second International East/West
Database Workshop, Klagenfurt, Austria, 25-28 September 1994. - (Workshops in
Computing Series)
   I. Eder, Johann II. Kalinichenko, Leonid A.
   III. Series
   005.74
ISBN 3-540-19946-2

Library of Congress Cataloging-in-Publication Data
International East/West Database Workshop (2nd : 1994 : Klagenfurt, Austria)
   East/West Database Workshop : Proceedings of the Second
International East/West Database Workshop, Klagenfurt, Austria,
25-28 September 1994 / J. Eder and L.A. Kalinichenko (eds.).
     p. cm. - (Workshops in computing)
  "Published in collaboration with the British Computer Society."
  Includes bibliographical references and index.
  ISBN 3-540-19946-2 (acid-free paper)
   1. Database management-Congresses. I. Eder, J. (Johann), 1958-
  II. Kalinichenko, L.A. (Leonid Andreevich) III. British Computer
Society. IV. Title. V. Series.
QA76.9.D3I5596 1994
005.74-dc20
                                                    94-49417
                                                      CIP

Apart from any fair dealing for the purposes of research or private study, or criticism or
review, as permitted under the Copyright, Designs and Patents Act 1988, this publication
may only be reproduced, stored or transmitted, in any form, or by any means, with the
prior permission in writing of the publishers, or in the case of reprographic reproduction
in accordance with the terms of licences issued by the Copyright Licensing Agency.
Enquiries concerning reproduction outside those terms should be sent to the publishers.

© British Computer Society 1995
Printed in Great Britain

The use of registered names, trademarks etc. in this publication does not imply, even in the
absence of a specific statement, that such names are exempt from the relevant laws and
regulations and therefore free for general use.

The publisher makes no representation, express or implied, with regard to the accuracy of
the information contained in this book and cannot accept any legal responsibility or
liability for any errors or omissions that may be made.

Typesetting: Camera ready by contributors
Printed by Athenæum Press Ltd., Gateshead
34/3830-543210 Printed on acid-free paper

Preface

This volume results from the four-day scientific Second International East/West Database Workshop which took place 25th–28th September 1994, in Klagenfurt, Austria, continuing a series of workshops started in Kiev in 1990 (Lecture Notes in Computer Science No. 504, Springer, "Next Generation Information System Technology"). The aims of this workshop are twofold: first, to provide a forum for the presentation and in-depth discussion of scientific achievements in the field of advanced databases that will effectively improve the building and use of future information systems; second, to establish and increase communication between research communities which were formerly separated and, therefore, had only rare opportunities to interact. It should establish contacts between researchers from the East and from the West to make exchange of ideas possible and to trigger collaborations.

However, it is not only political borders which change their perviousness as a result of – or giving rise to – new autonomies or new possibilities for interaction and collaboration. The same happens with the borders between scientific areas, in particular in the dynamically evolving areas of computer science. Databases and programming languages are integrated in object oriented databases, database and information retrieval technology form together the basis for modern (multimedia) information systems. Furthermore, the borders between different information systems change and allow various forms of collaboration while maintaining different degrees of autonomy. Heterogeneous and distributed databases are enabling technologies for these systems. So the main theme of this workshop is to question borders and to overcome restrictions posed by political, traditional, organizational, scientific, or technical borders to extend information systems technically and to extend the information systems of scientists geographically.

The technical contributions to this workshop present scientific achievements in areas of database research that will greatly influence future information systems. Special attention is given to the following list of topics.

- rules in databases
- special aspects like query optimization and security
- theoretical issues

- databases languages and specification languages
- information engineering, integrating information retrieval and databases
- data models and database standards
- design of databases and information systems
- heterogeneous and distributed information systems
- applications and interfaces

The workshop was sponsored by the following institutions: Department of Computer Science, University of Klagenfurt, Austria, Austrian Computer Society, Austrian Federal Ministry for Science and Research, Esprit Network of Excellence IDOMENEUS, Foundation for Extending Database Technology (EDBT), Rome, Italy, Association for International Scientific and Technical Communication and Cooperation (ASSISTANCE), Vienna, Austria, Friends of the Department of Computer Science, Klagenfurt, Austria. Without their support, the organization of this workshop would not have been possible.

We express our warmest thanks to Joachim Schmidt, University of Hamburg, the "Good Spirit" behind this workshop series, for his encouragement, his advice and his great support. Our special thanks are due to Anneliese Michael, University of Klagenfurt, for her tremendous support in all organizational issues of this workshop. The workshop participants were most appreciative of the support provided by the organization team (Michael Dobrovnik, Heinz Frank, Alex Krumpholz, and Walter Liebhart) of the Department of Computer Science, University of Klagenfurt. We gratefully acknowledge the support of Rosie Kemp, Springer-Verlag London, for her support in preparing these proceedings.

Finally, on behalf of all the workshop participants we would like to express our sincere thanks to everybody who helped make this second "East/West Workshop" in the area of databases a success.

Johann Eder, Klagenfurt, Austria
Leonid A. Kalinichenko, Moscow, Russia

Contents

Rules in Databases

Chimera: A Model and Language for Active DOOD Systems
S. Ceri and R. Manthey 3

Updates by Reasoning About States
G. Lausen and B. Ludäscher 17

Theoretical Issues

On the Theory of Relational Data Bases with Incomplete Information
M.Sh. Tsalenko 33

Constraint Satisfiability in Object-Oriented Databases
A. Formica, M. Missikoff and R. Terenzi 48

Objects Within a Conceptual Shell
V.E. Wolfengagen 61

Special Aspects

Comparison of Clustering Algorithms in a Single User Environment Through 007 Benchmark
K. Koc, A. Dogac and C. Evrendilek 77

Security as an Add-On Quality in Persistent Object Systems
A. Rudloff, F. Matthes and J.W. Schmidt 90

Optimization of Object-Oriented Queries by Inverse Methods
J. Eder, H. Frank and W. Liebhart 109

Database Languages

F-Bounded Polymorphism for Database Programming Languages
S. Alagić 125

OODBMS's Query and Programming Languages: What Do They Provide and What Do We Need
S.D. Kuznetsov 138

A Meta-Language for Specification of Evolving Class and Object Lattices in OODB
H.-M. Haav 147

A Stack-Based Approach to Query Languages
K. Subieta, C. Beeri, F. Matthes and J.W. Schmidt 159

Information Engineering

Identifying Internet-Related Database Research
P.M.G. Apers 183

Integrating Text and Database Systems: Possibilities
and Challenges
W.B. Croft 194

Logical and Conceptual Models for the Integration of
Information Retrieval and Database Systems
N. Fuhr 206

Models

Composition Models of Databases
I.A. Basarab, B.V. Gubsky, N.S. Nikitchenko and V.N. Red'ko 221

Could the OODB Standards be Better if More Grounded?
I. Chaban, L. Kalinichenko and V. Zadorozhny 232

Version Support for CAD/CASE Databases
W. Wieczerzycki and J. Rykowski 249

Design

A General Framework for Database Design Strategies
B. Thalheim 263

Towards Foundations of Database Schema Independent
Modelling of Concepts
R. Gustas 275

Inheritance of Object Behavior – Consistent Extension
of Object Life Cycles
G. Kappel and M. Schrefl 289

Specification

Visual Specification of Complex Database Actions
G. Engels and P. Löhr 303

The Database Specification Language Ruslan: Main Features
A.V. Zamulin 315

Heterogeneous and Distributed Systems

Structural and Behavioral Abstractions of the Multiactivities
Intended for Their Concretizations by the Pre-Existing
Behaviors
L. Kalinichenko 331

Management and Translation of Heterogeneous
Database Schemes
P. Atzeni and R. Torlone 346

Federated Schemata in ODMG
R. Busse, P. Fankhauser and E.J. Neuhold 356

ADDS Transaction Management System
Y. Breitbart 380

Persistent Object Systems and Interoperability: Linguistic
and Architectural Requirements
K. Subieta 394

Applications and Interfaces

CSCW – Paradigm of Modern Applied Informatics and
Problem of East-West Relationships
S.S. Azarov and A.A. Stogny 411

Model Based User Interface Constructor with
Consistency Checking
Z. Kouba, J. Lažanský, Vl. Mařík, O. Štěpánková and
T. Vlček 426

Author Index 437

Rules in Databases

Chimera: A Model and Language for Active DOOD Systems*

Stefano Ceri
Dip. di Elettronica e Informazione
Politecnico di Milano
Piazza L. Da Vinci - I-20133 Milano
Italy

Rainer Manthey
Department of Computer Science
University of Bonn
Römerstrasse 164, D-53117 Bonn
Germany

Abstract

Chimera is a novel database model and language which has been designed as a joint conceptual interface of the IDEA project, a major European cooperation initiative aiming at the integration of object-oriented, active and deductive database technology. In this paper, we present a view of the main features of Chimera and discuss the design choices made. The most remarkable characteristic of Chimera is the fact that fully developed rule languages for both active and deductive rules have been integrated in an object-oriented context. Rules are in the center of interest of the IDEA project, which aims at developing prototypical components of a future "intelligent" DBMS.

1 Introduction

In this paper, we introduce a major attempt towards integrating active, deductive and object-oriented data modeling and manipulation techniques within a unified framework. The resulting model and language, called Chimera, has been designed as a joint conceptual interface for our work within the IDEA project, a four-years activity sponsored by the ESPRIT program of the Commission of the European Community. The project consortium involves partners from Belgium, France, Germany, Italy and Spain. The overall aim of the IDEA project has been the design and prototyping of an "intelligent database system", offering a conceptual interface that supports a variety of novel features proposed and developed recently within the DB research community: an object-oriented data model, deductive rules (for the definition of derived concepts), static integrity constraints (for the definition of legal DB states) and active rules (for the definition of reactive behaviour of the system in addition to the methods of the data model). Systems integrating deductive and object-oriented functionality have been called "DOOD systems" for some time now. Active DOOD systems in addition provide the concept of an active rule, thus naturally extending representation power and operational strength.

---

*This work was supported in part by the Commission of the European Community under ESPRIT project number 6333 (IDEA)

Chimera is the name of a famous mythical creature composed from a lion, a goat and a serpent. When designing Chimera, we often felt like creating such a monster indeed! On the one hand, the integration of concepts from three of the most active and productive areas of current research caused a lot of problems, because there are so many possible choices and design parameters to be considered. On the other hand, doing such an exercise within the context of a European research consortium composed of a very heterogeneous set of partners - from different nations, from industry and academia, with very different background and interests - is a difficult and exhausting affair. However, we feel that this effort has been worthwhile as we finally came up with a solution that we do not regard as too much of a compromise, but as a rather well-balanced and solid piece of design that might be of interest to others outside the consortium as well.

We did not attempt to invent any exciting or exotic new features, but instead aimed at a proper selection of important and well-established concepts and a good and seamless blend into a unified framework. Thus, the value of Chimera does not so much depend on the originality of its individual ingredients (though some new solutions have been developed, particularly wrt active rules), but on the way how these features have been combined and how potential conflicts have been resolved.

Chimera consists of a conceptual model (called **Chimera Model**, short: CM), providing object-oriented modelling facilities, and of a conceptual language (called **Chimera Language**, short: CL), providing data definitions, declarative queries, procedural primitives for database manipulation, as well as various forms of rules and constraints. Chimera has been designed in such a way, that it can either serve as an interface to a stand-alone database system or as a database sublanguage embedded in various procedural host languages. Due to the diversity of programming environments present in the IDEA consortium (ranging from C/C++ to PROLOG), aspects of procedural, general-purpose programming have been omitted from CL as far as possible. This issue has been left to the respective programming language into which Chimera will be embedded by the various partners. Certain basic linguistic decisions in CL, such as primitive value types, syntax of primitive values, conventions for distinguishing variables, constants or functors, and so on, may vary from one embedding to the other due to the particular conventions of the host language.

This paper is mainly aimed at providing a brief account of the spectrum covered by the Chimera design. The main ingredients of model and language are reviewed and some key decisions are highlighted. Representative examples, collected in the Appendix due to space limitations, will illustrate the flavor of the language.

2 CM: Chimera's Data Model

First we will introduce Chimera's data model in form of a "bird eye's view" of the concepts to be found in CM. Each of the concepts is briefly introduced and the relationships between the individual parts of the model are sketched and discussed. A more precise, formal definition of the model (as well as of CL) is beyond the scope of this overview paper and can be found in [GBB94].

2.1 Objects and Values

CM is an object-oriented data model. **Objects** are abstractions of real world entities (such as persons, companies, or machines). Every entity of an application domain should be modeled as an object. Objects are distinguished from each other by means of unique **object identifiers** (OIDs), automatically generated by the DBMS on object creation. Objects are the essential components of a database, representing real world entities that are characteristic for the respective application domain. In contrast, values serve as a means of describing objects, but are not essential components of a database.

A **value** can be either atomic or structured. Atomic values are atomic, printable symbols, such as numbers or strings, or OIDs (i.e., references to objects). Structured values are built from atomic values by recursively applying one of the predefined constructors for sets, lists, or records. Chimera provides a number of predefined **operators** applicable to values, such as arithmetic operators (e.g., *, +, or sqrt) applicable to numbers, or selectors (like head and tail), applicable to constructs.

Attributes are functions mapping an object to a uniquely defined value. Any semantically meaningful information about a particular object has to be associated with that object by means of one of its attributes. Attribute values of an object may change over time, without changing the identity of that object. The collection of all attribute values associated with an object is called the **state** of that object. The state of an object is represented in Chimera as a record of attributes.

Objects can be manipulated by means of **operations**, defined and implemented by the designer of a particular application according to needs. An operation is essentially one of the procedural primitives offered by Chimera or a procedure written in the procedural host language of the environment in which Chimera is embedded. Rather than identifying Chimera operations and procedures one to one, a level of indirection has been introduced: operations are related to procedures by means of "guarded" declarations. When invoking an operation, the corresponding procedural code is executed only, if the "guard" (a declarative condition) is satisfied in the state of the database reached when the call is processed. In this way, operations are clearly separated from procedures conceptually, and control over operation invocations is assigned to the Chimera run-time system. Note that values cannot be described by means of attributes and cannot be manipulated by means of operations.

2.2 Types and Classes

Chimera supports both the notion of type and of class, with a one-to-one relationship between them. Whereas the notion of "type" emphasizes the structural and behavioural similarity of objects, the notion of "class" emphasizes membership of these objects in a common set of instances. In Chimera, most types remain implicit, while classes are defined, populated, and deleted explicitly, thus underlining the database character of Chimera: the main purpose of the language and the model is to provide an interface to a persistent store of collections of elements of the same type.

All objects of a Chimera application must belong to an **object class**. Classes must be defined first, and then objects may be inserted into classes. Type definitions (i.e., definitions of structure and behaviour) are inferred automatically from class definitions. Whereas those attributes introduced in the previous subsection associate values with individual objects, Chimera provides a means for associating values with entire classes as well. **Class attributes** are functions mapping an entire class to a unique value. Examples of possible class attributes are cardinalities or statistical values such as average age or average salary for a class of person objects. Analogously, **class operations** manipulate an entire class rather than individual instances.

Object classes may be recursively specialized into **subclasses**, resulting in a taxonomic hierarchy of arbitrary depth. Multiple superclasses are possible, but multiple inheritance is subject to restrictions. A subclass inherits all attributes and operations from its superclasses, but may redefine their implementation. Moreover, a subclass may introduce additional attributes which are applicable to the objects in that subclass only. Subclass definitions are acceptable only if the corresponding (implicit) types are compatible. A set of subtyping conditions have to be satisfied whenever a class is defined as being subclass of another class.

Values are organized by means of types and classes as well. Most atomic values, such as integers, reals, or characters, are predefined and provide a (possibly infinite) "pool" of possible atomic symbols. These values cannot be manipulated by the database user, i.e., they cannot be inserted or deleted. Therefore, we do not regard concepts like *integer* or *string* as classes of Chimera, but as types only. Similarly, structured values are described by means of type constructors (record, set, and list) applied to value types. Structured value types also provide a (possibly infinite) "pool" of structured values. Once a type is defined, it is available in Chimera (for reuse in other object descriptions).

Chimera users may in addition introduce application specific collections of values, called **value classes**. These are populated explicitly, by means of insert operations, according to the needs of applications. In analogy to object classes, value classes are associated with a unique, but implicit type; they do not have attributes or operations. Value classes are used in Chimera as **active domains**: whenever the attribute of an object has a type which corresponds to a value class, the only allowed attribute values for that object must belong to the resp. value class.

2.3 Object Identifiers and Object References

In order to be able to express object-valued attributes as well as operations and constraints accepting objects as parameters, Chimera explicitly distinguishes between objects and object identifiers. **Object identifiers** are concrete symbols referencing a particular (abstract) object, but are not identical with that object. Thus, an object-valued attribute, e.g., managers of employees (being employees themselves) is in fact "OID-valued". OIDs do not carry any meaning, but serve purely as internal surrogates. They are generated and manipulated by system software and cannot be retrieved by database users. In addition to OIDs, users of a Chimera application may, however, define their own **external names** for individual objects of particular interest.

This design choice leads naturally to an *object sharing semantics for object-valued attributes* (in which multiple objects may reference one and the same object by means of different attributes), rather than a copy semantics (in which objects referred to by attributes of a given object would have to be copied in the state of that object).

2.4 Targeted and Untargeted Definitions

A **schema definition** in CL is a collection of targeted and untargeted definitions. Each type or class definition is a **target**, that is, a unit of abstraction and modularization. Features (such as attributes and operations) which are defined in the context of a given target have a scope that is limited to that target. Thus, targets enable a modular design and some degree of information hiding that is typical of object-oriented design (this is further supported by the separation between the definitions of signatures and implementations of each target, see later).

However, some information in the schema cannot be targeted; for instance, views combining information from several classes, or triggers affecting multiple classes, or constraints relating the state of objects from several classes. Therefore, some definitions cannot be expressed in the context of types and classes; these are called **untargeted definitions**.

Given that targeted definitions are usually easier to understand, control, and evolve, a good design principle for Chimera applications is to choose an appropriate collection of targets, so that most of the definitions in the schema can be targeted.

2.5 Derived Attributes, Derived Classes, Views

Passive rules of the CL language may be used for deriving information, as is normally done in deductive databases. Passive rules can be applied in the following situations:

- **Derived attributes**, can have values which are defined by means of rules instead of individual update operations over time. Derived attribute values are part of the object's state as well.

- In the context of hierarchies of object classes, populations of some subclasses, called **derived classes**, may also be defined by means of passive rules, which generate the subclass population implicitly when certain properties of the superclass hold.

- Finally, untargeted **views** are always defined by means of passive rules which combine information from one or more classes of Chimera. Each view is introduced independently of a particular type or class definition and is "implemented" by one or more passive rules.

2.6 Constraints and Triggers

In addition to the basic structural and behavioural concepts of attribute and operation, Chimera provides two more concepts: constraint and trigger. Both concepts can be either targeted or untargeted.

Constraints are a means of restricting the contents of the database. Constraints consist of declarative conditions (expressed in CL). They have a name, and they may have output parameters. In case of a violation of a constraint, these output parameters return values specific to the cause of the particular violation. Constraints that are targeted to a particular class may either restrict the extent of the respective class or restrict the set of legal values of its attributes; some constraints may be targeted to value types. Untargeted constraints restrict the set of legal database states and usually relate two or more classes. Constraints are checked after a commit command, issued by a transaction; if they are violated, then the transaction is rolled back.

Triggers are a means of introducing specific reactions to particular events relevant to the database. Such events are currently restricted to database specific operations (i.e. queries and updates) and operation calls. Other events, currently not supported in the language, could be time-related or external events. Reactions are calls to procedures written in either CL or the embedding host language. The execution of reactions is subject to conditions on the database state reached whenever an event is monitored; further, triggers are prioritized, so that when several of them can be fired a partial order is imposed. Triggers are named like constraints, but do not have parameters. A trigger that refers to a single class in each of its components (i.e., event, condition, and reaction part) can be introduced together with the definition of that particular class, as a targeted concept. All other triggers have to be introduced individually. Triggers are synonymously referred to as **active rules** within this document, because both notions are commonly used in the active database community, and in order to emphasize there relationship with passive rules (the former being imperative, the latter declarative specifications of certain autonomously initiated behaviour of the database system).

2.7 Signature and Implementation

When defining a new class, all attributes and operations of the new class have to be specified together with the corresponding domains (i.e., the class from which the attribute values or the operation parameters have to come). In addition, names and parameters of those constraints and triggers targeted to the particular class have to be introduced. The entirety of these name and domain definitions makes up the **signature** of the respective class.

Concepts are first introduced and "typed" in the signature of a class, then they have to be "implemented". There are different ways of implementing a concept, depending on its particular nature. Classes can be populated either by explicit, individual creation of all instances, or by implicitly and collectively defining their instances by means of passive rules. The same applies in principle for attributes and class attributes: attribute values can either be introduced individually during object creation, or collectively by means of passive rules. Constraints (and class constraints) are always implemented by passive rules. Operations are implemented by means of a "guarded procedure body", as mentioned earlier. Finally triggers are implemented by active rules. The association of attributes, classes, constraints, operations, and triggers with the expressions implementing them is performed after the respective signatures have been introduced. All concept definitions related to a particular class form the **implementation** of that class.

Both signature and implementation are considered part of the class definition. However, CL provides different data definition operations for introducing signature and implementation, in order to reflect that implementations are usually introduced after signatures have been defined.

3 CL: Chimera's Conceptual Language

CL serves two main purposes. It offers data definition facilities for implementating CM schemas (expressed by means of passive rules, active rules, and operation implementations). In addition, it provides for the manipulation of data by means of queries, updates and transactions (expressed by means of the declarative and procedural expressions of the language). CL comes in two slightly different versions, the one aimed at providing an interactive database language (supporting a "user-friendly interface" - UFI), the other to be used as embedded database sublanguage within a general-purpose programming language (forming an "application programming interface" - API). This section provides a brief summary of the concepts to be found in CL together with remarks concerning the rationale behind our design choices.

3.1 Declarative Expressions

CL is a logic-based language, supporting declarative queries, declarative (passive) rules for data definition as well as declarative conditions for controlling imperative (active) rules and imperative operations. Logical languages are classically composed of two main syntactic categories: terms and formulas.

Terms denote individuals in the respective domain of interpretation of the language. In the Chimera context this means that a CL term denotes either a value or an object. Atomic terms include constants and variables (starting with an uppercase letter). Complex terms are made from constructors (set, list, record) or by means of functions available in Chimera (attributes, selectors, predefined operators). Attributes are applied in postfix dot notation to variables denoting objects.

Formulas express propositions about individuals, being either true or false. In CL, there are five categories of atomic formulas:

- Class (and type) formulas are used for typing variables denoting objects or values.

- Membership formulas state that an object or a value is contained in a set.

- Comparison formulas provide means of comparing terms for equality or by means of a standard comparator.

- Constraint formulas serve as a means to access parameters of individual constraint violations (for compensation or repair, e.g.).

- Event formulas appear in conditions of active rules (see below).

Complex formulas are constructed from atomic ones by means of conjunction and negation. Formulas are evaluated over a database state according to the classical assumptions of first-order semantics. In order to avoid syntactically valid formulas which denote infinite set of instances, we impose that formulas be range-restricted. When compared to other Datalog-like logic languages, CL offers a richer collection of mechanisms for building terms and formulas; these however enable us to implement and use all the features available through CM, which is a rich object-oriented data model.

3.2 Passive Rules

Passive rules are one of the key concepts of CL. They are used for declaratively defining class instances or attribute values, and for the implementation of views and constraints. A **passive rule** is an expression of the form $Head \leftarrow Body$ where the *Head* is an atomic formula, the *Body* is an arbitrary formula, and each variable in the head occurs positively in the body. Rules are stratified with respect to sets and negation, thereby ensuring that the computation of their fixpoint converges to a unique, minimal model. These limitations do not allow us to express certain semantics by means of rules (for instance, we exclude locally stratified rules). Moreover, our choice for a "standard" semantics for stratified rules excludes the possibility of choosing other semantics for more general rules, such as inflationary semantics. However, our design choice is motivated by the fact that stratified rules satisfy the requirements of most applications and have a more intuitive meaning than nonstratified rules.

3.3 Procedural Expressions

CL does not aim at being a full-fledged programming language. However, there is the need for expressing certain database-related imperative actions under the control of the database system, and thus for incorporating a certain degree of procedural syntax into CL.

Procedural expressions in CL are composed of primitive database statements, i.e., of updates, queries and operation calls. Chimera supports rather conventional notions of query, update, and transaction.

Queries in the UFI mode include *display* and *find*; queries supported from an API include *select* and *next*. In essence, all four query primitives are very similar. Each of them consists of a Chimera formula F and a target list T. In all cases, the formula F is evaluated over the current state of the database, returning either individual bindings to the variables in T (in the case of *find* and *next*) or the set of all the bindings to these variables (in the case of *display* and *select*). Thus, the rationale of query primitives is to provide both instance-oriented and set-oriented access from both kinds of interfaces.

Updates in Chimera support object creation and deletion, object migration from one class to another, state change or change of persistency status of objects, and value class population and modification. This collection of primitives enables all possible class and persistency updates which can be envisioned in Chimera, with the only exception of turning an object from persistent to temporary.

The only general means of forming more complex statements is to build chains of primitive statements. Due to the database nature of these primitives, CL provides two different chaining operators: one for passing sets of variable bindings from one component statement to the other (the *sequence* operator) and one for passing individual bindings (the *pipe* operator). In addition, the UFI mode of interaction provides two syntactic variants which express iteration over sets of objects either explicitly or implicitly.

Finally, Chimera supports a conventional notion of **transaction**, where user-controlled *commit* and *rollback* primitives allow to either atomically execute all changes defined inside the transaction boundaries, or to restore the transaction's initial state.

3.4 Active Rules and Operation Implementations

Similarly to the way how passive rules serve as a declarative means of implementing certain Chimera concepts, there are two categories of imperative constructs for implementing other concepts of CM: triggers are implemented by means of **active rules**, whereas operations are defined by means of an **operation implementation**. Both categories of constructs contain a procedural CL expression as their "body", expressing a sequence of database actions that are to be executed. In both cases, trigger as well as operation, this execution only takes place, if a certain declarative (pre-)condition is satisfied over the current state of the database. The difference between the two categories of constructs is the style of invocation. In case of operations, an explicit invocation (operation call) is required and control is locally transferred from one operation call to the next. In case of triggers, invocation is implicit, controlled by a system component monitoring actions and determining appropriate reactions.

3.5 Triggers

Chimera supports *set-oriented triggers*, which are activated by database operations and perform reactive computations. The distinguishing choice of Chimera is to map an object-oriented data model with set-oriented triggers, e.g., triggers responding to collective operations. Triggers in Chimera follow the *event-condition-action* paradigm of active databases:

- *Events* correspond to database accesses for retrieval or manipulation.
- Each *condition* is a declarative formula, to be evaluated in the state before activation of the reaction.
- Each *reaction* is a chain (sequence or pipeline) of one or more procedure calls, which can perform any computation on the database.

Events are a uniform interface for defining patterns of actions the observation of which can trigger a reaction. Such patters can be:

- *Queries* performed over object classes. A query is any retrieval operation which occurs during the evaluation of a term in the context of a passive rule. Events are denoted by the name of the target of the query (either a class or an attribute of a class).
- *Updates* performed over object classes. Events are denoted by the name of the resp. update operation and the target (class name, possibly attribute name) of this operation.

Each trigger is defined on a set of triggering events; the set is associated to a disjunction semantics (the trigger becomes active if *any* of its triggering events occurs). We exclude, for the time being, to support within Chimera a more complex event calculus. Note that we do not support triggers on value classes.

The **condition** is a declarative formula written in CL; it serves the purpose of monitoring the execution of the reaction part. The **reaction** is a chain of procedure calls; procedures can be either update primitives of Chimera, or *display* primitives, or operations, or externally defined procedures, or the transactional command *rollback*. Conditions and reactions may share some *atomic variables* that are used in order to relate them; in addition, conditions may use special formulas *occurred* and *holds* in order to identify objects which have been the target of one of the above events. **Event formulas** in the condition part of a trigger are provided as a means of referring to triggering events occurring within a transaction declaratively. Event formulas referring to updates are evaluated with respect to the *net effect* of a transaction. References to the state before and after a transaction can be made within the condition part as well.

Syntactically, active rules must be *safe*, that is, the variables occurring as input parameters of some procedures in the reaction part of the rule must be present in some positive literals of the condition part of the same rule (or be defined as output parameters of precedent procedures).

Execution of Chimera triggers may be controlled by means of a few control options (such as "coupling modes" or "event consumption modes"). Priorities can be given in order to partially order triggers relative to each other. A complete description of triggers in Chimera can be found in [CFPT94]; their formal semantics is presented in [FPT94].

4 Conclusion

In this paper we outline the main characteristics of Chimera, the conceptual interface to various implementations produced by the partners of the IDEA consortium within the ESPRIT III program of the CEC. Chimera consists of an object-oriented data model and a database sublanguage that supports a fully declarative query language, data definition and data manipulation primitives, passive and active rules, constraints and operations. Thus Chimera is one of the first attempts of combining concepts developed in active, deductive and object-oriented databases in a systematic manner. Chimera implementations are under development within the IDEA consortium and a rich variety of applications written in Chimera is currently designed and implemented by the application partners within IDEA. In addition, Chimera will be used as a standard conceptual model in the context of design methodologies and tools for supporting the development of active DOOD applications; assisting applications design will be a major objective of the second part of the IDEA project (June 1994 - June 1996).

Chimera is a joint effort of a group of researchers from various institutions. We would like to acknowledge the valuable contributions of Elena Baralis, Elisa Bertino, Stefano Crespi-Reghizzi, Claudia Roncancio, Christoph Draxler, Ulrike Griefahn, Piero Fraternali, Danilo Montesi, Stefano Paraboschi, Giuseppe Psaila, Andrea Sikeler, and Letizia Tanca.

Appendix

Due to space limitations we cannot include extensive examples in the text. Instead we provide a coherent set of example definitions in this appendix prototypically demonstrating all major concepts of CM and CL.

- An object class definition:

```
define object class person
    attributes    name:string(20)
                  birthday:date
```

```
                         vatCode:string(15)
                         age:integer
                         income:integer
                         profession:string(10)
         operations      changeIncome(Amount:integer)
         constraints     tooLowIncome(N:name)
                         key(V:vatCode)
         c-attributes    averageAge:integer
                         lifeExpectancy:integer
         c-operations    changeLifeExpectancy(Delta:integer):integer
         c-constraints   invalidLifeExpectancy(I:integer)
```

- Its implementation:

```
define implementation for person
   attributes     Self.age=X <- X=1994 - Self.birthday.year
   operations     changeIncome(Amount):
                     integer(New),New=Self.income+Amount ->
                     modify(person.income,Self,New)
   constraints    tooLowIncome(N) <-
                     Self.income<500000, N=Self.name
   c-attributes   Class.averageAge=Y <-
                     integer(Y), Y=avg(X.age where person(X))
   c-operations   changeLifeExpectancy(Delta):
                     integer(New), Delta<10,
                     New=Class.lifeExpectancy + Delta ->
                     modify(person.lifeExpectancy,Class,New),
                     return(New)
   c-constraints  invalidLifeExpectancy(I) <-
                     I = Class.averageAge - Class.lifeExpectancy,
                     abs(I) > 5
```

- A view on the class person:

```
define view marriage: record-of(husband:person,wife:person)
   marriage((husband:X,wife:Y)) <- X.spouse=Y, X.sex=male
```

- An untargeted constraint:

```
define constraint tooLowLiability(Name: person.name,
                                  Plate: car.plate,
                                  Liability: integer)
tooLowLiability(Name, Plate, Liability) <-
                  person(X), car(Y), X = Y.owner,
                  Name = X.name, Plate = Y.plate,
                  Liability = Y.insuranceLiability*0.7,
                  Liability < 500000
```

- An untargeted trigger:

```
define trigger raiseBudget
   events      create(employee)
               modify(employee.salary)
               modify(dept.members)
               modify(dept.salaryBudget)
   condition   dept(D), integer(I),
               I=sum(E.salary where employee(E), E in D.members),
               I>D.salaryBudget
   actions     modify(dept.salaryBudget,D,I)
   after       employee.adjustSalary
```

- A display query:

```
display(X.name,Y.make where person(X), car(Y), Y.owner=X)
```

- A create primitive:

```
create(project,
       (name:"Intelligent DB Environment for
              Advanced Applications",
        acronym:"IDEA",
        number:6333,
        duration:4,
        commencement:(day:1,month:6,year:1992)),X)
```

- A transaction:

```
begin transaction;
  select(X where employee(X), X.mgr.name="Manthey"),
  modify(employee.salary, X, X.salary + 5000);
commit
```

References

[AG88]   S. Abiteboul and S. Grumbach: "COL: a Logic-based Language for Complex Objects", Proc. EDBT 1988, Venezia, March 1988

[AK89] S. Abiteboul and P.C. Kanellakis: "Object Identity as a Query Language Primitive", Proc. SIGMOD 1989, Portland, April 1989

[MANI89] M. Atkinson, F. Bancilhon, D. De Witt, K. Dittrich, D. Maier and S. Zdonik, "The Object-Oriented Database System Manifesto", Proc. DOOD 1989, Kyoto, December 1989, 40–57

[B90] C. Beeri: "A formal approach to Object-Oriented Databases", *Data and Knowledge Engineering*, 5:353-382, 1990

[C88] L. Cardelli, "A semantics of multiple inheritance", *Information and Computation*, 76:138-164, 1988.

[CCC+90] F. Cacace, S. Ceri, S. Crespi-Reghizzi, L. Tanca, R. Zicari: "Integrating Object-Oriented Data Modeling with a Rule-Based Programming Paradigm", Proc. SIGMOD 1990, Atlantic City, May 1990

[CCCT92] F. Cacace, S. Ceri, S. Crespi-Reghizzi and L. Tanca: "Designing and Prototyping Data-Intensive Applications in the Logres and Algres programming Environment". *IEEE Transactions on Software Engineering*, June 1992

[CFPT94] "Active Rule Management in Chimera" in *Active Databases*, (S. Ceri, U. Dayal, and J. Widom eds.), Morgan-Kaufmann, 1995 (to appear).

[CGT90] S. Ceri, G. Gottlob and L. Tanca: *Logic Programming and Databases*. Springer Verlag, 1990

[CFPT92] S. Ceri, P. Fraternali, S. Paraboschi and L. Tanca: "Automatic generation of production rules for integrity maintenance", Technical Report 92-054, Politecnico di Milano - Dipartimento di Elettronica e Informazione, 1992. To appear in *ACM Transactions on Database Systems*

[CM93] S. Ceri and R. Manthey: "Consolidated specification of Chimera, the conceptual interface of IDEA", Technical Report IDEA.DD.2P.004, ESPRIT Project 6333 IDEA, June 1993

[GBB94] G. Guerrini, E. Bertino, R. Bal: "A Formal Definition of the Chimera Object-Oriented Data Model", IDEA.DE.2P.011.01, May 1994.

[FPT94] P. Fraternali, G. Psaila, L. Tanca: "A Framework for the Design of Active Rules Semantics and its Application to Chimera" IDEA.DE.2P.007.02, May 1994.

[CBB+89] S. Chakravarthy, B. Blaustein, A. P. Buchmann et. al.: "HiPAC: A research project in active, time-constrained database management", Technical Report XAIT-89-02, Xerox Advanced Information Technology, July 1989

[GJ91] N. Gehani and H.V. Jagadish. "ODE as an active database: Constraints and triggers", Proc. VLDB 1991, Barcelona, Sept. 1991, 327–336

[WF90] J. Widom and S.J. Finkelstein: "Set-oriented production rules in relational database systems", Proc. SIGMOD 1990, Atlantic City, May 1990, 259–270

[WCL91] J. Widom, R. J. Cochrane and B. G. Lindsay. "Implementing set-oriented production rules as an extension to Starburst", Proc. VLDB 1991, Barcelona, Sept. 1991, 275–285

Updates by Reasoning about States

Georg Lausen   Bertram Ludäscher
Institut für Informatik, Albert-Ludwigs-Universität
D-79104 Freiburg, Germany
{lausen,ludaesch}@informatik.uni-freiburg.de

Abstract

We present a language extension to Datalog which allows to specify deterministic update procedures in a declarative way. Existing update languages either rely on procedural aspects of program evaluation or leave the framework of deductive databases and logic programming. In contrast, we show that declarative update semantics can be attained by incorporating state terms into the language. Since the resulting language corresponds to a certain class of logic programs, well-known semantics and evaluation techniques can be applied to it.

1 Introduction

While Datalog [20], the most prominent deductive database language, has proven to be very powerful as a *query language*, it lacks means to specify database *dynamics*. The model of a Datalog program statically describes one state of the modelled world. However, updating the contents of a database — like querying — is one of the most fundamental operations that a database system must provide. Consequently, numerous extensions to Datalog have been proposed to integrate the required update concepts.

Clearly, in order to express updates, the expressiveness of Datalog has to be increased. In [1] it is argued that *update = logic + control*, i.e. additional expressiveness is attained by additional control. However, the proposed extensions rely on procedural aspects of program evaluation and incorporate updates into a (bottom-up) evaluation procedure [1, 2]. Consequently, the resulting semantics can only be understood procedurally and a major advantage of logic-based languages, viz their declarative semantics is lost.

In contrast, we propose to increase expressiveness by incorporating *state terms* into the language. This allows to specify complex and deterministic update "procedures" by referring to different database states, yet a declarative semantics is retained. Since the proposed language *Statelog* stays within the well-known framework of logic programming, a plethora of semantics and evaluation techniques can be applied.

We continue work started in [12] where a fixpoint semantics was defined for an update language which could only process a constant number of intermediate states. In contrast, by the use of state variables, Statelog allows to refer to arbitrary database states, which results in greater expressiveness. It turned out that Statelog is closely related to the temporal deductive database language $Datalog_{1S}$ [9]. In fact, we use the same notion of periodicity to define the final state of an update (cf. section 5.1).

The structure of the paper is as follows. In section 2 we introduce the basic ideas of our approach. We continue with a discussion of various examples in section 3. Section 4 presents the syntax and a general framework for the semantics of Statelog. As an important example, we consider the perfect model semantics and its computation in section 5. In section 6 we summarize our approach and compare it to related work.

2 Basic Ideas

Statelog is based on the following two observations. First, the evolution of a database is given by a sequence of database states. Thus, in order to describe the transition from one state to another declaratively, the *language* must allow to refer to different states. Second, in order to describe deletions declaratively, facts which are implied by a logic database may not be removed at will. Instead, some information (a delete request) has to be added which prevents the derivation of the to be deleted facts. This requires a nonmonotonic formalism like the use of negation in logic programming. Statelog allows for exactly these requirements by incorporating *state terms* into the language and by the use of a *frame rule* which handles delete requests.

More precisely, every state in the database evolution is identified by a natural number, where 0 refers to the initial state and $S+1$ to the immediate successor state of S. The transition of a database from state S to $S+1$ is then given by the following simple frame axiom:

$$True(S+1) = True(S) \backslash Del(S+1) \cup Ins(S+1) \qquad (1)$$

The first part $True(S)\backslash Del(S+1)$ indicates that atoms which were true in the predecessor state S and which are not "marked for deletion" in $S+1$ continue to be true in $S+1$. Additionally, the newly inserted atoms $Ins(S+1)$ are true in $S+1$. $True(S)$ constitutes the actual logical model of state S. All atoms which are not in $True(S)$ are considered false. In order to represent (1) within Statelog, it is sufficient to partition every state S into the set $True(S)$ of true atoms and the set $Del(S)$ of atoms which are to be deleted. $Ins(S)$ is then given implicitly by the corresponding update program.

Intuitively, for an atom R, the expression $[S]+R$ corresponds to the *goal* $R \in True(S)$, if it occurs in the body of a Statelog rule, or to the *assertion* $R \in True(S)$, if it occurs in the head. In the latter case, the rule specifies an insert operation. For brevity we usually write $[S]R$ instead of $[S]+R$. Similarly, the expression $[S]-R$ corresponds to $R \in Del(S)$. In particular, if $[S]-R$ occurs in the head of a rule, the rule specifies a delete operation.

Given an n-ary relation R, the part of (1) which preserves the "old information" $True(S)\backslash Del(S+1)$ can be expressed in Statelog by the *frame rule* for R:

$$[S+1]\ R(\bar{X}) \leftarrow [S]\ R(\bar{X}), \neg[S+1]-R(\bar{X}). \qquad (2.1)$$

Here, S is a distinguished *state variable* which may only be bound to a state identifier (a natural number), while $\bar{X}$ is a vector $X_1, \ldots, X_n$ of ordinary (data) variables.

A Statelog database consists of an extensional database EDB and an intensional database IDB which are defined as usual and describe the initial state 0 of the database. A corresponding frame rule (2.1) is used for all EDB relations and may be applied to derived relations as well (cf. section 3).

Additionally, there is a *transition base* TB which contains *update rules* describing the possible transitions of the database from a current state s via intermediate (virtual) states $s+1, s+2, \ldots$, to a new final state s'. Usually update rules are blocked by certain goals, so-called *events* which act as *guards*.

An event is conceived as a built-in predicate whose validity in a state s is asserted externally. The set of occurred events is recorded as a finite set of ground facts, the *event base* EB. To distinguish symbols denoting events from "ordinary" predicate symbols, we stipulate to prefix them with a special character ∇ (pronounced "occurs"). Whenever an event ∇E occurs in a state s, a ground fact $[s]\nabla E$ is added to EB. This may trigger update rules which generate new database states through the insertion or deletion of EDB or IDB atoms until the final state s' is reached. s' is defined using the periodic structure of the model of the database (section 5.1).

3 Statelog by Example

In the following, we present some simple examples which demonstrate how updates may be specified in Statelog.

EDB Updates Consider the proverbial (and oversimplified) "employee-salary" example. Assume the EDB contains facts es(E,Sal) describing the initial employee-salary relation in state 0. We want to allow the user to issue a request raise(E,F) with the desired effect of increasing E's salary by a factor F. We can use the following update rule[1]

$$[S+1] \ \text{es}(E,\text{Sal1}), \ [S+1]\text{–es}(E,\text{Sal}) \leftarrow \\ [S] \ \nabla\text{raise}(E,F), \ [S] \ \text{es}(E,\text{Sal}), \ \text{Sal1} = \text{Sal} \cdot F. \tag{3.1}$$

Assume the current database state is s, and es(john,1000) is true in the current state. In order to raise john's salary by 7%, we have to assert that ∇raise(john,1.07) is true in s. This can be given explicitly by the user, e.g. in a query shell: `[s]> raise(john,1.07)`.

Such a shell allows to assert events for the current state and to query a window of predecessor states. The occurrence of the event ∇raise(john,1.07) triggers rule (3.1), and a new database state $s+1$ is created: the first atom in the head causes the insertion of es(john,1070), while the second results in the deletion of es(john,1000). The frame rule for es

$$[S+1] \ \text{es}(E,\text{Sal}) \leftarrow [S] \ \text{es}(E,\text{Sal}), \ \neg \ [S+1]\text{–es}(E,\text{Sal}). \tag{3.2}$$

guarantees that the other employees' salaries remain the same in the new state.

Integrity Constraints One way to express integrity constraints in deductive databases is in the form of *denials*. Since Statelog allows to refer to different

---
[1] Rules with multiple heads like (3.1) are an abbreviation for several rules with the same body, thus the head denotes a conjunction.

states, not only static but also dynamic integrity constraints may be expressed. The following rule states that salaries may never decrease.

$$[S+1] \text{ false} \leftarrow [S] \text{ es}(E,Sal), [S+1] \text{ es}(E, Sal1), Sal1 < Sal \qquad (3.3)$$

Whenever the salary of an employee in state $S+1$ is less than in S, false is derived in $S+1$ which indicates a violation of the integrity constraint.

Another possibility is to use rules to *enforce* integrity constraints, e.g. by undoing the effect of an update: assume we want to reject a salary raise if some employee earns more than 2100. We use the rule

$$[S] \text{ undo\_raise} \leftarrow [S] \text{ es}(E,Sal), Sal > 2100. \qquad (3.4)$$

In order to enforce this constraint, we add rule (3.5) to the program.[2]

$$\begin{aligned}[S+2] \ (\text{es}(E,Sal), &-\text{es}(E,NewSal)) \leftarrow \\ [S] \ (&\nabla\text{raise}(E,F), \text{es}(E,Sal)), \\ [S+1] \ (&\text{es}(E,NewSal), \text{undo\_raise}).\end{aligned} \qquad (3.5)$$

If undo_raise is true in state $S+1$ a new final state $S+2$ is created where the effect of the update rule (3.1) is undone. In a sense (3.4) expresses the negation of a *post-condition*, which says that after an update on es all employees' salaries must be less or equal to 2100.

Finally, rule (3.5) also allows a kind of *what-if* reasoning by always undoing a salary raise, or equivalently, by removing the subgoal undo_raise. Then querying $S+1$ yields the (hypothetical) es relation *after* the update on es, while the final state $S+2$ holds the *original* es relation, i.e. *before* the raise.

IDB Updates One possibility to handle updates to IDB relations in Statelog is to apply the frame rule (2.1) to derived relations as well. Consider the following example (cf. [6]): assume we want to represent a relation flight(Flight_No, Day, Departure, Arrival). Since departure and arrival times of flights often coincide for different days, it is advantageous to use rules of the form

$$\text{flight}(\text{lh4356},Day,0725,0900) \leftarrow \text{day}(Day), Day \neq \text{sunday}. \qquad (3.6)$$

The flight relation is propagated to subsequent states (modulo insertions and deletions) by the frame rule (2.1). (3.6) states that there is a flight lh4356 between 7:25 and 9:00, which operates daily except for Sundays. In a sense, (3.6) derives a default relation in state 0 for flight, while subsequent changes by update rules act as *exceptions* to (3.6) (this resembles the approach for deterministic IDB updates [13]). The update rule

$$\begin{aligned}[S+1] \ (\text{flight}(F,Day2,D,A), &-\text{flight}(F,Day1,D,A)) \leftarrow \\ [S] \ (&\nabla\text{move}(F,Day1,Day2), \text{flight}(F,Day1,D,A)).\end{aligned}$$

when triggered by the event ∇move(lh4356,saturday,sunday) moves the flight lh4356 from Saturday to Sunday. A different way to handle IDB relations is shown in the following paragraph.

---

[2] Here parenthesis are used to group literals with the same state term.

Update Procedures The last example is a variant of the *game of life* (cf. [2]) and shows how more complex update procedures can be formulated using Statelog. Assume the EDB contains a symmetric binary relation neighbor(C1,C2) describing which cells are neighbors and a relation alive(C) to record the living cells. The IDB contains rules to determine whether a cell has (at least) 2 respectively 3 neighbors that are alive:

has2neighbors(C) ←
    neighbor(C,N1), neighbor(C,N2), N1 $\neq$ N2,
    alive(N1), alive(N2).

has3neighbors(C) ←
    neighbor(C,N1), neighbor(C,N2), neighbor(C,N3),
    N1 $\neq$ N2, N2 $\neq$ N3, N1 $\neq$ N3,
    alive(N1), alive(N2), alive(N3).

The relation has2neighbors(C) has to be derived anew in every state S in order to reflect the changes of alive(C). Hence, instead of applying the frame rule to has2neighbors(C), we use the following rule (analogously for has3neighbors(C)):

$[S]$ has2neighbors(C) ←
    $[S]$ (neighbor(C,N1), neighbor(C,N2), N1 $\neq$ N2),   (3.7)
    $[S]$ (alive(N1), alive(N2)).

The update procedure for alive consists of rules which define when a living cell dies or when a new cell is born. This is accomplished by corresponding delete and insert operations. The event ∇next_gen is used to guard the activation of rules. Since at any moment only finitely many events may have occurred, the program terminates (cf. section 5.1). A new generation is computed by asserting ∇next_gen in the final state.

% less than 2 neighbors: cell dies
$[S+1]$−alive(C) ←$[S]$ (∇next_gen, alive(C), $\neg$ has2neighbors(C)).

% more than 2 neighbors: cell dies   (3.8)
$[S+1]$−alive(C) ←$[S]$ (∇next_gen, alive(C), has3neighbors(C)).

% exactly 2 neighbors: cell is born
$[S+1]$ alive(C) ←$[S]$ (∇next_gen, has2neighbors(C), $\neg$ has3neighbors(C)).

4   A Statelog Framework

In this section we define the syntax and a general framework for the semantics of Statelog. By mapping Statelog programs to a certain class of standard logic programs, declarative semantics like the perfect model semantics [17], the well-founded semantics [22] and the stable semantics [10] can be applied to Statelog.

4.1   Syntax

Definition 4.1 (Signature) The Statelog language $\mathcal{L}$ is built using the following standard items: the set of predicate symbols $\mathcal{P}$, the set of function symbols $\mathcal{F}$ and the set of data variables $\mathcal{V}$. $\mathcal{C} \subseteq \mathcal{F}$ is the set of constants (function symbols with arity 0). We partition $\mathcal{P}$ into two disjoint sets: the set $\mathcal{R}$ of "ordinary" relation symbols and the set $\mathcal{E}$ of *event symbols* (built-in predicates). By convention event symbols start with a special character ∇.

Additionally, we have the following non-standard items: a set $\mathcal{S}$ of *state variables*, where $\mathcal{V} \cap \mathcal{S} = \emptyset$, a distinguished constant $0 \notin \mathcal{C}$ and a distinguished unary function symbol $+1 \notin \mathcal{F}$ (usually written in postfix).

From 0 and +1 we build the set of *state identifiers* $\Sigma = \{0, (0)+1, ((0)+1)+1, \ldots\}$ which may be identified with the set of natural numbers $\mathcal{N}_0$. Thus 2 is the same as $((0)+1)+1$ etc. □

In the context of deductive databases, usually $\mathcal{F} = \mathcal{C}$, but we may also allow a restricted (safe) use of function symbols.

Definition 4.2 (State Terms) A *state term* is of the form $[S+k]+$ or $[S+k]-$, where $S \in \mathcal{S} \cup \{0\}, k \in \mathcal{N}_0$. $S+k$ stands for the k-fold application of the function symbol +1 to S. State terms without state variable are called Σ-*ground*. □

State terms $[S+k]+$ and $[S+k]-$ are used to refer to the two parts $True(S+k)$ and $Del(S+k)$ of a state $S+k$. For notational convenience, we write $[S+k]\pm$ to denote either $[S+k]+$ or $[S+k]-$. $[S+k]$ is a shorthand for $[S+k]+$. The Σ-ground state terms $[0+k]\pm$ are abbreviated to $[k]\pm$.

Definition 4.3 (Statelog) From the set of data variables $\mathcal{V}$ and function symbols $\mathcal{F}$ we build *data terms* in the usual way.

A Statelog *atom* is of the form $\tau\ p(t_1, \ldots, t_n)$ where τ is a state term, p is an n-ary relation or event symbol from $\mathcal{P}$ and t_i are data terms. A *literal* is an atom A or its negation $\neg A$.

A *rule* r is of the form $H \leftarrow B_1, \ldots, B_n$ where H is an atom and each B_i is a literal. If $n = 0$, r is called a *fact*, if the head H is omitted r is a *query*. The rule $H_1, \ldots, H_k \leftarrow B_1, \ldots, B_n$ is an abbreviation for k rules $H_i \leftarrow B_1, \ldots, B_n$, i.e. $H_1, \ldots, H_k$ denotes a conjunction.

If r contains no state variables it is Σ-*ground*, if it contains no variables at all it is called *ground*. A Σ-ground rule r^* which is obtained from a rule r by substituting state variables by state identifiers is called a Σ-*instance* of r.

A Statelog *program* P is a finite set of range restricted[3] rules. P is partitioned as follows: facts and rules where only state terms $[0]+$ occur, define the initial state of the database and make up the EDB and IDB. Since we allow to omit $[0]+$, EDB and IDB constitute a Datalog program.

Ground facts, where the predicate symbols are events ∇E build the *event base* EB, all other rules describe database transitions and belong to the *transition base* TB. □

4.2 Semantics

Statelog models the evolution of a database as a sequence of states. Therefore rules have to be interpreted *progressively*, i.e. it is not possible to change past states or make assumptions about future states.

---
[3] Every data variable occurring in a rule occurs in at least one positive literal in the body.

In the frame axiom (1), $True(S+1)$ depends on $Del(S+1)$. This induces a natural order $Del(0), True(0), \ldots Del(n), True(n), \ldots$ on the sets $True(s)$ and $Del(s)$. Formally, we define an order on the set of Σ-ground state terms by a mapping $ord : \tau \mapsto |\tau|$ into the set of natural numbers

$$|\tau| = \begin{cases} 2s & \text{if } \tau = [s]-,\ s \in \Sigma \\ 2s+1 & \text{if } \tau = [s]+,\ s \in \Sigma \end{cases} \qquad (2)$$

Given this ordering the meaning of a Statelog rule is defined as its *progressive extension*:

Definition 4.4 (Extensions) A Σ-ground rule $\tau_0 H \leftarrow \tau_1 B_1, \ldots, \tau_n B_n$ is called *progressive* if $|\tau_0| \geq |\tau_i|$ for $i = 1, \ldots, n$; *strictly progressive* if $|\tau_0| > |\tau_i|$.

The *extension* $[\![r]\!]$ of a rule r is the set of all *progressive* Σ-instances which can be constructed from r. We say that r is *progressive* if $[\![r]\!] \neq \emptyset$, *strictly progressive* if additionally all rules in $[\![r]\!]$ are strictly progressive.

r is called *local* if for every rule $r^* \in [\![r]\!]$, all τ_i are equal, i.e. r^* only refers to one state. The extension $[\![P]\!]$ of a Statelog program P is the union of all extensions of rules of P. □

Example 4.5 Due to the progressive reading of rules, the meaning of the progressive but not strictly progressive rule $[S]$ p $\leftarrow [T]$-q is *"for all $S \geq T$: if q was deleted in T then p is true (inserted) in S"*.
The rules $[S]$ p $\leftarrow [S+1]$ q and $[S]$-p $\leftarrow [S]$ q are not progressive. The frame rule (2.1) and $[S]$ p $\leftarrow [S]$-q are strictly progressive rules, (3.7) is a local rule.

The semantics of a Statelog program P is defined using Herbrand structures. The Herbrand universe $\mathcal{U}_P$ is the set of all ground data terms which can be constructed from P, the Herbrand base $\mathcal{B}_P$ is the set of all ground atoms $p(t_1, \ldots, t_k)$ where $t_i \in \mathcal{U}_P$ and p is a predicate symbol occurring in P. In the sequel, we assume that $\mathcal{B}_P$ is finite, i.e. P contains no function symbols (apart from state terms).[4]

Definition 4.6 (Σ-Interpretation) A Σ-*interpretation* I^Σ is a mapping from Σ to $2^{\mathcal{B}_P} \times 2^{\mathcal{B}_P}$, i.e. to each state identifier $s \in \Sigma$ two Herbrand interpretations $Del(s), True(s) \subseteq \mathcal{B}_P$ are assigned $I^\Sigma : s \mapsto (Del(s), True(s))$, which hold the to be deleted respectively true atoms of state s.

$I^s = (Del(s), True(s))$ is called the *snapshot* of I^Σ at s. A (possibly infinite) sequence of successive snapshots $I^s, I^{s+1}, \ldots, I^{s+w-1}$ where $w \in \mathcal{N} \cup \{\infty\}$ is called a *window* of I^Σ. It is denoted $I^{\langle s,w \rangle}$, where s is the *start* and w the *width* of $I^{\langle s,w \rangle}$. □

Definition 4.7 (Models) Given a Σ-interpretation I^Σ, $s \in \Sigma$ and $R \in \mathcal{B}_P$ we define $I^\Sigma \models [s]-R$ iff $R \in Del(s)$ and $I^\Sigma \models [s]+R$ iff $R \in True(s)$,
For a Σ-ground rule $r^* : \tau_0 H \leftarrow \tau_1 B_1, \ldots, \tau_n B_n$ we define $I^\Sigma \models r^*$ iff $I^\Sigma \models \tau_i B_i$ for $i = 1, \ldots, n$ implies $I^\Sigma \models \tau_0 H$.

---
[4] We may relax this restriction and admit programs with the *bounded term size property* [21]. Then for every query Q with maximal term size k, it is sufficient to consider derivations where the size of terms is bound by a function of k. Consequently, if we include Q in the program P, a finite subset of the Herbrand universe is sufficient to answer Q. Since it is in general undecidable whether a given program has the bounded term size property one has to define some decidable criterion which approximates it [21].

$I^\Sigma \models r$ for a Statelog rule r iff $I^\Sigma \models r^\star$ for all $r^\star \in [\![r]\!]$. Finally, I^Σ is a *model* of a program P iff $I^\Sigma \models r$ for all $r \in P$. □

Statelog programs can be regarded as a syntactic variant of a class of logic programs augmented by the concepts which are required in our framework for database updates, viz the *progressive reading of rules*, *bipartite states* and rules with *events acting as guards*. By mapping Statelog to "ordinary" logic programs it is possible to apply well-known declarative semantics and evaluation techniques to Statelog.

Definition 4.8 (State Reification $P^\star$) The *state reification* of a Statelog program P is the set of rules $P^\star = \{r^\star \mid r \in [\![P]\!]\}$, where $r^\star$ is the result of substituting atoms $[s] \pm p(t_1, \ldots, t_k)$ in r by $p_\pm(s, t_1, \ldots, t_k)$. □

Note that the language $\mathcal{L}_{P^\star}$ of the reified program contains two relations p_+ and p_- denoting the true, respectively to be deleted tuples instead of the relation p of the original Statelog program.

The Herbrand universe $\mathcal{U}_{P^\star}$ of the reified program $P^\star$ consists of $\mathcal{U}_P \cup \Sigma$. Since we are only interested in certain Herbrand interpretations, we define as the Herbrand base of the reified program the set of all ground atoms $p_\pm(s, t_1, \ldots, t_k)$ for every $(k+1)$-ary $p_\pm$ of $P^\star$, $s \in \Sigma$, $t_i \in \mathcal{U}_P$. The following is a straightforward consequence of the previous definitions and links P and $P^\star$:

Proposition 4.9 *Every model M^Σ of P defines a Herbrand model $M^\star$ of $P^\star$ and vice versa by defining for all $s \in \Sigma$, $p(t_1, \ldots, t_k) \in \mathcal{B}_P$:*

$$p_-(s, t_1, \ldots, t_k) \in M^\star \quad \textit{iff} \quad p(t_1, \ldots, t_k) \in Del(s) \textit{ and}$$
$$p_+(s, t_1, \ldots, t_k) \in M^\star \quad \textit{iff} \quad p(t_1, \ldots, t_k) \in True(s)$$

Due to proposition 4.9 we may use M^Σ and $M^\star$ synonymously in the sequel.

5 Perfect Model Semantics

The perfect model semantics is generally accepted to be the "right" respectively "intended" semantics for the class of locally stratified programs [17]. Since it restricts the use of negation in a certain way (no recursion through negation is allowed), the meaning of a (locally) stratified program can be easily grasped by a programmer. Even more important, it is amenable to efficient implementation provided a stratification can be easily computed.

In the presence of state terms, the usual notion of stratification which only considers predicate symbols is not sufficient and a slightly generalized version called Σ-*stratification* is necessary. To see why, consider rules (3.1) and (3.2) from section 3. The atom $-\text{es}(\text{E},\text{Sal})$ in the head of rule (3.1) depends on the goal $\text{es}(\text{E},\text{Sal})$ which in turn depends negatively on $-\text{es}(\text{E},\text{Sal})$ due to frame rule (3.2). However, looking at the state terms one easily verifies that this negative cycle is not present in the extension of the program; in fact, the reified program is locally stratified.

This leads to the following observation which is crucial for our definition of Σ-stratification: given a Σ-instance of a progressive rule r, the literals in the body of r refer to the same state s as the head of r or to predecessor states of s. As a consequence, cyclic dependencies between atoms can only occur *within*, but never *across* states. Therefore, strictly progressive rules including frame rules need not be considered when computing the dependency graph of a Statelog program.

Definition 5.1 (Σ-Stratification) Let P be a Statelog program, P' the subset of rules of P which are progressive but *not strictly progressive*. The *dependency graph* $\mathcal{D}_P$ is a directed graph whose nodes correspond to the rules of P'. Given two rules $r, r' \in P'$ with disjoint variables

$$r : \quad \tau_0 A_0 \leftarrow \tau_1 B_1, \ldots, \tau_n B_n$$
$$r' : \quad \tau_0' A_0' \leftarrow \tau_1' B_1', \ldots, \tau_m' B_m'$$

there is a *positive arc* from r' to r, denoted $r' \to r$ iff there are Σ-instances $r^* \in [\![r]\!], r'^* \in [\![r']\!]$ of the form

$$r^* : \quad s_0 A_0 \leftarrow s_1 B_1, \ldots, s_i B_i, \ldots s_n B_n$$
$$r'^* : \quad s_o' A_o' \leftarrow s_1' B_1', \ldots, s_m' B_m'$$

such that $s_i = s_0'$ and $B_i \Theta = A_0' \Theta$ for some substitution Θ. There is a *negative* arc $r' \overset{\neg}{\to} r$, if B_i is a negated atom, i.e. of the form $\neg A_i$ and $A_i \Theta = A_0' \Theta$. P is called Σ-*stratified* if $\mathcal{D}_P$ contains no cycles with negative arcs. $\square$

The next theorem implies that every Σ-stratified program P has a unique perfect model $\mathcal{M}$.

Theorem 5.2 *If a Statelog program P is Σ-stratified then the state-reified program $P^\star$ of P is locally stratified.*

Proof We show: if $P^\star$ is not locally stratified then P is not Σ-stratified.

If $P^\star$ is not locally stratified then the dependency graph built from the rules $r^\star$ of $P^\star$ contains a cyclic dependency with a negative arc. Let $r_1^\star \to \ldots \to r_k^\star \to r_1^\star$ be this negative cycle and $r_i^\star \to r_j^\star$ an arbitrary arc thereof. Given $r_i^\star \to r_j^\star$ let s_i^h be the state identifier occurring in the first argument of the head of $r_i^\star$, and let s_j^b be the state identifier of a literal of the body of $r_j^\star$. We have $s_i^h = s_j^b$ and, since all rules in the negative cycle are progressive, the states occurring in it satisfy the following inequalities:

$$s_1^h = s_2^b \leq s_2^h = s_3^b \leq \ldots \leq s_k^h = s_1^b \leq s_1^h$$

Therefore s_1^h occurs in the head of all rules $r_i^\star$. This implies that no rule of the cycle is strictly progressive. Hence, the cycle is also present in the subset P' of rules of P which are not strictly progressive. It follows that P is not Σ-stratified. ∎

If $P^\star$ is locally stratified it has a unique perfect model $\mathcal{M}^\star$ [17] which according to proposition 4.9 corresponds to a model $\mathcal{M}^\Sigma$ (or $\mathcal{M}$ for short) of P. For the rest of the paper we assume that a Σ-stratified Statelog program is given and that $\mathcal{M}$ is its perfect model.

5.1 Termination and Periodicity of $\mathcal{M}$

Although $\mathcal{M}$ consists of infinitely many snapshots it can be finitely represented due to its periodic structure. Note that by assumption (the relevant part of) $\mathcal{B}_P$ is finite. We need a few definitions.

Definition 5.3 A Σ-interpretation M^{Σ} is called *ultimately periodic* if there exist $s_0, T \in \mathcal{N}_0$ such that $M^{s+T} = M^s$ for all $s \geq s_0$. Given the least such s_0 and T, we define as the *final state* of M^{Σ} the last snapshot M^{s_0+T-1} of the periodic window $M^{\langle s_0, T \rangle}$. □

Definition 5.4 A Σ-interpretation M^{Σ} is called *progressively deterministic* if there exist $s_0, w \in \mathcal{N}_0$ such that for all $s \geq s_0$ the snapshot M^s functionally depends on its w predecessor states, i.e. $M^s = f(M^{\langle s-w, w \rangle})$ for all $s \geq s_0$ and some function $f : (2^{\mathcal{B}_P})^w \to 2^{\mathcal{B}_P}$. □

The following proposition is a direct consequence of the previous definitions.

Proposition 5.5 *Every progressively deterministic Σ-interpretation M^{Σ} is ultimately periodic.*

Obviously, an ultimately periodic model is characterized by an initial window $M^{\langle 0, s_0 \rangle}$ and a periodic window $M^{\langle s_0, T \rangle}$ and thus can be finitely represented. In the presence of negation, such a periodicity cannot be guaranteed for all common semantics: e.g. the program with the two rules $[S]$ p $\leftarrow [S]$ ¬ q and $[S]$ q $\leftarrow [S]$ ¬ p has two different stable snapshots {p} and {q} for *every* state $s \in \Sigma$. Consequently, not all stable models of P are periodic. However, for the perfect model $\mathcal{M}$ we have the following result.[5]

Theorem 5.6 *The perfect model of a Σ-stratified Statelog program is ultimately periodic.*

Proof *(sketch)* We show that $\mathcal{M}$ is progressively deterministic. Clearly, Σ-instances of rules with at most one state variable only refer to a fixed number of states. Since only progressive rule extensions are considered, the state s in the head of the rule is defined using predecessors of s and s itself. It can be shown that literals with state variables different from the one in the head can be eliminated [14]. Since every true atom in $\mathcal{M}^s$ is supported by a rule, the perfect model semantics defines a unique snapshot $\mathcal{M}^s$ given the input of w predecessors $\mathcal{M}^{\langle s-w, w \rangle}$. ∎

Given a progressive rule $[S + k_0] \pm H \leftarrow [S + k_1] \pm B_1, \ldots, [S + k_n] \pm B_n$ the *range* $w = \max_{0 \leq i \leq n}(k_0 - k_i)$ is the number of predecessor states on which the derivation of H depends. If the rule contains several state variables the derivation of H also depends on such a fixed range w (for sufficiently large states). In the above proof, w is the maximal range of rules of the program P.

---

[5] A similar result has been established in [7]. A difference is, that we need not consider strictly progressive rules when computing the dependency graph, which generalizes the usual notion of stratification. This is due to the progressive reading of rules, which in addition allows a simpler proof.

5.2 Computing the Perfect Model

The actual computation of $\mathcal{M}$ can be accomplished along the lines of the well-known *iterated fixpoint computation* [3].

First, the dependency graph $\mathcal{D}_P$ of rules P' which are progressive but not strictly progressive is computed using a straightforward modification of unification (essentially, one has to take into account state terms and the progressive reading of rules). Next, the strongly connected components (SCCs) are determined. If a SCC contains a negative arc, P is not Σ-stratified. Otherwise, a topological sort of the SCCs yields a partition of P', the stratification $L_1, \ldots, L_k$.

After these preprocessing steps, the computation of $\mathcal{M}$ proceeds by successively computing the snapshots $\mathcal{M}^0, \mathcal{M}^1, \ldots$ until the period is detected: given the range w of P, one has to check for the earliest repetition of a window $\mathcal{M}^{\langle s,w \rangle}$ during the computation of $\mathcal{M}$.

For a given state s, the computation of the snapshot $\mathcal{M}^s = (Del(s), True(s))$ is accomplished as follows: the $Del(s)$ part is computed before $True(s)$ since it is smaller according to the order on state terms (cf. (2) in section 4.2). In a first step the strictly progressive rules which define $Del(s)$ are iterated until a fixpoint is reached (note that each snapshot is finite). These rules correspond to the lowest stratum L_0 w.r.t. the current state s, since they solely depend on already computed predecessor states of s. The next step consists in iterating the remaining (not strictly progressive) rules which define $Del(s)$ according to the stratification $L_1, \ldots, L_k$, until the $Del(s)$ part of the snapshot is computed. $True(s)$ is computed in the same way, i.e. first the strictly progressive rules (including frame rules), then the remaining rules according to the given stratification are iterated.

5.2.1 State Transitions between Final States

We now turn to the question how the transition from the current to a new final state is modelled in our framework. It turns out that we can view the database evolution as an incremental computation of $\mathcal{M}$.

Given a Statelog program P we assume that the EDB, IDB and the update procedures in TB are fixed while the event base EB is successively enlarged by the occurrence of events. In other words, we conceive the event base as a parameter of the perfect model. In order to emphasize this, we write $\mathcal{M}(EB)$ for the perfect model of P.

Assume that at a certain time instant the event base is EB_{t_i}. Since $\mathcal{M}(EB_{t_i})$ is ultimately periodic, a unique final state s_f is defined by EB_{t_i}. We require that when new events occur, these occurrences are assigned to the final state s_f or some $s > s_f$, thereby extending EB_{t_i} to $EB_{t_{i+1}}$. It is easy to see that $\mathcal{M}(EB_{t_{i+1}})$ and therefore a new final state can be computed as an *extension* of $\mathcal{M}(EB_{t_i})$: in order to compute $\mathcal{M}(EB_{t_{i+1}})$, it is sufficient to remember a window of w predecessor states of the final state s_f. Earlier states have no influence on $\mathcal{M}(EB_{t_{i+1}})$ because (i) events may not occur in the past (i.e. for some $s < s_f$) and (ii) rules only effect the present and future states due to their progressive reading.

5.2.2 Guarded Programs

As already mentioned, the computation of a snapshot $\mathcal{M}^s$ depends on a fixed window of w predecessors of s. While for a given transition base, w is a constant,[6] the length T of the periodic window may be exponential in the size of the EDB (this can be seen using a program from [8] whose semantics coincides with our semantics $\mathcal{M}$, cf. [14]). Thus detecting the period may require storing exponentially many snapshots of $\mathcal{M}$. Clearly, it is desirable to identify program classes which allow to detect and store the periodic window efficiently. An example for such a class are the *guarded programs* defined below. The main idea is that rules which define a new state are guarded by some event in the body and that events are not defined by rules. While such user-definable events allow event-based programming similar to [23], they make detection of the period difficult. Although guarded programs are less expressive than general Statelog programs, many practical update procedures including the examples from section 3 can be expressed with guarded rules.

Definition 5.7 (Guarded Rules) A non-local Statelog rule r with head $[S+k]\pm H$ is *guarded* if there is a *positive* occurrence of some event $[S+k']\nabla E$ in the body of r for some $k' \leq k$. $[S+k']\nabla E$ is called a *guard* for r.

A Statelog program is called guarded if all of its non-local rules, apart from frame rules, are guarded. □

Although local rules and frame rules are not guarded, they have no influence on the period if all other rules are guarded:

Theorem 5.8 *The perfect model of a guarded Σ-stratified program P is ultimately periodic with period $T = 1$.*

Proof *(sketch)* It is easy to see that the perfect model has a period of one, if only local rules are considered. By adding frame rules the period of one is retained [14]. Intuitively, this is due to the fact that frame rules copy only already derived information from state s to $s+1$. Since the event base is always finite, all but finitely many Σ-instances of guarded rules are blocked. Therefore, for all sufficiently large s the snapshot $\mathcal{M}^s$ of the perfect model of P only depends on local and frame rules. ■

6 Conclusion and Outlook

We have presented Statelog, an extension of Datalog which allows to specify deterministic procedures for EDB and IDB updates, as well as static and dynamic integrity constraints. By incorporating state identifiers into the language, declarative, model-based semantics such as the well-founded or stable semantics can be applied to it. In this paper, we have concentrated on the perfect model semantics for Σ-stratified programs. The periodic structure of the perfect model is used to define the final database state and termination of the update program. We have introduced the class of guarded programs which allow efficient computation of the final state.

---

[6]Typically, rules refer only to few predecessor states, e.g. in section 3 the maximal range w of rules is 2.

In [23] an approach to unify deductive and active databases is presented. The way updates are treated is similar to our approach. Update requests to EDB relations are stored in a so-called *event-queue* and processed successively. In addition to events which allow the insertion and deletion of facts, the user may define new event types. While this results in great flexibility, guaranteeing program termination seems to be more difficult than in Statelog and may lie in the responsibility of the programmer.

From a logic point of view, Statelog is closely related to the temporal deductive database language $Datalog_{1S}$ [9]. In [7] it is shown that the perfect model of a stratified $Datalog_{1S}$ program is ultimately periodic. However, [9] do not deal with database updates but use $Datalog_{1S}$ for temporal reasoning. The main difference between Statelog and $Datalog_{1S}$ is that Statelog interprets rules by their progressive extension. This seems to be a natural prerequisite in our context and allows to model database evolution as an incremental computation of the perfect model semantics.

The Datalog extensions proposed in [2] have a procedural semantics which is defined by a bottom-up evaluation and which does not coincide with model-based semantics known from the area of logic programming. [15, 16] use dynamic logic to define semantics of updates but also rely on a certain evaluation strategy (top-down). [4] propose *Transaction Logic*, a very general and powerful *framework* for numerous phenomenons of state change including database updates and planning and consequently leave the standard framework of logic programming. In contrast, we have presented a "minimal" extension of Datalog which is sufficient to specify updates in much the same way as queries.

Future work will focus on alternative ways for the treatment of IDB updates, e.g. by integrating intensional updates [5]. Another important issue is the identification of tractable program classes like the class of guarded programs, for which the overhead of update evaluation is small.

Statelog may be implemented on top of existing deductive systems like XSB-Prolog [19] or Coral [18]. Alternatively, the techniques from the database programming language Heraclitus[Alg,C] [11] which supports *deltas* as first class citizens, multiple virtual states, active rules and a wide variety of semantics, may be useful for an efficient implementation of state transitions.

Acknowledgments We wish to thank Jürgen Frohn, Paul Th. Kandzia, Heinz Uphoff and Klaus Ries for fruitful discussions and comments.

References

[1] S. Abiteboul. Updates, a new frontier. In *ICDT'88 (Second Intl. Conf. on Data Base Theory), Bruges, LNCS 326*, pages 1–18. Springer–Verlag, 1988.

[2] S. Abiteboul and V. Vianu. Datalog extensions for database queries and updates. *Journal of Computer and System Sciences*, 43, 1991.

[3] K. Apt, H. Blair, and A. Walker. Towards a theory of declarative knowledge. In J. Minker, editor, *Foundations of Deductive Databases and Logic Programming*, pages 89 – 148. Morgan Kaufmann, 1988.

[4] A. J. Bonner and M. Kifer. Transaction logic programming. Technical Report CSRI-270, Computer Systems Research Institute, University of Toronto, 1993.

[5] F. Bry. Intensional updates : Abduction via deduction. In *Proc. of the Intl. Conference on Logic Programming*, 1990.

[6] F. Bry. Towards intelligent databases. In *Proc. of the Intl. Symposium on Methodologies for Intelligent Systems*, LNCS. Springer, 1993.

[7] J. Chomicki. *Functional Deductive Databases: Query Processing in the Presence of Limited Function Symbols*. PhD thesis, Rutgers University, 1990.

[8] J. Chomicki and T. Imieliński. Temporal deductive databases and infinite objects. In *Proc. of the ACM SIGACT-SIGMOD-SIGART Symposium on Principles of Database Systems*, 1988.

[9] J. Chomicki and T. Imieliński. Finite representation of infinite query answers. *ACM Transactions on Database Systems*, June 1993.

[10] M. Gelfond and V. Lifschitz. The stable model semantics for logic programming. In R. Kowalski and K. Bowen, editors, *Proc. of the Intl. Conference on Logic Programming*, pages 1070–1080, 1988.

[11] S. Ghandeharizadeh, R. Hull, D. Jacobs, J. Castillo, M. Escobar-Molano, S.-H. Lu, J. Luo, C. Tsang, and G. Zhou. On implementing a language for specifying active database execution models. In *Proc. of the Intl. Conference on Very Large Data Bases*, 1993.

[12] M. Kramer, G. Lausen, and G. Saake. Updates in a rule-based language for objects. In *Proc. of the Intl. Conference on Very Large Data Bases*, 1992.

[13] D. Laurent, V. Phan Luong, and N. Spyratos. Updating intensional predicates in deductive databases. In *Proc. of the IEEE Intl. Conference on Data Engineering*, 1993.

[14] G. Lausen and B. Ludäscher. Updates by reasoning about states. Technical Report 59, Universität Freiburg, Institut für Informatik, Sept. 1994.

[15] S. Manchanda and D. S. Warren. A logic-based language for database updates. In J. Minker, editor, *Foundations of Deductive Databases and Logic Programming*, pages 363–394. Morgan-Kaufmann, Los Altos, CA, 1988.

[16] S. Naqvi and R. Krishnamurthy. Database updates in logic programming. In *Proc. of the ACM SIGACT-SIGMOD-SIGART Symposium on Principles of Database Systems*, pages 251–262, 1988.

[17] T. C. Przymusinski. On the declarative semantics of deductive databases and logic programs. In J. Minker, editor, *Foundations of Deductive Databases and Logic Programming*, pages 191 – 216. Morgan Kaufmann, 1988.

[18] R. Ramakrishnan, D. Srivastava, S. Sudarshan, and P. Seshadri. Implementation of the coral deductive database system. In *Proc. of the ACM SIGMOD Conference on Management of Data*, 1993.

[19] K. Sagonas, T. Swift, and D. S. Warren. XSB as an efficient deductive database engine. In *Proc. of the ACM SIGMOD Conference on Management of Data*, 1994.

[20] J. D. Ullman. *Principles of Database and Knowledge-Base Systems, Volume I*. Computer Science Press, New York, 1988.

[21] A. Van Gelder. Negation as failure using tight derivations for general logic programs. In J. Minker, editor, *Foundations of Deductive Databases and Logic Programming*, pages 149–176. Morgan Kaufmann, 1988.

[22] A. Van Gelder, K. Ross, and J. Schlipf. The well-founded sematics for general logic programs. *JACM*, 38(3):620 – 650, 7 1991.

[23] C. Zaniolo. A unified semantics for active and deductive databases. In *Proceedings of the Workshop on Rules in Database Systems*, Workshops in Computing, Edinburgh, U.K., 1993. Springer.

Theoretical Issues

On the Theory of Relational Data Bases with Incomplete Information

M.Sh.Tsalenko*
Russian State University for Humanities,
Moscow, Russia

Abstract

In many applications the information stored in relational databases is incomplete. Database designers and users quite often face difficulties due to the inadequate consideration of incomplete information. In this paper we present a theory for the treatment of incomplete information in relational databases using L-relations and algebras of L-relations. We show that the main results of the theory of relational databases like the theory of functional and mulivalued dependencies remain valid for L-relations. Furthermore, it is shown that in order to solve the decomposition problem for L-relations we have to investigate systems of equations with coefficients in L which express specific properties of L-relations.

1 Introduction

Any relation R between sets $M_1, M_2, \ldots, M_n$ is by definition a subset of the cartesian product $M_1 \times .M_2 \times \ldots \times .M_n$. There are at least two other points of view on relations. The relation R can be considered as a set of functions $f : \{1, 2, \ldots, n\} \to \cup_{i=1}^n M_i$ such that $f(i) \in M_i$ for all $i = 1, 2, \ldots, n$. A generalization of this point of view leads us to an algebra of files (see,e.g.,[8]).

Instead of the relation R we can consider a $n-$ary predicate

$$P_R : M_1 \times M_2 \times \ldots \times M_n \to B_2 = \{0, 1\}.$$

Again a generalization of this point of view enables us to replace the Boolean algebra B_2 by any complete Heyting algebra, or cH-algebra (necessary definitions are given in the section 2). We can't replace B_2 by arbitrary lattice L because the well-known multiplication of binary L-relations is associative iff L is a cH-algebra [7].

However we can replace B_2 by any distributive lattice L with 0 and 1 if L-relations have finite carriers (see section 2). It is worth to mention two well-known examples of L-relations. In [2] N.Belnap suggested that computers have to deal with B_4-relations where B_4 is the four-elements Boolean algebra. In the case of $L = [0, 1]$ we obtain fuzzy relations due to L.Zadeh [10].

---

[0]The research was supported by the Russian Basic Research Foundation, grant number 94-01-01479-a

E.F.Codd [4] suggested consider instead of B_2 three-element chain $0 < \omega < 1$ which is the simplest non-boolean distributive lattice. Of course all finite distributive lattice are cH-algebras. However E.Codd extended all domains adding the null value ω instead of considering L-relations.

An algebra of L-relations was described in many publications; some references can be found in [8]. The main purpose of this paper is to extend some essential results concerning relational algebras and relational data bases to algebras of L-relations and L-relational data bases.

The paper is organised as follows. In section 2 we remind necessary definitions and constructions. Then the extended version of some results obtained by T.Imieliaski and W.Lipski [5] are stated. We describe more precisely connections between algebras of L-relations and generalized cylindric algebras.

In section 3 and 4 we show that the theory of functional and multivalued dependencies remains valid for L-relations.

In section 4 we describe briefly tableau for L-relations following [2].

2 Algebras of L-relations

Let
$$T \subseteq N \times V \tag{1}$$

be any binary relation between an infinite countable set N of "names" and an arbitrary set V of "values". As usual $im_T A$ where $A \in N$ denotes the set

$$im_T A = \{v | (A, v) \in T\}. \tag{2}$$

Two names A and A' are called *equivalent* if $im_T A = im_T A'$. Instead of $im_T A$ we shall use an usual notation $Dom A$, i.e. $Dom A = im_T A$. In subsequent we assume that $N \cap V = \emptyset$ and that any equivalence class in N is infinite countable.

Definition 2.1. A lattice L is called a *complete Heyting algebra*, or cH-algebra, if L is a complete lattice and in L the following distributive law

$$\omega \bigcap (\bigcup_{i \in I} \omega_i) = \bigcup_{i \in I} (\omega \bigcap \omega_i) \tag{3}$$

holds for every set I of indices and for all elements $\omega, \omega_i \in L$.

Remind that in every complete lattice L there exist the least element 0 and the greatest element 1.

Every finite distributive lattice, in particular every finite Boolean algebra, is a cH-algebra.

Every linear ordered set in which there are sup and min for all familiex of elements is a cH-algebra. In this case sup and min coincide with joins and meets respectively. In particular the closed interval $[0, 1]$ is a cH-algebra. Codd's three element chain $0 < \omega < 1$ [4] is the simplest non-trivial example of a cH-algebra. In general every finite chain is a cH-algebra but not Boolean one.

For every set X the set of all mappings $f : X \to L$ from X into any cH-algebra L is again a cH-algebra $Map(X, L)$. The operations of this algebra are defined as follows. If $f_i : X \to L$, $i \in I$, then for all $x \in X$

$$(\bigcup_{i \in I} f_i)(x) = \bigcup_{i \in I} f_i(x); \tag{4}$$

$$(\bigcap_{i \in I} f_i)(x) = \bigcap_{i \in I} f_i(x). \tag{5}$$

In particular if $X = M_1 \times M_2 \times \ldots \times M_n$ mappings $f : M_1 \times M_2 \times \ldots \times M_n \to L$ are called $L-relations$ between $M_1, M_2, \ldots, M_n$.

Let us return to the binary relation $T \subseteq N \times V$ (see(1)). Let $U = \{A_1, A_2, \ldots, A_n\} \subset N$. Denote by $\Pi(U)$ the cartesian product $DomA_1 \times DomA_2 \times \ldots \times DomA_n$:

$$\Pi(U) = DomA_1 \times DomA_2 \times \ldots \times DomA_n.$$

By $Rel_L(U)$ we denote a set of L-relations

$$R : \Pi(U) \to L$$

with finite carrier $suppR$. Here $suppR$ denotes the set

$$suppR = \{r \in \Pi(U) | R(r) \neq 0\}.$$

As usual each L-relation R with finite carrier can be represented as a table with $(n + 1)$ columns:

R	A_1	A_2	...	A_n	L
	a_{11}	a_{12}	...	a_{1n}	ω_1
	a_{21}	a_{22}	...	a_{2n}	ω_2
	...	...	...	...	...
	a_{m1}	a_{m2}	...	a_{mn}	ω_m

where $R(a_{i1}, a_{i2}, \ldots, a_{in}) = \omega_i \neq 0$, i.e. $(a_{i1}, a_{i2}, \ldots, a_{in}) \in suppR$.

Every set $Rel_L(U)$ is a distributive lattice under operations (4) and (5). A *natural join* of two $L-$relations $R_1 \in Rel_L(U_1)$ and $R_2 \in Rel_L(U_2)$ is defined as follows: if $U = U_1 \cup U_2$ and $r \in \Pi(U)$ then

$$(R_1 \circ R_2)(r) = R_1(r[U_1]) \bigcap R_2(r[U_2]) \tag{6}$$

A *projection* $R[V]$ of the L-relation $R \in Rel_L(U)$ on a subset $V \subseteq U$ is defined as follows: if $r \in \Pi(V)$ then

$$R[V](r) = \bigcup_{r_i \in \Pi(U), r_i[V] = r} R(r_i) \tag{7}$$

Notice that the right side of (7) contains finite number of operands which depends on a tuple r if $suppR$ is finite.

Definition 2.2. A lattice L with 0 is called a *cylindric algebra of the dimension n without diagonals* or *dfc*-algebra if the unary operations $c_i : L \to L$, $i = 1, 2, \ldots, n$, are given in L in such a way that the following axioms are satisfied:

$CA1.$ $\quad 0c_i = 0$, $i = 1, 2, \ldots, n$.
$CA2.$ $\quad \forall x \in L \ (x \cap xc_i) = x$, $i = 1, 2, \ldots, n$.
$CA3.$ $\quad \forall x, y \in L \ (x \cap yc_i)c_i = xc_i \cap yc_i$, $i = 1, 2, \ldots, n$.
$CA4.$ $\quad \forall x \in L \ (xc_i)c_j = (xc_j)c_i$

The operations c_j are called *cylindrifications*. An usual definition of a cylindric algebra requires that L is a Boolean algebra. We omit this requirement.

Let $U = \{A_1, A_2, \ldots, A_n\} \subset N$ be any finite set. Denote by $\overline{Rel_L(U)}$ a set of all functions

$$R : \Pi(U) = DomA_1 \times DomA_2 \times \ldots \times DomA_n \to L.$$

Hence $Rel_L(U) \subseteq \overline{Rel_L(U)}$. As we know the algebre $\overline{Rel_L(U)}$ is a cH-algebra. In addition formulas (6) and (7) define natural joins and projections for algebras $\overline{Rel_L(U)}$ as well.

Now we define cylindrifications $c_i : \overline{Rel_L(U)} \to \overline{Rel_L(U)}$, $i = 1, 2, \ldots, n$: for each $R \in \overline{Rel_L(U)}$ and each $r \in \Pi(U)$

$$(Rc_i)(r) = R[U \setminus A_i](r[U \setminus A_i]). \tag{8}$$

This definition means that

$$(Rc_i)(r) = \bigcup_{x \in DomA_i} R(a_1, \ldots, a_{i-1}, x, a_{i+1}, \ldots, a_n),$$

where $r = (a_1, \ldots, a_{i-1}, a_i, a_{i+1}, \ldots, a_n)$.

Theorem 2.1. *For any finite subset $U \subset N$ with n elements the cH-algebra $\overline{Rel_L(U)}$ is a dfc-algebra of dimension n.*

Let $X \subseteq U$ be any subset of U, Define a mapping $h : \overline{Rel_L(X)} \to \overline{Rel_L(U)}$ as follows:

$$(h(R))(r) = R(r[X]) \tag{9}$$

for all $r \in \Pi(U)$.

For every subset $X = \{A_{i_1}, A_{i_2}, \ldots, A_{i_k}\} \subseteq U$ and for every L-relation $R \in \overline{Rel_L(U)}$ define

$$Rc_X = Rc_{i_1}c_{i_2}\ldots c_{i_k}. \tag{10}$$

Theorem 2.2. *Let X, X_1, Y be three subsets of U and $Y \subseteq X$. Then the following statements are valid:*
1. For any $R \in Rel_L(X)$

$$h(R[Y]) = h(R)c_{U \setminus Y}.$$

2. For two L-relations $R_1, R_2 \in Rel_L(X)$

$$h(R_1 \bigcup R_2) = h(R_1) \bigcup h(R_2),$$

$$h(R_1 \bigcap R_2) = h(R_1) \bigcap h(R_2).$$

3. For L-relations $R_1 \in Rel_L(X)$, $R_2 \in Rel_L(X_1)$

$$h(R_1 \circ R_2) = h(R_1) \bigcap h(R_2).$$

Denote by $E(X)$ the greatest element of $\overline{Rel_L(X)}$, i.e.

$$E(X)(r) = 1$$

for all $r \in \Pi(X)$.

Theorem 2.3. Let $X_1, X_2 \subseteq U$ be two subsets of U and $R_1 \in Rel_L(X_1), R_2 \in Rel_L(X_2)$. The equality $h(R_1) = h(R_2)$ holds iff $R_1 = R_2$ or $R_1[X] = R_2[X]$, $R_1 = R_1[X] \circ E(X_1 \backslash X)$, $R_2 = R_2[X] \circ E(X_2 \backslash X)$, where $X = X_1 \cap X_2$.

Theorems 2.1, 2.2, 2.3. were obtained in collaboration with my graduate student M.A. Babushkin. All proofs were included in his thesis [1].

3 Functional dependencies

In order to clarify a subsequent definition of functional dependencies for L-relations we begin with some remarks concerning ordinary binary relations. Let $R \subseteq A \times B$ be a binary relation between two sets A and B. By $R^\# \subseteq B \times A$ we denote an *involution* (or *inversim*) of R:

$$R^\# = \{(b, a) \mid (a, b) \in R\} \qquad (11)$$

By $\triangle_A (\triangle_B$ respectively) we denote a diagonal of $A \times A$ ($B \times B$ respectively):

$$\triangle_A = \{(a, a) | a \in A\}. \qquad (12)$$

A relation R is called *functional* iff

$$R^\# \bullet R \subseteq \triangle_B. \qquad (13)$$

The sign $\bullet$ denotes the well-known multiplication of binary relations. The last inclusion expresses in pure algebraic terms the assertion that for every $a \in A$ there exists at most one element $b \in B$ such that $(a, b) \in R$.

Consider now L-relation $R : A \times B \to L$. In this case $R^\# : B \times A \to L$ can be defined as follows:

$$R^\#(b, a) = R(a, b). \qquad (14)$$

It is easy to check that for L-relation R the inclusion (13) can be equivalententry rewritten as a set of equlities

$$R(a, b_1) \cap R(a, b_2) = 0 \qquad (15)$$

where $a \in A, b_1, b_2 \in B$ and $b_1 \neq b_2$.

Example 3.1. Let $A = B = B_4$ where the Boolean algebra B_4 is shown below:

$$B_4: \quad \begin{array}{c} 1 \\ \diagup \quad \diagdown \\ \omega_1 \qquad \omega_2 \\ \diagdown \quad \diagup \\ 0 \end{array}$$

A table

R	A	B	B_4
	ω_1	ω_1	ω_1
	ω_1	ω_2	ω_2
	ω_2	ω_1	ω_1
	ω_2	ω_2	ω_2

represents a functional relation $R : A \times B \to B_4$ because equalities (15) are satisfied.

Return now to a L-relations R on scheme $U = \{A_1, A_2, \ldots, A_n\}$. We will say that A_i *functionally determines* A_j in R (or A_j *functionally depends* on A_i in R) if the projection $R[A_i, A_j]$ is a functional L-relation. Extending this definition we introduce a general notion of functional dependency $X \to Y$ in R for arbitrary subsets $X, Y \subseteq U$.

Definition 3.1. Let X, Y be two subset of $U = \{A_1, \ldots, A_n\} \subset N$ and let $R \in \overline{Rel_L(U)}$. The functional dependency $X \to Y$ holds in R if the projection $R[X \cup Y]$ is a functional binary relation between $\Pi(X)$ and $\Pi((X \cup Y) \setminus X)$.

Let $R \in \overline{Rel_L(U)}$ and $r \in \Pi(U)$. We'll write $r = (x, y, z)$ if $x = r[X]$, $y = r[Y]$, $z = r[Z]$ and $X \cup Y \cup Z = U$. We shall not assume that subsets X, Y, Z are pairwise disjoint.

Proposition 3.1. *The functional dependency $X \to Y$ holds in L-relation $R \in \overline{Rel_L(U)}$ iff the equality*

$$R(x, y, z) \cap R(x, y_1, z_1) = 0 \tag{16}$$

holds for every pair of tuples $r_1 = (x, y, z)$, $r_2 = (x, y_1, z_1) \in \Pi(U)$ *such that* $y \neq y_1$.

Denote by $FD(R)$ the set of all functional dependencies in L-relation $R \in \overline{Rel_L(U)}$.

Proposition 3.2. *Let $R \in \overline{Rel_L(U)}$. The set $FD(R)$ satisfies following two axioms:*

F1. If $X, Y \subseteq U$ and $X \supseteq Y$ then $X \to Y$.
F2. If $X \to Y$ and $(Y \cup Z) \to V$ then $(X \cup Z) \to V$.

Theorem 3.3. *The set of axioms F1 and F2 is sound and complete for functional dependencies in L-relations.*

Soundness follows immediately from the proposition 3.2 and completeness follows from Armstrong's theorem because for every lattice L we can consider an usual n-ary relation $R \subseteq \Pi(U)$ as a function from $\Pi(U)$ to L which takes value 1 for tuples r belonging R and takes value 0 for the remaining tuples.

Suppose now that the cH-algebra (or distributive lattice) L has the following property: if $\omega_1 \neq 0$ and $\omega_2 \neq 0$ then $\omega_1 \cap \omega_2 \neq 0$. In other words

$$\omega_1 \cap \omega_2 = 0 \; iff \; \omega_1 = 0 \; or \; \omega_2 = 0. \tag{17}$$

It is obvious that every chain satisfies this condition. However there exist distributive lattices that are not chains but have the indicated property.

Example 3.2. The lattice

$$L: \quad \begin{array}{c} 1 \\ / \; \backslash \\ a \quad b \\ \backslash \; / \\ c \\ | \\ 0 \end{array}$$

is distributive and satisfies the condition (17).

Proposition 3.4. *If the cH-algebra L satisfies (17) then the functional dependency $X \to Y$ holds in L-relation $R \in Rel_L(U)$ iff it holds in suppR.*

Proposition 3.4 follows immediately from (15) and (17). It shows that for lattices that satisfy (17) we don't get non-standard functional dependencies.

Now suppose that the lattice L doesn't satisfy the condition (17). It means that in L there are at least two elements ω_1 and ω_2 such that $\omega_1 \neq 0$, $\omega_2 \neq 0$ but $\omega_1 \cap \omega_2 = 0$. In this case we can construct very simple L-relations with non-standard functional dependencies.

Example 3.3. Assume that $\omega_1 \cap \omega_2 = 0$ and $\omega_1 \neq 0$, $\omega_2 \neq 0$ in lattice L. Then L-relation R shown below satisfies the functional dependency $X \to Y$:

R	X	Y	L
	x	y_1	ω_1
	x	y_2	ω_2.

Notice that $X \to Y$ doesn't hold in supp R.

Let us interpret DomX as a set of objects and DomY as a set of their properties. Furthermore we interpret meets in L as conjuctions. Under this interpretation the functional dependency $X \to Y$ states that every object x can't possess different properties simultaniously.

4 Multivalued dependencies

Definition 4.1. Let $R \in \overline{Rel_L(U)}$ be any L-relation and $X, Y \subseteq U$. A multivalued dependency $X \twoheadrightarrow Y$ holds in R if

$$R = R[X \bigcup Y] \circ R[X \cup Z], \tag{18}$$

where $Z = U \backslash (X \cup Y)$.

Proposition 4.1. *MV-dependency $X \twoheadrightarrow Y$ holds in R iff*

$$R(x,y,z_1) \bigcap R(x,y_1,z) \leq R(x,y,z) \tag{19}$$

for all tuples $r_1 = (x,y,z_1)$, $r_2 = (x,y_1,z)$, $r = (x,y,z) \in \Pi(U)$

Remark 1. We can assume in addition that in (19) $y \neq y_1$ and $z \neq z_1$ because inequalities

$$R(x,y,z) \cap R(x,y,z_1) \leq R(x,y,z),$$

$$R(x,y,z) \cap R(x,y_1,z) \leq R(x,y,z),$$

are always valid.

Corollary 4.2. *MV-dependencies $X \twoheadrightarrow Y$ holds in L-relation R iff*

$$R(x,y,z) \cap R(x,y_1,z_1) = R(x,y_1,z) \cap R(x,y,z_1) \tag{20}$$

Proofs of prepositions 4.1 and 4.2 can be found in [9].

For any L-relation $R \in \overline{Rel_L(U)}$ we introduce a relation $R^+ \subseteq \Pi(U)$ as follows:

$$R^+ = \{(a_1, \ldots, a_n) \in \Pi(U) | R(a_1, a_2, \ldots, a_n) = 1\} \tag{21}$$

Proposition 4.3. *If $R_1 \in \overline{Rel_L(U_1)}$, $R_2 \in \overline{Rel_L(U_2)}$ then*

$$(R_1 \circ R_2)^+ = R_1^+ \circ R_2^+. \tag{22}$$

The proof is obvious.

Proposition 4.4. *For every L-relation $R \in \overline{Rel_L(U)}$ the set of all MV-dependencies in R has the following properties:*

MVD1. *If $X \supseteq Y$ then $X \twoheadrightarrow Y$.*
MVD2. *If $X \twoheadrightarrow Y$ and $(Y \cup Z) \twoheadrightarrow V$ then $(X \cup Z) \twoheadrightarrow V \backslash (Y \cup Z)$.*
MVD3. *If $X \twoheadrightarrow Y$ and $X \twoheadrightarrow Z$ then $X \twoheadrightarrow (Y \cup Z)$.*
MVD4 *$X \twoheadrightarrow Y$ iff $X \twoheadrightarrow Z$ where $Z = U \backslash (X \cup Y)$.*

All proofs are modifications of corresponding proofs in [7] that use Proposition 4.1 instead of well-known definition of MV-dependencies.

Theorem 4.5. *The set of axioms MVD1–MVD4 is sound and complete for MV-dependencies in L-relations.*

Soudness follows immediately from Proposition 4.4. Completeness follows from the classic result for MV-dependencies because any relation $R \subseteq \Pi(U)$ is always L-relation for arbitrary cH-algebra L.

Proposition 4.6. *Let L-relation $R \in \overline{Rel_L(U)}$ satisfies MV-dependency $X \twoheadrightarrow Y$. If the cH-algebra L satisfies the condition (17) then suppR satisfies the MV-dependency $X \twoheadrightarrow Y$.*

Proof. If $(x,y,z), (x,y_1,z_1) \in suppR$ then $R(x,y,z) \neq 0$ and $R(x,y_1,z_1) \neq 0$. Hence $R(x,y,z) \cap R(x,y_1,z_1) \neq 0$ because L satisfies (17). By condition the MV-dependency $X \twoheadrightarrow Y$ holds in R. Applying Proposition 4.1. we get $R(x,y,z_1) \cap R(x,y_1,z) \neq 0$ and consequently $R(x,y,z_1) \neq 0$, i.e. $(x,y,z_1) \in suppR$, g.e.d.

The Proposition 4.6 shows that non-trivial new MV-dependencies arise only for cH-algebras L in which there are at least two elements ω_1 and ω_2 such that $\omega_1 \neq 0$, $\omega_2 \neq 0$ but $\omega_1 \cap \omega_2 = 0$. The example 4.1. illistrates this observation.

Before considering examples we introduce some useful notations. Let $Y \subseteq U$ and $x \in suppR[X]$ for some L-relation $R \in Rel_L(U)$. We denote by Y_x the set

$$Y_x = \{r[Y] | r \in suppR \land r[X] = x\} \tag{23}$$

Similar notation Z_x denotes the set

$$Z_x = \{r[Z] | r \in suppR \land r[X] = x\} \tag{24}$$

If Y_x contains m elements and Z_x contains n elements then from the equality (20) we get $C_m^2 \cdot C_n^2$ equations for given x. Solving these equations we find (up to isomorphism) all decomposable L-relations.

Example 4.1. Let L be the Boolean algebra B_4, $m = n = 2$. In this case we have only one equation

$$R(x, y, z) \cap R(x, y_1, z_1) = R(x, y_1, z) \cap R(x, y, z_1).$$

For simplicity we'll write $u_{00}, u_{11}, u_{10}, u_{01}$ instead of $R(x, y, z), R(x, y_1, z_1), R(x, y_1, z), R(x, y, z_1)$ respectively. Hence we have to find all solutions of the equation

$$u_{00} \cap u_{11} = u_{10} \cap u_{01}. \tag{25}$$

Of course there are three trivial solutions:

$$u_{00} = u_{11} = u_{10} = u_{01} = \omega_1,$$

$$u_{00} = u_{11} = u_{10} = u_{01} = \omega_2,$$

$$u_{00} = u_{11} = u_{10} = u_{01} = 1.$$

Now we consider two cases.

Case 1: $u_{00} \cap u_{11} = \omega_1$, $u_{00} \cup u_{11} \cup u_{10} \cup u_{01} = 1$. It is easy to check that all solutions are given in the following table:

u_{00}	u_{11}	u_{10}	u_{01}
ω_1	ω_1	ω_1	1
ω_1	ω_1	1	ω_1
1	ω_1	ω_1	ω_1
ω_1	1	ω_1	ω_1
1	ω_1	1	ω_1
1	ω_1	ω_1	1
ω_1	1	1	ω_1
ω_1	1	ω_1	1

(26)

Another set of solutions we get if we replace ω_1 by ω_2.

For example the first row of the table (26) gives B_4-relation

R_1	X	Y	Z	B_4
	x	y	z	ω_1
	x	y_1	z_1	ω_1
	x	y_1	z	ω_1
	x	y	z_1	1

and the fifth row gives B_4-relation

R_5	X	Y	Z	B_4
	x	y	z	1
	x	y_1	z_1	ω_1
	x	y_1	z	1
	x	y	z_1	ω_1

Case 2: $u_{00} \cap u_{11} = 0$, hence $u_{10} \cap u_{01} = 0$ and $u_{ij} = \omega_1$ or $u_{ij} = \omega_2$, $i, j = 0, 1$.

All solutions are represented in the next table:

u_{00}	u_{11}	u_{10}	u_{01}
ω_1	ω_2	ω_1	ω_2
ω_1	ω_2	ω_2	ω_1
ω_2	ω_1	ω_1	ω_2
ω_2	ω_1	ω_2	ω_1.

(27)

Again for example the first row of the table (27) gives B_4-relation

R	X	Y	Z	B_4
	x	y	z	ω_1
	x	y_1	z_1	ω_2
	x	y_1	z	ω_1
	x	y	z_1	ω_2

Remark 2. Notice that elements $0, \omega_1, 1$ in B_4 constitute Codd's three-elements chain L. Therefore the table (26) gives simultaneously all non-trivial solutions for the three-element chain.

Remark 3. Substitute in the table (26) 0 instead of ω_1. The equality (25) is still valid for all rows. It is easy to see that we get all possible ordinary relations with one or two rows in which $Y \to Z$ or $Z \to Y$ and therefore the MV-dependency $X \twoheadrightarrow Y$ holds.

If we replace ω_1 by 0 and 1 by ω_1 we get all "degenerating" L-relations and B_4-relations.

Example 4.2. Let L be the three element chain $0 < \omega < 1$, $Y_x = \{y, y_1\}$, $Z_x = \{z, z_1, z_2\}$. In this case we have the system of three equations

$$\begin{cases} R(x,y,z) \cap R(x,y_1,z_1) = \\ \qquad = R(x,y_1,z) \cap R(x,y,z_1), \\ R(x,y,z) \cap R(x,y_1,z_2) = \\ \qquad = R(x,y_1,z) \cap R(x,y,z_2), \\ R(x,y,z_1) \cap R(x,y_1,z_2) = \\ \qquad = R(x,y_1,z_1) \cap R(x,y,z_2). \end{cases} \tag{28}$$

This system has six unknowns. Of course we have two trivial solutions

$$R(x,y,z) = R(x,y_1,z) = \ldots = R(x,y_1,z_2) = \omega,$$

$$R(x,y,z) = R(x,y_1,z) = \ldots = R(x,y_1,z_2) = 1.$$

Case 1: The left-side of one equation in (28) is equal 1. Suppose that

$$R(x,y,z) \cap R(x,y_1,z_1) = 1.$$

Then

$$R(x,y_1,z) \cap R(x,y,z_1) = 1.$$

and

$$R(x,y,z) = R(x,y_1,z_1) = $$
$$= R(x,y_1,z) = R(x,y,z_1) = 1.$$

Substituting these values in (28) we get

$$\begin{cases} R(x,y_1,z_2) = R(x,y,z_2) \\ R(x,y,z_2) = R(x,y_1,z_2). \end{cases} \tag{29}$$

Non-trivial solution is

$$R(x,y,z_2) = R(x,y_1,z_2) = \omega. \tag{30}$$

Hence the L-relation R has the following representation:

R	X	Y	Z	L
	x	y	z	1
	x	y_1	z_1	1
	x	y_1	z	1
	x	y	z_1	1
	x	y	z_2	ω
	x	y_1	z_2	ω

Case 2: all left sides of equation in (28) are equl ω.
Suppose that

$$R(x,y,z) = R(x,y_1,z) = \omega.$$

It is easy to check that all possible solutions are listed in the following table:

$R(x,\ y,z)$	$R(x,\ y_1,z)$	$R(x,\ y,z_1)$	$R(x,\ y_1,z_1)$	$R(x,\ y,z_2)$	$R(x,\ y_1,z_2)$
ω	ω	1	ω	ω	ω
ω	ω	ω	1	ω	ω
ω	ω	ω	ω	1	ω
ω	ω	ω	ω	ω	1
ω	ω	1	1	ω	ω
ω	ω	1	ω	1	ω
ω	ω	ω	1	ω	1
ω	ω	ω	ω	1	1

Suppose now that
$$R(x,y,z) = R(x,y,z_1) = \omega.$$

Then we get
$$\begin{cases} R(x,y_1,z) \cap R(x,y,z_2) = \omega \\ R(x,y_1,z_1) \cap R(x,y,z_2) = \omega. \end{cases} \quad (31)$$

If $R(x,y,z_2) = \omega_1$ then $R(x,y_1,z_1)$, $R(x,y_1,z_1)$, $R(x,y_1,z_2)$ can take arbitrary values. If $R(x,y,z_2) = 1$ then $R(x,y_1,z) = R(x,y_1,z_1) = \omega$ and $R(x,y_1,z_2)$ takes again arbitrary values. All solutions are represented in the following table:

$R(x,\ y,z)$	$R(x,\ y_1,z)$	$R(x,\ y,z_1)$	$R(x,\ y_1,z_1)$	$R(x,\ y,z_2)$	$R(x,\ y_1,z_2)$
ω	1	ω	1	ω	1
ω	1	ω	1	ω	ω
ω	1	ω	ω	ω	1
ω	ω	ω	1	ω	1
ω	1	ω	ω	ω	ω
ω	ω	ω	1	ω	ω
ω	ω	ω	ω	ω	1
ω	ω	ω	ω	1	ω
ω	ω	ω	ω	1	1

Again if we replace ω by 0 we get "degenerating" solutions which correspond to the functional dependency $Z \to Y$ (see Remark 3).

5   Tuple Generating Dependencies

Remind that the set $Rel_L(U)$ is a distributive lattice. Hence we can apply a general scheme for investigations of data dependencies described in [8].

Let S be an ordered set. Call a mapping $q : S \to S$ *reflexive* if $x \leq q(x)$ for any $x \in S$ and *monotone* if $x_1 \leq x_2$ implies $q(x_1) \leq q(x_2)$ for all $x_1, x_2 \in S$.

All the reflexive monotone mappings of the set S into itself constitute a monoid $RM(S)$ that contains in particular all the closure operators.

Call a set S *weakly noetherian* if in S every increasing chain of elements has only finite number of different members provided that there exists an upper bound for the given chain. Lattices of finite subsets of any set are weakly noetherian. Consequently many data models satisfy the condition of weak noetherness.

Now we shall interpret mappings $q : S \to S$ as static integrity constraints. Introduce a binary relation

$$sat \subseteq RM(S) \times S \qquad (32)$$

containing pairs (q, x) such that $x = q(x)$. In other words an element x satisfies the constraint q if x is a fixpoint of q.

Proposition 5.1. *The relation (15) has the following properties:*
RMD1. $(I_S, x) \in sat$ for any $x \in S$ (I is the identical mapping on S).
RMD2. $(q_1, x), (q_2, x) \in sat$ imply $(q_1 q_2, x) \in sat$.
RMD3. $(q, x) \in sat$ and $q_1 \leq q$ imply $(q_1, x) \in sat$ ($q_1 \leq q$ iff $q_1(x) \leq q(x)$ for all $x \in S$).

Let $Q \subseteq RM(S)$ be an arbitrary semigroup. A set

$$orb_Q(x) = \{q(x) | q \in Q\}, x \in S,$$

is called *an orbite* of x *with respect to Q*. An element x is called *a fixpoint* of the semigroup Q if $orb_Q(x) = \{x\}$. This definition claims that $x = q(x)$ for all $q \in Q$.

Theorem 5.2. *Let S be a weakly noethrian set, $q_1, \ldots, q_m \in RM(S)$, c be a closure operator, $q_i \leq c$ for $i = 1, \ldots, m$, Q be a semigroup generated by $q_1, \ldots, q_m$. Then the orbite of an arbitrary element $x \in S$ contains an unique fixpoint element of Q which is the greatest element of the set $orb_Q(x)$.*

Under the conditions of theorem 5.2 denote by $chase_Q(x)$ the greatest element of $orb_Q(x)$. The mapping $chase_Q : S \to S$ appears a closure operator such that $q_i \leq chase_Q \leq c$ for all i.

Let $\Sigma = \{q_1, \ldots, q_m\} \subseteq RM(S)$. The constraint $q \in RM(S)$ is a *semantic implication* of Σ if $(q_1, x), \ldots, (q_m, x) \in sat$ imply $(q, x) \in sat$. Proposition 5.1 shows that the set Σ^* of all implications of Σ is a monoid containing semigroip Q generated by Σ. Moreover Σ^* contains together with q all the q_i's such that $q_1 \leq q$.

Proposition 5.3. *Under the conditions of theorem 5.2*

$$\Sigma^* = \{chase_Q\}^*.$$

Proposition 5.3 shows that the set of constraints Σ is equivalent to one constraint $chase_Q$. It can be treated as a dual assertion to the existence theorem for Armstrong relations.

Return now to the set $Rel_L(U)$ where $U = \{A_1, A_2, \ldots, A_n\}$ and suppose that $Dom A_i \cap Dom A_j = \emptyset$ for all pairs $A_i \neq A_j$. Following [2] we call a pair

$(\mathcal{T}, w)$ *tableau* if $\mathcal{T}$ is a finite subset of $\Pi(U)$, $w \in \Pi(U)$ and $w[A_i] \in \mathcal{T}[A_i]$ for all $A_i \in U$. A partial mapping

$$\beta : \bigcup_{i \in I} Dom A_i \to \bigcup_{i \in I} Dom A_i$$

is called *evaluation* if β has a finite domain and $\beta(Dom A_i) \subseteq Dom A_i$ for all $A_i \in U$.

Let $R \in Rel_L(U)$ be any L-relation. For any evaluation such that $\beta(\mathcal{T}) \subseteq suppR$ we assign a truth value for the tuple $\beta(w)$ as follows:

$$t(\beta(w)) = \bigcap_{r \in \beta(\mathcal{T})} R(r) \tag{33}$$

Now we introduce a relation $\mathcal{T}(R) \subseteq \Pi(U)$:

$\mathcal{T}(R) = \{r \in \Pi(U) | r = \beta(w) \text{ for some evaluations } \beta \text{ such that } \beta(\mathcal{T}) \subseteq suppR\}$.

The relation $\mathcal{T}(R)$ can be extended to L-relation in a following way:

$$(\mathcal{T}(R))(r) = \bigcup_\beta t(\beta(w)), \tag{34}$$

where the union is taken over all evaluations β such that $r = \beta(w)$.

Proposition 5.4 *The mapping $R \mapsto \mathcal{T}(R)$ is reflexive and monotone.*

It is easy to see that the sets $Rel_L(U)$ are weakly noetherian if the lattice L is weakly noetherian. For example the set N of natural numbers is weakly noetherian.

The proposition 5.4 shows that we can use the same technique as in [2] for L-relations in order to investigate tuple generating dependencies.

6 Conclusion

It was shown in this paper that main theoretical results concerning relational algebras and data dependencies in data bases are valid for L-relational data bases where L is a cH-algebra. In addition it was shown that in order to solve the decomposition problem for L-relations we have to investigate systems of equations with coefficients in L which express specific properties of L-relations.

An open question concerns the semantics of elements in cH-algebra L. They constitute an extended set of truth values instead of 0 and 1 and the choice of a corresponding lattice depends on a universe of discourse.

References

[1] M.A.Babushkin. Heyting categories with involution and their applications. Ph.D.Thesis.-Moscow State Pedagog.Inst., 1988.

[2] C.Beeri, M.Y.Vardi. Formal systems for tuple and equality generating dependencies. SIAM J. Comput., 1984, v. 13 , NI, pp.76 - 98.

[3] N.D.Belnap. How a computer should think. In: Contemporary aspects of philosophy. Proc. of the Oxford Int. Symposium, 1976.

[4] E.F.Codd. Extending the Database Relational Model to Capture More Meaning. ACM Trans on Datebase Systems, 1979, v.4, N4, pp. 397-434.

[5] T. Imielinski, W. Lipski. The relational model of data and cylinric algebras. J. of Comp. and Syst. Sci., 1984, v. 28, pp. 80 - 102.

[6] D.Meier. The theory of relational databases. Comp. Sci. Press. 1983.

[7] M.Sh.Tsalenko. Modeling semantics in data bases. Moscow, Nauka, 1989 (in Russian).

[8] M.Sh.Tsalenko. Database theory in Russia (1979–1991)(an overview). Lect. Notes in Comp. Sci., 1992, v. 646, pp. 50–70.

[9] M.Sh.Tsalenko. Functional and multivalued dependencies for L-relations. ADBIS'94. Proc. of Int. Conf., Moscow, 1994, pp. 228–234.

[10] L.A.Zadeh. The concept of a linquistic variable and its application to approximate reasoning. N.Y., Elsevier Publ. Comp., 1973.

Constraint Satisfiability in Object-Oriented Databases

Anna Formica and Michele Missikoff
IASI, CNR
Rome Italy

Roberto Terenzi[*]
IFSI, CNR
Frascati Italy.

Abstract

Database design is one of the main concerns in developing data intensive applications. In this paper, we investigate the problem of designing Object-Oriented database (OODB) schemas, enriched by integrity constraints. In particular, we concentrate on the problem of verifying satisfiability of semantic integrity constraints defined by using comparison operators. To this end, we relay on the technology of theorem provers. Our work starts from the theorem prover Satchmo, selected among those available in literature. Since the performance was not suited for our purpose, we propose a new theorem prover, called **SaRTer**, that improves the performance of Satchmo allowing for the verification of the satisfiability of a wide class of OODB schemas in an efficient way.

1 Introduction

The success of relational databases is due, among other reasons, to the intuitiveness and the relative simplicity of the underlying data model. The features of the model greatly simplify the design of relational databases. Nevertheless, wide research activities have been carried out to supply principles and methodologies for relational database design [1]. With the advent of more expressive database models and, in particular, Object-Oriented databases (OODBs) enriched by semantic integrity constraints (IC), the problem of designing a correct database schema becomes harder. Even if we concentrate on the static part of the model, neglecting the behavioral part, we have powerful mechanisms to structure data and, therefore, the possibility of defining complex (and error prone) schemas. In this perspective, new methodologies are required to support the database design phase [6].

In this paper, we focus on the problem of verifying the satisfiability of an OODB schema enriched by semantic IC and we propose to solve this problem by means of a theorem prover (TP). In particular, the work presented originates within the project MOSAICO [13], an environment for conceptual modeling and rapid prototyping of Object-Oriented database applications. A database schema, modeled under MOSAICO, is a set of type-definitions specified by using the design language $\mathcal{TQL}$++ [3], [5]. An interesting property, that follows from the formal semantics of $\mathcal{TQL}$++ [4], is that the problem of verifying the

---

This work has been partially supported by "Progetto Finalizzato Trasporti 2" of CNR, theme n. 3.2.1: "Railways Traffic Control".

[*]Currently at Division AT, CERN, Geneva Switzerland.

satisfiability of the static component of a $\mathcal{TQL}$++ schema corresponds to verify the satisfiability of a set of Range-restricted First Order Logic (RFOL) clauses with functions [10].

For this reason, among the theorem provers proposed in literature, we started by selecting Satchmo [9], [10]. In fact Satchmo is a theorem prover implemented in Prolog, based on the Hyperresolution *inference* rule [2] and conceived to check unsatisfiability of RFOL clauses in an efficient way. However, there are still some open problems: in formulating IC, equality is needed and a TP in general does not handle equality in a very efficient way.

There are two different ways to cope with equality in Hyperresolution based theorem provers. If S is the set of clauses representing the database schema, it is possible to add:

1. *all* the equality axioms to S;

2. the Paramodulation rule [2] to Hyperresolution and a reduced set of equality axioms to S.

Both solutions are unsatisfactory.

In fact, solution 1 leads to inefficient proofs[1] due to the combinatorial explosion of clauses derived from the e the effect is even amplified in using theorem provers like Satchmo, where additional predicates have to be introduced [9] to handle the equality axioms that are not in RFOL.

Solution 2 has been investigated in [15] where a new theorem prover, obtained by adding the Paramodulation rule to Satchmo, called Satchmo-P, is presented. Even though Satchmo-P performs better than Satchmo [15], we will see that the achieved improvement is still not satisfactory. The main problem is due to the fact that Paramodulation does not replace all the equality axioms (the reflexive ones are still required) and this leads to inefficient refutations.

In this paper, we propose a new and more efficient solution based on a set of inference rules, referred to as **HaRT** (**H**yperparamodulation **a**nd **R**eflex on **T**erms) that can handle equality *without requiring any equality axioms*. In particular, when equality occurs in the IC formulation, the problem of verifying the satisfiability of a $\mathcal{TQL}$++ schema corresponds to verifying the satisfiability of a set of Equality Range-restricted First Order Logic (ERFOL) clauses (a subclass of the RFOL clauses class). Informally speaking, ERFOL clauses show restrictions on equality predicate occurrences similar to those required for the *built-in* predicates in deductive databases [16], where database rules hindered to create infinite relations starting from finite ones[2]. ERFOL clauses will be formally defined in section 3.1.

It has been shown [15] that <**HaRT**, ERFOL> is a sound and (refutation) complete logical calculus.

Based on **HaRT** and by using the general frame of Satchmo, **SaRTer** (**Sa**tchmo-P and **R**eflex on **Ter**ms) theorem prover has been developed.

SaRTer shows much greater efficiency than both Satchmo and Satchmo-P in refutations of input clauses with equality predicate. Therefore, it can be effectively used as a building-block for IC checking in MOSAICO.

---
[1]In this paper, proofs or refutations efficiency is measured in terms of the number of clauses produced in the inference process.
[2]We stress the fact that in our formulation *functional terms* are allowed, while in [16] they are not considered.

SaRTer, developed for satisfiability checking of $\mathcal{TQL}$++ schemas, can be used as a general purpose theorem prover for ERFOL formulas. Furthermore, provided that the reflexive and functional reflexive axioms are added to input clauses, **SaRTer** can be also used as a theorem prover for full First Order Logic (FOL).

The rest of the paper is organized as follows. The next section starts by showing an example of the static component of a $\mathcal{TQL}$++ schema and its translation into a set of ERFOL clauses, as required by the proposed approach. Then, in Section 3 we will introduce the new set of inference rules, called **HaRT**, that are the basis of the **SaRTer** theorem prover, shown in Section 4. The **SaRTer** procedure represents the kernel of the Semantic Verifier Module of MOSAICO [7], [12]. At the end of the paper, in the conclusion, we will compare some refutations derived by **SaRTer** against the same refutations derived by Satchmo and by Satchmo-P.

This introduction ends reporting a few notations used in the paper.

1.1 Notations

Boolean connectives *and*, *or*, *not*, *implies* will be respectively denoted by ",", ";", "¬", "→". Equality, when intended as a FOL predicate, will be represented by a binary predicate, "*equ*" being the functor:

$$\text{equ}(x, y)$$

Clauses will be represented in implication form:

$$L_1, \ldots, L_n \to P_1; \ldots; P_m$$

where L_i are the negative literals (or negative *atoms*) and P_j are the positive literals (or *atoms*). Positive clauses are represented by using *true* in the clause antecedent, while the negative ones have *empty* in the clause consequent.

Positive clauses will be also called *satellites*, while all other clauses will be called *rules* (or *nuclei*).

Given a set P containing predicates, $\text{arg}(P)$ is the set of all the arguments of predicates in P, while $T(P)$ is the set of all the terms in $\text{arg}(P)$ (therefore, including the function arguments as well).

A term or argument is said *ground iff* it contains no variables.

For reader's convenience, in Appendix B a few definitions of well-known inferences rules and the related terminology used in the paper are reported.

2 The Static Component of a $\mathcal{TQL}$++ Schema

The language $\mathcal{TQL}$++ allows the description of both the static and behavioral component of a database application. As already mentioned, in this paper we focus on the static aspects of the language. In this section, we briefly recall the syntax and the semantics of the static component of a $\mathcal{TQL}$++ schema, referred to as $\mathcal{TQL}$+ schema. For a complete and formal presentation of the language see [3].

A $\mathcal{TQL}+$ schema consists of a set of type-definitions. Each type-definition has a structural part and, possibly, a set of semantic IC. The structural component is represented by a labeled tuple of typed properties. Each property can be typed by means of a basic type (e.g., *string* or *integer*), a nested tuple, or the label of a type-definition. Properties can be functional or multi-valued, i.e. they allow the association of one (and only one) object or a set of objects to a given property, respectively. Recursive type-definitions are allowed. A semantic integrity constraint has a label and imposes θ-relationships (θ is a comparison operator, such as: $=, >, <, \ldots$) between two values or, more in general, the elements of two sets of objects. Each term of a comparison is defined by using a sequences of properties (path) expressed by means of the dot notation formalism. Below, we recall the definition of a $\mathcal{TQL}+$ schema.

Definition 2.1 *A $\mathcal{TQL}+$ schema is a set of type-definitions with no dangling type labels, i.e. each label used in the right hand side of a type-definition must be defined.*

EXAMPLE 2.1 *A simple $\mathcal{TQL}+$ schema:*

```
employee  := [salary:integer, vehicle:car],
    ic1:    this.salary > this.vehicle.price,
    ic2:    this.vehicle.owner = this
car       := [price:integer, owner:employee],
    ic3:    this.price > this.owner.salary,
    ic4:    this.owner.vehicle = this
```

According to the formal semantics defined for $\mathcal{TQL}+$ [4], the tuple of a type-definition can be seen as a set of implicit IC. Therefore, an object complies with a type-definition if and only if it satisfies both the implicit and semantic IC specified in it. In the above example, there are two type-definitions whose labels are *employee* and *car*, respectively. Let us consider, for example, the first one. In the tuple there are two functional properties, i.e. an object *employee* must have one (and only one) *salary* of type *integer*, and one (and only one) *vehicle* of type *car*. Furthermore, the integrity constraint ic1 requires that the *salary* must be greater than the *price* (all the prices, if more than one) of the *vehicle*. The integrity constraint ic2 is satisfied if the *owner* of the *vehicle* is the same object that references it.

The set of objects satisfying a type-definition will be referred to as the *class* of that type-definition. The key-word "this" refers to the "current" object for which the constraint must be satisfied. Since each constraint must be verified by all the objects belonging to a class, "this" can be seen as a pseudo-variable ranging over the entire class.

In the following, we recall the notion of satisfiable $\mathcal{TQL}+$ schema.

Definition 2.2 *A $\mathcal{TQL}+$ schema is satisfiable if and only if there exists at least one database state such that all the type-definitions of the schema have a non-empty class.*

The above schema can be translated into a set of clauses by a two steps translation:

- first from $\mathcal{TQL}+$ schemas into FOL formulas [4]:

$(\forall x)\text{employee}(x) \rightarrow \quad (\exists w, v)(\text{salary}(x, w) \land \text{vehicle}(x, v) \land$
$\qquad\qquad\qquad\qquad\quad \text{integer}(w) \land \text{car}(v) \land$
$\qquad\qquad\qquad\qquad\quad (\forall y)(\text{price}(v, y) \rightarrow \text{greater}(w, y)) \land$
$\qquad\qquad\qquad\qquad\quad (\forall z)(\text{owner}(v, z) \rightarrow \text{equ}(z, x)))$

$(\forall x)\text{car}(x) \rightarrow \quad (\exists y, v)(\text{price}(x, y) \land \text{owner}(x, v) \land$
$\qquad\qquad\qquad\qquad \text{integer}(y) \land \text{employee}(v) \land$
$\qquad\qquad\qquad\qquad (\forall w)\text{salary}(v, w) \rightarrow \text{greater}(y, w)) \land$
$\qquad\qquad\qquad\qquad (\forall z)(\text{vehicle}(v, z) \rightarrow \text{equ}(z, x)))$

$(\exists x)\text{employee}(x)$
$(\exists x)\text{car}(x)$

The last two formulas require that both the classes associated to *employee* and *car* must be non-empty.

- Then the above set of formulas is transformed into clauses. The result of the transformation is represented by F3 set[3] in Appendix A.

  The predicates *integer*, *greater* and *equal* are assumed to be axiomatized or interpreted, according to the cases.

Note that, the universal quantification on the right-hand side of the formulas is required since in $\mathcal{TQL}+$ multi-valued properties are allowed. Here we do not elaborate about this transformation, since the issue falls outside the scope of the paper.

3 HaRT

In this section the set of inference rules, referred to as **HaRT**, is presented and its soundness and completeness (in ERFOL) are briefly recalled [15].

3.1 ERFOL clauses

When the equality predicate occurs in the antecedent of a RFOL clause, it may result an unsafe clause. For example, let us consider the following clause:

$$p(x, y), \text{equ}(z, w) \rightarrow q(z, w)$$

According to the definition (see Appendix, definition B.1), the above clause is in RFOL, but one could instantiate $\text{equ}(z, w)$ over the whole Herbrand Universe, without any restriction: just unify z with w and instantiate w to any ground term. Due to the equality properties, there are no restrictions on the domain over which the variables To overcome these kind of problems, further restrictions on equality occurrences are required.

We will adopt restrictions similar to those in [16], in defining the ERFOL formulas in clausal form.

Definition 3.1 *A clause* $(A \rightarrow C)$ *is in ERFOL iff:*

---

[3] in F3 "employee" is written as "emp", "greater" as "grt" and "integer" as "intg".

1. $(A \rightarrow C)$ is in RFOL;

2. if A_S is the set of all the predicates in A and given:

$$E = \{\text{equ}(\tau_1, \tau_2) | \text{equ}(\tau_1, \tau_2) \in A_S\}$$

than either:

  (a) τ_1 and/or τ_2 are ground;

  (b) $\arg(E) \subseteq T(A_S \setminus E)$ i.e. the arguments of the equ predicates in A_S are terms appearing in some predicates (other than equ) in A_S.

A set S of clauses is in ERFOL *iff* all its clauses are in ERFOL.

3.2 Hyperresolution and Paramodulation in RFOL Class

Hyperresolution is an inference rule derived from resolution [2]. It applies to a set of clauses and produces a clause called hyperresolvent (for specific terminology, see Appendix B).

If all clauses are in RFOL, then *all* the positive clauses are *ground* and so are the derived hyperresolvents. Therefore, in unifying satellites and nucleus antecedent, variables are substituted by *ground* terms. This means that no *occur check* is needed in the unification algorithm and Prolog built-in unification can be successfully used [8].

Paramodulation is an inference rule introduced by Robinson and Wos [14] in order to handle equality more efficiently than by simply adding equality axioms to input clauses (see Appendix B for definitions).

Dealing with input clause sets in RFOL, one can usefully restrict the application of Paramodulation as in Slagle's corollary [2], i.e. one needs only to apply Paramodulation from a positive clause containing the *equ* predicate only, *into* a positive clause. In this case, Hyperresolution plus Paramodulation is called Hyperparamodulation [2]. Since in RFOL all the positive clauses are *ground*, Paramodulation simply becomes a substitution of ground terms into ground terms [15].

Hyperparamodulation is refutation complete if the set $E_R(S)$ of reflexive axioms [2] is added to the input clause set S. These axioms have the form:

$$\text{true} \rightarrow \text{equ}(x, x) \tag{1}$$

and

$$\text{true} \rightarrow \text{equ}(f(x_1, \ldots, x_n), f(x_1, \ldots, x_n)) \tag{2}$$

for every n-ary function f occurring in S.

The set $E_R(S)$ is *not* in RFOL, but it is possible to transform it into the set $E_R^*(S)$ that is in RFOL. In fact, any clause set S can be transformed (preserving unsatisfiability) into RFOL by using an auxiliary predicate *dom* ($\mathcal{D}$-transform) [9]. The *dom* predicate directly allows the variables in S, that are not range-restricted, to range over the whole Herbrand Universe of S.

3.3 Proof Procedures based on Hyperresolution and Paramodulation

Using RFOL properties, Hyperresolution has been implemented in Satchmo [10], and Paramodulation has been added in the theorem prover called Satchmo-P [15].

We stress the fact that, for refutations of an input clause set S showing equality predicate occurrences, Satchmo requires *all* the equality axioms to be added to S. On the other hand, by using Satchmo-P, due to the presence of the Paramodulation, on the equality reflexive axioms are needed. To assure completeness, both procedures work in a *level saturation* fashion: calling S_i the set of clauses in the i-level ($i \geq 0$), S_i^+ all the positive clauses in S_i, S_i^- all the rules in S_i, then in the $(i+1)$-level Satchmo produces all the hyperresolvents $\mathcal{H}(S_i)$ having S_i^+ as satellites and S S_0 is the input clause set S augmented by the set $E_A^*(S)$ of all the equality axioms. Then for every $i \geq 0$, it results:

$$S_{i+1} = S_i \cup \mathcal{H}(S_i) \quad \text{where} \quad S_0 = S \cup E_A^*(S)$$

Satchmo-P works as Satchmo, but the input clause set S has to be augmented only by $E_R^*(S)$. In the $(i+1)$-level, apart from $\mathcal{H}(\hat{S}_i)$, it also produces all the paramodulants $\mathcal{P}(\hat{S}_i)$ obtained by Paramodulation from all the *equ* in $\hat{S}_i$ into all the positive clauses $\hat{S}_i$. Then for every $i \geq 0$ we have:

$$\hat{S}_{i+1} = \hat{S}_i \cup \mathcal{H}(\hat{S}_i) \cup \mathcal{P}(\hat{S}_i) \quad \text{where} \quad \hat{S}_0 = S \cup E_R^*(S)$$

Please, note that:
$$|\hat{S}_0| < |S_0|$$
Therefore, we have a saving in refutation cardinality.

3.3.1 Adding equality axioms

Let us consider an input clause set S in RFOL with equality occurrences. Then, the reflexive equality axioms $E_R(S)$, transformed into $E_R^*(S)$, have to be added to S.

We note that multiple applications of Hyperresolution and Paramodulation to $E_R^*(S)$ produce, among others, two sets of clauses: $D = \{\text{dom}(\tau)\}$ and $E = \{\text{equ}(\tau, \tau)\}$, where τ represents ground terms of the Herbrand Universe of S.

In a level saturation procedure, this means that in each derivation level n, reflexive *equ* whose arguments are *all* the terms in the Herbrand Universe of level n are produced. But for clauses in RFOL this is redundant, because the predicates in the clauses are *restricted*, that is their arguments can only range over a subset of the Herbrand Universe (though *a priori* unknown). Starting from this consideration, it would be desirable to produce only the reflexive *equ* whose terms are also terms of other ground predicates. Ths

3.4 Reflex Rule

Reflex on Terms (Reflex for short) is an inference rule defined in order to produce reflexive *equ* from RFOL clauses. It applies to a clause $(A \rightarrow C)$ and produces positive unit clauses whose predicate is a reflexive *equ*, as follows:
For every ground term τ in $(A \rightarrow C)$ Reflex infers the clause:

$$\text{true} \rightarrow equ(\tau, \tau)$$

The set $\mathcal{R}(S_i)$, where S_i is a set of clauses, contains all the reflexive *equ* that can be generated by applying the Reflex rule to all the clauses in S_i:

$$\mathcal{R}(S_i) = \{\text{equ}(\tau,\tau) | \tau \text{ ground}, \tau \in T(S_i)\}$$

3.5 HaRT Soundness and Completeness

HaRT is the set of inference rules: $\{Hyperparamodulation, Reflex\}$.

HaRT is sound in ERFOL since the Reflex rule produces from any set of clauses S a subset of the reflexive *equ* predicates that can be derived by Hyperresolution from S augmented by all the equality axioms.

About **HaRT** completeness in ERFOL, a formal proof is given in [15]. Here, we emphasize the following facts.

1. Given an unsatisfiable set S of clauses in ERFOL, there is a R_S level-saturation refutation obtained by Hyperresolution and Paramodulation from $S \cup E_R^*(S)$, having a *refutation level* equal to N (i.e., N is the level where the empty clause $\square$ is produced). Then, in the Nth-level of R_S all the reflexive *equ*, say E_N, instantiated over the Nth-level of the Herbrand Universe, are produced.

2. It can be shown that given N, there exists a number n such that all the reflexive equ $\in E_N$ that are ancestors of $\square$ in R_S are derived by applying n levels of **HaRT** inference rules starting from S (only).

4 SaRTer theorem prover

SaRTer is a sound and refutation complete theorem prover for ERFOL clauses. It is based on **HaRT** inference rules and is implemented in Prolog [15]. **SaRTer** works on a level saturation fashion: given a set S of ERFOL clauses, in each level $i \geq 0$ the following clauses are produced:

$$\check{S}_{i+1} = \check{S}_i \cup \mathcal{H}(\check{S}_i) \cup \mathcal{P}(\check{S}_i) \cup \mathcal{R}(\check{S}_i) \quad \text{where} \quad \check{S}_0 = S$$

Then, we have:

$$|\check{S}_0| < |\hat{S}_0| < |S_0|$$

i.e., the cardinality of the input clause set required by **SaRTer** is strictly less than the cardinality of the input clause set required by Satchmo-P and by Satchmo.

The structure and the back-track mechanism used to handle non-unit hyperresolvents is similar to that implemented in Satchmo [9].

The refutations derived by **SaRTer** have been compared against those derived from the same input clause sets by Satchmo and by Satchmo-P.

In all the tests performed, **SaRTer** is more efficient than Satchmo or Satchmo-P. This is mainly due to the fact that in a level i, Satchmo and Satchmo-P produce all the reflexive ground *equ* instantiated over the whole Herbrand Universe of level i. On the other hand, **SaRTer** produces only ground *equ* instantiated over terms that occur in arguments of the ground predicates derived up to the level i. We point out that even a single extra reflexive *equ* produced in a level i could become ancestor of a great number of derived predicates in levels $j > i$. This effect is particularly important when the input clause set is not function-free. In fact, Paramodulation in Satchmo-P or full equality axioms in Satchmo significantly amplify the number of clauses derived from a single reflexive *equ* as the level i increases.

In the table that follows the conclusion, we summarize a few tests related to unsatisfiable input clause sets (F1 through F4) derived from some MOSAICO schemas. F1 is quite simple: it has two functions, while F2, F3 and F4 are more complex, showing four functions (see Appendix A).

In the table, N is the refutation level, and n_p is the number of clauses derived up to that level. The numbers in parenthesis, when reported, are the numbers of reflexive *equ* derived (for Satchmo and Satchmo-P these numbers have been *computed* from the cardinality of the Herbrand Universe of level N).

In our experiments, we stopped the derivation performed by the TPs when more then 2000 clauses were produced (F2, F3 and F4 for Satchmo and F3 and F4 for Satchmo-P). In these cases the number of reflexive *equ* produced is generally much less than the total number of derived clauses, since one has to add all the hyperresolvents and paramodulants produced up to level N. These numbers are not easy to comput one can see that they are much higher than the shown number of reflexive *equ*.

As already stated, from the table it results that **SaRTer** is more efficient with respect to Satchmo and Satchmo-P, and the improvement is even greater as the number of functions and the refutation level (i.e. the level where □ is derived) increase. Tests on additional schemas have been performed and they show similar results.

5 Conclusion

In this paper, we have presented the **SaRTer** theorem prover that is based on the **HaRT** inference rules. These rules have been defined in order to verify the satisfiability of sets of clauses derived from OODB schemas enriched by semantic integrity constraints. According to a set of tests performed, **SaRTer** resolves unsatisfiability more efficiently than, for example, the theorem prover Satchmo, from which we started our work.

The work developed in this paper represents a starting point for the activities, carried on within the project MOSAICO, aimed at the verification of correctness of OODB schemas. In fact, as future work, we mean to concentrate on another fundamental problem that arises when verifying the satisfiability of schemas: the axioms of infinity [11]. This is a critical issue that is at the basis of the undecidability of the constraint satisfiability problem. To this end, we first intend to characterize the $\mathcal{TQL}+$ axioms of infinity. Successively, the goal is to extend the Semantic Verifier of MOSAICO by means of a module that allows the system to recognize the $\mathcal{TQL}+$ axioms of infinity before using the theorem prover.

Clauses Set	Satchmo	Satchmo-P	SaRTer
F1	$N=4$ $n_p=43$	$N=4$ $n_p=43$	$N=4$ $n_p=25$
F2	$N>3$ $n_p>2000\ (\geq 170)$	$N=3$ $n_p=161$	$N=3$ $n_p=64$
F3	$N \geq 5$ $n_p > (682)$	$N \geq 5$ $n_p > (682)$	$N=5$ $n_p=92\ (16)$
F4	$N \geq 7$ $n_p > (10922)$	$N \geq 7$ $n_p > (10922)$	$N=7$ $n_p=187\ (20)$

APPENDIX

A Input clause sets examples

The following examples are translations of $\mathcal{TQL}+$ schemas into clausal form. In addition to the listed clauses, we have the clauses necessary to handle the comparison operators. For example, the *greater* predicate (grt) is represented by:
grt(X,X)--->empty.
grt(X,Y),grt(Y,X)--->empty.
grt(X,Y),grt(Y,Z)--->grt(X,Z).
In the examples, *integer, employee, person* are represented, respectively, by intg, emp and pers.

In particular, below the set F1, there is the related $\mathcal{TQL}+$ schema. Furthermore, both the sets F2 and F3 derive from the schema in Example 2.1. In particular, since in such a schema all the properties are functional, in the last four clauses of F3 the universal quantifications of the variables Z, Y, W, K have been substituted in the set F2 by Skölem functions. Obviously, as it is shown in the table at the end of the paper, the number of produced clauses is definitively lower than that of F2. Finally, the set F4 refers to a schema slightly different from the one in the Example 2.1. The property *owner* in the type-definition *car* is typed by *any type* (i.e. TOP).

```
***********************          *******************
F1                               * F2
***********************          *******************
true--->pers(e).                 true--->emp(e).
pers(X)--->age(X,a(X)).          true--->car(v).
pers(X)--->child(X,c(X)).        car(Y)--->owner(Y,o(Y)).
pers(X)--->pers(c(X)).           car(Y)--->price(Y,p(Y)).
pers(X)--->grt(a(X),a(c(X))).    emp(X)--->salary(X,s(X)).
pers(X),child(X,Y)--->equ(a(X),a(Y)).  emp(X)--->vehicle(X,c(X)).
pers(X)--->intg(a(X))            car(Y)--->emp(o(Y)).
                                 emp(X)--->car(c(X)).
                                 emp(X)--->intg(s(X)).
                                 car(Y)--->intg(p(Y)).
person:= [age:integer,child: person],  emp(X)--->equ(X,o(c(X))).
ic1:this.age>this.child.age,     emp(X)--->grt(s(X),p(c(X))).
ic2:this.age=this.child.age      car(Y)--->grt(p(Y),s(o(Y))).
                                 car(Y)--->equ(Y,c(o(Y))).
*******************              *******************
F3                               * F4
*******************              *******************
true--->emp(e).                  true--->emp(e).
true--->car(v).                  true--->car(v).
emp(X)--->salary(X,s(X)).        emp(X)--->salary(X,s(X)).
emp(X)--->vehicle(X,c(X)).       emp(X)--->vehicle(X,c(X)).
emp(X)--->intg(s(X)).            emp(X)--->intg(s(X)).
emp(X)--->car(c(X)).             emp(X)--->car(c(X)).
car(Y)--->emp(o(Y)).
car(Y)--->intg(p(Y)).            car(Y)--->intg(p(Y)).
car(Y)--->price(Y,p(Y)).         car(Y)--->price(Y,p(Y)).
car(Y)--->owner(Y,o(Y)).         car(Y)--->owner(Y,o(Y)).
emp(X),owner(c(X),Z)--->equ(Z,X). emp(X),owner(c(X),Z)--->equ(Z,X).
emp(X),price(c(X),Y)--->grt(s(X),Y). emp(X),price(c(X),Y)--->grt(s(X),Y).
car(Y),salary(o(Y),W)--->grt(p(Y),W). car(Y),salary(o(Y),W)--->grt(p(Y),W).
car(Y),vehicle(o(Y),K)--->equ(Y,K). car(Y),vehicle(o(Y),K)--->equ(Y,K).
```

B Definitions

In the following, there are the definitions of the Hyperresolution and Paramodulation inference rules, and related terminology, formulated as needed in **HaRT**.

B.0.1 Hyperresolution

Given a rule N and a set G of positive clauses, a hyperresolvent K can be produced, providing that the following conditions are fulfilled [2]:

1. for every literal A_i in the antecedent of N there is a literal P_i in one of the positive clauses in G such that A_i and P_i are *unifiable* by an unifier σ_i;

2. all the σ_i must be compatible, i.e. a *most general unifier* (mgu) λ has to exist that allows for the unification of all the A_i in the antecedent of N and all the related P_i in the satellites simultaneously.

In this case, the hyperresolvent is a positive clause obtained by disjunctively conjoining the consequent of N with those satellites that do not occur in the antecedent of N. All the literals in the resulting positive clause are transformed by applyi

B.0.2 Paramodulation

In the following, a given literal L having an argument containing a term t will be denoted by $L[t]$. If a single occurrence of t in $L[t]$ is replaced by s, the result will be denoted by $L[s]$.

Given a literal or, more in general, a disjunction of literals C and a substitution λ, then $C\lambda$ is the result of applying the substitution λ to C.

Paramodulation[2] applies to two clauses (*parents* clauses) and produces a third clause called *paramodulant*.

Since we are in RFOL clauses, we can apply Paramodulation starting from positive clauses, according to Slagle's corollary [2]. Then, we can formulate the Paramodulation inference rule as follows.

Given two positive clauses (true $\to C_1$) and (true $\to C_2$), a paramodulant (true $\to C_3$) is produced, providing that the following conditions are fulfilled:

1. C_1 and C_2 are, respectively:

   $\text{equ}(t_1, s); C_1^*$

   $L[t_2]; C_2^*$

   where C_1^* and C_2^* are disjunctions of literals;

2. a most general unifier λ exists such that:

   $$t_1 \lambda = t_2 \lambda$$

Then the inferred paramodulant is:

$$(\text{true} \to L\lambda[s\lambda]; C_1^* \lambda; C_2^* \lambda)$$

B.0.3 RFOL formulas

RFOL is defined for FOL formulas in clausal form as follow [9]:

Definition B.1 *A given clause $(A \to C)$ is in RFOL iff every variable in the consequent occurs in its antecedent as well.*

A set of clauses S is in RFOL *iff* all its clauses are in RFOL. According to definition B.1, a positive clause in RFOL is necessarily ground.

B.0.4 Herbrand Universe of level i

Given a set of clauses S, we define the *Herbrand Universe of level i* of S as follow[2]:

Definition B.2 *Let H_0 be the set of constants appearing in S. If no constant appears in S then $H_0 = \{a\}$, where 'a' is a symbol not appearing in S. For $i = 0, 1, 2, \ldots$ let H_{i+1} be the union of H_i and the set of all terms of the form $f(\tau_1, \ldots, \tau_n)$ for all n-place functions symbols occurring in S, where τ_j, $j = 1, \ldots, n$ are members of the set H_i. Then each H_i is called the* Herbrand Universe *of level i, and H_∞, or $\lim_{i \to \infty} H_i$, is called the* Herbrand Universe *of S.*

References

[1] C.Batini, S.Ceri, S.B.Navathe: *Conceptual Database Design - An entity-relationship approach*; Benjamin-Cummings Publ., 1992.

[2] Chin-Liang Chang, R. Char-Tung Lee: *Symbolic Logic and Mechanical Theorem Proving*; Academic Press Publ., London 1987.

[3] A.Formica, M.Missikoff: *Integrity Constraints Representation in Object-Oriented Databases*; in *Information and Knowledge Management*, T.W.Finin, C.K.Nicholas, Y.Yesha eds., Lecture Notes in Computer Science (LNCS) 752, Springer-Verlag, pp. 69-85, 1993.

[4] A.Formica, M.Missikoff: *Logical foundations of the $\mathcal{TQL}+$ Object-Oriented design language*; Technical Note, IASI-CNR, Rome, November 1993.

[5] A.Formica, M.Missikoff: *Correctness of ISA Hierarchies in Object-Oriented Database Schemes*; Proc. of the 4th Int.Conf. on Extending Database Technology 94 (EDBT 94); Lecture Notes in Computer Science (LNCS) 779; Cambridge, March 1994.

[6] M.Jarke: *DAIDA: Conceptual Modelling and Knowledge-Based Support for Informaton Systems*; Technique et Science Informatique, v.9, n.2, 1990.

[7] H. Lam, M.Missikoff: *On Semantic Verification of Object-Oriented Database Schemes*; Proc. of Int. Workshop on New Generation Information Technology and Systems - NGITS, Haifa, pp. 22-29, June 1993.

[8] J.W. Lloyd:*Logic Programming*; Springer Verlag, Berlin, Heidelberg, New York, 1993.

[9] R. Manthey, F. Bry: *Satchmo: a theorem prover implemented in Prolog* in *Proceedings of CADE 88 (9th Conference on Automated Deduction)* Argonne Illinois; 1988.

[10] R. Manthey, F. Bry: *A Hyperresolution-Based Proof Procedure and its Implementation in Prolog* in *Proceedings 11th Workshop on AI (GWAI 87)*, September 28th - October 2nd 1987.

[11] F.Bry, R.Manthey: *Checking Consistency of Database Constraints: a Logical Basis*; Proc. of 12th Int Conf. on Very Large Data Bases (VLDB), Kyoto, August 1986.

[12] M.Missikoff, M.Toaiti: *Safe Rapid Prototyping of Object-Oriented Database Applications*; Proc. of 5th Int. Workshop on Rapid System Prototyping; Grenoble, France, June 1994.

[13] M.Missikoff, M.Toiati: *MOSAICO- A System for Conceptual Modeling and Rapid Prototyping of Object-Oriented Database Application*; Proc. of the 1994 ACM SIGMOD Int. Conference on Management of Data; Minneapolis, May 24-27, 1994.

[14] G. Robinson, L. Wos: *Paramodulation and theorem-proving in First-Order Theories with Equality*, in *Machine Intelligence 4*, 135-150, Edinburgh University Press (1969).

[15] R. Terenzi: *HaRT: a Sound and Complete Logical Calculus for Range-restricted Formulas with Equality*; Technical Note, IFSI-CNR, Frascati (Rome), September 1994.

[16] J. D. Ullmann: *Database and Knowledge-Base Systems*, vol. I; Computer Science Press, Rockville, Maryland, USA (1988), ISBN 0-7167-8069-O.

Objects within a Conceptual Shell †

V.E.Wolfengagen

Kashirskoe Shosse, 31, Cybernetics Department,
Moscow Engineering Physical Institute
Moscow, 115409, Russian Federation
E-mail:krylov@jurinf.npimsu.msk.su

Abstract

The notion of a *shell* is established to involve the objects and their environment. Appropriate *methods* are studied as valid *embeddings* of refined objects. The refinement process determines the linkages between the variety of possible representations giving rise to variants of computations. The case study is equipped with the adjusted equational systems that validate the initial applicative framework.

Introduction

Computation is sure to become one of the dominant trend in computer research especially to carry out object derivation processes.

Objects. The notion of an object arises for different purposes, especially in specific applied systems and often inspired by accidents. Issue where the objects come from usually is distinct from exact development and tends to mathematical consideration. The remarks here can be taken as a suggestion to group numerous aspects of 'object' to result in a general computational framework that gives a suitable scheme. This scheme can be useful as a *primitive frame* to put important ideas of object modelling in a certain order.

Representation. Applications involve the excessively complicated *representations* of objects that are equipped with the *methods*. An idea of object generalizes the experimental or theoretical observations concerning the behaviour of the selfcontained couples of data. Among other representations the 'data' is less of all understood. Attempts to capture the most important features of data lead to various mathematical ideas that are distant from the selected model of computation and result in a spectrum of far distant models. The proposals here are to fill the gaps between them.

Individuals. The domain under discussion contains atomic, or primary objects. Compound, or derived objects are generated from the atomic by the rules of generation. The problem domain is a general couple of objects D. Objects of D are *possible* with respect to prespecified theoretical framework. The set D is augmented with *virtual* objects: they are 'indirect' and produced by the computational model.

---

† *This research is supported by Russian Basic Research Foundation (project 93-01-00943)*

The mode of specification the objects results in a distinction of *actual* objects that produce the subset of possible objects. Specifications individualize the objects and specified objects are individual objects, or *individuals*. The mathematical tool in use gives the descriptions as 'the unique <object> that <logical formula>'. The calculus of descriptions is embedded into higher order theory.

Concepts. A generic idea of a concept usually deals with the selfcontained couples of individuals. Indeed, the family of individuals captures more meaning of the generic nature of a concept. Namely, 'the family' presupposes some kind of parameter that enforces the concept to generate its particular representation. Enforcing concepts to generate individuals may be achieved by different ways. The sound ground may be given by a pure theory of functions that is successively 'refined'. The refinements would be done equationally.

Theory of functions. Often the researchers in the field agree that a *theory of functions* matches the goal. This inquires some additional conditions concerning: (1) kind of a theory, (2) its selective capabilities, (3) relations with other theories, and (4) ability for design and applications. The basis for sound reasoning consists of a minimal amount of functional entities, or objects. These primitive objects are equipped with the mode of combining to generate compound objects. A theory with those properties is known as *combinatory logic* and primitive objects are named *combinators*.

Combinatory logic. Combinatory logic represents a theory of functions over *arbitrary* objects. This is significant to generate flexible data models [4],[1]. Even more: combinatory logic is known as a sound amount of theoretical and applied knowledge related to the ground nature of objects [3]. It supports: (1) basic representation of arbitrary objects, (2) computational ideas with the objects, (3) integrity of both syntax and semantic.

This *was* known to computer science theoreticians, but *was not* used in applications at almost any scale.

Valid mathematical objects would be *embedded* into combinatory logic. As embedding of an object is the main verification procedure within combinatory logic then it is ready made for compiling an arbitrary object into 'computational instructions' [2], that in turn are combinators.

Those observations enforce the researcher to establish the regular scheme to reconstruct all the vital entities by the objects with useful mathematical properties. In applications this is known as determining the *method*.

A brief outline of the refinement is observed as follows. Imagine the fixed class of primary and derived objects that is prescribed by the set of equations. The proposal is to define the properties of the objects by adjusting the initial set. The effect observed tends to capture more meaning by the refined objects, and the process of refinement evolves along distinct computational *methods*.

The first and second sections of the paper contain a suitable formulation of a (higher order) theory of functions. It is based on combinatory logic and the relative computation theories referred as *shell*, or conceptual theory. The process of embedding, or creating the method, is exemplified by a minitheory, or individual theory of list processing. The process of refinement is covered mainly in the third section. The connections of applicative and imperative modes of computation are explicated. The refined objects are embedded into the shell. Some improvements to evaluate expressions are made in the fourth section. The final section gives a brief sketch of logical language to support concepts and individuals.

1 Postulates

To carry on with computation shell the minimal set of equations has to be postulated. An easy start gives the triple of primary objects I, K, S and the metaoperator of *application*. This triple is power to maintain an *applicative computation system* with the higher order functions.

1.1 Applicative system

Let I, K, S to be the (mathematical) objects. Also an infinite set of the indeterminants is added to support the supply of *variables*. All the variables are included into the class of objects. The objects determine the set of generic objects, or atoms. The definition of derived objects is as follows by induction on the complexity.

Definition 1.1 (Objects) *(i)* I, K, S *and the variables are the objects.* *(ii) If* a, b *are the objects so is* $(a\ b)$.

The step of induction needs the intuitive understanding. Thus, the binary *application* operator $(\cdot\ \cdot)$ is taken into game:

$$(\cdot\ \cdot) : \text{object} \times \text{object} \to \text{object}.$$

It is the object generating operator that ranges over the objects. A first object is viewed as the 'function' while the second is the 'argument'. Hence the application operator enables function to be applied to an argument that results in a generating of some new object, or result of applying function to its argument, and without application there is no chance to take a resulting value.

To compare objects with other objects some (binary) relation is to be defined. Usually this relation is referred as the *conversion* and is determined by the *postulates* (CL):

(I) $Ia = a$, (K) $Kab = a$, (S) $Sabc = ac(bc)$,

(σ) $a = a$, (ρ) $\dfrac{a=b}{b=a}$, (τ) $\dfrac{a=b,\ b=c}{a=c}$,

(μ) $\dfrac{a=b}{ca=cb}$, (ν) $\dfrac{a=b}{ac=bc}$,

where a, b, c indicate the arbitrary objects and '=' is the conversion relation.

1.2 Alternative formulation

Note that the class of objects above has the unique metaoperator, namely application. For convenience the second metaoperator of *abstraction* would be added:

$$(\lambda \cdot ..) : \quad \text{variable} \times \text{object} \rightarrow \text{object}.$$

It is also object generating operator but it ranges over variables and objects. After that the previous definition of an object may be augmented by the additional step: (*iii*) *If x is a variable, a is an object then $\lambda x.a$, or $(\lambda x.a)$ is the object.*

For convenience the agreement is added – the left associated parentheses may be omitted (or recovered) if needed. The recent abstraction operator would be avoided.

1.3 Basis

To avoid the excessive objects the basis of disassembling is needed. The following metatheorem validates the triple I, K, S to be the basis.

Metatheorem 1.1 (Disassembling) *Any object $\lambda x.M$ may be disassembled by case studying (according to induction on complexity):*

$$(i)\ \lambda x.x = \mathsf{I};\ (ii)\ \lambda x.y = \mathsf{K}y,\ y \neq x;\ (iii)\ \lambda x.M'M'' = \mathsf{S}(\lambda x.M')(\lambda x.M'').$$

In fact, this metatheorem determines the primary basis.

2 Creating a shell

To verify the useful properties of basis I, K, S consider an example of *embedding*. To be more rigorous add to postulates (CL) above the following schemes:

(α) $\lambda x.a = \lambda y.[y/x]a$, $y \overline{\in} a$ (congruency); (β) $(\lambda x.a)b = [b/x]a$ (substitution);

$$(\xi)\ \frac{a=b}{\lambda x.a = \lambda x.b}; \qquad (\eta)\ \lambda x.bx = b,\ x \overline{\in} b.$$

(Note that (η) determines b as a concept.) The extended set of postulates will be referred as $(CL\eta\xi)$.

2.1 Embedding

To demonstrate the expressive power of $(CL\eta\xi)$ let to specify the set of functional concepts

$$\{Append,\ Nil,\ Null,\ List,\ Car,\ Cdr\} \qquad (Lisp)$$

as follows.
For arbitrary objects $x_1, \ldots, x_n$ a finite sequence (list) $< x_1, \ldots, x_n >$ is specified equationally as:

$$\begin{aligned}
Append\ a\ (Append\ b\ c) &= Append(Append\ a\ b)c, \\
Append\ Nil\ a &= Append\ a\ Nil = a, \\
Null\ Nil &= \underline{1}, \\
Null\ (Append(List\ a)b) &= \underline{0}, \\
Car(Append(List\ a)b) &= a, \\
Cdr(Append(List\ a)b) &= b.
\end{aligned}$$

(Here: if A, B, C are the finite sequences then

$A \frown (B \frown C) = (A \frown B) \frown C$; $Nil =< >$ (empty sequence);

$A \frown < > = < > \frown A = A$; $List\ x = < x >$;

$$Null\ A = \begin{cases} \underline{1} & \text{for } A = Nil, \\ \underline{0} & \text{otherwise}; \end{cases}$$

$Car < x_1, \ldots, x_n > = x_1$; $Cdr < x_1, \ldots, x_n > = < x_2, \ldots, x_n >$.)

2.2 The stages of embedding

The verification is straightforward. It may be shown that the set $Append =$ B, $Nil =$ I, $Null = $ D$\underline{0}$(K(K $\underline{0}$)), $List = $ D, $Car = $ DcK, $Cdr = \lambda xy.xy\underline{0}$ matches the goal, where 'c' is arbitrary object, $\underline{0} = \lambda xy.y$, $\underline{1} = \lambda xy.xy$, B $= \lambda xyz.x(yz)$ (composition), D $= \lambda xy.\lambda r.rxy$ (pairing).

Note that each of the λ-expressions may be disassembled, e.g. $\underline{0} = $ KI, $\underline{1} = $ I etc. Pay attention that $(CL\eta\xi)$ is used. The spirit of computation would be captured during the verification of *Append*.

It is easy to establish that Ba(Bbc)$x = $ B(Bab)cx for any variable x, $x\bar{\in}a, b, c$, and Ba(Bbc) $= $ B(Bab)c. Note that to avoid 'x' in the equation above one needs to reverse the scheme (ν). This is all right iff x is a variable because of:

$$\frac{z_1 x = z_2 x}{\lambda x.z_1 x = \lambda x.z_2 x}\ (\xi), \qquad \frac{\lambda x.z_1 x = \lambda x.z_2 x}{z_1 = \lambda x.z_1 x;\ z_2 = \lambda x.z_2 x}\ (\eta,\ \eta),$$

$$\frac{z_1 = \lambda x.z_1 x;\ \lambda x.z_1 x = \lambda x.z_2 x;\ z_2 = \lambda x.z_2 x}{z_1 = z_2}\ (\tau,\ \tau),\text{so,} \qquad \frac{z_1 x = z_2 x}{z_1 = z_2}\ (\nu^{-1})$$

and $\nu^{-1} = \xi \eta^2 \tau^2$. These reasons complete the embedding of $(Lisp)$ into $(CL\eta\xi)$ with the refined postulate ν^{-1}.

3 Augmenting the shell

The initial shell was described by (CL) with the single metaoperator $(\cdot\ \cdot)$ of application. The enhanced version $(CL\eta\xi)$ was equipped with the additional metaoperator ($\lambda \cdot \cdot \cdot$) of abstraction. The main previously extracted result was of embedding the set ($Lisp$) of functional concepts into ($CL\eta\xi$). Note that the properties of ($Lisp$) determine the finite sequence $< x_1, \ldots, x_n >$ as a valid object. Next efforts will be undertaken to further augmenting of ($CL\eta\xi$).

3.1 Restrictions

The ($CL\eta\xi$) formulation is given equationally, i.e. the binary relation '=' of conversion can be specified as a kind of equality. The additional equations seem to capture more features of practically helpful objects. Up to the current stage the consideration was purely syntactical. Now an attempt to generate 'the embedded applications' that essentially contain semantics will be done.

For purely mathematical reasons the additional (and not generic) combinators would simplify the notations. Here some combinators are axiomatized by the following equations:

$$\mathsf{I}x = x, \; \mathsf{C}xyz = xzy, \; \mathsf{B}xyz = x(yz), \; \mathsf{K}xy = x, \; \mathsf{S}xyz = xz(yz),$$
$$\mathsf{D}xy \equiv [x,y] \equiv \lambda r.rxy, \; < f, g > \equiv \lambda t.[ft, gt],$$
$$\Phi xyzw = x(yw)(zw), \; \Psi xyzw = x(yz)(yw), \; \mathsf{B}^2 \equiv \mathsf{BBB}, \; \mathsf{C}^2 xyzw = xwyz,$$
$$Curry \equiv \lambda h.\lambda xy.h[x,y], \; p[x,y] = x, \; q[x,y] = y.$$

They will be used below to refine the properties of the initial shell.

3.2 Application

Consider the set ($CL\eta\xi$) of postulates with the additional equation:

$$\mathsf{B} = \Psi(\Phi \; \mathsf{I}) \qquad\qquad (\cdot(\cdot) =)$$

The resulting set will be referred as ($CL\eta\xi$) + ($\cdot(\cdot) =$). To study the expressive power of this *conceptual equation* take the indeterminants V, M, N, ρ (possibly, variables, or, at least, objects).

The left and right part application respectively gives:

$$\mathsf{B}\mathsf{V}MN\rho \stackrel{(\mathsf{B})}{=} \mathsf{V}(MN)\rho \qquad \Psi(\Phi \; \mathsf{I})\mathsf{V}MN\rho \stackrel{(\Psi)}{=} \Phi \; \mathsf{I}(\mathsf{V}M)(\mathsf{V}N)\rho$$
$$\equiv \|MN\|\rho \qquad\qquad\qquad\qquad\qquad \stackrel{(\Phi)}{=} \mathsf{I}(\mathsf{V}M\rho)(\mathsf{V}N\rho)$$
$$\stackrel{(\mathsf{I})}{=} \|M\|\rho(\|N\|\rho)$$

with the agreement $\mathsf{V}(\cdot) \equiv \|\cdot\|$, that enables V as *evaluation* mapping. The direct observation gives the equation

$$\|MN\|\rho = \|M\|\rho(\|N\|\rho)$$

that is implied by ($\cdot(\cdot) =$).

3.3 Ordered pair

Consider the equation

$$\mathsf{CB}^2\mathsf{D} = \Psi(\Phi\ \mathsf{D}) \qquad\qquad ([\cdot,\cdot] =)$$

in a context of $(CL\eta\xi)$, i.e. use the augmented shell $(CL\eta\xi) + ([\cdot,\cdot] =)$. The left and right part concepts for V, M, N, ρ generate respectively the conversions as follows:

$$\mathsf{CB}^2\mathsf{D}VMN\rho \overset{(C)}{=} \mathsf{B}^2VDMN\rho \quad \Psi(\Phi\ \mathsf{D})VMN\rho \overset{(\Psi)}{=} \Phi\mathsf{D}(VM)(VN)\rho$$
$$\overset{(B^2)}{=} V(DMN)\rho \qquad\qquad\qquad \overset{(\Phi)}{=} \mathsf{D}(VM\rho)(VN\rho)$$
$$\overset{(D)}{=} \|[M,N]\|\rho, \qquad\qquad\qquad \overset{(D)}{=} [\|M\|\rho,\|N\|\rho].$$

Thus the equation

$$\|[M,N]\|\rho = [\|M\|\rho, \|N\|\rho]$$

is derived.

Discovering the conceptual equations $(\cdot(\cdot) =)$ and $([\cdot,\cdot] =)$, as may be shown below, refines the properties of the initial shell (CL) up to *computational model* of general purpose. For explicit studying the computational properties of $(CL\eta\xi)$ and $(CL\eta\xi) + (\cdot(\cdot) =) + ([\cdot,\cdot] =)$ the refined (and partially conversed) consideration would be helpful. The concepts of main interest are *constants* that gives rise to the *object constructor*.

3.4 Constant object

Often the formal systems involve the *constants*. The notion or idea of a constant is assumed to be intuitively clear. When the constants are viewed as the *relative entities* with respect to some presupposed objects this idea is not so self-evident. Let the *valuation* V and the *environment*, or *assignment* ρ are selected to be the point of relativization.

Definition 3.1 (constant object) $\mathcal{K}$ *is defined to be the constant object relative to the valuation* V *and the environment* ρ *if and only if it is not dependent on the valuation* V *and the environment* ρ:

$$\|\mathcal{K}\|\rho \equiv V\mathcal{K}\rho = \mathcal{K} \qquad\qquad (\mathcal{K})$$

Thus the equation $(\mathcal{K})$ captures some important aspects and *does* enrich our intuitive idea of a constant. Moreover, provided V and ρ are as above and $\mathcal{K}$ is a constant object we have to assume for arbitrary object x:

$$\begin{aligned}\mathcal{K}(Vx\rho) &= (V\mathcal{K}\rho)(Vx\rho) \qquad \text{by } (\mathcal{K})\\ &= V(\mathcal{K}x)\rho.\end{aligned}$$

The last equation reflects a very natural principle that 'the valuation of application is the application of valuations'. Similarly, one concludes:

$$(\mathsf{V}x\rho)\mathcal{K} = (\mathsf{V}x\rho)(\mathsf{V}\mathcal{K}\rho) \quad \text{by } (\mathcal{K}))$$
$$= \mathsf{V}(x\mathcal{K})\rho.$$

The observations being accumulated result is the following working rule: *the constant is extracted through the valuation within some environment*. The importance of the equation $(\mathcal{K})$ erases into a special *equational* principle of constant $(\mathcal{K})$. Actually, it would be better to construe the equation $\mathsf{V}\mathcal{K}\rho = \mathsf{C}\mathsf{V}\rho\mathcal{K}$ for the combinator C, thus the principle $(\mathcal{K})$ would be reformulated as $\mathsf{C}\mathsf{V}\rho\mathcal{K} = \mathcal{K} = \mathsf{I}\mathcal{K}$.
Let $\mathcal{K}$ be constructed as a variable by means of $(CL\eta\xi)$. Then the equation $(\mathcal{K} =)$ is derivable:

$$\mathsf{C}\mathsf{V}\rho = \mathsf{I} \qquad\qquad (\mathcal{K} =)$$

This equation is intended in the desirable property of being a constant. On the other hand using the equations

$$\mathsf{V}\mathcal{K}\rho = \mathcal{K} = \mathsf{K}\mathcal{K}\rho,$$

and solving the equation $(\mathcal{K} =)$ for the evaluation V one obtains $\mathsf{V} = \mathsf{K}$. The immediate consequence of this equation gives

$$\| \mathcal{K} \| \rho =' \mathcal{K}\rho,$$

and hence $\| \mathcal{K} \| =' \mathcal{K}$ for $' = \mathsf{K}$. The symbol ' $'$ ' is the *quotation function* that is analogous to the function *quote* in *LISP*. For this solution of the equation $(\mathcal{K})$ the following conclusion is valid:
the evaluation K gives the 'constant' computational system, i.e. evaluation views all the objects as ordinary constants.

3.5 Object constructor

3.5.1 Valuation of application

Let x, y be the objects evaluated as follows:

$$\begin{aligned}
\| xy \| \rho &= \| (p[x,y])(q[x,y]) \| \rho \\
&= \| \mathsf{S}pq[x,y] \| \rho & (\mathsf{S}) \\
&= \mathsf{S}pq(\| [x,y] \| \rho) & (\mathcal{K}) \\
&= \mathsf{S}pq[\| x \| \rho, \| y \| \rho] & ([\cdot,\cdot]) \\
&= (p[\| x \| \rho, \| y \| \rho])(q[\| x \| \rho, \| y \| \rho]) & (\mathsf{S}) \\
&= (\| x \| \rho)(\| y \| \rho) & (p,q)
\end{aligned}$$

Here: S is a combinator, p and q are the first and second projections respectively. The principles $(\mathcal{K})$ and the 'valuation of pair' are used in this derivation. Therefore the principle 'valuation of application' is derivable from the principles $(\mathcal{K})$ and 'valuation of pair'.

3.5.2 Valuation of pair

Let to analyze separately the derivation of principle the 'valuation of pair'. The steps are analogous to those from the above:

$$\begin{aligned}
\| [x,y] \| \rho &\equiv \| \mathsf{D}xy \| \rho \\
&= \| \mathsf{D}x \| \rho (\| y \| \rho) & (\cdot(\cdot)) \\
&= \mathsf{D}(\| x \| \rho)(\| y \| \rho) & (\mathcal{K}) \\
&= [\| x \| \rho, \| y \| \rho] & (\mathsf{D})
\end{aligned}$$

Here: D is a pairing combinator. The principle 'valuation of pair' is derived from the 'valuation of application' and ($\mathcal{K}$). Hence the principle 'valuation of pair' is derivable from the principles ($\mathcal{K}$) and 'valuation of application'.

3.5.3 Redundancy of computational principles

As was observed above the principles ($\mathcal{K}$), $\cdot(\cdot)$ and $[\cdot,\cdot]$ are mutually dependent. Thus some redundant entities would be eliminated. The possible postulates are the principles as follows:
(1) $\| \mathcal{K} \| \rho = \mathcal{K}$;
(2) either 'valuation of application' or 'valuation of pair'.

4 Equational notation

Now let apply the computational principles to the combinators. Suppose V, M, N, ρ are the variables.

$$\begin{aligned}
\| MN \| \rho &= (\| M \| \rho)(\| N \| \rho) = \mathsf{V}(MN)\rho = (\mathsf{V}M\rho)(\mathsf{V}N\rho) \\
&= \mathsf{B}\mathsf{V}MN\rho = \Phi\mathsf{I}(\mathsf{V}M)(\mathsf{V}N)\rho \\
&= \Psi(\Phi\mathsf{I})\mathsf{V}MN\rho.
\end{aligned}$$

From the equation $\mathsf{B}\mathsf{V}MN\rho = \Psi(\Phi\mathsf{I})\mathsf{V}MN\rho$ given above the characteristic equation $(\cdot(\cdot)=)$ is derivable:

$$\mathsf{B} = \Psi(\Phi\mathsf{I}) \qquad (\cdot(\cdot)=)$$

This equation is understood as the *equational* notation for the principle 'evaluation of application' whereas V is the valuation, M, N are the objects, and ρ is the environment or assignment.

The same reasons are applied to the equational notation of the 'evaluation of pair':

$$\begin{aligned}
\| [M,N] \| \rho &= [\| M \| \rho, \| N \| \rho] = \mathsf{V}[M,N]\rho = [\mathsf{V}M\rho, \mathsf{V}N\rho] \\
&= Curry\, \mathsf{V}MN\rho = \mathsf{D}(\mathsf{V}M\rho)(\mathsf{V}N\rho) = \Phi\mathsf{D}(\mathsf{V}M)(\mathsf{V}N)\rho \\
&= \Psi(\Phi\mathsf{D})\mathsf{V}MN\rho
\end{aligned}$$

The immediate consequence is the equation $([\cdot,\cdot]=)$:

$$Curry = \Psi(\Phi\mathsf{D}) \qquad ([\cdot,\cdot]=)$$

The modified equation takes into account $Curry = \mathsf{CB}^2\mathsf{D}$. Thus
$$\mathsf{CB}^2\mathsf{D} = \Psi(\Phi\mathsf{D}) \qquad ([\cdot,\cdot] =)$$

4.1 Modified equation to evaluate the application

The following observation would be fruitful for further derivations. The evaluation of $\| xy \| \rho$ is likely to involve the definition of ε. From $xy = \varepsilon[x,y]$ the following equations are valid:

$$\begin{aligned}
\| xy \| \rho &= \| \varepsilon[x,y] \| \rho = \varepsilon(\| [x,y] \| \rho) \\
&= \varepsilon[\| x \| \rho, \| y \| \rho] &&\text{(by } [\cdot,\cdot]) \\
&= (\| x \| \rho)(\| y \| \rho) &&\text{(by } \varepsilon)
\end{aligned}$$

4.2 Currying, application and product

Let z be equal to the ordered pair i.e. $z = [u,v]$. Of course, from the equations $u = pz$ and $v = qz$ we derive $z = [pz, qz] = <p,q> z$. Having in mind the equation $z = \mathsf{I}z$ and ignoring the *type* considerations it is easy to show:

$$<p,q> = \mathsf{I} \qquad (\times =)$$

Suppose $h = \varepsilon$ in the definition $h[x,y] = Curry\ h\ xy$. The immediate consequence is the following:

$$\varepsilon[x,y] = xy = Curry\ \varepsilon\ xy, \text{ and } Curry\ \varepsilon = \mathsf{I}$$

The equation above interconnects the currying $Curry$ and the explicit application ε. The following is derivable from the equation $(\times =)$:

$$\begin{aligned}
hz &= h[pz,qz] \\
&= Curry\ h(pz)(qz) &&\text{(by } (\times =)) \\
&= (Curry\ h \circ p)z(qz) &&\text{(by } \circ) \\
&= \varepsilon[(Curry\ h \circ p)z, qz] &&\text{(by } \varepsilon) \\
&= (\varepsilon \circ <Curry\ h \circ p, q>)z, &&\text{(by } <\cdot,\cdot>)
\end{aligned}$$

For arbitrary variable z in the equations above one concludes:

$$h = \varepsilon \circ <Curry\ h \circ p, q> \qquad ([\cdot,\cdot])$$

The last equation gives characteristics of the computations with the *ordered pairs*.

The modified derivation gives the following:

$$\begin{aligned}
kxy &= \varepsilon[kx, y] = (\varepsilon \circ <k \circ p, q>)[x,y] \\
&= Curry(\varepsilon \circ <k \circ p, q>)xy
\end{aligned}$$

The derivation above generates the equation $(\cdot(\cdot))$:

$$k = Curry(\varepsilon \circ <k \circ p, q>) \qquad (\cdot(\cdot))$$

that characterizes the computations with the *applications*. Combinators and combinatory logics produce some additional entities, e.g. *product* and *coproduct*. For instance, it can be verified that the above results in $\varepsilon = \mathsf{S}pq$.

5 Logic, individuals and concepts

Linkage of individuals and formulae is established in a logical language.

5.1 Language

The *language* tends to define and manipulate the objects of different kinds and gives a logical *snapshot*. This snapshot does not depend on any external parameters the same way as in a database theory:
   Object::=Atom | Complex
   Atom::=Constant | Variable
   Complex::=Constant_function(Object)|
      |[Object,Object]
      | Object(Object)
      | Object ∈ Object
   Logical_formula::=Equation | Compound
      Equation::=(Variable=Complex)
      Compound::=Logical_formula ∧ Logical_formula |
         | Logical_formula ∨ Logical_formula
         | Logical_formula ⇒ Logical_formula
         | ∃Variable.Logical_formula
         | ∀Variable.Logical_formula

The objects with the proper computational aspects are, as usually, pairs [·, ·], applications ·(·), and inclusions · ∈ · which generate a class of equations. The equations are counterparts in the compounds. The target of this is to support the object of a special kind, namely the concept.

5.2 Building the concepts

Concepts are mainly the basic building blocks. They are separated into generic concepts and indexed concepts. Note that new concepts generate the *definitional dimension* and are introduced by the descriptions like:

$$New\_concept \;=\; \mathcal{I}y : Power\_sort \\ \forall x : Sort \\ (y(x) \leftrightarrow Logical\_formula(x))$$

Generic concepts are often used as a kind of the *representation*. They are intentional objects – and are correspondent to *sort* or *type* symbols – which are interpreted as sets. Initially the generic concepts are established to represent generic ideas of physical or abstract objects that are distinct and understood in a problem domain.

5.3 Computational model

Language has to be enforced by the external parameters, or stages of knowledge, or assignments etc. Assignments enable language to capture a family of snapshots, or *view*. This view is partially analogous to the view in a database theory, but only partially. The computational model with views is the following.

$$
\begin{aligned}
Concept &= individual^{assignment} \\
individual &= state^{assignment} \\
individual &= Concept(assignment) \\
state &= individual(assignment) \\
Logic &= Logical\_formula^{assignment} \\
Logical\_formula &= Logic(assignment) \\
&= Truth\_value \\
Truth\_value &= \{true, false\} \\
Logic &= Truth\_value^{assignment}
\end{aligned}
$$

To explicate the advantages of the approach the links between logic and concepts are to be established.

5.4 Logical revelation of the concepts

Logical formulae generate the concepts by the definitions:
$Concept = \{individual \mid Logical\_formula\}$
The concepts are fixed in a language by the descriptions with the comprehension captured from a higher order logic. Think of objects as having being described.

To manipulate *objects* the computational tool is needed. The basic set of the objects is the following: $\perp$ (the logical constant), g (the functional constants), $(\cdot(\cdot))$ (the application operator, or the functional variable), $\in$ (the set constructor).

The *model* is to be constructed to reflect the resulting evaluations by the induction on the object complexity:

Objects:

$$
\begin{aligned}
\|\perp\| \, I &= false \\
\| x = y \| \, I &= \| x \| \, I = \| y \| \, I \\
\| gx \| \, I &= g \circ \| x \| \, I \\
\| [x, y] \| \, I &= [\| x \| \, I , \| y \| \, I] \\
\| x(y) \| \, I &= (\| x \|_{1_A} I)(\| y \| \, I) \\
\| y \in x \| \, I &= \| y \| \, I \in \| x \|_{1_A} I
\end{aligned}
$$

Logical objects:

$$
\begin{aligned}
\| (\Phi \wedge \Psi) \| \, I &= \| \Phi \| \, I \wedge \| \Psi \| \, I \\
\| (\Phi \vee \Psi) \| \, I &= \| \Phi \| \, I \vee \| \Psi \| \, I \\
\| (\Phi \Rightarrow \Psi) \| \, I &= f : B \to I \, \& \, \| \Phi \|_f B \\
& \Rightarrow \| \Psi \|_f B \\
\| \forall x. \Phi \| \, I &= f : B \to I \, \& \, b \in H_T(B) \\
& \Rightarrow [b/x] \| \Phi \|_f B \\
\| \exists x. \Phi \| \, I &= \exists a \in H_T(I).[a/x] \| \Phi \| \, I
\end{aligned}
$$

Computational model gives rise to the syntactic-and-semantic object $\| \cdot \| \cdot$, the evaluation map. To understand its properties the idea of variable domain is needed, e.g. $H_T(I) = \{h \mid h \to T\}$ where T is the *type*. Note that the construction separates the system of concepts and the managing of them.

In the above the notation $[a/x](\| \cdot \| \cdot)$ means the valuation $\| \cdot \| \cdot$ as fixed so that a matches x. The notation $\| \cdot \|_f \cdot$ means the valuation that matches $\| x \|_f$ with each of the relevant variables x for f-shifted valuation.

Conclusions

Main results are briefly summarized as follows.
1. Varying with different researches the nature of 'object' from a computational point of view would be captured, represented and embedded into a kind of primitive frame. This scheme operates within a theory of functions concerning *combinatory logic* and generates a primary conceptual shell.
2. Combinators give a sound *substrate* to produce a data object model. The objects in use inherit both syntax and semantic of the initial idea of object. This leads to and object-as-functor computations and generates a refinement process to capture the *methods* for individual objects.
3. The concepts are embedded into the shell and inherit the logical properties of the objects. The higher order theory (with *the descriptions*) is in use.
4. The refinement process suits the equational conditions. The distinct methods are to be studied within an equational framework.

References

[1] S. Clue, C. Delobel, A general framework for the optimization of object-oriented queries, In **Proc. SIGMOD**, San Diego, California, USA, June 1992, pp. 383-392

[2] G. Cousineau, P.-L. Curien, M. Mauny, The categorical abstract machine. **LNCS, 201, Functional programming languages computer architecture**, 1985, pp. 50-64

[3] D.S. Scott, Lambda calculus: some models, some philosophy, **The Kleene Symposium**, Barwise, J., et al.(eds.), Studies in Logic 101, North– Holland, 1980, pp.381-421

[4] V.E. Wolfengagen, Computational aspects of data objects, **Proceedings of the workshop on advances in database and information systems**, ADBIS'93, May 11-14, Moscow, 1993, pp. 1-12

Special Aspects

Comparison of Clustering Algorithms in a Single User Environment through OO7 Benchmark

Kadir Koc   Asuman Dogac
Cem Evrendilek

Software Research and Development Center
Scientific and Technical Research Council of Türkiye
Dept. of Computer Engineering,
Middle East Technical University
06531 Ankara Türkiye

Abstract

In this paper, we present a new clustering algorithm called the High Fan Out algorithm and then give the performance comparison of the High Fan Out (HFO) algorithm, Kernighan-Lin based algorithms, and the Probability Ranking Partitioning algorithm for a persistent C++(C**) implementation in a single user environment where the global request stream follows a pattern most of the time. The global request stream is obtained through OO7 Benchmark. It is shown than HFO algorithm performs the best when object sizes are uniform and the cache sizes are relatively large. We conclude with a table that indicates the best clustering algorithm to be used depending on the characteristics of the database application at hand and the restrictions imposed by the computer system. It is also indicated that, the performance of a clustering algorithm can not be based solely on the communication cost, or on the amount of internal fragmentation. On the contrary both of the measures should be taken into account to predict the number of cache misses.

1 Introduction

In object-oriented databases, without effective clustering, following a reference from one object to another may involve a disk I/O. Thus the performance of the system may be severely limited if objects that reference one another are not clustered together.

Clustering can be visualized as a hypergraph partitioning problem [TN91]. The nodes of the graph are the objects, and the edges represent the references between objects. It has been shown that the problem of finding the best clustering is an NP-complete problem [Hu91]. Several heuristic clustering algorithms have been developed [Sta84, BD90, DK90, YW73]. Stochastic clustering defined in [TN91] works by assuming that the workload is generated by some stochastic process. Statistics from the training trace is gathered, and parameters of the stochastic process is determined. To partition the object graph into pages, Kernighan-Lin (KL) [KL70] graph partitioning algorithm is used. KL algorithm achieves the pairwise optimality, i.e., there will be no two nodes belonging to two different partitions that can be exchanged and result in a lower total partitioning cost.

Recently a performance comparison of the clustering algorithms for client-server environments through simulation revealed the fact that stochastic clustering based upon Kernighan's heuristic graph partitioning algorithm [KL70] performs the best [TN92]. The clustering algorithm in this study assumes the object sizes to be equal. Another important result of [TN92] is that Probability Ranking Partitioning [YW73] performs nearly optimal although its computational cost is a lot less than that of KL algorithm.

In this paper, two clustering algorithms based on Kernighan's heuristic graph partitioning algorithm, a clustering algorithm based on Probability Ranking Partitioning, and a new clustering technique called High Fan-Out have been designed and implemented in a single user environment for a persistent C++ implementation, namely C**. The implementation of the algorithms are general enough to be used with any persistent programming language or Object-Oriented DBMS. The performance of the system for these algorithms has been evaluated for the work load described in [CDN93a, CDN93b]. Since there are no system specific constraints, the observations are general.

The contributions of the paper are as follows:

- A new fast clustering algorithm, called High Fan-Out (HFO), is designed and implemented. The HFO algorithm performs the best when object sizes are uniform and the cache sizes are relatively large.

- Main observation of the performance comparison is that although the computational complexity of KL is higher than that of PRP and HFO, the KL based algorithms perform better than PRP and HFO, for request streams following a pattern which is the most common case in single user environments. It should also be noted that the clustering algorithms are executed off-line, and thus do not degrade the performance of the programs written in a persistent programming language for database applications.

- The algorithms are designed and implemented to handle variable object sizes under the page size hard constraint.

- A table is prepared to indicate the best clustering algorithm depending on the characteristics of the database application at hand and the restrictions imposed by the computer system.

2 Implementation of the Algorithms

2.1 Working Environment

The clustering algorithms developed, are integrated to a persistent C++ implementation running on DOS environment in single user mode. Persistency is added to Borland C++ version 3.0 as a storage class through a preprocessor and a class library [EDG92].

2.2 The Formation of Object Graph

In the presence of reference strings, clustering algorithms form a Statistical Object Graph (SOG) by assuming a model approximating Simple Markov Chain (SMC), and partition the network into cluster units(pages). The pages are assigned to the secondary storage according to the Probability Ranking Model [TN91].

Object Graph (OG) of each object base is formed such that the vertices in the graph are the objects, and the edges represent total inter object reference counts. Given an object reference string, the weights of the corresponding vertices in the OG are incremented by the total number of occurrences of the corresponding objects in the string. The weight of an edge a–>b in the OG is incremented each time ... a, b,... occurs in the given reference string. This gives an approximate SMC model OG.

2.3 The Implementation of KL Based Clustering Algorithms

The KL clustering algorithm, is based on the well-known Kernighan-Lin [KL70] graph bisection algorithm. The algorithm has been implemented to handle variable size objects under page size hard constraint.

Let S denote the object graph with an associated cost matrix $C = (c_{ij})$ $i,j=1, ...$, N where N is the total number of objects for an object base and c_{ij} denotes the total number of accesses from object i to j, and vice versa. If an edge of a node crosses the partition boundary, it is termed as an external edge, otherwise it is called an internal edge. The gain of a node i, when it is moved to another partition X, is defined to be the difference between the total costs of external (Ei) and internal (Ii) edges emanating from node i towards partition X and the current partition respectively. This gain value gives a measure of the change at the cut-size, when this vertex is moved to another partition.

Initially, to partition the object base into two, the graph is partitioned randomly into two sub-graphs. In each partition, the nodes are assigned to bins corresponding to their initial gain values. The gain values of all nodes in the initial random partition is referred to as the initial gain values. KL algorithm, at each iteration, looks for a vertex having the greatest gain in the source partition to be moved to other partition. To avoid the sorting overhead at each step, a bin is associated with each vertex such that the vertices having larger gains are placed in larger numbered bins. The node at the top bin of the partition having greater total cluster size is moved to the other side, and it is locked not to be moved again. After the node with the maximum gain is moved to other side, the gains of all the nodes which are adjacent to the moved node, are updated. All the moves are made temporarily and the moving procedure is repeated until no other unlocked node is found in the source partition. The sequence of the moves maximizing the total gain are made permanent in the real structure. Finally, all the nodes are unlocked, and the new partition scheme is input as the initial configuration to the whole algorithm. This process continues until either the cut size decreases or it does not decrease but the load difference gets improved.

The second of the KL (KLFM) based algorithms follows the same implementation technique with the exception that a balance ratio reflecting the page size is set at the beginning and it is preserved at each iteration [FM 82]. As the first step, the weight balance is achieved between the partitions to get a ratio r, $0 < r < 1$, $|A|/(|A| + |B|) = r$ where $|A|$ ($|B|$) is the sum of the sizes of the objects assigned to partition A (B). Once this ratio is set, an initial pass is made by moving the objects between the partitions to conform to the ratio r. The balance ratio obtained from the initial pass is maintained with every move. After the formation of a cluster of a page size, the balance ratio is set anew.

2.4 Implementation of Probability Ranking Partitioning Algorithm

In this algorithm, the objects are sorted in ascending order of their reference counts. A bin is associated with each reference count. During the bin sorting process, objects in each bin are kept sorted in ascending order of their sizes. This in turn enables us to minimize internal fragmentation.

PRP (head,depth)

- initialize bin pointers
- do for all objects

- place into the bin corresponding to object's total reference count preserving object sizes
- do for all objects in descending order of reference counts
    - if the object at hand can be placed into the current page
        * map the object at hand into current logical page
    - else
        * get a new page and place the object into this page

2.5 Implementation of High Fan-out Algorithm

This algorithm is very similar to the PRP algorithm except that the objects are sorted in ascending order of their fan-outs (total number of references from this object to the other objects) . A bin is associated with each fan-out. During the bin sorting process, objects in each bin are kept sorted in ascending order of their sizes. This in turn enables us to minimize internal fragmentation.

HFO (head,depth)

- initialize bin pointers
- do for all objects
    - place into the bin corresponding to object's total fan-out preserving object sizes
- do for all objects in descending order of fan-outs
    - if the object at hand can be placed into the current page
        * map the object at hand into current logical page
    - else
        * get a new page and place the object into this page

3 Experimental Results

In order to make a performance study of clustering algorithms, object traces are needed. Instead of producing object traces randomly, we wanted to use object reference strings derived from applications having object-oriented features and therefore we obtained the object traces from the work load described in [CDN93a, CDN93b].

The OO7 benchmark [CDN93a, CDN93b] models an engineering design database: The key element in the OO7 database is the composite part. A composite part has a couple of attributes, such as id and buildDate, and two important relationships. The first relationship is a bidirectional relationship to a Document object. A document object holds a variable amount of text describing the composite part. The second relationship is with a set of atomic parts.

The connection of atomic parts within each composite part is random. However, random connections do not ensure complete connectivity. To ensure complete connectivity, one connection is initially added to each atomic part to connect the parts in a ring; more connections are then added at random.

The composite parts, along with their associated atomic parts, connections, and documents form the bulk of the database. To support OO7's wide range of operations, however, the composite parts are further grouped into an "assembly hierarchy".

At the first level of the hierarchy, composite objects are grouped within base assembly objects. The base assembly objects consist of some data describing the assembly plus references (bidirectional relationships) to composite parts. Base assembly objects can also be grouped into complex assembly objects. Complex assemblies can then be grouped into a tree, representing a hierarchy of design objects, with each level being built from lower levels.

Finally, this tree of assembly objects is logically grouped to form a module. Modules are intended to model the largest sub-units of the database application. Each module also has an associated Manual object, which is a larger version of a document.

Two access styles are defined in OO7: Lookup and Traversal.

Lookups: They represent the random accesses. K objects are selected among N with uniform probability, and subsequently each one of them is visited.

Traversals: An assembly object is chosen randomly. Each such object becomes the root of a recursive DFS traversal of the assembly hierarchy. Once a base assembly is reached during this traversal, each of the composite parts of this base assembly is visited. In each of the composite part, an atomic part is selected randomly and a DFS traversal is performed for a specific number of times. This process continues recursively until the required number of traversals are performed.

We have generated an object graph from OO7 benchmark for lookup and traversals. Then the object graph is traversed to form 16 object reference strings both for lookup and traversals as explained above. Each trace contains approximately 1300 objects. The first trace is used to form the clustering graph by processing the object graph with the clustering algorithms and to assign the objects to pages. The remaining 15 traces are used to record cache misses and the average of all is taken as the representative of total number of cache misses produced. Running time of the clustering algorithm, total number of pages that objects have mapped to, average internal fragmentation in the pages and the total inter-page communication costs of the resulting clustering are also recorded.

We have tested the clustering algorithms for unit size or variable size objects. For variable size objects, we have two methods to assign sizes to objects. In the first method, object sizes are randomly selected and uniformly distributed between 0 and the page size while in the other, object sizes are uniformly distributed between 0 and half the page size.

Note that, Figures 1 through 4 are not scaled with respect to cache size due to space limitation.

When queries representing random accesses are performed on the object graph, it has been observed that all the clustering algorithms perform almost the same as seen in Figure 1. However, in object-oriented databases, small fraction of queries perform random accesses.

In Figure 2, where the object sizes are uniform, KL algorithm performs the best up to a certain cache size, after which HFO algorithm gets the lead. HFO and PRP algorithms behave similar for small cache sizes. KLFM algorithm performs the worst. This unexpected behaviour of KLFM may be due to the handling of page size constraint in this algorithm. Because of the balance ratio constraint, the high gain moves may not be performed and thus the algorithm may get stuck in a local minimum. Additionally, for unit size objects, the internal fragmentation caused by HFO and PRP algorithms are zero. This implies that objects may spread out over probably more pages for KL(FM) causing more page faults which is justified in figure 7.

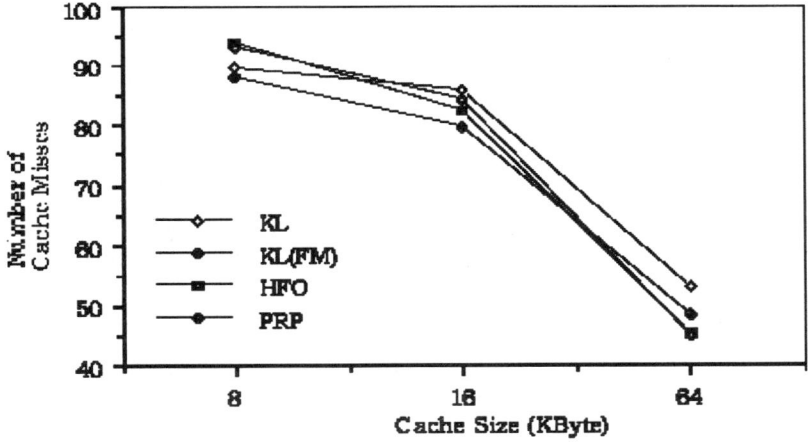

Figure 1. Cache Miss Rates for Random Access Patterns

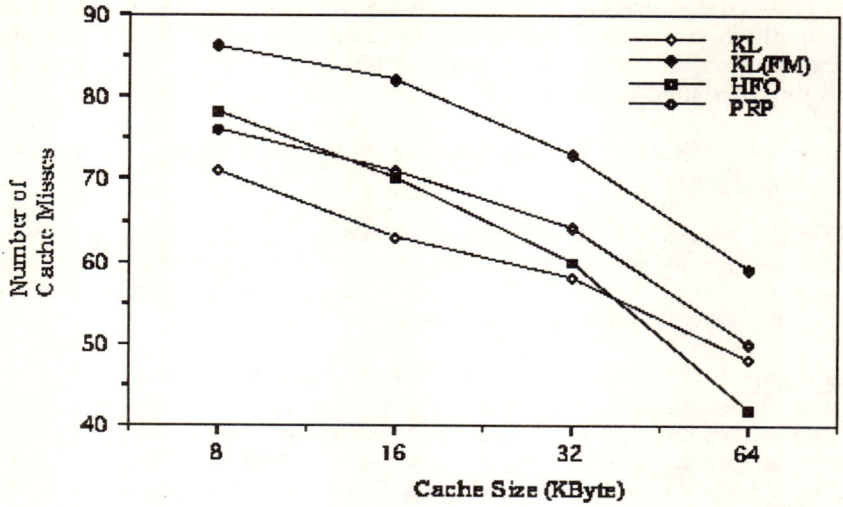

Figure 2. Cache misses for uniform object sizes

When the object sizes are randomized with respect to the whole page size, KLFM algorithm performs the best as seen in Figure 3. KLFM takes into account the weight of objects before moving them between partitions. In KLFM, an initial pass is made to set a balance ratio which is maintained throughout the partitioning process. This explains the superior behaviour of KLFM for variable size objects.

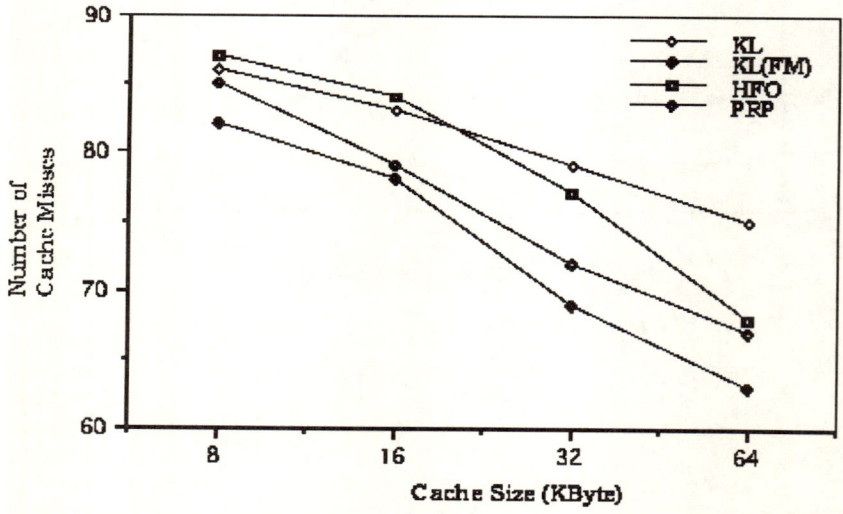

Figure 3. Cache misses for variable size objects randomized wrt page size

When the object sizes are randomized with respect to half the page size, KL algorithm outperforms the others as seen in Figure 4. KLFM is the second best algorithm since the variable size objects are handled better than the greedy algorithms.

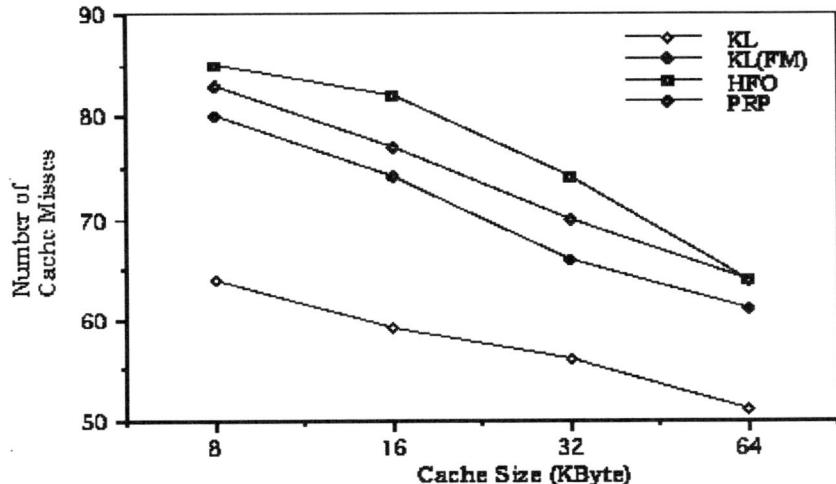

Figure 4. Cache misses for variable size objects randomized wrt half the page size

As noted from figures 3 and 4, KL(FM), PRP and HFO algorithms behave similarly for variable size objects randomized either with respect to full page size or half the page size. The change in the performance of the KL algorithm in figures 3 and 4 confirms the expected fact that when the object sizes gets larger close to a page size, this algorithm does not cluster the objects succesfully.

As observed from Figure 1 through 4, KL based algorithms generally perform better than the PRP and HFO algorithms. When the variance of size of the objects in the database gets larger, KLFM becomes the most effective. PRP and HFO algorithms are more stable in the sense that they are not as sensitive to object sizes as KL based algorithms.

In terms of execution times shown in Table 1, the order of the algorithms are as follows: KLFM > KL> PRP > HFO. It should be noted HFO, proposed in this paper, performs slightly better than PRP in terms of execution time. At first sight, this execution time order of algorithms may seem to unfavour KLFM and KL. However it should be noted that reruns of KL based algorithms take the previous partition as the input and therefore executes faster since the topology of the object-graph does not change much with similar access patterns.

Number of Objects	PRP	HFO	KL	KL(FM)
60	0.00	0.00	0.50	0.16
150	0.00	0.00	1.83	3.00
200	0.00	0.00	4.66	4.66
300	0.16	0.09	7.00	8.00
400	0.18	0.12	9.33	15.33
500	0.19	0.15	13.00	17.00

Table 1: Execution Times of the Algorithms (Tick Count)

The inter-page communication cost between two pages is defined to be the total number of references between these two pages. The total communication cost is the sum of the communication costs between all pair of pages.

Total communication cost of a clustering algorithm represents the degree of clustering achieved by the algorithm. The lower the total communication cost, the probability of an object being referenced from another page is smaller. However, it does not always ensure fewer cache misses. For example KL has the minimum communication cost as seen in Figure 5, however as observed from Figure 3, PRP performs better than KL for objects with sizes randomized with respect to full page.

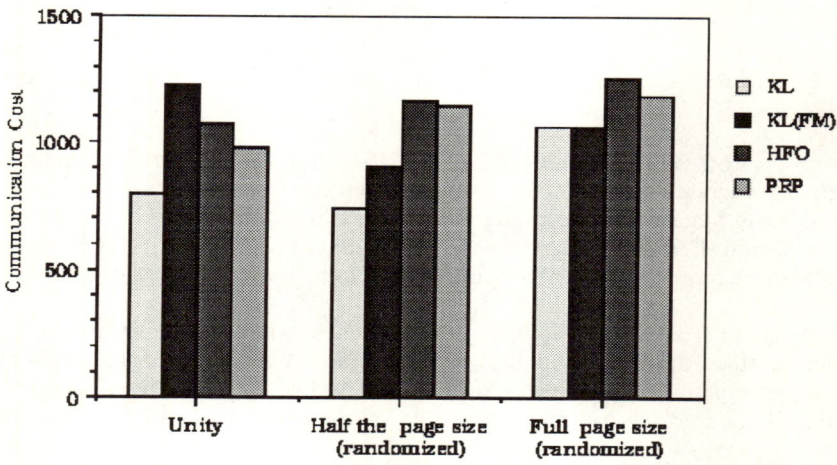

Figure 5. Total Communication Costs Between Pages for Lookup

Also note that the success of the clustering algorithm depends on the internal fragmentation. The internal fragmentation is defined as the proportion of the space not used in a page to the page size. As seen in Figure 6, internal fragmentation is higher in KL based algorithms than that of PRP and HFO although the inter-page communication cost is lower. Figure 6 also implies that as the object sizes increases, the internal fragmentation in HFO and PRP algorithms also increase, to the contrary of KL based algorithms.

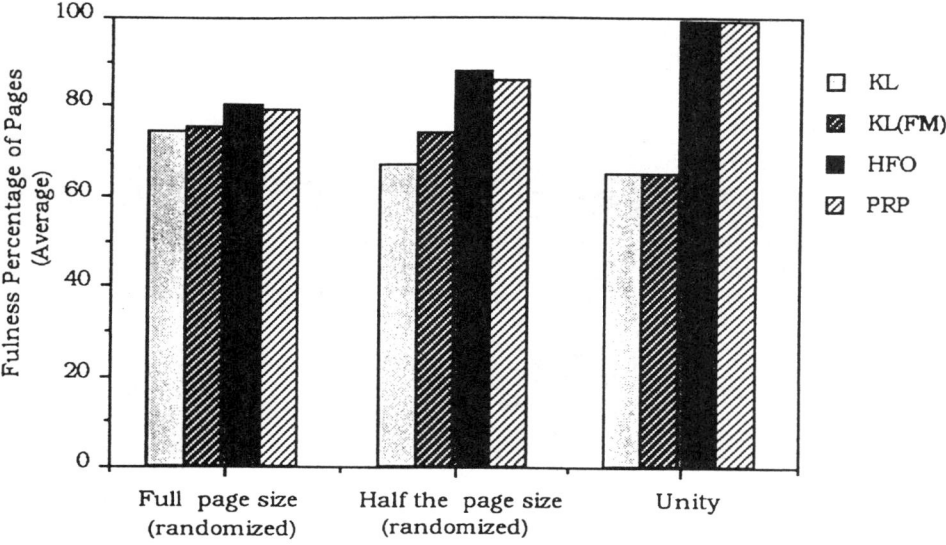

Figure 6. Fullness Percentage of Pages for the Algorithms

KL based algorithms map the objects to more pages as seen in Figure 7. This is due to the fact that, they do not try to fill a page greedily in contrast to PRP and HFO algorithms.

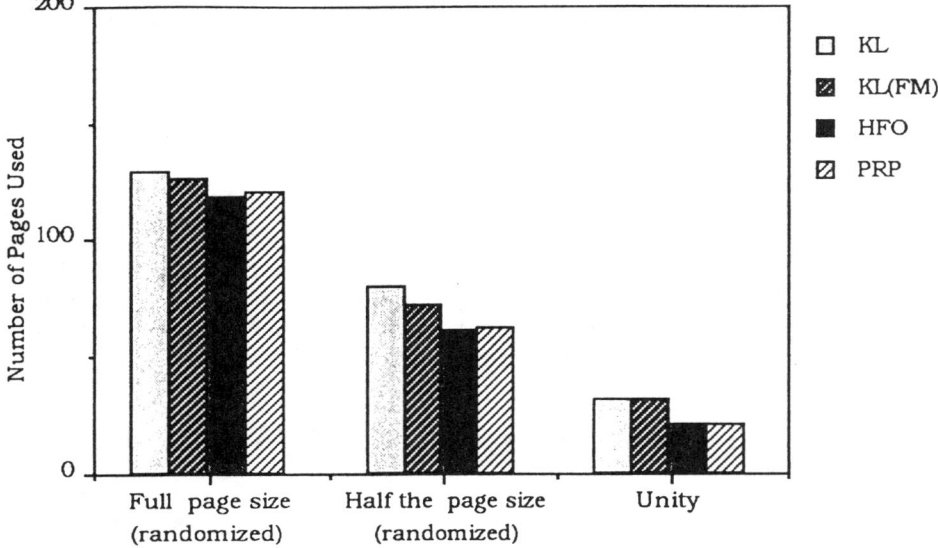

Figure 7. Total Number of Pages used by the Algorithms

Figure 8 summarizes results obtained in this paper in a schematic way. The table in this figure indicates the best clustering algorithm to be used depending on the cache size and the variance of object sizes.

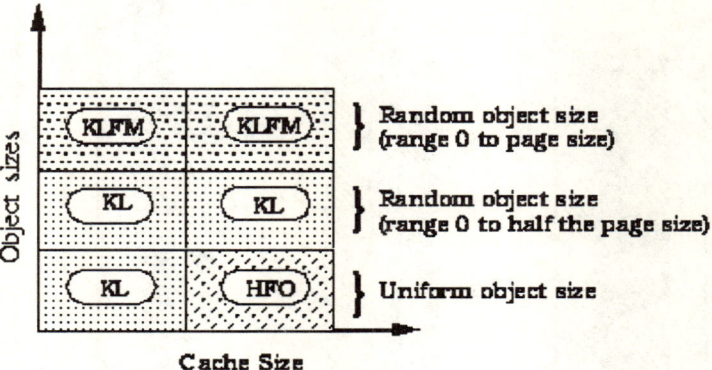

Figure 8. The Best Clustering Algorithm Depending on the Cache Size and the Variance of Object Sizes

4 Conclusions

In this study, we have suggested a new clustering algorithm, called HFO and implemented four clustering algorithms, namely, KL, KLFM, HFO and PRP for a persistent C++, called C**, in single user environment. A previous study [TN92], has compared the performance of clustering algorithms through simulation for the client-server architecture. We have considered the best performing algorithms of this study as the candidates to our study and showed that the observations for client-server environment [TN92] is valid in single user environment for most of the time. However there are the following additional observations:

1. Lookups in a single user environment is a representative of the combined reference stream for client-server architectures. When we consider this fact together with the observations obtained from Figure 1, we conclude that greedy algorithms like HFO are more promising for client server architectures. We plan to improve HFO by taking weights of edges into account.

2. In forming the object graph, the reference string is used as an approximation. This reduces the time to form the object graph.

3. For single user environments with the conventional characteristics of small cache sizes, when the request stream follows a pattern and clustering is performed offline, KL based clustering algorithms perform the best.

4. The performance of a clustering algorithm can not be based solely on the communication cost, or on the internal fragmentation. On the contrary,

both of the measures have to be taken into account to predict the number of cache misses.

5. In implementing Probability Ranking Partitioning (PRP) algorithm, to prevent internal fragmentation, the objects are also sorted according to their sizes when storing on disk.

References

[BD90] V. Benzaken and C. Delobel, "Enhancing Performance in Persistent Object Store: Clustering Strategies in O2 ", Proceedings of the fourth workshop on persistent object systems, pages 403-412, July 17, 1990.

[CDN93a] M. J. Carey, D. J. DeWitt, and J. F. Naughton, "The OO7 Benchmark", University of Wisconsin ,Technical Report, April 1993.

[CDN93b] M. J. Carey, D. J. DeWitt, and J. F. Naughton, "The OO7 Benchmark", in Proc. of the ACM SIGMOD Int. Conf. on Management of Data, June 1993.

[DK90] P. Drew, and R. King, "The Performance and Utility of the Cactis Implementation Algorithms", Proceedings of the 16th VLDB Conference, pages 135-147, Australia 1990.

[EDG 92] Evrendilek, C., Dogac, A., Gesli, T., " A Preprocessor A pproach to Persistent C++", Submitted for publication.

[FM82] C. M. Fiduccia and R. M. Mattheyses, "A Linear-Time Heuristic for Improving Network Partitions", 19th design Automation Conference, 1982.

[Hu91] J. G. Hughes, Object-Oriented Databases, Prentice Hall, 1991.

[KL70] B. W. Kernighan and S. Lin, "An efficient Heuristic Procedure for Partitioning Graphs", Bell System Technical Journal, 49(2), pages 291-307, February 1970.

[Sta84] J. W. Stamos, "Static Grouping of Small Objects to Enhance Performance of a Paged Virtual Memory", ACM Transactions on Computer Systems, 2(2):155-180, May 1984.

[TN91] M. M. Tsangaris and J. F. Naughton, "A stochastic Approach for Clustering in Object Stores", In Proceedings of the SIGMOD International Conference on Management of Data, pages 12-21, Denver, Colorado, May 1991.

[TN92] M. M. Tsangaris and J. F. Naughton, "On the Performance of Object Clustering Techniques", In Proceedings of the SIGMOD International Conference on Management of Data, pages 144-153, San Diego, California, June 1992.

[YW73] P. C. Yue and C. K. Wong, "On the Optimality of the Probability Ranking Scheme in Storage Applications", JACM,20(4), October 1973.

Security as an Add-On Quality in Persistent Object Systems[1]

Andreas Rudloff   Florian Matthes
Joachim W. Schmidt

University of Hamburg, Dept. of Computer Science,
Vogt-Kölln-Straße 30, D-22527 Hamburg, Germany
rudloff@informatik.uni-hamburg.de

Abstract

System security services like authentication, access control and auditing are becoming increasingly critical for information systems particularly in distributed heterogeneous environments. Since information system architectures are moving rapidly from centralized, *grand unifying architectures* towards open, service-oriented and communication-based environments ("Persistent Object Systems") constructed with well-organized component technologies it is essential that such structural changes are reflected adequately in the architecture of system security services.

In this paper we present an open, library-based approach to the security of Persistent Object Systems which generalizes and unifies the protection mechanisms that traditionally come bundled with database, communication or operating system services. More specifically, we illustrate how polymorphic typing can be exploited to abstract from particular commercially available security services, such as Kerberos, and how higher-order functions allow the user to add value to existing security services. Furthermore, we demonstrate how higher-order functions, first-class modules and reflection provide a technical framework for the realization of domain-specific security policies and for the systematic construction of security-enhanced activities.

1 Introduction

Customer demands on information systems in the commercial, public and private sectors require an ever-increasing number of services such as bulk data storage, data persistence, transactions, network data communication, window-based data visualization or data retrieval. Consequently, there is a strong market pressure to factor-out such services into generic libraries and to facilitate the safe use and free combination of such services. Furthermore, the required functionality is offered through a variety of service providers such as operating systems, database systems, language processors, directory servers, communication services or "middleware" toolkits.

---

[1]This research is supported by ESPRIT Basic Research, Project FIDE, #6309 and by a grant from the German Israeli Foundation for Research and Development (*bulk data classification*, I-183 060).

The Tycoon[2] *Persistent Object System* addresses this situation and combines a higher-order polymorphic language (**Tycoon** Language TL) with orthogonal persistence to implement directly the desired services and to integrate existing external services via type-safe interfaces to foreign libraries (written in languages like C or C++). Tycoon achieves thereby type-safe "plug and play" interaction between objects on screen, objects in memory, objects on disk, and objects on the wire in open heterogeneous environments. This freedom in the manipulation of persistent objects immediately raises security issues like the protection of sensitive or personal data held in shared repositories or the control and billing of resource consumption (time, space, communication bandwidth).

Traditionally, the security mechanisms required for authentication and authorization came hard-wired with a specific service provider like a database management system. Since it is impossible to cover an entire application domain that involves different service providers with a unique security model and it is also impossible to tailor a hard-wired security mechanism to specific application requirements. In this paper an add-on approach to security is proposed based on generic security libraries. It is clear that an add-on approach to security requires a certain degree of built-in security support in an integrated framework that contains all computational objects like values, functions and threads.

Section 2 introduces basic security notions. A presentation of the Tycoon framework is given in section 3 including an insecure example of a classical database application. The reinterpretation of security in the Tycoon framework and its integration is shown in section 4 together with a secure version of the example presented above. Since all this is done on a purely application level, the underlying built-in system support is described in section 5. Using the library-based security capabilities of Tycoon the correct development of secure applications can be simplified using generators as detailed in section 6. Final conclusions are discussed in section 7.

2 Basic Security Notions

Security[3] in persistent application systems is based on *authentication* and *authorization*. The semantics of these terms can be explained by the example of a distributed environment. In such an environment active entities can be identified (and named) uniquely on a purely logical level not restricted by machine or application boundaries. These active entities which are mainly users or processes (acting for itself or on behalf of a user) are the *principals* [BAN89] of the environment. Their counterparts are the passive entities which are part of an application having an identity only inside their application and which are controlled by a principal. A typical passive entity is a table in a relational database controlled by a database management system.

An active environment is characterized by the interaction of its principals. Since this may happen across machine boundaries via open potentially insecure networks there is no identity guaranteed by an operating system. This raises the need for a trusted authentication mechanism [SNS88, Lin93] between the

---

[2] Typed Communication Objects in Open Environments
[3] Security aspects like availability and integrity are not covered by this paper.

principals. The heart of such a mechanism is an *Authentication Server* administered by a (environment-) global authority. Using these protocols based on cryptographic algorithms [DES77, RSA78] each and every principal can construct a *credential* [FL93] containing the cryptographic information allowing another principal to verify the claimed identity. In addition, this information enables the creation of passive entities labeled with the identity of their creating principal which guarantees the provability of origin and lack of modifications. On a technical level this is done by adding a cryptographic checksum as *signature* to the entities. These *safe* objects can further more be made *private* through enciphering.

Authentication is a necessary requirement for answering the central security question of as to whether a *principal has the authorization to execute an action on an entity*. While the desired access can be done only by an active entity, a principal, the accessed entity can be either an active one (another principal) or a passive one. It is not necessary, however, that every principal has to be able to be both accessor and accessee. For this reason, authorization distinguishes between *subjects* which are principals in the role of an accessor, and *objects* [Mul91], which are active or passive entities in the role of an accessee. Assuming a successful authentication, it is the task of the principal representing or controlling the object the object to decide whether this access is to be granted or not. This task requires an internal information base structured by rules describing a specific *access control model (security model)*.

If an access control model allows the *creator* of an entity to decide on the subjects to which entity access will be granted, the model realizes *discretionary access control* [DRKJ85, Vin85]. A typical example of discretionary access control models are *access control lists*. They are attached to the object where access should be controlled and contain subjects and the type of access which will be allowed for these subjects.

This is in contrast to *mandatory access control models* [BL73, BN89, Mil89, TCS85] where a system-wide security model defines the allowed access patterns without further influence of the entity creators. Most of these models define a partially ordered set of security levels and assign a security level to every object and every subject. Read access will only be granted if the security level of the accessing subject dominates the security level of the accessed object; write access will only be granted if the security level of the object dominates the security level of the subject. One main difference in the mandatory access control models is that they require strict enforcement of the security model in the whole system environment whereas discretionary access control is restricted to the application environment. Therefore, discretionary access control can be used on top of a system guaranteeing mandatory access control.

3 The Rationale Behind Tycoon

The Tycoon Persistent Object System is an example of a software system that gives users flexible, problem-oriented, safe access to large sets of long-lived objects of various types [SM93, Mat93]. In Tycoon, the main abstractions necessary for the construction of such systems, namely functions, polymorphic types and persistence, have been identified and generalized. The system consists of three layers related hierarchically.

The *top layer* consists of Tycoon's higher-order language TL where *functions* and types are treated as first-class language objects thus allowing the user to write generic libraries and generators without leaving Tycoon's language framework. The semantic model of Tycoon is based on higher-order type theories [Car88]. The core semantic entities of Tycoon are values, types, bindings and signatures [BL84, Car89]. Values and types can be named in bindings for identification purposes and in order to introduce shared or recursive structures at the value and type levels. Signatures act as (partial) specifications of static and dynamic bindings. Bindings are embedded into the syntax of values, i.e. they can be named, passed as parameters, etc. Accordingly, signatures appear in the syntax of types to describe these aggregated bindings.

Higher-order functions imply *function parameterization* which enables programmers to pass functions dynamically as arguments to other functions and *function generation*, i.e., the possibility of returning functions as the result of functions. In supplying generic data structures like relations or stacks in the application framework, user-defined higher-order type operators are provided. They denote parameterized type expressions that map types or type operators to types or type operators. For example, the type operator *Pair* takes any type X that is a subtype of the trivial type **Ok** and returns a tuple type with two fields of type X:

Let Pair=**Oper**(X <:**Ok**) **Tuple** fst:X snd:X **end**   type operator binding

These generic types can be instantiated later with type parameters to construct application-specific types like

Pair(Int), Pair(String), Pair(Pair(Int))   type operator applications

Large TL programs are typically divided into modules, interfaces and hierarchically nested libraries with support for separate compilation and dynamic linking by the language processor. They are translated to *TML* (Tycoon Machine Language) [GM94] thereby entering the *second layer*. TML is a minimal intermediate language based on an untyped lambda calculus and extended with imperative constructs that serve as a low-level, portable TL program representation in distributed heterogeneous environments. TML was designed to support efficient host-specific target code generation as well as dynamic optimizations analogous to query and transaction rewriting in database systems. Execution is performed by the Tycoon Machine, TM, represented by a set of *threads* that act as the unit of execution for TML code. These threads are first-class objects and as such they are available as TL-values and can also be made persistent [MS94].

Finally, persistence of all *values* is realized in the *third layer* via *TSP* (Tycoon Store Protocol), a data-model-independent object store protocol based on the notion of a *persistent heap* that shields TML evaluators (and TL programmers) from operational aspects of the underlying persistent store like access optimization, storage reclamation, concurrency or recovery. By forcing all higher levels of the system to use the TSP (software) protocol, it provides a starting point to add system functionality at the object store level (e.g. distribution transparency). A key contribution of the TSP to the overall Tycoon system functionality is support for *orthogonal persistence* [AB87]: data of any type (including functions) can exist for any length of time or as short as required by the application. Programmers do not need to write explicit code to move data between persistent and volatile store.

A classical persistent application is the storage of bulk data. For example, a database storing personal records consisting of a name and an address can be modeled by an abstract data type (ADT) `Person.T` and implemented in Tycoon as follows:

```
interface Person
  T <: Ok
  new(name :String  address :String) :T
  get(name :String) :T
  name(person :T) :String
  address(person :T) :String
end
```

It is assumed that the corresponding implementation of this interface does not contain any security mechanisms. Furthermore, the application requires that access to the personal data is restricted to authorized users and that the set of authorized users for the name attributes differs from the set for the address attributes of a specific person tuple (of type `Person.T`). The use of the Tycoon security libraries (see section 4.2) will be demonstrated by securing this simple application.

4 An Add-On Approach to Security

Traditionally, security is being handled as a *built-in* system feature. This can be observed in the fact that security is not a feature where it is up to the user to apply it or not but it is a *restriction* that must be enforced, especially with respect to users who want to circumvent this restriction intentionally. The high cost of the the built-in approach has as a consequence that only a few systems, mainly database and operating systems, possess integrated security components.

Another key disadvantage of built-in security components is their lack of flexibility and exchangeability in cases where they do not fit the application requirements. In addition, it is a much too narrow view that only values in a database or operating system objects must be put under access control. In a programming environment access to every creatable object regardless of its type has to be controllable by a matching access control model. This requirement leads to the development of an open add-on approach to security as exemplified in the following sections by the Tycoon security model.

4.1 Tycoon's View on Security

In section 2 security control is defined as the task of defining and deciding whether *a principal has the authorization to act on an entity*. This *security task* is tackled in the Tycoon framework by relating the security concepts introduced in section 2 (i.e., principal, action, entity) to Tycoon's computational entities as outlined in section 3 (i.e., thread, function, value).

Intuitively speaking in Tycoon the three central security questions are answered as follows:

Who is active principal? All application activities are represented and controlled by Tycoon *threads*.

What action is performed? Application actions are abstracted by Tycoon *functions*.

Which entity is involved? All abstractions of Tycoon are *values* and have first-class status.

This leads to a reformulation of our security task:

Has the TL thread at hand the right to apply the intended TL function to a given TL value?

In the example in section 3 a principal is a client's application program being executed by a thread (on behalf of a user) that accesses an ADT-value (of type **person.T**) with ADT-functions.

In section 4.2 we present the security concepts introduced in section 2 as Tycoon add-on libraries. The central issue of how such security libraries can be *securely* added to a Tycoon kernel and which basic security support must already be built-in remains open until section 5.

4.2 Add-On Security Libraries

In the Tycoon environment with its inherent add-on approach [MS93] the applications security needs are realized by implementing the basic security concepts presented in section 2 as polymorphic libraries which are described in this section. It should be noted that activities needing security in a distributed environment are characterized by at least two principals, one client and one server. For activity execution they have to communicate with each other in a secure way. The underlying communication abstractions (interprocess communication, RPCs, ...) including details of the authentication protocols on top of the security libraries are outside the scope of this paper and will not be discussed in the following.

4.2.1 Authentication

Authentication in a distributed programming environment requires agreement on a protocol and a supporting infrastructure which consists mainly of authentication servers administered by a trusted authority. On the one hand all of these services could be implemented completely in Tycoon itself but, on the other hand existing standardized authentication systems with a C-API (like, for example, the Kerberos system [SNS88]) are to be preferred. In the latter case, access to the authentication services is done via a type safe TL-interface using the C-call mechanism of the Tycoon system. In both cases the authentication services are presented to the application programmer by a common interface with exchangeable implementations.

Under the assumption of an existing authentication infrastructure, the libraries have to contain abstractions for principals and their credentials as described below. Since all authentication is based on cryptographic algorithms, an abstraction for these algorithms must also be made available. In combination with a credential they can be used to make arbitrary objects *private* or *safe*.

Component Principal The principal abstraction contains two type definitions for principals according the two different roles in which a principal can be used (`Principal.T` and `Identity.T`). This distinction on the type level helps to increase the correctness of the application programs.

```
interface Principal export
  T <: Ok
  Identity <: Ok
  get(name :String) :T
  proveIdentity(p :T  secret :String) :Identity
  ...
end;
```

- A principal is simply an identifier of an active entity. Such an identifier is described by the type `Principal.T`. Values of this type, called *simple principals* in the following, support the management of principals but do not include the possibility of acting on behalf of a principal.

- If a user wants to act as the named principal he/she has to get the *identity* of this principal (a value of type `Principal.Identity`). For proving that he/she really is the intended principal a *secret* has to be presented which normally is a password. Internally this is used for authentication against the authentication server or unlocking stored encryption keys depending on the underlying authentication system. Only the owner of an identity can acquire credentials.

The most important functionality of the interface is to lookup a principal (function `get`) by giving the name of the desired principal and to obtain the identity of a principal by presenting the correct secret (function `proveIdentity`).

Components Credential and Encryption If a principal (in the role of a client) who has successfully received his identity has to prove this identity against a peer principal (in the role of a server) a credential is required. This contains the cryptographic information necessary for the peer to verify the claimed identity. This credential will be transported to the peer using the communication medium selected by the application.

```
interface Credential export
  T <:Ok
  new(p :principal.Identity) :T
  valid(p :principal.T  c :T) :Bool
  ...
end;
```

Credentials in the interface are described by values of type *Credential.T* which hides the specific structure of a credential used by the authentication system. The *new*-function takes a principal identity as parameter and returns the credential whereas the *valid*-function used by the server to check whether a received credential proves the claimed identity of a client returns only a simple principal. Additional functions are provided for credentials valid only for a specific server which are needed by some authentication protocols.

The encryption component contains the abstractions for encryption keys and functions for en- and decrypting. Since their use is restricted to the credential component and the safe/private components described below, they will not be discussed in detail here.

Components Private and Safe Following a successful authentication by the exchange of credentials these credentials are used to guarantee the safety or privacy of objects created by the principals. These objects can also be exchanged by a communication mechanism. The corresponding abstraction component in the Tycoon libraries uses the cryptographic information like encryption keys stored in the credentials and the corresponding cryptographic algorithms. The component **Safe** is described as an example:

```
interface Safe export
  Signed(A<:Ok) <:Ok
  Signature(A<:Ok) <:Ok
  signIt(A <:Ok c :credential.T object :A)    :Signed(A)
  signedBy(A <: Ok c :credential.T object :Signed(A)) :Bool
  contents(A <: Ok c :credential.T object :Signed(A)) :A
  ...
end;
```

The type operator **Signed** is parameterized with the type of objects to be signed and describes signed values. A signed value of type **Signed(Int)** is a pair of a value of type Int and a hidden signature. Signatures itself are described by values of type **Signature(V)** where V denotes the type of the signed value. The function **signIt** takes the credential of the signing principal as parameter and returns a signed object. The verification that a signed object was signed by a specific principal is carried out by the function **signedBy**, again using the credential of this principal (the match between a principal and a credential can be checked using the principal component); the function **contents** works similarly but returns the value and raises an exception if the value was not signed by the principal represented by the credential. Analogous functions using signatures only are also available.

Again, the use of type operators in combination with the static typing of TL enforces at a language level that arguments to functions are signed and that every access to a parameter value must be preceded by a call to a function that returns the value and checks its authenticity (and integrity). Polymorphic typing avoids a type loss during the **sign** operation.

4.2.2 Authorization

Authorization decides on the question of whether a subject is allowed to access an object or not. A subject can be a principal but authorization can be based also on other granularities. For example, in many systems access has to be granted to groups or roles.

In each of these cases, the *access granularity* is represented by a principal who is the basis of authentication. It is the task of the access control mechanism to decide whether a principal is a valid representative of its claimed access granularity.

Component Subject The subject abstraction of the Tycoon libraries built on top of the principal and credential abstractions supports multiple access granularities and describes subject values by a type operator `Subject.T` parameterized with the type of the accessing granularity.

```
interface Subject export
  By(B <:Ok) <:Ok
  new(B <:Ok
      equal(:B   :B) :Bool
      isPrincipal(:principal.T  :credential.T) :Bool
      representative(:B  :principal.T) :Bool) :By(B)
  T(B <:Ok) <:Ok
  Identity <:T
  get(B <:Ok  by :By(B)  baseEntity :B   p :principal.T) :T(B)
  prove(B <:Ok by :By(B) s :T(B) c :credential.T) :Identity(B)
  fromSystem() :Identity(principal.T)
  baseEntityOf(B <:Ok by :By(B) s :T(B)) :B
  principalOf(B <:Ok by :By(B) s :T(B)) :principal.T
  credentialOf(B <:Ok by :By(B) s :Identity(B)) :credential.T
  byPrincipal :By(principal.T)
  ...
end;
```

As is the case for principals (see section 4.2.1) it is necessary to distinguished between *simple subjects* and *subject identities*. Whereas a simple subject is only an identification for a subject, a subject identity proves its identity based on a claimed principal, a credential and a check that the principal belongs to the access granularity. The management of access rights can be done only on simple subjects, access granting decisions have to be based on subject identities. The twofold character of subjects is reflected by the additional type operator `Identity` which is a subtype of `T` and therefore also parameterized by the type of the accessing granularity.

Multiple access granularities are supported by the type operator `By`. A value describing the framework for a specific granularity is created with the `new`-function. This function takes three functions as arguments to describe the structure of a specific access granularity. All other functions must be parameterized with such a value; the coherence of the access granularity type of all parameters is guaranteed by the type parameter `B` expressing an inter-parameter constraint. For example, the function *prove* takes a granularity value, a simple subject and a credential restricted to the same access granularity type. It returns a subject identity, only if all necessary checks have been passed. The function `fromSystem` returns a subject identity based on the system authentication as described in more detail in section 5.

Access Control Models Based on the subject abstraction described above a wide range of access control models can be constructed. Access control lists are such an example for a discretionary access control model and will be described.

```
interface ACL export
  T(ObjectT, SubjectT <:Ok) <: Ok
  new(ObjectT, SubjectT <:Ok
      equal(:subject.T(SubjectT)
            :subject.T(SubjectT)):Bool)
          :T(ObjectT  SubjectT)

  addSubject(ObjectT, SubjectT <:Ok
             s :subject.T(SubjectT)
             acl :T(ObjectT  SubjectT)) :Ok

  deleteSubject(ObjectT, SubjectT <:Ok
                s :subject.T(SubjectT)
                acl :T(ObjectT  SubjectT)) :Ok

  grant(ObjectT, SubjectT <:Ok
        s :subject.Identity(SubjectT)
        acl :T(ObjectT  SubjectT)) :Bool
  ...
end;
```

An access control list is attached to the object to which access should be controlled. It simply contains the subjects to which access will be granted. The interface defines a type operator T describing access control list values. It is parameterized with the type of the controlled object as its first parameter ObjectT; as explained in section 4.2.2, a subject represents an access granularity that is defined by the second parameter SubjectT.

The interface contains functions to create access control lists for a given object and subject type and to add and delete subjects (of the correct access granularity type) from an access control list. These two functions still work on simple subjects whereas the grant function which checks whether a subject is contained in the access control list uses subject identities (requiring the use of an authentication check function of the subject component).

A major difference between the access control lists in the Tycoon libraries and traditional access control lists is the apparent lack of an access type specification (like *read* or *write*). In an environment where functions are one of the main abstractions and all activities are done by functions, the *application access type* is expressed by a function value and there is only one access type available on functions, namely to *execute* them.

The access control list above can be attached directly to the functions or objects to be controlled by the application developer. If this does not fit the application requirements, a predefined **access control list manager** can be used. This component manages pairs of objects and access control lists.

```
interface ACLManager export
 T(ObjectT, SubjectT <:Ok) <: Ok
 new(ObjectT, SubjectT <:Ok
     equal(:ObjectT   :ObjectT) :Bool
     equal(:subject.T(SubjectT)
            :subject.T(SubjectT)) :Bool)
             :T(ObjectT  SubjectT)

 addObject(ObjectT, SubjectT <:Ok
           manager :T(ObjectT  SubjectT)
   object :ObjectT) :Ok

 grant(ObjectT, SubjectT <:Ok
       manager :T(ObjectT  SubjectT)
       s :subject.Identity(SubjectT)
       object :ObjectT) :Bool
 ...
end;
```

Again the controlled objects can be of arbitrary type including function types. The necessary object-equality function can be constructed easily with the existing function-equality-test function of the Tycoon library. It should be noted that such a function can only exist in a homogeneous environment where functions are first-class values.

Other access control models can be realized in the same manner. This includes also mandatory access control models under the assumption of an adequate system environment. Activities controlled by some access control model can in turn be used by other activities which may be controlled by another model. This makes it possible to build up complex access control structures depending on the application needs.

4.3 Example: A Secure Person Database

In securing the person database of section 3 the first step is the identification of the objects to be protected following the application needs. These are the ADT-values like **peter** in

```
let peter = person.get("Peter")
```

The access types for these protected objects are defined on the application level by the ADT-functions **person.name** and **person.address**. The targets for the access control can be modeled in TL by the tuple **ObjectT**:

```
Let ObjectT = Tuple
  accessType :Fun(person.T) :String
  protected :person.T
end
```

The secured version of the **Person** database is now constructed on top of the existing **Person** module, the **Subject** component and an access control model. Since the application requires a differing authorization for **secureName**

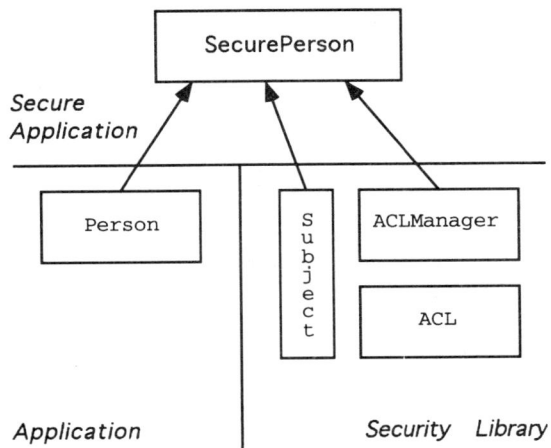

Figure 1: The component structure of **SecurePersons**

and **secureAddress** the **ACLManager** (see section 4.2.2) is chosen which uses itself ACLs. This results in a new component **SecurePerson** (see figure 1).

Access should be granted to principals determining them as access granularity. The authentication uses for simplicity the information gained during the system-authentication (see section 5). In the component **SecurePerson** an aclmanager (a value **personACLs** of type **ACLManager.T**) is created during the linking phase using the functions **objectEqual** and **principalAsSubjectEqual**:

```
let objectEqual(o1, o2 :ObjectT) :Bool = ...
let principalAsSubjectEqual = ...
let personACLs = aclManager.new(objectEqual
                                principalAsSubjectEqual)
```

For all security relevant functions **f** in **Person** the component **SecurePersons** contains a secure variant **secureF**, which combines security management with the base functionality of **Person**. The **secureNew**-function creates a new person using **person.new** and adds a value of type **ObjectT** denoting the protected person and the access type to the ACLs.

```
let secureNew(name :String  address :String) :person.T =
  begin
    let p = person.new(name  address)
    aclManager.addObject(personACLs
                         tuple person.name p end)
    aclManager.addObject(personACLs
                         tuple person.address p end)
    ...
  end
```

The secure access functions like `secureAddress` are responsible for authentication (reusing the system-authentication in this example) and the following authorization. Only if all checks have been passed successfully is the base access function called; otherwise an error is raised.

```
let secureAddress(p :person.T) :String = begin
  let subjectId = subject.fromSystem()
  if aclManager.grant(personACLs  subjectId
                      tuple person.name p end) then
    person.address(person)
  else
    raise authorizationError
  end
end
```

It should be remarked that this example neglects details of a possible communication context between client and server (requiring additional authentication) and the administration of the access rights.

5 System Security Support

The flexibility of authentication and in particular authorization mechanisms in Tycoon is in strong contrast to existing systems equipped with a hardwired security system. All security models must be protected against misuse and this cannot be done by a purely add-on approach. Since hardwiring *all* security mechanism is far too strong a mechanism, a measure of security support from the system will suffice to gain the flexibility of the add-on approach. Security can be enforced on three levels in the Tycoon environment.

Application Level The Tycoon security libraries following the add-on approach are discussed in detail in section 4.2.

Machine Level Execution of Tycoon code is finally done by the threads of the TM. During this execution access control to store objects based on access types determined by the used machine functions can be done.

Objectstore Level In a Tycoon environment all objects are allocated (and persistently stored) in a persistent object store. This gives the possibility of access control during access to the objects in the store.

The levels on which security support must be used are determined by the level on which the sphere of control over the execution unit switches from the client to the server depending on the configuration of the Tycoon system in a distributed environment. In principle all activities done under the control of the protected server or an execution unit trusted by the server can be considered as *security enforcing*, all activities controlled by clients must be considered as unsafe.

5.1 Configuration Scenarios

Different configurations are characterized primarily by configuration parameters determining

- single- or multi-user mode (clients and protected server are running concurrently on the same object store);
- who has control over the thread or the object store;
- whether arbitrary TML-code generated by the client can be executed by the server (remote code execution).

The consequences of different selections of parameters from the protected servers view should be clarified by a few examples. In the simplest case of a single-user Tycoon system without remote code execution the system can still be used as a server by using some communication mechanisms like RPCs or sockets. All execution takes place under the control of the server and a security mechanism on the application level is sufficient. With the additional possibility of remote code execution which is carried out by the server's thread additional security mechanisms on the machine level must be used.

In a multi-user system where the threads are under the control of a trusted Tycoon kernel the security mechanism on the application level must be enhanced by security mechanisms on the machine level. Otherwise unauthorized clients can try to directly access protected objects by circumventing the security enforcing functions of the application level. In the secure version of the person database this for example means that users must be forced not to use directly the person.address-function but only the secureAddress-function. If the threads are running under the control of the clients they again cannot be forced to use the security mechanisms of the thread. In this case security mechanisms on the store level are required. This in turn only works in a secure way if the store access is done under the control of the trusted Tycoon kernel. If they are done by the clients themselves no security can be guaranteed. It is possible to encrypt the store in this situation but the clients will have enough time to crack the ciphertext off-line without being detected.

5.2 Machine Level Security

Security on the machine level should only guarantee the enforcement of the application level security. There is no need for high flexibility with regard to different access control models. In the following the case of a multi-user Tycoon system with a tycoon-kernel controlled TM is considered. Access control information for all relevant thread operations is managed by the kernel. It consists of a principal denoting the owner of the object affected by the operation and one access right determining whether only this principal or all other principals may perform this operation. By default all operations affecting objects of linked application may only be executed by their owner.

In order to use the Tycoon Environment a client must request the initiation of a TM with an initial thread by the Tycoon kernel. During this start-up an authentication (*system authentication*) needs to be performed. This authentication on the machine level is not a substitute for authentication on the application level. In combination with the access control described below it only defines a set of reachable objects for the applications. Inside this set the applications can perform their own authorization based on their own authentication. This gives the application the freedom to switch between different principals while the thread is still running under the same principal. Nevertheless the system authentication is still available as one of the possible authentications at the application level.

The activated TM and the first thread are marked with a *real principal* and an *effective principal* (similar to the user-ids of the Unix system), both are initialized with the starting principal. New threads inherit their principals from their parent thread. Since a thread can only execute functions owned by its effective principal there is to this point no possibility of creating servers. However, if a principal links an application as a server he has the opportunity to mark some functions as *secure*. As a consequence the access rights at the machine level for the machine operations executing these application functions are modified to allow access for all principals.

This marking can be done by extending the TL syntax with a corresponding keyword or through the use of higher-order functions which modify the kernel access control information. It is the responsibility of the application developer to mark only functions as secure which enforce the application level security mechanisms.

Only the functions marked as secure can be executed by all principals. The access rights of functions called by them remain unchanged, otherwise their security checks can be circumvented. This requires a change of the effective principal of the executing thread to the principal of the owner of the secure function directly after entering this function. This is followed by the security checks and eventually the function may be executed provided the security checks are positive.

5.3 Object Store Level Security

Security mechanisms on the object store level require a store designed by the client/server principle for realizing Tycoon kernel controlled store accesses. The strict enforcement of this is in contrast to the Tycoon environment's goal in supporting flexibly different stores and can only be done by a substantial extension of the TSP. There exists at present no need to investigate this aspect since Tycoon kernel controlled store accesses can be simulated by a thread, similarly under Tycoon kernel control, which checks access control information attached to the store objects at every access.

6 Securing Applications

The use of a Tycoon environment equipped with security mechanisms on the application and machine levels allows the application developer to create secure activities by using only the Tycoon security libraries. However, this forces him to deal with the correct implementation of the application semantics and the correct integration of the security model which leads to some disadvantages as follows:

1. Integration of a security model requires for the most part the securing of selected functions dedicated to the use by the intended clients. The repetition of this task contains the danger of inconsistencies and raises the possibility of programming errors.

2. Depending on the programming style of the developer it may be hard to exchange the security relevant code which is caused by a radical change in the security requirements. Also changes in the application semantics and the resulting updates of the implementation may unintentionally lead to modifications of the security relevant code. A special case is the introduction of a security model to an existing insecure application.

Of course all security mechanisms whether they are built-in or add-on can not guarantee security if they are used incorrectly. This can be avoided by automatic generation of the security relevant code which can be done in two alternative ways.

6.1 Generation by Higher-Order Functions

The capability of higher-order functions to take function values as parameters and to return function values opens up their use as *generators*. They directly fit the requirements securing a function by using a specific security model. In this context *securing* is a function which takes the function to be secured and a value representing the security model as input and returns the secured function which can be used by clients. As a side effect the securing function can call the functions necessary to set up the security mechanisms at the machine level (see section 5.2).

The dependence from the security model requires that the securing functions are part of the security model components and fixed in an interface. In the implementation of the securing functions function values of the type of the input functions have to be constructed. Inside the implementation the ariety of these function values and the types of their parameters have to be known. For this the signature of the securing function has to specify the input function type up to their ariety and only the parameter types itself can be parameterized. As consequence only securing functions for a fixed set of input function types with respect to their ariety can be realized. Of course this is no real restriction if this set is large enough.

6.2 Generation by Code-Generators

Generation using higher-order functions is completely done at the application level and allows easy securing of single functions. But this does not really reflect the process of developing secure applications which consists of creating components represented by interfaces where all functions should be secured. As a result an interface containing only secured functions should be produced. Although an interface in TL is simply a tuple type and its implementation a tuple value this cannot be realized by generator functions because the generator function implementation has to be aware of the single tuple fields for constructing the resulting tuple type. This knowledge consists of the name of the field and the type of its value. In the case of being a function type the restrictions mentioned in section 6.1 for the securing functions apply. Again this must be reflected in the signature of the generator functions thus disallowing the parameterization of them with the tuple type.

This problem can be solved by generating the source code of the implementation for the secured components (the interface remains unchanged). As input a code-generator function takes the interface to be secured and the interface of the security model to be used. From this it generates the source code for the secure interface and its implementation. The implementation primarily consists of calls to the secure function of section 6.1.

7 Concluding Remarks

A major goal of the Tycoon persistent object system is the realization of an add-on approach [MS93] to secure system construction. Security is expected to be a key requirement of tomorrow's *information highways* [YS93] and as such will become the next orthogonal dimension to be integrated into Tycoon and similar systems. This paper focuses on two aspects of security integration in Tycoon resulting from the add-on approach.

At first add-on security requires a kernel security support to be built into system environments. For this authentication and minimal access control information is attached to the threads [MS94] executing the Tycoon applications in varying distributed configurations. The task of this system security support is to enforce security mechanisms defined independently on the application level by Tycoon's security libraries. For the development of these generic libraries, the second aspect of add-on security, the full power of Tycoon's higher-order polymorphic language is available for example avoiding a type loss during enciphering operations. Customizable and exchangeable security models can now be added safely on application demands supported by Tycoon's generating facilities.

While basic security mechanisms for authentication and authorization are already available as higher-order polymorphic libraries in the current multi-threaded version of the Tycoon system, future work will concentrate on the development of high-level security abstractions. These include sophisticated and flexible access control models, discretionary or mandatory, allowing the definition and enforcement of uniform environment-wide security policies.

References

[AB87]   M.P. Atkinson and P. Bunemann. Types and persistence in database programming languages. *ACM Computing Surveys*, 19(2), June 1987.

[BAN89] M. Burrows, M. Abadi, and R. Needham. A logic of authentication. Technical report, DEC System Research Center, 1989.

[BL73]   D.E. Bell and L.J. LaPadula. Secure computer systems: Mathematical foundations. Technical Report ESD-TR-73-278, Vol. 1, The MITRE Corporation, Bedford, Massachusetts, 1973.

[BL84] R. Burstall and B. Lampson. A kernel language for abstract data types and modules. In *Semantics of Data Types*, volume 173 of *Lecture Notes in Computer Science*. Springer-Verlag, 1984.

[BN89] D.F.C. Brewer and J.W. Nash. The chinese wall security policy. In *Proceedings 1989 IEEE Symposium on Security and Privacy*, Oakland, California, 1989. IEEE Computer Society Press.

[Car88] L. Cardelli. Structural subtyping and the notion of power type. In *Proceedings of the Fifteenth ACM Symposium on Principles of Programming Languages, San Diego, California*, 1988.

[Car89] L. Cardelli. Typeful programming. Technical Report 45, Digital Equipment Corporation, Systems Research Center, Palo-Alto, California, May 1989.

[DES77] Data encryption standard. Federal Information Processing Standards, no. 46, National Bureau of Standards, U.S. Department of Commerce, 1977.

[DRKJ85] D.D. Downs, J.R. Rub, C.K. Kung, and C.S. Jordan. Issues in discretionary access control. In *Proceedings 1985 IEEE Symposium on Security and Privacy*, pages 208–218, April 1985.

[FL93] W. Fumy and P. Landrock. Principles of key management. *IEEE Journal on Selected Areas in Communications*, 11(5):785–793, May 1993.

[GM94] A. Gawecki and F. Matthes. The Tycoon machine language TML: An optimizable persistent program representation. FIDE Technical Report FIDE/94/100, Fachbereich Informatik, Universität Hamburg, Germany, August 1994.

[Lin93] J. Linn. Practical authentication for distributed computing. In *Proceedings 1990 IEEE Symposium on Research in Security and Privacy*, pages 31–40. IEEE Computer Society Press, 1993.

[Mat93] F. Matthes. *Persistente Objektsysteme: Integrierte Datenbankentwicklung und Programmerstellung*. Springer-Verlag, 1993. (In German.).

[Mil89] J.K. Millen. Models of multilevel computer security. *Advances in Computers*, 29:1–45, 1989.

[MS93] F. Matthes and J.W. Schmidt. System construction in the Tycoon environment: Architectures, interfaces and gateways. In P.P. Spies, editor, *Proceedings of Euro-Arch'93 Congress*, pages 301–317. Springer-Verlag, October 1993.

[MS94] F. Matthes and J.W. Schmidt. Persistent threads. To appear in the Proceedings of the Twentieth Conference on Very Large Databases, VLDB, 1994, Santiago, Chile, 1994.

[Mul91]   S.J. Mullender. Protection. In S.J. Mullender, editor, *Distributed Systems*, chapter 7, pages 117–132. ACM Press, 1991.

[RSA78]   R. Rivest, A. Shamir, and L. Adleman. A method for obtaining digital signatures and public key cryptosystems. *Communications of the ACM*, 21(2), 1978.

[SM93]   J.W. Schmidt and F. Matthes. Lean languages and models: Towards an interoperable kernel for persistent object systems. In *Proceedings of the IEEE International Workshop on Research Issues in Data Engineering*, pages 2–16, April 1993.

[SNS88]   J.G. Steiner, B.C. Neumann, and J.I. Schiller. Kerberos: An authentication service for open network systems. In *Proceedings of the Winter 1988 Usenix Conference*, February 1988.

[TCS85]   Trusted computer system evaluation criteria. Department of Defense, DOD 5200.28-STD, 1985.

[Vin85]   S.T. Vinter. Extended discretionary access controls. In *Proceedings 1988 IEEE Symposium on Security and Privacy*, pages 39–49, April 1985.

[YS93]   M. Yap and D. Sng. Building public concurrent engineering frameworks on a national information infrastructure. In *Proceedings of 2nd IEEE Workshop on Enabling Technologies Infrastructure for Collaborative Enterprises*, West Virginia, U.S.A., April 1993.

Optimization of Object-Oriented Queries by Inverse Methods

Johann Eder, Heinz Frank, Walter Liebhart
Institut für Informatik, Universität Klagenfurt
Klagenfurt, Austria
e-mail: {eder, heinz, walter}@ifi.uni-klu.ac.at

Abstract

For object-oriented databases we propose a new technique for optimizing queries containing method invocations. This technique is based on the definition of inverse methods and query rewriting. It can be viewed as providing computed inverted access structures like (secondary) indexes provide stored inverted access structures. This technique can be applied to methods which can be fully specified as functions and to the usual comparison operations in queries. We introduce an extension to ODMG-93 [1] to define inverse methods and present the optimization algorithm for homogeneous as well as for heterogeneous collections. The application of this technique can reduce the cost of query-evaluation by orders of magnitude.

1 Introduction

Automatic optimization of queries is crucial for the applicability of declarative database query languages. The development of powerful query optimizers using efficient physical access structures was essential for the success of the relational data model. Therefore, also the optimization of queries for object-oriented databases is intensively researched [2,3,4]. However, most of the approaches proposed so far concentrate on the structural dimension of object-oriented databases while optimization of queries involving method calls has attracted comparatively little attention. Our work on schema integration [5] and view definition for object-oriented databases [6,7] made us aware of the great demand for effective optimization of such queries.

Optimization techniques reported recently include to estimate the cost of method invocation for cost-based query optimizers[2,8] and the precomputation of method calls [9,10,11] following the lines of view-materialization. The essence of the latter approach is to convert computed data (i.e. the result of method calls) to stored data so that all access structures and optimization techniques for stored data can be employed. Obviously, this technique requires considerable overhead for update operations and can only be applied to a very restricted class of methods. In particular, methods with parameters can hardly be materialized.

The approach presented here introduces computed inverted access to computed data through inverse methods. Let us introduce this technique with a small example taken from an usual schema integration problem where the scaling conflict between temperature values in degree Fahrenheit and Celsius are solved by conversion functions.

Suppose an object-oriented database to handle materials with their melting point for European and American users. During the schema integration process you decided to store the melting point of a material as degree Celsius and provide a conversion function, temp_fahrenheit, to get the temperature in Fahrenheit. If an user would like to know the names of all materials with a melting point less than 100 degree Fahrenheit, he would write the following statement (according to ODMG-93):

```
SELECT    m.name
FROM      m in Materials
WHERE     m→temp_fahrenheit () < 100
```

Traditionally, this query requires a full scan of the Materials class and an invocation of the method temp_fahrenheit for each object. With the introduction of the inverse method[1] temp_celsius, which transfers Fahrenheit to Celsius, we are able to rewrite the above query as:

```
SELECT    m.name
FROM      m in Materials
WHERE     m.melting_point < Material→temp_celsius (100)
```

This has the following advantages which can reduce the cost of query evaluation by orders of magnitude:

- ☐ The inverse method has to be computed only once, while the original method would have to be evaluated for each object.
- ☐ Access structures (indexes) can be used to avoid loading all objects from the disc into the main memory.

Obviously it is not possible to define inverse methods for all methods in the database - it is up to the database designer or tuner to decide whether it is possible and worthwhile to introduce an inverse method, like he decides for indexes. Until now the user or application programmer would have to rewrite the query instead of a query optimizer. For this purpose he needs detailed information about the internals of the objects. However, this would jeopardize view concepts and sacrifice encapsulation for performance. Using our optimization strategy protects encapsulation and view concepts and relieves the users of knowledge about internal data representation. In particular, in the case of multi-database systems, the user

---

[1] In section 2 we will argue why inverse methods have to be type methods.

even might not have access to the necessary information. In the example the users has to know whether the temperature is stored as degree Celsius or as degree Fahrenheit.

2 Definition of Inverse Methods

2.1 Optimizable Methods

Not every kind of method is appropriate for our optimization process. Most important, optimizable methods have to be side-effect free functions. Such methods can formally be defined as a family of functions:

For the following discussion let m be a method of the object-type C with parameter(s) P and return type Z. The method m is optimizable with an inverse method, if it can be fully specified as the following family of functions:
$$\forall P: m_P: C \to Z$$

A special subclass of these optimizable methods are those which use exactly one (distinguished) attribute for the computation. This class of methods are further characterized by the following condition:

Let a be an attribute of type A, o and o' be objects of type C, then:
$$\forall P \,\forall o, o': o.a = o'.a \Rightarrow o \to m_P = o' \to m_P$$

Such methods can be described as the following family of functions:
$$\forall P: m_P: A \to Z$$

2.2 Inverse Methods

For deciding which queries containing invocations of such methods can be optimized and for choosing the appropriate rewriting rules we need further information about properties of the methods, in particular about injectiveness and monotonicity.

2.2.1 Injective Functions

Injective functions have an inverse function. According to the above classification the inverse functions m^{-1} can be specified more precisely as:

☐ with distinguished attribute:
$$m^{-1}_P: Z \to A, \text{ with } \forall a, P: m^{-1}_P(m_P(a)) = a$$
☐ without distinguished attribute:
$$m^{-1}_P: Z \to C, \text{ with } \forall o, P: m^{-1}_P(m_P(o)) = o$$

To optimize inequality comparisons, we are interested in strict monotonous functions, a subclass of injective functions. The definition of the inverse of strict monotonous functions is the same as for injective functions.

2.2.2 Non Injective Functions

Non injective functions have no one-to-one inverse functions. Nevertheless, we are able to optimize non injective functions by the definition of an inverse method which maps its results into power set $\wp$. According to the above classification we again specify such methods more formally as:

- with distinguished attribute:
    $m^{-1}_P: Z \rightarrow \wp(A)$, with $\forall\, a, P: m^{-1}_P(m_P(a)) = \{\, a' \mid m_P(a) = m_P(a')\,\}$
- without distinguished attribute:
    $m^{-1}_P: Z \rightarrow \wp(C)$, with $\forall\, o, P: m^{-1}_P(m_P(o)) = \{\, o' \mid m_P(o) = m_P(o')\,\}$

2.3 Integration in ODMG-93

According to the above considerations we extend ODMG-93 with a special language construct to create an inverse method (similar to an index definition):

> **inverse operation** <return_type> <operation_name> (<argument_list>)
> **on** <type_name>
> **for** <operation_name> [**injective** | **increasing** | **decreasing**]
> [**based on** <attribute_name>] [<raises_expr>] <context_expr>

The definition of an inverse method starts with the keyword *inverse operation* followed by the return type, the name of the inverse method and its argument list, similar to the construct for defining a method in ODMG-93. The type, where the inverse method is attached is specified with the property *on*. The name of the corresponding original method is stated after the keyword *for*. To characterize the kind of the method (injective, strict monotonous increasing or strict monotonous decreasing) the optional keywords *injective*, *increasing* and *decreasing* are used. If the inverse method refers to a non injective method none of these parameters are allowed, but the return type of the inverse must be a set of the return type of the original method. The existence of a distinguished attribute is specified with the keyword *based on* followed by the name of the attribute. The parameter *raises_expr* is necessary for the treatment of exceptions raised by methods. According to ODMG-93 the definition of an inverse method ends with the method body, indicated with *context_expr* [1] in our language construct.

The definition of an inverse method underlies several constraints which can be checked automatically:

- The return type of the inverse method must be of the same type as the type of the corresponding attribute defined with the keyword *based on* or a set of this type. Without an distinguished attribute the return type of the inverse must be equal with the type specified with the *on* property (or a set of this type).

- The arguments of the inverse method must be equivalent to the argument list of the original method. Additionally, a further parameter is needed for the comparison operand. This parameter has to be the first in the argument list and its type must be the same as the result type of the original method.
- If the result type of the inverse method is a set of the type , or a set of the type of the distinguished attribute, respectively, then none of the optional parameters *injective*, *increasing* or *decreasing* is allowed.

Inverse methods are realized as type methods rather than as object methods. What are the reasons for this decision? Inverse methods could be invoked on elements of the codomain of the original method. We do not place it as (normal) method in the type of this codomain, because this type is frequently a value type (e.g. numbers) such that we cannot define methods there. Moreover, the semantic context of the inverse method is the original type. If the type of the codomain already has a suitable method, then the body of the inverse method can simply consist of a call of that method. Furthermore, the inverse method is not invoked on on an object of the type but rather results in an object (or a distuinguished attribute) such that we cannot define it as object method of the type.

Consider the small example from the introduction. The extended ODMG-93 definition of the inverse method temp_fahrenheit would be:

```
inverse operation real temp_fahrenheit (in real)
on Material
for temp_celsius increasing
based on melting_point  <context_expr>
```

We consider inverse methods as access structures belonging to the internal level of a database as they are used for optimization purpose only. Like indexes they can be added and dropped at runtime affecting the performance of the system only. Queries do not have to be reformulated when inverse methods are defined or deleted (physical data independence).

3 The Optimization Process

3.1 Rewriting Rules

We first present the rewriting rules for the optimizing queries for homogeneous collections. In the following sections we will extend this algorithm to heterogeneous collections and discuss all aspects of inheritance.

We optimize the following generic kind of queries:

```
SELECT       ....
FROM         objectVar in Type_Extent
WHERE        objectVar→Method(Parameter) RelOp ComparisonOperand
```

RelOp are the usual comparison operators, such as *equal, greater, less* and *in*. *ComparisonOperand* can be, for instance, a constant, a set or a subquery.

The condition part of the query is rewritten into:

    WHERE   FirstPart RelOp' SecondPart

The *FirstPart* of the rewritten query depends on the existence of a distinguished attribute, specified with the *based on* property. If there is one, then the FirstPart is rewritten to *objectVar.Attributename* otherwise only to *objectVar*.

The rewriting rules for *RelOp'* and *SecondPart* depend on the original relational operator *RelOp* and the kind of the method, as specified in table 1.

Method Kind	RelOp	RelOp'	SecondPart
injective	=	=	$T \rightarrow m^{-1}$ (CO, P)
	IN	IN	FOR x IN (CO) $\{T \rightarrow m^{-1}(x,P)\}^2$
strict monotonous increasing	$<, \leq$ $>, \geq$	$<, \leq$ $>, \geq$	$T \rightarrow m^{-1}$ (CO, P)
strict monotonous decreasing[3]	$<, \leq$ $>, \geq$	$>, \geq$ $<, \leq$	$T \rightarrow m^{-1}$ (CO, P)
non injective	=	IN	FOR x IN (CO) $\{T \rightarrow m^{-1}(x,P)\}$
	IN	IN	FLATTEN[4] (FOR x IN (CO) $\{T \rightarrow m^{-1}(x,P)\}$)

  T   type where the inverse method m^{-1} is defined, stated by the *on* property
  CO ComparisonOperand, e.g. a constant, a subquery, an object
  P   parameters of the original method

Table 1: Rewriting Rules

---

[2] As the inverse method must be performed on all members of the set it is necessary to use an iteration operator, which until now is not defined in ODMG-93 but for instance in O_2 [12].

[3] Strict monotonous decreasing methods require to switch the relational operators.

[4] As the result of the iterator operation is a set of sets, it is necessary to flatten the result. For this purpose we use the flatten operator defined in ODMG-93.

There may exist comparison operands, which are not valid for the inverse method, although they can be used in the original query (e.g. non surjective functions). For such operands the inverse method has to raise the special exception *inverse_exception*, which must be known by the query optimizer. If the optimizer recognizes such an exception the original statement has to be executed. The efficient treatment of such queries is subject of ongoing research.

3.3 Examples

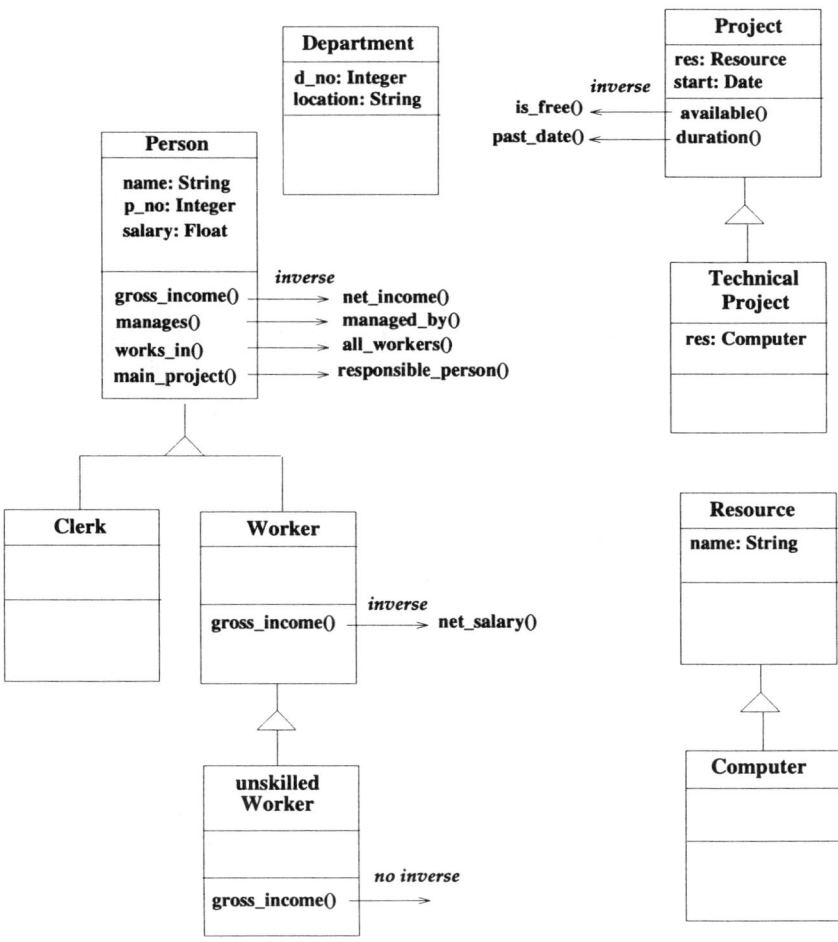

Figure 1: A Small Database Schema

Figure 1 shows an example of a small database schema in OMT-like syntax [13]. You can see a type Person with its subtypes Clerk, Worker and unskilled Worker. Each type has some attributes and methods. The inverse methods are shown with an arrow. There are also some other types, Project with the subtype Technical Project, Department and Resource with the subtype Computer.

All further query examples are based on this small schema. An informal description of each method is given in the query examples. We are aware that essential parts (such as relationships) are missing in our example. Moreover we do not consider implementation aspects of methods but concentrate only on the necessary parts to present our optimization strategy.

In the following examples we concentrate only on the condition part of the queries because of space limits.

Injective methods: We want to know the manager of the department 27 using the method manages. The inverse method is called managed_by and is based on the attribute p_no:

p→manages () = 27	p.p_no = Person→managed_by (27)

Non injective methods: We want a list of all persons working in the department 27. The method works_in in the example of figure 1 is based on the attribute p_no and returns for each person the corresponding department. However, the inverse method all_workers produces a set of values, exactly all persons being engaged in that department.

p→works_in () = 27	p.p_no IN Person→all_workers (27)

Strict monotonous decreasing methods: Compute a list of all projects running longer than 30 days. The method duration computes the duration time of a project, which is based on the attribute start. The inverse method past_date computes the date minus n days.

p→duration () > 30	p.start < Project→past_date (30)

Usage of the IN operator in a non injective method: We want to know all persons working in a department which is located in Austria.

p→works_in () IN
   (SELECT d.d_no
    FROM d in Departments
    WHERE d.location = "Austria")
	p.p_no IN FLATTEN (FOR x IN
	   (SELECT d.d_no
	    FROM d in Departments
	    WHERE d.location ="Austria")
	   {Person→all_workers (x)})

Method without distinguished attribute: Compute a list of all persons, who have their main project located in Austria. The method main_project returns the main project of a person. The inverse method responsible_person computes the responsible person of a project.

p→main_project () IN
   (SELECT pro
    FROM pro in Projects
    WHERE   pro.location = "Austria")
	p IN (FOR x IN
	   (SELECT pro
	    FROM pro in Projects
	    WHERE pro.location = "Austria")
	   {Person→responsible_person(x)})

3.3 Advantages

The difference in the evaluation costs between the original and the rewritten query depends on the following:

- ☐ evaluation cost of the original method and its inverse
- ☐ the number of objects in the collection
- ☐ the existence of indexes
- ☐ the selectivity of the distinguished attribute
- ☐ whether the method is injective
- ☐ the cardinality of the result of the inverse method for non injective methods
- ☐ the cardinality of the comparison operand for IN comparisons
- ☐ whether the parameter of the method is independent of the object variable
- ☐ whether the comparison object depends on the object variable (correlated subquery)

A quantitative model is beyond the scope of this paper. For applying this technique the rewriting rules of a cost-based query optimizer should be extended. The advantage of this optimization technique, however, can be several orders of magnitude. For an example take an injective method (without distinguished attribute), equality comparison, and a non-correlated comparison operand. For a collection of cardinality N it would be necessary to retrieve N objects and invoke the method N times, while the inverse method is evaluated only once and a single object is fetched from secondary memory. If the execution costs of the methods are about the same this results in a reduction of the evaluation costs of the queries by the factor N. For such methods and queries our optimization technique can even be integrated in rule based optimizers. On the other hand, if the comparison object is a correlated subquery the evaluation costs of the rewritten query might be higher, since the inverse method then has to be executed for each object of the collection. Such queries should only be optimized with a cost-based optimizer.

4 Aspects of Inheritance

4.1 Inheritance of Inverse Methods

Inverse methods are inherited, too. However, the scope of an inverse is tied to the scope of its method. If a method is overridden, neither the overridden method nor its inverse method are inherited, irrespective whether an inverse of the overriding method has been defined or not. However, it is possible to override inverse methods without overriding the original method, although this will rarely be necessary.

This general concept of inheritance is very useful for our optimization process. It may be necessary to optimize queries, whose target type is a subtype of the type where the inverse method has been defined, for instance consider a query which computes a list of clerks with a gross income greater than 30000. We can optimize this query by using the inverse method net_income defined within the type Person. To handle such queries, the optimizer needs to collect the necessary information about the inverse method, e.g. by searching the type hierarchy backwards.

4.2 Method Overriding

Our optimization technique can also be applied to heterogeneous collections, i.e. collections of objects of different types. If neither the method to be optimized nor the inverse method are overridden, then the optimization process presented in section 3 can be applied without change. Overriding of methods and inverses leads to a more complex optimization process dealing with overridden methods and therefore, with the existence of different inverse methods. Additionally, an overridden method may have no corresponding inverse method.

In our example we have three subtypes of Person, the types Clerk, Worker, and unskilled Worker (with the corresponding extents Clerks, Workers and unskilled Workers). Each of these types inherits an attribute salary, where the net income of a person is stored and a method gross_income, which computes the gross income based on the salary. As the computation of the gross salary differs between clerks and workers the method gross_income is overridden in Workers. Obviously there exist different inverse methods called net_income and net_salary. Additionally, the gross income is overridden in unskilled Worker without defining an inverse method.

To rewrite queries over heterogeneous collections we have to distinguish the objects according to their types. Depending on the existence and the kind of inverse methods it is not always possible to fully optimize the whole query. To produce an optimized query, the condition is rewritten with a disjunction of clauses - one clause for each pivot type, i.e. the type T of the extent defined in the query and all (direct and indirect) subtypes of T, where either the method or its inverse is overridden. Let ST be the set consisting of the name of a pivot type T and all its (direct and indirect) subtypes which neither override the method m nor its inverse. For each pivot type we create the following clause:

ObjectVar.Type.Name IN ST AND
<optimized statement>

The *<optimized statement>* is the rewritten query based on the kind of the inverse method as explained in section 3. If an optimization is not possible, because of an inadequate relational operator or the overridden method has no inverse method, the original condition is used.

Consider the following condition part of a query based on our small example:

p→gross_income () > 10000	(p.Type.Name IN {Person, Clerk} AND
	    p.salary > Person→net_income (10000)) OR
	(p.Type.Name IN {Worker} AND
	    p.salary > Worker→net_salary (10000)) OR
	(p.Type.Name IN {unskilled_Worker} AND
	    p→gross_income () > 10000)

As you can see method overriding decreases the advantages of our optimization strategy. Now it is necessary again to scan the whole collection, as the type of each object is necessary within the optimized query. But still the number of method calls is significant smaller than with the origin query. Obviously the advantage of our approach decreases the more methods are redefined within the type hierarchy.

4.3 Attribute Overriding

In the object-oriented paradigm the overriding of attributes is possible as the redefinition of methods within the type hierarchy. However, the overridding of attributes is restricted by the concept of covariance which is supported by ODMG-

93. The type of an attribute's redefinition must be a subtype of its original inherited definition. In the case of overridding the distinguished attribute we have to analyze possible constraints to our approach.

Suppose the following query, which computes all projects, whose resource is available on the 1st of October. The method available returns the date when the resource of the corresponding project is not any more used.

p→available () = "1.Oct. 1994"	p.res IN Project→is_free ("1.Oct. 1994")

The inverse method is_free returns a set of resources. As technical projects also belongs to the extent projects (by instance inheritance) and the attribute resource is overridden in type technical project we have to deal with the comparison of different types (in our example we have to compare objects of type Computer with objects of type Resource).

Although ODMG-93 does not consider that problem explicitly, such a query can be written in O_2. Regarding to our approach, we are able to optimize queries with an overridden distinguished attribute without any restrictions.

5 Conclusions

We presented a novel technique for the optimization of queries against object-oriented databases with method calls in the condition part of the query. Our approach introduces inverse methods as computed inverted access structures. We consider these inverse methods to somehow belong to the physical level of database systems. They can be added and dropped like stored access structures (indexes).

These inverse methods can then be used to rewrite the condition part of queries. For a significantly large class of queries our approach reduces the cost of query evaluation by orders of magnitude and our approach can be directly integrated into rule based optimizers. For other classes the cost of the original and the rewritten query have to be estimated, such that we recommend the integration only into cost-based optimizers.

Best results are obtained, when our technique is applied to queries against homogeneous collections or to heterogeneous collections, where the method used in the condition part is not overridden. Our approach has been extended to all heterogeneous collections with overridden methods too. However, the necessary type case distinction reduces some of the advantages.

References

1. Cattell R. The Object Database Standard: ODMG-93. Morgan Kaufmann Publishers, San Mateo, 1993
2. Mitchell G., Zdonik S., Dayal U. Optimization of Object-Oriented Queries: Problems and Approaches In: Dogac A., Özsu T., Biliris A., Sellis T. (ed) Proceedings of the NATO ASI Object-Oriented Database Systems, Kusadasi, Turkey, 1993, pp 30-66
3. Graefe G. Query Evaluation Techniques. ACM Computing Surveys, Vol. 25, No. 2, June 1993, pp 73-170
4. Freytag J., Maier D., Vossen G. Query Processing for Advanced Database Systems. Morgan Kaufmann Publishers, San Mateo, 1994
5. Eder J., Frank H. Schema Integration For Object Oriented Database Systems. In: Tanik M., Rossak W., Cooke D. (ed) Proceedings of Software Systems in Engineering, New Orleans, USA, 1994, pp 275-284
6. Dobrovnik M., Eder J. View Concepts for Object-Oriented Databases In: Proceedings of the 4th International Symposium on System Research, Informatics and Cybernetics, Baden, 1993
7. Dobrovnik M., Eder J. A Concept of Type Derivation for Object-Oriented Database Systems, In: Gün, Onvural R. Gelenbe E. (ed) Proceedings of the Eight International Symposium on Computer and Information Sciences (ISCIS VIII), Istanbul, 1993
8. Graefe G., Ward, K. Dynamic Query Evaluation Plans. SIGMOD Proceedings, ACM, 1989, pp 358-366
9. Bertino E. Method Precomputation in Object-Oriented Databases. SIGOIS Bulletin, 12(2,3), 1991, pp 199-212
10. Kemper A., Kilger C., Moerkotte G. Function Materialization in Object Bases. SIGMOD Proceedings, ACM, 1991, pp 258-267
11. Kemper A., Kliger C., Moerkotte G. Function Materialization in Object Bases: Design, Realization and Evaluation. IEEE Transaction on Knowledge and Data Engineering, Vol. 6, No. 4, August 1994, pp 587-608
12. The O_2 User Manual, Version 4.2, January 1993
13. Rumbaugh J. et al. Object-Oriented Modeling And Design. Prentice Hall, Englewood Cliffs, New Jersey, 1991

Database Languages

F-Bounded Polymorphism for Database Programming Languages

Suad Alagić*

Department of Computer Science, Wichita State University
Wichita, KS 67260-0083, USA, e-mail: alagic@cs.twsu.edu

Abstract

The relevance of F-bounded polymorphism for database programming languages (object-oriented in particular) is investigated. Two different kinds of object types are proposed as a solution for the controversy between inheritance and subtyping. It is with this duality that complex, recursive object types so typical for database application environments are constructed and the relationship with F-algebras and F-coalgebras hinted in the literature established. Surprisingly enough, the covariant (and thus unsafe) ordering for object types is shown to play an important role in interpreting formally the contravariant (type-safe) subtyping for object types. These results are established in a formal framework based on a variety of kinds (of types) of a polymorphic database type system which serves as a basis for a typed database technology. In addition to the formal theory, application-oriented and database system-oriented illustrations of the usage of F-bounded polymorphism are also presented.

1 Introduction

A fundamental issue in object-oriented database type systems is the subtype ordering of object types. While the covariant subtype ordering that matches inheritance for classes has been adopted in the O2 data model and the associated database programming language [16] and Eiffel [18], and claimed to be more natural, it has been proved that such ordering is not type safe [13]. The subtype ordering for object types contravariant in the argument types is known to be type-safe with respect to substitution of an instance of a subtype where an instance of its supertype is expected. As such it has been adopted in Galileo [5], Machiavelli [19] and other (related) approaches to object types for database programming languages [6]. It has been argued that this controversy shows that subtyping should not be identified with inheritance ([12], [13]), contrary to [16] and [18].

Recursive object types that arise naturally in many standard database application environments show that the contravariant (type-safe) subtype ordering does not produce results that one would intuitively expect. The reason is the interplay of the contravariant subtyping for methods and recursion. Bounded subtyping, so important for object-oriented type systems such as those for

---

*System-oriented implications of this research are made possible by a grant No. 33741-MA-RIP from the DOD Defense University Research Instrumentation Program

Modula-3 [10], Modulex [2] and Eiffel [18], also does not produce the expected results for recursive object types with contravariant subtype ordering. F-bounded polymorphism [11] has been proposed as a solution for the typing problems of recursive object types.

In F-bounded polymorphism, F is a function mapping object types into object types. In order to understand F-bounded polymorphism, we first establish formally the domain and the codomain of the type function F axiomatizing the properties of a variety of kinds (of object types in particular). Kinds for data-oriented languages have been introduced in [9]. There also exists a recent interesting proposal for an extensible typed database technology based on kinds [15].

A kind is a preordered collection of type signatures. Two kinds prove to be particularly relevant for F-bounded polymorphism. Those are dual kinds of F-bounded polymorphic types that correspond to F-algebras and F-coalgebras ([17],[14]). We prove that recursive object type signatures require completeness of these two dual kinds in the sense that appropriately defined initial resp. terminal F-bounded polymorphic types exist. This clarifies the relationship with F-algebras and F-coalgebras hinted in [11].

While these observations hold for a variety of recursive types typical for database application environments, they do not carry over to the object-oriented paradigm. The problem there is that the type function F is not subtype preserving (i.e., it is not covariant or monotone) if the subtype ordering for object types is type safe (contravariant). While fixed points of such functions do exist [12], the question is how can that be the case for Fs which are not even monotone?

We show that with the appropriate duality theory these issues may be resolved in a formally correct manner and that a solution requires two different kinds of object types. While F-bounded subtyping has been studied, we introduce its dual notion and prove that it is in fact required in order to explain why F-bounded polymorphism works for the type-safe subtyping of object types.

Our results apply to other kinds that are not necessarily kinds of object types and we show how F-bounded polymorphism is relevant beyond the area of object-oriented database type systems. In fact, our duality theory is motivated by the duality of two other kinds: the kind of record types and the kind of variant types that are shown to have relevance of their own for database programming languages.

The paper is organized as follows. In section 2 we introduce kinds (types of types), particularly those relevant to database programming languages. We then present briefly our approach to polymorphism based on kinds (section 3). Types of complex, recursive objects without encapsulation are discussed in sections 5 and 6 where we show how they are constructed using covariant type functions. Those complex (and recursive) object types are used as motivation for introducing the kinds of F-bounded polymorphic types and their limits (sections 6 and 7). The formal approach to object-oriented F-bounded polymorphism is then established in section 8. Section 9 outlines situations in which application of F-bounded polymorphism is appropriate. Finally, we analyze the results of the paper, compare them with some other approaches and discuss some possible generalizations.

2 Kinds

A kind is a preordered set of type signatures. TYPE is a collection of all type signatures $T1, T2, ..., Tj, ...$, of a particular type system together with the subtype relationships among those types denoted as $<:$.

TYPE is constructed inductively as a disjoint union (coproduct) of kinds as: TYPE $\cong \coprod K_i$ where each K_i is a preorder.

$K_0 = SIMPLE$ is a discrete preorder, i.e. a kind whose only subtype relationships are of the form $T <: T$. Objects of SIMPLE are simple types such as **Integer**, **Boolean**, **String** and **Real**. If $T1$ and $T2$ are simple types then neither $T1 <: T2$ nor $T2 <: T1$ holds. But once we start constructing structured types, subtyping relationships will be introduced accordingly.

RECORD is a set of all record type signatures of the form:

$R =$ **Record** $A1 : T1, A2 : T2, ..., An : Tn$ **End**

where Ai are attribute (field) identifiers and Ti are their corresponding types. $Ai \neq Aj$ for $i \neq j$ and the ordering of attributes is irrelevant.

Let $Attr(R) = \{A1, A2, ..., An\}$ be the set of attribute names of R and

$Type(R.Ai) = Ti$ be their corresponding types, elements of TYPE.

Then $R2 <: R1$ iff $Attr(R1) \subset Attr(R2)$ and $Type(R2.Ai) <: Type(R1.Ai)$ for $Ai \in Attr(R1)$.

This subtype ordering corresponds to [9]. RECORD is equipped with the terminal type (the empty record type) which has the property that every other record type is its subtype.

VARIANT is a collection of all type signatures of the form:

$V =$ **Variant** $A1 : T1 \mid A2 : T2 \mid ... \mid An : Tn$ **End**

where Ai are variant identifiers and Ti are their corresponding types. $Ai \neq Aj$ for $i \neq j$ and the ordering of variants is irrelevant. Let now:

$Attr(V) = \{A1, A2, ..., An\}$ be the set of variant names of V and

$Type(V.Ai) = Ti$ their corresponding types, elements of $TYPE$.

Then $V2 <: V1$ iff $Attr(V2) \subset Attr(V1)$ and $Type(V2.Ai) <: Type(V1.Ai)$ for $Ai \in Attr(V2)$.

VARIANT is equipped with the initial type (the empty variant type) which is a subtype of any other variant type.

SET is a kind consisting of a collection of type signatures of the form **Set**(T) where T is a type signature. $\mathbf{Set}(T2) <: \mathbf{Set}(T1)$ iff $T2 <: T1$.

FUNCTION is a collection of all function type signatures of the form

Function (A1, A2, ..., An): A where $A1, A2, ..., An, A$ are type signatures. Given types F =**Function** (A1, A2, ..., An): A and G = **Function** (B1, B2, ..., Bn): B, $F <: G$ holds iff $B1 <: A1, B2 <: A2, ..., Bn <: An$ and $A <: B$ [9].

3 Polymorphic demands on a database type system

The model of polymorphism in this paper is based on signatures for kinds and subtyping relationships of kinds that appear as parameters of polymorphic functions. This approach leads to a specific typed database technology in which not only strong, but even static type checking is possible. In order to accomplish that goal type computation performed at compile time is sometimes required, as in the case of the equi and the natural join operators. The following four functions illustrate the requirements imposed on a type system for database programming:

(i) A generic (polymorphic) projection and restriction function has two type parameters. T2 is the underlying record type of input set S and T1 is the output record type obtained from T2 by projection. Thus T2 $<:$ T1. *Predicate* is a parametric polymorphic restriction function on input records.

Function Select [T2,T1: RECORD | T2 $<:$ T1]
       (S: **Set**(T2), Predicate: **Function**(T2): **Boolean**
       ): **Set**(T1)

(ii) A generic sort function also has two type parameters in the subtyping relationship. T2 is the record type of the input set S and T1 is the record type which consists of sort fields of T2 so that T2 $<:$ T1. *LessThan* is a polymorphic comparison function.

Function Sort [T1,T2: RECORD | T2 $<:$ T1]
       (S: **Set**(T2), LessThan: **Function**(T1,T1): **Boolean**
       ): **Set**(T2)

(iii) Generic join has three type parameters. T1 and T2 are record types of the input sets S1 and S2 respectively. T3 is the underlying record type of the output set. There are also two restriction conditions on the input relations expressed in a polymorphic manner. The function *Match* provides the join condition and the function *Output* constructs the output records. Both are specified in a polymorphic fashion.

Function ThetaJoin [T1,T2, T3: RECORD]
       (S1: **Set**(T1), S2: **Set**(T2),
       Restriction1: **Function**(T1): **Boolean**,
       Restriction2: **Function**(T2): **Boolean**,
       Match: **Function**(T1,T2): **Boolean**,
       Output: **Function**(T1,T2): T3,
       ): **Set**(T3)

(iv) A generic natural join function requires type computation. In order to specify the type of the output, the join operation (in the RECORD kind) on the input record types must be applied. This type computation (denoted as T1 $*_{T0}$ T2) occurs at compile time. There are three type parameters. T1 and

T2 represent record types of input relations and T0 the record type consisting of the join fields. This condition is expressed by two subtyping relationships T1 <: T0 and T2 <: T0.

Function EquiJoin [T0,T1,T2: RECORD | T1 <: T0, T2 <: T0]
(S1: **Set**(T1), S2: **Set**(T2)): **Set**(T1 $*_{T0}$ T2)

Alternative and related approaches to the typing problems of database operators are compile-time linguistic reflection [20] and type inference [19].

4 Covariant type functions

The typing solution for the equi and the natural join requires a type operator. In this paper we show that such type functions play a key role in database type systems. They are the formal basis of a variety of recursive types so typical in database application environments. In section 8 we explicate the role which such type functions play in object-oriented type systems.

An example of a covariant (monotone) type function is TYPE $\longrightarrow$ SET defined as: T $\longrightarrow$ **Set**(T). Recall that T2 <: T1 implies **Set**(T2) <: **Set**(T1).

Perhaps contrary to the expectations, many type functions that come up in the typing problems of polymorphic database functions are not monotone. In order to give some important database examples, we first observe that if K is a kind, we can construct another preorder denoted as $K^{<:}$. The elements of $K^{<:}$ are the signatures T : Tj <: Ti that represent the subtyping relationships of K. Given another such signature R: Rj <: Ri, a subtyping relationships T <: R exists in $K^{<:}$ iff the pair of subtyping relationships Tj <: Rj and Ti <: Ri exists. With these definitions, we will regard $K^{<:}$ as a kind.

The following two examples are not covariant type functions:

IndexFunction: $RECORD^{<:} \longrightarrow$ FUNCTION defined as
IndexFunction($R2 <: R1$)= **Function** (R1): **Set**(R2)

R2 above represents the record type of the extent that is indexed and R1 a subset of the indexing attributes.

Projection: $RECORD^{<:} \longrightarrow$ FUNCTION defined as follows:
Projection($R2 <: R1$)=**Function**(**Set**(R2)): **Set**(R1)

The second example demonstrates typing of a generic projection function which takes a set of records of type R2 and returns a set of records of type R1, where R1 corresponds to a subset of the set of attributes in R2.

5 Recursive types as kinds

Covariant type functions lead to recursive type signatures according to the following formal properties.

Proposition Given a kind K with the terminal type $\top$, a covariant F : $K \longrightarrow K$ determines a linearly ordered kind:
$$\ldots F^{n+1}(\top) <: F^n(\top), \ldots, F^2(\top) <: F(\top) <: \top$$

Dually, given a kind K with the initial type $\bot$, a covariant $F : K \longrightarrow K$ determines a linearly ordered kind:
$$\bot <: F(\bot) <: F^2(\bot), \ldots, F^n(\bot) <: F^{n+1}(\bot) \ldots$$

Example. Consider a mapping $F : RECORD \longrightarrow RECORD$ defined as follows:

F(T) = **Record** name: **String**; price: **Real**;
              parts: **Set**(T)
    End

It is easy to verify that $T2 <: T1$ implies $F(T2) <: F(T1)$. In doing that we have to use the fact that **Set** is monotone.

Consider now a covariant $G : RECORD \longrightarrow RECORD$:

G(T) = **Record** name: **String**;
              parts: **Set**(T)
    End

We have $T2 <: T1$ implies $F(T2) <: G(T1)$ and thus $F^n(\top) <: G^n(\top)$ for all n. The recursive type specified by F is thus a subtype of the recursive type specified by G. Formal results related to recursive subtyping are given in section 7.

Dually, consider a covariant F: VARIANT $\longrightarrow$ VARIANT defined as:

F(T)= **Variant** part: Part |
              product: **Record** name: **String**; price: **Real**;
                          parts: **Set**(T)
              End
    End

These examples are illustrations used in the subsequent two sections for dual kinds of F-bounded polymorphic types and their limits that correspond to recursive type specifications.

6 Kinds of F-bounded polymorphic types

It has been hinted [11] that F-bounded polymorphism bears some relationship with the notion of F-coalgebra. Yet, in the context presented in [11] it is not possible to see what the actual relationship is. The relationship is established by constructing two dual preorders for a covariant F: K $\longrightarrow$ K for some kind K. The elements of the first are the signatures of the form $T <: F(T)$. These signatures are in fact F-coalgebras ([17], [14]). We will call this preorder the kind of F-bounded subtypes. The subtyping relationships of that kind are defined as follows:

Proposition The collection of F-bounded subtypes of a covariant F: K $\longrightarrow$ K is a kind whose subtyping relationships are defined as:
$$((T2 <: F(T2)) <: (T1 <: F(T1)) \text{ iff } (T2 <: T1) .$$

Example. For F: VARIANT $\longrightarrow$ VARIANT defined above and

T2= **Variant** part: Part |
          product: **Record** name: **String**; price: **Real**;
                          parts: **Set**(Part)
                  End
    End

T1= **Variant** part: Part |
          product: **Record** name: **String**;
                          parts: **Set**(Part)
                  End
    End

We have T2 <: T1 implies F(T2) <: F(T1). Furthermore, T1 <: F(T1) and T2 <: F(T2).

The elements of the dual preorder are signatures of the form $F(T) <: T$. If we regard them as type signatures, we get what we call F-bounded supertypes for lack of a better term. The subtyping relationships are defined as follows:

Proposition The collection of all F-bounded supertypes with the subtyping relationships defined as
   $((F(T2) <: T2)) <: (F(T1) <: T1))$ iff $(T2 <: T1)$
is a kind.

Example: F(T) defined as above and
T2=**Record** name: **String**; price: **Real End**
T1=**Record** name: **String End**.
We have T2 <: T1 implies F(T2) <: F(T1) and furthermore F(T2) <: T2 and F(T1) <: T1.

7 Limits of F-bounded polymorphic types

Recursive type signatures such as:

Type Product=
Record name: **String**; price: **Real**;
        parts: **Set**(Product)
End

Type Product=
Variant part: Part |
        product: **Record** name: **String**;
                        parts: **Set**(Product)
                End
End

are justified by the following two formal results:

Proposition If the kind of all F-bounded supertypes of a covariant $F : K \longrightarrow K$ has the initial type $F(\bot_F) <: \bot_F$ then $F(\bot_F) \cong \bot_F$.

In other words, if $F(\bot_F) <: \bot_F$ is the initial F-bounded supertype, then $F(\bot_F) <: \bot_F$ is type equivalence (isomorphism).

Dually, we have the following result:

Proposition If the kind of all F-bounded subtypes of a covariant $F : K \longrightarrow K$ has the terminal type $\top_F <: F(\top_F)$, then $F(\top_F) \cong \top_F$.

In other words, if $\top_F <: F(\top_F)$ is the terminal F-bounded subtype, then $\top_F <: F(\top_F)$ is type equivalence (isomorphism).

One familiar rule that can be proved from the introduced assumptions is the induction rule for recursive subtyping [12]. But that rule can be generalized in the sense that it has its dual. This completes the considerations presented in section 5.

Proposition If $F : K \longrightarrow K$ and $G : K \longrightarrow K$ are covariant type functions such that $T2 <: T1$ implies $F(T2) <: G(T1)$ then
(i) $\bot_F <: \bot_G$ if both $\bot_F$ and $\bot_G$ exist.
(i) $\top_F <: \top_G$ if both $\top_F$ and $\top_G$ exist.

Proposition Let K be a kind and $F : K \longrightarrow K$ covariant. If the kind of all F-bounded supertypes has the initial type $\bot_F$ and the kind of all F-bounded subtypes has the final type $\top_F$, then $\bot_F$ is a subtype of $\top_F$.

The proposition says that the initial F-bounded supertype is a subtype of the terminal F-bounded subtype, if both of them exist.

8 Object-oriented F-bounded polymorphism

The kind of all object types OBJECT is defined as a collection of type signatures of the form

Object MethodList **End**

The types in the method list are required to be function types. The subtype ordering is the same as for RECORD. This is a well-known approach to modeling of object types ([10],[6]) that has in particular been accepted in papers on F-bounded polymorphism ([11],[12]).

Many object types are naturally recursive such as the following typical database example:

Type Product=
Object name: **Function**(): **String**;
       Parts: **Function**(): **Set**(Product);
       IsPart: **Function**(Product): **Boolean**
End.

This type definition produces a type mapping $F : OBJECT \longrightarrow OBJECT$ such that Product $\cong$ F(Product).

F(T)= **Object** name **Function**(): **String**;
        Parts: **Function**(): **Set**(T);
        IsPart: **Function**(T): **Boolean**
    End.

Although Product $\cong$ F(Product), F is not covariant (monotone), i.e. $T2 <: T1$ does not imply $F(T2) <: F(T1)$. F is not contravariant either. None of the already established results in this paper seem to apply. A further problem is that intuitively we might expect the following type to be a subtype of Product:

Type CommercialProduct=
Object name: **Function**():**String**; price: **Function**():**Real**;
        Parts: **Function**():**Set** (CommercialProduct);
        IsPart: **Function**(CommercialProduct):**Boolean**
End.

While admittedly natural from the point of view of software reuse, the definition of CommercialProduct has the property that CommercialProduct is not a subtype of Product (CommercialProduct$\not<:$ Product) because of the contravariance of the subtype ordering for methods in the argument types. Failing to realize this produces programs that satisfy the static type check and fail at run-time due to a type error. For example:
    p1,p2: Product; cp: CommercialProduct;
    Let p1 = cp; p1.IsPart(p2)
The problem comes from the local nature of type-checking and dynamic binding. p1.IsPart(p2) type checks. But at run time, the redefined version of IsPart will be chosen since the method is applied to an instance of type CommercialProduct (dynamic binding) and will get the actual argument of the supertype, contrary to the principle of subtyping where only an instance of a subtype may be substituted in place of its supertype.
    The observations made above for F hold for G defined as: $G : OBJECT \longrightarrow OBJECT$

G(T)=**Object** name **Function**():**String**; price:**Function**():**Real**;
        Parts: **Function**():**Set**(T);
        IsPart: **Function**(T):**Boolean**
    End

The solution is in a different kind of object types $OBJECT^{co}$ with the ordering for function types which is covariant (and thus unsafe) in the argument types. It has the same type signatures as OBJECT but the ordering, denoted by $:\rightarrow$, is defined as:
    Function(A1,A2,..., An):A $:\rightarrow$ **Function**(B1,B2,..., Bn):B iff
    A <: B and A1 <: B1, A2 <: B2,..., An <: Bn.

Now: $F : OBJECT^{co} \longrightarrow OBJECT^{co}$ and $G : OBJECT^{co} \longrightarrow OBJECT^{co}$ are covariant and we can speak of F-bounded and G-bounded polymorphic types as defined in this paper.

A fundamental observation is that isomorphism in theses two kinds coincides.

Proposition Two object types are type equivalent ($T1 \cong T2$ holds in OBJECT) iff they are inheritance equivalent ($T1 \cong T2$ holds in $OBJECT^{co}$)

If indeed $T2 \cong T1$, then there is no need to specify further what ordering we mean, as it will be necessarily the case with both. This means that if F has a fixed point in $OBJECT^{co}$, it has the same fixed point in OBJECT, and vice verse. One more result is needed in order to clarify formally why CommercialProduct is an F-bounded subtype of Product.

Proposition If $G(T) \cong T$ and $G(T) <: F(T)$ for all T, then $T <: F(T)$.

The proof is obvious. According to the above proposition CommercialProduct is an F-bounded subtype of Product since $CommercialProduct <: F(CommercialProduct)$ holds.

9 Applications

Applications of F-bounded polymorphism are restricted to languages supporting parametric polymorphic types and subtyping. Parametric polymorphic types are in fact type functions. For example:

Type Part[T: OBJECT]= **Object** name: **Function**():**String**;
   Parts: **Function**():**Set** (T);
End.

Part items are now required to have at least the methods *name* and *Parts*, but possibly some others. This condition is expressed using an F-bounded subtyping constraint:

Type PartItem [T: OBJECT | T <: Part[T]]=
Object ...
End.

Now PartItem[Product] and PartItem[CommercialProduct] are both type correct. By contrast, if Item is defined as

Type Item= **Object** name: **Function**():**String**;
   price: **Function**():**Real**
End.

then PartItem[Item] is not type correct.

F-bounded polymorphism is also required in strong and static typing of low-level database system abstractions. Here is a typical illustration:

Type Index[T, T0: OBJECT | T <: T0, T0 <: Order[T0]]=
Object ...
access: **Function**(T0):**Set**(T)
End.

The type parameter T represents the object type of the elements in the extent which is indexed, and T0 a collection of the indexing attributes, hence T <: T0. The other constraint guarantees that there is an ordering on T0. More precisely, the F-bounded constraint T0 <: Order[T0] guarantees that T0 has all the methods Order has. Order might be defined as:

Type Order [T: OBJECT]=
Object LessThan: **Function**(T): **Boolean**
End.

10 Conclusions

While some hints on the possible relationships of F-bounded polymorphism and F-coalgebras may be found in [11], to our knowledge this paper is the first to establish formally those relationships together with the duality results that we proved to be particularly relevant (kinds of F-algebras and F-coalgebras) for database programming languages.

While F-bounded subtypes have been studied in [11], we proved that the dual notion of F-bounded supertypes (F-algebras) is needed in order to understand F-bounded polymorphism. It is only with this duality that object-oriented F-bounded subtypes may be interpreted as F-coalgebras.

Our formal approach also explains the relationship between type safe, contravariant subtype ordering ([9], [6]) and unsafe, covariant subtype ordering ([16], [18]) that caused so much recent debate [13].

While it has been claimed ([16], [18]) that the covariant ordering, although unsafe, is more natural and more intuitive, our formal reasoning shows that it has its precise place in the theory of F-bounded polymorphic types and in fact makes F-bounded polymorphism coherent.

Our solution for the controversy between object subtyping and inheritance is in two different kinds of object types. Although they share the same set of object type signatures, their orderings are different. The subtype ordering enjoys the substitutability property and the inheritance ordering does not. For type safety to be preserved, those two kinds must be distinguished.

There is one other proposal that we are aware of that distinguishes these two different orderings in an object-oriented programming language [7]. The difference is that the object-oriented language presented in [7] does not support parametric polymorphism, nor any other higher-order features such as kinds or F-bounded polymorphism.

The main limitation of the presented approach is its syntactic nature since in this paper we consider type signatures only. The semantic model for a type system that supports F-bounded polymorphism does exist [8]. It is admittedly quite sophisticated (based on partial equivalence relations (PERs) over suitably defined complete partial orders), and we do not deal with it in this paper.

In separate papers ([3], [4]) we elaborate the role which F-bounded polymorphism plays in an object-oriented type system which is enriched with logic-based executable specifications of the semantics of methods.

References

[1] S. Alagić, Object-Oriented Database Programming, Springer-Verlag, New York, 1989

[2] S. Alagić, Toward Multiparadigm Database Interfaces. In: J. W. Schmidt and A. A. Stogny (eds), Next Generation of Information Systems Technology, Springer-Verlag, 1991, (Lecture Notes in Computer Science Vol. 504)

[3] S. Alagić and R. Sunderraman: Expressibility of Typed Logic Paradigms for Object-Oriented Databases, Proceedings of BNCOD-12, pp. 73-89, Springer-Verlag, 1994 (Lecture Notes in Computer Science Vol. 826)

[4] S. Alagić, R. Sunderraman and R. Bagai: Declarative Object-Oriented Programming: Inheritance, Subtyping and Prototyping, Proceedings of ECOOP '94, pp. 236-259, Springer-Verlag, 1994, (Lecture Notes in Computer Science Vol. 821)

[5] A. Albano, L. Cardelli and R. Orsini, Galileo: A Strongly Typed, Interactive Conceptual Language, ACM Transactions on Programming Languages and Systems Vol. 10, pp. 230-260, 1985

[6] A. Albano, G. Ghelli and R. Orsini, Objects for a Database Programming Language, In: P. Kanelakis and J. Schmidt (eds): Proceedings of the Workshop on Database Programming Languages, pp. 236-253, Morgan-Kaufmann Publishers, 1991

[7] K. B. Bruce, Safe Type Checking on a Statically Typed Object-Oriented Programming Language, Proceedings of the ACM Conference on Principles of Programming Languages, pp. 285-298, ACM, 1993

[8] K. Bruce and J. Mitchell, PER Models of Subtyping, Recursive Types and Higher-order Polymorphism, Proceedings of the ACM Conference on Principles of Programming Languages, pp. 316-327, ACM, 1992

[9] L. Cardelli, Types for Data Oriented Languages, In: J.W. Schmidt, S. Ceri and M. Missikoff (eds), Advances in Database Technology - EDBT '88, pp. 1-15, Springer-Verlag, Berlin, 1988 (Lecture Notes in Computer Science Vol. 303)

[10] L. Cardelli, J. Donahue, M. Jordan, B. Kalslow and G. Nelson, The Modula-3 Type System, In: Conference Record, ACM Symposium on Principles of Programming Languages, pp. 202-212, ACM, 1989

[11] P. Canning, W. Cook, W. Hill, W. Olthoff and J.C. Mitchell, F-Bounded Polymorphism for Object-Oriented Programming, In: Proceedings of the Conference on Functional Programming Languages and Computer Architecture, pp. 273-280, ACM, 1989

[12] W. R. Cook, W. L. Hill and P. S. Canning, Inheritance Is Not Subtyping, In: Proceedings of the ACM Conference on Principles of Programming Languages, pp. 125-135, ACM, 1990

[13] W. R. Cook, A Proposal for Making Eiffel Type Safe, The Computer Journal Vol. 32, pp. 305-311, 1989

[14] P. Freyd. Algebraically Complete Categories, In: A. Carboni, M.C. Pedicchio and G. Rosolini (Eds): Category Theory: Proceedings of the International Conference (Como), pp. 95-104, Springer-Verlag, 1991, (Lecture Notes in Mathematics Vol. 1488)

[15] R. H. Guting, Second-Order Signature: A Tool for Specifying Data Models, Query Processing and Optimization, Proceedings of the ACM SIGMOD Conference, pp. 277-286, ACM, 1993

[16] C. Lecluse and P. Richard, The O2 Database Programming Language, Proceedings of the 15th International VLDB Conference, pp. 411-422, Morgan-Kaufmann Publishers, 1989

[17] E. G. Manes and M. A. Arbib, Algebraic Approaches to Program Semantics, Springer-Verlag, 1986.

[18] B. Meyer, Eiffel: The Language, Prentice-Hall, 1992.

[19] A. Ohori, P. Buneman and V. Breazu-Tannen, Database Programming in Machiavelli - a Polymorphic Language with Static Type Inference, Proceedings of the ACM SIGMOD Conference, pp. 46-57, ACM, 1989.

[20] D. Stemple, L. Fegaras, T. Sheard and A. Socorro, Exceeding the Limits of Polymorphism in Database Programming Languages, In: F. Bancilhon and C. Thanos (Eds), Advances in Database Technology - EDBT '90, pp. 269-285, Springer-Verlag, 1990 (Lecture Notes in Computer Science Vol. 416)

OODBMS's Query and Programming Languages: What Do They Provide and What Do We Need

Sergei D. Kuznetsov

The Institute for System Programming, Russian Academy of Sciences

Moscow, Russia

Abstract

We propose in this paper an approach toward a non-navigational query language for object-oriented database systems. This language would be closed under the notions of class and type. We strictly separate these notions and give a set-theoretical meaning to the notion of class. We then describe a variant of algebra of classes which is closed under the notion of class. In the last part of the paper, we describe preliminary ideas that might help us to avoid the impedance mismatch between such a query language and an object-oriented database programming language.

1 Introduction

There are several main reasons making object-oriented (OO) approach so attractive in the area of information systems. First, the relational data model is too restricted for a number of advanced applications and development tools. Second, OO programming languages and systems are more and more widely used (in particular, C++). Third, the inconvenience of separate modeling of real world structure and behavior is widely recognized. Fourth, the impedance mismatch [1] between programming languages and relational database languages prevents developers from using a natural style of application development.

At the same time, many researchers recognize that the current level of OO DBMSs is far from the best [2],[5],[7],[9]. Let us observe what is more or less satisfactory for application developers who use recently available OO DBMSs.

Note that though relational systems allow arbitrary queries based on relationships not defined by referential integrity rules, in most cases those joins are actually in use that are related by explicit references. Being expressed in terms of objects, this means that in most cases an explicit or implicit unnest operation is sufficient. In other words, in querying OODB it's almost always sufficient to use those classes which are defined statically [3],[4],[6],[8].

Although a new relational scheme is produced when two relations are joined, we actually deal with controlled schema production in the cases when statically defined references are used. In fact, we deal in these cases with nested complex objects modelled with the use of flat relations.

It seems that the majority of OODB users are satisfied with querying only objects of one class (and all its subclasses) at any moment. But even if this is really true, it would be desirable to understand what is the subset of objects of one class that satisfy some condition. Is this a class or something else? If it is a class, what is its place in the class hierarchy?

An even more interesting question is why relational DBMSs actually allow arbitrary joins? Probably this is because sometimes one cannot define statically all possible relationships between different entities. But if this is true for relational data bases why something analogous might not be needed for OO DBMSs?

However, it is not so easy to provide such features in OO DBMSs. There are several problems to be solved. Some of these problems are natural for OO databases, some are raised mainly by historical reasons.

OO databases have inherited too much from programming languages (languages with abstract data types, OO languages, etc.) and too few from DBMSs (keeping in mind second generation DBMS, i.e. relational systems). In particular, OO DBMSs have inherited from OO languages an overloaded notion of class and an underloaded notion of type. In fact, the notion of class has been absolutely deprived of features that are peculiar to databases; the class is actually considered only as the type of some objects stored within a database. Additional notions are used to refer to object sets, a class extension or simply a collection.

There is quite an opposite situation in relational databases. There are also an underloaded notion of type and an overloaded notion of relation but the semantics of a relation generally reflects its set-theoretical nature. To introduce some analogy of type, an additional notion of a relational scheme is used (it is only an analogy because a relational scheme does not have its own name, and only one "variable" of this "type" with the same name is declared).

Following these differences, relational databases allow the existence of advanced declarative manipulative languages but are not well suited for application programs (the well known effect of impedance mismatch). On the other hand, specific features of existing OO DBMSs allow their easy and efficient use (although in restricted modes) in applications but actually prevent any possibility of advanced declarative query languages.

We believe that to design, develop and implement a declarative OODB query language and corresponding OODB programming language (without new effects of impedance mismatch), we should solve the following problems:

1) defining a minimal set of orthogonal notions that would be enough and convenient for OODB modeling, OODB querying, and application development.

2) developing an algebraic framework for declarative OODB manipulations.

3) specifying an approach for OODB programming language organization, that does not contradict the declarative nature of an OODB query language.

4) understanding how to optimize OODB queries specified in a declarative manner.

In this paper we are not going to give complete solutions for all these problems. Rather, we are trying to find some ways to get such solutions in future. Some ideas of this paper were discussed at the workshops of Moscow ACM SIGMOD Chapter [10],[11].

The rest of the paper is organized as follows. In the first section we briefly consider some of related works. The second section contains informal definitions of main notions used in the paper. In the next section we propose (again informally) some variant of algebra of classes. The forth section is dedicated to the problem of impedance mismatch in object-oriented database systems. The last section of the paper is a short conclusion.

2 Related work

The topic of data model and query languages for object-oriented database systems has been very popular during the last years. A huge number of publications in the subject exists. Our list of references is only a small subset of papers that are the most characteristic (and interesting) from our point of view.

One can do several different classifications of published papers. For example, there are approaches that are based on statically defined relationships between objects (object-preserving approaches) [14],[15]. Other authors propose query languages (and corresponding features of data models) that allow the dynamic creation of new objects [8],[9].

Another way to classification is based on object encapsulation. Some authors prefer not to support object encapsulation in query languages. Such query languages (and data models) are closer to complex objects, nested relations, or even semantic data model approaches [3],[6],[13]. Other authors believe that the feature of object encapsulation is one of the most fundamental features of OO approach and support this feature in query languages [12],[15].

The majority of researchers recognize the importance of the property of closure. This property implies the existence of some basic concept in a query language under which this language is closed, i.e. the nature of input and output of queries is the same. Consequently, one query may be applied to the result of another query, and so on. But this concept is not OO itself in most cases. For example, a set of values is such an additional concept in O2 [8]. Some other authors are trying to provide the closure property based only on pure OO concepts [12],[15]. Of course, to make this more precise and close to databases, a specific semantics of OO notions is required. Ideas of this paper are very close to those of [12, 15], but we are trying to introduce more orthogonal notions of type and class.

One can consider a number of other ways to classification of OO data models and query languages. For example, there are different approaches for the integration of query and programming languages of OO database systems. But we feel that such a short overview is sufficient for the purposes of this paper.

3 Main notions

We will generally use the widely accepted ideas of object-oriented system with multiple inheritance. Some notions most important in the context of this paper will be refined.

We represent an OODB as directed acyclic graph with a root (DAG) each vertex of which represents some class of objects, and each arc corresponds to some relationship of inheritance. Let call this DAG the static DAG of OODB.

Each object has its type and immediately belongs to some class, and also belongs to any superclass of this class. All objects of the same class have the same type (the type of immediate objects of this type), so one can speak about the immediate type of a class.

For any class, the type of any its superclasses is the supertype of the type of this class. Thus one object may have different types in different classes. The immediate type of an object is the type of its immediate class. We also allow the existence of several classes in OODB's DAG which are not related by class-superclass relationship but have the same type.

The type of an object (class) characterizes not only its syntax but also semantics. Two objects (classes) with a common type have a common nature. In particular, if two classes have the same type then it is reasonable to perform the set-theoretical operations of union and intersection for them. We consider that two classes have the same type if they have the same immediate type or if there exists some supertype that is common for both class types. In the last case we'll consider this supertype as the type of both classes.

We distinguish between a static DAG of classes (OODB as such) and a dynamic DAG of classes appearing during processing (interpreting) a query to OODB. These dynamic classes are analogous to temporal relations that may be created during processing a query to relational database.

Any dynamic DAG is local for a given query (more correct, for a given transaction). During query evaluation, objects may change their immediate classes in a given dynamic DAG. In some sense, a dynamic DAG represents a dynamically created view of a database schema. The result of a query is some class of objects in dynamic DAG, too. To get some values from these objects, an application should use their methods. The lifetime of such a class depends on specific features of the programming language.

We suppose that each type has a functional signature, i.e. an external type specification has the form of a set of function prototypes with specified parameters. Each parameter is typed, i.e. if some parameter of a function prototype is an object, then an object type is specified rather than a class. In a special case, a function prototype in a type signature can have no parameters at all, and this may be treated as a possibility to have a direct access (read) to the attributes of type values. A function of a type may return an object of some type; the class of such an object is not specified.

The separation of notions of class and type generally results in existence of different DAGs for classes and types of one OODB. These graphs have different structures because (1) we allow the existence of different classes of the same type without inheritance relationship, and (2) subclass may have the same type as its class.

In the most general case, it should be possible to create an object of any given type in any class of this type. It should be noted that it might be very reasonable to have different classes of the same type. The name of a particular class may be considered as some additional implicit attribute that is common for all objects of this class. For example, there might be subclasses of the class "Citizen" - "Moscow Citizen" and "Petersburg Citizen" (all three classes are of the type CITIZEN). Now, if we want to find somebody from Moscovits we need not include the predicate "is Moscovit" into the search condition; it is sufficient to seek within the class "Moscow Citizen".

Therefore, there may exist different DAGs of classes and types (static and dynamic). For any given OO database, the DAG of types is similar to the DAG of classes but not necessary the same.

4 Algebraic framework

Above notions allow us to construct an algebra of objects that is closed with respect to the notions of class and type. Each algebraic operation takes one or two classes of given types as arguments and produces a new class the type of which is defined by the operation. We here present an interpretation of set-theoretical operations (UNION, INTERSECT and cross-product) and also operations of selection and projection. For each operation we specify conditions of its application, the type of its result (more precise, the signature of this type), the place of this type in the dynamic DAG of types, and the place of the result class in the dynamic DAG of classes.

4.1 UNION of classes

The operation of union has two argument classes which must have the same type.

The type of a result class is the same as the type of arguments. The resulting class becomes a superclass for both classes-arguments. If arguments are denoted as A and B and result is denoted as C, then all objects of classes A and B (including objects of their subclasses) immediately belong to the class C in the given dynamic DAG.

4.2 INTERSECTION of classes

The operation of intersection has two argument classes which must have the same type.

The type of a result class is the same as the types of arguments. The resulting class becomes a subclass for both classes-arguments. If arguments are denoted as A and B and result is denoted as C, then all objects that immediately belong to class C also belong to both classes A and B in the given dynamic DAG.

4.3 Cross-product of classes

The operation of cross-product has two arguments and can be applied to any two classes of a DAG (static or dynamic).

The signature of a result type is produced by concatenation of signatures of argument types. Possible function name collisions are resolved using qualification by type name. Resulting class C produced by cross production of classes A and B includes each object that can be produced by "pairing" objects of classes A and B. Objects of class C are newly created temporal objects of OODB and have their own identities. The type of class C is a subtype of immediate types of classes A and B. The class C is, however, not a subclass of either class A or class B. The only place for class C in the dynamic DAG of classes is immediately under the root superclass of the static DAG.

It should be noted that even if classes A and B do have a common subclass of the same type as C, this subclass can not be considered as class C because objects of this class may have quite another origin.

4.4 Selection of class

The operation of selection has two arguments. The first argument is a class A from a DAG of classes (static or dynamic). The second argument is a Boolean expression F constructed from simple conditions wich include invocations of functions from the class A type signature.

A resulting class C has the same type as the class A, it a subclass of A in the dynamic DAG of classes. It immediately includes each object of A for which the value of F is true.

4.5 Projection of class

The operation of projection has two arguments. The first argument is a class A from DAG of classes (static or dynamic). The second argument is a subsignature S of the class A type signature, typically a list of function names from this signature.

The type of a resulting class C is a supertype of the class A type. The signature of this type is constructed by the deletion of all functions, listed in S, from the class A type signature. Objects of the class C are newly created temporal objects of OODB and they have new identities. Class C is not a super- or subclass of class A. The only place for class C in the dynamic DAG is immediately under the root class of the static DAG of classes.

Using the above set of operations, one can construct algebraic expressions. The fixed semantics of elementary operations allows us to interpret these expressions unambiguously if natural priorities of operators are defined: selections and projections have the highest priority, cross-products have the next level of priority, unions and intersections have the lowest priority.

It should be noted that it would be generally needed to check the structural equivalence of types of intermediate classes during expression interpretation (to determine, for example, the possibility of performing a set-theoretical operation). This task is quite solvable if functional signatures are used.

Of course, one can define the join operation based on cross-product, selection, and projection.

It's also should be noted that we do not say anything about cross-product and projection implementation. It's clear that cross-product constructs a class of objects that have properties of objects of both argument classes. Whether this composite objects are built by simple concatenation of component objects or some other techniques is used is an optimization issue. Similarly, projection may be implemented either by denying the access to a part of object functions or by reducing the object internal structure.

5 How to avoid a new situation of impedance mismatch?

The ideas of the previous section give some chances to develop a really declarative powerful query language for OODBs. To implement such a language (and even to define it precisely), we need, however, to solve a large number of technical problems, some of which are very complicated.

Before trying to solve these problems, it's desirable to estimate chances of avoiding a new impedance mismatch situation between a declarative query language and an OODB programming language. In this section, we propose some preliminary ideas of OODB programming language features which seem to be useful for avoiding the impedance mismatch. They are the following:

(a) to extend the semantics of class in OO programming languages to make stronger its set-theoretical aspect;

(b) to allow the construction of new classes from existing ones using a "query language";

(c) to allow the use of not only newly created objects and objects-parameters in a program but also objects of existed classes (selected from the database).

Any program written in such a language starts its execution in the context of two kinds of DAGs of classes and types. Classes of the first DAG are defined within the program and are initially empty. Classes of the second DAG are defined in the external environment of a program (e.g. OODB) and may already contain objects. A new object created in some class (probably it is more precise to speak about putting new object of a given type into a given clas) is stored in this class. The duration of object lifetime is defined by locality of the corresponding class (where this class has been defined). All visible classes (and objects of these classes) are available in any part of the program.

The name of any class is actually the name of a set of typed objects with a known place in the class hierarchy. Classes may be explicitly constructed by specifying both the type of objects and the place of this class in the static DAG of classes. They can be also specified by querying the set of existing and visible classes. In the last case a new (in general not empty) class is produced for which the type of its objects, the place of this type in the (dynamic) DAG of types, and the place of the class itself in the (dynamic) DAG of classes are known at compile time. Of course, we suppose that the "scheme" of the external environment is known and accessible at compile time.

Such an implicitly created class can either be unnamed if it's used absolutely locally, or be named as a local class of a program, or be specified as a class of an external environment. Thus one can construct a new class in any part of a program. In all cases, this class will be visible in that part. It can be used later either for the construction of additional new classes or for the retrieval of objects of this class.

Since one can always construct a class which includes only objects with desirable properties, one can see two ways of using the objects of a class: (a) any object of a given class is suitable, or (b) it is needed to operate in some manner with each object of a given class. To provide the both ways, it is sufficient to have operators of fetching an arbitrary object of a given class and of organizing an iteration to operate with all objects of this class sequentially.

Of course, these initial ideas are too far from a real language. We hope, however, they demonstrate an approach towards an OO language which includes a declarative OODB query language without impedance mismatch.

6 Conclusion

In this paper we have presented some ideas which can be useful for the declarative OODB query language development. We have also proposed an approach to the OODB programming language development which includes a declarative query language which is free from impedance mismatch.

We do not discuss implementation problems in this paper. These problems are hard enough, it is not reasonable to hope they may be solved soon. It is, however, very important to understand which approach to query languages for OO databases is really required before solving technical problems.

References

[1] Malkolm Atkinson, Francois Bansilhon, David DeWitt, Klaus Dittrich, David Maier, Stanley Zdonik. The Object-Oriented Database System Manifesto. 1st Int. Conf. Deductive and Object-Oriented Databases, Kyoto, Japan, Dec. 4-6, 1989

[2] Francois Bancilhon. Query Languages for Object-Oriented Database Systems: Analysis and Proposal. Datnbanksyst. Buro, Tech. and Wiss.: GI/SI - Fashtag., Zurich, Marz. 1-3, 1989, pp.1-18

[3] Timothy Andrews, Craig Harris. Combining Language and Database Advances in an Object-Oriented Development Environment GemStone Object-Oriented DBMS. Proc. OOPSLA'87, Orlando, Fla, USA, Oct. 4-8, 1987, pp.430-440

[4] Christophe Lecluse, Philippe Richard, Fernando Velez. O2, an Object-Oriented Data Model. Proc. ACM SIGMOD Int. Conf. Manag. Data, Chicago, Ill, USA, June 1-3, 1988, ACM SIGMOD Record, V. 17, No. 3, 1988, pp.424-433

[5] Francois Bancilhon. Query Languages for Object-Oriented Database Systems: Analysis and Proposal. Datanbanksyst. Buro, Tech. and Wiss.: GI/SI - Fashtag., Zurich, Marz. 1-3, 1989, pp.1-18

[6] E. Laenens, F. Staes, D. Vermeir. Browsing a la carte in Object-oriented Databases. Computer J., V. 32, No. 4, 1989, pp.333-340

[7] Catriel Beeri. A Formal Approach to Object-Oriented Databases. Data and Knowledge Eng., No. 5, 1990, pp.353-382

[8] Sophie Cluet, Claude Delobel, Christophe Lecluse, Philippe Richard. RELOOP: An Algebra Based Query Language for an Object-Oriented Database System. Data and Knowledge Eng., No. 5, 1990, pp.333-352

[9] Gail M. Shaw, Stanley B. Zdonik. A Query Algebra for Object-Oriented Databases. 6th Int. Conf. Data Eng., Los Angeles, Calif., USA, Febr. 5-9, 1990, pp.154-162

[10] S.D. Kuznetsov. Towards Non-Navigational Query Languages for Object-Oriented Database Systems. Proc. of ADBIS'93, Moscow, Moscow ACM SIGMOD Chapter, 1993, pp.44-53 (in Russian)

[11] Sergei Kuznetsov. Object-Oriented Database Programming Languages and Query Optimization. Proc. of ADBIS'94, Moscow, Moscow ACM SIGMOD Chapter, 1994

[12] Reda Alhajj. A Query Model and Object Algebra for Object-Oriented Databases. Bilkent University, Tech. Rep. CIS-9312, Ankara, Turkey, 1993

[13] S.Y.W. Su, M. Guo, and H. Lam. Association Algebra: A Mathematical Foundation for Object-Oriented Databases. IEEE Trans. on Knowledge and Data Engineering, V. 5, No. 5, October 1993, pp.775-798

[14] Michael Kifer, Won Kim, Yehoshua Sagiv. Querying Object-Oriented Databases. Proc. of 1992 ACM SIGMOD Int. Conf. on Manag. of Data, San Diego, Calif., June 2-5, 1992, pp. 393-402

[15] J. Banerjee, W. Kim, and K.C. Kim. Queries in Object-Oriented Databases. 4th Int. Conf. Data Eng., Los Angeles, Calif., USA, Febr. 1988, pp. 31-38

A Meta-language for Specification of Evolving Class and Object Lattices in OODB

Hele-Mai Haav

Institute of Cybernetics, Estonian Academy of Sciences
Akadeemia tee 21, EE0026 Tallinn, ESTONIA
Email: helemai@cs.ioc.ee

Abstract. The purpose of the paper is to describe the design of logic-based meta-language for representing constraints on managing evolution of class and object lattices in OODB. It will be prototypically incorporated to the object-oriented environment and language NUT. One of the goals of the paper is also to propose clean solutions to the integration of the procedural object-oriented programming language and declarative logic based language for representing evolution in OODB.

1 Introduction and Motivation

The fundamental problems of object-oriented (OO) database design and class lattice evolution have been discussed by several authors [1, 2, 3, 4, 5, 6]. We consider the following problems of managing constraints on class and object lattices and try to solve these problems on the basis of the meta-language described in this paper:

• *type subsumption problem.* This problem is well investigated in different fields of computer science [1, 6, 7]. Following our notation in this paper, the type is equivalent to the notion of class definition. The class definition ClassDef(C1) subsumes ClassDef(C) iff ClassDef(C1) is more general than ClassDef(C) i.e., C1 is a superclass of the class C. Complexity of decision, whether the class definition is subsumed by another class definition depends on the language used for representation of class definitions. Several languages are proposed to find a type representation language which has both a reasonable expressive power and a reasonable computational complexity [7, 8, 9]. We provide two integrated languages for type representation: OO specification language and declarative meta-language based on it.

• *constraint derivation problem.* Given a set of constraints on class and object lattices, new constraints can be derived using corresponding inference rules. A user can be interested in queries on class lattice or its evolution invariants. A user can also ask whether the certain change (evolution) is allowed and under what circumstances. In the latter case, conditional answers can be provided as we have proposed in [10, 11], where we used partial deduction techniques for that purpose.

- *undesirable properties of a class lattice*. They occur in the process of class lattice design (evolution). We can consider the following undesirable properties of a class lattice:

1. *Inconsistency* appears if the class lattice is defined so that one class is a subclass of two or more disjoint classes. Then that class definition cannot have an instance i.e. this class is empty.
2. *Cyclic structures* in the class lattice should be avoided.
3. *Redundant inheritance relationships* should be avoided. They are considered as inheritance relationships that can be derived from other inheritance relationships by transitivity.

In addition to problems mentioned above, we consider managing constraints on class and object lattice evolution called *evolution invariants* in this paper. Usually, evolution invariants depend on the implementation of an object-oriented system and language and as such cannot be defined in general.

There are some well-known approaches proposed by several authors [1, 2, 12] to solve problems concerning evolution of class and object lattices. We can distinguish at least two successful implementation issues: versioning [3, 12] and updatable views [13]. On the other hand, formal concept analysis based on lattice theory can be useful when representing and analysing different aspects of OODB schema and underlying object base. This has been recognized by several object-oriented programming and database researchers during the few last years [7, 8, 9, 14]. As a result, a number of logic languages of complex objects inspired by deductive database and logic programming research have been proposed [7, 2, 8, 15, 4].

In contrast to both pure object-oriented and logic based approaches we believe in multi-paradigm approach, where features of different paradigms are integrated. To solve the main problems of managing class lattice constraints and evolution invariants we propose a logic based meta-language for representing constraints on class and object lattices and provide a set of corresponding inference rules. The meta-language differs from other logic based languages for complex objects in its intention to be used on the top of the object-oriented language NUT and in tight relationships with underlying object-oriented specifications of classes and objects. This makes the language very simple but also practically useful. The meta-language will be prototypically incorporated to the object-oriented language and system NUT developed at the Institute of Cybernetics of the Estonian Academy of Sciences [16].

The paper is organised as follows. In the Section 2 we give an overview of the object-oriented system and language NUT used as a basis for the meta-language proposed. This Section also contains the definition of our object model. The Section 3 presents formal definition of the logic-based meta-language considered as a layer on the top of OO language and mainly used for specifying evolution invariants and reasoning on class and object lattices. In the Section 4 we introduce a set of inference rules for constraints on class and object lattices as well as for evolution invariants. Finally, we conclude our discussion in the Section 5.

2 The NUT System and its Data Model

2.1 General Description

The NUT programming system is an object-oriented environment, where two different programming paradigms - propositional logic programming and procedural programming are integrated. The language of the NUT system (called also NUT) combines features of declarative and procedural languages into an unified language based on object-oriented approach. The main feature of the NUT language is automatic synthesis of methods based on proof-as-program paradigm, where intuitionistic propositional calculus has been used as underlying formalism. The basic concepts of the NUT language are objects, classes and rules [16, 17]. Comparing to the other object-oriented languages the NUT language includes more logic based mechanisms.

First of all, for supporting synthesis of methods the parameters of methods must be state variables of a class in the NUT language. This makes state variables and methods interconnected. That allows to consider methods as specifications of computations represented by them and thus perform synthesis of some of the methods by the specifications of the others.

Second, Horn clauses are introduced to the language for meta-level reasoning about problems and specifications. Correspondence between classes (or objects) and meta-specifications is implemented by means of certain transformations.

The NUT environment contains the NUT language compiler, interpreter, program synthesiser, production system, interactive graphics, run-time support. The NUT system also supports compatibility with the C language that can be used for writing the implementation part of methods besides the procedural part of the NUT language itself. The NUT system operates on workstations (SUN etc.) running UNIX OS and the X Windows System.

2.2 The Data Model

In general, our data model used within the NUT system is a traditional object-oriented data model. Although the OO system and language NUT includes most of all concepts and features needed for OO data modelling, it is intended to be mainly an OO environment equipped with certain declarativeness. To make it also serve as OO data modelling tool needs some additional concepts and features to be added to.

First of all, classes in the NUT language are not containers of objects belonging to them. Classes describe only common interface and components of all instances of that class. Usually, in OO data models class is considered as a set of objects of certain type. Therefore, in that case the class is not used only for creating objects belonging to that class but also for managing the collection of objects. Thus, to provide NUT with notion of collection of objects of a class is important for making NUT a data modelling tool as well. We are working now on persistency of objects and on collection of persistent objects in the NUT environment, but this topic is out of the scope of this paper.

Since we consider multiple inheritance, also implemented now in the NUT environment, classes with these mutual relationships form a distributive lattice. We introduce as many others [2, 7, 9] top and bottom elements of this lattice to our data model. Top element is defined as a superclass of all classes and it is called *any*. Bottom element of the lattice is defined as a subclass of all classes and it is called *nil*.

Considering classes as collections of objects (actual instances of the class) together with the type (class) of these objects gives two different semantics to the definition of the class lattice. On the one hand, it represents class inheritance (set inclusion). On the other hand, it represents type inheritance (type inclusion) i.e. inheritance of components (attributes) and methods applicable to the instances of the class. We as well as in [2] separate such different semantics by introducing two types of lattices as follows: class lattice and object lattice (class instance lattice).

Definition 1. The lattice $<C, \leq>$ is called *class lattice*, where C is a finite set of class names including special elements for denoting the top (a least upper bound of the lattice - *lub*) and bottom classes (a greatest lower bound of the lattice - *glb*) in the class lattice. It contains also names of built-in primitive classes. Class names in C represent corresponding class definitions.

Definition 2. The lattice $<O, \subseteq>$ isomorphic to the class lattice $<C, \leq>$ is called *object lattice*, where a set O consisting of object identifiers for the class names in C is the basic domain for instances of class definitions denoted by class names in C.

Each class name c from C has associated a non empty subset of O, the domain of c denoted as Dom(c). Dom(c)=glb({Dom(c_1),...Dom(c_n)}) iff c = glb({c_1,...,c_n}). For a given class name c, there can be instances which do not belong to its subclasses. For them is defined a set of proper object identifiers i.e. a subset of Dom(c). The sets of proper object identifiers for the class names are pairwise disjoint.

The inheritance relationship between class definitions causes inclusion relationships among sets of instances. Thus, all instances of all class definitions are also instances of the class *any* and objects may be instances of more than one class definition.

2.3 An Example

Let us consider as a running example a class lattice that contains such classes as *person, stud, empl* and *stud_empl* together with these properties (attributes and methods) and inheritance relationships. The following picture represents the class lattice of our running example.

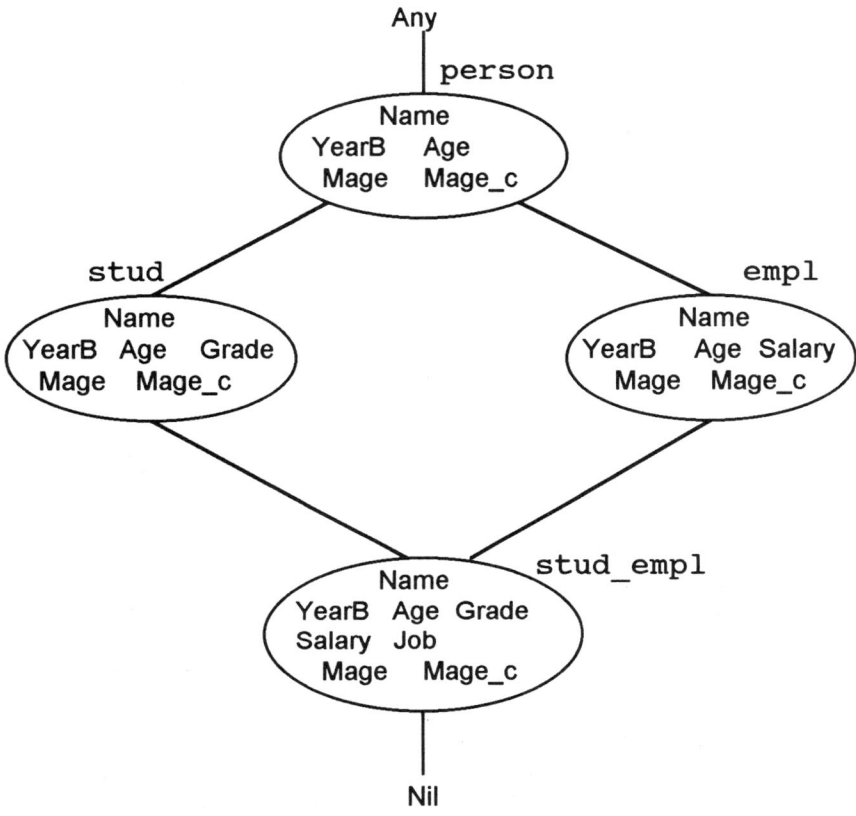

Picture 1. Class lattice of the example for the NUT environment

Let us represent our running example (see also Pic 1) in the OO language NUT as follows. Let *person, stud, empl* and *stud_empl* be user-defined class names (i.e. not built-in class names). Classes for which superclasses are not defined are considered as subclasses of most general class *any* (top element of the lattice). The statement *super <classname>* describes superclass of the class under consideration. Keyword *var* indicates the description of state variables and keyword *rel* description of methods with these signature and body enclosed to brackets. Keywords *text* and *num* denote built-in primitive classes (i.e. they are built-in class names). Also *any* and *nil* are built-in class names. The following set of classes describes class lattice for our example also illustrated in Pic 1.

person (// by default *super any* is assumed
  var Name:*text*;
      YearB: *num*;
      Age:*num*;

rel
      Mage: YearB->Age { age:= cur_year( ) - YearB};
      Mage_c: YearB->Age {*spec*};   // implicit method is described by *spec*
)

empl   (*super* person;
        var   Salary: *num*;
)

stud   (*super* person
        var   Grade:*text*;
)

stud_empl   (*super* stud;
                super empl;
                var   Job:*text*;
)

3   The Meta-language for the OO Language NUT

First, we define a very simple language based on Horn clauses without function symbols to represent class and object lattices. Second, we introduce a set of inference rules for expressing class lattice constraints and evolution invariants.
    An alphabet of the meta-language is defined as follows:

1. Set of constants **N** that consists of the set of object identifiers (names) **O**, names of class definitions (inc. special class names **any** and **nil**) **C**, methods' identifiers **M**, values of state variables.
2. Set of variable names **V**, which contains also names of state variables and methods used in OO specification and special variable Oid corresponding to an object identifier. Uppercase letters denote the variables in **V**.
3. Set of predicate symbols **P** contains the set **C** of names of class definitions, names of abstract predicates denoted by the symbol $ (inc. predefined predicate symbol $super), names of executable predicates denoted by the symbol !.

By this definition, the names of class definitions used in the OO specification have dual role in the meta-language: they can be either constants or predicate names.
    Terms are either constants or variables. An atom (atomic formula) is a formula of the form $p(t_1,...,t_n)$, where p is a predicate symbol and $t_1,...,t_n$ are terms.

Definition 3. Atoms with predicate symbols denoting names of class definitions are called *class atoms*.

Class atoms can be ground or non ground. A set of non ground class atoms represents a collection of class definitions in a class lattice. Non ground class atoms can be mapped into an object-oriented language as follows: if $p(Oid, S_1,...,S_n, M_1,...,M_m)$ is a class atom, then Oid denotes an object name, $S_1,...,S_n$ are names of state variables and $M_1,...,M_m$ are methods names. The first argument of the class atom is always reserved for an object identifier. Arguments of the predicates are not typed on the level of meta-language, but the type of an argument is taken into account when generating ground instances of these atoms on the basis of object-oriented language using transformations.

Set of all ground class atoms corresponds to an object base i.e. a collection of objects from object lattice. Every ground class atom of the form $p(o, s_1,...,s_n, m_1,...,m_m)$ corresponds to an unique object with the name o, with state (values of corresponding state variables) $s_1,...,s_n$, and methods code $m_1,...,m_m$. The set of all ground class atoms associated with certain class represents its proper instances.

Definition 4. Atoms with predicate symbols denoted by symbol $ are called *abstract atoms*. They are used in the inference rules and there is no transformations defined for generation of abstract atoms except for superclass atoms.

Definition 5. Atoms with predicate symbols denoted by symbol ! are called *executable atoms*. They are names of pre-programmed procedures.

Definition 6. Abstract atoms with predefined predicate symbol $super and of the form $super(SuperClass,This) are called *superclass atoms*.

Non ground superclass atoms define that the class definition denoted by the variable *SuperClass* is an immediate superclass of the class denoted by the variable *This*. Every ground superclass atom corresponds to particular super/subclass relationship between two classes in the class lattice. Collection of all ground superclass atoms represents set of immediate superclass relationships in the class lattice.

The methodology proposed in [10, 11, 18] provides transformations for obtaining a collection of non ground class atoms and ground superclass atoms from the object-oriented class definitions dynamically during the compile time of class definitions and object creating statements. Transformation rules for generating superclass atoms are as follows. During the compile time of the class definition with the name c, the variable *SuperClass* of the superclass atom gets the value of the name of a superclass of this class and variable *This* has the value c. If no any superclasses are defined for the class c, the nonground superclass atoms $super(**any**,c) and $super(c,**nil**) are generated.

Example 1. For example, the set of ground superclass atoms generated on the basis of class lattice given above is as follows:
$super(**any**,person)
$super(person, empl)
$super(person, stud)
$super(stud,stud_empl)
$super(empl,stud_empl)
$super(stud_empl, **nil**)
The set of ground class atoms that represents an object base (lattice) can be also generated automatically on the basis of object creating statements or objects states.

It is undesirable to generate all possible ground class atoms, because usually there is a huge number of objects in object base. Thus, we get a large number of ground class atoms (facts) that make our logic program also large. So, we do not generate ground class atoms first at the compile time. We do it later and only for such class atoms (non ground) that appear in the body of rules. In order to get knowledge about these non ground class atoms for what we have to generate (if possible) ground class atoms we use partial deduction (opening of predicates) as proposed in [10, 11].

Example 2. Set of non ground class atoms generated on the basis of class descriptions given in the example 1 is as follows:
person(Oid, Name, YearB, Age, Mage, Mage_c)
empl(Oid, Name, YearB, Age,Mage, Mage_c ,Salary)
stud(Oid, Name, YearB, Age, Mage, Mage_c,Grade,)
stud_empl(Oid, Name, YearB, Age, Mage, Mage_c, Grade, Salary, Job)

Example 3. A set of ground class atoms (facts) can be generated from the object creating statement as follows. Suppose, we create and object that corresponds to person, whose name is Lauri using the following statement in the NUT language:
o1:= *new* person Name = 'lauri', YearB = 1976 ;
The following ground fact corresponding to this statement can be generated by transformation rules:
person(o1, lauri, 1976, nil, mage, mage_c) ←,
where mage and mage_c are methods' identifiers. The set of all ground atoms associated with the class definition *person* represents all proper instances of that class definition. No inheritance is taken into account when generating these atoms from the statement of the object-oriented language. In order to take into account instance inheritance we use special inference rules stated in the next Sections.

Definition 7. Inference rules are formulas of the following form:
$A \leftarrow A_1, A_2,...,A_n$,where $A_1, A_2,...,A_n$ is conjunction of atoms A_i, i=0,...,n .

Inference rules are used to define class lattice constraints and evolution invariants. Most inference rules are predefined and built into the system. Users are also provided to specify constraints in the form of rules.

An interpretation for the meta-language is defined as a set of ground atoms constructed from predicate names in **P** and constants in **N**. A top-down method of computation based on a variant of resolution method [17] is used for reasoning .

4 Using the Meta-language for Managing Evolution in OODB

Class lattice design is the most important step of OO database design process. In order to keep the database schema correct and consistent during its evolution several constraints have to be checked dynamically. The user is specifying the collection of class definitions together with inheritance relationships among them using an OO language (the NUT language in our case). The OO specification is a source for generating the corresponding set of constraints during compilation of class definitions. Also conflicts caused by multiple inheritance can be resolved using special set of conflict resolution rules. In the NUT system, the preorder for names of instance variables and methods' names is defined. On the other hand, conflict resolution rules can be considered as evolution invariants for changes on class definition and as such represented using the meta-language proposed.

The set of constraints generated from the OO specification of the class lattice is a collection of all ground superclass atoms corresponding to this specification (see example 1 above). We define a set of inference rules for solving constraint derivation problems as well as for verification modifications on constraints in the following subsections.

4.1 Inference Rules for Class Lattice Constraints

We do not consider type subsumption problems in the form as it is done in most of work oriented to creating a general object-oriented logic languages [7, 8, 15]. We can generate a set of class atoms on the basis of given class definitions, but we do not define mechanism for deciding subsumption between class atoms. We use reflexivity and transitivity properties of inheritance relationship to decide subsumption between class definitions using superclass atoms and inference rules for inheritance constraints described as follows:

- *inference rules for inheritance of class definitions*

$inherits(Subclass,Class) ← $super(Class,Subclass)
$inherits(Subclass,Class) ← $inherits(Subclass,Subclass1),$super(Class,Subclass1)
The predicate $inherits(Subclass,Class) says that the class Subclass inherits its properties from class Class through sub/superclass chain.

- *inference rules for the lowest superclass (or greatest subclass) definition for a pair of class definitions*

   $lub(A, B, C) ← $super(A, B), $super(A, C)
   $glb(A, B, C) ← $super(B, A), $super(C, A)
The predicate $lub(A, B, C) means that the class A is the least upper bound of two class definitions B and C. The predicate $glb(A, B, C) means that the class A is the greatest lower bound of two class definitions B and C.

- *inference rules for avoiding undesirable properties of class lattice*
   1. inconsistency of a class lattice
   $empty(A) ← $glb(A, B, C),$disjoint (B,C), where the predicate $empty(A) denotes that the class A cannot have instances.
   2. redundant classes can be checked when deriving all ground instances of the predicate $inherits(Subclass,Class) for a certain class c (i.e. answering the goal ←$inherits(c,Class)). If the fact $inherits(c,c) is derived, then the class c is redundant class in the class lattice.

3. redundant inheritance relationship can be checked when before adding a new superclass atom $super(c,a) for certain classes c and a, the fact $inherits(a,c) is already derivable from the initial set of superclass atoms.

4.2 Inference Rules for Object Lattice Constraints.

Inference rules for object lattice constraints are as follows:
- *inference rules for disjointness constraint on classes (extents).* The user of the NUT language is not provided to define explicitly disjointness of classes, but it is assumed implicitly that immediate subclasses of the most general class **any** are disjoint. The following rules are built into the system for that purpose:

   $disjoint (A,B) ← $lub(**any**, A, B)
   $disjoint (C,B) ← $inherits(C,A), $disjoint (A,B)

The predicate $disjoint (A,B) means that two classes A and B are disjoint. It means that there is no common instances of class definitions A and B. The second rule says that disjointness is propagated to subclasses of disjoint classes.

- *inference rules for object lattice*

   !inst_of(Oid, B) ← !inst_of(Oid, A), $inherits(A, B)
   !inst_of(Oid, C) ← !inst_of(Oid, A),!inst_of(Oid, B), $glb(C, A,B)

The executable atom !inst_of(Oid,B) denotes that an object with identity (name) Oid is an instance of the class definition B.

4.3 Inference Rules for Evolution Invariants.

Evolution invariants are used to maintain consistency of class and object lattices during their evolution. They are declarative definitions of constraints that should hold for any evolution in a consistent OO database. We do not provide here a complete set of all possible evolution invariants, but we present in the following some typical rules for class and object evolution.

- *evolution invariants for class lattice*
   1. changes on class definition

   !add_inst_var(Var, Class) ← !not_defined(Var,Subclass),
                              $inherits(Subclass, Class)
   !not_defined(Var,**nil**) ←
   !add_method(M, Class) ← !not_defined(M,Subclass),
                           $inherits(Subclass, Class)
   !not_defined(M,**nil**) ←

These rules say that adding a new state variable or method name to a class definition is allowed if it is not already defined in its subclasses.

   2. changes on class lattice (e.g. adding or dropping a class definition). If a new class definition is added to the class lattice, then the corresponding ground superclass atom and non ground class atom are added to the initial

set of superclass atoms and class atoms. If some of class definitions are removed, then these atoms are removed from initial set of atoms. No special inference rules are needed for that purpose.

- *inference rules for maintaining class instances (object base) under class lattice changes.* There are two changes on class lattice that have to be reflected on instances of class definitions: add a new class or drop an existing class. In general, we use application specific or user defined rules for partitioning of the instances of the superclass, because we consider this case as a case when an object is changing its class definition (see the example 4)

- *user can add application specific rules* e.g. to describe conditions for changing class of an object during computations or when reflecting changes on class lattice to objects. In this case, class atoms are used together with superclass or inheritance predicates to define rules.

Example 4. For example, consider constraints on changing a class definition of instances of the *person* class to the *empl* class. Let the subclassing condition be that all persons, who were born earlier than 1985 are employees. The corresponding rule can be defined as follows:

!change_class(Oid, empl) ← person(Oid, Name, YearB, Age, Mage, Mage_c),
 !lt(YearB, 1985), $super(person,empl)

The inference rule system used for constraint derivation should be complete and sound. In general, the soundness and completeness of the inference rules for inheritance (single and multiple) constraints and disjointness constraints are proved by several researchers as discussed in [1].

5 Conclusion

The metalanguage for representing constraints on class and object lattices was presented and a set of corresponding inference rules was provided. The metalanguage differs from other logic based languages for complex objects in that it is intended to use on the top of the OO language NUT and is tightly related to underlying OO specifications of classes and objects. This fact makes our language very simple but on the other hand, practically useful.

Acknowledgements

I would like to thank all my colleagues, who have taken part in design and implementation of the NUT system. I acknowledge the Nordic Council of Ministers, who supported this work in part by the Grant 1993-8341-2 and Technical University of Denmark for making me available its library, equipment and working atmosphere.

References

1. Kim H-J, Algoritmic and Computational Aspects of OODB Schema Design,In: R. Gupta, E. Horowitz (Eds), Object-Oriented Database wirh Applications to CASE, Networks, and VLSI CAD, Prentice Hall, 1991, pp 26-62
2. Heuer A. and Sander P, The LIVING IN A LATTICE rule language, Data & Knowledge Engineering No 9 (1992/93) 249-286
3. Hem J. A. and Sloth L, Object-Oriented Database management Systems. A Design for Schema Evolution in Beta-Flex, Technical Report AoOOP-nr 33, Aarhus University, Dept. of Computer Science, October 1992.
4. Tsuda K, Tanaka M.Yamamoto K , etc., MORE: An Object-Oriented Data Model with a Facility for Changing Object Structures,IEEE Transactions on Knowledge and Data Engineering, Vol 3 No 4, 1991, pp 444-460
5. Bergstein P. L., Object-Preserving Class Transformations, In: SIGPLAN NOTICES, Vol 26, No 11, 1991
6. Kangassalo H, COMIC: A system and methodology for conceptual modelling and information construction, Data & Knowledge Engineering No 9 (1992/93) 287-319
7. Kifer M. and Lausen G., F-logic: A Higher-order Language for Reasoning about Objects, Inheritance, and Schema, In: Proceedings, ACM-SIGMOD Intl. Conf. on Management of Data, June 1989 pp. 134-146
8. Bancilhon F. and Khoshafian S., A Calculus of Complex Objects, J. of Computer and Systems Sciences 38, 326-340 (1989)
9. Fischer Nilsson J., An Algebraic Logic for Concept Structures, In: Information Modeling and Knowledge Bases V, IOS Press, Amsterdam 1994 pp 75-85
10. Haav H-M, Specifying Semantics of Evolution in Object-Oriented Databases Using Partial Deduction, In: U. W. Lipeck, B. Thalheim (eds.), Modelling Database Dynamics. Selected Papers from the Fourth International Workshop on Foundations of Models and Languages for Data and Objects, Volkse, Germany, Springer-Verlag, London, 1993 pp 48-63
11. Haav H-M, Matskin M. Using Partial Deduction for automatic propagation of changes in OODB, In: Information Modelling and Knowledge Bases IV: Foundations, Theory and Applications, IOS Press, Amsterdam, 1993 pp 339-353
12. Kim W and Chou H-T, Versions of schema for object-oriented databases, In: Proc. of the 14th VLDB Conference, Los Angeles, California 1988
13. Scholl M. H., Laasch C. and Tresch M., Updatable Views in Object-Oriented Databases, DOOD'91, LNCS 566, 1991
14. Kifer M.and Wu J., A Logic for Programming with Complex Objects, J. of Computer and Systems Sciences 47, 77-120 (1993)
15. Greco S, Leone N and Rullo P, COMPLEX: An Object-Oriented Logic Programming System, IEEE Transactions on Knowledge and Data Engineering, Vol 4 No 4, 1992 pp 344-359
16. Tyugu E, Matskin M, Penjam J, Eomois P. NUT-An object-oriented language, Computers and Artificial Intelligence 1986, 6:521-542
17. Eomois P. Knowledge Representation and Deduction in extended PRIZ, In: Plander J. (Ed.) Artificial Intelligence and Information Control Systems of Robots, Elsevier Science Publishers B. V., North-Holland , 1984 pp 123-127
18. Komorowski J. and Matskin M, Reasoning and Synthesis in an Object-Oriented Environment by Partial Deduction, In: Proceedings of Norwegian Conference on Informatics NIK'94, Molde, 14-16 November, 1994 (to appear)

A Stack-Based Approach to Query Languages[*]

Kazimierz Subieta
Institute of Computer Science, Polish Academy of Sciences,
Ordona 21, 01-237 Warszawa, Poland
subieta@wars.ipipan.war.pl

Catriel Beeri
Hebrew University, Institute of Computer Science,
Givat Ram, Jerusalem 91904, Israel
beeri@cs.huji.ac.il

Florian Matthes
Joachim W. Schmidt
University of Hamburg, Department of Computer Science,
Vogt-Kölln-Straße 30, D-22527 Hamburg, Germany
matthes@dbis1.informatik.uni-hamburg.de

Abstract

Scoping, naming and binding are central concepts in the definition and understanding of programming languages. With the introduction of sophisticated data models, these issues become important for query languages as well. Additionally, the goal of integrating query and programming languages requires a common basis for their operational semantics. We offer here an approach to the definition of the operational semantics of query languages based on an abstract machine, in which names, their bindings, and scopes defined by query and data structure are central. The machine has own simple data model for its store, and has a stack for dealing with scopes. We argue for the generality of the approach and illustrate it by defining the semantics of many query language primitives. Finally, we briefly consider how assignment and procedures can be neatly added.

1 Introduction

A major theme of database research in the last decade is the relationship between declarative, high level query languages and procedural, general purpose programming languages. The standard solution, namely embedding a query language (typically SQL) in the programming language suffers from

---

[*]Work partially supported by a grant from the German-Israel Foundation for Scientific Research and Development.

problems that have been amply recorded in the literature and collectively called *impedance mismatch*. Alternative approaches that have been proposed and extensively investigated include persistent programming languages and database programming languages such as Pascal/R [13], Galileo [1], DBPL [14, 7], Napier88 [8], Machiavelli [12], Taxis [10], and O_2C [11]. The emergence of object-oriented databases is also due, in part, to the feeling that classical database systems do not provide the functionality desired and required for data intensive application development.

Despite their limited algorithmic expressive power, query languages are one of the major achievements of the database domain [2, 15, 16]. This is not only because they are the means for *ad hoc* interactive querying and updating of a database, but rather because they are the basis for high level, declarative, data independent data definition and manipulation. In data manipulation, declarative queries are much easier to optimize than procedural programs. Queries are also potentially parallelizable. The use of queries and set-oriented updates increases programmers' productivity, and program reliability, readability and modifiability. In data definition, queries are used to express integrity constraints, access restrictions, views, snapshots, database procedures, and active rules. However, despite continuous advances in research and development of database languages and object-oriented database systems, the ideal of "seamless integration" of a programming language with a query language is still elusive.

A primary goal of this paper is to contribute to the understanding of the relationship between query and general programming languages. A major thread in the development of programming languages concerns facilities for modularity, as expressed, e.g., in procedural abstraction in the form of functions and procedures, and data abstraction in the form of ADT's and objects. The use of such facilities emphasizes the relationships between names used in a program, their scope of definition, and the bindings they receive at compile and run-time. We believe that the study of *names, scopes, and bindings* is also important for the design and use of query languages. Understanding of the relevant issues is a crucial step towards the successful integration of query and programming languages. The issue is important even if one is interested in query languages only for the relational model, since a query may use a relation name or an attribute more than once with different meanings. However, in the last decade many query languages for more sophisticated models have been defined and studied. In such models, the meaning of a name depends both on where it is defined and where it is used.

This paper proposes an approach to the definition of the operational semantics of query languages centered around the naming-scoping-binding theme. Specifically, we present an abstract machine that we claim to be suitable for the definition of program data bindings. An important component of the machine, that distinguishes it from other machines, is its store, modelling the database as a collection of related entities associated with names to which they can be bound. The store can also contain volatile objects. It is defined in terms of a simple object model. We argue that the simplicity of the model makes our work applicable to a variety of current data models.

The actual binding of names appearing in queries to store objects is achieved by the use of *environments*, where an environment is a collection of local scopes and rules used for associating names with programming objects. The common approach, which we follow here, is that the scopes are organized in a stack, with the "search from the top" rule. Some extensions to the structure of stacks used in the definition and interpretation of programming languages are necessary to accommodate, e.g., the fact that in a database we have bulk data structures, hence possibly multiple simultaneous bindings for a name. This environment stack, and a procedure for evaluation of queries, are the backbone of our approach. An important aspect of the evaluation is parallelism which is inherent in many query primitives, and important for proper definition of update semantics.

The machine and the semantics of a query language are derived from a language implemented in the system LOQIS [17]. However, majority of constructs that we considered exists also in other query languages. In the paper we illustrate how the machine can be used to provide a precise definition of the semantics of some query constructs. (A more comprehensive presentation can be found in [18]). We also illustrate the design of a query language that is directly influenced by the stack-based discipline of scoping and binding. Finally, we briefly consider updates and procedures, thus supporting our claim that this approach facilitates the integration of declarative and procedural constructs.

The rest of the paper is organized as follows. In Section 2 we discuss the abstract store model and present preliminary formal definitions. In Section 3 we discuss the abstract machine model, introducing details of the operational semantics used for the specification of language constructs. In Section 4 we present and discuss various query constructs. In Section 5 we discuss updates and procedures. Section 6 concludes.

2 An Abstract Store Model

The store is the component of the abstract machine that models the database. The operational semantics of queries is defined to a large extent in terms of accesses and manipulations of its elements. The store model and its relationship to other data models are described below.

2.1 The Goals

The primary goal is to serve as a basis for defining the operational semantics of query languages. The model does not include details of physical data organization, indices, storage hierarchies, and buffer management. We view a database as a large collection of (possibly interrelated) entities, as it can be found in modern persistent object stores [9, 3]. The store may contain both persistent and volatile entities; we strive to treat them uniformly.

Current implemented or proposed data models include a large variety of features: data types such as records and arrays; bulk data types such as sets, bags, lists, maps and trees; object features such as identity, *is-a* relationships, methods and encapsulation. We want our approach to semantics to be applicable to a wide range of query languages. One possible approach to addressing this diversity of concepts is to define a rich model that contains "all" features. We have chosen the opposite approach of a very simple model, where various conceptual models, from value-based to object-based, can easily be mapped to it. Semantics for a specific query language over a given model can be defined by a mapping to our model, and by providing the semantics in our model.

Although some features found in existing models have no direct mapping to our model, it covers a large variety of features and can be easily extended. The approach presented in this paper can also be adapted directly (without translation) as another data model.

The ideas treated in the paper do not require a specific (monomorphic, polymorphic) type discipline nor precise data representation details. Types are very important for enforcing static constraints on the use of queries and procedures; however, they are irrelevant to the goals of this paper, hence are not discussed.

2.2 The Model

Intuitively, a stored database (at a given point of time) consists of a collection of stored entities which we call *store objects*[1]. There are three components in a store object: (1) its location; (2) the name that can be used to denote it; (3) the value stored there, i.e., its content. As we are not interested in physical organization, we represent locations abstractly, using the concept of *l*-value from programming language semantics. Atomic values, records, components of records, conceptual objects, are all store objects: each one of them resides somewhere in memory and needs location for internal identification, in order to be retrieved, updated or deleted. For us, these locations have no structure or meaning, except that they can be used to access objects; queries do not refer to them or use their values in any way. In the sequel, to emphasize their abstract nature, locations are called identifiers.

Names are among the basic building blocks of queries and, in general, of program expressions. Their bindings are an important component of semantics, and a central topic in this paper. While for general programming languages names used in a program are normally defined in the program itself, most of the names used in queries are defined in the database. That is, we are dealing with persistent data where names are an inherent part.

The contents (i.e., the *r*-value) can be an atomic or complex value, or a location. As for the names, we assume that each store object contains one value. As seen below, more than one value associated with an object is modelled by creating many objects.

Formally, let I be a set of *identifiers*, N be a set of *names*, and V be a set of atomic values. We make no assumption about V; it may contain numerals, strings, graphics, compiled procedures, and so on. Atomicity of the elements of V means that we do not assume the existence of operations that refer to their parts. We assume $I \cap (V \cup N) = \emptyset$; however, N and V are not required to be disjoint. It is possible, even common, that programs compute values, then use them as names, e.g., integers are used as array indices. Generally, some stored values can be used as names of store objects; this property supports genericity of programming. In many languages, for example Ingres/Windows 4GL [4], LOQIS [17] and F-logic [6], data names are first-class citizens.

A *store object* is a triple $< i, n, \vartheta >$, where $i \in I, n \in N$, and ϑ are its identifier, name, and value, respectively. We say that i identifies this object. The value ϑ can be one of the following:

- An atomic value from V.

---

[1] These should not be confused with the conceptual objects of object-oriented models.

- An identifier from I. This identifier, as the value of the store object, serves as a (logical) pointer to another store object.

- A set of objects.

We refer to these three types of objects as *value-objects, pointer-objects,* and *set-objects,* respectively. Objects of the first two types are called *atomic,* those of the third type are called *complex.* Nesting of set-objects allows us to represent arbitrarily complex objects with hierarchical structure. Below is an example of a complex object, consisting of three atomic objects.

$$< i_5, EMP, \{ < i_{51}, NAME, Smith >,$$
$$< i_{52}, SAL, 2000 >, < i_{53}, WORKS\_IN, i_6 > \} >$$

In the following, "object" always means store object, unless specifically noted otherwise.

A *store* is a set S of store objects, and set R of identifiers of designated *root* objects. We make no assumption that elements of R refer to the top hierarchy level of store objects: sometimes elements of R refer to objects nested in other objects. We assume that S satisfies the obvious constraints: An element $i \in I$ is used in it at most once as an identifier; that is, there is a one-to-one correspondence between the set of identifiers used in a database, and the set of objects in it. If an identifier is used as a pointer, then it is also used as an identifier (referential integrity). We also assume that each root identifier actually identifies an object in S. By definition, objects inaccessible from R (directly or indirectly) do not exist. As we will see later, we build over the set R some structure which we will call *environment stack*. The persistence status of objects is irrelevant in our approach; indeed, there is no essential semantic property that can make distinction between querying persistent and volatile data. (The orthogonality of types, queries and persistence is assumed in many modern DBPLs [1, 7, 8, 12, 14, 17].)

We re-emphasize that the identifiers are *internal* – they are not used in queries or programs, and are not printable. A one-to-one mapping of all identifiers to another collection of identifiers cannot be recognized from the outside. The names are *external* in the sense that they are used in queries – they are part of the users' model.

Example 2.1 The following is an example store. The root objects are

$\{i_1, i_5, i_9, i_{13}, i_{17}\}$.

```
              MyDatabase:
< i₁,   EMP,    {< i₂, NAME, Brown >,
                 < i₃, SAL, 2500 >, < i₄, WORKS_IN, i₁₃ >} >

< i₅,   EMP,    {< i₆, NAME, Smith >,
                 < i₇, SAL, 2000 >, < i₈, WORKS_IN, i₁₇ >} >

< i₉,   EMP,    {< i₁₀, NAME, Jones >,
                 < i₁₁, SAL, 1500 >, < i₁₂, WORKS_IN, i₁₇ >} >

< i₁₃,  DEPT,   {< i₁₄, DNAME, Toy >,
                 < i₁₅, LOC, Paris >, < i₁₆, LOC, London >} >

< i₁₇,  DEPT,   {< i₁₈, DNAME, Sales >,
                 < i₁₉, LOC, Berlin >} >
```

Note that an object WORKS_IN stores an identifier of a department object. If instead it contained, say, a department name, the example would be value-based. If additionally we disallow multiple LOC objects for a department, we obtain a relational database. □

In examples we also use the schema presented in Fig.1. It has redundancy allowing us to demonstrate different styles of querying, e.g. relational and navigational. Arrows denote pointers, and symbols 1 and n denote a 1:n relationship. For example, EMPLOYS denotes pointer-objects inside DEPT objects; a DEPT objects can contain many EMPLOYS objects. Similarly, LOC and PREV_JOB are multi-valued attributes.

2.3 Discussion

Having defined the model, let us now consider how databases given in one of the common conceptual models can be represented in it. In the relational model, to represent information about employees, we may use a relation, i.e., a set of tuples, called EMP. Considering the execution of the query **select SAL from** EMP, we can see that the name EMP gets *bound to each tuple* of the relation. As we are interested in names in the context of binding, in our model the name EMP is associated not with the relation, but rather with each of its tuples. This holds in general for any named set: in our model the name is associated with each of the elements of the set; see, e.g., LOC of DEPT in MyDatabase.

Speaking in terms of programming languages, a tuple defines a local environment: each attribute is a name that, *in the context of this tuple*, can be bound to the associated object – attribute value. Note that we do not have *tuple* as a data structure in our model – as just seen, a tuple is represented by the set of its named components. Also note that the identifier of the object representing the tuple is internal and has nothing to do with the conceptual model, in which this tuple is a value, not an object. It is just an abstract

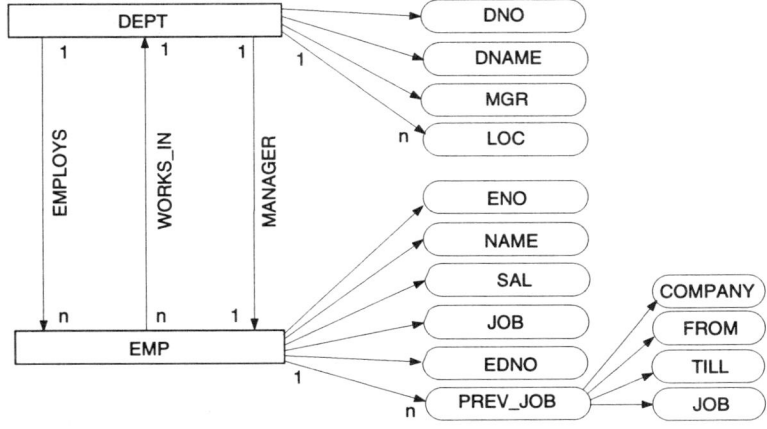

Figure 1: A database schema used in examples

representation of the fact that the tuple is an identifiable store object. (Many relational systems indeed use tuple-id's internally.)

Names can be numbers. For example,

$< i_1, A, \{< i_2, 1, Monday >,$
$\qquad < i_3, 2, Tuesday >, \ldots, < i_8, 7, Sunday >\} >$

represents an *array*. Thus, tuples and arrays have essentially the same representation. Indeed, both are essentially local environments, and the differences have to do only with the type and generation of the names that can be used in the environment. As already noted, names used in arrays are also values, and can be calculated during run-time.

We do not impose constraints requiring that objects with the same name should have the same structure. This allows us to represent *variants*, as in the following database fragment:

$< i_1, EMP, \{< i_2, NAME, Brown >, < i_3, SAL, 2500 >\} >$
$< i_6, EMP, \{< i_7, NAME, Smith >, < i_9, IS\_STUDENT, TRUE >\} >$

Similarly, we can represent *null values*, when they mean lack of stored information. Since the definition of a store does not include any concept of format, a null value is represented simply by the absence of a binding. For example, in the database fragment above, the SAL field for Smith is null-valued. We do not associate any semantics with this absence. As far as we are concerned, Smith may have no salary, or his salary may be unknown, or it may be determined in another way, e.g., by using the information that he is a student. The interpretation of the absence of information is part of the semantics of the data, but is *outside* of the scope of our model. Of course, we need the ability to test for the lack of a stored object with a given name, so that the query evaluator can interpret this and apply the appropriate semantics.

To generalize to the nested relational, or complex object models, we need to be able to represent sets, and obviously we have that in the model. We can also represent bags. For example, the object $< i_1, N, \{< i_2, M, 5 >, < i_3, M, 5 >\} >$ represents the bag $\{5,5\}$. Similarly one can represent lists, trees, and generally, instances of recursively defined data types.

Let us now consider a conceptual object. It has an identity, and an updatable state. The mapping is straightforward – an object is represented as a store object. Object sharing and relationships between objects can be easily mapped by using internal object identifiers as values of pointer sub-objects, as seen in *MyDatabase* above.

In summary, this simple model allows one to represent a variety of data structures and concepts, and their combinations, including tuples, arrays, sets, bags and lists, variants, null values; objects, object sharing, and instances of recursive types. For object-oriented models some simple extensions are needed; we discuss them in [18]. However, we believe that the simplicity of the model is an advantage: it allows us to explain the meaning of query constructs without having to deal with a variety of special cases.

3 An Abstract Machine Model

In this section we present an abstract machine model, on which query language expressions can be evaluated. A component of a state of the machine is a store, as described above. Other components include an environment stack and a result stack for the store of intermediate results. We discuss some commands of the machine, and its facility for parallel execution.

3.1 The Environment Stack

The atomic components of queries are the names and constants. The evaluation of names means binding them to data units, depending on the context. Consider, for example, a query in a relational database that asks for the names of employees satisfying some condition:

     select *NAME* **from** *EMP* **where** ...

The evaluation of the query involves finding a set of bindings for *EMP*, then removing some of them which do not satisfy a predicate after *where*. Each binding for *NAME* is then determined in a context associated with one of the bindings to *EMP*; it is bound to the appropriate *NAME* sub-object inside an EMP object.

3.1.1 Stack Organization

While bindings for simple relational queries, such as the one above, seem to be well understood, this is not the case for more complex queries. For example, in a query that selects the salaries of employees that earn more than their managers, *SAL* is used three times, and there is a need to define how each occurrence is bound. The problem is aggravated in models that admit deeply nested structures, possibly, with repeated (sub) attributes. The binding of a name to its meaning may then depend both on the positions of the name in the data structure, and its use in the query.

To deal with this issue, we propose a well known concept of *environment*. Abstractly, an environment is an association of names and objects. It is constructed incrementally, by accumulating local scopes and the scope added last is the first to be visited in a search. Thus, the environment is subdivided into parts, called *sections*, which form the *environment stack*, denoted ES.

We assume that each section of ES stores identifiers of store objects. Given an identifier, the complete object can be retrieved. In particular, the name stored in the object can be retrieved, to be compared with the name for which a binding is requested. Thus, storing identifiers suffices for establishing bindings.

In a (run-time) stack in programming languages a stack section typically contains local data such as parameters and local variables of a procedure. Such local data *lives* on the stack. In contrast, we are dealing here with global data, that live in the database, and continue to exist not only when a stack section is removed, but also when query evaluation has terminated and the complete stack has disappeared. Thus the objects themselves will be stored in the store, and their identifiers stored in the appropriate stack section(s). This scheme allows the same object to be referenced from several sections (in contrast to the runtime stack where an object occurs in precisely one section). The semantics we are going to deal with depends on this property. Note that in a run-time stack a name occurring in a program is bound to one object. In contrast, we allow a section in ES to associate several objects with a name, as e.g. for the EMP name.

In summary, our proposal generalizes the environment stack as used in programming languages in two major ways: (1) The stack contains identifiers of both persistent and volatile store objects, which exist outside the stack; (2) Binding is a multi-valued, rather than a single-valued. This is intimately related to the set orientation and parallelism inherent in query semantics.

In an implementation based on our semantics many optimizations are possible, such as storing names with the identifiers in sections, avoiding long lists of identifiers of objects having the same name, and performing some bindings during compilation. Some of these optimisations are implemented in LOQIS; they are not discussed here.

We assume that at the beginning of the evaluation of a query the environment stack consists of one section containing identifiers of all persistent *root* database objects, such as the EMP and $DEPT$ objects in $MyDatabase$.

3.1.2 Binding via Stack Operations

Binding a name n is performed by a search for one or more objects associated with that name in the environment stack. The search follows *scope rules*. The simplest rule is to strictly follow the structure of the stack, from the top down towards the bottom. The search terminates when it finds a section that contains one or more bindings for the given name. In that case, the set of *all* objects associated with the name in that section is returned as the result of the search. The result we denote by *search(n)*. If no section with bindings for the given name exists, the search terminates at the bottom of the stack, returning an empty set. This simple search strategy will be changed to accommodate more sophisticated scope rules, e.g., skipping irrelevant stack sections for binding names used inside a procedure.

Changes to the environment have to update the stack by adding or removing sections at its top, using the traditional operations *push* and *pop*. These operations correspond to opening a new scope and closing a scope, respectively.

In programming languages, opening a new scope corresponds to an activation of a block or a procedure. In a query language, it corresponds also to the evaluation of a query component in a context determined by another component. In the general case, this operation depends on both the structure of the query and the structure of the data. Consider, for example, the query $DEPT.LOC$. Each possible binding for LOC is determined by a binding for $DEPT$. That is, first $DEPT$ is bound, in general to many identifiers $i_1, i_2, ..., i_k$ (one for each department). Each identifier i_j identifies a department object, and this object defines a scope in which names such as DNO, DNAME, MGR, LOC are associated with the objects that make up the department object. The semantics of the dot operation is that bindings for LOC are determined in each of these scopes.

Let $o = <i, n, v>$ be an object, with identifier i. We denote by $nested(i)$ the following set of identifiers: If o is a set object, then $nested(i)$ is the set v; if o is a pointer object $<i, n, j>$, then $nested(i) = \{j\}$; if o is a value object, $v \in V$, then $nested(i) = \emptyset$. For uniformity, we extend the function $nested$ for values $v \in V$: $nested(v) = \emptyset$. Then we extend the function to sequences of identifiers and values by defining the result to be the union of the value of the function on the components. For example (c.f. *MyDatabase*), $nested(i_1) = \{i_2, i_3, i_4\}$, $nested(i_4) = \{i_{13}\}$, $nested(i_3) = nested(1800) = \emptyset$, and $nested(<i_1, i_{13}>) = \{i_2, i_3, i_4, i_{14}, i_{15}, i_{16}\}$.

Going back to the evaluation of $DEPT.LOC$, we see that for a given binding i for $DEPT$, the scope in which it makes sense to look for a binding for LOC is $nested(i)$. If this set is pushed as a new scope on the stack then the search for bindings for LOC will find the objects representing the location(s) of the given department, as required. As will be shown, this approach is a core of the definition of many query operators, including *where*, dot, join, and quantifiers.

3.2 The Query Result Stack

In addition to the environment stack ES, we also need a place for intermediate query results. These are kept on another stack, called the *query result stack* $(QRES)$. In particular, at the end of evaluation its top holds the answer to the query. We assume that an intermediate result is always a *table*, where a table is a multi-set (bag) of *rows*, all of the same width. Rows may contain atomic values or identifiers, i.e. their elements belong to $V \cup I$. For uniformity, we represent single values or identifiers as tables having one row and one column (1×1 tables), and do not distinguish between such a table and the element in it. An example table, referring to *MyDatabase*, is presented below; it may represent an answer to the query "Get employee names, their department's names, and 10% of their salary".

i_2	i_{14}	250
i_6	i_{18}	200
i_{10}	i_{18}	150

A table is not in the form we want to see for printed query results. We assume, however, that the visualisation of it, if necessary, can be done by a some procedure (e.g. *display*) taking the table as an argument.

3.3 Set Orientation and Parallelism

The query *DEPT.LOC* illustrates an important characteristic of queries, namely parallelism. The bindings for *LOC* are to be performed *for each* binding found for *DEPT*. In principle, choosing a binding for *DEPT* and then searching for bindings for *LOC* can be done in any order, even in parallel. For queries, there is no difference between a parallel or a sequential execution in some arbitrary order; however, there is a significant difference when updates are considered. Consider, for example, the update 'increase the salary of each employee by 10% if smaller than the average of the employees' salaries.' In a parallel execution, the average is the same for all updates. In a sequential execution, each update changes the average and thus may influence the next update. To precisely define the semantics of a bulk updates, parallelism is a very useful notion, even if the real implementation will be sequential.

We assume that our machine has sequencing, denoted by ';', parallel loops denoted by *foreach i in C do in parallel...end foreach*, and regular sequential loops denoted similarly, without "in parallel'.' The degree of parallelism is determined by a specified collection: each element i in the collection corresponds to, or generates an evaluation stream. The element i is available for use, as a parameter, in the stream. We assume that when a parallel loop is started, a separate processor is allocated to each stream. Each processor has its own stacks: $QRES$ is initially empty, and ES is a copy of the common stack. Each branch of the parallel loop continues as a process running one of these processors, and the processors execute concurrently and asynchronously. The streams merge into one stream when they terminate. The store is shared among the parallel streams.

There are issues that we need to worry about in this idealized parallel execution. One is how these streams are merged when they terminate. We assume that when a branch terminates, ES returns to its state at the time just before the loop started; thus, at the end environment stacks are identical for all streams. Considering QRES, when a parallel stream executes, it does not change any part of the stack below the level at the starting time, and that at the end the local stack contains one cell storing the partial result. When the parallel branches merge, these tables are merged, forming one table at the top of the common $QRES$. The merge function depends in general on on the query operator being actually evaluated.

4 The Language SBQL

In this section we illustrate how the semantics of query language primitives, and hence also complete query languages, can be defined on our machine. We sketch here the definition of an untyped language, called **SBQL** (Stack-Based Query Language). For lack of space, we present only some of the constructs. A few update and procedural constructs are presented in the next section.

4.1 The General Framework

The structure of the language is simple: Any constant or name is an *atomic query*. From such queries we build complex queries by applying unary or binary operators. For example, EMP, SAL, 1800 and 2 are queries, from which we can build such queries as EMP *where* $(SAL > 1800)$ and $2*2$. With the exception of typing constraints (e.g., one cannot multiply two sets of strings), we assume full orthogonality of operators. Parentheses are allowed, precedence rules are not discussed here.

To define the semantics of the language, we introduce a recursive procedure *eval* that maps a syntactically correct query and a machine state to a result. The state consists of a store and a state of the environment stack. The procedure is defined by cases, one for each operator. It may change the environment stack; however, the state of the stack after evaluation is always the same as before evaluation. The result of a query is left as a new cell at the top of $QRES$.

4.2 Atomic Queries

We start with atomic queries, namely constants and names. We assume that constants that denote some elements of V are available in the language. For the query c, where c is a constant, $eval(c)$ leaves the 1×1 table $\{c\}$ at the top of $QRES$. For the query n, where n is a name, $eval(n)$ searches for bindings for n is ES, and leaves the result, $search(n)$, at the top of $QRES$. For example, the query EMP, applied to $MyDatabase$, returns a single-column table containing identifiers i_1, i_5, i_9.

4.3 Compound Queries: Algebraic Operators

An operator is called *algebraic* if its effect is defined purely in terms of its argument(s), and is independent of the environment. By convention, such an operator takes its argument(s) from $QRES$ (popping the cells that contain them) and pushes its result there. Examples of algebraic operators include operations on atomic values such as arithmetic operations and comparisons, string operations, boolean operations, and equality tests of identifiers. They also include aggregates applied to collections, and set operations such as set union, product, tests for containment, emptiness, and so on.

The semantics of a binary algebraic operator Θ is defines as follows:

    case *query* is $q_1 \Theta q_2$ (Θ algebraic):
      begin
        $eval(q_1)$;
        $eval(q_2)$;
        $apply(\Theta)$
      end

By our assumption on the state of ES before and after a call to *eval*, both queries are evaluated in the same environment. We assume that *apply* is defined without any use of the environment. The semantics of operations such as set union or product may be defined using the same pattern. Dereferencing may be needed, dependening on the operator being applied; for example, $SAL > 2500$ requires dereferencing of an identifier returned by SAL. For the space limit we omit further discussion.

4.4 Compound Queries: non-Algebraic Operators

The general syntax for application of a non-algebraic operators is $q_1 \Theta q_2$, where q_1 and q_2 are (arbitrarily complex) queries, and Θ is an operator. The general pattern that defines a part of the *eval* procedure for queries with a non-algebraic operator is as follows.

> **case** query is $q_1 \Theta q_2$ (Θ non-algebraic):
> **begin**
> $eval(q_1)$;
>   for each row r in $top(QRES)$ do in parallel
>   push($ES, nested(r)$);   (* Open a new scope on ES *)
> $eval(q_2)$;
> $partial\_result := combine(r, top(QRES), \Theta)$;
>   pop(ES); pop($QRES$); (* Restore the state of local processors *)
>   end for each;
> $merged\_result := merge(partial\_results, \Theta)$;
>   pop($QRES$); (* Remove from QRES the table created by q_1 *)
>   push($QRES, merged\_result$);
> **end**

Before the evaluation of q_2, many parallel processors are activated, one for each row r from the table returned by q_1. Each processor opens an own new scope $nested(r)$, then evaluates q_2. A partial result returned by it depends on the result returned by q_2, r and Θ. Finally, partial results are merged; the merging function depends on Θ.

Note that the evaluation is not symmetric in the two subqueries, since q_2 is evaluated in environments determined by the result of q_1. In the rest of the section we define and illustrate various non-algebraic operations that exploit these environment stack dependencies.

4.5 Selection

The syntax for the selection operation is q_1 *where* q_2, where q_1 is any query, and q_2 is a boolean-valued query, i.e., a condition. The semantics is defined by the scheme above, where the function *combine* is defined by:

$combine(r, top(QRES), where) \equiv$ **if** $top(QRES) = TRUE$
                                                then return $\{r\}$ **else** return $\emptyset$

The *merge* function is the union of partial results.

Example 4.1 (C.f. *MyDatabase*).
Consider EMP *where* $(SAL > 1800)$ expressing the query"List employees earning more than 1800". We follow its execution. Initially, the environment stack contains one section containing identifiers of all root database

records:

$$i_1(EMP), i_5(EMP), i_9(EMP), i_{13}(DEPT), i_{17}(DEPT)$$

First, *eval* is called with the atomic query EMP. The name EMP is bound to three objects, whose identifiers are put in a single-column table in $QRES$:

$$\begin{array}{|c|} \hline i_1 \\ i_5 \\ i_9 \\ \hline \end{array}$$

Each row is processed by the body of *for each*. For the row containing i_1, we have $nested(i_1) = \{i_2, i_3, i_4\}$. This set is pushed onto ES:

$$\begin{array}{|l|} \hline i_2(NAME), i_3(SAL), i_4(WORKS\_IN) \\ i_1(EMP), i_5(EMP), i_9(EMP), i_{13}(DEPT), i_{17}(DEPT) \\ \hline \end{array}$$

Now $SAL > 1800$ is evaluated. The predicate $>$ is algebraic, so subqueries SAL and 1800 are evaluated with the same environment stack. The evaluation goes through the following states of local $QRES$ (which is assigned to a processor processing i_1):

$eval(SAL)$: $\quad$ $eval(1800)$: $\quad$ Dereferencing:
$\boxed{i_3}$ $\qquad\qquad$ $\boxed{\begin{array}{c}1800\\i_3\end{array}}$ $\qquad$ $\boxed{\begin{array}{c}1800\\2500\end{array}}$ $\qquad$ Comparison: $\boxed{TRUE}$

Since the predicate returns $TRUE$, the row i_1 is included into the result.

The same action is performed concurrently for the rows i_5, for which the predicate is also $TRUE$, and i_9, for which the predicate returns $FALSE$. At the end, upon exit from the *for each*, the environment stack will be the same as at the beginning. Merging individual results of parallel streams is collected at the top of $QRES$ as a table $\{i_1, i_5\}$. □

4.6 Joins

Using the product and the selection, we can define joins. Consider the query

$(DEPT \times EMP)$ *where* $(DNO = EDNO)$.

As described above, the query $DEPT \times EMP$ leaves on $QRES$ a two-column table where each row is a pair of identifiers of $DEPT$ and EMP objects. A stream in the evaluation of the *where* clause will push onto ES $nested(\{i,j\})$ for one such pair, then evaluate the condition. The top section now contains identifiers of objects whose names are the attributes of the $DEPT$ and EMP collections. The condition $DNO = EDNO$ is evaluated on attributes of the two objects. The final result is a set of pairs of identifiers, one from each collection, that identify pairs of objects for which the condition is true.

4.7 Projection, Navigation, Path Expressions

We need the ability to retrieve subobjects of previously identified objects. This is provided by the 'dot' operator. When used more than once, it allows navigation in an object graph using path expressions. The syntax is $q_1.q_2$, where q_1 and q_2 are queries. To avoid parenthesis in long path expressions, we assume association to the left. The definition of the semantics is very similar to the semantics of *where*, except that the *combine* function simply returns the table returned by q_2.

Example 4.2

$EMP.SAL$

returns a single-column table, in which each row is the identifier of a SAL object nested inside some EMP object, for example, i_3.

$(EMP\ where\ NAME = "Smith").WORKS\_IN.$

The evaluation of the first part terminates with ES containing only the initial section, and $QRES$ containing the table $\{i_5\}$. Now, to evaluate the '.$WORKS\_IN$' part, we push on ES the section $nested(i_5) = \{i_6, i_7, i_8\}$. The evaluation terminates with $\{i_8\}$ at the top of $QRES$. □

To find the name of the department where Smith works, we have to write

$(EMP\ where\ NAME = "Smith").WORKS\_IN.DEPT.DNAME$

An evaluation strategy requires $DEPT$ in the path expression to be able to access $DNAME$. This is a viable option, however, it makes path expressions longer. Most languages for object-oriented databases have chosen to interpret the "dot" operation so that $EMP.WORKS\_IN.DNAME$ is a legal query.

To follow this tendency, we could introduce a new function *nested*, which for a pointer object returns its r-value. However, this will make it difficult to treat updates. How do we define assignment of a new $DEPT$ identifier to the $WORKS\_IN$ attribute of Smith? We need the query that returns the l-value for the assignment, which in this case is i_8, but with the currently considered option the query returns the r-value, i_{17}. We can also consider elliptic syntax, which does not change semantics, but allows us in some contexts to omit some elements of a full query. These issues are not considered in this paper.

Example 4.3

$EMP\ where\ SAL > ((EMP\ where\ NAME = "Smith").SAL)$

This query combines nested *where* clauses with 'dot'. It expresses the query "List employees earning more than Smith". Note that the binding of the second occurrence of EMP is performed on ES containing two sections, e.g.

$i_2(NAME), i_3(SAL), i_4(WORKS\_IN)$
$i_1(EMP), i_5(EMP), i_9(EMP), i_{13}(DEPT), i_{17}(DEPT)$

and will again return $\{i_1, i_5, i_9\}$, and binding of the second occurence of SAL is performed on the stack containing three sections, e.g.

$i_{6(NAME)}, i_{7(SAL)}, i_{8(WORKS\_IN)}$
$i_{2(NAME)}, i_{3(SAL)}, i_{4(WORKS\_IN)}$
$i_{1(EMP)}, i_{5(EMP)}, i_{9(EMP)}, i_{13(DEPT)}, i_{17(DEPT)}$

and will return (in this case) i_7. □

It is easy to see that 'dot' is an associative operation: $(q_1.q_2).q_3$ is equivalent to $q_1.(q_2.q_3)$; thus, parentheses are not needed.

Example 4.4

$(EMP\ where\ NAME = "Smith").WORKS\_IN.$
$DEPT.EMPLOYS.EMP.(NAME \times JOB)$

returns a table containing (identifiers of) the name and job of the employees working in the same department as Smith. This query illustrates the use of product for constructing multi-component target list, which may be important in the context of multivalued attributes. □

Path expressions for navigation in object databases have been proposed in many papers, e.g. [5]. We believe that our approach is very general, fully orthogonal to other query operators, and semantically clean.

4.8 Navigational Join

The 'dot' operation allows one to 'walk' on a path, but the result is always the end point of the path. Another interesting operation is *navigational join*, that forms pairs containing the start and end points of a path. For example, we might want to create a set of pairs of employees and the departments they work in. In relational systems such an operator can be defined as a product followed by a selection, but in object-oriented systems it is often more natural to express it directly as a navigation through a pointer-valued attribute.

The syntax is $q_1 \bowtie q_2$. Let $\otimes$ denote the cartesian product generalized to bags. The semantics of the operation is defined by the same scheme as above, except for the *combine* function, which is defined as follows:

$combine(r, top(QRES), \bowtie) \equiv return(\{r\} \otimes top(QRES))$

Thus, each row r returned by q_1 is combined with each row returned by q_2 for this r. As previously, the final result is a union of partial results.

Example 4.5

$EMP \bowtie (WORKS\_IN.DEPT)$

returns a two-column table, where each row contains the identifiers of an employee and the identifier of his department.

$EMP \bowtie (DEPT\ where\ EDNO = DNO)$

is a relational variant of the previous example. It shows that the construct is general. In $q_1 \bowtie q_2$, the second component q_2 can be any query, in particular, a function of the elements returned by q_1.

$EMP \bowtie (WORKS\_IN.DEPT.(DNAME \times LOC))$

returns a three column table, where identifiers of EMP are associated with identifiers of $DNAME$ and LOC of the department in which the employee works.

$$DEPT \bowtie avg(EMPLOYS.EMP.SAL)$$

returns a table of pairs consisting of a department identifier and the average salary of its employees. In SQL this query requires the *group by* operator. In our approach we achieve the same goal using clean functional semantics and orthogonality. □

4.9 Quantifiers

The syntax is $Qq_1(q_2)$, where Q is either $\forall$ or $\exists$, q_1 is an arbitrary query, and q_2 is an arbitrary boolean-value condition. Thus, Q is regarded as a binary operation, similar to previous non-algebraic operations. The semantics is also defined similarly. The differences are in the *combine* function, and in how the results of the parallel evaluation streams are merged. The *combine* function simply returns the truth value returned by q_2. For $\forall$ the result is $TRUE$ if q_1 returns an empty table, or the boolean conjunction of all returned truth values otherwise; for $\exists$ the result is $FALSE$ in the first case, or the booloean alternative of partial results otherwise.

Example 4.6 Departments where all programmers used to work for IBM:

$$DEPT \text{ } where \text{ } \forall \text{ } (EMPLOYS.EMP \text{ } where \text{ } JOB = "programmer")$$
$$(\exists \text{ } PREV\_JOB \text{ } (COMPANY = "IBM")) \qquad \square$$

Usually quantifiers are associated with auxiliary variables. The next subsection addresses this problem.

4.10 Correlation Variables and Synonyms

Most logical calculi rely strongly on the use of variables; so do many query languages. However, the concept of variable as used in these languages is quite different from its standard use in programming languages as a cell used to hold an updatable value. In calculi and query languages, variables are used as temporary names: either to provide synonyms for stored relations (to avoid name conflict), or as iterators over sets. The SQL phrase *from EMP e*, introduces e for a similiar purpose.

Semantics of such auxiliary names is not always obvious. An example is the DBPL construct [14]:

$$FOR \text{ } EACH \text{ } x \text{ } IN \text{ } EMP : x.JOB = \text{``}clerk\text{''} \text{ } DO \text{ } x.SAL := 3000; \text{ } END;$$

where x is used both as a calculus variable and as a programming variable. Achieving all goals of auxiliary naming, (i.e. local synonyms for objects with statically determined scope, naming of a query result or its parts, iterators/cursors, updating via auxiliary names, easy and clean semantics, avoiding semantic anomalies) is difficult. The proposal below (implemented and tested in LOQIS) is a solution that in our opinion is very simple, universal, and free of many disadvantages of other solutions.

The basic idea is that an auxiliary name can be used to refer object temporarily, i.e., only in the context of a subquery. This blends naturally with our scoping-based approach. We distinguish two kinds of occurrences of auxiliary names in a query: declaration and use. The syntax for the declaration is $n \leftarrow q$, where q is an arbitrary query. The declaration associates the name n with each row in the result of q. For row r returned by q, $n(r)$ denotes the corresponding row returned by $n \leftarrow q$. We allow also such named rows to appear in ES. To be consistent with our previous definitions, we have to improve the function *nested*: for arguments $n(r)$ it is an identity function. This means that during opening a new scope such elements are copied to ES without changes. The binding works as usual, but with a small difference: when name n occured in a query is bound to the object $n(r)$ on ES, only r is pushed on $QRES$; name n is not propagated to the result.

Example 4.7 (C.f. MyDatabase.)

$$(x \leftarrow EMP) \text{ where } (x.SAL > 1800)$$

As before, the atomic query EMP returns a single-column table $\{i_1, i_5, i_9\}$. Application of $x \leftarrow$ changes this table into $\{x(i_1), x(i_5), x(i_9)\}$. Assume $x(i_1)$ is processed by the *where* operator. This means the application of *nested*, which pushes $x(i_1)$ without changes on ES. Name x in the predicate after *where* is bound to this element, but only i_1 is send to $QRES$; name x is not propagated. The dot operator in a subquery $x.SAL$ pushes $nested(i_1) = \{i_2, i_3, i_4\}$ on the top of ES; thus SAL can be bound, as usual, to i_3. Then, the dereferencing and comparison operators will return $TRUE$. In the result, the whole query will return a single-column table $\{x(i_1), x(i_5)\}$.

The reader can verify that the SQL-style query

$$(((x \leftarrow (EMP \text{ where } JOB = "clerk")) \times (y \leftarrow EMP) \times (z \leftarrow DEPT))$$
$$\text{where } (x.SAL > y.SAL \wedge x.EDNO = z.DNO \wedge z.MGR = y.ENO)).x$$

returns identifiers of clerks earning more than their managers. Besides the SQL style, this general mechanism of auxiliary names allows for many other styles (in particular, the domain calculus style). □

5 Updates and Procedures

In this section we briefly consider how bulk updates and procedures can be integrated into the language,

5.1 Assignment

The semantics of an assignment $l := r$ assumes that the left-hand side evaluates to an l-value, and the right-hand side evaluates to an r-value; the r-value is assigned as the new value associated with the l-value.

Our approach to assignment as a general operation generalizes the *update* statement of SQL. The general syntax is $q_1 := q_2$. It can be combined with previous queries in the form $q.(q_1 := q_2)$. To understand the issues in using such an operation, consider

(EMP where $SAL > 1800$).
($WORKS\_IN := (DEPT$ where $DNAME = "Toy"))$

The first part of the query terminates with $\{i_1, i_5\}$ on the top of $QRES$. The '.' evaluation starts streams, pushing the corresponding scopes on ES. Consider the stream for i_5. The first argument of the assignment evaluates to an l-value, i.e., to i_8. The second argument evaluates to the identifier i_{13}. The assignment updates the object $< i_8, WORKS\_IN, i_{17} >$ to $< i_8, WORKS\_IN, i_{13} >$. Note that it is crucial here that $WORKS\_IN$ returns a l-value for a $WORKS\_IN$ objects (i_8), not its r-value (i_{17}).

The example illustrates an issue that needs to be resolved for bulk updates to be well defined. To avoid semantic ambiguity we assume that each of parallel streams prepares only an intention list of updates to be performed, relying on a state before the updating, common to all parallel streams. When streams are merged, their lists are merged. During merging inconsistences can be discovered, e.g. more than one stream attempted to update the same object. To take into account a more complex case of nested updates (i.e. when the update is of the form $q.p$, where q is a query and p is an arbitrary updating program) we must assume the transactional semantics: each parallel stream can see only own updates, and any inconsistency or conflict between parallel stream reverts the database to the initial state.

We can easily do multiple updates in a single stream (';' denotes sequencing):

Example 5.1

(EMP where $JOB = "clerk"$).($SAL := SAL + 100; JOB := "officer"$)

□

5.2 Procedures

Since the semantics of procedures is also defined by using a stack, we can easily incorporate procedures into our framework. There are, nevertheless, many issues to be considered, e.g. methods of parameter transmission. For lack of space, we only illustrate the essential idea. A procedure can introduce local objects, which are removed when the procedure is terminated. Parameters are treated similarly. We assume static scoping, i.e., if p_1 calls p_2 then local objects of p_1 are not visible from the inside of p_2. Local objects can be easily implemented by storing them as volatile named objects, and storing the identifiers on a new cell of ES. When the cell containing an identifier is popped, the object is gone. Output from functional procedures is pushed onto $QRES$.

A procedure declaration has the usual format, with a header that contains a formal parameter list. A call has the form

<procedure name> ($p_1 : q_1; ...$),

where p_i is a name of the i'th formal parameter, and q_i is a query that provides a value for it. Local objects (i.e., variables) are declared by

create local < specification of the object >

Example 5.2 A functional procedure 'poor' has a list of jobs as a parameter. It returns pointers to names, salaries, and department names of employees, who do one of the specified jobs and earn less than the average.

    procedure *poor(JOBS)*
      begin
        create local AVERAGE(avg(EMP.SAL));
        (* Creating a set of pointer objects pointing poor EMPs *)
        create local pointers
          POOR(EMP where(JOB $\in$ JOBS $\wedge$ SAL < AVERAGE));
        return POOR.EMP.((N $\leftarrow$ NAME)
                      $\times (S \leftarrow SAL)$
                      $\times (D \leftarrow (WORKS\_IN.DNAME)))$;
      end *poor*;

A query that retrieves names of poor clerks and programmers from the department *"Sales"*:

$(poor(JOBS : \{"clerk", "programmer"\})\ where\ (D = "Sales")).N$

Increase salaries of poor programmers from the department *"Sales"* by 100:

$(poor(JOBS : "programmer")\ where\ (D = "Sales")).(S := S + 100)$
$\hfill\square$

Example 5.3 Define a view $MyView(Dname, AvgSal, Mgr(Name, Sal))$ containing information about department names, average salaries, and manager names and salaries for departments located in Paris.

    procedure *MyView()*
      begin
        return(DEPT where "Paris" $\in$ LOC).(
          (Dname $\leftarrow$ DNAME)$\times$
          (AvgSal $\leftarrow$ avg(EMPLOYS.EMP.SAL))$\times$
          (Mgr $\leftarrow$ (MANAGER.EMP.
                ((Name $\leftarrow$ NAME) $\times$ (Sal $\leftarrow$ SAL)))))
      end *MyView*;

A query on the view: Give manager name for the department with the highest average salary:

$(MyView\ where\ AvgSal = max(MyView.AvgSal)).Mgr.Name$

An update through the view: Increase by 200 the salary of the manager of the Sales department:

$(MyView\ where\ Dname = "Sales").Mgr.(Sal := Sal + 200)$
$\hfill\square$

6   Conclusions

We have presented an approach to query languages based on a modification of concepts that are well known in programming languages. It makes possible to build query languages for variety of data models, including relational and object-oriented models. The approach supports pragmatic universality, orthogonality, and precision of specification of semantics. We have shown that a modified stack-based mechanism can be used to define and process declarative queries, and that it makes possible seamless integration of query constructs with imperative constructs and programming abstractions.

For space limit, we do not discuss many issues relevant to this approach, in particular, static polymorphic typing, object orientation, general transitive closures, ordering, processing of null values and variants, various procedural constructs, methods of parameter transmission in procedures, optimization, active rules and event-driven programming. Many of them are implemented in LOQIS and they will be subjects of subsequent papers.

References

[1] A. Albano, L. Cardelli, R. Orsini. Galileo: A Strongly-Typed, Interactive Conceptual Language. ACM Transactions on Database Systems, Vol.10, No 2, 1985, pp.230-260

[2] C. Beeri. Formal Models for Object-Oriented Databases. Proc. 1st DOOD Conf., Kyoto, pp.370-395, 1989.

[3] A.I. Brown, R. Morrison. A Generic Persistent Object Store. FIDE, ESPRIT BRA Project 3070, Technical Report Series, FIDE/92/39, 1992

[4] Language Reference Manual for INGRES/Windows 4GL for the UNIX and VMS Operating Systems. INGRES Release 6, Ingres Corporation, August 1990.

[5] M. Kifer, W. Kim, Y. Sagiv. Querying Object-Oriented Databases. Proc. ACM SIGMOD Conf. pp.393-402, 1992.

[6] Kifer, M. and G. Lausen F-Logic: A higher-order language for reasoning about objects, inheritance, and scheme. *Proc. SIGMOD Conf.*, June 1989, pp. 134–146.

[7] F. Matthes, A. Rudloff, J.W. Schmidt, K. Subieta. The Database Programming Language DBPL, User and System Manual. FIDE, ESPRIT BRA Project 3070, Technical Report Series, FIDE/92/47, 1992

[8] R. Morrison, F. Brown, R. Connor, A. Dearle. The Napier88 Reference Manual. Universities of St Andrews and Glasgow, Departments of Comp. Science, Persistent Programming Report 77, July 1989.

[9] E.J. Moss. Design of the Mneme Persistent Object Store. ACM Transactions on Information Systems, Vol.8, No.2, April 1990, pp.103-139

[10] J. Mylopoulos, P.A. Bernstein, H.K.T. Wong. A Language Facility for Designing Database-Intensive Applications. ACM Transactions on Database Systems, Vol.5, No 2, 1980, pp.185-207

[11] The O_2 User Manual, Version 4.1. O_2 Technology, Versailles, France, October 1992

[12] A. Ohori, P. Buneman, V. Breazu-Tannen. Database Programming in Machiavelli - a Polymorphic Language with Static Type Inference. Proc. of ACM SIGMOD 89 Conf., 1989, pp.46-57

[13] J.W. Schmidt. Some high level language constructs for data of type relation. ACM Transactions on Database Systems, Vol.2, No 3, 1977, pp.247-261

[14] J.W. Schmidt, F Matthes. The Database Programming Language DBPL, Rationale and Report. FIDE, ESPRIT BRA Project 3070, Technical Report Series, FIDE/92/46, 1992

[15] M. Stonebraker, L.A. Rowe, and M. Hirohama. The Implementation of POSTGRES. IEEE Transactions on Knowledge and Data Engineering, 2:1, pp.125-142, 1990.

[16] M. Stonebraker, L.A. Rowe, B. Lindsay, J. Gray, M. Carey, M. Brodie, P. Bernstein, D. Beech: The Committee for Advanced DBMS Function. Third-Generation Data Base System Manifesto. ACM SIGMOD Record 19(3), pp.31-44, 1990.

[17] K. Subieta. LOQIS: The Object-Oriented Database Programming System Proc.1st Intl. East/West Database Workshop on Next Generation Information System Technology, Kiew, USSR 1990 Springer Lecture Notes in Computer Science, Vol.504, pp.403-421, 1991.

[18] K. Subieta, C. Beeri, F. Matthes, J.W. Schmidt. A Stack-Based Approach to Query Languages. Institute of Computer Science Polish Academy of Sciences, Report 738, Warszawa, December 1993.

Information Engineering

Identifying Internet-related Database Research

Peter M.G. Apers[†]

Computer Science Department, University of Twente
Enschede, the Netherlands

Abstract

With the arrival of the Information Society, which is getting great political support, computer science has to wonder whether the research efforts are focused on the right topics. Activities such as World-Wide Web are leading us the way to the "Information Superhighway". As a database community we have to ask ourselves what can we contribute to this field. By discussing various issues of finding relevant data on the Internet, Internet-related database research topics are identified.

1 Introduction

Rapidly our society is changing from an Industrial Society into an Information Society. Everybody is experiencing the changes caused by new technologies coming from Information Technology and Communication Technology. Currently more in our offices than in our homes, but this is just a matter of time.

Also politicians are getting interested. The National Information Infrastructure programme of US administration has as its goal the implementation of the "information superhighway", connecting universities, schools, libraries, hospitals, ministries, public agencies, and business [18, 23]. This plan received a lot of public attention. Besides that, the European Commission is ready to put this topic high on its agenda [6, 7].

From the infrastructure point of view, there will be an integration of networks currently provided by telephone companies, cable television companies, and Internet. The users will in future no longer be aware which underlying network is used, because all three are able to provide the same sort of services.

The main question is "what will be the important applications?" The most important application that is currently mentioned is: *interactive television*, such as video-on-demand, homeshopping or teleshopping, and entertainment. But also multimedia and education, on-line services, business-to-business on-line services, information about public administration *etc* are growing fields. IDOMENEUS [20] has as one of its missions to get SME's involved in the usage of Internet.

In computer science, research topics have been studied within the various disciplines such as telecommunications, distributed systems, software engineering, databases, application domains *etc.* Time has come to combine our efforts to work on topics relevant for our Information Society. Multidisciplinary

---

[†]e-mail address: apers@cs.utwente.nl
home page: http://www_is.cs.utwente.nl:8080/dolls.html

work on real problems is required to really have impact. A first sign of this multidisciplinary work is combining the efforts in Information Technology and Communication Technology into *Information Communication Technology, ICT* [7].

So, the question is what can each subdiscipline of ICT contribute to make the information superhighway work. In this paper we will address topics where the database community can contribute. In Section 2 a short history of Internet and the available services are given, followed, in Section 3, by posing the major problems when looking for relevant data. In Section 4 various Internet-related database topics are discussed. In Section 5 we conclude with some final remarks.

2 Internet

The history of Internet goes back to the late 60s with the start of the experimental computer network called ARPANET. In the beginning it only connected computers at universities in Los Angeles, Stanford, Santa Barbara, and Utah. In the 80s the ARPANET had turned into an interconnection of hundreds of LANs. And now it is an integral part of Internet, just like other networks, such as NSFnet and EUnet, interconnecting an evergrowing number of sites. Just some statistics: the number of connected networks is in the order of 10K, the number of connected machines roughly 2M, and the number of Internet users is well over 20M [15, 9].

Services that are provided can be split into tools to operate on Internet and information providers. We want to make this distinction because we expect an enormous growth for the latter. *Tools* that are available are: e-mail, news, ftp, telnet, WAIS, Gopher, WWW *etc* [12]. They mainly operate in client-server mode, which means that for all these tools there is a client and a server, most of the time with the same name. WAIS, which stands for Wide Area Information Server, facilitates indexing on large databases. It consists of two programs, one for indexing and one for searching. Gopher integrates the various services such as, retrieving files with ftp, access other computers with telnet, reading news, using WAIS databases. It started as a campus information system at the University of Minnesota.

Popularity of Internet has grown tremendously by the introduction of World-Wide Web [13, 16], which provides a relatively easy to use user interface to the whole network based on hypertext. The user does not have to be aware of the underlying technology, a simple click of the mouse is sufficient to retrieve data from the other end of the world. In a way it is similar to Gopher, the main difference is that it is based on hypertext and it integrates various media.

Information providers are newsgroups, Archie, Veronica, WAIS databases, meta-hyperdocuments, on-line library catalogs, electronic journals *etc* [12]. Archie, developed by the McGill University in Montreal, provides indexing of FTP archives. Anonymous-FTP sites periodically send data about the files they archive to Archie servers, which then becomes available via Archie. Veronica will help you find Gopher servers that maintain data that you are interested in. WAIS has a directory-of-servers to direct you to the right WAIS server.

Right now the majority of documents are text based. A growing number of documents include pictures, sound, and video. With broad bandwidth networks this will become standard [6, 7, 18, 23]. Therefore, WWW can be characterized as a *distributed hypermedia document storage system*.

With an evergrowing amount of data that is available — look at the statistics above — the major problem is *how to find relevant data*.

3 Major problems

Let us analyze this problem of finding relevant data. There are many aspects involved, which we will discuss in turn.

- How to **store** and **update** data? Currently the data is primarily stored as flat files in various formats or as hypertext documents. No distinction is made between schema and instance. Also information about the files is encoded in their names, prohibiting the placement of a file in another domain. Constraints, such as referential constraints, are not maintained. If one has a reference to a document and this document is deleted an error occurs when following that reference.

- Where to **look for** data? With the evergrowing number of users the amount of data grows even faster. To still be able to find relevant files, index services such as Archie, Veronica, and WAIS databases *etc* are created. They are a kind of yellow pages, but at a lower level than one would expect. Also, the query facility of most index services is rather limited.

- How to obtain **relevant** data? Finding relevant data is not easy. Index services mainly use titles of document, and we all know that this is not a good basis to decide whether a document is relevant or not. WAIS indexes are an exception, they are based on the content of documents.

- How to find data in a **reasonable amount of time**? All tools on Internet are set up as a client-server architecture. So, in general this means that one has to retrieve files from servers and investigate them on clients. Due to the enormous number of files this will not work. However, there are exceptions, where tools maintain indexes on servers and queries on them are also processed there. Such servers are often overloaded. Also, robot-based searches, an alternative for indexes, may overload the resources of the network, so administrators of systems may forbid them entering their systems.

- What is the **quality** of the data? Because everyone can put everything on the network, there is no quality control. As experienced researcher, one knows which journals and proceedings to look at and to keep track of what particular groups are doing.

- How to **bill** consumers for the provided service? The usage of the Internet will not be for free for ever. Also not many companies will be interested in providing information if they cannot charge for it. So, therefore we will have to cope with charging for services.

4 Database research

In this section we will identify Internet-related database research. Either existing techniques are applied to new problems or new ideas are formulated.

4.1 Database support

Relational DBMSs have penetrated the administrative domain strongly, but still there are many fields in which database support is obvious, but not realized. Most of the structured data is still not maintained by DBMSs [24], let alone unstructured data. We have to ask ourselves why. Several reasons come to mind:

- Interface is too complex. SQL is a rather difficult language to learn, therefore it is hidden most of the time. Also the strong distinction between schema and instances is not appreciated by everybody. Simple, intuitive interfaces such as spreadsheets and hypertext are more popular.

- The commercial DBMSs are too complex for simple applications and most of the time too expensive. Furthermore, do all applications need the full functionality of DBMSs, e.g. strict concurrency control, transaction management, etc? Probably not.

So, answering the question whether database support of Internet is wanted, we have to ask ourselves the question whether the strong points of database technology are applicable to this field of Internet and can help overcome some of its weaknesses.

Examples of such points are:

- logical and physical data independence

- data model

- query facility to formulate declarative queries

- distributed query optimization and data allocation

- constraint maintenance

- interoperability

In the following sections these topics will be addressed. The first two in Subsection 4.3, the topics related to queries in Subsection 4.4, constraint maintenance in Subsection 4.5, and interoperability in Subsection 4.6. But first we start with a new perspective of looking at DBMSs.

4.2 DBMS-support

The trend in database technology is to provide more and more functionality. This obviously has consequences for performance. So, the first question when applying database technology to a new field is whether all this functionality is required, given the performance penalty. However, even if we choose not to use the complete functionality, we are faced with the problem that current DBMSs are black boxes.

A new approach to providing database technology to new application fields is to open up DBMSs and make the components available as building blocks [24]. The advantage of this is that a selection of the available building blocks can be made to get the right functionality. Examples of building blocks are: low level object server, data dictionary, query interface, concurrency control, and transaction management. For a DBMS to be an open system, it means that the interfaces and functionality of the building blocks are publicly available, allowing for competition between vendors. In this way one can choose the appropriate building blocks from various vendors. A consequence is that database technology will have far more impact, because it can be used in a wide variety of application domains. Note that this approach is different from extensible databases; there the interfaces are not publicly available, so still resulting in a closed system.

4.3 Data description

Internet itself is just a distributed file system with a protocol to exchange files, so it has no data model. Various types of files are stored in Internet and a certain level of expertise is required to know which tool to use for which type of files. WWW tries to overcome this problem by providing a uniform interface. By clicking on the mouse, a file is retrieved and based on the format the WWW-client knows which tool to use for presentation. In contrary to what is a custom in databases, knowledge about the format and the appropriate tool is encoded in the file name and its URL address (the address under which it can be accessed via WWW). For example,

```
file://ftp.cs.utwente.nl/pub/doc/TM/TM20manualRevC.ps.Z
```

is the file TM20manualRevC.ps.Z on the ftp-server ftp.cs.utwente.nl in directory pub/doc/TM. This way of creating object identifiers prohibits the transfer of a file to another domain, unless the name of the file is changed. When this file is retrieved the WWW-client knows that it first has to decompress the data and then to open a ghostview window. This knowledge about when to use what can be seen as a very rudimentary form of a schema. Because for all objects belonging to the class POSTSCRIPT a method to present it to the user calls ghostview.

Although WWW does not make use of a real data model, it is, however, a hypermedia system and in that sense it has a rather trivial schema consisting of *nodes*, representing files, and *edges*, representing the links between the nodes. However, the full functionality of data models is not used. This lack of a data model means for example that no query language is available and that no constraints, such as referential integrity, can be formulated, and hence cannot be maintained. The same is true for triggers.

One of the advantage of having a data model is that a distinction can be made between the conceptual and physical level, with well-known advantages, such as logical and physical data independence. A schema architecture also allows for different views of the data for different users [15]. Also, storage and index structures can be used to improve the performance of search queries. Various types of indexes become important if *ad hoc* queries are allowed.

If an object-oriented data model is used, various types of nodes and edges can be distinguished, such that specific attributes and methods can be assigned to a particular type of node or edge. For example, an edge may have an attribute ABSTRACT containing an abstract of the document it refers to and a video node may have a method MATCH to see whether a picture given as input parameter appears in that video node. In this way a form of necessary standardization is enforced, and at the same time enough flexibility is available.

The field of active databases provides an interesting, and in this context quite useful, concept, namely triggers. For example, one can specify that one wants a subscription on reports that are produced by the database group in Twente on the language TM [5]. So, every time a new document is placed in the directory /pub/doc/TM one is notified of that and automatically receives an abstract.

A query language should be expressive enough to be able to formulate queries that include conditions in terms of both the schema and the instances, such as "give me all directory nodes in Twente that contain files related to databases". An additional advantage of having a data model is that query processing can be improved, because schema information can be used to limit the search space.

4.4 Query formulation and processing

Various aspects of queries are discussed. First, we start with index services, followed by forms of interaction. We finish with query optimization.

4.4.1 Index services

With the growing number of Internet users, the amount of available data has become gigantic. In a normal library, if there is no catalogue, one might as well throw away the books. The same is true in our electronic library. If we cannot find the data we are looking for, it becomes useless to put more data on the Internet.

Some of the index services that are available are: Archie for FTP-archives, Veronica for Gopher servers, and WAIS for WAIS databases, plus meta-hyper-documents such as The Global Network Navigator, EINET Galaxy, Virtual Library, The Mother-of-all BBS, ALIWEB, the GNA Meta-Library. Most of them are based on keywords with references to particular servers, files, or documents. This means that there is a layered approach. First one accesses a directory-of-servers to find the relevant server, which is then accessed in search of relevant documents.

The main problems are that:

- the index services are always (slightly) out-of-date;

- the language to express the queries is rather limited (WAIS is an exception);

- it requires some skill to formulate the right question (at the directory level the question is different from the one at the server level);

- it also requires some skill to interpret the result of a query;

- often the sites providing the services are overloaded.

The index services are created automatically, mainly based on titles of documents. One can imagine the problem, if information about the actual content of files is included, as is the case in WAIS. The quality of WAIS indexes and searches is good, but it is not expected to scale up. We seriously have to ask ourselves whether this process of classifying can be completely automated. Classifying books, so that they show up in literature searches, is something with which librarians are familiar with. However, for large volumes of data, it is impossible to make use of librarians, therefore, (semi-)automatically classifying texts based on abstracts becomes important, based on existing, community-specific taxonomies [15].

Higher-level index services are needed. In real life, in yellow pages there is a relationship between a product and a shop, between a service and a service provider. One can imagine the same in Internet: under the topic "research on object-oriented databases" one will find all the research groups that are willing to provide information about OODB. Given this list we should be able to formulate a distributed query in a high-level language about all the documents produced by these groups. Part of this query will be executed at the servers of the groups that provide this information. Therefore, there will not be a tendency to put oneself on too many lists, because all these queries will eat up CPU-cycles of ones servers.

Also the index services can be distributed and replicated. There is no reason to have the yellow pages of all disciplines on one server. If they are distributed the availability of the servers will increase.

The index services are all passive, in the sense that it requires action from the user side to use it. Although commercials are rather boring, it may be another way of informing users. The user may even subscribe to commercials in a particular area of interest, like newsgroups.

4.4.2 Forms of interaction

Lacking a decent data model also means that no query language is available. Because WWW is based on hypertext, browsing is the predominant way of accessing the documents. Although an interesting way of going through documents, there are some disadvantages [4, 11]:

- losing track of where one is ("lost in hyperspace" syndrome);

- not being able to return to a previously read document;

- not being able to indicate how much one has read of a document.

Paths and guided tours are proposed to guide the browsing.

It is to be expected that the future interaction will be a combination of *browsing* and *searching*. Searching will be used to find a couple of starting point from whereon browsing will be used. After having browsed for a while, there maybe a need to start a search again [19]. So, what we need are good search techniques to address the contents of documents. Therefore, search techniques from Information Retrieval have to be used to access the text data, using global and local index techniques; but also pattern matching techniques are required for matching pictures and video.

Another interesting approach are robot-based search techniques that start from a particular document and continue searching the space via the hyperlinks [10]. Various search strategies can be applied.

For whatever interaction, it is vital not to have a limited number of central resources to be accessed. These will definitely be overloaded as can be seen for Archie.

4.4.3 Query optimization and data placement

One of the main challenges in the field of optimization is optimization of queries addressing not only structured data, but also hypermedia data, such as text, pictures, video *etc*, especially in a distributed environment [4]. Until now multimedia objects are seen as pointers to blobs with a presentation facility as only operation on it. It is to be expected, if full-fledged hypermedia functionality need to be provided, queries will address the contents of objects. Simple examples are of course queries that address both the title of a text document and its contents [14], but more complex cases are where pattern matching between a given picture and a set of videos [19].

The question is how are we going to handle such queries. Currently, queries addressing both normal attributes and the contents of hypermedia documents are split, so that each part can be processed separately. The reason for this division is that the evaluation models seem to be incompatible. For example, IR techniques use a kind of ranking to indicate whether a document is appropriate; with pattern matching and with uncertain data fuzzy logic is used.

Is it possible to integrate existing query optimization techniques with IR techniques [21], pattern matching *etc*? Is it possible to create an open query optimizer in which knowledge about specific domains can be put such that queries addressing hypermedia searches can be handled in an integral way?

Another topic is the placement of data. A distinction should be made between index type of data and the actual documents. The index data should be partitioned as much as possible. A first approach would be to partition by discipline, but this might have a negative effect on multi-disciplinary documents. Existing data partition techniques can be used to determine rather independent parts of the index data. After that these parts should be allocated, probably redundantly, to various servers. Techniques are available to decide where [2]. The actual documents should be distributed as much as possible to avoid overloading of the servers.

If we look at the actual access pattern of data, we see that a client is accessing the same data, be it an index or an actual document, a number of times. For this reason, caching is extremely important to avoid overloading the network [15].

4.5 Constraint maintenance

In one of the previous sections we have already mentioned referential integrity constraints.

For this type of constraint we would like to make a distinction between hyper links that connect "local" hyper nodes that together form a "standalone" document and hyper links such as a hot list or a meta-hyperdocument.

For the former we would like to enforce strict constraint enforcement. No dangling pointers are allowed. So, a simple transaction management is required to maintain this type of constraint.

The other constraints are more difficult to maintain. Because there are more than 10M hotlists there is no way to enforce constraint maintenance in the traditional way. Currently, if one follows a dead-end one gets an error message, without an actual indication of what is wrong. The first step would be to generate an appropriate error message. Another solution is create a level of indirection. So, one does not directly access a file, but one accesses a kind of directory where information about local files is kept. If a file is thrown away, moved, or given another name, this local directory is updated so that queries accessing this file will find either an appropriate error message or are automatically redirected to the new version of the file, even if it is moved to another server.

Another type of constraint is caused by replication. One expects that copies are either identical or will be in the long run. Because copies are mainly for index data, the primary-secondary copy approach seems reasonable. If there are many secondary copies broadcasting techniques along a minimum spanning tree seem appropriate. If the copies are large incremental updates are required.

4.6 Interoperability

In a way WWW intends to solve an interoperability problem. The tremendous speed with which new developments take place means that we already have legacy systems in this field. Also rather independent developments are coming together, resulting in an interoperability problem. Work in the following areas will become important in the field of Internet:

- coupling of what we traditionally call databases and other data sources, such as document storage, multimedia, but also spreadsheets *etc* (the new databases) [24];

- query processing involving many data sources [1, 22];

- advanced distributed transactions [3, 8].

A lot of research effort is focused on coupling existing, heterogeneous databases. The problem is, however, broader. Only a small percentage of the electronic data is stored in databases, the rest is stored in spreadsheets, mailboxes, textprocessor files, hyper documents, or, and this is the majority, just flat files. To let database technology have impact it is important to provide a hypermedia query interface to a combination of data sources.

Advanced applications such as trip reservations require to access many data sources, and for example depending on the outcome of a flight reservation a hotel reservation must be made. This problem of distributed transactions has some similarities with computer cooperative work, because both require a coordination of tasks and transactions. Languages are required to specify this type of distributed transactions that access rather independent, probably heterogeneous, data sources. In [8] a first attempt is made based on the object-oriented database specification language TM [5] and LOTOS, a protocol specification language.

5 Conclusion

The database field is a mature research area, with major contributions to industry, such as database management systems. At the same time we have to realize that only a very small portion of computerized data is stored in databases. With the arrival of the Information Age, which once more has become clear by discussions about the Information Superhighway, we have to ask ourselves what we, as database researchers, can contribute.

Just looking at the current status of Internet, an incomplete list of Internet-related database topics has been identified: open database management systems, schema architecture and data models, query formulation and processing, constraint maintenance, and interoperability. Although identifying was more important than solving, we sometimes applied available techniques to new problems, sometimes suggested new solutions.

To conclude, for our research to have impact in this field, but probably in any other field, we have to get rid of the idea that database management systems are black boxes. Open database management systems, based on building blocks and publicly available interfaces, so that customers can tailor their database management system to their problem (and not the other way around) is vital.

References

[1] S. Abiteboul, S. Cluet, and T. Milo, Querying and Updating the File, Proc. VLDB 1993, Dublin, pp. 73-84.

[2] P.M.G. Apers, Data Allocation in Distributed Database Systems, ACM Transactions on Database Systems, Vol 13, No 3, September 1988, pp. 263-304.

[3] P. Attie, M. Singh, A. Sheth, and M. Rusinkiewicz, Specifying and Enforcing Intertask Dependencies, Proc. VLDB 1993, Dublin, pp. 134-145.

[4] V. Balasubramanian, State of the Art Review on Hypermedia Issues And Applications,
http://www.csi.uottawa.ca/~ dduchier/misc/hypertext_review/

[5] Herman Balsters, Rolf A. de By and Roberto Zicari, "Typed Sets as a Basis for Object-Oriented Database Schemas," Proc. of the Seventh European Conf. on Object-oriented Programming (ECOOP'93), Kaiserslautern, Germany, July 1993, Springer-Verlag, pp 161–184.

[6] M. Bangemann, "Information Technology in Europe: The EC Commission's View", EITO94, pp 10-15.

[7] M. Bangemann et al., Europe and the global information society, Brussels, May 1994.

[8] Rolf A. de By and Hennie J. Steenhagen, "Interfacing Heterogeneous Systems through Functionally specified Transactions," Proc. DS-5 Semantic interoperability, Lorne, Australia, November 1992, Elsevier Science Publishers.

[9] NLnet, NLUUG, and TUNIX, Werken met Internet, http://gammix.tunix.kun.nl/boek/index.html, in Dutch.

[10] P. De Bra and R. Post, Information Retrieval in the World-Wide Web: Making Client-based searching feasible, WWW-94 Conference, CERN, May 1994.

[11] P.M.E. de Bra, Hypermedia, structures and systems, http://www.win.tue.nl/win/cs/is/debra/cursus/

[12] E. Braun, "The Internet directory", Fawcett Columbine, New York, January 1994, ISBN 0-449-90898-4.

[13] T. Berners-Lee, R. Cailliau, A. Luotonen, H. Frystyk Nielsen, and A. Secret, The World-Wide Web, CACM Vol. 37, No. 8, August 1994, pp. 76-82.

[14] E. Bertino, F. Rabitti, and S. Gibbs, Query processing in a multimedia document system, ACM TOIS, Vol. 6, No. 1, Jan. 1988, pp. 1-41.

[15] C.M. Bowman, P.B. Danzig, U. Manber, and M.F. Schwartz, Scalable Internet Resource Discovery: Research Problems and Approaches, CACM, Vol. 37, No. 8, August 1994, pp. 98-107.

[16] CERN, presentation on World-Wide Web, http://info.cern.ch/hypertext/WWW/Talks/General.html

[17] EITO, "Information Technology: The State of the Art and the Key Technology Factors of Evolution", EITO94, pp. 72-109.

[18] A. Gore, Telecommunications Policy Forum, speech, January 1994.

[19] W.I. Grosky, Multimedia information Systems - A Tutorial, IEEE Multimedia Vol.1, No 1, 1994.

[20] IDOMENEUS, Information and Data on Open MEdia for NEtworks of USers, ESPRIT Network of Excellence, No. 6606, http://idom-www.informatik.uni-hamburg.de/

[21] F. Rabitti and P. Savino, An Information Retrieval Approach for Image Databases, Proc. VLDB '92, Vancouver, pp. 574-584.

[22] K. Shoens, A. Luniewsky, P. Schwarz, J. Stamos, and J. Thomas, The Rufus System: Information Organization for Semi-Structured Data, Proc. VLDB 1993, Dublin, pp. 97-107.

[23] US Industrial Outlook 1994, US Dept of Commerce, 35th Annual addition, An Almanac of Industry, Technology and Services, January 1994.

[24] D. Vaskevitch, Database in Crisis and Transition: A Technical Agenda for the Year 2001, Proc SIGMOD 1994, Minneapolis, May 1994, pp. 484-489.

Integrating Text and Database Systems: Possibilities and Challenges

W. Bruce Croft
Computer Science Department
University of Massachusetts
Amherst, MA, 01003 U.S.A.

Abstract

Text-based applications typically require the ability to handle structured data and provide effective text access. In this paper, we review approaches to the integration of database systems and text retrieval systems. We also describes some new areas of text analysis research that are related to this problem.

1 Introduction

Many new applications of information systems, such as document production and management in organizations, involve data with complex structure and content. Textual data, in particular, has become much more common and there has been a significant increase in the development of text-based information systems[1]. Text-based systems require both the ability of database systems to model, store and maintain data with complex structure, and the ability of information retrieval (IR) systems to provide effective access to the textual part of the data. The integration of these two types of system is difficult, however, and a number of approaches to building text-based systems have been developed almost independently by the IR, database, and hypertext communities.

IR systems provide a means of representing the content of text, specifying queries, and retrieving text in response to a given query. To support the development of text-based information systems, they will typically provide the ability to define simple structure in the text database through additional attributes, such as document creation date, author, etc., that can be used as part of the query. In addition, some systems provide a gateway to a backend database system (through SQL queries, for example).

Database systems provide robust, long-term storage of objects and maintain the validity of the data through recovery and concurrency control mechanisms. They have the ability to model and query data with complex structure, but text retrieval capabilities, if they exist at all, are limited to selection based on Boolean combinations of simple predicates (such as a string match on a text attribute).

---

[1]We shall use the term "text-based" to refer to data which is mostly text, or for applications in which text is of primary importance.

Hypertext systems are designed to provide access to information through "navigation" or browsing. Structure in these systems is captured using links between hypertext "nodes". As these systems are scaled-up to handle larger databases, they are confronting the same problems that have been studied in the context of database and IR systems. Indeed, some experimental hypertext applications are being developed using database and IR systems.

None of these approaches represent a complete solution to the problem of developing text-based information systems. Different approaches emphasize different aspects of the overall system, but what is really needed is an integrated system that provides effective techniques for all aspects of defining, maintaining, and accessing text-based information. In this paper, we will discuss some of the issues involved with the integration of IR and database systems. The discussion is based on current projects in the Center for Intelligent Information Retrieval at the University of Massachusetts.

In the next section, we present the main features of an IR system, with an emphasis on what makes these systems different from database systems. We then discuss approaches to integration and cover the following topics:

- *Object Management* - supporting the creation, indexing and maintenance of text objects.

- *Optimization* - improving the efficiency of query processing for text-based queries.

- *Query Language and Data Models* - combining IR and database query languages, and representing complex objects.

- *Distributed Systems* - locating databases and merging results in a distributed text-based environment.

- *Heterogeneous Data* - accessing databases with different formats and degrees of structure.

- *Text Extraction* - extracting structure from text.

- *Data Mining* - supporting analysis of text databases.

- *Digital Libraries and Multimedia* - supporting new applications and data types.

2 Characteristics of IR

The basic processes in an information retrieval system are text representation, representation of a user's information need, and comparison of these two representations. Given that, the major research issues in IR fall into four broad categories:

1. What makes a good text representation? What are retrievable objects and how are they organized? How can a representation be generated from the text of an object? These issues, under the general heading of *indexing*[2], has been a major part of IR research over the last 30 years and has included a substantial amount of work on the use of natural language processing techniques.

2. How can we represent the user's information need and how can we acquire the representation from a description (a query) or through interaction with the user? The research in this area includes work on user interfaces, query languages, and relevance feedback [18].

3. How can we compare representations to judge likelihood that a document matches an information need? Algorithms for comparison are based on a *retrieval model*, such as the vector space model [19] or probabilistic models such as the inference net [10].

4. How can we evaluate the effectiveness of the retrieval process? Recall and precision are well-known measures of retrieval effectiveness, but many others have been discussed [19].

These issues have similarities to those addressed by database systems research, but there are significant differences. In the area of representation, for example, the database community has focused on the representation of the structure and operations associated with complex objects, while the IR community has emphasized the representation of the content of one particular data type. In the area of query languages, the IR community has focused on the difficult process of acquiring an accurate query, whereas the database community has generally regarded the query as being a precise specification (with some exceptions, for example, [17]). Finally, in the important area of retrieval models, IR has emphasized approaches that reflect the uncertainty that is inherent in the retrieval process, whereas the database community has assumed that Boolean logic is appropriate.

3 Approaches to Integration

A variety of approaches to integrating IR and database systems have been considered. A number of papers have looked at how a conventional relational system could be used to implement text retrieval [15, 1]. These approaches typically use very simple retrieval techniques and long sequences of SQL to resolve queries, and do not lead to efficient solutions. More recently, extensible or object-oriented database systems have been used to implement IR systems [20, 14, 8, 13], but these too have used simple text-based techniques and have not addressed all of the issues raised above. Finally, there have been attempts

---

[2]Note that indexing is used in a somewhat different sense to database literature, which uses it to refer to the process of generating secondary indexes such as B-trees on specific data attributes.

to define unified conceptual frameworks for integration [12, 11, 9]. One of these, the inference net [9], is the conceptual basis for our work on integration. These unified frameworks address the issue of how probabilities which arise in text operations can be incorporated into the overall retrieval process. This leads to the definition of mechanisms where database attributes, such as date of publication or author name, can also have probabilities associated with them and retrieve ranked output.

In terms of implementing an integrated system, we can characterize two basic approaches. We call these approaches "loose" and "tight" integration. The term "loose" indicates that the text retrieval capabilities are layered upon the database system, and "tight" indicates that those capabilities have been integrated into the database system.

A "loose" integration gives the user the illusion that the system is completely integrated, without actually providing a total integration of text retrieval algorithms within the internal database system. "Loose" integrations fail to provide correct query semantics because the text retrieval indices are maintained either externally to the database management system, or external to the normal access method control of the system. Many standard features of DBMS are ignored by circumvention of the controls put in place to ensure integrity of data and optimized access.

In these types of integrations, the application itself manages the text retrieval algorithms, and the DBMS has no control over that part of the application. Simple features like recovery may not properly keep textual index structures synchronized with data because the database management system has no knowledge that the index structure is semantically tied to other data residing within the system. The database management system in this case simply acts as a data store, not as a data manager; and the integrity of the data can be compromised. Other side effects of this type of "loose" integration are as follows: low levels of concurrency control, a consistency model which is less robust, no query optimization model, and a backup/recovery mechanism which is not fully integrated. A heterogeneous database system which provides access to a range of different database and text systems falls into this category.

The "tight" integration allows text to be fully supported as a datatype within a database management system. The text retrieval queries are placed within the framework of an extended database model, modifying the corresponding database management system to effectively use the text specific information which is supplied. In this type of integration, the DBMS has knowledge of text retrieval at each layer of the query processor; in effect, there is a new type of access method by which the system retrieves textual data. Ranked or probabilistic results are combined with database query results and the query optimization phase is modified to correctly use the information provided within the text retrieval portion of the query.

In a "tight" integration, a database management system can be utilized to manage all parts of the application, including the indexing and retrieval of text; and the relationships between the data and the index structures can be maintained by the system. Very few DBMSs exist today which can do content based retrieval on text, and there exist no systems which have implemented a "tight" integration.

4 Object Management

A crucial part of any text-based system are the indexes created to support efficient and flexible searching. Typically, this is done through a fully inverted index on all words (or stems) in the collection of text objects. The huge number of words in a large text database, the extreme variation in the size of the inverted lists, and the number of operations that must be supported by the index has made it extremely difficult to support text indexes in conventional database systems. There is also the problem that the information in the indexes comes from scanning and tokenizing the text using techniques that could be dependent both on the IR system and the domain of the collection. For example, some systems use stemming, some store positional information (word in sentence, paragraph, etc.), some store statistical information (term frequency in object), and some recognize "concepts" from domain-specific thesauri. On the other hand, IR systems have usually assumed that text databases are relatively static and have not paid much attention to concurrency and techniques for rapid updating.

In two recent papers [3, 2], we have shown that a persistent object store can provide competitive performance with custom data management software, and that the extensibility of an object store, together with its capabilities for controlling caching, file allocation, recovery and concurrency control provide significant benefits to the IR system designer.

We are currently working on providing fast delete and update capability for the indexes. Although this is a well-known problem for inverted files, it is made more difficult by the fact that there is typically no index on document number to the words in the documents. This is despite the fact that algorithms such as relevance feedback could make use of such an index. In relevance feedback, the words in documents identified as relevant are used to expand and reweight the original query. In the absence of a document-based index, the relevant documents must be re-parsed to extract the words. The main disadvantage of a document-based index is that it would entail a considerable storage overhead. It may be possible that with the decreasing cost of storage, appropriate compression techniques, and multiple benefits for updating and relevance feedback, these indexes would become practical.

In another project, we have been studying the implementation of an IR system using an extensible relational database system. Using BLOBs for such an implementation is similar to the implementation using the persistent object system, but with less flexibility. We are also looking at tighter integrations using relational tables and new index structures.

5 Query Optimization

Query optimization is a well-defined problem in the database community. With IR, the goal of query optimization is to reduce the total response time required to produce the particular document ranking defined as optimal by the retrieval model being used. Each system may have a different "best" ranking and use different information to produce that ranking, so optimization techniques will vary. There are, however, some commonalities. Optimization techniques can be described as either "safe" or "unsafe" depending on whether they are guaranteed to produce the "correct" ranking or an approximation to the ranking. Examples of work in this area include [4, 22, 16].

We are currently studying a range of safe techniques for optimizing the more complex, tree-structured queries used in the INQUERY system, which is based on the inference net [5]. These include redesigning the inverted file to make it possible to "skip" portions during reading, separating proximity information, maintaining lists of the documents with the most occurrences of particular words, and combining list-at-a-time processing (that is, accessing all of the inverted list associated with a query term) with document-at-a-time processing (accessing all inverted lists associated with query terms simultaneously).

6 Query Language and Data Models

One of the fundamental problems in the integration of text and database systems is the fact that while IR systems are designed to deal with uncertainty, database systems are not. This means that in a database environment, it is difficult to deal with uncertainty in the specification of a query, the representation of the meaning of an object, and the process of inferring answers to queries. As mentioned above, these are essential features of a text-based system and must be supported in an integrated system. It is appealing to think of redesigning the underlying data model so that uncertainty becomes a fundamental part of the information system, including the database attributes [12, 11, 9]. This may indeed be the correct long-term approach, but in the short term, uncertainty must be incorporated into existing database frameworks. In systems where this has been attempted, the solution has been to truncate the ranked list of text objects by taking the top n or all those with scores greater than some value. This subset is then treated as a normal relation, or sometimes as a sorted relation.

The query languages designed for database systems are cumbersome to use for text-based operations. Some of the SQL extensions proposed for handling text are too simple for advanced techniques, whereas other proposals essentially bury the complexity of text in user-defined functions that cannot be optimized by the system. Implementing a text ADT in an object-oriented database framework addresses some of the problems of integration, but it does not answer the query language issues.

In designing solutions to integration, it is important to remember that an

IR query language does not consist only of the operators AND, OR and NOT, nor are all queries written in simple natural language. A query language for a sophisticated IR model can have a range of operators with very different properties. As an example, Table 1 lists the operators currently available in the INQUERY system. All of these operators are probabilistic and produce rankings. They may also be combined in a variety of ways.

OPERATOR	ACTION
#and	Specifies that all terms should be present in the document.
#or	Specifies that any of the specified terms should be present.
#not	Specifies that the term should not be present.
#band	Boolean version of #and.
#bandnot	Boolean version of #not.
#sum	Specifies that the more terms present, the better.
#wsum	Specifies that some terms are more important than others, but also that the more present, the better.
#max	Specifies that the term with the highest associated probability is the most important. A form of synonym operator.
#n	Specifies that the terms should be present, in order, with at most $n-1$ words between them.
#uw$n$	Specifies the terms should be present, in any order, in a text window of size n.
#phrase	Specifies that the terms should be present as a simple noun phrase. The way that probabilities are combined for these terms depends on the statistics for the phrase in the document collection [7].
#syn	A synonym operator where all terms are treated as equivalent.
#passage$n$	Specifies that as many of the terms as possible be present in a text window of size n.
#field	Specifies that a particular document field should contain terms as modified by a field comparison operator

Table 1: The operators in the INQUERY query language.

One part of the query language issues that we have been studying involves probabilistic attribute searching. This has involved extending the inference net framework used for text retrieval to include database attribute or field retrieval. Although this is a common facility in commercial IR systems, we have extended the notion of fields to incorporate ranking in field matching and include fields extracted from the text content. As an example, we have a DATE recognizer that converts all references to dates and times in texts to canonical forms that could be stored as an attribute in a relational schema. The #field operator in INQUERY supports conventional queries such as

```
#field( DATE 1952 )
#field( DATE  #range 19880101 19880301)
```

where the first query finds documents that mention 1952 and the second finds documents mentioning dates between 1st January, 1988 and 1st March, 1988. In addition, the #field operator can accept any INQUERY query such as

```
#field( DATE #wsum( 1.0 1951 3.0 1952 2.0 1953))
```

In this case, documents are retrieved ranked by the relative weight of the years they contain.

Another research area related to the data model is representing the complex structure of text objects. Many of the documents stored in text databases will contain some form of markup language that describes the structure and layout of the document. These markup languages, such as SGML, are becoming increasingly prevalent and an integrated information system must be able to handle them. One issue is how the tags or structure in the document can be used to assist indexing. Some parts of the documents will be more appropriate to index than others, whereas other parts may be impossible to index, such as a compressed representation of an image. The difficulty will be in developing a scheme where potentially thousands of domain-specific tags could be registered and used by document parsers that are dealing with a heterogeneous mix. The alternative is imply to ignore the markup for indexing purposes, but this may not always be possible.

Another issue is how the structure indicated by these tags is represented in the database environment and how it is used in the query language. It is possible that every document component indicated in the markup structure could be represented as an object in the database. This is, however, unlikely, given the enormous number of objects that would be created. Between representing all objects and representing the document as a single object, there are a lot of other possibilities (e.g. [8]) and approaches need to be developed that combine flexibility with efficiency.

An example of the importance of structure in queries is retrieval from databases containing large amounts of text in the form of table captions. If a user is looking for a table of China's exports, they do not want get back hundreds of tables where China is one of the entries of the table rather than the subject of the whole table. The text in the table should be indexed, but the caption should receive special treatment since it gives the main topic. Note that part of this problem could be handled through the markup structure (distinguishing a caption from the body of the table) and part through analysis of the caption text.

7 Distributed Systems

One of the crucial aspects of any practical integrated information system is that it must deal with a wide range of databases and information sources. Even from the point of view of scalability, it is unlikely that a database of 100 GBytes will be treated as a single database in a practical system architecture. Searching multiple, distributed databases, therefore, is a central area of research.

The most important issue conceptually is guaranteeing a consistent global result from the combination of many local searches. In a system like INQUERY, the probabilities that are the basis of the document ranking are calculated using global statistics of word occurrence. If a given database is broken up into many pieces and each of those pieces is searched separately and the results combined, the ranked list produced will typically not be the same as that produced by searching the single large database. Although for a small number of distributed databases it would be possible to maintain global statistics, when the number of possible databases grows to hundreds or thousands, this would probably not be practical. Instead, it seems better for each database to be treated as a separate source, and for the source outputs to be combined using a weighted function (such as #wsum in INQUERY). The relative weights could be learned through user feedback and would be different for different profiles, individuals and groups.

¿From the architecture point of view, it is important to do more work to understand what the tradeoffs are between different client-server implementations. Important factors include whether the search is being done over a local network, the INTERNET, multiple instantiations of the same system or different systems, and the capabilities of the client machines. We are studying this issue using data collected from operational systems and simulations.

8 Heterogeneous Data

Heterogeneous systems have been studied by database researchers for some time. They will continue to be important in the design of integrated systems since much of the available information will reside in other systems. The possible contribution that could be made by IR systems in this area would be the notion of cascaded filtering. In this approach, relatively simple queries would be used to pull large amounts of information from heterogeneous systems. The retrieved information would then be made available for more precise searching using a more sophisticated local text search engine.

Another important aspect of heterogeneity for integrated systems is that in many real applications, related information occurs in many different formats. The classic example of this is in medical information systems, where the same information is stored in many different ways both within and between institutions. Document markup can help to some extent, but people will not agree on markup in the same way they disagree on database schemas. Some information is very difficult to codify using structured approaches. Text indexing and extraction techniques are part of the solution to this problem, since they can make information available regardless of the field it has been recorded in.

9 Text Extraction

Text extraction refers to the identification of entities, attributes and relationships in free text. In typical text extraction scenarios, a template or schema of the desired information is used and relations are generated by the extraction software. For example, if someone was interested in joint ventures, they may want to search a relation with attributes such as the names of the companies participating, their locations, the name of the new company, the amount of money involved, the product that will be produced, etc. The aim of text extraction is to populate this database by analyzing text such as the Wall Street Journal.

In our work we have concentrated on building extraction software for objects that are of general interest, such as company names, people names, dates, monetary amounts, and locations [5]. The extracted information is indexed in a similar fashion to words and is then available for use in queries and in other analysis software, such as data mining. We plan to extend this approach to a library of common extraction routines.

Other people have used more sophisticated techniques to identify relationships and roles ([21]). These techniques tend to be more knowledge and computation-intensive. We are working with two such groups to see how extraction techniques can be incorporated into an integrated system.

10 Data Mining

Data mining can refer to many things, but one is the discovery of relationships that are not explicitly represented in databases. As an example of what can be done with text-based techniques, we carried out a project where company and people extraction was combined with calculations of statistical associations. In this system, it is then possible to query against automatically constructed company and people databases, including retrieving by activity. Given a company or person as a starting point, ranked lists of related companies or people can then be retrieved. When interesting associations are found, the relevant texts can be retrieved [6].

Another important form of discovery is automatic thesaurus generation and support for concept browsing. We have obtained very promising results in this area using an approach called PhraseFinder [23], which represents concepts by words that occur in the same context.

11 Digital Libraries and Multimedia

Much of what has been described as an integrated text-based information system is essential as part of a platform for digital libraries. The definition of a digital library is rather loose, and incorporates essentially any application that involves access to distributed information. The multimedia aspect of digital libraries, which is often mentioned, is just one more aspect of storing and querying complex objects. Text has a central role in such an application because it serves as the "glue" to hold together disparate sources of information such as tables, images, video, and audio. The database framework is important because of the robustness and flexibility it provides. The challenge is to produce an integrated system that is efficient and combines the best aspects of both types of system.

References

[1] David C. Blair. An extended relational retrieval model. *Information Processing and Management*, 24(3):349–371, 1988.

[2] E. Brown, J. Callan, and B. Croft. Fast incremental indexing for full-text information retrieval. In *Proceedings of VLDB 94*, 1994.

[3] E. Brown, J. Callan, B. Croft, and E. Moss. Supporting full-text information retrieval with a persistent object store. In *Proceedings of EDBT 94*, pages 365–378. Springer-Verlag, 1994.

[4] Chris Buckley and Alan F. Lewit. Optimization of inverted vector searches. In *Proceedings of the Eighth Annual International ACM SIGIR Conference on Research and Development in Information Retrieval*, pages 97–110, New York, NY, 1985. ACM.

[5] J. P. Callan and W.B. Croft. An evaluation of query processing strategies using the TIPSTER collection. In *Proceedings of ACM SIGIR International Conference on Research and Development in Information Retrieval*, pages 347–356, 1993.

[6] J.G. Conrad and M.H. Utt. A system for discovering relationships by feature extraction from text databases. In *Proceedings of ACM SIGIR International Conference on Research and Development in Information Retrieval*, pages 260–271, 1994.

[7] W. B. Croft, H.R. Turtle, and D.D. Lewis. The use of phrases and structured queries in information retrieval. In *Proceedings of the ACM SIGIR Conference on Research and Development in Information Retrieval*, pages 32–45, 1991.

[8] W. Bruce Croft, Lisa Smith, and Howard Turtle. A lossely coupled integration of a text retrieval system and an object-oriented database system. In *Proceedings of SIGIR 92*, pages 223–232, 1992.

[9] W. Bruce Croft and Howard Turtle. Retrieval of complex objects. In *Proceedings of EDBT 92*, pages 217–229, 1991.

[10] W. Bruce Croft and Howard R. Turtle. Text retrieval and inference. In P. Jacobs, editor, *Text-Based Intelligent Systems*, pages 127–156. Lawrence Erlbaum, 1992.

[11] Norbert Fuhr. A probabilistic framework for vague queries and imprecise information in databases. In *Proceedings of VLDB 90*, pages 696–707, 1990.

[12] H. Garcia-Molina and D. Porter. Supporting probabilistic data in a relational system. In *Proceedings of EDBT*, pages 60–74, 1990.

[13] D. Harper and A. Walker. ECLAIR: An extensible class library for information retrieval. *The Computer Journal*, 35(3):256–267, 1992.

[14] C. A. Lynch and M. Stonebraker. Extended user-defined indexing with applications to textual databases. In *Proceedings of the Very Large Database Conference*, pages 306–317, 1988.

[15] I.A. Macleod and R.G. Crawford. Document retrieval as a database application. *Information Technology: Research and Development*, 2:43–60, 1983.

[16] A. Moffat and J. Zobel. Fast ranking in limited space. In *Proceedings of the 10th IEEE Conference on Data Engineering*, pages 428–437, 1994.

[17] Amihai Motro. VAGUE: A user interface to relational databases that permits vague queries. *ACM Transactions of Office Information Systems*, 6(3):187–214, July 1988.

[18] Gerard Salton and Chris Buckley. Improving retrieval performance by relevance feedback. *JASIS*, 41:288–297, 1990.

[19] Gerard Salton and Michael J. McGill. *Introduction to Modern Information Retrieval*. McGraw-Hill, 1983.

[20] H.J. Schek. Methods for the administration of textual data in database systems. In C.J. Van Rijsbergen, R.N. Oddy, and P.W. Williams, editors, *Research and Development in Information Retrieval*, pages 218–235, 1981.

[21] B. Sundheim, editor. *Proceedings of the Third Message Understanding Evaluation and Conference*. Morgan Kaufmann, Los Altos, CA, 1991.

[22] W.Y.P. Wong and D.L. Lee. Implementations of partial ranking using inverted files. *Information Processing and Management*, 29:647–669, 1993.

[23] J. Yufeng and W.B. Croft. An association thesaurus for information retrieval. In *Proceedings of RIAO 94*. to appear.

Logical and Conceptual Models for the Integration of Information Retrieval and Database Systems

Norbert Fuhr*
Informatik VI, University of Dortmund
44221 Dortmund, Germany

Abstract

We present two new approaches to the problem of integrating information retrieval (IR) and database (DB) systems. On the logical level, IR is based on uncertain inference, which is a generalization to the certain inference process employed in DB systems. As an implementation of this concept, we present a probabilistic relational algebra. On the conceptual level, we distinguish between the logical, layout and content structure of DB objects. In the past, DB research used to focus on the logical structure of objects, whereas IR research dealt with the content of documents. By combining these two approaches and incorporating also the layout structure of objects, a conceptual model for integrated IR and DB systems is outlined.

1 Introduction

The integration of information retrieval (IR) and databases (DB) has been discussed for many years now, but without satisfying results. However, in the past, there was little need for integrated IR-DB systems, since the application fields were rather different: Whereas database management systems (DBMS) were in widespread use, IR systems were applied almost exclusively by online providers running large bibliographic databases. Currently, the situation is changing very fast. In scientific as well as in commercial environments, most documents are available now in electronic form, and so there is an interest in storing them in an IR system. However, especially in the commercial area, storing factual and textual data in separate system is not a reasonable solution, since there are often close relationships between the two different types of data, which cannot be modelled by using two specialized systems. For this reason, there is a clear trend towards integrated systems. For example, several (commercial) relational DBMS are offering text retrieval capabilities now. From a theoretical point of view, however, these systems offer very poor IR functions, since they are based on Boolean retrieval. The poor retrieval quality and the user-unfriendliness of this retrieval method are well-known (at least in the IR field, see e.g. [Salton et al. 83]).

---

*This work was supported in part by ESPRIT BRA 8134.

So there is a need for developing integrated IR-DB systems based on a better theoretical foundation. Let us first consider the classical view of the two fields (to which we referred implicitly above): A short characterization consists in the statement that databases contain formatted data (or facts), while IR systems deal with unformatted data, i.e. texts. For formatted data, powerful data models and query languages have been developed, whereas for texts, robust text analysis (i.e. stemming) methods, statistical term weighting and retrieval models with ranking have been the focus of research. In addition, due to the rather different application environments, the DB field has developed methods for coping with database integrity, security, concurrency and recovery. In IR, these topics have become an issue only recently. From this point of view, there is little overlap between the two fields, and so there is no common basis from which an integration could be started.

In this paper, we will discuss two different views on the fields of IR and DB, which are located at different abstraction levels, namely the logical and the conceptual level. Each of these views can be used as a starting point for developing an integrated system. In the following section, we will first present an approach based on the logical level, regarding IR as uncertain inference. Section 3 discusses the problem of conceptual modelling of complex objects, where we claim that IR and DB have different views on the same objects, and propose methods for combining these views. Finally, we give an outlook on further work in this area.

2 The logical level

In the logical view on databases, computing the answer to a query q from a database means to find all objects o for which the logical formula $q \leftarrow o$ is true. If one would take the same approach to document retrieval, then a document d should be retrieved in response to a query if $q \leftarrow d$ can be shown to be true. In fact, this is exactly what Boolean retrieval does. However, since IR has to deal with vagueness and imprecision, this approach is not adequate. For this reason, it is argued in [Rijsbergen 86] that IR should be regarded as an uncertain inference process instead. By using probability theory as basis, Rijsbergen shows that document retrieval is equivalent to computing the probability $P(q \leftarrow d)$ for a document d.

Comparing the two types of inference, one can see that uncertain inference used in IR is just a generalization of the inference mechanism employed in DBMS. So an integration of IR and DB on the logical level seems to be feasible. However, this view just sets the frame for a set of possible solutions. In order to arrive at a model which can both be implemented and is also applicable in practice, one has to take a data model from the DB field and generalize it in a way such that it also comprises probabilistic inference.

In [Fuhr & Rölleke 94], a probabilistic relational algebra (PRA) is described which generalizes standard relational algebra; this way, it fulfills the requirements for forming the basis of an integrated IR-DB system. In the following, we give a brief description of the PRA.

Unlike similar approaches, PRA is based on intensional semantics, which is the key to a probabilistic data model that is a real generalization of relational algebra. Let $\bar{R}$ denote an instance of an ordinary relation, and δ a tuple from the corresponding domain. Then we have either $\delta \in \bar{R}$ or $\delta \notin \bar{R}$. In probabilistic relations, we assume that δ is associated with a binary stochastic event η, where $\eta = $ true, if $\delta \in \bar{R}$, and $\eta = $ false, otherwise. So we regard the probability $\beta = P(\delta \in \bar{R})$ as additional information belonging to a tuple in a probabilistic relation. We distinguish between basic events and complex events. The actual database relations (called base relations in the following) only contain basic events. Complex events are Boolean combinations of basic events. They are formed as a by-product of relational operators. By keeping track of the basic events leading to a tuple in a derived relation, we implement intensional semantics.

DocTerm

η	β	DocNo	Term
DT(1, IR)	0.9	1	IR
DT(2, DB)	0.7	2	DB
DT(3, IR)	0.8	3	IR
DT(3, DB)	0.5	3	DB
DT(4, AI)	0.8	4	AI

Figure 1: Example probabilistic relation

So a tuple t of a probabilistic relation is a triple (η, β, δ) where $t.\delta$ is the data tuple containing the values for the different attributes, $t.\eta$ gives the event expression and $t.\beta$ is the probability of the event being true. For base relations, $t.\beta$ is given explicitly, whereas for derived relations, it is computed from $t.\eta$ as the probability of the corresponding Boolean expression of the basic events being true. An example probabilistic relation representing probabilistic document indexing is given in figure 1.

η	β	Term
DT(1, IR) $\vee$ DT(3, IR)	0.98	IR
DT(2, DB) $\vee$ DT(3, DB)	0.85	DB
DT(4, AI)	0.8	AI

Figure 2: $\Pi_{\text{Term}}(\text{DocTerm})$

Now the five basic operations of relational algebra are redefined in PRA such that in addition to the manipulation of the attribute values, we also form Boolean combinations of the event expressions of the tuple involved: For union

η	β	DocNo
DT(1, IR)	0.9	1
DT(2, DB)	0.7	2
DT(3, IR) ∨ DT(3, DB)	0.9	3

Figure 3: $\Pi_{\text{DocNo}}(\sigma_{\text{Term}='IR'}(\text{DocTerm})) \cup \Pi_{\text{DocNo}}(\sigma_{\text{Term}='DB'}(\text{DocTerm}))$

DY

η	β	DocNo	Year
DY(1,1980)	0.8	1	1980
DY(1,1981)	0.2	1	1981
$\hat{E}$	1.0	2	1990
DY(3,1985)	0.4	3	1985
DY(3,1986)	0.4	3	1986
DY(3,1987)	0.2	3	1987

Figure 4: A probabilistic relation for the imprecise attribute Year

and projection, the disjunction of the corresponding event expression is formed, cartesian product leads to the conjuntion of the event expression, and for difference, we form the conjunction of the first argument and the negation of the second argument; the selection operation does not change the event expressions of the tuples selected. For example, figure 2 gives the result of projecting DocTerm (DocNo, Term) on the attribute Term, and figure 3 shows the answer to a query asking for documents about IR or DB.

Here we have assumed that the basic events are independent of each other. This assumption is reasonable for most applications. Then we can compute the probability for any event expression from the probabilities of the basic events only by applying the well-known sieve formula.

PRA also can be used for representing imprecise attribute values. For that, we model imprecise attribute values as probability distributions over the corresponding domain. As an example, the probabilistic relation DY depicted in figure 4 shows some documents for which the publication year is not known precisely: document 1 was published either in 1980 or 1981, document 2 certainly in 1990 ($\hat{E}$ denotes the certain event here) and document 3 in 1985, 1986 or 1987. Obviously, not all tuples in DY represent independent events. Here the events DY(1,1980) and DY(1,1981) are disjoint to each other, in the same way as the three events DY(3,1985), DY(3,1986) and DY(3,1987). On the other hand, we would like to assume that tuples belonging to different document numbers represent independent events. In order to describe the disjointness of events in such a probabilistic relation, we introduce the concept of a *disjointness key*, where two tuples represent disjoint events if they agree on the values of this key (i.e. the attribute DocNo in this example). If the disjointness key is empty, then all tuples of the base relation represent disjoint events. On the other hand, if the disjointness key contains all the attributes of the relation scheme (which is the default), then there are no dependent tuples within the relation.

For example, the PRA expression $\Pi_{DocNo}(\sigma_{YEAR>1985}(DY))$ searches for documents published after 1985; as result, we get for DocNo=3 the event expression (DY(3,1986) $\vee$ DY(3,1987)), with a probability of $0.4 + 0.2 = 0.6$.

Q1

η	β	Term
Q1(DB)	0.7	DB
Q1(IR)	0.3	IR

Figure 5: Query term weighting

$\Pi_{DocNo}(Q1 \bowtie DocTerm)$

η	β	DocNo
Q1(IR) $\wedge$ DT(1, IR)	$0.3 \cdot 0.9$	1
Q1(DB) $\wedge$ DT(2, DB)	$0.7 \cdot 0.7$	2
Q1(IR) $\wedge$ DT(3, IR) $\vee$ Q1(DB) $\wedge$ DT(3, DB)	$0.3 \cdot 0.8 + 0.7 \cdot 0.5$	3

Figure 6: Result of query term weighting

Another important application of disjoint events is query term weighting in text retrieval. If we represent the set of query terms as a relation of disjoint events, then we achieve a specific form of query term weighting. For example, a query with the terms DB and IR could be represented as shown in figure 5. Then the expression $\Pi_{DocNo}(Q1 \bowtie DocTerm)$ would yield the result depicted in figure 6. Since in Q1 the terms represent disjoint events, but in DocTerm they stand for independent events, the probabilities in the result relation are computed as the scalar product of the corresponding weights.

PRA also allows for modelling of vague conditions in queries. For example, a customer looking for PCs with a price less than $1000 may be willing to pay a little more in certain circumstances. In literature databases, a person searching for relevant publications from the past 3 years may also be interested in a highly relevant paper published 4 years ago.

In [Fuhr 90], we have developed a probabilistic interpretation of vague predicates. E.g., in the first example from above, there is a certain probability that the customer will pay a specific price higher than $1000. This phenomenon can be modelled by means of a probabilistic relation with two attributes containing the values to be compared, and the associated probability that a

LT

η	β	A	Price
$\hat{E}$	1.0	1000	900
$\hat{E}$	1.0	1000	950
LT(1000,1000)	0.99	1000	1000
LT(1000,1050)	0.90	1000	1050
LT(1000,1100)	0.60	1000	1100

Figure 7: A probabilistic relation for the vague predicate $\tilde{<}$

user formulating a query with this vague predicate will accept a specific pair of values. Figure 7 shows some tuples of the relation for the example from above. Given this relation, it is obvious that we could express a vague selection condition like "Price $\tilde{<}$ 1000" on a relation R by means of the PRA expression R $\bowtie \Pi_{\text{Price}}(\sigma_{A=1000}(\text{LT}))$.

The relation corresponding to a vague predicate need not be given explicitly — in many cases, the tuple probability could also be specified as a function of the two values to be compared. In [Fuhr 90], it is shown how this type of function can be derived from empirical data.

Obviously, events in relation LT are neither independent nor disjoint to each other. However, we only run into problems if we get an event expression which contains two different events from this relation; in this case we would need appropriate dependence information. Without additional effort, we can only process queries which do not lead to event expressions containing pairs of dependent events.

With the different features as described above, PRA extends relational database systems for coping with uncertainty and vagueness. It is the first model of this kind for which all equivalences from ordinary relational algebra hold. Due to the latter fact, we can exploit the connection between relational algebra and relational calculus: We use the same transformation process from calculus to algebra but apply the algebraic expression to probabilistic relations. So we have a probabilistic relational calculus which yields probabilistic relations as answers.

From an IR point of view, PRA allows for modelling document indexing and search term weighting. On the DB side, we have the standard relational model plus imprecise attribute values and vague queries. So PRA is not only a combination of probabilistic IR with relational databases, it also offers additional features for modelling imprecision in databases.

3 Conceptual modelling of objects

In [Meghini et al. 91], conceptual modeling of multimedia documents is discussed. In electronic publishing, one distinguishes between the logical structure and the layout structure of documents. For example, for the document type "letter", there is a logical structure containing sender, recipient, salutation, several paragraphs, closing and signature. The layout structure may consist of several rectangular regions placed on the top, the bottom, centered or flushed left or right on a page. However, the logical and the layout structure are not sufficient for performing IR on document bases. For this reason, the conceptual structure is added which permits the representation of the meaning of documents. For example, a letter may belong to the conceptual document type "offer", consisting of frame (with sender and recipient) and content, where the latter is a set of product infos with name, description and price.

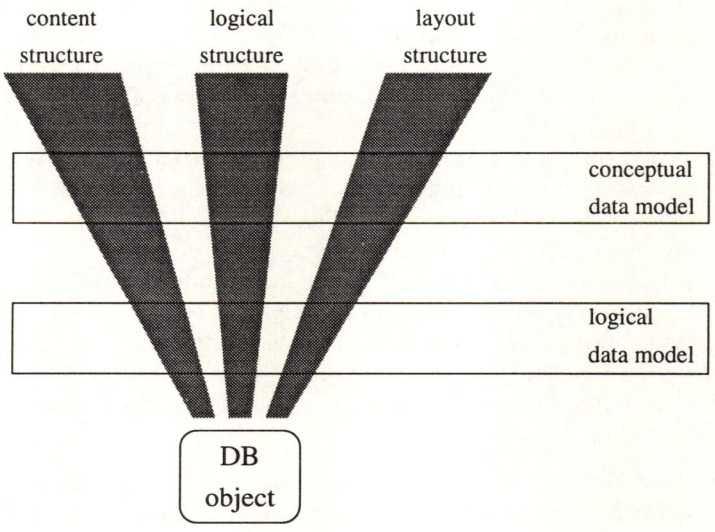

Figure 8: Abstraction levels and views on objects

In this model, the conceptual structure is a higher-level view (namely from the conceptual level) on multimedia documents. However, we think that in general, the semantic content of a document should also be represented at the logical level, in order to access this content in the same way as elements of the logical structure (e.g. attribute values). For this reason, we will use the term "content structure" instead of conceptual structure in the following. The relationship between the three structures and the two abstraction levels is depicted in figure 8.

In [Fuhr 92], this approach is extended from documents to all kinds of database objects. It is claimed that for databases comprising a large number of different object types, there is a need to support all three types of structures. Typically, the DB field only deals with the logical structure of objects. There are powerful data models for representing a broad range of possible object structures, for retrieving and manipulating these structures. Recently, there is also increasing interest in data models supporting the complex logical structure of text documents (see e.g. [Loeffen 94]). However, the more complex the logical structures are, the more rises the need for considering also the content structure. For example, assume that we have an object-oriented DBMS as part of a CASE tool. In a bank application, the software manager might search for all modules affected by a new tax law. Since the modules were developed with different tools and in different programming languages, their logical structure will vary to a great extent; even two modules performing the same task may have a very different logical structure. As another example, consider an environmental information system where a user seeks information about the pollution of ground water with nitrate. There may be text documents, maps or relations containing relevant information. A traditional DBMS would force the user to ask specific queries for the different types of objects.

Generally speaking, if there is a large number of object types, then there is a certain need for supporting queries which are independent of specific logical structures. This issue leads us to the introduction of a content structure (or view) of objects. In the following, we want to describe some of the characteristics of the content view.

The major task of the content structure is to offer a unified view on a large number of object types with varying logical structures. In general, this goal cannot be achieved without sacrifying precision. A major reason for different logical structures is due to the variety of the objects to be modelled. If we want to map different logical structures onto a single content structure, then we are losing precision. This can affect details of the (logical) structure as well as the values stored within this structure. A simple example for this process is text indexing: Whereas a document may have a complex logical structure, most IR methods represent its content by a simple set of terms with associated weights. As another example, in materials databases, the properties of a certain material also depend on the product form (e.g. bar, tube or sheet metal) and on form-specific parameters (e.g. thickness of sheet metal). In response to a query for materials with certain properties, it should be possible to receive answers without specifying additional parameters first (because these parameters are mostly material-specific). This could be achieved by applying appropriate aggregate functions (e.g. minimum, maximum or both) to the values of a single property in the different materials variants.

One can also regard the content structure as a certain abstraction from the logical structure. So the content structure is derived from the logical structure — similar to a view in a database. Generally, updates to the content view are not possible, since it is not clear how such an update should affect the logical structure. For example, if we had a document and we would add a certain term to its content view, how should its logical structure change in order to reflect the new content structure?

The most important problem is the definition of the mapping from the logical structure onto the content structure. For the case of text documents, this has been (and is still) a major issue of IR research. Here a very simple data model has been used for the content structure, and the mapping involves mainly statistical methods. For other types of objects, more complex data models will become necessary, in order to cover at least certain aspects of the logical structure. Unfortunately, little work has been done in this area (e.g. the universal relation model [Maier et al. 84]).

Besides logical and content structure, there is also a layout structure for documents. So we might ask whether there also should be a layout structure for objects in general. For older data models, there was no need for bothering about this point, since some generic output formats were sufficient. However, for complex objects, CAD applications or in geographic information systems, the presentation of objects is an important issue. Currently, this problem has to be solved in the application programs. But we think that the layout structure can and should be integrated in the database, in order to provide object-type-specific presentation mechanisms. A first step in this direction is the "print" method in object-oriented systems (e.g. Smalltalk), which has different implementations in different classes (by means of method overloading). For an implementation of the layout view, this method should become more flexible, e.g. allowing for displaying only certain parts of an object, or different presentations depending on the display context.

Recent studies in the field of IR and human-computer interaction have shown that small changes in the layout have a significant impact on the performance of humans when using such a system (see e.g. [Allen 94]). When databases with complex object structures are used in interactive mode, then layout structure also will be an important issue.

Based on these considerations, we propose a new conceptual model for integrated IR-DB systems. Figure 9 shows our conceptual model. Here real world objects are mapped onto database objects. A DB object consists of a logical structure and a layout structure. Furthermore, it has a content structure which is derived from its logical structure.

For performing retrieval on objects, each object has an object description which can be addressed by queries. Only properties of an object which are represented here can be used to qualify it as an answer to a query. This view is an important point when we are dealing with textual or multimedia objects. From a user's point of view, these objects have a rich semantics, but only a small fraction of it can be modelled in the database. For this reason, the description of such an object will be rather poor, and its semantics becomes only visible to the user once it is retrieved. Furthermore, it also may be reasonable not to represent the complete logical or layout structure in the description, since these structures may be very complex, and there is little need to be able to answer queries referring to all properties of these structures. Such a statement may be rather unusual in the DB area. However, we should bear in mind that there is a huge deficit in constructing useful content structures, and we should rather try to resolve this imbalance than aiming at perfect modelling of features nobody is interested in.

The object description should contain features of all three structures, since queries may also specify conditions relating to the different structures. Assume

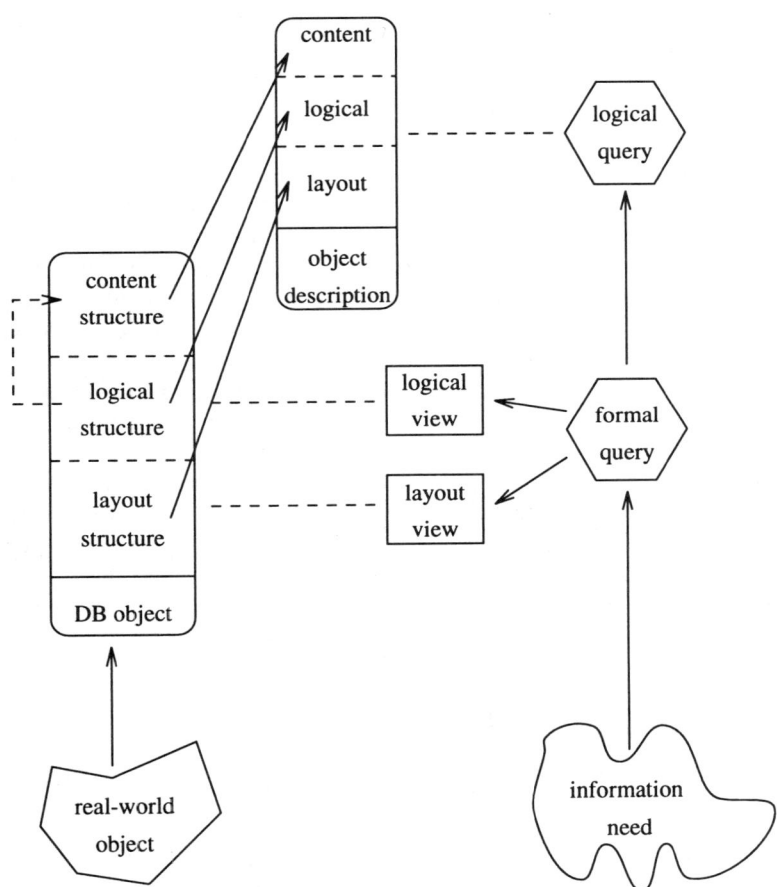

Figure 9: Conceptual model

that we have an office information system, then a query about information concerning computer equipment would relate to the content structure, a search for the last letter from Miller & Co. refers to the logical structure, and looking for a letter with two tables on the first page addresses the layout structure.

On the query side of our conceptual model, we first have an information need of a user. By formulating this need specified in a language which is accepted by the system, we get a formal query. From this statement, the logical query is derived, which specifies the conditions that an object must fulfill in order to be considered as an answer to the query. As described above, conditions can only address properties which are represented as part of object descriptions.

In addition, the formal query also may specify the parts of the relevant objects the user is interested in, and how these parts should be displayed. The first aspect refers to the logical view of objects, whereas the second one addresses the layout view. Information concerning these aspects may be contained explicitly in the formal query, or some useful defaults should be applied. For example, in a fulltext document, only the relevant passages may be interesting, plus the bibliographic information about the document. From a map stored in the system, the geographic region that is referred to by the query and some additional context should be presented.

As mentioned before, imprecision and vagueness play an important role in an integrated IR and DB system. On the object side, a major source for imprecision is due to the problems of deriving the content structure. However, also the real world data may be imprecise, thus we need mechanisms for representing this imprecsion in the logical structure. On the query side, we have to cope with vagueness, since information needs often cannot be specified as precisely as expected by today's DBMS. So the system should allow for the formulation of vague conditions as part of the formal query, and represent vagueness also in the logical query.

4 Conclusions and outlook

In this paper, we have outlined two new approaches for the integration of IR and DB systems.

On the logical level, IR can be seen as a generalization of the DB approach, replacing certain inference by an uncertain one. As one possible model implementing this view, we have described a probabilistic relational algebra. In principle, it should be possible to develop probabilistic generalizations for most data models, thus offering a variety of solutions to the IR-DB integration problem.

The conceptual level gives us a deeper understanding of the integration problems. As there are three different types of views on objects, it seems that currently each of the fields of IR, DB and human-computer interaction focuses on one of these views. A truly integrated system should aim at a closer integration of the different views, and for that, knowledge from all three fields is necessary. Our new conceptual model aims to clarify the situation, and it points out some of the problems that have to be solved.

The PRA is a logical data model. It makes no distinction between logical and content structure. This may be reasonable at this level. However, PRA also offers no possibility for deriving the content structure from the logical structure. So this mapping must happen outside of PRA — which is not what we would really like to have. One possible solution is to extend the deductive capabilities of PRA towards a probabilistic version of Datalog. Currently, we are investigating this approach.

Instead of starting with a classical data model, one can also use more powerful knowledge representation formalisms for combining logical and content structure. In [Meghini et al. 93] and [Sebastiani 94], an approach based on terminological logic is presented. However, this introduces a computationally expensive inference process, and thus may not be feasible for large databases.

So the conceptual model is a framework which can be filled by very different approaches. The choice of the appropriate model should not only depend on theoretical considerations, but also on the actual needs of the application in mind.

References

Allen, B. (1994). Perceptual Speed, Learning and Information Retrieval Performance. In [Croft & Rijsbergen 94], pages 71–80.

Croft, W. B.; van Rijsbergen, C. (eds.)(1994). *Proceedings of the Seventeenth Annual International ACM-SIGIR Conference on Research and Development in Information Retrieval*, London, et al. Springer-Verlag.

Fuhr, N.; Rölleke, T. (1994). *A Probabilistic Relational Algebra for the Integration of Information Retrieval and Database Systems.* (Submitted for publication).

Fuhr, N. (1990). A Probabilistic Framework for Vague Queries and Imprecise Information in Databases. In: McLeod, D.; Sacks-Davis, R.; Schek, H. (eds.): *Proceedings of the 16th International Conference on Very Large Databases*, pages 696–707. Morgan Kaufman, Los Altos, Cal.

Fuhr, N. (1992). Konzepte zur Gestaltung zukünftiger Information-Retrieval-Systeme. In: Kuhlen, R. (ed.): *Experimentelles und praktisches Information Retrieval*, pages 59–75. Universitätsverlag Konstanz.

Loeffen, A. (1994). Text Databases; A Survey of Text Models and Systems. *Sigmod record 23(1)*, pages 97–106.

Maier, D.; Ullman, J.; Vardi, M. (1984). On the Foundations of the Universal Relation Model. *ACM Transactions on Database Systems 9(2)*, pages 283–308.

Meghini, C.; Rabitti, F.; Thanos, C. (1991). Conceptual Modeling of Multimedia Documents. *IEEE Computer 24(10)*, pages 23–30.

Meghini, C.; Sebastiani, F.; Straccia, U.; Thanos, C. (1993). A Model of Information Retrieval Based on a Terminological Logic. In: Korfhage, R.; Rasmussen, E.; Willett, P. (eds.): *Proceedings of the Sixteenth Annual International ACM/SIGIR Conference on Research and Development in Information Retrieval*, pages 298–308. ACM, New York.

van Rijsbergen, C. J. (1986). A Non-Classical Logic for Information Retrieval. *The Computer Journal 29(6)*, pages 481–485.

Salton, G.; Fox, E.; Wu, H. (1983). Extended Boolean Information Retrieval. *Communications of the ACM 26*, pages 1022–1036.

Sebastiani, F. (1994). A Probabilistic Terminological Logic for Modelling Information Retrieval. In [Croft & Rijsbergen 94], pages 122–131.

Models

Composition Models of Databases

Ivan A. Basarab Bogdan V. Gubsky
Nikolaj S. Nikitchenko Vladimir N. Red'ko

Faculty of Cybernetics, Kiev State University
Vladimirskaja 64, Kiev-17, Ukraine
e-mail: tp@inp.kiev.ua

Abstract

Special models of databases are constructed based on principles of composition programming. The determinacy, subordination and separation principles define a semantic-syntactic style of approach proposed, and the naming, functionality and compositionality principles define the algebraic method of formalization of informational and manipulational aspects. The informational model is considered to be the special subclass of named data, satisfying integrity constraints, and the manipulational model is defined by sets of basic manipulational functions and compositions. Computational completeness of the constructed models for general classes of named data, tabular and quasirelational data is studied.

1 Introduction

Modern technologies of integrated information system development should be based on adequate models of programs, programming constructs and databases (DB). It is important to build such models on a unified methodological basis, eliminating the distinction between programming languages (PL), which are primarily oriented towards computational data processing, and database systems, which are oriented towards manipulational data processing. The majority of investigations of PL and DB problems covers mainly extensional questions. Disconnection of theoretical platforms and concepts, looseness and inadequacy of terminological systems have led to additional difficulties in the development of the area. All these points could not but tell negatively on intentional character of PL and DB studies.

The most important pragmatic DB aspects are informational and manipulational ones. Their essence concerns the methods of representation of informational content of application domains in DB states and the tools of manipulating their components.

The informational aspect of DB in comparison with the manipulational one is more simple, is easier to formalize and consequently is easier to investigate. Hence, it is no wonder that this aspect takes the central place in theoretical

investigations on DB. The most well-known questions, connected with informational aspects are the following:
- relational, hierarchical and net data representations and their various generalizations;
- structures of dependencies (functional, multivalued, hierarchical and others) in relational DB;
- physical organization of data and methods of their representation in computer memory.

The nature of manipulational aspect is more complex because its specification demands rigorous and adequate data models. Besides, specification of data manipulations as certain transformations turns into the problem of revealing the essence of operators and programs. And this problem, as is well known, is difficult itself. Within the bounds of the manipulational aspect the following questions were traditionally studied:
- Codd's relational algebra and special languages, related with it;
- completeness of query languages;
- applied query and update languages;
- procedural tools of DB integrity support;
- methods of physical organization of data.

Investigation of DB based on composition approach [1, 2] displays that specification of the mentioned DB aspects leads, on the one hand, to principally new models, and on the other hand, permits to use the results obtained in traditional fields of DB theory.

In this article the composition approach to DB models is considered. Models constructed are called composition models. Their distinctive feature in comparison with other approaches is the goal-directed and conscious use of naming relations, which allows informational and manipulational aspects of DB to be formalized adequately. Computational completeness of such models is investigated.

2 Main Principles of Composition Programming

Composition programming (CP) aims to develop adequate tools and methods for program construction. This approach is based on a collection of general and special principles. The most important is the *determinacy* principle which proclaims that all structures of programs are determined by their genesis structures. In other words, the description of programs by their derivation history rather than by their computational properties is a conscious choice of CP. As a consequence of this principle, program construction is considered on different levels of abstraction. Other principles specify various program structures.

The *subordination* principle suggests that the pragmatic aspect is of primary importance among the three main aspects of programs; the semantic aspect is subordinated to the pragmatic aspect, while the syntactic aspect is derived from the other two aspects. The *separation* principle makes it possible to focus separately on the semantic aspect, abstracting from the syntactic aspect. The *functionality* principle treats the program semantics as a function that associates results with input data. The *compositionality* principle reduces tools of program constructions to algebraic operations (compositions) on certain functions.

Specific CP systems are thus determined by the set of data that the programs manipulate (informational aspect) and by the set of functions, representing the program semantics, and the set of compositions, formalizing the program construction tools (manipulational aspect). Therefore, the semantic aspects of programs are specified in CP by algebras of programs. The advantages of this approach are simple semantics, clear hierarchical structure of programs and wide applicability of algebraic methods to program analysis and construction.

3 Named Data and Type Structures of Named Data

Analysis of various informational structures reveals, that they use a property of data to be sets, consisting of named elements. Such sets are called named sets. More precisely, finite sets of the form $\{(v_1, a_1), (v_2, a_2), ..., (v_n, a_n)\}$ with pairwise distinct elements $v_1, v_2, ..., v_n$, are called *named sets*. In other words, named sets are finite functional relations. Elements $v_1, v_2, ..., v_n$ are called *names*, and elements $a_1, a_2, ..., a_n$ are called *values* (*denotations*) of the names. The notion of named set is widely used not only in DB, but in programming in general.

On the base of named sets, the class D of *named data* is defined [2]. Let V and W be nonempty sets, the elements of which are considered as names and basic values, respectively. The class D is defined inductively. It is supposed that $W \subset D$. Other elements of D are generated by the following rules:

P1: if $v_1, v_2, ..., v_n \in V$, all these names are pairwise distinct and $d_1, d_2, ..., d_n \in D$, then the named set $\{(v_1, d_1), (v_2, d_2), ..., (v_n, d_n)\}$ belongs to D, $n \geq 0$;

P2: if $d_1, d_2, ..., d_k \in D$, then the set $\{d_1, d_2, ..., d_k\}$ belongs to D, $k \geq 0$.

Various data types used in relational, hierarchical, net, object-oriented and deductive DB can be represented adequately by named data structures [3–9].

The formalization of informational aspects of DB requires the development of tools which are able to construct complex data types from simple ones. Such tools have to reflect properties of informational structures, which appear when various fragments of the real world are represented in DB. More precisely, it is necessary to develop an algebraic formalism, which permits to define a class of derived named data types on the base of given sets of basic types.

In CP, data types are understood as subsets of the set of named data D with operations, defined over such sets. Different operators of data type constructions are introduced. Let us mention the following operators, which are used to describe types in traditional DB:

1) types of *named sets* $NSET(V, T) = \{r \mid r \subseteq V \times T, r \text{ is a named set }\}$,

2) types of *finite sets* $SET(T) = \{s \mid s \subseteq T, s \text{ is a finite set }\}$,

3) types of *records*

$REC(v_1 : T_1, ..., v_n : T_n) = \{\{(v_1, t_1), ..., (v_n, t_n)\} \mid t_1 \in T_1, ..., t_n \in T_n\}$,
where $v_1, ..., v_n$ are pairwise distinct names, which are considered as parameters of the operator, and operands $T_1, ..., T_n$ are arbitrary data types;

4) types of *sequences* $SEQ(T) = \{<t_1, ..., t_n> \mid t_1 \in T, ..., t_n \in T, n \geq 0\}$, where the sequence $<t_1, ..., t_n>$ is considered as a named set of the form $\{(1, t_1), ..., (n, t_n)\}$.

It is clear that the power set of D is closed under the operators described above and consequently it forms together with these operators an algebra of data types.

The general named data type D with a set of names V and a set of basic data W is defined in the algebra of types by the following recursive definition:
$D = W \cup NSET(V, D) \cup SET(D)$.

Any subset of W defined constructively can be taken as a basic data type. Usually, the set of basic types consists of types *string*, *boolean*, *integer* and so on.

Expressions over a type algebra are called *type expressions*. Such expressions are used to define interesting classes of data types. For example an expression of the form $REC(v_1 : t_1, ..., v_n : t_n)$, where $t_1, ..., t_n$ are symbols of basic types, defines a type of one-level records. The expression itself may be considered as a schema of records.

Another interesting type of named data is the *tabular* type. Tabular structures are widely used in various application domains. Tabular type is defined by type expressions of the form $SET(rec)$, where rec is a schema of records. If we wish to have hierarchical tabular structures considered, then the consistency relation $\simeq$ on D should be introduced by the following definition:

1) relation $\simeq$ on W is based on some given equivalence relation on W;

2) named sets $\{(v_i, d_i) | 1 \leq i \leq n\}$ and $\{(u_j, b_j) | 1 \leq j \leq k\}$ are consistent if and only if $n = k$, $v_l = u_l$ and $d_l \simeq b_l$ for $1 \leq l \leq n$;

3) nonempty sets $s_1, s_2 \in SET(D)$ are consistent if all named data of the union $s_1 \cup s_2$ are pairwise consistent.

Consistent data are characterized by the same named structure. Using the consistency relation we can define a general tabular type
$TD = \{t \mid t \in SET(ND), r_1, r_2 \in t, r_1 \simeq r_2\}$,
where $ND = NSET(V, W \cup ND)$.

The names used in sets of tabular types are called *attributes* (similar to relational DB). In standard syntactic representation of such sets (tables), attributes, subordinated according to the named structure, are put into the header of the table.

We can generalize the notion of table to quasirelation, permitting any sets of consistent data as values of names (attributes). Quasirelation type QD is defined by the following definition:

$QD = \{q \mid q \in SET(RD), r_1, r_2 \in q, r_1 \simeq r_2\}$,
where $RD = NSET(V, W \cup SET(W) \cup RD \cup SET(RD))$.

Object-oriented programming extends the described notion of type in the following respects: classes of objects are considered as sets of named records with special operations, connected with them; inheritance may be viewed as a form of a parameterized type construction operator that creates a composite type from the parent type.

Strictly speaking, we should consider type T as a sequence of the form $< S, nf_1 : f_1, ..., nf_n : f_n >$, where S is a sort (subset of D), $nf_1, ..., nf_n$ are the names of operations, connected with T, and $f_1, ..., f_n$ are the operations themselves, which are defined on sorts.

These lead to new type expressions: $CLASS(V_{obj}, v_1 : T_1, ..., v_n : T_n; nf_1 : f_1, ..., nf_k : f_k)$ and $INHERITS(T, v'_1 : T'_1, ..., v'_l : T'_l; nf'_1 : f'_1, ..., nf'_m : f'_m)$. The first expression defines a type, called class, which consists of objects of type $REC(v_1 : T_1, ..., v_n : T_n)$, named by the elements from V_{obj}. The operations with names $nf_1, ..., nf_k$ are defined by the expressions $f_1, ..., f_k$, respectively. The second expression defines a new class, built by inheritance from class T (superclass). This new class consists of objects, obtained by expanding states of objects from T by components with names (attributes) $v'_1, ..., v'_l$. The operations are obtained by overlaying operations of T and operations $nf'_1, ..., nf'_m$. Operations from class T should be redefined on the new subclass. It should be noted, that the operations are introduced as polymorphic functions, because they depend upon types, which are used as parameters of the operations. From a syntactic point of view these definitions of classes and inheritance are very close to the definitions of an order-sorted algebra [10].

Similar definitions can be written for other data structures, used in DB. So, the algebra of data types and schema languages built over it can represent adequately informational aspects of various DB.

4 Named Functions and Compositions of Functions

The formalization of manipulational aspect of DB requires functions, reflecting this aspect, to be specified. Since the informational aspect is represented by classes of named data, the manipulational aspect will be represented by functions, defined over the class of named data D. Such functions are called *named functions*. Moreover, a special class of named functions is used. These functions are called denotation preserving functions [3]. More precisely, a function $f : D \to D$ is called a *denotation preserving function* if there is a finite set $H \subseteq W$ such that for any d of the domain of f $den(f(d)) \subseteq den(d) \cup H$, where den is a function collecting basic data of a named set. Such functions will be also called data manipulation functions (DM-functions).

The following functions are DM-functions ($v \in V$ is a parameter, $d \in D$):
- naming $\Rightarrow v(d) = \{(v, d)\}$,
- denaming $v \Rightarrow (d) = d'$, where $\{(v, d')\} \in d$,

– removal $\setminus v(d) = d \setminus \{(v, d(v))\}$,
– "empty" function $\bar{\emptyset}(d) = \emptyset$,
– overlaying function ∇, which given two named sets d_1 and d_2 yields named set $d_1' \cup d_2$, where d_1' consists of those components of d_1, names of which do not occur in d_2. Functions, used in DB languages, are also defined [3, 4, 6].

Data manipulation functions are constructed by means of compositions. *Compositions* are specified as operations over named functions. We consider three levels of compositions: the abstract, set and named level.

Let us mention the following compositions [6]:
– abstract compositions: multiplication $\circ$, branching IF, iteration $*$;
– compositions on set level: set limitation DIS and internal application INA;
– compositions on named level: overlaying ∇, loop $WHILE$, superposition S^n.

Abstract compositions do not use properties of data structures. Composition $\circ$ is a usual functional composition, branching IF and iteration $*$ formalize traditional conditional and iteration statements.

Compositions on the set level consider data as finite sets.

The set limitation composition is defined by the formula
$DIS(p)(s) = \{d \mid d \in s, p(s)\}$, where $s \in SET(D)$.

In other words, elements of set s, which satisfy predicate p, are selected.

This composition is used for the formalization of operators of the form $SELECT\_FROM\_WHERE$.

The composition of internal application INA is defined by the formula $INA(f)(s) = \{f(d) \mid d \in s\}$.

Compositions of the named level consider data as named sets.

The overlaying composition (we use the same sign as for the definition of the overlaying function) is defined by the formula $f \nabla g(d) = f(d) \nabla g(d)$.

Various compositions formalizing methods of function constructions were defined on the named level. It is proved that compositions considered preserve the class of MD-functions [3].

5 Database Models

Database models, reflecting informational and manipulational aspects of DB, can be constructed on the base of the composition approach described above.

The *informational model* of DB is defined as a pair $\Im = <S, \Sigma>$, where S is a data type, describing possible states of DB, and $\Sigma = \{\sigma_1, ..., \sigma_n\}$ are integrity constrains of DB, limiting the class of possible DB states to the class of admissible states.

The *manipulational model* of DB is defined as a pair $A = <F, K>$, where F is a set of basic DM-functions and K is a set of compositions. The closure of the set of basic functions under the set of compositions contains functions, which describe the required processing of data.

Integrating informational and manipulational models, we can define the *composition model* of DB as a quadruple $< S, \Sigma, F, K >$ with the components described above.

Such composition models are built for various types of DB, including object-oriented databases [6, 9].

Introduction of formal models stimulates questions of their completeness, which play an important role in DB theory. Speaking about completeness of composition models, we can focus our attention on informational or manipulational completeness. The first aspect of model completeness is of informal character, because it touches the adequacy of representations of real world objects through named data structures. The second aspect has various formulations depending on pragmatic requirements. In this article we investigate computational completeness of composition models. The requirement of computational completeness was even declared in "The object-oriented database system manifesto" [11].

6 Computational Completeness of Composition Models

Usually computability is understood as computability of n-ary functions defined on integers or strings. Such computability may be called Turing computability. But data manipulation functions are defined on more complex data structures such as tables, relations, quasirelations and so on. In this case it is difficult to use Turing computability and a new notion of computability over complex data structures should be introduced.

Many results are currently available in this area. However, despite the richness of the available results, the attempt to apply them to our problems runs into various difficulties. To investigate the computational completeness of DB models we shall use the approach developed in [12]. The computability defined is an abstract one and can be applicable to an arbitrary finite data structure.

In order to formalize computability of a function over a finite data structure, we first need to define such data. This is a difficult question, and we will accordingly adopt the following strategy: we will first define a special form of finite data structure and subsequently reduce data of other forms to this special form.

Our intuitive notion of finite data structure is the following: any such datum d consists of several basic (atomic) components $b_1, ..., b_m$, organized (connected) in a certain way. If there are enumerably many different forms of organization for finite data structure, each of these data can be represented in the (possibly non-unique) form $(k, < b_1, ..., b_m >)$, where k is the datum code and the sequence $< b_1, ..., b_m >$ is the datum base. Data of this form are called *natural* data [12]. More precisely, if B is any set and Nat is the set of natural numbers, then the set of natural data over B is the set $Nat(B) = Nat \times B^*$.

A set D is called a set of *finite data structure* (over B with respect to nat), if a set B and a total multi-valued injective mapping $nat : D \to Nat(B)$ are given. This mapping nat is called the *naturalization* mapping, and the partial single-valued inverse mapping $nat^{-1} : Nat(B) \to D$, denoted by $denat$, is called the *denaturalization* mapping.

The introduction of natural data and naturalization mappings enables us to reduce computability over D to special computability over $Nat(B)$, which is called code computability. To define this type of computability we should recall that in natural data the code collects all known information about datum components, and code computability should be independent of any specific processing tools of the elements of the set B and can use only those tools which are independent of B and are explicitly exposed in natural data. The only explicit information in natural data is the datum code and the length of datum base. Therefore in code computability the datum code plays a major role, while the elements of the datum base are "extras" that virtually do not affect the computations. The elements of a datum base may be only used to form the base of the resulting datum.

The function $g : Nat(B) \to Nat(B)$ is called *code computable* if there exists a partial recursive multi-valued function $h : Nat^2 \to Nat \times Nat^*$ such that for any $k, m \in Nat$, $b_1, ..., b_m \in B$, $m \geq 0$ $g(k, < b_1, ..., b_m >) = (k', < b_{i_1}, ..., b_{i_l} >)$, if and only if $h(k, m) = (k', < i_1, ..., i_l >)$, $1 \leq i_1 \leq m, ..., 1 \leq i_l \leq m$, $m \geq 0$.

In other words, in order to compute g on $(k, < b_1, ..., b_m >)$, we have to compute h on (k, m), generate a certain value $(k', < i_1, ..., i_l >)$, and then try to form the value of the function g by selecting the components of the sequence $< b_1, ..., b_m >$ pointed to by the indexes $i_1, ..., i_l$. Functions of the type $Nat^2 \to Nat \times Nat^*$ will be called code-index functions.

We are ready now to give the main definition of this section.

The function $f : D \to D$ is called *naturally computable* (with respect to given B and nat) if there is code computable function $g : Nat(B) \to Nat(B)$ such that $f = denat \circ g \circ nat$.

We may consider natural computability as a generalization (relativization) of enumeration computability. In fact, for $B = \emptyset$ code computability reduces to partial recursive computability on Nat, and natural computability reduces to enumeration computability (wrt nat). Natural computability may be also considered as computability of polymorphic functions. Therefore, the notions of code and natural computability defined above are quite rich.

Finally, these notions are instantiated to specific finite data structures, such as tuples, sets, bags, lists, mapping, trees etc. Simple algebraic representations of complete classes of computable single-valued and multi-valued functions and compositions over these structures are constructed [13, 14, 15, 16].

Here we present only three such results: complete classes of computable functions over named data, tabular data and quasirelations. A set of names V is supposed to be a countable set, e.g. $V = \{v_0, v_1, ...\}$.

Appropriate naturalization mappings, reflecting their properties, can be defined for these three cases. In order to describe complete classes over named data, we should use additional functions: successor $succ_V$, predecessor $pred_V$ and constant $\bar{v}_0$ (enumeration functions over V), equality predicates $=_W, =v_0, = \emptyset$, predicates $\in_V, \in_W, \in_{SET}$, binary functions as (naming), cn (denaming), ex (removal) and predicate ec (existence of named component), such that for $v \in V$, $d \in D$ $as(v,d) = \Rightarrow v(d)$, $cn(v,d) = v \Rightarrow (d)$, $ex(v,d) = \backslash v(d)$, $ec(v,d) = v!(d)$. We also need functions set and elm such that $set(d) = \{d\}$ and $elm(\{d\}) = d$.

Theorem 1. The complete class of computable functions over the set of named data D coincides precisely with the class of functions, obtained by the closure of the set of functions $\{\Rightarrow v_0, \Rightarrow v_1, \in_V, \in_W, \bar{v}_0, = v_0, succ_V, pred_V, as, cn, ex, ec, \sqcup, \backslash, \times, =_W, set, elm, = \emptyset, \in_{SET}\}$ under the set of compositions $\{\circ, *, \nabla, INA\}$.

A class of named and unnamed tabular data TND is defined by the following definition

$$TND = TD \cup NSET(V, TD),$$

where set TD was described in section 3. Here we consider W as a countable set.

We shall use the following functions: union of consistent tables $\sqcup$, join function $\bowtie$, equality $=$, removal (selection) of the table with the minimal name E (π), naming by the minimal name $\leftarrow$, constructing of the initial table $\{\{(v_0, w_0)\}\}$ C, incrementing of the names of named tables ST, incrementing of the names in a table ST_V (ST_W), removal of the column with minimal name in a table U, naming of the rows of a table by the minimal name $\Leftarrow$.

Theorem 2. The complete class of computable functions over the set of tabular data TND coincides precisely with the class of functions, obtained by the closure of the set of functions $\{\sqcup, \bowtie, =, E, \pi, \leftarrow, C, ST, ST_V, ST_W, U, \Leftarrow\}$ under the set of compositions $\{\circ, *, IF, \nabla\}$.

Let us define the set of named and unnamed quasirelational data by the definition

$$QND = QD \cup NSET(V, QD),$$

where the set QD was defined in section 3.

To describe the complete class over QND it is necessary to redefine the described tabular functions over the set QND and introduce a function $<\equiv$ such that for any $d \in D$ $<\equiv (d) = \{\{(v_0, d)\}\}$.

Theorem 3. The complete class of computable functions over the set of quasirelational data QND coincides precisely with the class of functions, obtained by the closure of the set of functions $\{\sqcup, \bowtie, =, E, \pi, \leftarrow, C, ST, ST_V, ST_W, U, \Leftarrow, <\equiv\}$ under the set of compositions $\{\circ, *, IF, \nabla\}$.

7 Conclusion

During the last years various DB models were proposed. The composition approach described above is based upon a number of general and special principles and allows to construct adequate DB models which have such advantages as simplicity of their construction, clear hierarchical structure and wide applicability of mathematical methods to their analysis and transformation.

The determinacy, subordination and separation principles define composition models as semantic-syntactic models. Principles of functionality and compositionality induces algebraic structure of semantics, and principle of naming takes into consideration the "name-denotation" relation, reflecting fundamental properties of data and their processing.

Composition models are highly parameterized on data structures, basic functions and compositions, which allows to adapt them according to different requirements. That is why composition models can be used in the construction of adaptive information systems.

Much attention was paid to the mathematical investigation of composition models. The notion of computational completeness was introduced and simple representations of complete classes of data manipulation functions over various data structures were constructed.

Acknowledgements

The authors would like to thank Prof. Rainer Manthey for many helpful comments and suggestions.

References

[1] V.N. Red'ko, Composition of programs and composition programming, Programmirovanie, No 5, 3-24 (1978). In Russian.

[2] V.N. Red'ko, Fundamentals of composition programming, Programmirovanie, No 3, 3-13 (1979). In Russian.

[3] I.A. Basarab, V.N. Red'ko, A logical-functional approach to databases, Programmirovanie, No. 2, 53-67 (1984). In Russian.

[4] B.V. Gubsky, V.N. Red'ko, Semantics of data manipulation languages: composition approach, Proc. 12th international seminar on DBMS, Suzdal, USSR, Oct. 17-20, 65-76 (1989).

[5] N.S. Nikitchenko, V.I. Zadorozhny, An algebraic approach to deductive databases query languages formalization, Programmirovanie, N. 6, 29-47 (1992). In Russian.

[6] I.A. Basarab, N.S. Nikitchenko, V.N. Red'ko, Composition data bases, Kiev, Lybid', 192 p. (1992). In Russian.

[7] F. Bancilhon, S. Khoshafian, A calculus for complex objects, Proc. SIG-MOD 86, 53-59 (1986).

[8] M. Atkinson, P. Richard, P. Trinder, Bulk data types for large scale programming, Technical report 7, FIDE project, University of Glasgow, Glasgow G128QQ, Scotland, 26 p. (1991).

[9] I.A. Basarab, B.V. Gubsky, N.S. Nikitchenko, Composition models of object-oriented databases, International workshop on advances in databases and information systems ADBIS'94, Collection of abstracts, Institute for Problems of Informatics of the Russian Academy of Sciences, Moscow, p. 25 (1994).

[10] J.A. Goguen, J. Meseguer, Order-sorted algebra I: equational deduction for multiple inheritance, overloading, exceptions and partial operations, Theoretical Computer Science, 105, 217-273 (1992).

[11] M. Atkinson, et. al. The object-oriented database system manifesto, DOOD'89, 40-57 (1989).

[12] N.S. Nikitchenko, On the construction of classes of generalized computable functions and functionals, UkrNIINTI, techn. report No 856 Uk-84, Kiev (1984). In Russian.

[13] V.N. Red'ko, N.S. Nikitchenko, Composition aspects of programmology, Kibernetika, part 1, No 5, 49-56 (1987), part 2, No 1, 28-34 (1988). In Russian.

[14] D.B. Buj, B.V. Gubsky, V.N. Red'ko, Universality problems in the classes of computable named functions, Kibernetika, No 4, 58-65 (1988). In Russian.

[15] B.V. Gubsky, E.V. Krapiva, I.V. Red'ko, Computable functions on relations and tables in countable and finite alphabets, Docl. Acad. Nauk. Ukr.SSR, Ser. A, No 10, 74-76 (1988). In Russian.

[16] B.V. Gubsky, I.A. Basarab, Computable functions in the tabular data bases, Kibernetika, No 2, 24-25 (1989). In Russian.

Could the OODB standards be better if more grounded?

Inessa Chaban   Leonid Kalinichenko
Vladimir Zadorozhny
Institute for Problems of Informatics
Russian Academy of Sciences
Vavilova 30/6, Moscow, V-334, 117900
e-mail: leonidk@ipian23.ipian.msk.su

Abstract

The paper is devoted to the analysis of the basic features of the object database standard ODMG-93. We analyze ODMG-93 type system under requirements of systematically clear definition of type lattice (including type generators, definition of subtyping relationship for built-in and user defined types, interrelationship of mutable and immutable values, axiomatization of relationships) and of clean multi-level user type creation operations.

We analyze ODMG-93 query language under the requirements for clean support of the object creating queries treating types as algebraic systems. Such requirements lead to the necessity of providing of a well-defined type inferencing and integrating of the derived types into the type lattice. Cartesian product and binary set expression operations applied to sets of objects need more precise definition based on the interpretation of such sets as algebraic systems.

We conclude that more systematic and uniform way of type lattice, type inferencing and set operations definition is required and show possible ways how such definition could be reached [1].

1 Introduction

General situation in the object-oriented data bases (OODB) may be characterized still as chaotic. OODB vendors continue development of the systems supporting various, non-standardized object models that sometimes continue to be under the influence of relational legacy, no general consensus has been reached on what should be considered a sound foundation of the object models, providers of the relational DBs start their transition towards OO models tired to wait until SQL3 will be completed. Several years ago such situation might be considered natural: at that time the researchers were not ready to introduce justifiable concepts sufficient for explaining of various sides of the object models. Now the situation looks differently. During last few years the basic results were obtained (such as e.g., [4, 21, 22, 13]) making possible to conclude that now object models could be as well grounded as the relational data models were in 70s.

---

[1] This work was supported by the Russian Basic Research Foundation grant (93-012-618)

Though these results are well known among the research community, they are to much extent ignored by the industry that prefer to follow ad hoc proprietary solutions. Such solutions are reflected eventually in the standards of the corresponding level [23].

In this paper we analyze some decisions adopted in recently published object database standard ODMG-93 [23] focusing on the issues of the well-defined object model. We provide a correspondence with the features of the SYNTHESIS object model [13] intended for the semantic interoperation [12]. In the SYNTHESIS project we use a theory of algebraic systems developed by A.I. Maltsev [20] as a basic foundation for object model definition. Related works that influence the area will also be indicated.

The paper is organized as follows. Next two sections deal with the related works and elaborate a little on basic notions of algebraic system theory. In the forth section we consider ODMG-93 standard from the point of view of more sound approach. In the fifth section we characterize briefly SYNTHESIS object model, which is based on the notion of algebraic systems.

2 Related Works

The basic decisions on SYNTHESIS object model and in particular on its type system are inspired by Maltsev's algebraic system theory [20] and works on TIGUCAT object model [22]. The TIGUCAT object model is characterized by a purely behavioral abstraction of types and a uniform approach to objects. Everything in TIGUCAT model (including types, classes, functions and meta-information) is a first class object with well-defined behavior. It should be emphasized that the notion of cartesian product of algebraic systems that plays the central role in the Maltsev's theory and is used in the SYNTHESIS model also plays significant role in the TIGUCAT model. Taking into account independence of these two solutions, this fact may be considered as a natural trend in the development of object models.

Publications on abstract data types (ADT) semantics based on initial algebras by Goguen et al [8], on order-sorted algebra by Goguen and Meseguer [9] and works on expressiveness of algebraic languages by Beeri and Milo [4] greatly contributed to better understanding of the basic concepts of the object models.

In [21] it was noted that the relational model conceptualizes databases as sets of objects, which captures structural aspects of objects while existing object models conceptualize databases as algebras of objects, which captures behavioral aspects of objects.

In [4] issues related to deduction using negation and recursion considering ADT specification as a deductive program with '=' being the only predicate is investigated. A database is considered as a collection of named sets (every set is a database 'relation'). Each set is represented by a named constant, and its content is specified by equations. The semantics has the initial algebra of the type specifications as the domain, and additionally has relations that satisfy the formulas of the database and query specifications.

3 On theory of algebraic systems

The theory of algebraic systems [20] resulted from application of the methods of mathematical logic to algebra. So it takes frontier place between algebra and logic.

3.1 Basic definitions

Algebraic system (or simply system) is an object $U = <A, O_f, O_p>$, consisting of some non-empty set A, set of operations $O_f = \{F_1, ..., F_n\}$ defined on a set A, set of predicates $O_p = \{P_1, ..., P_m\}$ defined on A. In this case the *type* of the algebraic system is the object $< farity_1, ..., farity_n; parity_1, ..., parity_m >$, where $farity_i, parity_i$ are arities of an operation F_i and a predicate P_i correspondingly. [1].

The set A is called a carrier or the basic set of the system U and its elements are elements of U. The power of A is the power of U. Assuming $O = O_f \cup O_p$ we can write the system U in a shorter notation: $U = <A, O>$.

An algebraic system $U = <A, O>$ is called *an algebra* if $O_p = \emptyset$, and it is *a model* if $O_f = \emptyset$.

The mapping of algebraic system U_1 into the algebraic system U_2 is the mapping of system U_1 carrier A_1 into the system U_2 carrier A_2.

3.2 Cartesian product of algebraic systems

First we consider the case of a product of the systems having the same type.

Consider some non-empty set A, whose elements will be called indexes. For each index $\alpha \in A$ an algebraic system
$$U_\alpha = < M_\alpha, O_f{}^\alpha, O_p{}^\alpha >$$
of the given type τ is put in correspondence.

Cartesian product $\prod M_\alpha$ of indexed system of sets M_α under indexes from A is a set of functions f from A to union $\bigcup M_\alpha$, satisfying following condition:
$f(\alpha) \in M_\alpha$ $(\alpha \in A)$.

Very often the set N of natural numbers serves as the set of indexes. In this case the function f is defined by the sequence of its values $f(0), f(1), ..., f(k), ...$ and so may be equated with it.

We define operations O_f and predicates O_p on $\prod M_\alpha$ giving the algebraic system
$$U = < \prod M_\alpha, O_f, O_p >$$
of the same type as the type of the system U_α. Let $f_1, ..., f_n$ be some elements of $\prod M_\alpha$.

We assume

---

[1] Generally sets O_f and O_p may be infinite, however we shall consider here only finite sets of operations and predicates of algebraic systems

$P_i(f_1, ..., f_n) = true$
iff for every $\alpha \in A$
$P_i{}^\alpha(f_1(\alpha), ..., f_n(\alpha)) = true$.

In the same way we will call the value of $F_j(f_1, ..., f_m)$ the element $f \in \prod M_\alpha$, which is defined by the following condition:
$f(\alpha) = F_j{}^\alpha(f_1(\alpha), ..., f_m(\alpha))$ $(\alpha \in A)$.

The algebraic system $U = <\prod M_\alpha, O_f, O_p>$, constructed in such a way is called cartesian product of systems U_α under set of indexes A and is denoted as $\prod U_\alpha$. If the set A contains only numbers $1, 2, ..., k$, then cartesian product $\prod U_\alpha$ may be denoted as $U_1 \times ... \times U_k$, and its elements are equated with sequences $<c_1, ..., c_k>$ $(c_i \in U_i)$.

To define products of the systems having different types we consider once more the product $U = \prod U_\alpha$ of some algebraic systems U_α $(\alpha \in A)$. For every fixed $\alpha \in A$ the mapping $\pi_\alpha : f \to f(\alpha)$ $(f \in \prod M_\alpha)$ is a mapping of $\prod M_\alpha$ on M_α.

The system of mappings δ_α $(\alpha \in A)$ of some algebraic system U into an algebraic system U_α is called complete, if it allows to distinguish any two different elements in U. It means that for any a, b from U if the equality $a\delta_\alpha = b\delta_\alpha$ is true for every $\alpha \in A$ then $a = b$.

The product of systems
$U_\alpha = <M_\alpha, O_f{}^\alpha, O_p{}^\alpha>$
of different types will be a system
$U = <\prod M_\alpha, \delta_\alpha>$
where δ_α $(\alpha \in A)$ is a complete system of mappings $\pi_\alpha : f \to f(\alpha)$ $(f \in \prod M_\alpha)$ for every fixed $\alpha \in A$.

4 ODMG-93 in frame of more sound approach

Object Database Management Group (ODMG) published recently an ODMG-93 specification [23] and thus made an important step in the process of developing of Object Database Management Systems (ODBMS) standards required by the object database industry and users. "Although in its infancy, ODMG-93 is an important and positive contribution to industry-wide efforts to define a standard object-oriented database language" [17]. Five object database providers - Object Design, Ontos, O2 Technology, Versant and Objectivity (members of ODMG) are commited to supporting the standard expecting the proposal to become a de-facto standard for the industry. First widely published critical reactions to the standard are well known [18, 16, 17].

Here we use the ODMG-93 specification as an example to show how it might be improved if it would be more grounded.

We shall focus on some aspects of the type system and OQL proposed.

4.1 Object creation and model uniformity

The ODMG-93 model can be considered uniform in the sense that "Operations are always defined on a single object type. There is no notion of an operation independent of an object type, or of an operation defined on two or more object types".

So, the domain of operations is the set of the types' objects. ODMG-93 does not systematically clarify how this principle is applied to the type creation operations. Indeed, for example all built-in types are defined as instances of type *Type*. However, "Type *Type* is itself both a subtype and an instance of type *Atomic_Object*" (Fig. 4.1) [23].

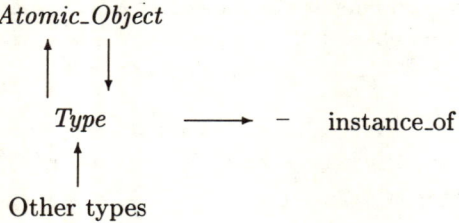

Following the principle above we have no way to create instances of type *Type* as in this case *create_instance* operation which is defined on type *Type* is not applicable to *Type* itself. We have no formal right to include it into type hierarchy and ask for its supertypes or instances. This kind of controversy should be clarified in [23].

For the sake of uniformity it would be better to define *Type* as the instance of itself. It would make the model extensible in obvious manner and self-descriptive. Currently (as far as we understand) such extensibility in ODMG-93 is supported using *create* operation defined on type *Object* by which we can create arbitrary objects, in particular, types. However, the model does not support the notion of the abstract data type as the general type constructor.

In SYNTHESIS model ADTs based on algebraic systems are introduced and defining the operations on type means that the domain of the operation should be the carrier of the corresponding to ADT algebraic system. In such model meta-types including object creation operations for instances of their instances are naturally defined.

4.2 Types and type generators

"We acknowledge the problem that types and types generators have been intermixed in the diagram (i.e., in built-in type hierarchy). Formally a type generator such as *Collection<T>* cannot be a subtype of a type. Nor can a type be a subtype of a type generator ... . In the interests of simplicity, we have folded them into the same hierarchy ..." [23].

Type generators are, in fact, parameterized types. Parameterized data type is a way to deal with generic operations adopted in some languages mainly for efficiency reasons (i.e., to allow type checking to be performed at compile time, rather then at run time).

These idea can be naturally incorporated into the lattice structure. We put into correspondence to each type constructor a sub-lattice rooted in the most general type. For example for set constructor we will have a sub-lattice

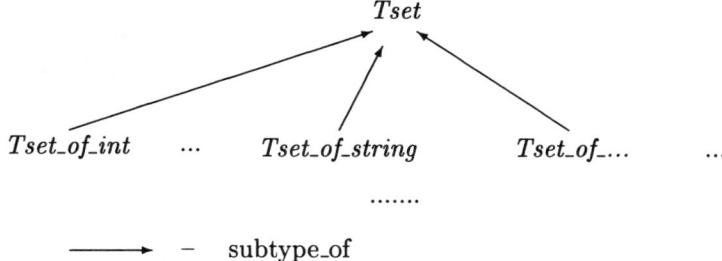

⟶ - subtype_of

Here *Tset_of_integer* is a subtype of *Tset* that reflects additional information on type element which allows static (compile-time) type checking. Declaring some value to be of type *Tset* (thus decreasing the information) we assume more run-time type checking context. In ODMG-93 it would be possible to introduce the general type for collection with undefined type of elements.

Another aspect concerning ODMG-93 type generators as they were defined in type hierarchy is that in the standard there is no definition of the explicit way to integrate concrete composite types with the existing lattice. For example consider two types:
    set<struct(men:Person, student:Student, number:Integer)>
and
    set<struct(men:Person, student:Person)>.
No explicit way of their interrelation in the existing type lattice of ODMG-93 is clearly indicated, though we believe that such interrelation is intended.

This issue and related problems are considered in more details in the section 4.5 dealing with query language.

4.3 Interrelation of mutable and immutable values

The ODMG-93 specification introduces a group of mutable (object) built-in types and a group of immutable (literal) built-in types providing no attempt to interrelate them. Such approach resulted in:

- absence of the notion of the abstract data type (as the general immutable type constructor in the language);

- duplication of the structured types (collection, set, bag, list, array, structure) as mutable and immutable without any relationship between them;

- difficulties with the clean type lattice definition.

For instance, there are two kinds of sets in the standard: mutable set and immutable set. "Immutable collections behave just like their mutable counterparts, except that they may not be modified. It is not possible to insert a member into an immutable collection or to remove a member from such a collection" [23].

How can we get an agreement between such polar definitions in one lattice? In SYNTHESIS we interrelate mutable and immutable types using the following sub-lattice:

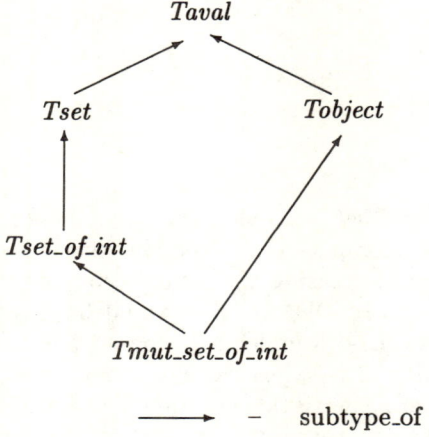

The root of the lattice is the *Taval* type corresponding to all abstract values considered in the model. All immutable types obtain properties of *Taval* type, all mutable types obtain properties of *Tobject* type. Values of the *Tobject* type specialize abstract values with new properties main of which is an ability to have a unique identifier. Therefore any mutable type is considered to be a subtype of the corresponding immutable type. Type *Tint_set* corresponds to immutable sets of integers, while type *Tmut_int_set* corresponds to immutable ones.

For justification we consider a case that is considered usually as an argument against the possibility of definition of mutable types as subtypes of immutable types:

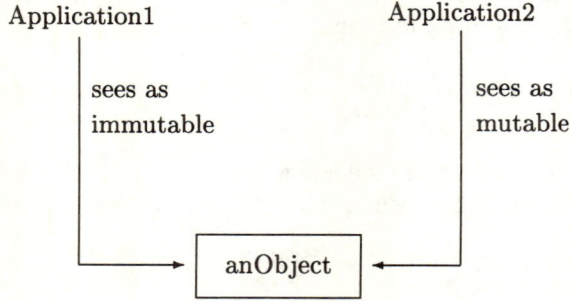

If Application1 and Application2 see one and the same instance of a certain type as immutable value (Application1) and mutable value (Application2) then what might be the specification of behaviors of the values having different nature ?

The following table presents immutable and mutable interfaces of the same value showing sharing of the results.

	immutable view	mutable view
create (immut.)	*value*	id: *value* + other object properties
delete (immut.)	*NULL*	id: *NULL* + other object properties
create (mut.)	*value*	id: *value* + other object properties
delete (mut.)	*NULL*	*NULL*
modify (only mut.)	*value1*	id: *value1* + other object properties

We believe that application of such approach to the systematic interrelated definition of immutable and mutable types will lead to more consistent type lattice of the language. At the same time, the result of the definition will be mostly consistent with the current treatment by the ODMG-93 of mutable/immutable values semantics.

4.4 Axiomatization of the relationships

ODMG-93 introduces concept of binary one-to-one and one-to-many relationships defined between mutable object types. The relationships rediscover CODASYL sets that were well studied in 70ies and 80ies. Semantics of CODASYL sets were dependent on the kind of set membership declared (such as OPTIONAL MANUAL, MANDATORY AUTOMATIC, etc.). Set membership influenced the semantics of set member (owner) creation, deletion, modification operations to preserve the referential integrity constraints imposed by the kind of the set membership declared. Partial order could also be imposed on the set type.

ODMG-93 says: "Relationships maintain referential integrity. If an object that participates in a relationship is deleted, a subsequent attempt to traverse the relationship in either direction will raise an exception." This sentence shows how incomplete current concept of ODMG relationship is. Really, ODMG-93 imposes no clear semantics on the relationship type (e.g., what is this - total or partial function and if partial, what kind of a function is it, how the semantics of remove/delete operations depend on the type of the function assumed, etc.).

In well-known CODASYL model semantics of sets membership influence the semantics of set member (owner) creation, deletion and modification to preserve the referential integrity constraints imposed by different kinds of set membership declared:

- for creation: *MANUAL, AUTOMATIC*
- for deletion and modification: *FIXED, MANDATORY, OPTIONAL*

In fact ODMG-93 supports only rather weak constraint, namely *OPTIONAL MANUAL*.

The contemporary approach for the relationship modeling could have used declarative axiomatization of the CODASYL sets that was provided in [15] for mapping of CODASYL sets into the relational representation. Such declaration treats the relationship as a total or as a partial function with imposed partial order that lead to true maintenance of the referential integrity (preserving the axioms declared - e.g., total or different kinds of partial functional dependencies for one-to-many relationship). It is important also that the relationship ordering should be declared as partial order imposing an order for a collection of objects associated with one and the same "owner" object in one-to-many relationship.

We believe that further the concept of the relationship of ODMG-93 should be improved along this direction. In the SYNTHESIS there is no specific subdivision of properties into attributes and relationships. We use one and the same notion of attribute. If attribute should behave like a relationship (more precisely, as any kind of CODASYL set or alike) it is sufficient to associate with the attribute corresponding constraints clearly indicating what type of functional dependency this attribute should interpret and how partial order for such association should be declared. Such declaration determines the imperative semantics of the operations applied to objects - constituents of the relationship.

Below is an example of SYNTHESIS support of relationships. These are three SYNTHESIS class declarations. The *mandatory_automatic* class is an attribute class (so called metaclass of associations). Attribute *teaches* of class *Professor* is declared to be an instance of the *mandatory_automatic* class with corresponding inverse attribute *taught_by* of class *Section*. Using metaclasses of associations we can define arbitrary semantics of attributes as relationships.

{ *mandatory_automatic*;
  in: *metaclass, association*;
  inverse: *automatic_mandatory*;
  instance_section:
    {association_type: {{*0, inf*}, {*1, 1*}};
    domain: *class*;
    range: *class*}
}

{ *Section*;
  in: *class*;

{ *Professor*;
  in: *class*;

```
       instance_section:                    instance_section:
         {taught_by: Professor;               {teaches: set_of Section;
          metaslot                             metaslot
            in: automatic_mandatory;             in: mandatory_automatic;
            inverse: Professor.teaches;          inverse: Section.taught_by;
          end}                                 end}
       }                                    }
```

4.5 Query language

Here we consider some problems associated with deriving of new types in OQL queries:

"An OQL query is a function which, when applied to this input (i.e., to denotable objects), delivers an object whose type may be inferred from the operator contributing to the query expression." ([23], page 66).

Traditionally two kinds of operators are distinguished: object-preserving and object-creating ones. The object-preserving operators are limited to returning existing objects from an object base while object-creative operators may create new objects during their execution [22]. The object- creating operators can form new types that were not integrated with the types from which they were formed.

Consider the following example ([23], page 66):
select distinct struct(name: x.name, hps: (select y
                from y in x. subordinates
                where y.salary > 100000))

The result of this query is a literal of the following type:
set<struct(name:string, hps:bag<Employee>)>

Based on the notion of well-defined type lattice we should have a systematic possibility to integrate this type into the existing lattice. ODMG-93 standard, however, does not address this problem at all. At this point the research results of [22] could be helpful which, in particular, consider procedures for deriving new types for all operators and investigate how to integrate them into the existing type lattice.

We believe that ODMG-93 model should contain type inferencing mechanism similar to those included into the [22, 13] models. The mechanism is based on type construction operations that are modeled as behaviors defined on the type T_type, which is type of types. These operations are used in type expressions giving for each operator a type of its result. To relieve the integration of the resulted type in the lattice *the product type* is defined, which is a behavioral abstraction of traditional tuple constructor. It is based on the notion of a cartesian product of algebraic systems (sect. 3.2). Product values replace the notion of tuple (or record) which is the basic for the relational model. They allow to compose objects preserving pure behavioral approach. Below we define product type more accurately.

A product type T is a composition of a number of other types $T_1, ..., T_n$ (including other product types). It may be defined using the following type expression

$$T = T_1 * ... * T_n,$$

where $*$ - denotes product type construction operation. Product type T defines as operational interface of its values by the system of mappings δ_α ($1 \leq \alpha \leq n$) (see above) which allows to distinguish any α^{th} component of the product value.

We emphasize the importance of using of the product type as making compositions of the algebraic systems (this is not the same as the cartesian product of pure sets).

Product type $T_1 * ... * T_n$ is located in the type lattice as a subtype of a type $T'_1 * ... * T'_k$ if $k \leq n$ and T_i is a subtype of T'_i. It is located in the type lattice as a supertype of a type $T''_1 * ... * T''_m$ if $n \leq m$ and T_i is a supertype of T''_i. If a product type cannot be located as a subtype of other product type it is located as a subtype of $Taval$ (if it is immutable) or $Tsynt\_object$ (if it is mutable).

The necessity of type inferencing can be shown for the OQL binary set operators (the same can be shown for the "cartesian product" operation mentioned in the explanation of ODMG-93 OQL query semantics). The ODMG standard does not clearly specify the admissible member types of set operands of such operations and what are the types of the members of resulting sets they produce. It would be more appropriate if ODMG-93 considered for such operations collections not as pure sets but as algebraic systems (especially in case when a type is considered together with its extent). It is not clear also how should we compare literals of different types in case of such binary set expressions.

To explicate our proposal consider a specific case, e.g., the *union* operator as it was defined in [22]. For union of collections P and Q with types of members correspondingly T_P and T_Q the membership type of the result collection is $T_P \sqcap T_Q$, where $\sqcap$ is the *meet* operation returning type T whose interface is defined as the intersection of T_P and T_Q interfaces. The *meet* operation produces a resulting type that is integrated into the type lattice as a supertype of its arguments.

For example, assume that P and Q are sets of objects of type *Student* and *Employee* correspondingly. Their union member type will be *Person*, which is a nearest common supertype of *Student* and *Employee* (i.e., *Person = Student $\sqcap$ Employee*). Generally location of such common supertype may be not so obvious.

Another issue which should be explicitly specified is a way of comparing of set members having different types. While for mutable objects we can use the unique identifiers for immutable values special policy should be adopted. In particular, in SYNTHESIS model we assume that the common supertype must contain some comparison operator allowing such immutable values to be compared.

Thus we see that more systematic and uniform way of type lattice, type inferencing and set operations definition in ODMG-93 is required and we show how such definition might be provided.

5 SYNTHESIS object model

Working on the SYNTHESIS object model we tried to get pure behavioral model which would be well-grounded and free of inconsistencies mentioned above and alike. The fundamental concept of the SYNTHESIS object model [13] (and early version in [14]) is *an abstract value*. All data components in SYNTHESIS are abstract values. Abstract values are instances of abstract data types (ADT) which are algebraic systems. So all the abstract values are typed. The model includes a consistent object-oriented subset – objects are considered as a kind of mutable values. The model is functional in the sense that all access to objects and all manipulation of objects is based on the application of functions to objects. Being based on the notion of the algebraic system SYNTHESIS object model is purely behavioral. In particular the basic for relational model notion of a tuple (or a record) type is replaced by more general notion of *a product type*. We believe that the product type should play a key role in object models, providing object compositions while preserving pure behavioral approach.

5.1 SYNTHESIS type system

The SYNTHESIS type system was formed under the influence of the following main basic principles:

- *data abstraction* principle (using of behavioral model for encapsulation of data values);

- *uniform representation* of various forms and kinds of data principle;

- *type extensibility* principle;

- *type orthogonality* principle;

- *primacy of specifications* over implementation principle (important for HIRE).

SYNTHESIS type system core lattice is given on Fig. 1.

Links in the lattice represent subtyping relationship. The root of the lattice is the *Taval* type corresponding to all abstract values considered in the model. Its base is *Tnone* type provided for representation of values with no semantics. For instance, the value *none* belongs to *Tnone* and may be returned by functions producing null result of any type.

All immutable types of the language obtain properties of *Taval* type, all mutable types obtain properties of *Tsynt_object* type. Values of *Taval* type are characterized by interfaces having function signatures with typed arguments. The basic property of an abstract value is a capability of executing of the interface functions requiring the abstract value itself as its first parameter.

Objects are a particular case of abstract values. Values of the *Tsynt_object* type specialize abstract values with new properties - an ability to have a unique

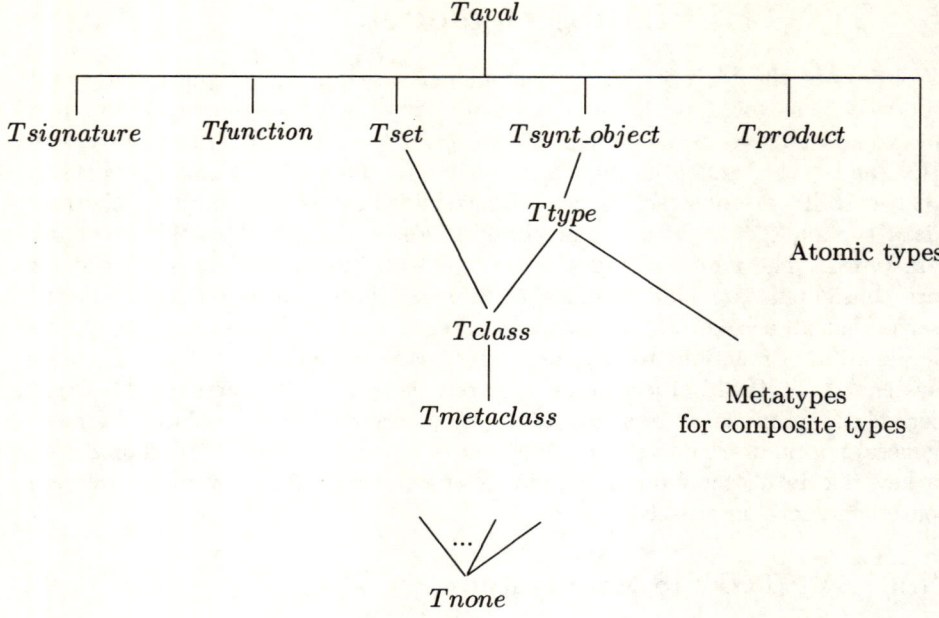

Figure 1: SYNTHESIS type system core lattice

identifier and a potential ability to belong to some class (classes). Therefore any mutable type is considered to be a subtype of the corresponding immutable type.

A type in the language is treated as the first-class value. Such values may be defined in specifications, on typing of variables, may be produced by type functions and type expressions.

Class in SYNTHESIS is treated as a subtype of the set type. It provides for using these generally different constructs homogeneously: a class may be used everywhere where a set defined on ADT may be used. This property simplifies reaching of the SYNTHESIS calculus and algebra closure. It should be noted that SYNTHESIS abstract values algebra is defined as operational interface in type $Tset$.

Class and type specifications are abstract and completely separated of their implementations. A number of various correct implementations (concretizations) may correspond to such specifications. Correspondence of an implementation to a specification may be established by means of the metadata repository.

Orthogonal to the generalization/specialization class dimension is their *classification* dimension formed by metaclasses.

A function type defines a set of functions, each of them being a mapping of the function domain into its range. Functions may be passed as parameters and returned as values.

A product type T is a composition of a number of other types $T_1, ..., T_n$ and has been already defined.

As the sound foundation we use for SYNTHESIS a model-based specifications providing the proof of the initial consistency of the model and the preservation of the invariants by the operations. The foundation leads also to a provable way of development of programs from specifications by proper *concretization (refinement)* of abstract data types and operations of the specification by concrete data types and programs satisfying strict concretization conditions. In particular, we focus on the Abstract Machine Notation (AMN) [1] that is in good correspondence with the algebraic system theory.

5.2 SYNTHESIS query language

The SYNTHESIS query language is defined as *object calculus* on an abstract value domain. It should be noted that traditionally lots of object model features are incorporated in calculus as specific axioms, or even as a part of calculus semantics [11, 19, 24]. In this case various interpretations of object features in different models should be taken into account. The fact that all the abstract values are typed according to *well-defined* [8, 4] SYNTHESIS abstract type system allows to support quite abstract style of "calculus-domain interaction". Data can be accessed only through interfaces defined in the corresponding abstract types. Under this approach we have quite natural generalization of "relational" Datalog-like deduction.

Also the SYNTHESIS object calculus is naturally integrated with type system. In particular, there is a number of type operations defined in the interface of type *Ttype* (such as type union, intersection and production). These operations allow to form and calculate various type expressions. It should be noted, that traditionally the calculus and type system are considered independently. SYNTHESIS *object algebra* is defined as operational interface in type *Tset* which simplifies reaching of the SYNTHESIS object calculus and algebra closure.

6 Conclusion

We believe that the basic theoretical and practical results that have been obtained during last years provide for object models well groundness. To our opinion these results can improve the situation in the object models and, in particular, in producing of ODBMS standards. We made some remarks considering well-known ODMG-93 standard from the position of algebraic system theory as proper foundations for the object models:

- ODMG-93 does not systematically clarify how the principle of operations being defined on a single type is applied to the object creation operations. Also current state of ODMG-93 model definition make unclear semantics of *Type* type which leads to contradictions. Providing the model uniformity in more consistent manner (as far as object creation is concerned) it would be better, for example, to define *Type* of ODMG-93 as the instance of itself. It would make the model extensible and self-descriptive.

- Type generating can be treated in the way which is more coherent with the type lattice definition. In this case each type generator corresponds to a collection of types forming a sub-lattice which is rooted in the most general type. In particular, dynamic and static type checking can be naturally considered in such context. It would allow more easy binding to languages with different strategies for type checking. Also it relieves integrating of concrete composite types with the existing lattice.

- Explicit provision of interrelationship between mutable and immutable types would allow to define type lattice in consistent and unambiguous way. The way how it could be done in ODMG standard is shown.

- Axiomatization of relationships introduced in ODMG-93 would provide for clear referential integrity constraints definition and for operational semantics preserving the declared constraints.

- Query language should be based on the well defined object calculus naturally integrated with the type system. In particular, some approach for deriving new types for all operators and integrating them into the existing type lattice should be adopted. To relieve the integration of the resulted type in the lattice *product type* could be used which is a behavioral abstraction of the conventional tuple constructor and is based on the notion of a cartesian product of algebraic systems. Proper type inferencing would also allow to define binary set operators in consistent manner. We showed how this could be applied to ODMG-93.

We refer to the SYNTHESIS object model as to an example of the model based on the algebraic system concept. It takes into account all remarks listed above. Being based on the notion of the algebraic system SYNTHESIS object model is purely behavioral. The model naturally integrates the object calculus with the type system.

The paper does not pretend to be exhaustive. It allows, however, to get general flavor of how results of the latest researches in ODBMS can be applied to the object models and languages standardization activity. We feel that additional attention is worthwhile of being attracted to get real synergy of industrial-strength and research projects that could bring significant benefits to both of them.

References

[1] Abrial J.-R. B-Technology. Technical overview. BP International Ltd., 1992, p. 73.

[2] Atkinson M., et al The object-orientad database system manifesto, DOOD'89, 1989, pp. 40-57.

[3] Beeri C. A Formal Approach to Object Oriented Databases. Data and Knowledge Engineering, 5 (1990), p. 353-382.

[4] C. Beeri, T. Milo. On the power of algebras with recursion. Proc. of the 1993 ACM SIGMOD Int. Conf. on Management of Data, 1993, pp. 377-386.

[5] Bjorner D., Jones C.B., Formal specification and software development. Prentice-Hall Series in Computer Science. Prentice-Hall, 1982

[6] Borgida A., Mertikas M., Schmidt J.W., Wetzel I. Specification and refinement of databases and transactions. DAIDA Deliverable, ESPRIT 892, Universitaet Hamburg, Germany, 1990.

[7] Carrington D., Duke D., Duke R., King P., et al Object-Z: an object-oriented extension to Z. FORTE'89, Vancouver, Dec. 1989

[8] Goguen, J. Thatcher, J., Wagner, E. An Initial Algebra approach to the Specification, Correctness and Implementation of Abstract Data Types. In Current Trends in Programming Methodology, IV, Yeh, R. (ed.). Prentice-Hall, 1978, p. 80-149.

[9] Goguen, J., Meseguer, J. Order-sorted algebra I: equational deduction for multiple inheritance, overloading, overloading, exeptions and partial operations. Theoretical Computer Science, 105, 1992, pp 217-273.

[10] A. Haxthausen, J.S. Pedersen, Prehn S. Raise overview. Computer Resources International A/S, 1992

[11] Jeusfeld, M., Staudt, M. Query Optimization in Deductive Object Bases. In Query Processing for Advanced Database Systems. Freytag, J., Maier, D., Vossen, G. (ed.), 1994, p. 146-176.

[12] L.A. Kalinichenko Emerging semantic-based interoperable information system technology. Proc. of the IISF/ACM Japan Int. Symposium, 1994, pp. 205-215.

[13] L.A. Kalinichenko SYNTHESIS: a languge for description, design and programming of interoperable information resource environment. Institute for Problems of Informatics of the Russian Academy of Sciences, September 1993, p. 113 (in Russian).

[14] L. Kalinichenko, V. Zadorozhny A generalized information resource query language and basic query evaluation technique, Proc. of the Second Int. Conf. on DOOD, Munich, December 1991, LNCS, N. 566 , p. 546-566.

[15] L. Kalinichenko Methods and tools for equivalent data model mapping construction. Proc. of the EDBT'90 Conference,1990,Springer Verlag,p.92-119.

[16] M. Kay. A peg in the ground: a review of the object database standard: ODMG-93. First Class. The OMG Newsletter, 2(4), 1994, pp. 13.

[17] W. Kim. Observations on ODMG-93. First Class. The OMG Newsletter, 2(4), 1994, pp. 14-15.

[18] W. Kim. Observations on ODMG-93 Proposal. SIGMOD Record, 23(1), 1994, pp. 4-9.

[19] Lausen, G., Marx, D. Evaluation Aspects of an Object-Oriented Deductive Database Language. In Query Processing for Advanced Database Systems. Freytag, J., Maier, D., Vossen, G. (ed.), 1994, p. 178-200.

[20] A.I. Maltsev. Algebraic Systems. Nauka Publ., 1970, p. 392. (in Russian)

[21] J. Meseguer, X. Qian. A logical semantics for object-oriented databases. Proc. of the 1993 ACM SIGMOD Int. Conf. on Management of Data, 1993, pp. 89-98.

[22] R. J. Peters, A. Lipka, M.T. Ozu, D. Szafron. The Query Model and Query Languge of TIGUCAT. University of Alberta, TR 93-01, June 1993, p. 95.

[23] The Object Database Standard: ODMG-93. Ed. by R.G.G. Cattell, Morgan Kaufmann Publ., 1994, p. 169.

[24] Yokota, K., Tsuda, H., Morita, Y. Specific Features of a Deductive Object-Oriented Database language Quixote. SIGMOD'93 Workshop on Combining Declarative and Object-Oriented Databases (WCDOOD), Washington, 1993.

Version Support for CAD/CASE Databases

Waldemar Wieczerzycki, Jarogniew Rykowski
Franco-Polish School of New Information
and Communication Technologies, Poznań, Poland

Abstract

In the paper new functionalities for *CAD/CASE* databases are proposed which are necessary to improve the co-operative work of the design team members. These functionalities mainly concern versioning aspects of the design environments. First, typical project life-cycles are studied to determine the requirements for supporting efficient merge operation for different design environments. Next, the original extensions of so called database version model are proposed. Finally, the implementation of merge operation is discussed.

All the functionalities mentioned above are currently implemented in the multiversion database prototype.

1 Introduction

Recently databases address non-traditional domains of application, such as computer aided design (*CAD*) and computer aided software engineering (*CASE*). Databases devoted to these domains need to support new functions. Most of them are provided by databases that have adopted object-oriented paradigm. They are called *object-oriented databases* (*OODBs*). *OODBs* combine the features of object-oriented languages, such as object identity, object encapsulation, complex objects, class inheritance, message exchange communication, etc., and traditional databases, such as persistence, concurrency, data consistency, recovery, access authorization, data distribution, etc.

CAD and *CASE* applications require complex data structures to represent schemas, pictures, photos, graphs, sounds etc., as well as modelling mechanisms which may express complex relationships between data. Very efficient graphical workstations recently released, on one hand, and the high level of modelling expression offered by *OODBs*, on the other hand, support sufficiently those requirements. In parallel, *CAD* and *CASE* applications also require the mechanisms which can precisely reflect particular stages of the design process and its typical elements, such as decision alternatives, revisions, feed-backs, etc. Unfortunately, *OODBs* currently available do not support these mechanisms or they support them in an unsatisfactory range.

One of the most important notions that must be supported in design databases is the notion of *object version*. *CAD* (*CASE*) project is typically very long: it may take several years to complete. During this time, many versions of different parts of project are usually developed. Their creation is a direct or an indirect consequence of an error fixing, changes of requirements (e.g. implied by more efficient hardware or new software tools), etc. A particular type of versions, called *variants*, may be distinguished. Variants reflect the parallel ways of the project development. Both complex and atomic objects have usually variants. Some of them are public, which means that they are available to all the members of a design team, while the other are private. Private versions, accessed exclusively by designers, are used in early stages of the design process. They are usually temporary - after updates, when ripe enough, they are promoted to public versions. The final public versions, commonly accepted by all the team members, are usually frozen and promoted to historical ones. Historical versions are public versions which cannot be changed or removed.

Not only the design artifact and its parts are versioned. During project development one can observe the dynamic modifications of:
- the working team composition (in very long projects the working team may change completely),
- the working team structure,
- work organization rules, task scheduling,
- project strategy (e.g. during compilation time, save CPU time instead of memory use),
- basic requirements (new hardware, new ideas, etc.),

Different versions of relationships between project components should also be supported. Objects created in *CAD/CASE* systems are usually very complex. Their internal structure is expressed not only by the composition hierarchy, but also by component dependency graphs, common origin and derivation relationships, etc.

Finally, the whole working environment should be versioned according to particular designer requirements. Typically, designers tend to work in parallel at the same time. Each of them requires, however, the system to be viewed as a private one, dedicated to his/her session, with no restrictions imposed by other users. The environments may evolve independently of each other until they reach a point in which they should be merged (preferably automatically) into a single, consistent environment reflecting common efforts of the design team.

Merging private design environments into a single public one is, on one hand, one of the most important functionalities which must be supported in every *CAD/CASE* system. On the other hand, it is also one of the most difficult problems which has not been solved satisfactory yet.

Various aspects of version management have been considered in the literature: version identification and manipulation, change notification and propagation, version primitives, functions, histories and structures of version graphs. These aspects have been considered separately for design databases [1, 2, 3, 4, 5, 6, 7, 8]. The obvious difference between the approaches proposed is the versioning granularity and the way of assuring consistency of the multiversion database.

In [8] a single object is the unit of versioning. All the versions of a particular multiversion object constitute a set which is called *generic object*. Both generic object and object versions have unique identifiers. Thus, it is possible to create explicit references (bindings) between object versions and generic objects. Two binding techniques are used: early and late. In early binding, object versions point directly to each other. In late binding, object versions point to generic objects. Exactly one version of each generic object is marked as the *current* one. It is used to resolve the reference. The consistency checking depends on the type of binding. For late binding, at one time, only one set of consistent versions exists, namely the set composed of *current* object versions. For early binding, to obtain all consistent combinations of object versions it is necessary to navigate across all the references between object versions.

In [6] model, the composition hierarchy of an object, called *configuration*, is the unit of versioning. The creation of a new version of a composite object implies the creation of new versions of all its components, unless the sub-configurations are versioned independently. Configurations are also the units of consistency, which means that object versions included in a configuration are mutually consistent.

Finally, in [2] model the whole database is versioned. In this approach, a multiversion database is viewed as a set of logically independent *database versions*. Each database version is composed of one version of each object. Object versions collected in one database version are mutually consistent.

The model with database versions mentioned above seems to be the most appropriate for *CAD/CASE* requirements. First, it provides all the concepts necessary in design environments like variants, revisions, etc. Second, it fits to the nature of the design process, because the users addressing private (local) database versions may work independently of each other, while the users addressing public (common) database versions may co-operate.

To be used efficiently in *CAD/CASE* applications, the model with database versions, however, requires substantial extensions. In general, they concern supporting merge operation of different database versions and improving the management of long-duration transactions addressed to the same database version. On the other hand, there is also a lot of problems which must be resolved while implementing this versioning model.

The goal of the paper is twofold. First, typical project life-cycles are studied to determine the requirements for supporting efficient merge operation. The original extensions of database version model are proposed. Second, the implementation of merge operation is discussed. The authors have participated in the design and implementation of the multiversion database prototype *MOM* which incorporates the model with database versions at the level of objects. In parallel, the authors have collaborated with BULL Research Center, France, where the model with database versions is currently implemented on the level of physical pages.

2 Database Version Approach

The database version approach was originally proposed by W. Cellary and G. Jomier in [2]. The main concept of this approach is that of a *database version* which comprises a version of each multiversion object stored in the database. Some objects may be hidden in a particular database version by the use of the *nil* values of their versions. In the database version approach, a database version is a unit of consistency and versioning. It is a unit of consistency, because each object version contained in a database version must be consistent with the versions of all the other objects contained in it. It is a unit of versioning, because an object version cannot appear outside a database version. To create a new object version, a new database version has to be created, where the new object version appears in the context of versions of all the other objects and respects the consistency constraints imposed. Database versions are logically isolated from each other, i.e., any changes made in a database version have no effect on the others.

To operate on database versions, *dbv-transactions* are used, while to operate on object versions inside database versions, *object transactions* are used. A dbv-transaction is used to derive a new database version, called a *child*, from an existing one, called its *parent*. To derive a child means to make a logical copy of all the object versions contained in the parent. Once created, the child database version evolves independently of its parent; also its parent is not prevented from evolving if it is admitted to by the application.

To efficiently implement database versions, and to avoid version value redundancy, database versions are organized as a tree reflecting derivation history, and are identified by *version stamps*. A version stamp makes it possible to easily identify the path in the derivation tree from a given database version to the root, i.e. to identify all the ancestors of the given database version. If a node is the n-th child of its parent whose node stamp is p, then the child node is stamped $p.n$. The root node is stamped 0. A multiversion object is implemented as a set of object version values and a control data structure called *association table*. Each row of the association table of a multiversion object associates an object version value with one or several database versions. Some database versions are associated explicitly, i.e. their version stamps appear explicitly in the association table. Others are associated implicitly: if the version stamp of a database version does not appear in the association table, this means that it shares an object version value with its parent, which in turn may share it with its parent, etc. This rule gives an important advantage: to derive a new database version, it is sufficient to register its version stamp in the system. Just after derivation, this version stamp does not appear in any association table, so automatically the new database version shares version values of all the objects with its parent. As an example, consider a multiversion database given in Fig. 1. It is composed of seven database versions stamped 0, 0.1, $0.1.1$, $0.1.2$, $0.1.3$, $0.1.1.1$ and $0.1.1.2$. Two multiversion objects A and B are stored in the database. Object A exists in two versions: a_0 and a_1. Object version a_0 appears only in database version 0. Object version a_1 appears explicitly in database version 0.1 and implicitly in all its successors in the database version derivation tree. Object B exists in five versions: b_0, b_1, b_2, b_3 and b_4. Object versions b_0, b_3 and b_4 are not shared between database versions, and they appear in database versions 0, $0.1.3$ and $0.1.1.2$, respectively. Object versions b_1 and b_2 are shared: b_1 appears in database versions 0.1 and $0.1.2$, while b_2 appears in database versions $0.1.1$ and $0.1.1.1$. The association tables of objects A and B are given in Fig. 2.

To update shared version value in a database version d, the following simple algorithm is used. First, a new row is added to the association table, associating the new version value and the version stamp of the database version d. Then, in the original row concerning the old version value, the version stamp of d is replaced by the version stamps of those of its immediate successors (children) that do not explicitly appear in any row of the association table. The same algorithm is also used to create and delete objects in a database version. Creation of an object in a database version consists in updating its *nil* version value by a given one; deletion of an object in a database version consists in updating its value by *nil*. Creation of a new multiversion object in the database consists of the creation of its association table with one row associating the nil version value with the root database version.

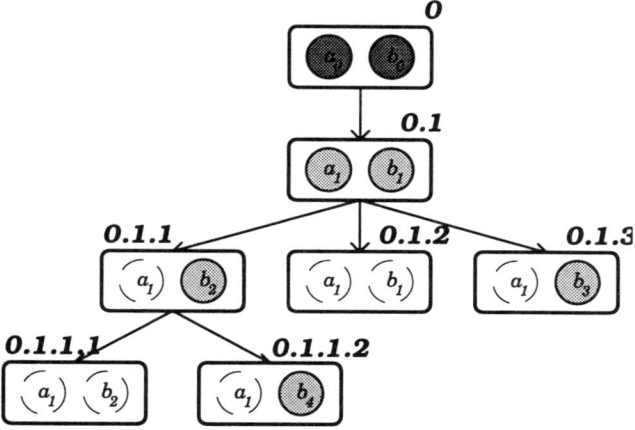

Figure 1. Database version derivation tree

Versions of A	Version stamps
a_0	0
a_1	0.1

Versions of B	Version stamps
b_0	0
b_1	0.1
b_2	0.1.1
b_3	0.1.3
b_4	0.1.1.2

Figure 2. Association tables of objects A and B

The versioning mechanism described above permits two object transactions addressed to two different database versions to run in parallel. They do not conflict and need not be serialized, even if both write the object version whose value is shared by both database versions addressed. This follows from the logical isolation of database versions: the update of a shared version value in one database version gives birth to a new one, while preserving the old one as explained above. The object transactions addressed to the same database version are serialized in exactly the same manner as in a monoversion database.

3 Merge Operation

In the database version approach (cf. Section 2) a new database version is derived from a single parent database version. Both database versions represent two different stages of the design process. During the co-operative design, however, the possibility of deriving a new database version from more than one parent database version should be supported. This kind of derivation, called *database version merging*, reflects an attempt to integrate objects developed separately by different designers.

In order to present typical co-operative project life-cycles we distinguish three different types of database versions:
- *private database version* - only one user can read and update it;
- *public database version* - several users can read and update it;
- *historical database version* - several users can read it, but nobody can update it.

Private database versions are used exclusively by designers. They are usually derived from a historical version and, when ripe enough, they are merged into public version. Merge operation can be performed several times until reaching the final state. Public version may be frozen and promoted into historical one.

3.1 Project life-cycles

In general we may distinguish two typical project life-cycles:
- with forward merge,
- with backward merge.

In the first case, designers start from the same historical version deriving their private database versions. Afterwards they work separately in corresponding private versions, and finally they merge them into a public version which is located at least one level below private database versions in the derivation tree. Merge operation may be done in several steps, creating more than one public version. Next, such public versions may be merged together or with other private versions to obtain a final one. After final merging, the most recently created public database version may be promoted to a historical one. Then, newly created historical version can be used as a starting point for creating new set of private versions, etc.

After merging updates made in private versions are not visible in other private versions from the same level. This life-cycle is illustrated in Fig. 3.

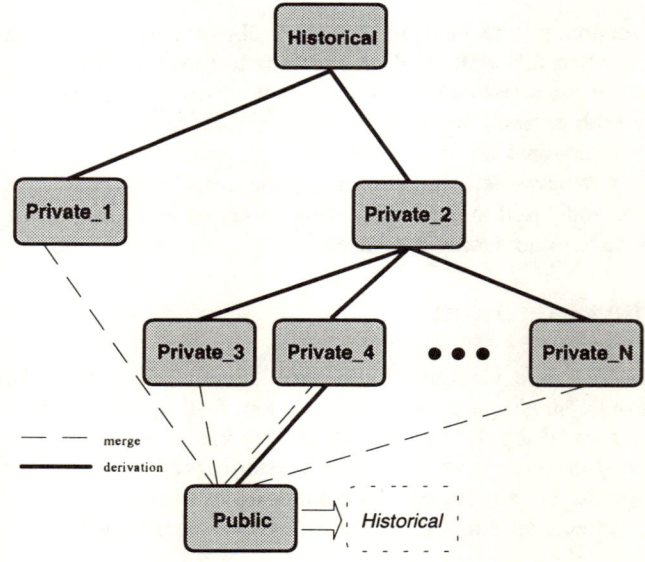

Figure 3. Life-cycle with forward merge

In the case of backward merge (cf. Fig. 4), several database versions are merged into an existing public version which is located one level (at least) above them in the database version derivation tree. Some of merged database versions may be "children" of the final public version.

Three particular types of backward merge may be distinguished.
- *No object percolation.* In this case versions of objects from public and private database versions are independent (in spite of the fact that they can be logical copies of each other). Merge operation does not imply any updates in private database versions.
- *Partial object percolation.* After merge operation, previously defined subset of objects from public database version is percolated to some private versions. This mechanism makes it possible to exchange particular updates between selected private database versions directly after merge operation.
- *Total object percolation.* After merge, the whole public database version is percolated to its children. As a consequence, the design process is cyclic. After its consecutive stages every designer (accessing private database version) has the same starting point. Then, the private versions evolve independently until the next merge operation, which again triggers percolation mechanism after which new design cycle (stage) is started.

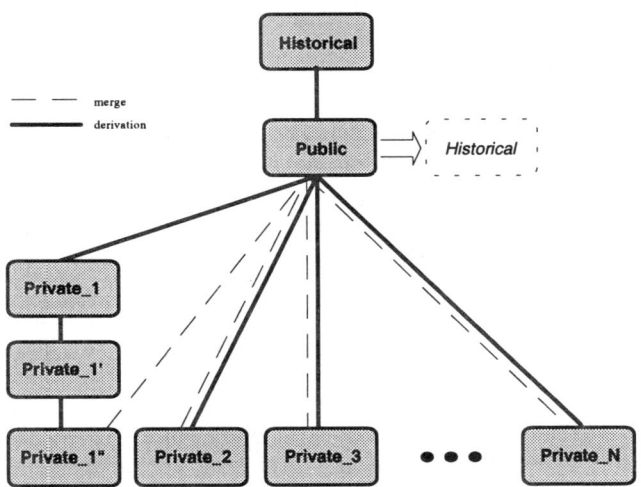

Figure 4. Life-cycle with backward merge

3.2 Merging database versions by object comparison

During merge operation one must decide which versions of objects to choose - at most one version of every object. If designers have not updated the schema of their private database versions, then a designer performing merge operation consecutively takes into consideration all multiversion objects (i.e. object by object) from private database versions and decides which version he wants to incorporate into the public database version. As a result of merging, a new set of object versions is generated and associated to the public database version.

This kind of merge operation seems to be a very slow and tedious process, in particular if database versions are composed of many objects. Thus, some automatization should be provided by the system. One of very useful embedded functionalities would be the possibility of comparing objects belonging to private database versions being merged.

Let us consider several private database versions which were derived from one "common point" of the design process (e.g. from the same database version) or from scratch. Assume that designers want to merge them into public database version. Some object versions are new - they have been created after last "common point". Some object versions are "old" - they were created before "common point" and they have not been updated since that time. When versions of particular object are compared, the possible cases are the following:
- object exists only in one of merged private database versions, i.e. there is only one object version to choose,
- object exists in several private database versions and:
  - is shared by these versions, i.e. version values are the same; as a consequence, the choice is trivial because in fact there is still one object version,
  - one or more object versions have been updated (or created) since last "common point"; then particular object exists in many versions, and the designer must choose one of them.

Designers should also have the possibility to define some default options of the merge operation, for example:
- if only one version of object exists, get automatically this one into final version;
- if there are exactly two object versions, get the newest one;
- choose all object versions existing in indicated database version and, if the version is *nil* (i.e. there is no object in it), choose not-*nil* object version from other database versions (the implementation of this case is discussed in Section 4).

Notice, that if sets of objects of every database version being merged are disjoined, then merge operation (using default options) can be done almost automatically, without user interference.

On the other hand, one must remember that some object versions are bound by different semantic relationships to versions of other objects (particularly in *CASE* systems). If a user wants to take such an object from one database version, he/she should also take the objects connected to the one considered from the same database version. Information about these connections sometimes is not stored explicitly in the database. In this case, after merge operation special tests should be performed to insure the correctness and consistency of the database. If the information about connections between objects is stored in the database (e.g. as an extension of a composition hierarchy), there should be a system tool for automatic detection of object inter-dependencies (even if types of connections are user-defined).

3.3 Merging database versions by *REDO* operation

After updating schema in private database versions merge operation is in general impossible to do. Only object versions being the instances of common parts of the schema can be compared and possibly merged. A partial solution of this problem could be the use of *REDO* operation instead of merging by object comparison.

To explain it, suppose that a designer derives a private database version from a public one and after making some updates he/she wants to incorporate those updates into public database version. Instead of copying objects, he/she can re-execute in the public database version the same operations he has executed in the private one (this is the *REDO* operation). For supporting this functionality, information about every transaction and sub-transaction committed in private database must be kept in a special file, called *log-file*. During *REDO* operation, the contents of *log-file* is interpreted and executed transaction by transaction in public database. After completing last transaction from *log-file* the *REDO* process is finished and database versions may be considered as merged. Of course, because of different context of transaction re-execution, some of its operations may not be performed correctly, especially if two database versions have different versions of schema. This implies new problem to be solved. In some cases the user intervention may be required.

The *REDO* operation is implemented as a single, multi-level transaction. Sub-transactions nested in it correspond to transactions committed in the private database version. Thus, there is a possibility to roll-back the whole transaction or any nested sub-transaction when an error occurs.

Using *REDO* operation is based on an optimistic approach. The designer supposes that, even if public database version has been changed by someone else, he/she can still repeat his operations and he will get the same result. It is very possible, if users work on different sets of objects and these sets are logically independent. Otherwise, errors may occur.

4 Implementation

For the purpose of merging database versions two different primitives for object version update are supported, database version derivation tree is extended to *DAG*, new transaction type is introduced, and object version identification rule is modified.

4.1 Primitives for Object Version Update

We distinguish two following primitive operations for updating object versions:

UpdateObject (oid, dbv, *NewValue),
LinkObject (oid, src_dbv, dst_dbv)

The first primitive derives new version of object *oid* associated with database version *dbv*. If the old version was not shared with other database versions - it is deleted, otherwise it still exists in other database versions.

The second primitive replaces version of object *oid* in database version *dst_dbv* by the version appearing in database version *src_dbv*. After this operation, database versions *src_dbv* and *dst_dbv* share the same version of *oid*.

As an example, consider object *A* with the association table given in Fig. 5 a). Database version *0.2.1* shares object version a_1 with database version *0.2*. Now assume that the following primitive is executed:

LinkObject (A, 0.3, 0.2.1)

As a result, database version *0.2.1* shares object version a_2 with database version *0.3*. Updated association table is given in Fig. 5 b).

a0	0
a1	0.1, 0.2
a2	0.3
a3	0.2.2

a)

a0	0
a1	0.1, 0.2
a2	0.3, 0.2.1
a2	0.2.2

b)

Figure 5. Association tables of object *A*

4.2 Database Version Derivation *DAG*

A single merge operation concerns two database versions only. To merge *n* database versions (*n>2*), one must repeatedly call merge operation for partially merged database versions.

As a consequence, instead of a database version hierarchy, we deal with rooted directed acyclic graph (*DAG*), whose nodes have at most two direct predecessors. If a particular node has two direct predecessors we distinguish *main* direct predecessor and *side* direct predecessor.

If node *n* has two direct predecessors stamped *ns1* and *ns2*, then node stamped *ns1* is a main predecessor if *ns1* contains smaller number on the first different element of its node stamp. For example, consider two nodes stamped *0.1.3.2.5* and *0.1.4.2*, respectively. The main predecessor is the one stamped *0.1.3.2.5*, because its node stamp contains *3* at the first different position in the number sequence (i.e. third position), which is smaller then *4*, being the third element of the second node stamp.

The main predecessor's stamp is taken as a prefix of a node stamp of merged database version. It is illustrated in Fig. 6, where merged database version is stamped *0.1.3.2.5.2*.

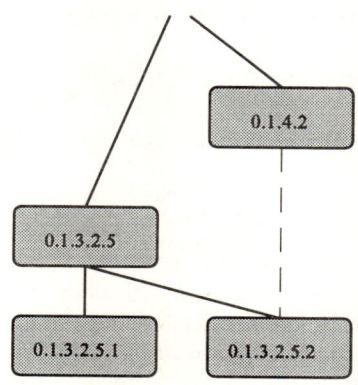

Figure 6. Database derivation *DAG*

The edge connecting the merged node with its main predecessor has greater priority then the one connecting it to the side predecessor. This priority influences the rule of object version identification presented in Section 4.4.

Originally, the database version derivation tree is implemented by the table in which each row represents single database version, and contains corresponding database version stamp and the number of child database versions. Now, the table has to be extended by a new column containing node stamp of a side predecessor. For the node *0.1.3.2.5.2* (cf. Fig. 7) the row given in Fig. 7 has to be included:

node version stamp	number of children	side predecessor
0.1.3.2.5.2	0	0.1.4.2

Figure 7. Row of derivation DAG table

Notice, that version stamps still preserve their main property: to find direct and indirect main predecessors one need not to consult database version table. It is sufficient to reduce node stamp from its right side. However, in the case of side predecessors one must consult the corresponding rows of the database version table.

4.3 New Transaction Type

A new transaction type, called *merging transaction*, has to be introduced. Merging transaction takes two arbitrary database versions, each one in a consistent state, and derives new database version, composed of the combination of object versions taken from source database versions. The contents of new database version is determined automatically according to the following rules:
- if an object exists only in one source database version it is logically copied to the merged database version,
- if an object exists in both: main and side database versions then, by default, the object version from the main database version is logically copied to the merged database version.

In both cases association tables need not to be modified.

If the resulting database version is not consistent, the merging transaction may use *UpdateObject()* primitive to introduce (derive) new versions of objects which violate integrity constraints. As a result, the merged database version no longer shares them with main or side predecessors. In particular case, the merging transaction may also override the default merging mechanism using *LinkObject()* primitive with the *src_dbv* argument pointing to the side predecessor. In both cases association tables must be modified.

4.4 Object Version Identification

The original rule of object version identification:

If the node stamp of the database version accessed does not appear in the association table then the database version shares object version with its parent database version is still valid for database versions having one direct predecessor.

In the case of merged database versions it must be extended to the following rule:
If the node stamp of the database version accessed does not appear in the association table then:
- *if the main predecessor contains not-nil object version, then the database version considered shares object version with its main predecessor;*
- *otherwise, i.e. if the main predecessor contains nil object version, then the database version considered shares object version with its side predecessor. It implies the necessity of consulting the database version table to find a stamp of the side predecessor.*

If node stamps of main or link predecessors do not appear in the association table, the rule given above is used recursively.

5 Conclusions

The extensions of database version approach presented in the paper support merging different database versions, corresponding to different designers of the team, into a single public database version representing common efforts of the team after particular stage of the design process. These extensions are currently implemented in *MOM* prototype.

Future work will mainly concern support of long-duration transactions in design database managed according to the database version approach.

References

[1] Atwood T., *An Object-Oriented DBMS for Design Support Applications*, Proc. IEEE COMPINT Conf., Montreal, 1985.

[2] Cellary W., Jomier G., *Consistency of Versions in Object-Oriented Databases*, Proc. 16th VLDB Conf., Brisbane, Australia, 1990.

[3] Chou H., Kim W., *A unifying Framework for Version Control in a CAD Environment*, Proc. 12th VLDB Conf., 1986.

[4] Katz R., Chang E., Bhateja R., *Version Modeling Concepts for CAD Databases*, Proc. ACM SIGMOD Conf., 1986.

[5] Katz R., Chang E., *Managing Change in a Computer Aided Design Database*, Proc. 13th VLDB Conf., 1987.

[6] Katz R., *Toward a Unified Framework for Version Modelling in Engineering Databases*, ACM Comouting Surveys, Vol. 22, No. 4, 1990.

[7] Kim W., Banerjee J., *Support of Abstract Data Type in CAD Database System*, Proc. COMPINT Conf., 1985.

[8] Kim W., Banerjee H., Garza J., Woelk D., *Composite Object Support in Object-Oriented Database System*, Proc. OOPSLA Conf., 1987.

Design

A General Framework for Database Design Strategies*

Bernhard Thalheim

Computer Science Institute, Cottbus Technical University, D - 03013 Cottbus
thalheim @ informatik.tu-cottbus.de

Abstract. Database design tools need to be adaptable to a wide range of designers.
This paper surveys the strategy support of the design system RADD and demonstrates how different database design strategies can be developed and supported.

1 Database Design

Database design methodologies and tools should facilitate database modeling, effectively support database processing, database redesign and transform a conceptual schema of the database to a high-performance database schema in the model of the corresponding DBMS. Since the late 1970's, various tools for database design have been introduced. Most of them, however, are dependent on the knowledge, comprehension and experience of the database analyst and their knowledge in normalization theory. The systems $(DB)^2$ and RADD (*R*apid *A*pplication and *D*atabase *D*evelopment) developed in our groups do not require the user to understand the theory, the implementational restrictions and the programming problems in order to design a database scheme. A novice designer can create a database design successfully using the system. These tools are based on an extended entity-relationship model. The entity-relationship model is extended to the *H*igher-order *E*ntity-*R*elationship *M*odel (HERM) by adding structural constructs and using integrity constraints and operations. The system RADD has a component which enables the user to choose his design strategy according to his experience and abilities. Different database design methodologies are developed based on the HERM approach.

The problem of *database design* can be stated as follows: Design the logical and physical structure of a database in a given database management system to contain all the information required by the user and required for an efficient behavior of the information system.

The implicit goals of database design are:

- to meet all the information (content) requirements of the entire spectrum of users in the given application area;

---

* This research has been supported by DFG Th 465/2.

- to provide a "natural" and easy-to-understand structuring of the information content;
- to conserve the whole semantic information of the designers for a later re-design;
- to achieve all the processing requirements and achieve a high degree of efficiency of processing;
- to achieve the logical independence for query and transaction formulation on this level.

While on the one hand the inputs to the process are so informal, the final output of the database design is a database definition with formal syntax and with qualitative and quantitative decisions regarding such problems of physical design like physical placement, indexing and organization of data. This adds additional complexity to the database design process. A formal design must be turned out from, at times, extremely informal available information. The main complexity of the design process is already given by the complexity and number of items included in the database scheme, and further by the semantics defined for the database and the operations.

The requirement acquisition is the most difficult step during database design. There are several reasons for that:

The designers start with vague ideas of the orderers. Those may have difficulty putting their ideas into words.
It may be difficult to obtain reliable requirements. Some of the participating orderers may tell the designer what they think the designer wants to hear.
There can be envisioned a functionality that is not consistent with the objectives that is accomplished from the system.
Objectives of different groups may compete or conflict.
Organizational interactions may impede among orderers.

The database design process can be described according to the information units which are necessary:

- The *requirement description* is an informal description of the application and the goals (mission) to be achieved.
- The *interface* is the description of the organizational structure and the distribution of the database.
- The *structure* of the database objects is described by different classes of objects and their typing systems.
- The *semantics* describes the static properties of objects and object classes. Thus, the semantics is used for restricting the set of possible databases.
- The *views* describes the different subschemata for different parts of the application.
- The *operations* describe how the database should operate.
- Based on the semantical, structural and view information *cooperating views* can be defined for the different sub-databases.

- Using abstraction *query forms* describe in general the database information retrieval processes for the user.
- The *behavior* specifies the dynamic constraints of a database.
- The *transactions* are used for the specification of database programs.
- Finally, the *database modul* collects and re-organizes the information.

These units are not independent. The description of views depends from the structural, semantical and interface information. The complete dependency graph is displayed in Figure 1. Based on these information units different design decisions can be generated.

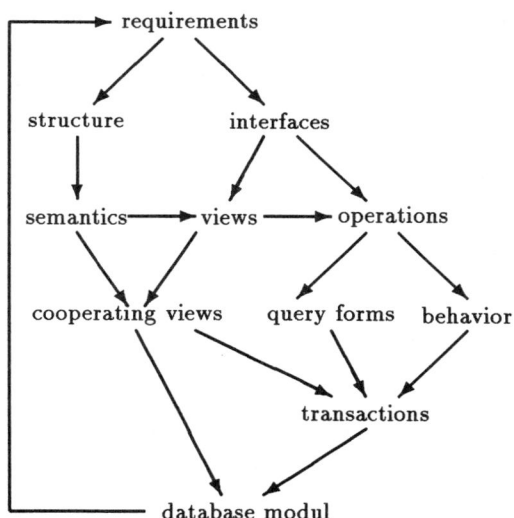

Fig. 1. The Information Acquisition in Database Design

Based on an analysis of systems supporting database design we developed a database design system $(DB)^2$ [6] which is supporting a high-level efficient database design. The system is using an extension of the entity-relationship model for the structural design and the graphical interface. Further, a high-level language for specification of integrity constraints and operations has been developed. At present, we are developing another tool RADD in a joint project in different groups [1] in Cottbus, Dresden, Münster and Rostock. The system is based on the experience of four year of extensive utilization of $(DB)^2$ in more than 100 different user groups. It has a better user support system especially for the more difficult design steps like design of integrity constraints, refinement and rebuilding the schema. Database design strategies are adapted to the model and the purposes of database design processes. This paper reports these results. For an automatic adaption of the design system to the chosen user strategy, known database design strategies have been generalized. Further, we developed our own database design strategy.

The paper is divided into five parts. In Section 2, properties of strategies is briefly discussed. Different classical design strategies are generalized to a framework in Section 3. We distinguish design directions, control strategies and modularity. Sections 4, 5, and 6 review this general framework.

2 Properties of Database Design Methodologies

A design methodology could be based on monotone reasoning. During design the information already modeled is not changed. This does not mean that structures, operations and constraints are not changed. However, the new design step does not abandon already obtained information. The methodology can be represented by the quadruple
$$(M, \Sigma_M, P, T)$$
where M is the metamodel, Σ_M is the set of metamodel constraints, P is the set of primitive steps that are available in the methodology, and T is the transition system.

Each design step is adding certain information. It can be modeled as a triplet
$$(s, d, a)$$
where s is the situation or environment of the step, d is the decision and a is the action. Each design step needs to satisfy certain restrictions:

- Each design step is *content-preserving*, i.e. there exists a query q such that for each database $db' \in SAT(S')$: $q(db') \in SAT(S)$ for S, S' and $Step(S) = S'$.
- Each design step is *constraint-preserving*, i.e. $\Sigma' \models \Sigma$ for $S = (Struc, Ops, \Sigma)$, $S' = (Struc', Ops', \Sigma')$ and $Step(S) = S'$.
- Each step is *minimally content-preserving*, i.e. the design step does not add derived types; there does not exist a query q such that for each database $db' \in SAT(S')$ there exists a database $db \in SAT(S)$ such that $q(db) = db'$ for S, S' and $Step(S) = S'$.

Furthermore, there are some desirable restrictions:

- Each step is *minimally constraint-preserving*, i.e. $\Sigma \models \Sigma' |_{Struc}$ for $S = (Struc, Ops, \Sigma)$, $S' = (Struc', Ops', \Sigma')$ and $Step(S) = S'$.
- Each step is *nearly free of path tuple-generating constraints*. When a path tuple-generating constraint is present it often requires that the path has to be computed to check whether the constraint holds in the database.

Notice, that inclusion constraints can be maintained in a database using only projections. Path inclusion constraints are still based on joins. The last restriction is often too strong. It can be replaced by the following restriction. This restriction requires an effective management of basic database operations.

- Each step is *update simplicity-preserving*, i.e. if for S the complete set of basic update operations is defined without join operations then $Step(S)$ has this property too.

A schema is *lexical-minimal* is it uses as few lexical units as possible. For instance, the attribute DepartmentName of the type *Department* is can be replaced by Name (the corresponding identifier is Department.Name).
It should be mentioned that several known normalization algorithms do not fulfill the above requirements. However, there are 4NF algorithms which preserve all properties.

A methodology needs also **rules** in which case which concept is going to be applied. One rule which could be considered as the basic rule is that independent objects are to be represented by entity sets.

A database design is similar to database lifetime. Each design step can be modeled by some transaction. The database is designed step by step using one of the given transactions. Each transaction commits or aborts the actions taken since the last last transaction committed. Therefore, the design strategy can be considered to be simple if the design is performed by a sequence of transaction. Often, design strategies are proposed which consists of one complex transaction. Such strategies are prone to errors. Errors and wrong assumptions made at the beginning are corrected only at the end. However, several implications have been derived during design from those assumptions. Therefore, error deletion or revision of assumptions lead in such cases to revision of the entire design process. We need to distingiush between wrong assumptions and errors. Wrong assumptions have several reasons. Errors are detectable at a certain stage of the design procedure. The princip should be that the detection should happen during the most early step.

- A database design step is *closed* if errors which could have been made during this step must be corrected before this step is going to be completed.

Checkpoints are an instrument to develop design strategies with closed steps.

In order to achieve closed design strategies a set of general **design bussiness rules** can be developed. Design consistency is maintained by enforcing these rules during database design.

3 Dimensions in Database Design

Database design has been based in the past on relational design techniques. Two main approaches have been developed: top-down approaches (decomposition) and bottom-up approaches (synthesis). The first strategy begins with a set of basic types and builds new types using decomposition. The second approach begins with a set of descriptions or attributes and then group those in types.

The relational decomposition approach starts with a given schema of relation types and decomposes it to smaller relation types until certain properties such as normal form and losslessness are satisfied. The starting schema can be a universal relation type or a near-normal-form set of types. In the synthesis approach to designing relational databases, we assume the application is described by a set of attributes and functional dependencies among them. The functional dependency (FD) is the main vehicle in synthesizing relation types out of lists of attributes. In this case, we start with a minimal cover of FDs. Normally, the two strategies are not applied in their pure form. Database design could be performed by mixing the two strategies which is sometimes called mixed strategy.

These two approaches could be considered as approaches with different design **directions**.

Design strategies can be distinguished also by their **control mechanism**. One control mechanism rules the step-by-step development of types. Control strategies decides which rules to use in a given situation. The inside-out strategy selects first one central type and then develops the associated type by a discrete neighborhood function. The next type to be developed is a new type with the smallest neighborhood value according to the central type. Another control mechanism exploits another more abstract schema of the database. This mixed strategy is controlled by a sketch of the database schema (the so-called skeleton). Alike in second-order grammars this control mechanism can be generated by another grammar. The skeleton schema is representing the control information of the database design.

Relational database design has been considered mainly for the design of conceptual schemata according to the three-level architecture of a database. The conceptual schema unifies the different views of external users. The database design could also begin with the view design [3]. The views are later composed into the conceptual schema. This approach can be useful for the design of homogeneous view sets. Since view integration is undecidable the applicability of this approach is limited. The **modular design strategy** *Design-by-units* extends this approach. For each subschema which could be considered to be a module similar to software technology the interface is defined for each unit. Units can be associated only by their units. We can define also other kinds of scoping rules in database design. This dimension of database design uses the **modularity** concept. Modularization is based on implementation abstraction and on localization abstraction. *Implementation abstraction* [4] is to selectively hide information about structures, semantics and the behavior of concepts defined by the previous two abstraction mechanisms. Implementation abstraction is a generalization of *encapsulation* and *scoping*. It provides *data independence* through the implementation, allowing the private portion of a concept to be changed without affecting other concepts which use that concept. *Localization abstraction* [4] is used to "factor out" repeating or shared patterns of concepts and functionality from individual concepts into a shared database / knowledge base application environment. Naming is the basic mechanisms to achieve localization. Parametrization can be used for abstraction over partial object descriptions.

Another dimension not represented in the figure is the **representation** form for design results. For instance, the ER model uses rectangles, diamonds as nodes of a graph. The IFO model uses more sophisticated node types and different

BCI = Bottom-up (, conceptual,) inside-out design
BCU = Bottom-up (, conceptual, uncontrolled) design
BCM = Bottom-up, (conceptual,) mixed design
BMI = Bottom-up, modular, inside-out design
BMM = Bottom-up, modular, mixed design
BMU = Bottom-up, modular (, uncontrolled) design
BVM = Bottom-up, view-oriented, mixed design
BVI = Bottom-up, view-oriented, inside-out design
BVU = Bottom-up, view-oriented (, uncontrolled) design
TCI = Top-down (, conceptual,) inside-out design
TCM = Top-down, (conceptual,) mixed design
TCU = Top-down (, conceptual, uncontrolled) design
TMI = Top-down, modular, inside-out design
TMM = Top-down, modular, mixed design
TMU = Top-down, modular (, uncontrolled) design
TVM = Top-down, view-oriented, mixed design
TVI = Top-down, view-oriented, inside-out design
TVU = Top-down, view-oriented (, uncontrolled) design

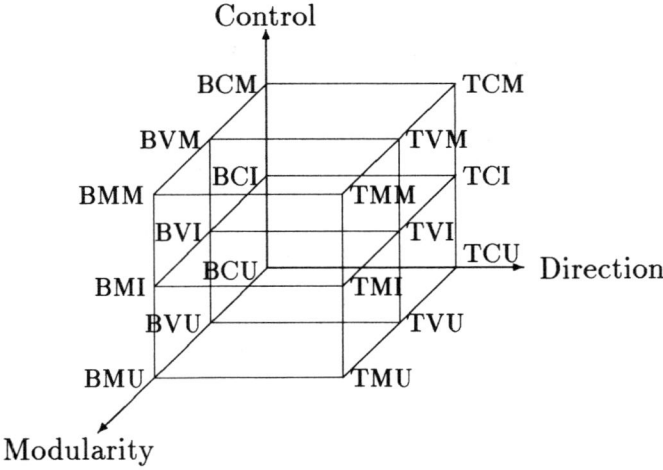

Fig. 2. Different Structure-Oriented Database Design Strategies

types of edges. The representation is more compact but also more complex. The graphical representation differs from model to model. The most important issue is, however, that the graphical representation has to be based on a well-founded semantics. Often, especially in the ER literature and for ER-based tools, design is considered as drawing graphs leaving semantic issues aside.

The power of abstraction principles comes from their orthogonality and their generality. All these mechanisms can be combined with more specialized mechanisms, like exception and default rules.

If we compare different strategies then we can relate them to known **search strategies** in AI. Search strategies are characterized by direction, topology, node representation, selecting rules and heuristic functions. Other design strategies can be developed based on this analogy. We could search forward or backward.

4 Directions of Database Design

4.1 The Top-Down Strategy in Database Structure Design

The pure top-down strategy is based on refinement of abstract concepts into more concrete ones. Each step introduce new details in the schema. The design process ends when all structural requirements are represented. According to the above discussed taxonomy of database design operations the following primitive operations can be used during top-down design:

$$decompose(t, e_0, e_1, ..., e_n, N_0, N_1, ..., N_n)$$
$$extend(E, A), \; extend(R, A), \; extend(R, E)$$
$$generate(E), \; generate(A)$$

The advantage of top-down design is the independent consideration of each type during a design step. The designer can analyse one concept ignoring the other concepts. However, top-down design requires from the designer the knowledge on the general picture of the design first. Therefore, complete top-down design can be performed only by experienced designers if the application area is not well-structured. Based on this approach, different primitives are developed.

4.2 The Bottom-Up Strategy Database Structure Design

Bottom-up design was first developed for the relational model. During bottom-up design each step introduces new concepts not considered before or modify existing ones. During each step the designer checks whether all features of requirements are covered. The designer start from elementary concepts and builds more complex out of them. The advantage of the bottom-up approach is its simplicity. The main disadvantage of the bottom-up approach is that this approach requires restructuring. Therefore, the strategy is not monotone.
The following primitive operations can be used during top-down design:

$$compose(t_1, ..., t_n, C, t)$$
$$extend(E, A), \; extend(R, A), \; extend(R, E)$$
$$generate(E), \; generate(A)$$

5 Control Strategies

5.1 The Inside-Out Strategy in Database Structure Design

The classical inside-out strategy restricts the bottom-up approach by controlling the order of primitives application. This strategy is still complete. We choose the most important concept first, design it and then proceed by moving as an oil stain does, designing first concepts that are conceptually closed to the already design. The order of refinements is disciplined. The designer navigates from the central type to the more distant ones. It is easy to discover new concepts which are to be designed next. However we loose abstraction capabilities. The global schema is built at the end only.

This strategy can be generalized now as follows:

Given a set of concepts C to be designed and a neighborhood function F on C, i.e.
$$F : C \times C \rightarrow NatNumber$$
This function is used for the design agenda. In this case we use the following algorithm for a given central concept c:

Algorithm   *Bottom-up version*

1. Agenda $:= \{c\}$; Designed $:= \emptyset$.
2. *Repeat until* Agenda $= \emptyset$
   (a) *Repeat until* Agenda $= \emptyset$
       i. *Choose* $c \in$ Agenda
       ii. *Design* c *using the bottom-up strategy*
       iii. Agenda $:=$ Agenda $\setminus c$
            Designed $:=$ Designed $\cup \{c\}$
   (b) $m := min\{F(c,c') \mid c \in C \setminus$ Designed, $c' \in$ Designed$\}$
       Agenda $:= \{c \in C \setminus$ Designed $\mid F(c,c') = m$ *for some* $c' \in$ Designed$\}$

For the top-down variant of the algorithm, step 2.(a).ii is used for the design in top-down fashion. This algorithm can be refined. For instance, if the set of concepts is unknown at the beginning then a substep is added to step 2 which looks for extensions of C and of F in each iteration.

5.2 The Mixed Strategy in Database Structure Design

Another controlled approach is the mixed approach. This approach mixes the top-down and the bottom-up approach. First, a skeleton schema is to be designed (using one of the previous approaches). This schema represents the main classes (or units) and their main associations. Then each of the units is refined and later integrated with other designed units. Using the skeleton schema the bottom-up integration of concepts is simpler. Since the complete requirements set is now partioned the design of each unit is less complex. The success of the strategy depends from the design of the skeleton schema. Therefore, this method is applicable if the application is already well-recognized.

5.3 Graph Grammars and Control

In RADD the control is based on graph grammars. Each graph grammar rule represents primitive operations. For instance, based on the extended entity relationship model the following primitives can be used:

$\mathbf{B}_1$ generate(E)
$\mathbf{B}_3$ compose($E_1,...,E_n,\cup,E$)
$\mathbf{B}_4$ compose($R_1,...,R_n,\cup,R$)
$\mathbf{B}_5$ compose($A_1,...,A_n,\cup,E$)
$\mathbf{B}_7$ compose($K_1,...,K_n,\times,R$)
$\mathbf{B}_8$ compose($A_1,...,A_n,\times,A$)
$\mathbf{B}_9$ compose($A_1,\{\}, A$)
$\mathbf{T}_{12}$ extend($K,A_1,...,A_n$)

For example, the modified bottom-up design can be modeled by the following production system:

S → b_6 b_4 end
b_6 → b_6 b_6 | $\mathbf{B}_1$ b_7 Generate entities.
b_7 → $\mathbf{T}_{12}$ b_7 | $\mathbf{T}_{12}$ b_8 Extend entities by atomar attributes.
b_8 → ε | $\mathbf{B}_5$ b_8 | $\mathbf{B}_8$ b_8 | $\mathbf{B}_9$ b_8 | b_4 Generation of complex attributes, generalization of attributes.
b_4 → b_4 b_4 | $\mathbf{B}_3$ | $\mathbf{B}_7$ | $\mathbf{B}_7$ b_5 Generalization of entities, generating relationship types.
b_5 → $\mathbf{B}_4$ | $\mathbf{B}_4$ b_5 Generalizing relationship types.

6 Modular Design by Units

6.1 Design by Units - Structural Design

In [7, 6] another new recursive design methodology was developed: **Design-by-units**. It promotes extensibility, reuse and inheritance as well as behavioral extension. To some extend, this approach is similar to modular design known in software engineering. The orientation is different only. We are first interested in the data representation part and then in the processing part since a part of the processing part is based on generic operations which are defined according to the structure. However, if we consider modularization, parametrization and inheritance to be the kernel concepts of object-oriented design then this design approach can be considered to be completely object-oriented.

This methodology is not following the classical waterfall model with iterations but rather supporting a high level inside-out-strategy [2]. Experience in utilization of (DB^2) has shown that this methodology was the most often choosen for practical design.

Algorithm   *Design-by-units*

1. *Basic step.*
   Design the types for the independent kernel object classes.

2. *Recursion step.*
   Repeat until the schema is not changed.
   Either reification :
   - *Refine the units introducing subtypes (in HERM represented by unary relationship types).*
   - *Refine the relationship types according to the subtypes.*
   or generalization of units:
   - *If there are associations among units then introduce a new unit containing the associated units and the relationship type according to the association.*
   - *Add other relationship types if there exist new associations.*

6.2 Design by Units - Process Design

As already discussed in the previous section, the data design and the process design can not be separated from each another. We need the process information as well as the structural information. For this reason the process design and the structural design need to be integrated. We use a dataflow approach [2]. One of the difficult tasks in processing modeling is to evaluate whether the designed data structures are appropriate for an effective processing of data. It is known already that relational normalization can contradict effective processing. Sometimes unnormalized relations can be used simpler. For handling this we use a cost model for processes which is based on models of complexity for operations and on priority functions for queries and transactions.

6.3 Modular Object-Oriented Design Based on Top-Down-Directions

Modular object-oriented design is based on a database model which encorporates structural, semantical, and behavioral model. The model developed and used in [5] could be used as one of such. The designer specifies the types, classes and methods of the given application. Similar to the previous strategy, we assume that kernel types and classes are specified. Then the specified scheme is refined by adding information on the database and changing the structure of the database or refining types in the schema. This change can be considered [5] as reification of the scheme and its types. This approach allows the development of generic class libraries for application areas. The types in the library are general enough to be used again after reification according to the specific applications of the given application area. This approach quickens the development of schemes. For modular developement of schemes, we specify the type, its interface, its semantics and meaning and its behavior within the database. The reification follows that specification. Therefore we can distinguish the following categories of reification:

Reification by Specialization. Refinement by specialization introduces new subclasses and reorganizes associated relationships. Moreover, it may involve to replace a structure expression such that the new type will be a subtype of the old type and the new implicit and explicit constraints will imply the old ones.

Reification by Splitting. Refinement by splitting also leads to new types. But their type corresponds to parts of an existing type which in turn is replaced by references.

Reification by Completion. Refinement by completion means the definition of new types, constraints, methods, and behavioral constraints.

Reification by Instantiation. The schema may contain undefined parameters, attributes, and types. Refinement by instantiation provides definition for those concepts. The same applies to class parameters. Reification by instantiation may introduce new parameters as well.

7 Conclusion

The system *RADD* [1] which is currently developed is intended to become a toolbox for the interactive, object-oriented design of databases. The solution of RADD is to build a *toolbox* that is *configurable* with respect to a variety of aspects, to different database design strategies and to different users.

This paper discusses the strategy support of the design system.

References

1. P. Bachmann, W. Oberschelp, B. Thalheim, and G. Vossen. The design of RAD: Towards an interactive toolbox for database design. RWTH Aachen, Fachgruppe Informatik, Aachener Informatik-Berichte, 90-28, 1990.
2. C. Batini, S. Ceri, and S. Navathe, Conceptual database design, An entity-relationship approach. Benjamin Cummings, Redwood, 1992.
3. C.C. Fleming and B. von Halle, Handbook of relational database design. Addison-Wesley, Reading, 1989.
4. J.W. Schmidt and F. Matthes. Language technology for post-relational data systems. LNCS 466, 1990, 81–114.
5. B. Schewe, K.-D. Schewe, and B. Thalheim, Object-oriented design of data intensive business information systems. Proc. 23 German Computer Science Conference, Dresden 1993. (In German)
6. B. Thalheim. The higher-order entity-relationship model and $(DB)^2$. LNCS 364, Springer 1989, 382–397.
7. M. Yaseen and B. Thalheim. Practical Database Design Methodologies. Kuwait University, Faculty of Science, 1989, 256p.

Towards Foundations of Database Schema Independent Modelling of Concepts

Remigijus Gustas
Information Systems Department,
Kaunas University of Technology, Lithuania
and
Swedish Institute for Systems Development
e-mail: gustas@if.ktu.lt , gustas@sisu.se

Abstract

The paper focuses on the investigation of special kind of dependencies and operations which allow to specify semantics of concepts by not considering database schema. The negative side of data dependencies exploited in relational database theory is that, in order to understand data semantics, we can not disregard schema of relation. The characteristic feature of constraints at conceptual level is that they abstract from any particular logical data representation aspect, while concentrating on the aspects which are common to all logical representations. It means that critical assumption about Universal Relation could be relaxed at the conceptual design phase. This study of conceptual dependencies and operations among concepts is based on the investigation of semantics of relationships which are defined independently from database logical schema.

1 Introduction

The data modeling primitives applied for specification of database conceptual schema, usually are based on Entity - Relationship like graphical notations. These constructions are not defined strictly and semantically poor. Nevertheless the Entity - Relationship approach based database design methodologies are comparatively user friendly. The main shortages of them are the following:

- Ambiguity of modeling constructs and meta types such as entity, relationship, attribute. Using the same model, semantics of the same application domain can be described by separate users in different ways. It means that the same concept is interpreted differently in several database subschemas, e.g. as an entity or as a relationship.

- Design technology dependence on database schema. Relaxation of primitives from data modeling level is obligatory to build up comprehensive database modeling methodologies,

- Lack of theoretical grounds. E.g.: inference rules of dependencies introduced in relational database theory is significant achievement for data schema design and maintenance. Semantical normalization procedure of Entity-Relationship representation is usually performed by designer, but not defined theoretically.

- The basic primitives are ill-defined. It leads to the uncomfortable and alien design activities.

Nevertheless, Entity - Relationship approach based methods are very often applied by designers, and even a few widely accepted CASE tools in the area of information system conceptual design are based on them. To our opinion, the main success factor of Entity - Relationship models is, that they better support primitives which are closer to human understanding, i.e. constructs of conceptual level. Conceptual Design level is database schema independent and serves for the purpose of description of possible states of affairs of universe of discourse including the classifications, rules, laws, etc. The ideas of explicit representation and separation of conceptual structures from implementation structures are stated in ISO Report [18].

We assume that specifying requirements [6], the following abstract levels can be separated in information system engineering:
1) The implementation level,
2) The level of modeling of data representation and data processing structures,
3) The conceptual level [4].

The Conceptual level [10] (sometimes called epistemological [3] or essential [19]) is closer to human understanding. The implementation level is dependent on physical structures of computer and so, is adopted to computer 'understanding'. The logical (static and dynamic data schema design) level is going to be intermediate. It should be assumed as a level between implementation and conceptual structures. A characteristic feature of primitives at logical level is that they abstract from any particular implementation, concentrating on the aspects which are common to all physical realizations, for example, on efficient data representation and processing aspect. Characteristic feature of primitives at conceptual level is that they abstract from any particular logical data representation, while concerning on the aspects which are common to all logical structures, i.e. on business modeling aspects.

2 Modelling Problems at Conceptual Level

The specification of requirements at conceptual level is supposed to be provided by following properties [11], [18]:
1) Independence
Data representation or physical data organization and access aspects should be not included in the specification.
2) Abstraction
Only general conceptually relevant aspects of business should be included in requirements specification. It enable easy communication between designers and users.
3) Verifiability
Conceptual specification needs to be analyzed in order to determine whether it is:
- incomplete,
- ambiguous or
- inconsistent.
4) Formality
The business modeling primitives should have a well-defined formal theory in order to normalize, manipulate and infer new valid descriptions on a basis of specified ones.
5) Traceability
The consequences of modifications should be possible to trace.

All presented requirements are closely related to each other and can't be satisfied autonomously. In this paper we discuss the following difficult problems of Entity-Relationship based requirements specification:
- sharp interpretation of basic categories of the model,
- resolving of naming conflicts,
- derived relationships.
To our opinion these problems are strongly related to all five requirements for conceptual specifications.

Sharp interpretation of basic categories of the model could cause different conceptual representations for the same data base. Lacking of relativeness of interpretation of basic classes (categories such as entity, relationship, attribute, objective, activity, actor etc.) is one of the main shortages of ER like models applying them into practice of conceptual modeling. Sharp distinction of categories can be a reason of different representations of the same universe of discourse, even when the same modelling methodology is used. The interpretation of categories should be flexible, i.e. independent on modelling primitives. For example, several interpretations of concept JOB is presented in Fig.2.1., while the meaning of the concept is the same in each diagram.

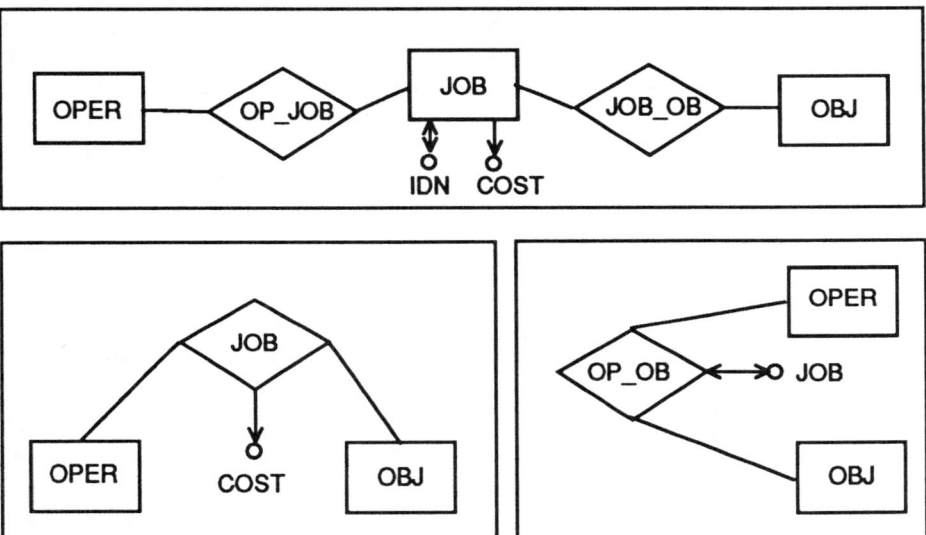

Fig.2.1. Relativeness of interpretation of concept JOB

The sharp distinction among categories can be a reason of artificial representation conflicts between several conceptual views. Sharp distinction of artifact categories injure the requirement of independence of conceptual specification.

We have another kind of conflicts when synonimic concepts have several names in different specifications of the same universe of discourse. They are known as naming conflicts [2]. Example of naming conflict between PERSON_PASSPORT_NUMBER and PASSPORT_NUMBER is presented in Fig.2.2.

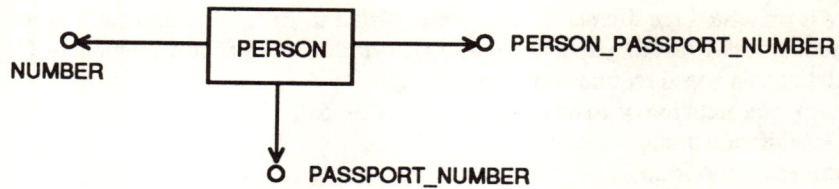

Fig.2.2. Example of naming conflicts

The origin of naming conflicts is quite natural. In order to distinguish the same concept among different names, conceptual dependencies among names of concepts should be specified very precisely. It allows to introduce automated procedures for generation of compound names of concepts which are supposed to be specializations or generalizations of specified simple names. Complex compound names could be derived according to the specified constraints. It means that specification should be based on well-defined primitives and inference rules on them. Inference rules are needed in order to derive more complex relationships. Also, in principle, it allows to introduce semantical normalization (minimization) procedure of conceptual specification.

The requirements stated using a language with ER type descriptions are ambiguous. Different people should not be able to interpret the specification differently. It leads to the conclusion that design methods should be based on theoretically well-defined models. The models have to ensure effective computer aided procedures for detection incorrectness, incompleteness, ambiguity, inconsistency of statements of specification in respect to each other.

3 Conceptual Dependencies

Semantic data models [9], [13] have been developed to capture some of the meaning, as well as the structure of data. Besides well-known types of relationships in the field of semantic data modelling, such as inclusion, inheritance (is-a), aggregation, generalization, association [14], [8] a number of additional types of relationships [16] have been identified by researchers in other disciplines (knowledge representation in artificial intelligence, logic and programming languages, linguistics, cognitive psychology). In this section the framework for analysis of various kinds of relationships will be introduced. Although conceptual [10] and semantic data models [9], [13] have been studied quite intensively, there is no formal basis and not even an agreement upon definitions of knowledge representation primitives (as generalization, aggregation, classification, inheritance, etc.). There are only a few models based on rigorous mathematical grounds [1], where these notions are relatively well-understood. But, as a rule, most of them, deal with data modelling level. For designer is highly inconvenient to keep in mind database logical schema, when business modeling aspects are considered. So, primary objective of this chapter to introduce the set of modeling primitives for definition of (static logical level independent) concept schema, i.e. relaxation from the assumption about Universal Relation [17] as a critical assumption in the area of data modelling, while concentrating on the epistemological [3] aspects, which are common to all logical realizations.

At the initial stage of requirements modeling, static requirements can be unambiguously expressed in terms of conceptual dependencies [7]. Conceptual dependencies are special kind of constraints which can be used in order to specify some basic semantics of concepts, without considering a database schemata. Using data (i.e. functional, inclusion, multivalued) dependencies of relational database theory [12] for description of data representation or data processing structures (i.e. logical level requirements) is possible, but is not - for specification of data semantics.

In general sense, relationships [5] represent their extensions and semantics of relationships can be expressed by set of constraints, which are valid regarding extensions of relationships. The constraints of binary relationships [16] can be defined as the min/max cardinalities represented by minimum and maximum number of occurrences of the concept B that can exist for each occurrence of the concept A, and vice versa. Types of preferable constraints for binary relationships are the following:

- (1,1;1,1) - bijection, will be denoted by (graphical and textual notatation of constraint between A and B, correspondingly)

$$A \Leftrightarrow B.$$

- (1,1;0,1) - injection, will be denoted by

$$A \Rightarrow B.$$

- (1,1;0,*) - total function (here meaning of ' *' is many), will be denoted by

$$A \rightarrow B.$$

- (1,*;0,1) - surjective partial function, will be denoted by

$$A \Rightarrow \{B\}.$$

- (1,*;0,*) - total multivalued dependency, will be denoted by

$$A \rightarrow \{B\}.$$

- (1,1;1,*) - surjection, will be denoted by

$$A \Leftrightarrow \{B\}.$$

- (1,*;1,*) - mutual multivalued dependency, will be denoted by

$$A \rightarrow \{B\} \text{ and } B \rightarrow \{A\}.$$

We can define constraints for any binary aggregation relationship denoted by $(A \triangle B)$. Here: $\triangle$ - operation of aggregation between concepts A and B.

The dependency of inclusion of instance A to the class B will denoted by

$$A \prec B.$$

Aggregation relationship denotes its extension, which is represented by the set of instances. For example, extension of aggregation relationship between PERSON and AGE can be represented as:

PERSON △	AGE
John	35
Petras	60

Aggregation relationship itself is constraintless, i.e. with cardinalities (0,*;0,*). It should be noted that presented types of constraints are classified according to abstraction of aggregation [14]. The generalization constraints are based on inheritance dependency.

If injection, total functional or total multivalued dependency is specified from concept X to Y then Y can be interpreted as an attribute of concept X. Let Y_i be a set of injectionally dependent attributes, Y_f - set of totally functionally dependent attributes, Y_m - set of multivalued attributes. The inheritance dependency is defined by

$$A \rightarrow B$$

if and only if $A \Rightarrow B$, $B_f =< A_f$, $B_i =< A_i$, $B_m =< A_m$. Here: ' =<' means subset.

It should be noted that

$$A \leftrightarrow B \text{ if and only if } A \rightarrow B \text{ and } B \rightarrow A.$$

4 Conceptual Operations

Specifying the business rules, it is highly important to define them unambiguously (with respect to the conceptual constraints presented in previous chapter). Our investigations show, that unambiguity depends on semantics of the relationship, which serves as the basis for the definition of a business rule. In other words, the relationship which constitutes the basis for the definition of the rule, must be semantic holeless. The relationship does not contain semantic holes if and only if it has no empty (undefined) instances. For example, let us have concepts PERSON, DRIVER, DRIVERS_LICENSE and LICENSE. Populations of classes of concepts are presented in Fig.3.1.

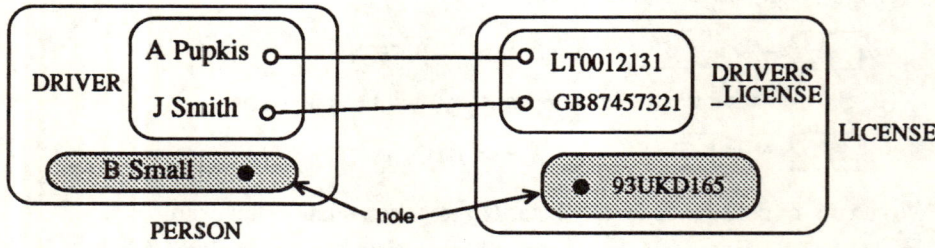

Fig.4.1. Example of Semantic Holes in two classes of Universe of Discourse

Empty instances should not be confused with incomplete instances [12]. According to the example, we may have many meaningful combinations of binary relationships between concepts PERSON, DRIVER, DRIVERS_LICENSE and LICENSE, but just one of them (DRIVER has DRIVERS_LICENSE) does not contain semantic holes. The examples of extensions of relationships are presented in figure Fig.4.2.

PERSON △	LICENSE
A Pupkis	LT0012131
J Smith	GB87457321
⊥	93UKD165
B Small	⊥

DRIVER △	DRIVERS LICENSE
A Pupkis	LT0012131
J Smith	GB87457321

Here: ⊥ - empty instance

Fig.4.2. Example of Extensions of Relationships

The rule will be safe against ambiguity, if it is defined on the basis of holeless relationships. Illumination of semantic holes can be performed using special operations of prefixing, grouping, specialization and negation. Expressions of definition of stores, agents, activities and business rules can be specified using operations of union, intersection, generalization and aggregation of concepts.

4.1 Operations for Elimination of Semantic Holes

- Operation of prefixing

Operation of prefixing is used for unambiguous identification of attributes with the same name specified for different entities in semantic data modelling [13].

Operation of prefixing (.) of B in the context A can be defined as A.B in the case of any dependency

$$(<=>, \rightarrow, =>)$$

from A to B. Operation of prefixing A.B gives us possibility to specify subclass of B instances having meaningful associations with instances of class A. Example of prefixing of concepts is presented in Fig.4.3.

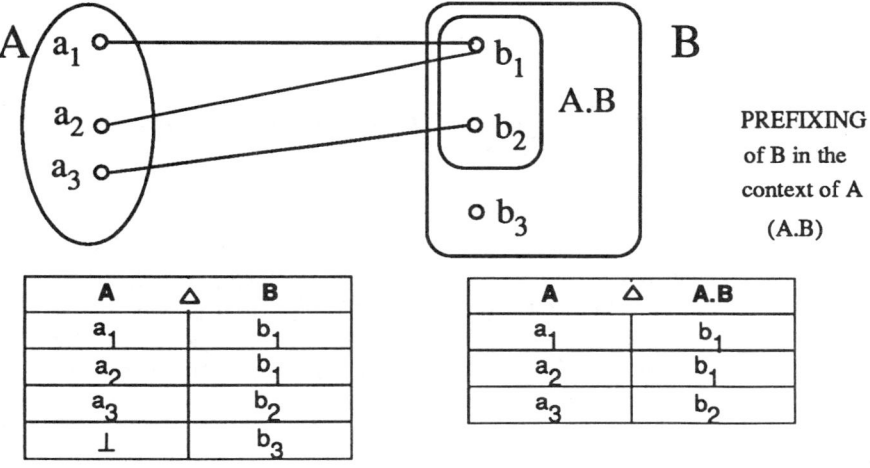

Fig.4.3. Operation of Prefixing of Concepts

Operation of prefixing serves as a means for generation of compound concepts in order to unambiguously specify their names.

- **Operation of grouping**

Operation of grouping can be realized as grouping of classes in Semantic Database Model [8].
Operation of grouping (:) of A in the context of B can be defined as A:B or A:{B} if there exist aggregation relationship between A and B, i.e.
$$(A \triangle B).$$
Operation of grouping A:B gives us a possibility to specify instances of concept A as a meaningful pairs of associations of instances between A and B. Example of grouping of concepts is presented in Fig.4.4.

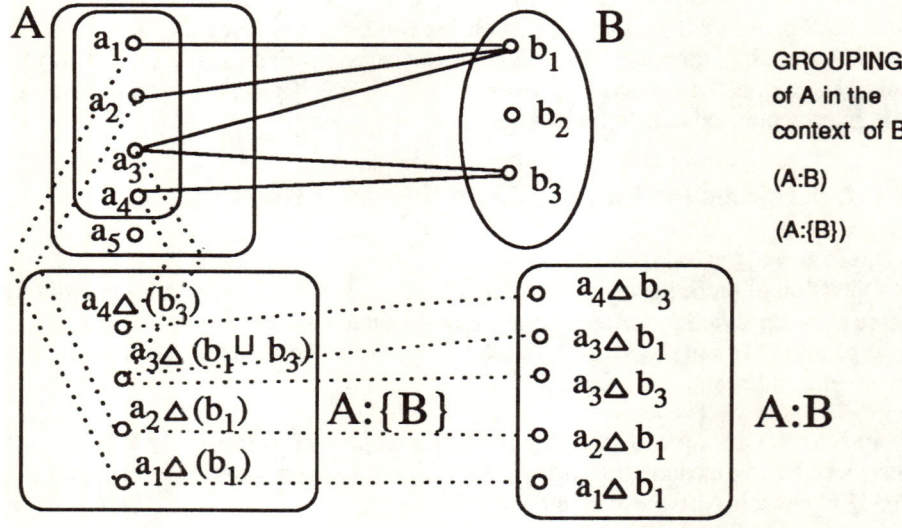

Fig.4.4. Operation of Grouping of Concepts

Operation of grouping serves as a means for illumination of semantic holes and unambiguously specify names of concepts.

- **Operations of Specialization and Negation**

If the concept B is an instance of concept X which is totally dependent from concept A and concept X has no correspondent name in natural language, then the semantic hole can be deleted by operation of specialization or negation.

Operation of specialization ([ ]) of A in the context B can be defined by A[B] if there exists exactly one association between B and every instance of subclass A. The example of specialization is presented in Fig.4.5.

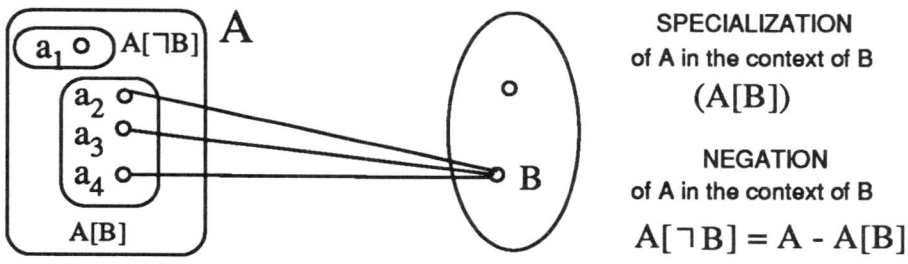

Fig.4.5. Operations of Specialization and Negation of Concepts

Negative information can be expressed using operation of negation. Operation of negation can be defined as follows:

$$A[\neg B] = A - A[B].$$

Using operation of specialization and negation, we are able to create names of more specific concepts. Thereby, we are able to illuminate semantic holes, i.e. to define more specific holeless structure of the relationship.

4.2 Aggregation and Generalization Operations

- Aggregation of Concepts

Operation of aggregation serves as a means of generation of adequate (according to the concept model) aggregation relationships, which can be assumed as definitions of stores or derived relationships. Valid aggregations of concepts can be constructed according to the following rules:
1) if X and X.Z then $(X \triangle X.Z)$,
2) if X.Y and X.Z then $X.(Y \triangle Z)$,
3) if X[Y] and X.Z then $(X[Y] \triangle X[Y].Z)$,
4) if X:Y and X.Z then $(X:Y \triangle (X:Y).Z)$.

It should be noted that, in general, X, Y and Z can denote complex definition (compound expression) of concept name.

- Intersection of Concepts

Conceptual intersection operation serves for definition of derivation rules of more complex concepts as a greater common specialization [15] of other ones and is similar to intensional sum primitive [10]. Any two concepts X and Y have their greater common specialization denoted by intersection

$$X \sqcap Y.$$

Operation of intersection satisfies the following axioms:
1) $(X \sqcap Y) \longrightarrow X$,
2) $(X \sqcap Y) \longrightarrow Y$,
3) $X \longrightarrow Y$ and $X \longrightarrow Z$ if and only if $X \longrightarrow (Y \sqcap Z)$.

Intersection of concepts is defined as intersection in extensional and in intensional sense. Interpretation of intersection in extensional sense is understood as intersection of extensions of classes X and Y and in intentional sense - as union of intensionals (attributes) of classes X and Y (see axioms). If the greater common specialization of intersection is empty element, then concepts X and Y are independent. Independence of concepts is denoted by expression

$(X \sqcap Y) = \bot$. The expression $X \rightarrow (Y \sqcap Z)$
denotes dependence of concepts Y and Z in comparison of concept X as their specialization.

- Union of Concepts

Conceptual union operation serves for definition of derivation rules of more complex concepts as a least common generalization [15] of other ones and is similar to intensional product primitive [10]. Any two concepts X and Y have their least common generalization denoted by intersection

$$X \sqcup Y.$$

Operation of intersection satisfies the following axioms:
1) $X \rightarrow (X \sqcup Y)$,
2) $Y \rightarrow (X \sqcup Y)$;
3) $X \rightarrow Z$ and $Y \rightarrow Z$ if and only if $(X \sqcup Y) \rightarrow Z$.

Union of concepts is defined (see axioms) as union in extensional and in intensional sense. Interpretation of union in extensional sense is understood as union of extensions of classes X and Y and in intentional sense - as intersection of intensionals (attributes) of classes X and Y.

- Generalization of Concepts

Generalization primitive gives us possibility to describe derivation rules of more general concepts using similar specialized ones and is consistent with abstraction of generalization [14] exploited in semantic data modelling for the definition of classes in terms of disjoint entities.

Generalization of two concepts X and Y as concept Z is defined by

$$Z \leftrightarrow (X \triangledown Y) \text{ if and only if } (X \triangledown Y) \rightarrow Z, \quad (X \triangledown Y) \leftarrow Z.$$

Here: $Z \leftarrow (X \triangledown Y)$ if and only if $(X \sqcup Y) \rightarrow Z$, $(X \sqcap Y) = \bot$,
$Z \rightarrow (X \triangledown Y)$ if and only if $(X \sqcup Y) \leftarrow Z$, $(X \sqcap Y) = \bot$.

Conceptual design operations of union, intersection, aggregation and generalization can be used among any number of concepts.

5 Derived Concepts

Conceptual dependencies could be interpreted as database integrity constraints. Constraints constitute the ground for definition of so called derivation rules which represent a conceptual dynamic relationships. Derivation rules usually correspond to queries or transactions at a logical database design phase. Elements of derivation rules are connected by aggregation and generalization (union, intersection) operators, and must be specified or derivable by special inference rules [7] due to specified conceptual constraints. Derived compound concepts serve as extension of specification of universe of discourse and are adequate according to conceptual schema.

Compound concepts are derived according to the following inference rules:
1) If A => B, B => C then A => B.C ;

Here, the additional dependencies could be derived, i.e.

If B.C then B.C => C and if B => C then B.C <=> B .
The example of derived entity PASSPORT.NUMBER is presented in Fig.5.1.

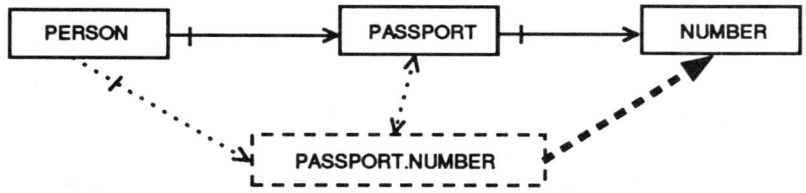

Fig.5.1. Example of derived entity PASSPORT.NUMBER

2) If A→ B , B→ C then A→ B.C ;

The example of derived entity CAR.GARAGE is presented in Fig.5.2.

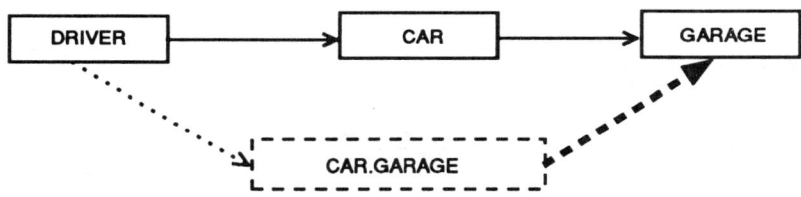

Fig.5.2. Example of derived entity CAR.GARAGE

3) If A → {B} , B → C then A:B → B.C ;

The example of derived entity TIME.LENGTH is presented in Fig.5.3.

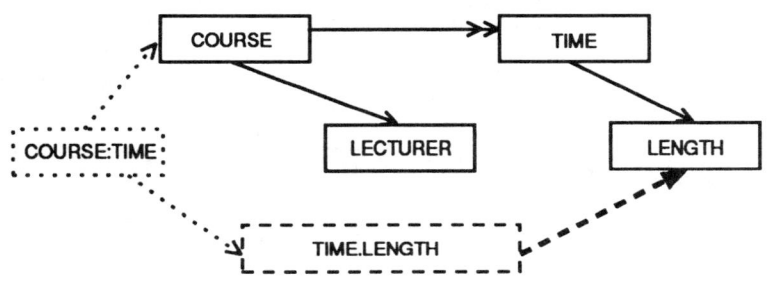

Fig.5.3. Example of derived entities COURSE:TIME and TIME.LENGTH

It should be noted that concept COURSE:TIME is populated by instances of COURSE combined by particular TIME instances. For example, let us have course of databases held in spring and autumn 1994. In that case, concept COURSE:TIME will be populated by two instances 'Databases Spring 1994' and 'Databases Autumn 1994'.

4) If A -< B , C → B then (C[A] ∇ C[¬A]) ←→ C ;

The example of derived entity PERSON[MALE] is presented in Fig.5.4.

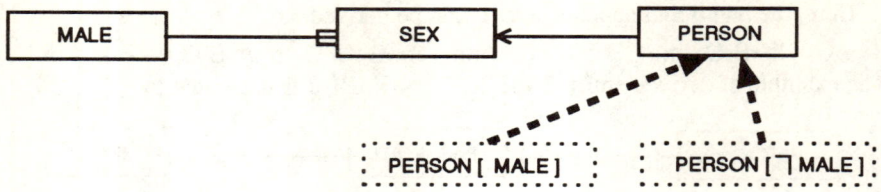

Fig.5.4. Example of derived entities PERSON[MALE] and PERSON[⌐ MALE]

Derivation of specialized entities make sense only in cases, if class of instance (SEX) has no correspondent name in natural language.

Using presented operations of prefixing, grouping, negation specialization, union, intersection, aggregation and generalization, in principle, is possible to define derivation rules of dynamic attributes, queries, data stores, business constraints and rules. Let us have the following specification of conceptual constraints for 'Telecom' application domain presented in Fig.5.5.

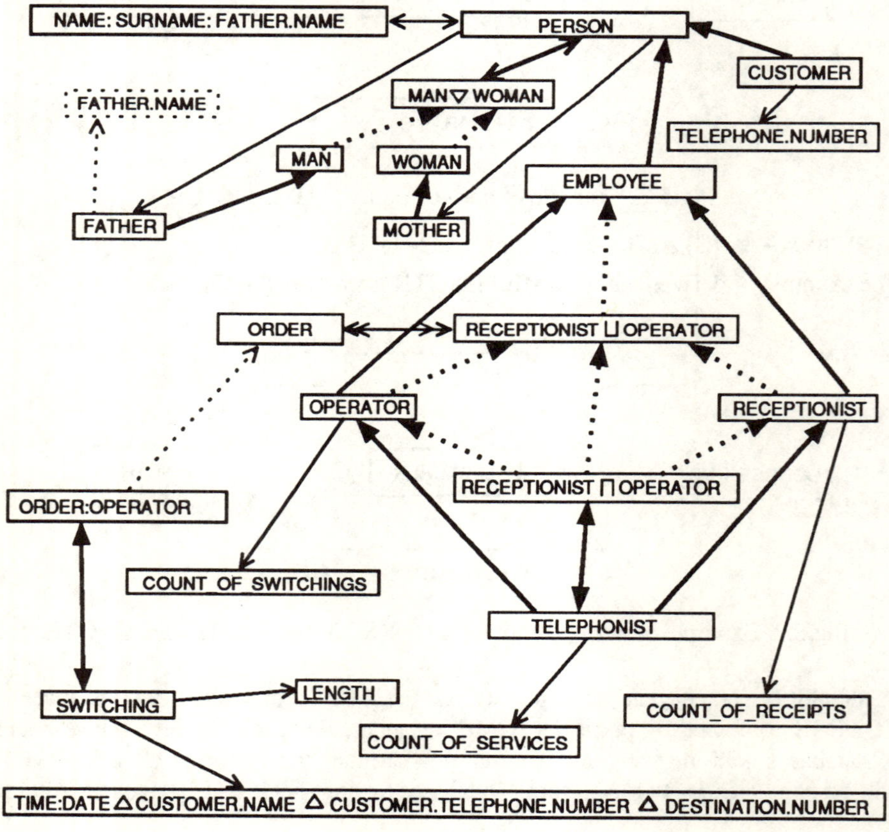

Fig.5.5. Examples of Conceptual Constraints

It is possible to describe dynamic rules by using specified or derived names of conceptual model. Sometimes, we have to specify several functions on classes in order describe semantics of business. The basic most primitive functions are the following: MIN, MAX, AVERAGE, TOTAL, COUNT, FIRST, LAST, NEXT, PREVIOUS, CURRENT. Actually, it is possible to introduce any number of well-defined functions, for example, such as arithmetical, i.e. +, -, x, /, ... The only requirement is that the semantics of particular function have to be implemented or specified on a basis of installed computer software. For example, one could have the following rules for definition of functional constraints:

1) TOTAL (COUNT_OF_SWITCHINGS) >TOTAL (COUNT_OF_RECEIPTS)
2) SWITCHING = ORDER:OPERATOR
3) TELEPHONIST.COUNT_OF_SERVICES =
TELEPHONIST.COUNT_OF_SWITCHINGS + TELEPHONIST.COUNT_OF_RECEIPTS
4) RECEIPT = ORDER:RECEPTIONIST
5) RECEPTIONIST.COUNT_OF_RECEIPTS = COUNT (RECEIPT:RECEPTIONIST)
6) OPERATOR.COUNT_OF_SWITCHINGS = COUNT (SWITCHING:OPERATOR)

These rules are defined on a basis of conceptual model, presented in Fig.5.5. The semantics of each rule is clear by definition.

6 Concluding Remarks

Lack of relativeness of interpretation of basic classes (categories such as entity, relationship, attribute, etc.) is one of the main shortages of semantic data models applying them into practice of business modeling. The sharp distinction of categories can be a reason of different representation of the same universe of discourse, even when the same modelling primitives are used. These ambiguities are artificial, i.e. representation primitives dependent. Other subset of ambiguities are known as a naming conflicts. They are usually arising when the business modeling is performed by separate designers independently. The origin of those ambiguities is quite natural. In order to avoid natural ambiguities, the names of concepts must be extended according to the special inference rules, using conceptual operations of prefixing, grouping specialization and negation.

The dependencies and relationships of conceptual model, constitute the basis for modeling of rules and complex constraints. The conceptual dependencies should be specified as precisely as possible. If the designer would define weaker primitives, then incomplete description of semantics of relationships can cause incompleteness in the specification of requirements. Constraints are of interest because they capture semantic detail about structure of relationships and control the procedure of definition of compound conceptual expressions, which are assumed as definitions of data stores, derived concepts, relationships, business rules and constraints in terms of most primitive elements.

7 References

1. S Abiteboul, R Hull A Formal Semantic Database Model. ACM Transactions on Database Systems, vol. 12, No 4, pp.525-565,1987.
2. C Batini, M Lenzerini, M Moscarini. Views Integration. In: Methodology and Tools for Data Base design, North-Holland Pub. Co., 1983, pp.57-84.
3. R Brachman On the Epistemological Status of Semantic Networks. Associative Networks, Academic Press, pp. 3-50, 1979.
4. J A Bubenko Extending the Scope of Information Modelling. Fourth International Workshop on the Deductive Approach to Information Systems and Databases, Polytechnical University of Catalonia, pp.73-97, 1993.
5. P P Chen The Entity-Relationship Model: Towards a unified view of data. ACM Transactions on database systems 1,1, 1976, pp. 9-36.
6. C Couvet, C Proix, C Rolland An Expert System for Requirements Engineering. Third Int. Conf. on Advanced Information System Engineering CAiSE'91,Springer-Verlag, pp.31-49,1991.
7. R Gustas Towards Understanding and Formal Definition of Conceptual Constraints. Proc. of the Fourth European - Japanese seminar on Information Modeling and Knowledge Bases, May 31 - June 03, Kista, Sweden, 1994.
8. M Hammer and D McLeod Database Description with SDM: A Semantic Database Model, ACM Transactions on Database Systems, Vol.6, No.3, pp.351-386, 1981.
9. R Hull and R King Semantic Database Modelling: Survey, Applications, and Research Issues. ACM Computing Surveys, Vol.19, No.3, pp.201-260,1987.
10. H Kangassalo Foundations of Conceptual Modelling: A Theory Construction View. Information Modelling and Knowledge Bases, IOS Press, pp.19-35, 1990.
11. P Loucopoulos Conceptual Modeling. In: Conceptual Modeling, Databases and Case: An Integrated view of Information Systems development, John Wiley, 1992, pp. 1-26.
12. D Maier The Theory of Relational Databases. Computer Science Press, Rockville, 1983.
13. J Peckham and F Maryansky Semantic Data Models. ACM Computing Surveys, Vol.20, No.3, pp.153-189, 1988.
14. J M Smith and D C P Smith Data Base Abstractions: Aggregation and Generalization, ACM Transactions on Database Systems, Vol.2, No2, pp.105-133,1977.
15. J Sowa Conceptual Structures. Addison-Wesley Publishing Company, 1984.
16. V C Storey Understanding Semantic Relationships. VLDB Journal, Vol.2, pp.455-487, 1993.
17. J D Ulman Principles of Database Systems. Computer Science Press, Rockville, 1982.
18. J J van Griethuisen (ed.) Concepts and Terminology for the Conceptual Schema and Information Base, Report ISO TC97/SC5/WG5, No 695, 1982.
19. E Yourdon Modern Structured Analysis, Prentice-Hall, Inc., 1989.

Inheritance of Object Behavior - Consistent Extension of Object Life Cycles

Gerti Kappel

Department of Computer Science, University of Linz
A-4040 Linz, Austria, email: gerti@ifs.uni-linz.ac.at

Michael Schrefl

Department of Information Systems, University of Linz
A-4040 Linz, Austria, email: schrefl@dke.uni-linz.ac.at

Abstract

Inheritance is one of the most prominent features of object-oriented design. Object types are organized in hierarchies in which subtypes inherit the structure as well as the behavior of supertypes. As inheritance of behavior is concerned, the discussion has mainly focused on inheritance of single activities in the past. Object behavior, however, is specified at two interrelated levels of detail: at the activity level *and* at the object type level. The latter is specified in terms of object life cycles that identify legal sequences of states and activities.

In this paper we treat inheritance of object life cycles in the realm of Behavior Diagrams, which are based on Petri nets. A behavior diagram of an object type models the possible life cycles of its instances by states, activities, and arcs corresponding to places, transitions, and arcs of Petri nets. In an inheritance hierarchy, subtypes usually specialize supertypes in two ways: by extension and by refinement. For Behavior Diagrams, extension means adding activities, states, and arcs; and refinement means expanding activities and states in subnets. The main contribution of this paper is a set of sufficient and necessary conditions to check whether a behavior diagram B' consistently extends another behavior diagram B.

1 Introduction

Much of the work on object-oriented system development deals with inheritance of object types to support reuse and, thus, to increase productivity. The prominence of inheritance is stressed by one of the most common definitions of object-orientedness which comprises objects, object types, and inheritance [26]. An object has an *internal structure* represented by a set of attributes and a certain *behavior* represented by a set of interrelated activities. An object is an instance of an object type, which specifies the structure and behavior of a set of similar objects. Inheritance defines a relationship between two object types, where one object type called the subtype inherits structure and behavior from the other one called the supertype. The inherited structure and behavior may be further specialized in the subtype.

Inheritance of object structure is analogous to the classical notion of specialization/generalization of attributes in semantic data models [8, 24], and will not be further discussed in this paper.

Inheritance of object behavior has mainly focused so far on inheritance of single, isolated activities (e.g., [25, 27]). For example, consider object type **RESERVATION** with activities checkAvailability and consume. The definition of legal execution sequences of activities - e.g., consume can only be invoked after checkAvailability on a reservation instance - is not part of object type definitions in object-oriented languages, where activities of an object type are implemented and inherited independently from each other.

With object-oriented specification methods, such as OMT [20], OOSA [7], OOAD [3] and OBD [11] to mention just a few, object behavior is specified at two interrelated levels of detail. For example, behavior diagrams [11] specify at the activity level the signature of an activity by identifying types and preconditions of input parameters, and the type and the postcondition of the return value. At the object type level, object behavior is specified in terms of object life cycles that identify legal sequences of states and activities. Preconditions and postconditions of activities are specified by their prestates and poststates, respectively. Continuing our example from above, the postcondition, i.e., the poststate, of the activity checkAvailability is at the same time the precondition, i.e., the prestate, of the activity confirm, thus stating that checkAvailability has to be successfully finished before confirm may be invoked.

Object behavior as well as inheritance of object behavior is specified at two interrelated levels of detail. Applying inheritance at the activity level resolves to inheriting signatures and specializing them, i.e., adding parameters, redefining types of parameters to subtypes, and strengthening pre- and postconditions. The notion of inheritance at the activity level is fairly well understood in literature [4, 25, 27]. Applying inheritance at the object type level resolves to inheriting object life cycles and specializing them. However, there exist no common understanding on how to specialize object life cycles and which criteria to follow. A solution to this problem is the main contribution of this paper.

Our research vehicle and representative of an object-oriented specification language are Object/Behavior Diagrams [11]. We discuss the inheritance of object life cycles in the realm of Behavior Diagrams which are based on Petri nets. A behavior diagram of an object type represents the possible life cycles of its instances by activities, states, and arcs corresponding to transitions, places, and arcs of Petri nets.

There are several possibilities to inherit and to specialize object life cycles ranging from no restriction at all, called *arbitrary inheritance*, to allowing no specialization at all, called *strict inheritance*. Whereas the former does not support any notion of substitutability in the sense that an instance of a subtype can be used when an instance of a supertype is expected [27], the latter prohibits the specification of new activities in the subtype at all. Whereas the former notion is too unrestricted to build reusable and reliable systems, the latter notion is too restrictive. Instead, we propose to inherit and consistently extend object life cycles based on the notion of *consistent extension*.

Object life cycles may be specialized by extension and by refinement. Extension means adding activities, states, and arcs. Refinement means expanding inherited activities and states into subdiagrams, which consist of newly added activities, states, and arcs in turn [12, 22]. In this paper we restrict our attention to consistent extension of object life cycles. Consistent extension requires that each possible life cycle of a subtype disregarding newly added activities and states must also be a life cycle of the supertype. Or in other words, consistent extension requires that a life cycle of the supertype reflects in each life cycle of the subtype. We propose rules for inheriting and consistently extending object life cycles in subtypes, and provide sufficient and necessary conditions for checking whether the behavior diagram of a subtype is a consistent extension of the behavior diagram of its supertype.

The paper is organized as follows: in the next section we give a short introduction to Object/Behavior Diagrams and provide a formal definition of the consistent extension of object life cycles based on behavior diagrams. In section 3, we proof that there exist sufficient and necessary rules for checking the consistent extension of behavior diagrams. Section 4 discusses related work and uncovers directions of further research.

2 Consistent Extension of Object Life Cycles

Object/Behavior Diagrams are an object-oriented graphical specification language developed for the design of object-oriented databases [10, 11]. Object/Behavior Diagrams represent the structure of objects in object diagrams and the behavior in behavior diagrams. For the scope of this paper we restrict our attention to behavior diagrams.

Behavior diagrams depict the behavior of (the instances of) an object type by a set of states, a set of activities, and a set of arcs connecting states with activities and vice versa. Each of the states represents a particular period, each of the activities an event in the life cycle of the instances of the object type. All possible life cycles of instances of an object type have a common start state called the *initial state*. The principle idea behind behavior diagrams stems from Petri nets [19]. States correspond to places of Petri nets, activities to transitions.

Definition 1 (Behavior Diagram) *A behavior diagram $B_O = (S_O, T_O, F_O, s_\alpha)$ of an object type O consists of a set of states S_O, a set of activities T_O, $T_O \cap S_O = \emptyset$, and a set of arcs $F_O \subseteq (S_O \times T_O) \cup (T_O \times S_O)$, such that $\forall t \in T_O : (\exists s_i \in S_O : (s_i, t) \in F_O) \land (\exists s_j \in S_O : (t, s_j) \in F_O)$. There is a distinguished state of S_O, the initial state s_α.*

Instances of an object type which reside in states correspond to individual tokens of a Petri net. We say an activity $t \in T_O$ *consumes* a token from a state $s \in S_O$ iff $(s, t) \in F_O$, and $t \in T_O$ *produces* a token into $s \in S_O$ iff $(t, s) \in F_O$. In addition, we say a state $s \in S_O$ is a *prestate* of an activity $t \in T_O$ iff $(s, t) \in F_O$, and $s \in S_O$ is a *poststate* of $t \in T_O$ iff $(t, s) \in F_O$. Due to the underlying Petri net semantics a behavior diagram determines the legal sequences of states and activities, and thus the legal sequences in which activities may be applied: an activity may be applied on an object if the object is contained in every prestate of the activity. If an activity on some object has been executed successfully, the object is contained in every poststate of the activity but in no prestate unless that prestate is also a poststate. Unlike Petri nets, where a transition is automatically fired if every prestate contains a token, an activity in a behavior diagram must be explicitly invoked for an object which is in every prestate

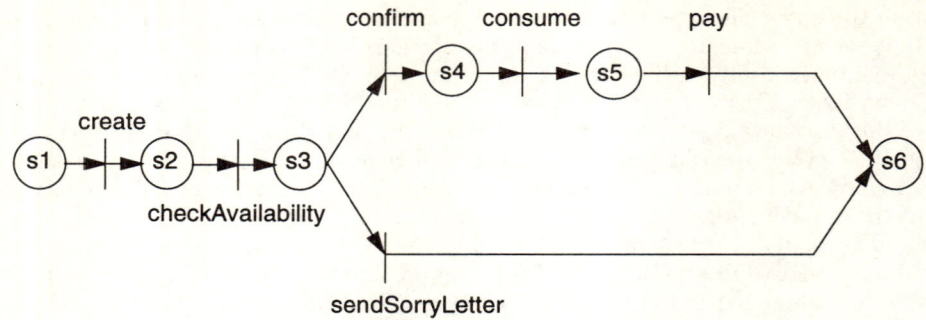

Figure 1: Behavior diagram of object type **RESERVATION**

of the activity. In addition, and unlike Petri nets, activities take some time. Therefore, during the execution of an activity on an object, the object resides in an implicit state named after the activity. This state is referred to as an *activity state*. Thus, we can say that every instance of an object type is at any point in time in one or several (activity) states of its object type, which is commonly referred to as *life cycle state* of the object type.

Definition 2 (Life Cycle State) *A* life cycle state (LCS) σ *of an object type* O *is a subset of* $S_O \cup T_O$.

Definition 3 (Start of an activity) *An activity* $t \in T_O$ *can be started on a life cycle state* σ, *if the set of prestates of* t, $\{s \in S_O \mid (s,t) \in F_O\}$, *is contained in* σ. *The start of activity* t *on LCS* σ *yields the life cycle state* $\sigma' = \sigma \setminus \{s \in S_O \mid (s,t) \in F_O\} \cup \{t\}$.

Definition 4 (Completion of an activity) *An activity* $t \in T_O$ *can be completed on a life cycle state* σ, *if* t *is in* σ. *The completion of activity* t *on* σ *yields the life cyclce state* $\sigma' = \sigma \setminus \{t\} \cup \{s \in S_O \mid (t,s) \in F_O\}$.

Example 1 Consider the behavior of object type **RESERVATION**, which generalizes the business processes of reservations of hotel rooms, theater tickets, and cars. The behavior diagram of **RESERVATION** is depicted in Figure 1. A state is depicted by a named circle, and an activity is depicted by a named vertical bar which is connected by a set of arcs to its pre- and poststates. (Note, to keep the example as small as possible we have simplified the graphical representation of behavior diagrams [11] using just abstract names for states.) □

A behavior diagram of an object type specifies all legal sequences of states and activities, i.e., all legal sequences of life cycle states. A particular sequence of life cycle states of an object type is referred to as *life cycle occurrence* of that object type.

Definition 5 (Life cycle occurrence) *A* life cycle occurrence (LCO) γ *of object type* O *is a sequence of life cycle states* $\sigma_1, \ldots, \sigma_n$, *such that* $\sigma_1 = \{s_\alpha\}$, *and for* $i = 1 \ldots n - 1$ *either* $\sigma_i = \sigma_{i+1}$, *or there exists an activity* $t \in T_O$ *such that either* t *can be started on* σ_i *and the start of* t *yields* σ_{i+1} *or* σ_i *contains* t *and the completion of* t *yields* σ_{i+1}.

Example 2 Given the behavior diagram in Figure 1. A possible life cycle occurrence of object type RESERVATION is [{s1}, {create}, {s2}, {checkAvailability}, {s3}, {confirm}, {s4}, {consume}, {s5}]. □

We restrict our discussion of inheritance of object behavior to a meaningful subclass of Behavior Diagrams, to activity reduced and safe behavior diagrams.

Definition 6 (Reachable life cycle states) *The set of reachable life cycle states $R(\sigma_\alpha)$ of a behavior diagram $B_O = (S_O, T_O, F_O, \sigma_\alpha)$ contains every LCS σ that can be reached from σ_α by starting or completing any sequence of activities in T_O.*

Definition 7 (Safe Behavior Diagram) *A behavior diagram $B_O = (S_O, T_O, F_O, \sigma_\alpha)$ is safe, if there exists no LCS $\sigma \in R(\sigma_\alpha)$ such that (i) some activity $t \in T_O$ can be started on σ which contains already t, or (ii) some activity $t \in T_O$ can be completed on σ, and σ contains already some poststate of t.*

Definition 8 (Potentially applicable activity) *An activity $t \in T_O$ is potentially applicable if there exists a life cycle occurrence $\gamma = \sigma_1 \ldots \sigma_n (n > 0)$ such that t can be started on σ_n.*

Definition 9 (Activity reduced behavior diagram) *A behavior diagram $B_O = (S_O, T_O, F_O, s_\alpha)$ is activity reduced if every $t \in T_O$ is potentially applicable.*

To restrict our discussion to activity reduced and safe behavior diagrams is meaningful in practice. First, activities which are not potentially applicable have no influence on object behavior. Such activities correspond to program statements never reached. Second, unsafe nets contradict the intention of behavior diagrams to identify by a state or an activity a single, specific processing state of an object.

Consistent extension of object behavior in type hierarchies requires that each possible life cycle of an instance of a subtype is, disregarding newly added activities and states, also a life cycle according to the supertype. To make two object life cycles comparable and to be able to check if one is a consistent extension of the other, we define the notion of restricted life cycle states and restricted life cycle occurrences.

Definition 10 (Restriction of a life cycle state) *The restriction of a life cycle state σ' of an object type O' to object type O, written σ'/O, is defined as $\sigma = \sigma' \cap (S_O \cup T_O)$.*

Definition 11 (Restriction of a life cycle occurrence) *The restriction of a life cycle occurrence $\gamma' = \sigma'_1, \ldots, \sigma'_n$ of object type O' to object type O, written γ'/O, is defined as $\sigma_1, \ldots, \sigma_n$, where for $i = 1 \ldots n$: $\sigma_i = \sigma'_i/O$.*

Example 3 Given the behavior diagram of object type CAR_RESERVATION in figure 2. A possible life cycle occurrence is [{s1}, {create}, {s2}, {checkAvailability}, {s3}, {confirm}, {s4, s7}, {s4, makeInsurance}, {s4, s8}, {consume, s8}, {s5, s8}]. The restriction of this life cycle occurrence to object type RESERVATION yields [{s1}, {create}, {s2}, {checkAvailability}, {s3}, {confirm}, {s4}, {s4}, {s4}, {consume}, {s5}]. □

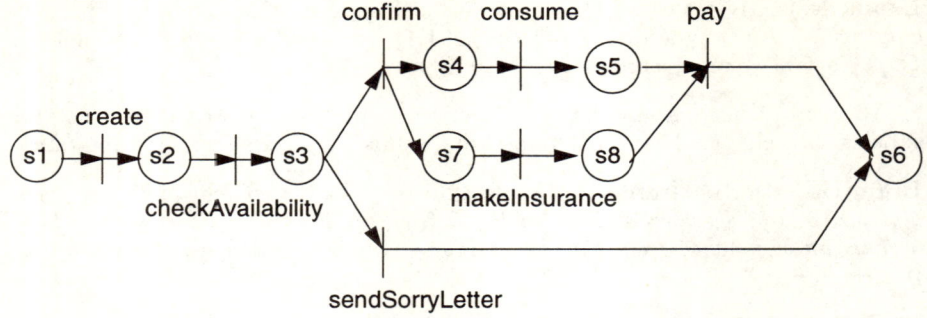

Figure 2: Behavior diagram of object type CAR_RESERVATION

Now we are ready for the formal definition of the consistent extension of object life cycles based on behavior diagrams.

Definition 12 (Consistent extension) *A behavior diagram* $B_{O'} = (S_{O'}, T_{O'}, F_{O'}, s'_\alpha)$ *is a* consistent extension *of a behavior diagram* $B_O = (S_O, T_O, F_O, s_\alpha)$, *if for every life cycle occurrence* γ' *of object type* O', γ'/O *is a life cycle occurrence of* B_O.

Example 4 The behavior diagram depicted in Figure 2 is a consistent extension of the behavior diagram depicted in Figure 1. Thus every life cycle occurrence of object type CAR_RESERVATION to object type RESERVATION is also a life cycle occurrence of object type RESERVATION (cf. example 2). This is shown for a particular life cycle occurrence in example 3. □

The question remains, how activities and states may be added in subtypes to comply to consistent inheritance? The next section provides an answer to this question. A set of sufficient and necessary rules to check whether a behavior diagram B' consistently extends another behavior diagram B is introduced.

3 Sufficient and Necessary Rules

The rule of inheritance requires that the initial state of the behavior diagram $B_{O'}$ of an object type O' is identical to the initial state of the behavior diagram B_O of its supertype O, and that every activity inherited by O' from O has in $B_{O'}$ at least the prestates and poststates as the activity has in B_O.

Rule 1 (Inheritance)
1. $s'_\alpha = s_\alpha$
2. $t \in T_{O'} \land t \in T_O \land (s, t) \in F_O \Rightarrow (s, t) \in F_{O'}$
3. $t \in T_{O'} \land t \in T_O \land (t, s) \in F_O \Rightarrow (t, s) \in F_{O'}$

The rule of immediate definition of prestates and poststates requires that no arc is added in $B_{O'}$ between two elements which already belong to B_O. (Note, an element is either a state or an activity.)

Rule 2 (Immediate Definition of Prestates and Poststates)
1. $(s,t) \in F_{O'} \land s \in S_O \land t \in T_O \Rightarrow (s,t) \in F_O$
2. $(t,s) \in F_{O'} \land s \in S_O \land t \in T_O \Rightarrow (t,s) \in F_O$

The rule of parallel extension requires that an activity added in $B_{O'}$ does not consume from an inherited state and does not produce into an inherited state.

Rule 3 (Parallel Extension)
1. $(s,t) \in F_{O'} \land t \in T_{O'} \land t \notin T_O \Rightarrow s \notin S_O$
2. $(t,s) \in F_{O'} \land t \in T_{O'} \land t \notin T_O \Rightarrow s \notin S_O$

The following theorem states that the rule of inheritance, the rule of immediate definition of prestates and poststates, and the rule of parallel extension are sufficient and necessary conditions to check whether some safe and activity reduced behavior diagram extends another safe and activity reduced behavior diagram.

Theorem 1 *Let $B_O = (S_O, T_O, F_O, s_\alpha)$ and $B_{O'} = (S_{O'}, T_{O'}, F_{O'}, s'_\alpha)$ be safe and activity reduced behavior diagrams. $B_{O'}$ is a consistent extension of B_O if and only if rules 1, 2, and 3 are obeyed.*

Proof:
I. (*if* direction; rule 1, rule 2, and rule 3 are sufficient)
To proof the if-direction we have to show that if rule 1, rule 2, and rule 3 hold then for every life cycle occurrence γ' object type O' it is true that γ'/O is a life cycle occurrence of O. The proof is by induction over the length n of the life cycle occurrence $\gamma' = \sigma'_1, \ldots, \sigma'_n$.
Induction basis (n = 1): $\gamma' = \{s_\alpha\}$. Then, by rule 1, $\{s'_\alpha\} = \{s_\alpha\} = \gamma'/O$ is a valid LCO of O.
Induction hypothesis (n > 1): Assume $\sigma'_1/O, \ldots, \sigma'_{n-1}/O$ is a valid LCO of object type O. Then, $\sigma'_1/O, \ldots, \sigma'_n/O$ is one, too.
Proof of induction hypothesis: As γ' is a LCO of O', σ'_n has been obtained from σ'_{n-1} by starting or completing some activity $t \in T_{O'}$. Activity t can also be in T_O or not. To proof the induction hypothesis, we consider each of the following four possible cases:

1. $t \in T_O$, start of t: By rule 1, all prestates of t in B_O are also prestates of t in $B_{O'}$. Thus, if t has been applicable in $B_{O'}$ on σ'_{n-1}, t can be applied in B_O on $\sigma_{n-1} = \sigma'_{n-1}/O$. Now, we have to show that applying t in B_O on $\sigma_{n-1} = \sigma'_{n-1}/O$ leads to $\sigma_n = \sigma'_n/O$. σ'_n is obtained from σ'_{n-1} by removing all prestates of t in $B_{O'}$ and by adding t. By rule 1, t in $B_{O'}$ removes from σ'_{n-1} *at least* all states that t in B_O removes from σ_{n-1}. By rule 2, t in $B_{O'}$ removes from σ'_{n-1} *at most* all states that t in B_O removes from σ_{n-1}. Thus, as the elements of $(S_O \cup T_O)$ in σ'_{n-1} are concerned, starting t in $B_{O'}$ removes from and adds to σ'_{n-1} the same elements as starting t in B_O removes from and adds to σ_{n-1}. Therefore, starting t in B_O on $\sigma_{n-1} = \sigma'_{n-1}/O$ leads to $\sigma_n = \sigma'_n/O$, and $\sigma'_1/O, \ldots, \sigma'_n/O$ is a valid LCO of O.

2. $t \in T_O$, completion of t: If t can be completed in $B_{O'}$ on σ'_{n-1}, t is in σ'_{n-1}. By assumption, $t \in T_O$. Thus, σ'_{n-1}/O contains t and t can be completed in B_O on $\sigma_{n-1} = \sigma'_{n-1}/O$. Now, we have to show that completing t in B_O on σ_{n-1} leads to $\sigma_n = \sigma'_n/O$. σ'_n is obtained from σ'_{n-1} by removing t and by adding all poststates of t in $B_{O'}$. By rule 1, t in $B_{O'}$ adds to σ'_{n-1} at *least* all states that t in B_O adds to σ_{n-1}. By rule 2, t in $B_{O'}$ adds to σ'_{n-1} at *most* all states that t in B_O adds to σ_{n-1}. Thus, as the elements of $(S_O \cup T_O)$ in σ'_{n-1} are concerned, completing t in $B_{O'}$ removes from and adds to σ'_{n-1} the same elements as completing t in B_O removes from and adds to σ_{n-1}. Therefore, completing t in B_O on $\sigma_{n-1} = \sigma'_{n-1}/O$ leads to $\sigma_n = \sigma'_n/O$, and $\sigma'_1/O, \ldots, \sigma'_n/O$ is a valid LCO of O.

3. $t \notin T_O$, start of t: By rule 3, starting t on σ'_{n-1} for gaining σ'_n means removing states not belonging to S_O and adding t not belonging to T_O. Thus, $\sigma'_{n-1}/O = \sigma'_n/O$, and $\sigma'_1/O, \ldots, \sigma'_n/O$ is a valid LCO of O.

4. $t \notin T_O$, completion of t: By rule 3, completing t on σ'_{n-1} for gaining σ'_n means removing t not belonging to T_O and adding states not belonging to S_O. Thus, $\sigma'_{n-1}/O = \sigma'_n/O$, and $\sigma'_1/O, \ldots, \sigma'_n/O$ is a valid LCO of O.

2. (*only if* direction; rule 1, rule 2 and rule 3 are necessary)
To proof the only-if-direction, we show by contradiction that rules 1, 2, and 3 are necessary.

1. **Rule 1, part 1** Assume part 1 of rule 1 is not obeyed, i.e., $\sigma'_\alpha \neq \sigma_\alpha$. σ'_α is a LCO of $B_{O'}$. But, as $\sigma'_\alpha \neq \sigma_\alpha$, σ'_α/O is no LCO of O.

2. **Rule 1, part 2** Assume part 2 of rule 1 is not obeyed. Then, there exist a state $s \in S_O$ and an activity $t \in T_O$, such that $(s,t) \in F_O$, but $(s,t) \notin F_{O'}$. We show, there is a LCO γ' for O' such that γ'/O is no LCO of B_O. As $B_{O'}$ is activity reduced, there exists some LCO $\gamma' = \sigma'_1, \ldots \sigma'_n$ ($n > 0$) for O' such that t can be started on σ'_n. Starting t leads to σ'_{n+1} which contains t and s. As $B_{O'}$ is safe, σ'_n/O does not already contain t. As σ'_n/O does not contain t and σ'_{n+1}/O does contain t, σ'_{n+1}/O can be reached from σ'_n/O in B_O only if t is started. But, starting t in B_O removes s from σ'_n/O and gives $\sigma'_{n+1}/O \setminus \{s\} \neq \sigma'_{n+1}/O$. Thus, $\sigma'_1/O, \ldots \sigma'_n/O, \sigma'_{n+1}/O$ is no LCO of B_O.

3. **Rule 1, part 3** Assume part 3 of rule 1 is not obeyed. Then, there exist a state $s \in S_O$ and an activity $t \in T_O$, such that $(t,s) \in F_O$, but $(t,s) \notin F_{O'}$. We show, there is a LCO γ' for O' such that γ'/O is no LCO of B_O. As $B_{O'}$ is activity reduced, there exists some LCO $\gamma' = \sigma'_1, \ldots \sigma'_n$ ($n > 0$) for O' such that t is in σ'_n. Completing t leads to σ'_{n+1} which does neither contain t nor s. As $B_{O'}$ is safe, σ'_n/O does not already contain s. As σ'_n/O does contain t and σ'_{n+1}/O does not contain t, σ'_{n+1}/O can be reached from σ'_n/O in B_O only if t is completed. But, completing t in B_O adds s to σ'_n/O and gives $\sigma'_{n+1}/O \cup \{s\} \neq \sigma'_{n+1}/O$. Thus, $\sigma'_1/O, \ldots \sigma'_n/O, \sigma'_{n+1}/O$ is no LCO of B_O.

4. **Rule 2, part 1** Assume part 1 of rule 2 is not obeyed. Then, there exist a state s and an activity t, such that $s \in S_O$, $t \in T_O$, $(s,t) \notin F_O$, and $(s,t) \in F_{O'}$. We show, there is a LCO γ' for O' such that γ'/O is no LCO

of B_O. As $B_{O'}$ is activity reduced, there exists some LCO $\gamma' = \sigma'_1, \ldots \sigma'_n$ ($n > 0$) for O' such that t can be started on σ'_n. Starting t leads to σ'_{n+1} which contains t, but not s. As $B_{O'}$ is safe, σ'_n/O does not already contain t. As σ'_n/O does no contain t and σ'_{n+1}/O does contain t, σ'_{n+1}/O can be reached from σ'_n/O in B_O only if t is started. But, starting t in B_O does not remove s from σ'_n/O and gives $\sigma'_{n+1}/O \cup \{s\} \neq \sigma'_{n+1}/O$. Thus, $\sigma'_1/O, \ldots \sigma'_n/O, \sigma'_{n+1}/O$ is no LCO of B_O.

5. *Rule 2, part 2* Assume part 2 of rule 2 is not obeyed. Then, there exist a state s and an activity t, such that $s \in S_O$, $t \in T_O$, $(t,s) \notin F_O$, and $(t,s) \in F_{O'}$. We show, there is a LCO γ' for O' such that γ'/O is no LCO of B_O. As $B_{O'}$ is activity reduced, there exists some LCO $\gamma' = \sigma'_1, \ldots \sigma'_n$ ($n > 0$) for O' such that t is in σ'_n. Completing t leads to σ'_{n+1} which does not contain t, but does contain s. As $B_{O'}$ is safe, σ'_n/O does not already contain s. As σ'_n/O does contain t and σ'_{n+1}/O does not contain t, σ'_{n+1}/O can be reached from σ'_n/O in B_O only if t is completed. But, completing t in B_O does not add s to σ'_n/O and gives $\sigma'_{n+1}/O \setminus \{s\} \neq \sigma'_{n+1}/O$. Thus, $\sigma'_1/O, \ldots \sigma'_n/O, \sigma'_{n+1}/O$ is no LCO of B_O.

6. *Rule 3, part 1* Assume part 1 of rule 3 is not obeyed. Then, there exist a state $s \in S_O$ and an activity $t \in T_{O'}$ such that $t \notin T_O$ and $(s,t) \in F_{O'}$. We show, there is a life cycle occurrence γ' of O' such that γ'/O is no life cycle occurrence of B_O. As $B_{O'}$ is activity reduced, there exists some LCO $\gamma' = \sigma'_1, \ldots \sigma'_n$ ($n > 0$) for O' such that t can be started on σ'_n. Starting t leads to σ'_{n+1} which contains t, but not s. We show, σ'_{n+1}/O can not be reached from σ'_n/O in B_O. As σ'_{n+1}/O does not contain s, σ'_{n+1}/O could be reached only from σ'_n/O in B_O by starting an activity t' with prestate s. Starting t' on $\sigma_n = \sigma'_n/O$ yields a LCS σ_{n+1} containing t'. Now, $t = t'$ or $t \neq t'$. $t = t'$ contradicts our assumption that $t \notin T_O$. If $t \neq t'$ and $t' \in \sigma'_n$, then $t' \in \sigma'_n/O = \sigma_n$ and starting t' on σ_n contradicts the assumption that B_O is safe. If $t \neq t'$ and $t' \notin \sigma'_n$, then $t' \notin \sigma'_{n+1}$ and, consequently, $t' \notin \sigma'_{n+1}/O$. Therefore, t' can not have been started on σ'_n/O to reach σ'_{n+1}/O. Thus, $\sigma'_1/O, \ldots \sigma'_n/O, \sigma'_{n+1}/O$ is no LCO of B_O.

7. *Rule 3, part 2* Assume part 2 of rule 3 is not obeyed. Then, there exist a state $s \in S_O$ and an activity $t \in T_{O'}$ such that $t \notin T_O$ and $(t,s) \in F_{O'}$. We show, there is a life cycle occurrence γ' of O' such that γ'/O is no life cycle occurrence of B_O. As $B_{O'}$ is activity reduced, there exists some LCO $\gamma' = \sigma'_1, \ldots \sigma'_n$ ($n > 0$) for O' such that $t \in \sigma'_n$ and, thus, t can be completed on σ'_n. Completing t leads to σ'_{n+1} which does not contain t, but does contain s. We show, σ'_{n+1}/O can not be reached from σ'_n/O in B_O. As $B_{O'}$ is safe, σ'_n does not contain s and $\sigma'_n/O = \sigma'_n \cap (S_O \cup T_O)$ does not either. Thus, σ'_{n+1}/O, which contains s, could be reached only from σ'_n/O in B_O by completing an activity t' with poststate s. Completing t' on $\sigma_n = \sigma'_n/O$ requires $t' \in \sigma_n = \sigma'_n/O$ and yields a LCS σ_{n+1} not containing t'. Now, $t = t'$ or $t \neq t'$. $t = t'$ contradicts our assumption that $t \notin T_O$. If $t \neq t'$ and $t' \in \sigma'_n$, then $t' \in \sigma'_{n+1}$ and, consequently, $t' \in \sigma'_{n+1}/O$. Therefore, t' can not have been completed on σ'_n/O to reach σ'_{n+1}/O. If $t \neq t'$ and $t' \notin \sigma'_n$, then $t' \notin \sigma'_n/O$ and t' can not be

completed on σ'_n/O. Thus, $\sigma'_1/O, \ldots \sigma'_n/O, \sigma'_{n+1}/O$ is no LCO of B_O.
q.e.d.

4 Related Work and Open Problems

Whereas inheritance of single activities is fairly well understood in literature, no common understanding of the inheritance of object life cycles exists. The main contribution of this paper has been to shed some light on the characteristics of object life cycles and how to specialize them. We have introduced a set of sufficient and necessary rules to check whether a behavior diagram B' consistently extends another behavior diagram B.

First of all, the problem of inheriting object life cycles has been discussed in the area of object-oriented specification methods (e.g., OMT [20] and OOSA [7]), however, without providing complete solutions. The articles by Ebert and Engels [5], and by Saake et al [21] provide inheritance rules for object life cycles, which are similar to our approach, however, in the realm of state diagrams. Their work is based on graph (homo-)morphisms, similar to the work of Ehrich and Sernads [6, 23] and Lopes and Costa [15]. An informal treatment of inheritance of state machines is provided in [17]. The work by Kalinichenko [9] deals also with the specialization of object life cycles based on Petri nets, however, a different set of specialization rules is provided. Recently, the inheritance of object life cycles has been also discussed in the area of concurrent object-oriented languages [2, 16, 18]. There, an object is defined as some process with a certain request/reply behavior.

The above list of related work leads to open research issues. First and most importantly, there is no common notion of object behavior that would allow a common definition of behavior inheritance taking into account the different approaches mentioned above. Second, consistent refinement of object behavior has to be considered next to consistent extension. Third, we have restricted the discussion in this paper to single inheritance leaving apart multiple inheritance. Last but not least, inheritance of object life cycles has to be discussed in the realm of contravariant and covariant inheritance rules [13, 14] aiming for a consistent notion of inheritance ranging from object-oriented specification to implementation.

References

[1] S. Alagic, R. Sunderraman and R. Bagai, "Declarative Object-Oriented Programming: Inheritance, Subtyping and Prototyping," in *Proc of the 8th European Conference on Object-Oriented Programming (ECOOP'94)*, ed. M. Tokoro and R. Pareschi, pp. 236-259, Springer LNCS 821, 1994.

[2] P. America, "Designing an Object-Oriented Programming Language with Behavioural Subtyping," in *Foundations of Object-Oriented Languages (REX School/Workshop Proceedings)*, ed. J.W. de Bakker, W.P. de Roever, and G. Rozenberg, pp. 60-90, Springer LNCS 489, 1990.

[3] G. Booch, *Object-Oriented Analysis and Design with Applications (2nd edition)*, Benjamin Cummings, 1994.

[4] P.S. Canningen, W.R. Cook, W.L. Hill and W.G. Olthoff, "Interfaces for Strongly-Typed Object-Oriented Programming," in *Object-Oriented Programming Systems Languages and Applications (OOPSLA), Special Issue of SIGPLAN Notices*, ed. N. Meyrowitz, vol. 24, pp. 457-467, Oct. 1989.

[5] J. Ebert and G. Engels, "Dynamic Models and Behavioural Views," in *International Symposium on Object-Oriented Methodologies and Systems (ISOOMS)*, ed. E.Bertino and S.Urban, Springer LNCS 858, 1994.

[6] H.-D. Ehrich, J.A. Goguen and A. Sernadas, "A Categorial Theory of Objects as Observed Processes," in *Foundations of Object-Oriented Languages (REX School/Workshop Proceedings)*, ed. J.W. de Bakker, W.P. de Roever, and G. Rozenberg, pp. 203-228, Springer LNCS 489, 1990.

[7] D.W. Embley, B.D. Kurtz and S.N. Woodfield, *Object-Oriented Systems Analysis - A Model-Driven Approach*, Yourdon Press, 1992.

[8] R. Hull and R. King, "Semantic Database Modelling: Survey, Applications, and Research Issues," in *ACM Computing Surveys*, vol. 19, pp. 201-260, Sept. 1987.

[9] L. Kalinichenko, "Structural and Behavioral Abstractions of the Multiactivities Intended for their Concretizations by the Pre-Existing Behaviors," in *Extending Information Systems Technology, Proceedings of the Second International East/West Database Workshop*, ed. J. Eder and L. Kalinichenko, Springer WSCS, 1994.

[10] G. Kappel and M. Schrefl, "Using an Object-Oriented Diagram Technique for the Design of Information Systems," in *Proceedings of the International Working Conference on Dynamic Modelling of Information Systems*, ed. H.G. Sol, K.M. Van Hee, pp. 121-164, North-Holland, 1991.

[11] G. Kappel and M. Schrefl, "Object/Behavior Diagrams," in *Proceedings of the 7th International Conference on Data Engineering*, pp. 530-539, IEEE Computer Society Press, Kobe, Japan, April 1991.

[12] G. Kappel and M. Schrefl, *Objektorientierte Informationssysteme*, Springer, Reihe Angewandte Informatik, Wien, New York, 1994 (in print).

[13] B. Liskov and J.M. Wing, "A New Definition of the Subtype Relation," in *Proc of the 7th European Conference on Object-Oriented Programming (ECOOP'93)*, ed. O.M. Nierstrasz, pp. 118-141, Springer LNCS 707, Kaiserslautern, 1993.

[14] B. Liskov and J.M. Wing, "Specifications and their Use in Defining Subtypes," in *Object-Oriented Programming Systems Languages and Applications (OOPSLA), Special Issue of SIGPLAN Notices*, vol. 28, pp. 16-28, Dec. 1993.

[15] A. Lopes and J.F. Costa, "Rewriting for Reuse," in *Proc. ERCIM Workshop on Development and Transformation of Programs*, pp. 43-55, Nancy (F), Nov. 1993.

[16] S. Matsuoka and A. Yonezawa, "Analysis of Inheritance Anomaly in Object-Oriented Concurrent Programming Languages," in *Research Directions in Concurrent Object-Oriented Programming*, ed. G. Aga, P. Wegner, and A. Yonezawa, pp. 107-150, ACM Press, 1993.

[17] J.D. McGregor and D.M. Dyer, "A Note on Inheritance and State Machines," ACM SIGSOFT Software Engineering Notes, vol. 18, no. 4, pp. 61-69, Oct 1993.

[18] O. Nierstrasz, "Regular Types for Active Objects," in *Object-Oriented Programming Systems Languages and Applications (OOPSLA), Special Issue of SIGPLAN Notices*, vol. 28, Dec. 1993.

[19] J.L. Peterson, "Petri nets," in *ACM Computing Surveys*, pp. 223-252, 1977.

[20] J. Rumbaugh, M. Blaha, W. Premerlani, F. Eddy and W. Lorensen, *Object-Oriented Modelling and Design*, Prentice-Hall, 1991.

[21] G. Saake, P. Hartel, R. Jungclaus, R.Wieringa and R. Feenstra, "Inheritance Conditions for Object Life Cycle Diagrams," in *EMISA Workshop*, 1994.

[22] M. Schrefl, "Behavior Modeling by Stepwise Refining Behavior Diagrams," in *Proceedings of the 9th Int. Conf. on Entity Relationship Approach*, pp. 113-128, Lausanne, Oct. 1990.

[23] A. Sernadas and H.-D. Ehrich , "What is an Object, After All?," in *Proceedings of the IFIP WG 2.6 Working Conference on Object-Oriented Databases: Analysis, Design and Construction (DS-4)*, ed. R. Meersman, W. Kent, and S. Khosla, pp. 39-70, North-Holland, 1991.

[24] J.M. Smith and D.C.P. Smith, "Database Abstractions: Aggregation and Generalization," in *ACM Transactions on Database Systems*, vol. 2, pp. 105-133, June 1977.

[25] A. Snyder, "Inheritance and the Development of Encapsulated Software Components," in *Research Directions in Object-Oriented Programming*, ed. B. Shriver and P. Wegner, pp. 165-188, The MIT Press, 1987.

[26] P. Wegner, "Dimensions of Object-Based Language Design," in *Object-Oriented Programming Systems Languages and Applications (OOPSLA), Special Issue of SIGPLAN Notices*, vol. 22, pp. 168-182, Dez. 1987.

[27] P. Wegner and S.B. Zdonik, "Inheritance as an Incremental Modification Mechanism or What Like Is and Isn't Like," in *European Conference on Object-Oriented Programming (ECOOP'88)*, ed. Gjessing S. and Nygaard K., pp. 55-77, Springer LNCS 322, Aug. 1988.

Specification

Visual Specification of Complex Database Actions

Gregor Engels
Leiden University, Dept. of Computer Science
P.O. Box 9512, NL-2300 RA Leiden
The Netherlands
engels@wi.leidenuniv.nl

Perdita Löhr
Quantum GmbH
Emil-Figge-Straße 83, D-44227 Dortmund
Germany
loehr@quantum.de

Abstract

The paper presents an approach to specify in an integrated way by visual, diagrammatic languages the structural and behavioural aspects of database applications. Hereby, well-known extended Entity-Relationship diagrams are employed to specify the structural aspects. The behavioural aspects of a database application are specified by using ViAL (Visual Action Language). ViAL specifications are a special kind of data (or better object) flow diagrams, where so-called elementary actions are used as basic building blocks. These elementary actions are automatically derived from a given EER diagram. They guarantee that after finishing their execution all inherent integrity constraints are fulfilled. The paper explains the features of the language ViAL and gives some illustrating examples.

1 Introduction

Nowadays, semantic data models are regarded as convenient means to specify database applications [11]. Most of these approaches offer corresponding visual specification languages which eases both to develop and to comprehend the specification. The most well-known representatives of such languages are languages based on the ER model and its extensions. They are widely used in scientific as well as commercial software development. Meanwhile, the ER approach can even be found in commercial products like ORACLE CASE, as well as in fully extended software development methods like Modern SA [17]. Additionally, the ER concepts impacted the development of object oriented approaches which partially adopted them for their structural specification parts, e.g., OMT [14] or OOA [3].

Since database applications besides structural parts tend to more and more encompass dynamic parts, suitable languages are needed to specify the application's behaviour and functionality. Those languages can be termed suitable if they fulfill the following two requirements:

1. Developped behaviour specifications are highly integrated with the structure specification, i.e., they obey the inherent integrity constraints imposed by the structure specification.

2. They are on the same language level as the language to define the structural part and are also visual, diagrammatic languages.

Usually, the classical approach to function specification, i.e., data flow diagrams, is added to the structure specification language. Unfortunately, this approach do not fulfill the first requirement. Thus, the well-known integration gap between conventional data and function specification arises.

An alternative approach to integrate data and function specification can be found in ACM/PCM [1]. There, the graphically specified data structures are also used to express data flow. For this purpose, the database schema is extended by basic operations referring to the object types. Since it is not possible to specify more elaborated control flow in these extended schemata, most of the remaining functionality has to be specified in a traditional, i.e., separate and textual, manner.

To our knowledge, such work on combining structural and behavioural modelling has not been continued in the semantic data modelling community. But, it has returned back as an interesting and important topic in the object-oriented modelling world. While industrial object-oriented methods like OMT [14] still lack a real integrated specification of structure and behaviour, some research results offer appropriate solutions. As an example, Petri net based approaches as for instance Object/Behaviour Diagrams [12] are mentioned here.

In this paper, we also propose an approach which offers a **visual specification language** to model actions **tightly bound** to the specification of a database schema, and thus fulfills the above mentioned two requirements. The language is called ViAL – Visual Action Language. It was developed during a DFG[1] project called CADDY (Computer-Aided Design of non-traditional Databases). In this context, ViAL is implemented as part of a prototype design environment for information systems [6]. In contrast to the above mentioned, non-integrated approaches ViAL focus on

- a specification of actions *highly integrated* with the database schemata. For this purpose, elementary actions are derived from the database schema and are automatically offered as graphic specification primitives in ViAL.

- *inclusion of arbitrary structured data* queried from the database. To support this facility, arbitrary queries can be separately defined and connected to a graphic symbol. In turn, this query symbol is offered in ViAL as a specification primitive. Furthermore, special constructs are available to handle the object sets delivered by the queries.

- an *intuitively comprehensible representation*. This is provided by using graphic symbols in ViAL which on the one hand, resemble the symbols of the used semantic data model, and on the other hand, adopt the well-known concepts of data flow diagrams.

---

[1]DFG is the abbreviation for the German Research Council - Deutsche Forschungsgemeinschaft

2 Specification of Conceptual Database Schemata

To show how to specify actions in terms of ViAL, we roughly introduce the specification of a database schema first, since ViAL's specification primitives base on it. For short: a specification of a database schema consists of three parts [5]: an extended Entity-Relationship (EER) diagram, definitions of application oriented data types and and definitions of static integrity constraints.

2.1 EER diagram

An EER diagram describes the object types of the database application and their relationships. It is an extension of the ER model by Chen [2] and enhances it by the well-known concepts of generalization/specialization, association, and aggregation. Figure 1 gives an EER diagram which models a simple aspect of flight reservation. You can see in this example schema that the basic constructs equal those of the classical ER model. Few concepts are denoted slightly different, for example, key attributes of an object type are marked by a black dot on the connecting edge, while optional attributes are marked by an hollow dot. A new construct, for example, is the type constructor which is denoted as a triangle in the schema. It describes the specialization of persons into the special object type PASSENGER. Attributes may be data-valued like Name or object-valued like AdrSet. Object-valued attributes (or components) are dependent on the existence of their owners. Futhermore, attributes may be multivalued like set, list, or bag, as, for instance, AdrSet. Further details on this data model can be found in [5].

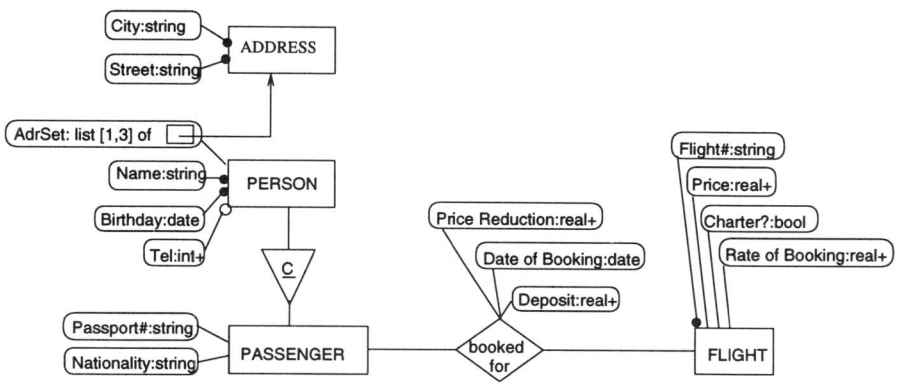

Figure 1: Example EER digram refering to booking of flights

2.2 Application-oriented Data Types

Data types are specified by using an algebraic approach. This allows to introduce application-oriented data types like **point, date, colour** besides the standard types like `int, real` into a specification, together with type specific operations.

2.3 Static Integrity Constraints and Queries

Static integrity constraints are expressed as formulas of an EER calculus. This calculus was especially developed for and adapted to the needs of an EER language. It allows to define variables and predicates over EER specific constructs [8].

On top of the EER calculus, an EER oriented query language is defined: SQL/EER [10]. This language facilitates to query the database on the same level as the defined EER diagram. An example of an SQL/EER query is:

SELECT pa.Name, (SELECT f.Flight#
                   FROM f IN FLIGHT
                   WHERE pa booked_for f)
FROM pa in PASSENGER
WHERE pa.Nationality = "Dutch"

This query selects for all Dutch passengers their names and the flight numbers they are booked for.

3 ViAL - Concepts and Syntax

Having the specification of the database schema on hand, we now introduce the visual language ViAL [4, 7, 9, 16]. ViAL enables to graphically specify complex (trans-)actions corresponding to the existing database schema. ViAL specifications are interactively executable by an interpreter, and, thus, offer the possiblity to test the specification of structure and behaviour of a database application in a prototype manner. For this purpose, ViAL offers the following concepts:

ViAL comprehends a set of **graphic symbols to express functionality**: the processing symbols. This set may be distinguished into two main groups of symbols: on the one hand, general symbols which include arbitrary actions or queries (cf. figure 3 and 4), and on the other hand, specific symbols which are derived from the existing database schema. The latter are shown in figure 2: rectangular symbols denoting operations on objects, diamond-shaped symbols for operations on relationships, and triangular symbols which represent the dynamic specialization/generalization of objects in type hierarchies.

Specifying an action in ViAL means to construct it from the **basic stock** of graphic symbols available. This basic stock encompasses the above standard operations for each object type, each relationship type and each specialization/generalization which are all automatically derived from the existing database schema. They are called **elementary actions** and are offered in ViAL like a construction kit with which to start the specification (cf. figure 2).

Each elementary action is (internally) composed of basic actions. Basic actions modify exactly one database object. There are basic actions

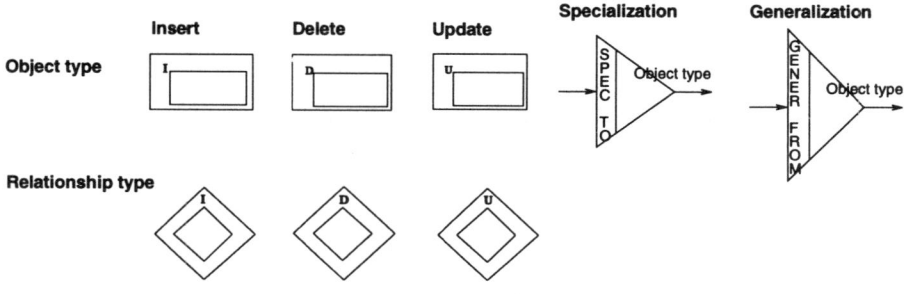

Figure 2: Graphical representation of elementary actions

- to insert or delete an instance of an object or relationship type
- to add or remove a component of an object
- to add or delete the membership of an object in a certain type construction
- to update attribute values of an existing object.

All these basic actions can automatically be derived from a given EER diagram. An important feature of elementary actions is that after the execution of an elementary action the database results in a consistent database state. Here consistency means that all EER diagram inherent integrity constraints are fulfilled.

Let us illustrate an elementary action by the example of the insertion of a new passenger. The automatically generated realization, here given in pseudo-code, is as follows:

```
elem_insert_PASSENGER (Name : string, Birthday : date) : PASSENGER
BEGIN
        /* check whether PASSENGER already exists */
        SELECT p
        FROM p IN PASSENGER
        WHERE p.Name = Name AND p.Birthday = Birthday

        IF p EXISTS
        THEN error
        ELSE /* check whether PERSON already exists */
              SELECT p
              FROM p IN PERSON
              WHERE p.Name = Name AND p.Birthday = Birthday

              IF p NOT EXISTS
              THEN /* insert new PERSON */
                    p := basic_insert_PERSON( Name, Birthday )
```

```
                        basic_add_comp_AdrSet( p )
                END IF;

                /* specialize PERSON to PASSENGER */
                basic_specialize_PASSENGER( p )
        END IF;
END elem_insert_PASSENGER;
```

The example shows that several basic actions, known as **update propagations** [15], are needed to yield a new consistent database state. Elementary actions describe minimal sequences of basic actions starting and resulting in a consistent database state [4]. All concrete data values have to be provided by the user during the interative execution of an elementary action. These are, for instance, the key values mentioned in the parameter list of this elementary action, as well as, for instance, concrete values for Passport# and Nationality, which have to be given by the user during the execution of basic_specialize_PASSENGER.

Besides the elementary actions, the basic stock includes so-called **existential queries**. Likewise, these queries are automatically generated for each object type (cf. figure 3). The issues of such a query is to check whether a particular object, determined by its key values, exists or not. If it exists, the query delivers, depending on the kind of edge (see below), either the object itself or a positive signal (along the edge marked by a black dot), otherwise a negative signal is sent (along the edge marked by a hollow dot).

These elements of the basic stock are provided for a ViAL specification from the beginning. This proceeding guarantees that all composed actions are highly integrated with the according database schema and obey all inherent integrity constraints.

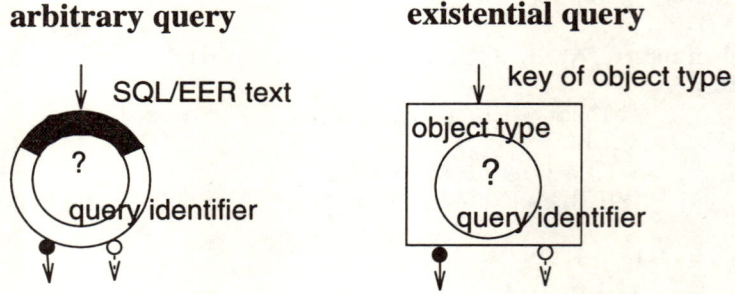

Figure 3: Graphical representation of queries

Furthermore, ViAL allows to include **arbitrary queries separately defined in SQL/EER** into an action specification. For this purpose, a particular symbol is offered which hides the textual representation of the query and may be used in a ViAL specification (cf. figure 3). The symbol for each such query is included in the basic stock of graphic ViAL symbols and, thus, available for each specification of an action. Such queries enable to process arbitrary combinations of data from the database and to incorporate them into a ViAL action. This proceeding supports one of the typical tasks of a database centered information system: processing of arbitrary data collections.

ViAL offers an **easy to handle abstraction concept**. Actions under development are identified by a name introduced by a declaration symbol (cf. figure 4). Such already specified (or even incompletely specified) actions can be (re)used in a currently developed action like calling a procedure in a conventional programming language (cf. figure 4). Like arbitrary queries, these procedure declaration and invocation symbols are included in the basic stock of graphic elements.

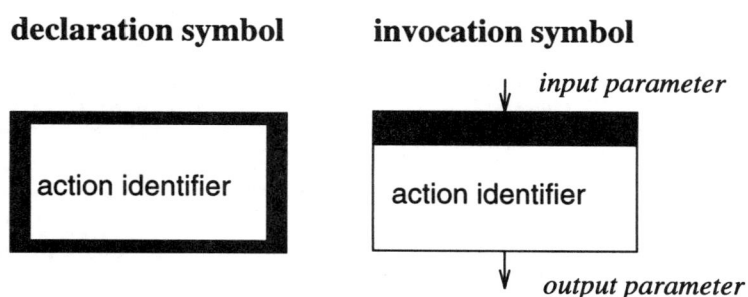

Figure 4: Graphical representation of procedures

To specify data flow and to connect the processing symbols, ViAL offers **data flow edges**. Three different types of such edges are available (cf. figure 5).

Via *object flow edges* (single or double arrow) objects or sets of objects flow through the specified processes. *Signal edges* handle boolean values, for example, the information whether an existential query has found an object or not. *Edges for error handling* connect an action with a standard error handling procedure in order to save a developer from tedious error handling details at the specification level.

ViAL supports **multivalue oriented data processing**. For this purpose, the double arrowed object edges are offered (cf. figure 5). Multivalued data are usually delivered by queries. From these, the data sets flow via the double arrowed object edges to the processing symbols. To handle these data sets conveniently, the processing symbols may be marked with an "asterisk" which means that they iteratively execute the data sets. The iteration need not be explicitly defined since the processing symbols are provided with an implicit cursor concept similar to those known from the combination of programming and database languages. Every element of figures 2 and 3 can be used in this context.

ViAL offers basic constructs to **control** the data flow (cf. figure 5).

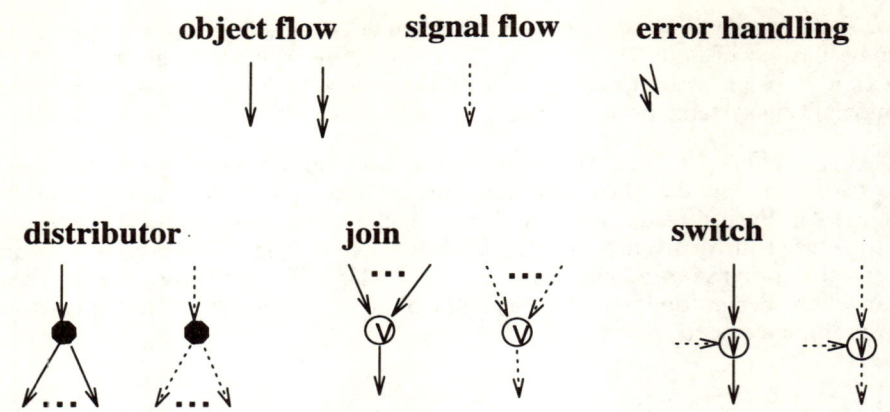

Figure 5: Data flow and control

The *distributor* takes one ingoing object or signal flow and distributes it to each of the outgoing edges. This allows to distribute data to parallel branches within one action.

The *join operator* joins different branches of information flow. Only one of the ingoing edges is allowed to carry information (exclusive or) which is then delivered to the outgoing edge.

Switch represents an operator to constrain data flow. The ingoing information (from the top of the operator) is delivered to the outgoing edge only if a constraint is satisfied represented by the left hand signal edge.

4 Example

Let us illustrate how a (more or less) complex action like **booking of a flight** can be specified using the ViAL construction kit (cf. figure 6). The action given in the figure refers to the introduced EER diagram in figure 1.

The complex action **booking of a flight** is constructed from two existential queries EQ_1 and EQ_2, another complex action **check data**, and the elementary action **elem_insert_booked_for**. Its input parameters are the **key:PERSON** and **key:FLIGHT**. At the beginning of the action, the two existential queries EQ_1 and EQ_2 ask interactively for the values of the key attributes of a PERSON and a FLIGHT. If the specified objects exist, the action continues, otherwise it stops, switching to the standard error handling. In case of continuation, one object for PERSON and one object for FLIGHT is delivered by the corresponding existential queries to the complex action **check data**. This action itself has to be specified as a ViAL action which is shown in the lower part of the ViAL diagram.

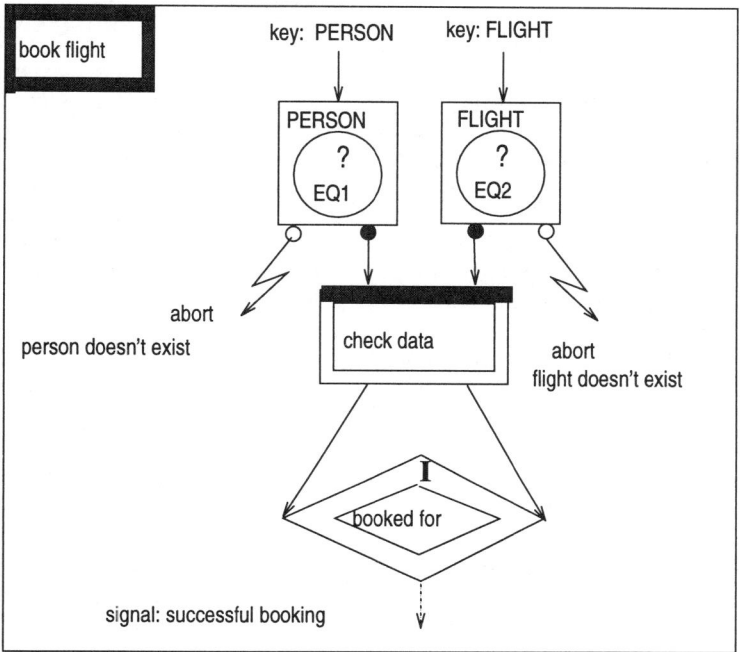
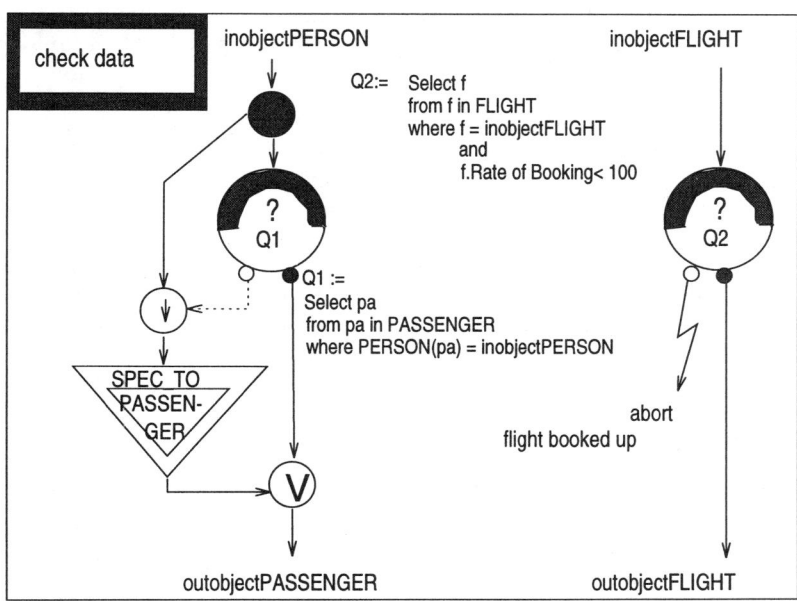

Figure 6: Example action **book flight**

Check data only starts to execute if every ingoing edge carries values. In such case, it checks whether the incoming object values are valid for the following action parts. This can be done in parallel. On the left hand side, the query Q_1 checks whether the delivered PERSON object already exists as a PASSENGER object. If not (outgoing negative signal edge of Q_1), the PERSON object is specialized to the required PASSENGER object, otherwise the PASSENGER object found by the former query Q_1 will be delivered. In parallel, the query Q_2 checks whether the flight corresponding to the specified FLIGHT object still has free seats. If not, is the flight booked up and the booking of a flight is aborted. Otherwise the FLIGHT object is delivered. The textual representation of the SQL/EER queries are only entered to support the comprehensibility of the diagram. In general, the text of a query is hidden and only shown to the user on request.

Then, check data delivers its outgoing objects to the elementary action elem_insert_booked_for which belongs to the relationship type booked_for of the EER diagram. To start its execution, the elementary action need both a PASSENGER object and a FLIGHT object in order to enter the corresponding relationship properly. If the booking action finished successfully, booking of a flight delivers a signal.

Even from this small example, it can be seen how the construction principle of ViAL works: elements of the basic stock like existential queries, user defined queries, and elementary actions may be chosen and combined to build a complex action. Other not yet defined actions like check data can be used as procedures. Since the primitive specification elements of the basic stock are automatically derived from the database schema, the integration and consistency between data and function specification is guaranteed. The graphic style of the language supports the understanding of the entire specification.

To gain experience, we began to use ViAL in small student projects at the university. In [13], ViAL was successfully employed to specify a complexer and larger application. By this practice, we learned that it is difficult to specify highly interactive applications with ViAL because no temporary variables exist which allow to hold information beside the data stored in the database. Positive experience was made with the concepts of procedural abstraction, the easy inclusion of database queries into the actions, and the convenient processing of multivalued data which in the whole lead to an easier specification of actions within a database application.

References

[1] M.L. Brodie and E. Silva. Active and Passive Component Modelling: ACM/PCM. In T. Olle, H.G. Sol, and A. Verrijn-Stuart, editors, *Information Systems Design Methodologies: A Comparative Review, Proc. IFIP WG8.1 Working Conference, Nordwijkerhout*, pages 41–92. North-Holland, 1982.

[2] P.P. Chen. The Entity-Relationship Model - Towards a Unified View of Data. *ACM Transactions on Database Systems*, 1(1):9–36, 1976.

[3] P. Coad and E. Yourdon. *Object-Oriented Analysis.* Yourdon Press Computing Series, Prentice Hall, Englewood Cliffs, New Jersey, 1990.

[4] G. Engels. Elementary Actions on an Extended Entity-Relationship Database. In *Proc. 4th Int. Workshop on Graph Grammars and Their Application to Computer Science, LNCS 532*, pages 344–362. Springer, Berlin, 1991.

[5] G. Engels, M. Gogolla, U. Hohenstein, K. Hülsmann, P. Löhr-Richter, G. Saake, and H.-D. Ehrich. Conceptual Modelling of Database Applications Using an Extended ER Model. *Data & Knowledge Engineering*, 9(2):157–204, 1992.

[6] G. Engels and P. Löhr-Richter. CADDY: A Highly Integrated Environment to Support Conceptual Database Design. In G. Forte, N. Madhavji, and H. Müller, editors, *Proc. 5th Int. Workshop on Computer-Aided Software Engineering, Montreal, Kanada*, pages 19–22. IEEE Computer Society Press, 1992.

[7] K. Gerlach. *Ein Interpreter für visuell spezifizierte komplexe Aktionen auf EER-Datenbanken.* Technical University of Braunschweig, Master Thesis, 1992.

[8] M. Gogolla and U. Hohenstein. Towards a semantic view of an extended Entity-Relationship model. *ACM Transactions on Database Systems*, 16:369–416, 1991.

[9] C. Hennemann and J. Schacht. *Entwurf und Implementierung einer Sprache zur visuellen Spezifikation von Aktionen auf erweiterten Entity-Relationship Databanken.* Technical University of Braunschweig, Master Theses, 1991.

[10] U. Hohenstein and G. Engels. Formal semantics of Entity-Relationship-based query language. *Information Systems*, 17(3):209–242, 1992.

[11] R. Hull and R. King. Semantic Database Modeling: Survey, Applications, Research Issues. *ACM Computing Surveys*, 19(3):201–260, 1989.

[12] G. Kappel and M. Schrefl. Object/Behaviour Diagrams. *Proc. 7th IEEE International Conference on Data Engineering*, Kobe, Japan, April 1991.

[13] P. Löhr-Richter. *Generische Methoden für die frühen Entwurfsphasen von Informationssystemen.* PhD thesis, Technical University of Braunschweig, 1993.

[14] J. Rumbaugh, M. Blaha, W. Premerlani, F. Eddy, and W. Lorensen. *Object-Oriented Modeling and Design.* Prentice Hall, Englewood Cliffs, New Jersey, 1991.

[15] P. Scheuermann, G. Schiffner, H. Weber Abstraction Capabilities and Invariant Properties Modelling within the Entity-Relationship Approach. In P.P. Chen (ed.): *Proc. of the 1st Int. Conference on Entity-Relationship Approach*, Los Angeles (California), 121–140, 1980.

[16] M. Wolff. *Eine Sprache zur Beschreibung Schema-abhängiger Aktionen in einem erweiterten Entity-Relationship-Modell.* Technical University of Braunschweig, Master Thesis, 1989.

[17] E. Yourdon. *Modern Structured Analysis.* Prentice Hall, 1989.

The database Specification Language Ruslan: Main Features

A. V. Zamulin

Institute of Informatics Systems
Siberian Division of Russian Academy of Sciences
630090, Novosibirsk, Russia
e-mail: zam@isi.itfs.nsk.su

Computer Science Section
School of Mathematics and Computer Sience
Universiti Sains Malaysia
11800 Penang, Malaysia
e-mail: zam@cs.usm.my

November 26, 1994

Abstract. The database specification language Ruslan is designed to provide tools for the formal specification of data models, databases, database programming languages, and application programs. A Ruslan database is regarded as a set of objects of definite data types. A database specification consists of formal specifications of all data types used, objects declared, and operations over database objects defined. The database specification is stored in the database and can be used for the specification of an application program operating with it. The biggest specification unit is a module generally consisting of kind, data type, type classes, object, and detached operation specifications. A module does not containing object declarations is a model module, representing a particular data model or database programming language. A model module can be later used for the specification of database modules. The specification of an application program is a specification of a function using and/or producing values stored in a database.

1 Introduction

The database specification language Ruslan is designed to serve the following purposes:

1. specification of data models,

2. specification of concrete databases,

3. specification of database programming languages,

4. specification of application programs.

Both a data model and a database programming language are regarded as collections of specific/generic data types and independent functions with facilities to declare mutable and immutable objects of different types. A concrete database is regarded as a collection of mutable/immutable persistent objects of specific types. An application program is regarded as a function processing transient and/or persistent data. The specification of a complex program can consist of a number of subspecifications defining the properties of constituting functions. The specification of a database object is stored in the database and can be used for the specification of an application program operating with this database.

To provide facilities for the specification of a large number of complex data models, databases, database programming languages, and application programs, the language provides tools for the specification of main building blocks which are data types, type kinds, type and kind classes, and detached operations. A data type serves to construct and manipulate data. Terms (expressions) composed of operators introduced in a type signature are data terms. Terms used to denote data types are type terms. A kind is a tool for constructing type terms. Actually, a kind is a "type of types" whose set of values is used to denote a set of lower-level data types [1]. A type class [2] characterizes a set of types (possibly of different kinds) with common operations. A kind class characterizes a set of kinds with common operations. A detached operation is an operation does not belonging to a particular kind or type and specified individually, therefore. Entity-structured signatures, algebras, and specifications are elaborated to provide a theoretical background for kinds, data types, type classes, and detached operations.

A certain collection of entity specifications is called a module. It is a persistent entity in Ruslan, i.e., each module specified can be later used for the specification of new modules. A module containing, among others, specifications of mutable (variable) and immutable (constant) objects specifies a particular database, it is called an object module. A module without object specifications is called a model module, it serves to specify object modules. A database programming language is a special sort of a data model module. Ruslan gives specifications of some important entities which are called built-in entities and provides tools for specification of new (used-defined) entities. A preliminary definition of Ruslan is given in [3].

The paper is organized in the following way. Entity-structured signatures, algebras, and specifications are introduced in Sections 2, 3, and 4. A special sort of an entity-structured signature, a kinded type-structured signature, is proposed in Section 5. The hierarchical nature of a kinded type-structured signature is used in Section 6 to extend entities with generic operations. The main specification unit of Ruslan, module, is discussed in Section 7. A short description of built-in modules is given in Section 8. Some related work is listed in Section 9. A conclusion is drawn in Section 10.

2 Entity-structured signature

Let

$\underline{S}$ be a set of (entity) names;
$\underline{Q}$ be a set of names (of entity classes),
an operation expression be either a name from $\underline{S}$ or $O1, ..., On \longrightarrow O$, where $O, Oi, i = 1, ..., n$, are operation expressions; Oi is called a domain unit and O is called a codomain unit;
an operation signature be a pair $op : O$, where op is an operator (function symbol) and O is an operation expression;
an entity class be a set of operation signatures constructed as above by extending the set $\underline{S}$ with the symbol "@" meaning "myself" and used at least once as domain and/or codomain unit in each operation signature;
an entity signature be a set of operation signatures constructed as above by extending the set $\underline{S}$ with the symbol "@" meaning "myself" and used at least once as domain and/or codomain unit in each operation signature;

then an entity-structured signature Σ is a tuple $< \underline{S}, \underline{Q}, \underline{\Theta}, \underline{\Phi}, \underline{\Delta}, int^t >$, where $\underline{\Theta}$ is a $\underline{Q}$- indexed set of entity classes, $\underline{\Phi}$ is a set of $\underline{\Theta}$-indexed entity signatures, $\underline{\Delta}$ is a set of (detached) operation signatures, and int^t is a function mapping $\underline{S}$ into $\underline{\Phi}$. For any $S \in \underline{S}$ and $\Phi \in \underline{\Phi}$, we say that Φ is denoted with S if $int^t(S) = \Phi$.

Notation: we write $op1, op2, ..., opn : O$ for $op1 : O, op2 : O, ..., opn : O$; separate operation signatures with semicolons and enclose an entity signature in square brackets.

3 Entity implementations

An algebra of a signature $\Sigma = < \underline{S}, \underline{Q}, \underline{\Theta}, \underline{\Phi}, \underline{\Delta}, int^t >$ is built by assigning

1. a set of elements to each name from $\underline{S}$;

2. a set of (partial) functions $|O1| \times ... \times |On| \longrightarrow |O|$ to an operation expression $O1, O2, ..., On \longrightarrow O$, where $|O|, |Oi|, i = 1, ..., n$, are sets assigned to the operation expressions O, Oi;

3. an element from the set associated with O to each operator $op : O$ from the set $S^\theta \cup \theta$, where θ is a class and S^θ is an entity signature denoted with the entity name S and indexed with the class θ, each occurrence of the entity name @ in O being replaced with S;

4. an element of the set associated with O to each operator $op : O$ from the set of detached operation signatures.

A set assigned to an entity name or operation expression is called the *set of values* of the entity. In this way, the notion of an entity is extended to include entities denoted with operation expressions, which are considered as void entities (entities without operations). The family of sets of entity values is called the *carrier* of the algebra. If op is an operator, then op^A is an element of the carrier assigned to the operator op in the algebra A. Note the difference between an entity and entity class made clear by entity implementations: an entity class is never provided with an implementation, its operators are implemented differently in entities indexed with it.

For a given signature Σ any number of algebras can be constructed. One special algebra, $W_\Sigma(X)$, called the *word algebra* is distinguished among them. Let X_O be a set of variables [1] indexed with an operation expression O. Then the elements of this algebra, which are called *entity terms*, are the following:

1. if x is a variable indexed with an operation expression O, then x is a term of entity O;

2. if S is an entity name and $op : O$ is an operation signature from the entity signature denoted with S, then $S'op$ is a term of entity O, each occurrence of the entity name "@" in O being replaced with S;

3. if S is an entity name, $op : O1, ..., On \longrightarrow O$ is an operation signature from the entity signature denoted with S, and $e1, ..., en$ are terms of entities $O1, ..., On$, respectively, then $S'op(e1, ..., en)$ is a term of entity O, each occurrence of the entity name @ in O being replaced with S;

4. if $op : O$ is a detached operation signature, then op is a term of entity O;

5. if $op : O1, ..., On \longrightarrow O$ is a detached operation signature and $e1, ..., en$ are terms of entities $O1, ..., On$, respectively, then $op(e1, ..., en)$ is a term of entity O;

6. if t is a term of entity O then (t) is a term of entity O.

Notation: we do not qualify an operator with an entity name where there is no ambiguity.

An entity term without variables is called a *ground* term. We denote the set of all terms of entity O by $|W_\Sigma(X)|_O$ and the set of ground terms of entity O by $|W_\Sigma|_O$, the sets of all terms and ground terms are denoted by $|W_\Sigma(X)|$ and $|W_\Sigma|$, respectively.

For any algebra A of a given signature, an evaluation function $eval^O = |W_\Sigma(X)|_O \longrightarrow |O|$ is defined in the following way:

1. for a variable $x \in X_O$ and a binding function $v : X_O \longrightarrow |W_\Sigma|_O$, $eval^O(x) = eval^O(v(x))$;

2. for an operator $c : O$, $eval^O(c) = c^A$,

---
[1] An algebraic variable, i.e. an identifier wich can denote any element of a given entity, is meant here.

3. for an operator $op : O1, ..., On \longrightarrow O$,
$eval^O(op(t1, ..., tn)) = op^A(eval^{O1}(t1), ..., eval^{On}(tn))$.

According to this definition of the evaluation function, all functions in the underlying algebra are *strict*.

4 Entity specifications

Let Σ be an entity-structured signature and E^θ, E^ϕ, and E^δ be sets of equations associated with each $\theta \in \Theta, \Phi^\theta \in \Phi$, and $\delta \in \Delta$, respectively, so that each equation in E^θ has at least one operator from θ, each equation in E^ϕ has at least one operator from $\Phi^\theta \cup \theta$, and each equation in E^δ uses δ. Then we get a *presentation*. A pair $< \theta, E^\theta >$ is called a *class specification*, a pair $< \Phi^\theta, E^\phi >$ is called an *entity specification*, and a pair $< \delta, E^\delta >$ is called a *detached operation specification*. We say a specification is *sound* if it uses only the operators from the corresponding signature and operators from its domain entities. We usually say "a theory" when actually have a presentation.

Thus, a theory is generally a set of class specifications, entity specifications and detached operation specifications. Note that at the level of presentation the function int^t binds entity names to entity specifications. An entity implementation must satisfy all equations of the corresponding entity specification and all equations of the indexing class.

For specification purposes, a notion of an axiom defined in the following way is used:

1. if $T1$ and $T2$ are terms of entity O, then $T1 = T2$ is an equation or axiom;

2. if A is an axiom, then **forall** $x1 : O1, ..., xn : On, A$ and **exist** $x1 : O1, ..., xn : On, A$, where xi is a variable and Oi is either an operation expression or the symbol @, are axioms;

3. an axiom does not contain other variables except those bounded by quantifiers **forall** and **exist**.

A *hierarchical* construction of entities is allowed in Ruslan. This means that each entity is specified using entities previously specified and no loops among entities are allowed. In this case, a partial order between entities can be defined. An entity $T1$ is called a *primitive entity* with respect to an entity $T2$ if $T1$ is used in the operation expressions of the signature of $T2$.

An entity specification is regarded as an abstract entity in the sense that any implementation satisfying the equations is allowed. This is known as *loose semantics* [4]. According to this, a specification methodology known as *behavioral approach* first advocated in [5] is used. In this case, the set of entity operations is divided into two groups: *constructors* and *observers*. The constructor yields a value of the entity being specified and the observer yields a value of a primitive entity. Constructors that can be used to create any value of the entity being specified are called *basic constructors*, others are called *secondary constructors*. Each observer in an entity specification is applied to each basic constructor and each secondary constructor is defined in terms of basic constructors.

An operation can produce an indefinite result in two cases:

1. its value is not defined for some arguments;

2. it is applied for an indefinite argument.

To cope with indefitity, Ruslan is based on algebras comprising strict partial functions. The clause **dom** in an entity specification defines the domain of a partial function; functions without explicitly indicated domain clause are considered total.

5 Kinded type-structured signature

Let $\Sigma\Lambda = <\underline{S}, Q, \Theta, \Phi, \Delta, int^t>$ be an entity-structured signature constructed as above and let $\underline{S} = S \cup Z$, where S is a set of names and Z is a subset of $|W_{\Sigma\Lambda}|$, where $|W_{\Sigma\Lambda}|$ is the set of ground terms of $\Sigma\Lambda$. Entity signatures are explicitly divided into two sorts in this case, *type signatures* and *kind signatures*. The constructors of type signatures produce *data terms*, they are not included in Z. The constructors of kind signatures produce either *type terms* or *kind terms*, both of them are elements of Z. Type terms serve to denote type signatures, kind terms serve to denote kind signatures. All names from S are used to denote kind signatures, they are *predefined kind terms*. In this way, a kind term denotes a kind signature whose terms can denote either kind signatures or type signatures, an so on. Some kind signatures may produce terms not denoting entity signatures, these are *void kind terms* used in the construction of other kind signatures. Two standard kinds are supposed to exist: KIND, uniting of all kind terms (kind units) except itself, and TYPE, uniting all type terms (type units).

A class from Θ indexing a data type signature is a *type class*, and a class from Θ indexing a kind signature is a *kind class*. Names from Q are *type class names* and *kind class names*, respectively. Elements constructed by kind operations are either *kind units* or *type units* and elements constructed by data type operations are *data*. The signature $\Sigma\Lambda$ is called a *kinded type-structured signature*.

Thus, the language of type terms is intermixed in Ruslan with the language of data terms. This corresponds to the normal practice of programming languages, in which these terms are also intermixed. When an algebra of a programming language is represented by an interpreter, both kinds of terms are evaluated interchangeably. When an algebra of a programming language is represented by a compiler, type terms are evaluated at compile time and data terms are evaluated at run time. Since both type units and data units can be used for construction of type units the so called *object-dependent* types in addition to generic data types can be specified with this technique.

6 Generic operations

Let

a *generic entity term* be a pair $< (q1^{\omega 1}, ..., qk^{\omega k}), oT^q >$, where $q1^{\omega 1}, ..., qk^{\omega k}$ are names (of parameters) indexed with entity terms $\omega 1, ..., \omega k$, respectively, and oT^q is an operation expression constructed by extending the set of terms of entities $\omega 1, ..., \omega k$ with $q1, ..., qk$ respectively;
a *generic operation signature* be a pair $op : goT$, where op is an operator and goT is a generic entity term.

We now redefine an entity signature as a set of operation signatures and generic operation signatures constructed by extending the set of entity terms with the symbol "@" meaning "myself" and used at least once in each operation signature and allow the set $\underline{\Delta}$ to contain generic operation signatures. **Notation**: if $q1, ..., qk$ are names of parameters indexed with entity terms $\omega 1, ..., \omega k$, respectively, and oTq is a type term, then **gen** $q1 : \omega 1, ..., qk : \omega k$ **op** oT^q is a generic type term.

The generic operators extend the set of entity terms in the following way:

1. for a generic operation signature $op^q :< (q1^{\omega 1}, ..., qk^{\omega k}), oT^q >$ from $T^c \cup C$, where C is an entity class and T^c is an entity signature indexed with the entity term T and entity class C, and entity terms $T1, ..., Tk$, such that each $Ti, i = 1, ..., k$, is a term of entity ωi, $T'op^q(T1, ..., Tk)$ is a term (*instantiated operator*) of operation type oT obtained from oT^q by replacing each qi with Ti and each @ with T;

2. for a detached generic operation signature $op^q :< (q1^{\omega 1}, ..., qk^{\omega k}), oT^q >$ and entity terms $T1, ..., Tk$, such that each $Ti, i = 1, ..., k$, is a term of entity ωi, $op^q(T1, ..., Tk)$ is a term (*instantiated operator*) of operation type oT obtained from oT^q by replacing each qi with Ti.

According to the extension of an entity signature and a detached operation set with generic operation signatures, an entity implementation is extended with:

1. a function map^{cq}, one for each generic operation signature $op^q :< (q1^{\omega 1}, ..., qk^{\omega k}), oT^q >$ from $T^c \cup C$, where C is an entity class and T^c is an entity signature indexed with the entity term T and entity class C, which binds an instantiated operator $op^q(T1, ..., Tk)$ to a function from the set of functions associated with oT, where oT is an operation type resulting from oT^q by replacing each qi with the type term $Ti, i = 1, ..., k$;

2. a detached operations implementation is extended with a function map^{dq}, one for each generic operation signature $op^q :< (q1^{\omega 1}, ..., qk^{\omega k}), oT^q >$ from $\underline{\Delta}$, each binding an instantiated operator $op^q :< (q1^{\omega 1}, ..., qk^{\omega k}), oT^q >$ to a function from the set of functions associated with oT, where oT is an operation type resulting from oT^q by replacing each qi with the entity term $Ti, i = 1, ..., k$.

The definition of the function *eval* is extended in the following way: for an instantiated operator $op^q(T11,...,T1k) : T1,...,Tn \longrightarrow T$,
$eval(op^q(T11,...,T1k)(t1,...,tn)) =$
$$map^q(op^q(T11,...,T1k))(eval(t1),...,eval(tn)).$$
(The operator *op* is here either a detached operator or a qualified operator, the function map^q is either one of map^{cq} or one of map^{dq}, depending on the set the operator belongs to.

7 Modules

Module is the largest specification unit in Ruslan. It is a *persistent* entity, i.e. its specification is stored on disk for an indefinitely long span of time. A module specification generally includes:

1. a collection of type specifications,
2. a collection of kind specifications,
3. a collection of class specifications,
4. a collection of object declarations,
5. a collection of object operation specifications,
6. a collection of integrity constraint specifications.

The collection of type specifications introduces specific data types known to the module. Each of them belongs to its own kind.

The collection of kind specifications introduces kinds, each of them specifying a set of related data types and a possible set of operations over them.

The collection of class specifications introduces classes defining operations common for a group of kinds or data types.

The collection of object declarations introduces constant and variable objects [2] of this module. An object declared in a module exists while the module exists or until an explicit dropping operation is executed. Objects marked with **priv** are private objects, which cannot be passed as operation arguments outside the module to ensure data integrity. Non-private objects declared in a module can be manipulated by the operations of the corresponding data types. Private objects may be manipulated only by operations defined in the object operation collection of the module. Operations marked with **priv** are private operations, which can be used only inside the module. Integrity axioms can be supplied to preserve the database integrity, they are checked each time a module variable is updated.

The collection of entity definitions and object declarations of a module is a *module signature*. A module algebra using the data types Memory, Variable,

---

[2] an object can be understood as a container with a value in it; a value associated with a variable object can be replaced with another value, a value associated with a constant object cannot be replaced; these notions should not be confused with the notions of algebraic constant and variable introduced in Section 3.

and Constant is specified in [3]. The *module word algebra* is the visible parent module algebra (if any) extended with the word algebra of entities and detached operations of this module and with the following:

1. if $vid : T := a$ is a variable declaration, then vid is a term of type $Var(T)$;

2. if $cid = T'c$ is a constant definition, then cid is a term of type $Const(T)$;

3. if K is a kind identifier bound to a kind signature, then K is a kind term;

4. if T is a type identifier bound to a type term of kind K, then T is a type term of kind K;

5. if T is a type identifier bound to a data type signature, then T is a type term of its own kind.

The *visible module word algebra* is the module algebra without terms using names of private objects.

A module with object declarations is an *object module* and a module without object declarations is a *model module*. A module can inherit the specification of some model module, which is called a *parent module* in this case. If the parent module is not indicated explicitly, the predefined module *Stand* is used. In this way, a hierarchy of modules is created. The module *Stand* is the root of the hierarchy. It specifies a database programming language like Atlant [6]. It is assumed that a number of model modules representing different *data models* are created at the next level of the hierarchy. Object modules representing particular databases are created at the lowest level.

8 Built-in modules

The biggest built-in model module in Ruslan specifies an imperative database programming language. It contains the specifications of the following kinds and data types:

1. data types Boolean, Natural, Integer, Rational, Character, Memory;

2. kind VARTYPE: types of variables which also serve as variable pointer types;

3. kind CONSTYPE: types of constants which also serve as constant pointer types;

4. kind SEQTYPE: types of sequences of one-type components;

5. kind ARRTYPE: types of Pascal-like arrays;

6. kind ENUTYPE: enumeration types;

7. kind RANTYPE: range types;

8. kind RECTYPE: record types;

    9. kind UNITYPE: union types;

    10. kind SUBTYPE: predicate subtypes;

    11. kind ROUTYPE: routine types;

    12. kind FILETYPE: Pascal-like file types;

the kind class EQUIV specifying type equivalence and approximation relations; the following type classes:

   1. EQUAL: all data types with the operation "=";

   2. ORDERED: all EQUAL-class data types with the operations " < ", " <= "," > "," >= ";

   3. ENUM: all ORDERED-class data types with the operations "$succ$", "$pred$";

   4. RENUM: all ENUM-class data types with the operations "$first$", "$last$";

   5. NUMERIC: all ORDERED-class data types with the operations " + ", " − "," ∗ "," / ".

the following detached operations:

   1. *if*: a conditional expression (conditional statement is a special case);

   2. *compound*: a compound expression (compound statement is a special case);

   3. *block*: a block expression (block statement is a special case);

   4. *while, repeat, for*: loop expressions (loop statements are special cases);

   5. *function*: a function creation operation (procedure is a special case);

   6. *program*: a program creation operation.

The next important built-in model module specifies a relational data model. It contains a specification of the kind RELTYPE with a specification of relation types and detached *join* and *natural join* operations. Full specifications of both modules can be found in [7].

9 Related work

A good deal of preliminary work in the field of database specification has been reported [8, 9, 10, 11, 12, 13]. The simplest approach was to consider a database schema as an algebraic data type [8, 9]. However, the approach was based on purely applicative concepts and did not take into account storage concepts like memory and variables. Since these concepts have been very important for databases, a model was suggested [10] which considered different database states as "possible worlds" in a modal system of algebras. This made the model more complex. The introduction of a special "object layer" above a conventional "data layer" [13] also did not contribute to the simplicity. The project ADAPTABLE [14] has attacked the problems of proving that a database transaction obeys certain integrity constraints. The above mentioned research has not lead to the development of a database specification language, however.

A number of general-purpose specification languages have also been reported. CLEAR [15], ACT ONE [16], ASL [17], OBSCURE [18], LARCH [19] are examples of them; SPECTRUM [20] is one of the latest developments in the field. Ruslan is distict by the possibility of declaring transient and persistent objects and by more powerful entity specification facilities. The technique of specification used was first introduced in [5] and further elaborated in [21]. It was also used in [22] where the symbol "@" meaning "myself" was proposed (it helped to separate a data type specification from its name). This paper extends the technique to include kinds and generic operations.

10 Conclusion

A new database specification language is proposed in the paper. The language is based on the concept of an entity-structured specification, which is a collection of specifications of data types, kinds, type and kind classes, and detached operations. This technique permits the specification of different data models, concrete databases, database programming languages, and application programs. A specification can be stored in a data base and used later for the specification of an application program. A database is specified with the use of such data types as memory, constant, and variable, which permit the creation and use of persistent objects of various types. An imperative database programming language is a built-in specification module of Ruslan. The imperative features of Ruslan enable the specification of real databases and provide for a smooth transition from database programming languages to database specification languages.

Two kinds of program specification, procedural specification and behavioral specification, are allowed in the language. The procedural specification of the task is much like a relational algebra query and the behavioral specification is much like an SQL query. By a process of step-wise refinement, a behavioral specification is transformed into a procedural specification, which is transformed into an executable program.

References

[1] Cardelli L. *Types for Data-Oriented Languages*. Lecture Notes in Computer Science, 1988, v. 303, pp. 1-15.

[2] Wadler, P. and Blott, S. *How to make ad-hoc polymorphism less ad-hoc*. Conf. Record of the 16th ACM Annual Symp. on Principles of Progr. Lang., Austin, Texas, January 1989.

[3] Zamulin, A.V. *The Database Specification Language RUSLAN (preliminary communication)*. Siberian Division of the Russian Academy of Sciences, Institute of Informatics Systems, Preprint 28, Novosibirsk 1994, 35 p. (Availaible electronically by anonymous ftp from math.tulane.edu, directory "pub/zamulin", file "Ruslan1.ps.Z").

[4] F.L. Bauer, R. Berghammer, M. Broy, ea. *The Munich project CIP. Volume I: The wide spectrum language CIP-L*. Lecture Notes in Computer Science, v.183, Berlin: Springer 1985

[5] Guttag, J., Hornung, J.J. *The algebraic specification of abstract data types.* Acta Informatika, 1978, v.10, No.1, pp. 27-52.

[6] Zamulin A.V. *The Database Programming Language Atlant.* University of Glasgow, Department of Computing Science, Research report CSC/89/R13, June 1989.

[7] Zamulin, A.V. *The Database Specification Language RUSLAN (specification examples)*. Siberian Division of the Russian Academy of Sciences, Institute of Informatics Systems, Preprint 29, Novosibirsk 1994, 54 p. (Availaible electronically by anonymous ftp from math.tulane.edu, directory "pub/zamulin", file "Ruslan2.ps.Z").

[8] Ehrig H., Kreowski H.J., Weber H. *Algebraic Specification Schemes for Database Systems*. Proc. 4th Int. Conf. on Very Large Data Bases, Berlin, 1978.

[9] Dosch W., Mascari G, Wirsing M. *On the Algebraic Specification of Databases*. Proc. 8th Int. Conf. on Very Large Data Bases, Mexico City, 1982.

[10] Golshani F., Maibaum T.S.E., Sadler M.R. *A Modal System of Algebras for Database Specification and Query/Update Language Support*. Proc. 9th Int. Conf. on Very Large Data Bases, Florence, 1983.

[11] Ehrich H.-D., Lipeck U.W., Gogolla M. *Specification, Semantics, and Enforcement of Dynamic Database Constraints*. Proc. 10th Int. Conf. on Very Large Data Bases, Singapore 1984.

[12] Khosla S., Maibaum T.S.E., Sadler M.R. *Database Specification*. Proc. IFIP Working Conf. on Database Semantics, R. Meersman/T.B.Steel (eds.), North Holland, Amsterdam, 1985.

[13] Ehrich H.-D. *Algebraic (?) Specification of Conceptual Database Schemata.* Recent Trends in Data Type Specification: Informatik Fachberichte, v. 116, 1984, p. 22-28.

[14] Sheard T. and Stemple D. *Automatic Verification of Database Transaction Safety*. ACM Transactions on Database Systems, v.12, No.3, p.322-368, September 1989.

[15] Sannella D. *A set-theoretic semantics for CLEAR*. Acta Informatika, v.21, No. 5, 1984, pp. 443-472.

[16] Ehrig H., Mahr B. *Fundementals of Algebraic Specifications*. Springer-Verlag, 1985.

[17] Sannella D., Wirsing M. *A Kernel Language for Algebraic Specification and Implementation*. LNCS, V.158, 1983, pp. 413-427.

[18] Lermen C.-W., Loeckx J. *OBSCURE, a New Specification Language*. Recent Trends in Data Type Specification: Informatik Fachberichte, v. 116, 1984, p. 28-30.

[19] Guttag, J. V., Horning, J.J., ea. *Larch: Languages and Tools for Formal Specification*. Springer Verlag, 1993.

[20] Broy M., Facchi C., Grosu R., ea. *The Requirement and Design Specification Language Spectrum, An Informal Introduction, Version 1.0*. Technische Universitaet Muenchen, Institut fuer Informatik, April 1993.

[21] Wirsing, M., Pepper, P., Partsch, H., ea. *On Hierarchies of Abstract Data Types*. Acta Informatica, 1983, v.20, p. 1-33.

[22] Nakajima, R., Honda, M., and Nakahara, H. *Hierarchical Program Specification: a Many-sorted Logical Approach*. Acta Informatika 14, pp. 135-155 (1990).

Heterogeneous and Distributed Systems

Structural and Behavioral Abstractions of the Multiactivities Intended for their Concretizations by the Pre-existing Behaviors

Leonid Kalinichenko
Institute for Problems of Informatics
Russian Academy of Sciences
Moscow, Russia

Abstract

An approach for the refinement of the information system activity (workflow) specifications by the pre-existing heterogeneous information resource behavior patterns is discussed. The proposed methodology is considered to be a part of the *semantic interoperation reasoning framework* [16]. The two-dimensionally uniform multiactivity specification [15] is assumed.

The paper is focused on the behavioral abstraction of the multiactivity specifications that are introduced as patterns of actions (Petri net firing sequences) generalized as regular expressions. Behavior concretization reasoning is based on the partial ordering of the patterns. Structural and behavioral abstractions of multiactivities work together to make their concretization feasible.

The technique is developed and used in frame of the SYNTHESIS project [1].

1 Introduction

The concepts of *semantic interoperation reasoning* (SIR) as a collection of basic procedures leading to the refinement of an information system specification by the pre-existing information resource patterns are defined in [16]. According to SIR, a basic schema of information system design and eventually of solving of a problem in an open environment [4] should include the procedures looking for the resources applicable to the problem, choosing among them of the most appropriate and coherent with the problem context, consistently composing of the chosen resources into a megaprogram [25], running the megaprogram to get a solution. Semantic interoperation reasoning framework (SIRF) [16] should provide necessary modeling, methodological and architectural capabilities for analysis, decision making, provable reasoning and implementation based on the pre-existing resource reuse.

It is assumed that a collection of pre-existing information resources is organized into heterogeneous interoperable information resource environment

[1]This work was supported by the Russian Basic Research Foundation grant (93-012-618)

(HIRE) (the resources in HIRE can technically interoperate according to some architecture, such as [21]).

Here we focus on provisions making feasible concretization of the information system design behavior by the HIRE. We use the generalized HIRE behavior modeling framework possessing two-dimensional uniformity of the specifications (horizontally for heterogeneous information resources and vertically for different layers of specification, design and implementation) [14, 15]. The SYNTHESIS framework can be equally applied to the specification and implementation of multiactivities, declarative interresource constraints and multiresource applications. An orthogonal set of language facilities that are necessary for the specification of the HIRE dynamics includes: 1) a high level Petri net-based script-oriented specification making possible definition of concurrent execution, data and control flow between the execution components (such as subactivities or software systems supporting the information resources); 2) function (object calculus-based) declaration facilities introduced to define actions and assertions over the heterogeneous information resources; 3) the object-oriented facilities used for specifying of class hierarchies where each class represents a relevant information resource model, uses inheritance, and provides for representing of specific resources (activities) as instances of the appropriate class.

Related researches for such specifications include areas of active databases, declarative specification of interdatabase constraints [23], multiactivity and multitransaction models [7, 9], flexible transaction specification and execution, multi-resource execution environment [22].

The paper continues development of the approach for refinement of an information sytem activity specification by the pre-existing information resource behavioral patterns. In [17] we showed how to use the same set of modeling facilities for capturing of structural aspects of the multiactivity modeling. The idea consisted in the localization of structural interactivity dependencies of megaprograms (such as introduced in [5]) in the concept of Generic Intercomponent Control Modules (GICM) capturing the semantics of the corresponding multiactivity (multitransaction) models. Such generic localization leads to the possibility of specification and generation of multiactivities (multitransactions) possessing necessary application (implementation) structural properties. But what is more important is that the localization leads to explicit separation of pure functional and concurrent behaviors. Such decomposition makes possible to apply well developed general functional refinement technique (leading to a possibility of reuse of the pre-existing behaviors, such as (atomic) transactions). Concurrency specification localized in GICM can be refined during the design separately leading finally to the specification of a multitransaction (new or combined of the pre-existing ones).

This paper goes further introducing an approach of getting of a behavioral abstraction of a script as patterns of actions (firing sequences) that can be instantiated by a script as a specific Petri net. Such patterns of actions are generically modelled as regular expressions implied by Petri net "grammar". Partial ordering of regular expressions makes possible to reason that a given abstraction of behavior can be considered a concretization of the abstraction of behavior assumed by the activity specification of requirements for the new information system.

The structural and behavioral abstractions introduced provide the methodological basis supporting the concretization of behaviors during the multiactivity design.

2 A uniform script-based multiactivity framework

An *activity* models an application and is defined as a computation over a collection of information resources intermitted by the interactions with the application environment of the information system. Multilevel collections of interrelated subactivities should be organized to represent complex, long-lived, collaborated *multiactivities*.

An activity is seen as a pattern of actions with their temporal ordering and behavioral relationships. According to *object-centric paradigm* activities can be seen as patterns of object communications [19]. An activity model is used for the declarative specification of object communication behavior, including temporal ordering of message exchanges within the object communications and the behavioral relationships between activity executions. Activity is defined in terms of participating object types, communication constraints, pre- and postconditions defining necessary relationships of the agents and the effect of the activity. An activity specification captures dynamic evolution and cooperation of a group of objects in solving of an application task.

Scripts are used in the SYNTHESIS language for the description of long-running activities (transactions) in terms of sequences of actions leading to changes of states of the information resources included into the HIRE. Our script model is based on the high level Petri nets [12]. Scripts are defined as classes that may be organized into the generalization/ specialization hierarchy. Each instance of a script class corresponds to a particular activation of an activity (transaction) defined by the script.

Like a Petri net, a script models the system behavior in terms of states and state transitions. As usual, a net is represented by a bipartite directed graph arcs of which connect nodes taken from two sets: set of states (places) and set of transitions. Each arc connects a state to a transition or vice versa. A transition is caused by input states that are connected to the transition by the arcs directed into the transition. A transition has the effect of activating the output states that are connected to the transition by the arcs directed out of the transition.

Script dynamics are determined by tokens that are put into the initial states of the script on its creation and transferred into the output states of each transition after the transition takes place or are passed into the external states of the script from the outside. The tokens are typed (as in the coloured Petri net [12]). Each state may contain several tokens of some type. One script instance may contain a number of tokens of different types simultaneously.

States are places where tokens waiting for conditions to move into transitions are accumulated. A state description of a script may include a definition of assertions that should be satisfied in order that a token which is placed into the state could be activated.

A description of each transition may include a list of transition conditions that should be simultaneously satisfied in order that a transition could be fired and a description of actions that should be taken on such firing. A transition actions are prescribed by the function description given inside of the transition specification in the *action* slot. In particular, an action may lead to the call of a transaction (an activity) that may conform to various transaction (activity) models. A type of input (output) tokens of a transition is agreed with the parameter types of the function prescribing the transition action. Tokens (input and/or output) may have no structure.

In the input states of a transition tokens may be accumulated and are considered in FIFO (or priority-based) order. For each of the tokens moved into a transition an action consists in a transition function call with actual parameters provided by the tokens. As the result, a token with a type defined by the function will be formed. One token (or prescribed number of tokens) formed will be directed to each state given by the list of the output states of the transition.

In a script an external states may appear to place tokens directed from other scripts or messages from objects. Such states are expressed as *gates* for the external *output* states of a script or as methods for the *input* states of a script that may be referenced externally. Hierarchical sripts are based on the idea of substitution of a transition by the whole (child) script of any complexity. Such facility is quite useful for the definition of complex activities.

Detailed definition of the script modeling facilities of SYNTHESIS is given in [17]. Specification of the script components is given in Appendix A. How to get to multiactivity (multitransaction) specificatons, declarative multi-resource constraint specifications and multi-resource interoperation programming using scripts is analyzed in [14, 15].

3 Localization of structural interactivity dependencies in megaprograms using scripts

Multiactivity modeling considering long-running application activities (*workflows*) with complex patterns of temporal, sequential, causal and other interactivity dependencies were discussed elsewhere [7, 9, 19]. First-order logic based formalism declaratively specifying component transaction and related objects dependencies that should be preserved was experienced in [5]. Thus intercomponent structural dependencies were declaratively specified.

Generalization of models contributes to the solution of the problem. For instance, rather general cooperative transaction model [20] is based on a structured set of cooperative transactions. *Operation machines* are introduced as the user definable synchronization mechanisms for specifying patterns and conflicts reflecting cooperative transaction structural dependencies.

To cope with the proper procedural control of the structural dependencies, dependency finite states automata were introduced [2]. Temporal propositional logic is used to specify the dependencies. The scheduler receives events corresponding to a possible task execution.

Transaction Specification and Management Environment (TSME) [10] is proposed as a facility to support the definition and construction of specific extended transaction models corresponding to application requirements. ECA rules are used for enforcing of the structural multiactivity dependencies.

In [17] a chunk-based model was proposed to abstract the structural aspects of the multiactivity specifications. *Chunk* is a code of a piece of an activity between "significant events" (such as termination of the current action, spawning of another (child or the same level) action or chunk, aborting of the current or a child action). On such call/return events (controlled by *chunk junction*) specific control depending on the multiactivity model may be applied. So, component activity is abstracted as a sequence of chunks with significant events in between. *Chunkpack* is a sequence of chunks separated by call/return of the components (actions and chunkpacks).

Chunk junctions (*Generic Intercomponent Control Modules (GICM)*) accumulate facilities for proper interpretation of significant events preserving *interactivity dependencies* defined for a *specific multiactivity model*. Using these simple abstractions, a multilayered structure can be specified where on each layer several chunkpacks may be located. In a nested case each two adjacent layers are parent layer and its direct child layer so that on the top level only one chunkpack is located.

A chunkpack is conveniently represented by hierarchical scripts [13] where the chunk junctions reflecting the specific features of a particular multiactivity (multitransaction) model are defined by the child scripts generated from the generic script once designed for each specific multiactivity model. The generation consists in providing of parameters for the generic script to communicate with concrete chunks and to call a child chunkpack and its compensation actions (if such child is required).

The application of this approach to the sequential SAGA model and to the closed nested model was shown in [17] where examples of generic junction scripts for such models were constructed.

Thus common features of the multiactivity (multitransaction) model and subactivity dependencies can be explicitely and generically introduced using the hierarchical script facility including such dependencies as commit-dependency, abort-dependency, weak-abort-dependency, termination-dependency, exclusion-dependency, compensation-dependency, begin-dependency, serial-dependency [5], etc.

3.1 Chunk model based approach for the concretization of multiactivities

A concretization of a multiactivity is a transformation of its specification into another one containing more details of concrete design or concrete implementation (eventually taking form of a specific multitransaction). In the semantic interoperation reasoning framework [16] the basic intention is to reuse pre-existing behaviors defined as the transaction (multitransaction) specifications. It means that the process of concretization should be based on the decisions that certain components of the original multiactivity specification can be refined as the pre-existing activities.

Chunk model introduced provides for making the process of multiactivity concretization reasoning constructive. Generally behavior reuse decisions are founded on the model-based approach [1, 24] for concretization (refinement) of functions that is quite well developed. Specification of a function (operation) consists of a definition of properties and relationships that state transitions caused by the function should satisfy. For that predicates relating values of state variables before and after operation (expressing *mixed pre- and post- conditions*) are defined. The notion of execution of a model-based specification consists of the proof of the initial consistency of the model and of the preservation of the invariants by the operations. There exist also a provable way of development of programs from specifications by proper *concretization* of abstract data types and operations of the specification by concrete data types and programs satisfying strict function concretization conditions. For particular function specification and the specification of its refinement (in our case the specification of the taken-of-the-shelf component) proof obligations should be generated and proved to justify that the reuse of such component for the original function is possible. Convenient tools of industrial quality now exist making such process of refinement practical [3, 1]. The problem is that the existing methodology works quite well for non-concurrent cases.

Chunk model provides for decomposition of the multiactivity concretization problem into subproblems for which the general function concretization methodology could become applicable. Such decomposition is based on the following principles:

- isolation of the pure functional type behavior of the concurrent type;
- structural localization of concurrency control in GICM (junctions);
- concretization - oriented specification abstraction of particular multiactivity model. The specification should be free of unnecessary details (imposed by efficiency, reliability and implementation constraints).

Application of these principles leads to the following general framework suitable for the multiactivity concretization:

1. treatment of chunks as pure functional behavior refining them using general functional refinement technique. In particular, this leads to a possibility of reuse of the pre-existing (atomic) transactions as chunks;

2. imposing of the refinement order on the various generic junction specifications;

3. separate refinement of junction specifications that leads finally to the specification of a multitransaction (new or combined of the pre-existing ones).

Detailed description of the approach for the localization of structural interactivity dependencies in megaprograms on the basis of the chunk model may be found in [17]. Further we present an idea of an approach intended for behavior concretization (refinement) reasoning based on the script behavior abstraction by regular expressions. This approach may be helpful also for the refinement of the chunk models specifications including junctions.

4 Activity concretization reasoning based on its regular expression abstraction

It was already noted that in the SYNTHESIS framework scripts are used for specification of dynamic features of the designed information system and of the pre-existing resources. The objectives of the specifications include: concretization of activities by pre-existing resource dynamics, checking of dynamic consistency of specifications (such as deadlocks and reachability of a certain state), multiactivity specification with certain dynamic interdependencies between subactivities, checking of the multiactivity consistency constraints and correctness dependencies. These specimens of the design procedures demonstrate the level of semantic interoperation reasoning necessary to deal with the information system dynamics. Here we continue to focus on the issues of concretization reasoning, that is how to decide whether the pre-existing dynamics (expressed by scripts) can be reused for a certain specification of an application activity under design.

It is clear that scripts are too complicated constructs to analyse them as a whole. Here we present an approach of getting a behavioral abstraction of a script as patterns of actions that are prescribed by a script (Petri net). The formal structure of a script specification in the SYNTHESIS language is given in Appendix A.

4.1 Script regular expressions

This approach is inspired by the Consistent Business Engineering of G.Dedene [8] proposed for objects to define *script regular expressions* as behavioral abstractions of scripts represented by the patterns of actions predetermined by the corresponding Petri nets "grammars". In [18] regular expressions are proposed for formal specifications of transaction -based information systems.

We restrict ourselves here with the consideration of deterministic activities [11] such that the behavior of an activity on its first $n + 1$ steps is determined by

the behavior of the activity on its first n steps only. Another restriction comes out of a class of behavior patterns representable by the regular expressions.
Script type is abstracted as a pair $<\alpha, e>$ where:

- α is the set of the event types which are relevant for the script type (the alphabet of the script type);

- e is a regular expression for the script type behavior (denoting all legal script firing sequences).

$., +, *, ||$ are basic primitives of the regular expressions *sequence, choice (selection), iteration, parallel composition*.
1 is a *do-nothing action type;* 0 - is the *deadlock* that prohibits any further action to happen in the life of a script.
Properties of sequence and selection primitives:

- *choice* (+) is *associative, commutative, idempotent;* 0 is neutral for + (0 + a = a + 0 = a)

- *sequence* (.) is *associative* (but not commutative), 1 is neutral for. (1.a = a.1 = a)

- (a + b).c = a.c + b.c (right distributivity)
  a.(b + c) = a.b + a.c (left distributivity)

A^* denotes all the finite sequences of action types belonging to A.
A script language L is formed by the set of all firing sequences of a labelled script (*names of transition actions* are used for the alphabet).
Selectors for script type N=$<\alpha, e>$ include:

- $S_A(N)= \alpha$ (a set of action types);

- $S_R(N)= e$ (a regular expression over α)

Projection of a regular expression e to alphabet B (label manipulation operator) is defined as e \ B that is equal to e with replacing of all action types in e not belonging to alphabet B by 1.

4.2 Ordering of script behaviors

Partial order on script behaviors (the same as in [8] for objects) is defined as:
  $N <= Q$ iff $N + Q \setminus S_A(N) = Q \setminus S_A(N)$
N and Q in this notation mean abstractions of scripts N and Q with a pair $<\alpha, e>$ as above.
Parallel composition of script types ([8]):
  $S_A(N||Q) = S_A(N) \bigcup S_A(Q)$
  $S_R(N||Q) = e$, where e is defined by the following expression specifying allowable patterns of actions constituting a script language:

$L(e) = L(N||Q) = \{s \in (S_A(N) \cup S_A(Q))^* | s \setminus S_A(N) \in L(S_R(N)) \land s \setminus S_A(Q) \in L(S_R(Q))\}$

Partial order relation for parallel composition of scripts (the same as in [8] for objects) is defined as:

$N \leq Q$ iff $(N||Q) \setminus S_A(N) = N$

N is smaller or equal to Q iff Q admits all traces from N in such way that in parallel lives of N and Q all possible N traces are possible.

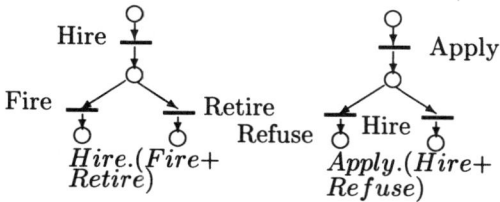

Fig. 1. JOB and APPLICATION scripts

4.3 Examples of regular expression abstractions of scripts

For an employment agency activities specifications (we used idea of examples from [8] and constructed script skeletons for them) scripts and their regular expressions are shown on Fig. 1, Fig. 2, Fig. 3.

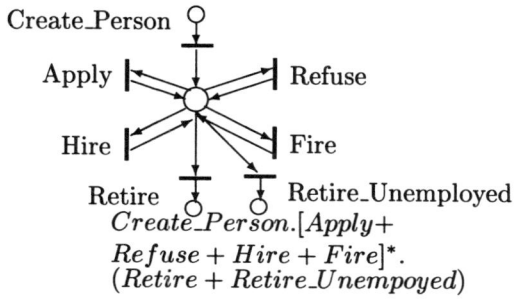

Fig. 2. PERSON script

4.4 Concretization of scripts

Now we can decompose the concretization problem and solve it on a piecemeal basis using the following script *concretization conditions* that should be checked when we are looking for a script Q that might be *reused* for concretization (refinement) of a script N. The notation used for denoting of the constituents of the script is defined in the Appendix A.

Q is a concretization of N iff:

1. $N \leq Q$ holds for script behavior abstractions that means:
$N + Q \setminus S_A(N) = Q \setminus S_A(N)$ and in particular that $S_A(N) \subseteq S_A(Q)$

2. *each transition* t_Q in projection $Q \setminus S_A(N)$ should be in *one-to-one correspondence with a transition* t_N in N. Each such pair (t_Q, t_N) should satisfy the following condition. Input places of t_Q should be in one-to-one correspondence with the input places of t_N. For output places of the pair (t_Q, t_N) it is required that to each output place of t_N an output place of t_Q should correspond. Corresponding places (p_N, p_Q) should be such that $C(p_q)$ *is a subtype* of $C(p_n)$ and $Ap(p_n) \to Ap(p_q)$. $F(t_Q)$ should be a *concretization* of $F(t_N)$ and $G(t_N) \to G(t_Q)$ for each pair of corresponding transitions (t_N, t_Q)

3. for corresponding pairs of transitions their ingoing and outgoing arcs (this follows from the second condition). For a pair of corresponding arcs (a_N, a_Q) $E(a_Q)$ should be a concretization of $E(a_N)$. It means that $E(a_Q).Par$ should be a concretization of $E(a_N).Par$, $E(a_N).Oce \to E(a_Q).Oce$ and $E(a_N).Z = E(a_Q).Z$

4. for *initial marking* M_N of N should correspond an initial marking M_Q of Q such that for corresponding pairs of places (p_N, p_Q) $M_Q(p_Q)$ *should be a concretization* of $M_N(p_N)$

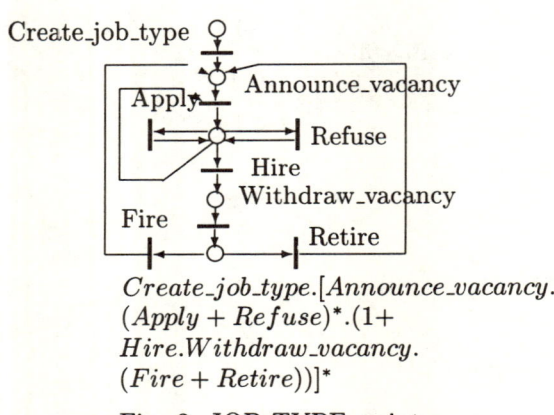

$Create\_job\_type.[Announce\_vacancy.$
$(Apply + Refuse)^*.(1+$
$Hire.Withdraw\_vacancy.$
$(Fire + Retire))]^*$

Fig. 3. JOB_TYPE script

For examples in Fig. 1, Fig. 2, Fig. 3 to reason on the possibility of concretizations it is sufficient to check only the first concretization conditions that are obvious for the examples:
JOB $\leq$ JOB_TYPE, JOB $\leq$ PERSON,
APPLICATION $\leq$ JOB_TYPE, APPLICATION $\leq$ PERSON
For concretization analysis we follow the procedure:

1. Look for scripts satisfying $N \leq Q$ behavioral condition (so that $N + Q \setminus S_A(N) = Q \setminus S_A(N)$ and in particular that $S_A(N) \subseteq S_A(Q)$). Regular

expression given for Q should correspond to the flat script (if Q is hierarchical).

2. In course of the search according to the first step analyse the incoherence and try to apply equivalent transformations to N and Q specifications to satisfy the behavioral condition. These may include decomposing of N and looking for scripts that can satisfy parts of N with subsequent hierarchical transformation of N.

3. If we get $N \leq Q$ conditions then we should check the complete set of concretization conditions given above.

5 Conclusion

Basic abstraction facilities needed for the application of the *semantic interoperation reasoning principles* to the concretization of an information system activity specifications by the pre-existing information resource behavior patterns are introduced. We are based on the generalized HIRE modeling framework possessing two-dimensional uniformity of the specifications (horizontally for heterogeneous information resources and vertically for different layers of specification, design and implementation).

Using the framework we apply its set of modeling facilities for capturing of structural aspects of the multiactivity modeling. Simple chunk-based multiactivity model leads to the localization of structural interactivity dependencies of megaprograms in the concept of Generic Intercomponent Control Modules (GICM) expressing semantics of the corresponding multiactivity (multitransaction) models. Generation (refinement) of a multiactivity with the pre-specified structural properties needed for the application becomes possible.

Separation of pure functional and concurrent behaviors opens the way for application of well developed general functional refinement technique (leading to a justifiable reuse of the pre-existing behaviors). Concurrency specification localized in GICM can be refined during the design separately leading finally to the specification of a multitransaction (new or combined of the pre-existing ones).

An approach of getting of a behavioral abstraction of a script as patterns of actions (firing sequences) that can be generated by a script as a specific Petri net is presented. Such patterns of actions are modelled as regular expressions implied by the Petri net "grammar". Partial ordering of regular expressions makes possible to reason that given abstraction of behavior can be considered a refinement of the abstraction of behavior taken from the specification of the activity.

Structural and behavioral abstractions of multiactivities work together to make their concretization feasible. The abstractions introduced make possible to decompose the hard activity concretization problem into manageable subproblems. The decomposition provides also for the possibility of using of the conventional well grounded function refinement technique.

References

[1] Abrial J.-R. B-Technology. Technical overview. BP International Ltd., 1992, 73 p.

[2] Attie P.A., Singh M.P., Sheth A., Rusinkiewicz M. Specifying and enforcing intertask dependencies, Proceedings of the 19th International Conference on Very Large Data Bases, September 1993

[3] Bjorner D. Prospects for a viable software industry. Computers as our better partners. Proceedings of the International IISF/ACM Symposium, Tokyo, World Scientific, 1994

[4] Brodie, M.L. The Promise of Distributed Computing and the Challenges of Legacy Systems. In P.M.D. Gray and R.J. Lucas (eds.) Advanced Database Systems: Proceedings of the 10th British National Conference on Databases, Springer-Verlag, New York/Heidelburg, July 1992

[5] P. P. Chrysanthis and K. Ramamritham. A Formalism for Extended Transaction Models. *Proceedings of the 17th International Conference on Very Large Data Bases*, September 1991.

[6] Chrysanthis P., Ramamritham K. ACTA: the SAGA continues. in [9]

[7] U. Dayal, M. Hsu, R. Ladin. A transactional model for long-running activities *Proceedings of the 17th International Conference on Very Large Data Bases*, September 1991

[8] Dedene G., Snoeck M. Object-oriented modeling: a new language for consistent business engineering, Proceedings of the International Conference EastEurOOPe'93, Bratislava, November 1993

[9] A. Elmagarmid, Ed. Database Transaction Models for Advanced Applications, Morgan-Kaufmann, 1992

[10] Georgakopoulos D., Hornick M., Krychniak P., Manola F. Specification and management of extended transactions in a programmable transaction environment. Proceedings of the 10th International Conference on Data Engineering, February, 1994

[11] Hoare C.A.R. Communicating Sequential Processes. Prentice Hall International, 1985.

[12] K. Jensen. Coloured Petri Nets: a High Level Language for System Design and Analysis. *High level Petri Nets. Theory and Application*. Springer Verlag, 1991.

[13] Kalinichenko L.A. SYNTHESIS: a language for description, design and programming of interoperable information resource environment. Institute for Problems of Informatics of the Russian Academy of Sciences, September 1993, 113 p. (in Russian)

[14] Kalinichenko L.A. A Declarative Framework for Capturing Dynamic Behavior in Heterogeneous Interoperable Information Resource Environment. Proceedings of the RIDE -IMS'93, Vienna, April 1993

[15] Kalinichenko L.A. Specification and implementation of dynamic behavior in the interoperable environment of information resources. Russian Academy of Sciences, IPIAN, Technical Report, October 1993

[16] Kalinichenko L.A. Emerging semantic-based interoperable information system technology. Computers as our better partners. Proceedings of the International IISF/ACM Symposium, Tokyo, World Scientific, 1994

[17] Kalinichenko L.A. Homogeneous localization of structural interactivity dependencies in megaprograms using scripts. Proceedings of the International Workshop on Advances in Databases and Information Systems (ADBIS'94), Moscow, May 1994

[18] Lustman F. Specifying transaction-based information systems with regular expressions. IEEE Transactions on Software Engineering, vol. 20, N 3, March 1994

[19] L. Liu, R. Meersman. Activity model: a declarative approach for capturing communication behavior in object-oriented databases. *Proceedings of the 18 International Conference on Very Large Data Bases,*Vancouver, August 1992.

[20] Nodine M.H., Zdonik S.B. Cooperative transaction hierarchies: transaction support for design applications. VLDB Journal, vol. 1, p. 41 - 80, 1992

[21] Object Management Group, "The Common Object Request Broker: Architecture and Specification", OMG Document Number 91.12.1, December 1991.

[22] M. Rusinkiewicz, S. Osterman, A. Elmagarmid, K. Loa. The Distributed Operational Language for Specifying Multisystem Application *Proceedings of the First International Conference on Systems Integration*, April 1990

[23] A. Sheth, M. Rusinkiewicz, and G. Karabatis. Using Polytransactions to Manage Interdependent Data. Chapter 14, in [9]

[24] Spivey J.M. The Z Notation. A reference manual. Prentice-Hall, 1989

[25] Wiederhold G., Wegner P., Ceri S. Toward megaprogramming. CACM, v. 35, N 11, November 1992

Appendix A

A Formal definition of a script type

Scripts are based on SYNTHESIS type system, object calculus and functions. Places are annotated with types and object calculus formulas, transitions - with object calculus formulas and functions. A binding is a term substitution replacing variables in formulas and input (output) parameters in transition functions with constants represented as tokens of the predetermined types. In a binding a type of a token should be in a subtyping relation with a type of the corresponding variable or parameter.

Script type may be abstracted as a variant of coloured Petri nets:

- (P,T,A;N) is a *net structure* (directed bipartite graph) with finite set of places P, finite set of transitions T, finite sets of arcs A and a node function N from A into $PxT \cup TxP$;

- $C : P \rightarrow$ Type is a *type function* mapping places into SYNTHESIS types (basically, abstract data types having mutable or immutable values). Each token belonging to a place must have a value of the given type or of its subtypes.

- Ap : P $\rightarrow$ Oce* is an *activity predicate function* mapping places into object calculus expressions defining formulas that should be satisfied for a token of the place to become active (only active tokens could be used in firing of the transitions);

- G : T $\rightarrow$ Oce is a *guard function* mapping each transition into an object calculus expression defining a predicate that should be satisfied for a transition to fire;

- F : T $\rightarrow$ Funct is an *action function* mapping each transition into a function definition determining a function to be applied on firing of a transaction; binding of input and output parameters of the function is given by an arc expression function;

- E : A $\rightarrow$ (Par x Oce x Z)* is an *arc expression function* mapping each arc into an object calculus expression defining a subset of transition input (output) sets of tokens that might be bind to some input (output) parameter of a transition function. This subset may be forwarded from (into) the state on transition firing. Additionally an integer may be added stating a number of tokens that might be consumed (produced) on transition firing in this particular binding;

- H : T$-> \sum$ is a *labelling function* mapping transitions into an alphabet that includes also an empty sequence;

- I : P$->$ (V x Z)* is an *initialization function* mapping each place into an expressions giving values of the token type defined for the place and a number of those values that should be created initially in the places.

Script dynamics is defined as follows. A token distribution in a script is a function M defined on P such that M (p) is an element of the powerset of the type C(p) values. A binding distribution is a function Y defined on T such that Y(t) is an element of all bindings for t (a binding is a proper substitution for variables and parameters for a transition).

A marking in a script is a token distribution and a step is a binding distribution. The set of all markings for a given script s is denoted by M_s and the set of all steps - by Y_s. M_0 is an initial marking.

When a step is enabled it transforms M into a directly reachable marking removing (adding) tokens from (to) places by concurrently enabled transitions included into a step. The direct reachability of M_2 from M_1 is denoted as $M_1[Y > M_2$.

A finite firing sequence of a script is a sequence of markings and steps:

$M_1[Y_1 > M_2[Y_2 > ...M_n[Y_n > M_{n+1}$

where M_1 is a start marking and M_{n+1} is an end marking.

Management and Translation of Heterogeneous Database Schemes*

Paolo Atzeni
Terza Università di Roma
c/o DIS, Via Salaria 113
00198 Roma, Italy

Riccardo Torlone
IASI–CNR
Viale Manzoni 30
00185 Roma, Italy

Abstract

We consider the problem of managing and translating schemes of different data models, in a framework that refers to a wide range of models. This can be at the basis of an integrated CASE environment supporting the analysis and design of information systems, allowing different representations for the same data schemes. We introduce a graph-theoretic formalism to define and compare models and schemes. This is based on a classification of the constructs used in the known data model into a limited set of types. Data models are represented by means of sets of patterns, a specific form of graphs. A lattice on sets of patterns is shown, which can be the basis for the formalization of translations froma a model to another.

1 Introduction

It is widely accepted now that a conceptual data model be used in the analysis phase and many tools exist that support the analysis and design of information systems [5]. At the same time, many data models have been defined [10], and each of the tools usually implements only one of the models. Incidentally, although it is true that most of the tools support the Entity-Relationship model [6], it is also true that there are in fact many versions of this model, which represent actually different models, often compatible only to a limited extent. It is reasonable that in a complex environment different models should coexist, for a number of reasons: (i) different subproblems have been analyzed independently (for examples by companies that later merged or got involved in a federated project); or (ii) different analysts prefer different models; or (iii) different subproblems are tackled with different models, because of the specific aspects of each.

We have already discussed the general ideas of our approach [3]. Our long term goal is an environment that allows the definition of "any reasonable data model," by means of a suitable formalism called a *metamodel*. Then, for any two models M_1 and M_2 defined in this way, and for each scheme S_1 (the *source scheme*) of M_1 (the *source model*), it should be possible to obtain a scheme S_2 (the *target scheme*) that be the translation of S_1 into M_2 (the *target model*). A major point in this plan is related to the expressive power of the metamodel, that is, the set of models that can be defined. In fact, the notion of a model is widely accepted and understood, but there is no general, formal

---

*This work was partially supported by Consiglio Nazionale delle Ricerche and by MURST.

definition. Therefore, it would be hopeless (and probably meaningless) to look for a "universal" metamodel, that is a metamodel that allow the description of every possible model. This problem can be overcome by noting that all the constructs used in most known models fall in a rather limited set of categories [10]: lexical type, abstract type, aggregation, generalization, function, grouping. Therefore, we have argued [3] that a metamodel can be defined by means of a basic set of *metaconstructs*, corresponding to the above categories. Then, a model can be described by defining its constructs by means of the metaconstructs in the metamodel. The generality and variety of the metaconstructs determine the expressive power of the metamodel. In a sense, this approach is "asymptotically" complete: if there is a model that cannot be expressed by means of the metamodel, because a construct in the model has no counterpart in the metamodel, then the metamodel can be extended by introducing a new, suitable metaconstruct. We believe that a wide class of models can be managed with a few extensions to the basic metamodel.

A second key point in our approach is that there is no clear notion of when a translation is correct: at first, one could think that the target scheme should be "equivalent" to the source scheme, that is, they should represent "the same information." A lot of research has been conducted in the last decades on scheme equivalence (or "comparison of information capacity") with reference to the relational model [2, 9, 15] or to heterogeneous frameworks [1, 11, 13, 14], but there is no general, agreed definition. Also, it is clear that the various models have different (often incomparable) expressive power, both in terms of actual representation capacity and in terms of understandability: we have observed [3] that the translation process may generate a *loss* and/or a *degradation* of information. In many cases, various possible translations may coexist, each preferable on some grounds and less desirable on others. Therefore, we can even claim that often there is no best translation.

To the best of our knowledge, there is not much literature related to the problem we tackle and the goal we set. Some work exists on the idea of a metamodel for the representation of models [4, 11], but the goal is more on the integration of heterogeneous databases in a federated environment [8, 16] than on the translation of schemes to generic target models.

On the basis of the above arguments, one of the conclusions of our preliminary discussion [3] was that it would be very difficult (if at all meaningful) to find general transformations that work for every pair of models and every scheme and satisfy all the possible requirements. Therefore, a pragmatic approach is needed: part of the translation has to be specified by a human (the *model engineer*) and the goal of this research becomes the support to be given to the model engineer, in terms of methodologies and tools. With respect to the methodology, the basic observation that a small set of metaconstructs is sufficient to describe the constructs of interest (in different models) can be exploited. As a matter of fact, the various constructs that correspond to the same metaconstruct can be assumed to have the same semantics (at least with respect to the translation process). As a consequence, the process of scheme translation can be based on translations of constructs (or simple combinations thereof) defined with respect to the corresponding metaconstruct. In this way, schemes and translations need not refer to specific models, but may be defined with respect to a *supermodel*, a model that has a construct for (each variant of) each metaconstruct. So, if translations from the supermodel to a given model are possible, then translations from any other model to such a model are also possible. The goal of this paper is to study formal properties of the translation process, obtained as the composition of elementary translation steps: we assume that a set of (correct) basic transformations is given and present criteria and techniques for finding "good" translations with respect to the involved models. The supermodel is the context of reference for the various models: each scheme, whichever be its actual model (if any) can be considered as a scheme according to the supermodel. Making one step further we could give an alternate (and more general) definition of a model: a model is a set of schemes—the schemes of the supermodel that are meaningful for such a model. In fact, in this paper we introduce a formalism to define models, based on the notion of graphs: we have the notion of a *structure*, a directed graph whose nodes have different types (corresponding to the basic metaconstructs we mentioned above, such as lexical, abstract, aggregation and function). Then, we use structures in two ways: we have *patterns*, structures where the edges have cardinalities as labels, and *schemes*, structures whose nodes and edges are labeled with names. Then a model M is defined by means of a set of patterns $\mathbf{P}$: a scheme S *belongs* to M if each of the elementary components (according to a specific, but natural notion) of S can be mapped (in a certain way) to one of the patterns in $\mathbf{P}$. In this way, there is a set of schemes associated with each model. Clearly, a scheme can belong to several models.

Let us now turn our attention to the translation process. An elementary translation (which refers to patterns) can be seen as a function from a set of schemes to a set of schemes. The main goal of this paper is to study how elementary transformations can be composed, in order to form complex translations: assuming that the basic transformations are correct, we study correctness and other properties of complex translations. In a sense, this could be called an "axiomatic" approach. This is coherent with the observation made above on the difficulty in defining correct translations: the model engineer has the responsibility (and the freedom) of choosing the most suitable basic transformations. Now, elementary transformations are described on the basis of the patterns they eliminate and the patterns they introduce: clearly, this is only part of their description (we say this is the *signature* of a translation step, as opposed to its *body* or *program*), but it is sufficient for our purposes. The main point of the approach is that if a transformation eliminates all components of a scheme that correspond to a pattern P_1 and replaces components corresponding to a pattern P_2, then, from an intuitive point of view, its application to a set of schemes described by a set of patterns $\mathbf{P}$ generates schemes described by another set of patterns (intuitively, $\mathbf{P} - \{P_1\} \cup \{P_2\}$, but things are more complex, since patterns are not really independent from one another). In this way, a translation from a model M_0 (described by the set of patterns $\mathbf{P}_0$) to another model M (described by $\mathbf{P}$) can be seen as a sequence of elementary translations $\tau_1, \ldots, \tau_k$ such that there is a sequence of sets of patterns $\mathbf{P}_1, \ldots, \mathbf{P}_k$ such that $\mathbf{P}_k = \mathbf{P}$ and τ_i applied to schemes described by $\mathbf{P}_{i-1}$ generates schemes described by $\mathbf{P}_i$. The main, interesting issue we consider in this paper is the observation that a partial order can be introduced on patterns that, suitably extended, becomes a lattice on sets of patterns. Then, properties of translations are based on lattice-theoretic operations.

An important point is that the supermodel is itself a model, and that it is the top element of the lattice, that is, the least upper bound of the set of all the models of interest. At the other extreme, the bottom element of the lattice is the empty set of patterns, and therefore it does not correspond to a significant model. However, it is reasonable to consider "minimal" models—sets of patterns that do not subsume any other (set of pattern representing a meaningful) model. In general, there may be several, incomparable minimal models. In this framework, it will be possible to study properties of translations, such as correctness, completeness, and minimality. This is the subject of current investigation.

The paper is organized as follows. In Section 2 we introduce a graph-theoretic formalism for the description of the various components of the metamodel, and show its properties. Specifically, patterns and sets thereof are studied. This formalism is used in Section 3 to define schemes, models and translations of schemes. Finally, in Section 4, we sketch some conclusions.

2 A graph-theoretic formalism

2.1 Structures and Patterns

A *structure* is a triple $S = (G, \mu, \epsilon)$ where $G = (N, E)$ is a digraph whose underlying graph is acyclic and μ and ϵ are *structuring functions*. The domain of μ is the set of nodes N and its range is the set of *node types* $\mathcal{N}$, whereas ϵ has the set of edges E as domain and the set of *edge types* $\mathcal{E}$ as range. The elements in $\mathcal{N}$ and in $\mathcal{E}$ correspond to the metaconstructs of the metamodel. In our examples, we will consider three types of nodes corresponding to *abstracts* (denoted by the symbol $\triangle$), *aggregations* ($\otimes$), and *lexicals* ($\square$); and five types of edges corresponding to *functions* (denoted by $\to$), *multivalued functions* ($\twoheadrightarrow$), *components of aggregation* ($\rightarrowtail$), *keys of aggregation* ($\bullet\!\!\rightarrow$) and *keys of abstract* ($\rightarrow\!\!\bullet$). Clearly, the structuring function must satisfy a number of conditions corresponding to the usual restrictions on the composition of constructs [10]. Note that for sake of simplification, we have assumed that a structure has no (directed or indirected) cycles. This is not a significant limitation in practice: intuitively, "cyclic" schemes can be obtained by composing structures, in the same way as in conceptual models cycles in the schemes appear, without recursive constructs (a formal justification for this argument was given by Kuper [12]).

Given two structures $S_1 = ((N_1, E_1), \mu_1, \epsilon_1)$ and $S_2 = ((N_2, E_2), \mu_2, \epsilon_2)$, a *mapping* Φ from S_1 to S_2 is a pair of functions $\theta : N_1 \to N_2$ and $\phi : E_1 \to E_2$. A mapping $\Phi = (\theta, \phi)$ is *structure-preserving* if: (1) for each $n \in N_1$, $\mu_1(n) = \mu_2(\theta(n))$, and (2) for each $e = (n, n') \in E_1$, $\epsilon_1(e) = \epsilon_2(\phi(e))$ and $\phi(e) = (\theta(n), \theta(n'))$. If θ and ϕ are bijections then we say that Φ is an *isomorphism* and that S_1 and S_2 are *isomorphic*.[1]

Let $\mathbf{N}$ be the set of natural numbers and $\mathbf{N}^+$ be the set of positive natural numbers. A *range of cardinality* (or simply, a *range*) is a pair (n, m) (*minimum* and *maximum* cardinality respectively) such that $n \in \mathbf{N}$, $m \in \mathbf{N}^+$ and $n \leq m$. If $x \in \mathbf{N}$ and $r = (n, m)$ is a range, then $x \in r$ if $n \leq x \leq m$.

A *(simple) pattern* is a pair $P = (S, \rho)$ where $S = (G, \mu, \epsilon)$ is a structure such that G is a rooted tree, and ρ is a function that associates a range with each edge of G. Two patterns $P_1 = (S_1, \rho_1)$ and $P_2 = (S_2, \rho_2)$ are *isomorphic*

---

[1]Note that two finite isomorphic structures are indeed identical.

if S_1 and S_2 are isomorphic and each edge of P_1 is associated with an edge of P_2 with the same range.

Before introducing the notion of instance of patterns we fix some terminology from graph theory. Given a digraph $G = (N, E)$ and a subset N' of N, the *subgraph of G induced by N'* is the graph $G' = (N', E')$ where E' is the subset of E whose edges have both head and tail in N'. Given a digraph G and a node n of G, the *subgraph of G generated by n* is the subgraph of G induced by n and all the nodes of G reachable from n. A *source* of G is a node of G with no incoming edge. A *component* of G is the subgraph of G generated by a source of G. It is easy too see that if the underlying graph of a digraph G is acyclic then every subgraph generated by a node (and so a component of G) is indeed a rooted tree. With a slight abuse of notation, in the following we will also speak of *substructure*, *subpattern* and *component of a structure*. In this case the various functions are always intended to be restricted to the involved nodes and edges.

Now, we say that a structure S *matches* with a pattern $P = (S', \rho)$ if there is a structure-preserving mapping $\Phi = (\theta, \phi)$ from S to S' such that for each edge e' of S', the number of edges e of S such that $e' = \phi(e)$ is contained in the range of e', that is, $|\phi^{-1}(e')| \in \rho(e')$. Note that a structure $S = (G, \mu, \epsilon)$ can match with a pattern only if G is a rooted tree. For this reason, the main definition of this section establishes correspondences between structures and sets of patterns (rather than single patterns). It is based on the notion of component of a scheme, as follows.

A structure S is an *instance* of a set of patterns $\mathbf{P}$ if for each component S_i of S there is a pattern $P \in \mathbf{P}$ such that S_i matches with P. Given a set of patterns $\mathbf{P}$, we will denote with $Inst(\mathbf{P})$ the set of all instances of $\mathbf{P}$.

A set of patterns $\mathbf{P}_1$ *is contained* in a set of patterns $\mathbf{P}_2$, in symbols $\mathbf{P}_1 \subseteq \mathbf{P}_2$, if $Inst(\mathbf{P}_1) \subseteq Inst(\mathbf{P}_2)$. If both $\mathbf{P}_1 \subseteq \mathbf{P}_2$ and $\mathbf{P}_2 \subseteq \mathbf{P}_1$ then we say that the two sets of patterns have *the same representation capacity* (in symbols, $\mathbf{P}_1 \equiv \mathbf{P}_2$).

Example 1 *Figure 1 shows a pattern and one of its instances. The pattern represents unary and binary aggregations of abstracts, and (optional) functions from abstracts to lexicals.*

2.2 Subsumption and Equivalence

In order to establish a partial order relationship among sets of patterns, we will consider patterns of a particular kind: we say that a pattern P is *unitary* if all the edges of P have range $(1, 1)$. Given a set of patterns $\mathbf{P}$, we say that the *decomposition* of $\mathbf{P}$, denoted with $\mathbf{P}^*$, is the set of patterns obtained by applying the following rules exhaustively, until no modification can be performed:

- if there is a pattern $P = (S, \rho)$ in $\mathbf{P}$ with an edge $e = (n_1, n_2)$ such that $\rho(e) = (0, y)$ then P is replaced by two patterns P_1 and P_2 such that: (i) $P_1 = (S, \rho_1)$ where $\rho_1 = \rho$ except that $\rho_1(e) = (1, y)$, and (ii) $P_2 = (S_2, \rho_2)$ where S_2 is the substructure of S induced by all the nodes of S but all the nodes of the tree generated by n_2, and ρ_2 is the restriction of ρ to S_2;

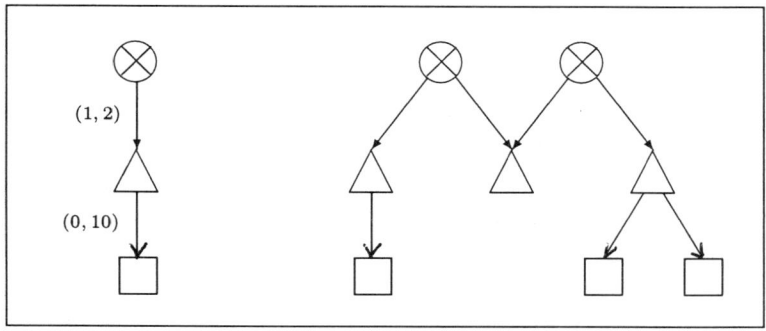

Figure 1: A pattern and one of its instances.

- if there is a pattern $P = (S, \rho)$ in $\mathbf{P}$ with an edge $e = (n_1, n_2)$ such that $\rho(e) = (x, y)$ and $x > 0$ then P is replaced by $y - x + 1$ patterns $P_0, P_1, \ldots, P_{y-x}$ such that each P_i coincides with P except that there are $x + i$ edges e_i in the place of e with $\rho(e_i) = (1, 1)$, that have attached at their tails a copy of the tree of $\mathbf{P}$ generated by n_2.

Lemma 1 *For every set of patterns $\mathbf{P}$, the decomposition of $\mathbf{P}$ (1) is unique, (2) contains only unitary patterns, and (3) has the same representation capacity as $\mathbf{P}$.*

A partial order relationship on sets of patterns is now defined as follows: we say that a set of patterns $\mathbf{P}_1$ is *subsumed* by a set of patterns $\mathbf{P}_2$ if for each pattern $P_1 \in \mathbf{P}_1^*$ there is a pattern $P_2 \in \mathbf{P}_2^*$ such that P_1 and P_2 are isomorphic. If both $\mathbf{P}_1 \preceq \mathbf{P}_2$ and $\mathbf{P}_2 \preceq \mathbf{P}_1$, we say that the two sets of patterns are *equivalent* (in symbols $\mathbf{P}_1 \sim \mathbf{P}_2$).

Theorem 1 *Let $\mathbf{P}_1$ and $\mathbf{P}_2$ be two sets of patterns. Then $\mathbf{P}_1 \preceq \mathbf{P}_2$ if and only if $\mathbf{P}_1 \subseteq \mathbf{P}_2$.*

Decomposition is at the basis of the operations on patterns, to be defined in the next section.

2.3 A lattice on sets of patterns

It is possible to show that the partial order relation $\preceq$ induces a *lattice* on the set of sets of (unitary) patterns, that is, every finite collection $\mathcal{P}$ of sets of patterns has both a *greatest lower bound* ($glb(\mathcal{P})$) and a *least upper bound* ($lub(\mathcal{P})$). Let us define two operations on sets of patterns. The *join* of a collection of a set of patterns $\mathcal{P} = \{\mathbf{P}_1, \ldots, \mathbf{P}_k\}$ is the set of unitary patterns obtained as the union of the decompositions of the elements in $\mathcal{P}$: $\cup_{i=1}^k \mathbf{P}_i^*$. The *meet* of $\mathcal{P} = \{\mathbf{P}_1, \ldots, \mathbf{P}_k\}$ is the intersection of the decompositions of the elements in $\mathcal{P}$ $\cap_{i=1}^k \mathbf{P}_i^*$.

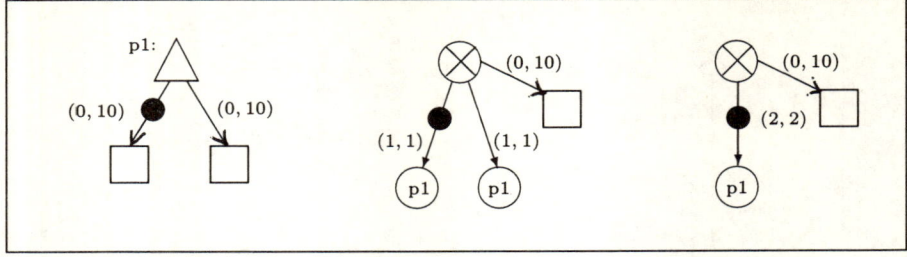

Figure 2: A set of patterns describing a version of the E-R model.

Lemma 2 *For each collection $\mathcal{P}$ of sets of unitary patterns there are a glb, equal to the meet of the elements in $\mathcal{P}$, and a lub, equal to the join of the elements in $\mathcal{P}$.*

We also define a difference operation on sets of patterns as follows. Given two sets of patterns $\mathbf{P}_1$ and $\mathbf{P}_2$ such that $\mathbf{P}_1 \preceq \mathbf{P}_2$, we have: $\mathbf{P}_2 - \mathbf{P}_1 = \mathbf{P}_1^* - \mathbf{P}_2^*$.

3 Models, Schemes and Translations

In this section we introduce several notions related to the activity of defining and manipulating schemes and models in our framework.

3.1 Models and Schemes

A *model description* (or simply a *model*) is a pair $M = (\mathbf{P}, \gamma)$ where $\mathbf{P}$ is a set of patterns and γ is a labeling function that maps each element of $\mathcal{N} \cup \mathcal{E}$ occurring in $\mathbf{P}$ to a label. These labels corresponds to the names associated to a construct in a specific model (e.g., the abstract construct is called *entity* in the E-R model).

Example 2 *In Figure 2, we show a set of patterns representing a version of the E-R model involving binary relationships with keys (with a limit of 10 key attributes and 10 non-key attributes for each entity and 10 attributes for each relationship). For the sake of conciseness, an identifier is used to refer to similar subpatterns that coincide with a pattern.*

A *scheme* is a pair $\mathcal{S} = (S, \lambda)$ composed by a structure S and by a *labeling function* λ that maps each node and each edge of S to a label, such that different labels are associated with different elements of the structure. These labels correspond to names associated to the various concepts in a specific scheme (e.g., persons, books and so on). We also associate with each scheme a label called the *name* of the scheme. Then, we say that a scheme $\mathcal{S} = (S, \lambda)$ *belongs* to a model $M = (\mathbf{P}, \gamma)$ if $S \in Inst(\mathbf{P})$.

Therefore, we can say that, in this framework, models are represented by sets of patterns, and schemes by instances of sets of patterns.

Let S be a structure and $\Delta(S)$ be the set of patterns $P = (S_i, \rho)$ such that S_i is a component of S and $\rho(e) = (1,1)$ for each edge e of S_i. The following result gives us an effective method to check whether a scheme belongs to a model.

Lemma 3 *Let $\mathcal{S} = (S, \lambda)$ be a scheme and $M = (\mathbf{P}, \gamma)$ be a model. Then, $\mathcal{S}$ belongs to M if and only if $\Delta(S) \preceq \mathbf{P}$.*

3.2 Translations of schemes

We say that a *structure transformation* T is a function from structures to structures. We are often interested in transformations between structures of a fixed model to structures of another fixed model. Then, we say that a structure transformation from a model M_1 to a model M_2 is a function $T : Inst(M_1) \to Inst(M_2)$.

Transformations should be defined by means of a specific language (for example a graph based database language [7]): a *translation program* is the specification of a structure transformation in such a language. For the goals of this paper, however, a simpler description is sufficient: a transformation can be effectively described by means of a pair of patterns representing respectively the components of the scheme that it eliminates and the components it introduces. This description can be considered as a high-level representation of the behavior of a transformation, completely described by a translation program.

Therefore, we introduce the notion of *translation rule* as follows. A *translation signature* σ for a translation program τ is a pair of unitary patterns $\sigma = (P_1, P_2)$ such that for each structure S and for each component S_i of S: (1) $\tau(S_i)$ is an instance of $\{P_2\}$ if S_i matches with P_1, and (2) $\tau(S_i) = S_i$ otherwise. We will denote with $\sigma[\tau]$ a *translation rule*, where τ is a translation program and σ is a translation signature for τ. A *translation specification* T (or simply a *translation*) is a sequence of translation rules $T = \sigma_1[\tau_1], \ldots, \sigma_k[\tau_k]$.

A nice property of a translation signature is that it can be used to characterize translations in terms of models. Let $\mathbf{P}$ be a set of patterns and $\sigma[\tau]$ be a translation rule where $\sigma = (P_1, P_2)$. In order to define the effect of σ on $\mathbf{P}$ we introduce the following sets of unitary patterns:(1) $Del(\sigma, \mathbf{P})$ is the meet of $\mathbf{P}$ and $\{P_1\}$; (2) $Add(\sigma, \mathbf{P})$ equals $\{P_2\}^*$ if $Del(\sigma, \mathbf{P}) \neq \emptyset$ and is the empty set otherwise. Then, we say that the *effect* of σ on $\mathbf{P}$, denoted by $\sigma(\mathbf{P})$, is the set of patterns obtained as the join of $\mathbf{P}^-$ and $\mathbf{P}^+$, where $\mathbf{P}^- = \mathbf{P} - Del(\sigma, \mathbf{P})$ and $\mathbf{P}^+ = Add(\sigma, \mathbf{P})$. We have the following result.

Theorem 2 *Let $\sigma[\tau]$ be a translation rule, $\mathbf{P}$ a set of patterns and S a structure such that $S \in Inst(\mathbf{P})$. Then, it is the case that $\tau(S) \in Inst(\sigma(\mathbf{P}))$.*

Let us consider a translation specification of the form $T = \sigma_1[\tau_1], \ldots, \sigma_k[\tau_k]$. Then, the *signature* σ_T of T is the sequence of signatures $\sigma_T = \sigma_1, \ldots, \sigma_k$, whereas the *body* τ_T of T is the composition of the translation programs in T: $\tau_T = \tau_k \circ \ldots \circ \tau_1$. The effect of the signature $\sigma_T = \sigma_1, \ldots, \sigma_k$ over a set of patterns $\mathbf{P}$ is the set of patterns $\sigma_k(\ldots \sigma_1(\mathbf{P}) \ldots)$. It turns out that the results above can be easily extended to entire translations.

Lemma 4 *Let T be a translation specification, $\mathbf{P}$ a set of patterns and S a structure such that $S \in Inst(\mathbf{P})$. Then, it is the case that $\tau_T(S) \in Inst(\sigma(\mathbf{P}))$.*

Corollary 1 Let $M_1 = (\mathbf{P}_1, \gamma_1)$ and $M_2 = (\mathbf{P}_2, \gamma_2)$ be two models and T be a translation such that $\sigma_T(\mathbf{P}_1) \preceq \mathbf{P}_2$. Then, τ_T is a structure transformation from M_1 to M_2.

4 Conclusions and further research

In this paper we have presented a formal approach to the problem of representing in the same context different database models and managing the translations between schemes of different models. We have introduced the notion of pattern as a graph-theoretic tool for the description of models and we have defined a partial order relationship among sets of patterns that induces a lattice on them. This lattice structure will allows to compare different data models and to define and characterize various interesting properties of translations.

We briefly sketch the basic definitions, which are currently inder investigation.

The first requirement for a translation is to be *correct*, that is, the output scheme should belong to the target model. We can say that a translation T is a *correct translation from a source model M_s to a target model M_t* if τ_T is a structure transformation from M_s to M_t.

A more general correctness criterion can be given by considering a *set* of source models for which a translation to a target model is valid. We say that T is a *correct translation from a set of source models $\mathbf{M}_s$ to a target model M_t* if it is a correct translation from each model $M_i \in \mathbf{M}_s$ to M_t.

Further criteria can be defined by giving a synthetic definition of the sets of models of interest, by means of a *supermodel* (an upper bound of all the relevant models) and a set of *minimal* models. In this way, if there exists a correct translation from the supermodel to each of the minimal models, then we can expect that translations between each pair of models in the set are possible.

References

[1] S. Abiteboul and R. Hull. Restructuring hierarchical database objects. *Theoretical Computer Science*, 62(3):3–38, 1988.

[2] P. Atzeni, G. Ausiello, C. Batini, and M. Moscarini. Inclusion and equivalence between relational database schemata. *Theoretical Computer Science*, 19(2):267–285, 1982.

[3] P. Atzeni and R. Torlone. A metamodel approach for the management of multiple models and the translation of schemes. *Information Systems*, 18(6):349–362, 1993.

[4] T. Barsalou and D. Gangopadhyay. M(DM): An open framework for interoperation of multimodel multidatabase systems. In *International Conference on Data Engineering*, pages 218–227, Tempe, AZ, February 1992.

[5] C. Batini, S. Ceri, and S.B. Navathe. *Conceptual Database Design, an Entity-Relationship Approach*. Benjamin and Cummings Publ. Co., Menlo Park, California, 1992.

[6] P.P. Chen. The entity-relationship model: toward a unified view of data. *ACM Trans. on Database Syst.*, 1(1):9–36, March 1976.

[7] M. Gyssens, J. Paredaens, and D. Van Gucht. A graph-oriented object database model. In *Ninth ACM SIGACT SIGMOD SIGART Symp. on Principles of Database Systems*, pages 417–424, 1990.

[8] D. Heimbigner and D. McLeod. A federated architecture for information management. *ACM Trans. on Inf. Syst.*, 3(3):253–278, July 1985.

[9] R.B. Hull. Relative information capacity of simple relational schemata. *SIAM Journal on Computing*, 15(3):856–886, 1986.

[10] R.B. Hull and R. King. Semantic database modelling: survey, applications and research issues. *ACM Computing Surveys*, 19(3):201–260, September 1987.

[11] L.A. Kalinichenko. Methods and tools for equivalent data model mapping construction. In *EDBT'90 (Int. Conf. on Extending Database Technology), Venezia, Lecture Notes in Computer Science 416*, pages 92–119, Springer-Verlag, 1990.

[12] G.M. Kuper. *The Logical Data Model: A New Approach to Database Logic*. PhD thesis, Stanford University, 1985.

[13] Y.E. Lien. On the equivalence of database models. *Journal of the ACM*, 29(2):333–362, 1982.

[14] R.J. Miller, Y.E. Ioannidis, and R. Ramakrishnan. The use of information capacity in schema integration and translation. In *Eighteenth International Conf. on Very Large Data Bases, Dublin*, 1993.

[15] J. Rissanen. On equivalence of database schemes. In *ACM SIGACT SIGMOD Symp. on Principles of Database Systems*, pages 23–26, 1982.

[16] A.P. Sheth and J.A. Larson. Federated database systems for managing distribuited database systems for production and use. *ACM Computing Surveys*, 22(3):183–236, 1990.

Federated Schemata in ODMG*

Ralph Busse, Peter Fankhauser, Erich J. Neuhold
Integrated Publication and Information Systems Institute, GMD–IPSI
Dolivostrasse 15, 64293 Darmstadt, Germany
email: {busse,fankhaus,neuhold}@darmstadt.gmd.de

Abstract

Due to the increasing acceptance of database management systems, many enterprises store most of their information in such databases. Unfortunately, the diversity of database management systems frequently leads to the situation, that different units of an enterprise use different systems or at least incompatible schemata, which makes it very burdensome to exchange data between these units. To increase efficiency of these existing databases, and to feed new applications in a homogenized fashion, it is getting more and more necessary to make the databases interoperable and to provide a unified access to them. This paper describes an approach to introduce the notion of *virtual classes* into the evolving object database standard ODMG–93. These virtual classes can be used to establish a federation database which is capable of importing and exporting data from and to other databases, to integrate (or just to provide in parallel) information from different data bases, and to tailor the overall schema for specific applications.

1 Introduction

In todays enterprises information is typically distributed among multiple database management systems. The databases are *heterogeneous*, i.e. they model information with differences in data model, naming, scaling, granularity, structure, and semantics, and they are autonomous, i.e. they cannot be modified for the purpose of integration, and their instances and schemata can evolve independently. To feed new applications in a homogenized fashion, and to exchange data between existing databases, these databases need to be made interoperable. For this purpose distributed data have to be structurally and semantically enriched, related data have to be recognized, and inconsistencies between them have to be resolved. The IRO–DB project (Interoperable Relational and Object-oriented DataBases – ESPRIT–III P8629) [17] aims at the provision of appropriate tools, to achieve interoperability between preexisting databases and applications.

One of the main obstacles to making existing systems interoperable is the heterogeneity of their data models. As pointed out in [26] an object-oriented data model can cover object-oriented and relational, as well as hierarchical and

---

*This work is partially supported by the European IRO–DB ESPRIT project (P8629). The project is developed in cooperation with GMD, GOPAS, IBERMÁTICA, EDS, GRAPHAEL, INTRASOFT, and O2 Technology.

network modelling concepts. We have chosen the data model proposed by the Object Database Management Group (ODMG) [6, 23] which is an extension of the OMG model for databases [19]. It supports types, classes, bidirectional relationships and operations, and provides an object-oriented query language OQL. The benefit of using an upcoming standard is the foreseeable availability of ODMG-compliant interfaces for many commercial database management systems.

On this basis IRO–DB will develop a layered approach to realize loosely and tightly coupled federations [31]. The *Local Layer* on top of each external database maps the individual data models onto ODMG, which serves as the canonical exchange data model. The *Communication Layer* provides means for accessing these databases through a network, and the *Interoperable Layer* allows for restructuring and merging of these data in order to provide a homogenized view to the end user and the applications.

The remainder of this paper is organized as follows: In Section 2 we present the overall structure of the IRO–DB project and sketch the ODMG–93 standard. After a general overview over the view concepts in object-oriented database systems, Section 3 describes the demands and restrictions for introducing such views into ODMG, leading up to our approach for representing federated schemata. Section 4 contains the specification of a meta schema that is capable of representing the whole view information, and Section 5 closes with conclusions and a short outlook.

2 Overall Framework

In this section we describe the overall architecture of the IRO–DB project and give a short overview over the ODMG data model [6, 23].

2.1 The IRO–DB System

Figure 1 presents the general architecture of the IRO–DB system. It consists of three layers. At the *Local Layer*, heterogeneous, existing databases are accessed. To overcome structural heterogeneities the local schemata are (partially) mapped to *export schemata* in the ODMG data model by means of *Local Database Adapters (LDAs)*. These can be composed from a toolbox consisting of C++ procedures including services to map standard data types and data type constructors of relational and object-oriented systems to the interchange format, to adapt local object identifiers, and to translate OQL queries into local queries.

At the *Communication Layer*, an object-oriented extension of the RDA (Remote Data Access) protocol is used to allow for method calls in queries, and to support object-identity and transfer of objects. This protocol is used to send, prepare, and execute database programs on remote export schemata.

The Local Layer and the Communication Layer give means to realize loosely coupled federations, where data have to be merged explicitly by the applica-

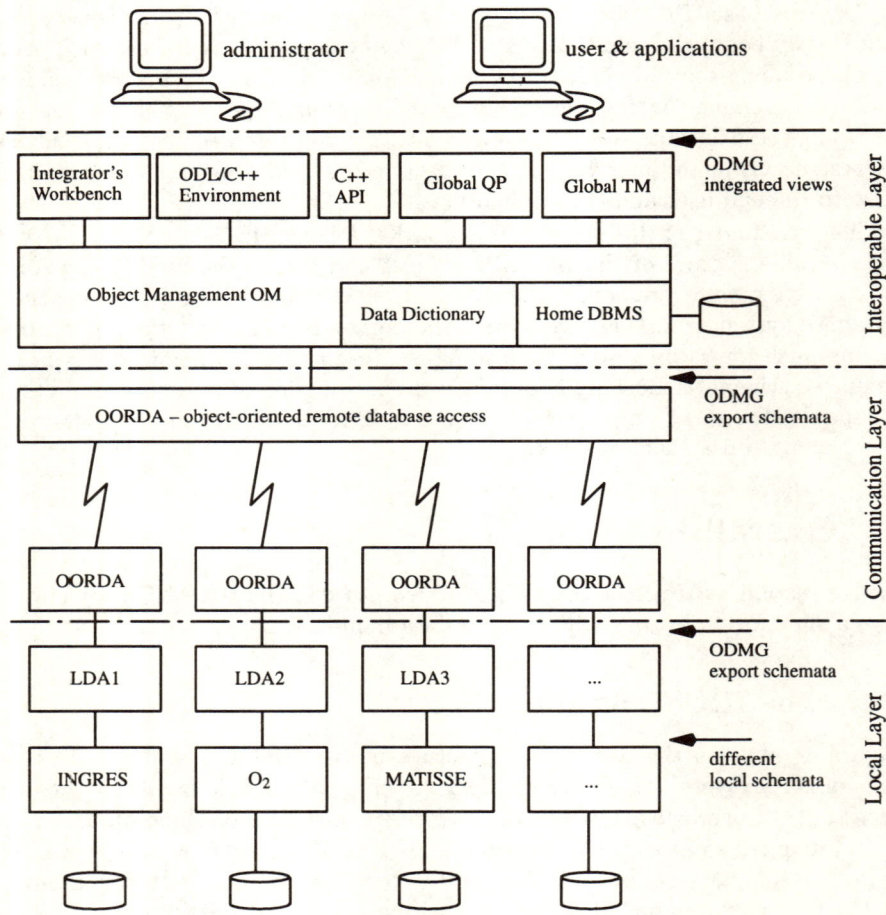

Figure 1: IRO–DB general architecture

tion. The *Interoperable Layer* [22] provides means to specify *federated schemata*, which support unified access to multiple databases with related data (*tightly coupled federations*). This layer provides a number of tools to actually interchange data between local databases and to provide new applications with integrated schemata on export schemata. In particular, an *Integrator's Workbench* is being developed, which consists of a graphical schema editor for multiple schemata, and which supports algorithms to detect possibly corresponding schema parts [15, 16], and to generate automatically federated schemata from correspondence assertions declared graphically by the user [13]. In addition, a dedicated repository on the *Home DBMS* stores federated schemata, integrated instances, and cross-reference tables. Global transaction management will be realized by the *optimistic ticket method* [18], and global query optimization will be implemented based on an algebraic approach.

2.2 The ODMG–93 Standard

The Object Database Management Group (ODMG) is an organization of object database vendors developing a standard for object-oriented databases, called ODMG-93 [6, 23]. The standard transfers the ideas of the Object Management Group (OMG) and their CORBA standard [19] from the entity-scoped programming environment to the set-scoped environment of databases. A powerful data model, a set of predefined interfaces, and both generic and language-bound specifications for data definition and manipulation provide the basis for product-independent interfaces and thus portable applications.

2.2.1 Data Model

The basic notion of the ODMG data model is the *denotable object*, which comprises both literals and objects. *Literals* are immutable, i.e. their contents cannot be changed. There will always be one integer 5, which is directly identified by its implementing bit pattern. Although a standard for *atomic literals* (Integer, Float, Boolean, Character), this is rather unusual for *structured values* (Set, Bag, List, Array, Structure). For example, instead of adding the integer 4 to the immutable set {1,2,3}, the whole set is replaced with a different set {1,2,3,4} – which resembles more the abstract mathematic approach (cf. [9]).

Objects, or *mutable objects*, on the other hand, are identified by a dedicated object identifier (oid) and can change their values. The structure (or *state*) of an object is defined as a list of attributes, having a name and a (literal) domain, and a list of *relationships* to other objects, guaranteeing referential integrity for any cardinality (1:1, 1:n, n:m). Attributes are not restricted to stored values (cf. [30]) – their implementation is hidden behind the corresponding access methods get_value and set_value. The behaviour is given as a list of method signatures that can be applied to the object. Both structure and behaviour of an object are specified as a *type* in the ODL syntax (see below). Thus, all instances of the type (called the type *extent*) have the same structure and behaviour. The types are organized in a *type hierarchy*. Each type inherits from all its supertypes, and the extent of a type is always a subset of each supertype's extent. The type of an object is determined at creation time, i.e. each object is a *direct instance* of exactly one type, and at the same time *indirect instance* [5][1] of all its supertypes. In ODMG it is impossible to move or copy an object into a different extent, unless a new object is created. Although the interfaces are the same for all instances of a type, their implementations may differ. A specific implementation of a type is called a *class*, and all classes that implement a type contribute to its extent. In addition, the lifetime of an object (**coterminus with procedure, process,** or **database**) is orthogonal to this classification.

2.2.2 Object Definition Language ODL

The Object Definition Language is based on OMG's Interface Definition Language IDL [19] and is used to define the structure and behaviour of objects, i.e. their types. A schema definition is a list of type definitions which look as follows:

interface *Mytype* : supertype_list {
  extent   *extentname*;
  keys   *att1*;
  attribute   Integer   *att1*;
  ...
  relationship Othertype   *relname* **inverse** *Othertype::invrel*;
  ...
  Integer   *compute_value* (**in** Integer *increment*) **raises** (ExOverflow);
  ...
};

In this example, *Mytype* is the name of the type, which inherits from all types given in **supertype_list**. *extentname* is an optional identifier (called an *entry point*) that provides access to the set of all instances of the type. **keys** allows to define a set of attributes which uniquely identifies each object of the type. The subsequent attribute, relationship and method signature definitions constitute the essential definition of the type. Note, that method implementations are not part of the type, and are thus not specified in ODL.

2.2.3 Object Query Language OQL

The query language provides declarative access to a database. First of all, the well known **select** ... **from** ... **where** ... construct has been adapted from relational databases. The range variables iterate over object sets, the **where** predicate may contain method calls and object expressions, and the **select** clause consists of object and value constructors, function calls and method invocations. In addition, the following object expressions are part of OQL:

---

[1] Abiteboul [1] calls them *real instances* and *virtual instances*, respectively. [3] refers to them as *instances* and *members*. However, most authors do not distinguish them at all.

- constants, variable names and entry points
  1, **true**, **nil**, "John", persons, ...

- object and literal constructors
  Person(name:"Pat", birthdate: "3/28/56"), **struct**(val:1, txt:"one"), ...

- arithmetic expressions
  not, +, −, *, **union**, ...

- quantifications and comparisons
  forall, **exists**, **in**, =, ...

- grouping, sorting, aggregation functions
  sort by, **group by**, **count**, **max**, ...

- indexing, de-referencing and method calls
  list[1], aPerson→name, myCompany→addEmployee(mable), ...

- conversions
  element, **listtoset**, ...

2.2.4 Object Manipulation Language OML

There is no generic object manipulation language. Objects are manipulated by calling member functions of the predefined types and by using constructs of the specific language bindings.

2.2.5 Language bindings

In addition to the generic data model and its definition language, [6] provides specific language bindings for C++ and Smalltalk. These bindings specify, how the datatypes should be implemented in the concrete language, and define a mapping from the generic specification syntax to a corresponding definition with the means of the language. The interfaces that are defined in the binding constitute the programming language specific OML.

3 Federated Schemata

In the remainder of this paper we focus on how to use ODMG for realizing federated schemata, which provide a more or less integrated access to more than one existing database. In the first subsection, we present an overview over the notion of *views* in object-oriented database systems. Then we give our schema architecture for federated systems, and finally we present the design choices and the resulting implementation. For the further discussions it is more convenient to talk about *classes* instead of *types*, as the term *class* is more usual in the framework of extension handling. From the viewpoint of ODMG each occurrence of *class* should be read as *type*, unless we assume a single implementation for each type, thus establishing a 1–to–1 correspondence.

3.1 Views in Object-Oriented Databases

The basic functionality for tailoring existing database information for specific needs is generally known as the *view* concept. In contrast to views in relational database systems, this notion is very obscure in the field of object-oriented databases. Although all definitions are based on a common understanding of the goals of a view, the proposed solutions and the assumptions made about the capabilities of the underlying object-oriented databases spread a wide range. Basically, there are three actions that are done via views: *hiding* information, that is unnecessary or confidential, *restructuring* information to fit better the needs of a user, an application, or an integration task, and *enriching* the information by adding new behaviour or computed (derived) values, by "objectifying" simple values, or by classifying the objects into generalizations or specializations. These kinds of data manipulation are combined to serve different purposes [1, 3, 10]. A view provides an *interface* to a user or to an application, which allows for *logical data independence*. It eliminates structural and behavioural heterogeneities and inconsistencies in the framework of *database integration*, like in this paper. It provides *security* by hiding confidential information. The interpretation of a view as a set of additional *integrity constraints* [24] is a facet of the security aspect, as well. At a more abstract level, views are just *data abstractions* from the original database [20], and looking at them from the viewpoint of a daily user, they allow an easy *re-use* of predefined queries.

The different implementations of views can be classified along several dimensions:

The kind of derivation: There are two ways how query results are obtained. The first is to evaluate a query on the original database, and the second one is to define the view class as a subclass or superclass of an original class and to use standard inheritance mechanisms for populating it [10].

The type of a "view result": In general, views provide the user with sets of objects. (Values are normally converted to objects for sake of closedness of the view.) These objects may be represented as a simple set, i.e. stored in a variable, or as the extent of a view class. The main difference is that only classes allow to change the objects' member functions[2]. If the results are stored in variables, any new behaviour must be implemented as global functions, which use a different invocation syntax, for example obj→getName() vs. getName(obj), and conflict with the "black box principle" of objects. This point is strongly related to the next one:

Availability of object migration: This is the most crucial point that divides all approaches into two camps. Most authors assume the availability of object migration, which means that an existing object may move up and down

---

[2]Unless the data model allows to define functions independently from a class definition, like in [1] and [8].

in the inheritance hierarchy (*restricted migration*) [2, 10, 11], or may be put into a totally different class, thus keeping the object identifier, but gaining a new behaviour (*free migration, multiple class membership/multiple instantiation*) [8, 20, 29]. Availability of object migration makes things easy. View results are just put into an appropriate class and obtain all the necessary behaviour. Absence of this feature, on the other hand, implies either the usage of global functions for changing behaviour, or the creation of *surrogate objects* (representation objects, proxy objects) for the result. The corresponding problems are discussed in Subsection 3.3.

If the system provides object migration, the type of the view result is normally classified into the hierarchy of existing types and classes. However, if we need to create surrogate objects, we must be very careful with this classification, because each new object will also be an (indirect) member of all the superclasses, thus changing the original classes. This is absolutely forbidden, when each object of such a class becomes part of the database. If we can distinguish between persistent and transient objects, this is in principle possible but should be treated very carefully. Furthermore, even if the system provides object migration, surrogate objects are still necessary when multiple objects are merged or values are converted to objects (*imaginary classes*) [2, 8, 11, 20].

Inclusion of relationships: According to [5], we can identify two different granularities of views: While *schema views* (eg [3, 27]) are capable of representing several classes in a view result, class views (eg [2, 20, 25, 32]) map only single classes and are thus unable to provide relationships between view classes.

In addition to this general characterization, there are a lot of specific features. [2, 8, 11] allow for the specification of parameterized classes, [3] defines a special derivation clause for relationships, and [11] defines a *may-be* relationship for classifying views in the class lattice. [34] follows a very different approach by defining one global class REF that manages all query results and performs method propagation in a generic way.

3.2 Schema Architecture

A system that implements federated schemata needs to provide the following functionality:

- importing external objects
- transforming class definitions
- merging different classes into one integrated class

Figure 2 shows an appropriate structure of a federated schema in more detail. We can distinguish four different kinds of classes that appear in such a system:

a) *External classes*
These are the existing classes that shall be made available to the federated

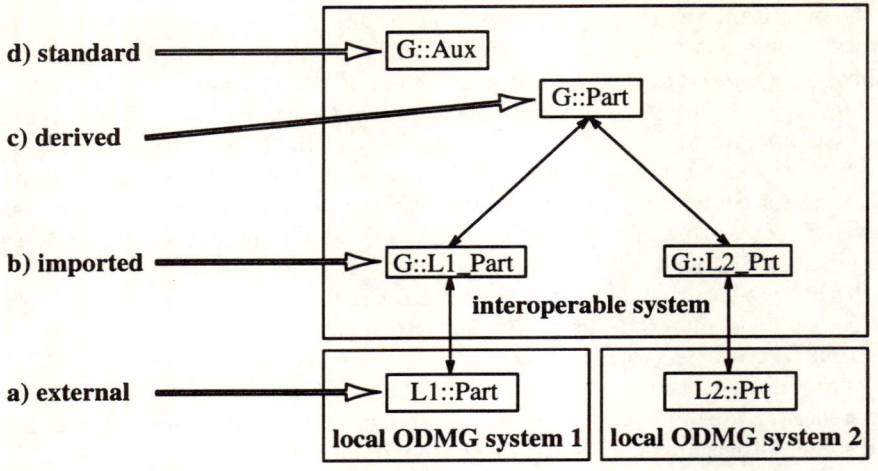

Figure 2: Different kinds of classes in a federated system

system. All their instances are located on an external (or *local*) node. They do not have any instances on the global node, because they are physically bound to the external node. When a local database is added to the interoperable system, it is extended with a *Local Layer*. This Local Layer is responsible for providing a uniform data model, by representing the local data in the form of an ODMG database. The corresponding ODMG schema, which is located at the local site, is called the *local schema* or *external schema*.

b) *Imported classes*

Imported classes are (partial) 1–to–1-copies of external classes. They exist on the global node and are instantiated on the global node, but all instantiations reflect only the external data of the corresponding external class. They provide only a means for hiding physical locations and for making the external data accessible from the global node (*location transparency*). A dedicated *Import Object Manager* handles the mappings between the imported and external classes. On the one hand it generates a global instance for each external object that needs to be accessed. On the other hand, it propagates accesses to the attributes of this global instance via the Communication Manager to the original external object.

c) *Derived classes*

To allow for interoperability between objects derived from several import class objects, and to overcome inconsistencies in representation between these import class objects, a further layer is added on top of the imported classes. In one or more steps, a *derived schema* combines the independent, imported schemata to a set of more or less integrated classes. One object of a derived class may be derived from objects of several imported or other derived classes. The corresponding objects are identified by some predicate. The derivation of the properties and relationships of a derived object may involve arbitrary mappings. The *Derivation Object Manager* handles the identification of corresponding base objects and their derivation to integrated global objects. Compared to the Import Object Manager it needs more sophisticated mapping facilities, but it is not concerned with remote data access.

d) *Standard classes*
In addition, it should be possible to store additional information that is not derived from external databases in some ordinary class.

The classes of type b) and c) are called *virtual* classes. These classes behave like ordinary object classes. They consist of an interface and an implementation. But unlike ordinary classes, which store their objects directly, the implementation of a virtual class *derives* its objects from the objects of other classes. In IRO-DB these virtual classes are maintained by a home database system, which imports objects from external database systems and combines them into a uniform representation.

3.3 Virtual Classes

3.3.1 Design Choices

Before we present our final realization of virtual classes in ODMG, we explain our design choices that are strongly related to ODMG's capabilities.

Distribution needs surrogate objects: The first thing to mention is the distribution. The original objects reside on a local host, whereas an application expects the objects of a federated schema on the global node, in order to execute their methods. As ODMG is mapped onto C++, these objects are just memory areas together with executable code in some object file or library. Consequently, these objects are bound to the memory and run-time environment of the local site and cannot be moved to the global node. Therefore, we need to create surrogate objects on the global node that provide the physical objects for the application and propagate all accesses to the original local objects.

Merging needs surrogate objects: When we want to merge different objects into a single one, we need an additional object to represent the union, because a set of objects (perhaps together with some data) is not an appropriate object by itself. Although Chen and Shan describe an approach of representing view objects and, as a consequence, ordinary objects as sets of oids [7], this is not feasible in the C++ environment, and would even impose the need to change the external databases.

Value objectification needs surrogate objects: Especially in the preparation of a merge, it is often necessary to convert literals into objects, because they correspond to objects in another database and shall be integrated in the final schema. Again, we need to create surrogates.

Derivation needs surrogate objects: Most other object-oriented database systems allow for run-time classification of objects. In that case, a view can be defined as a query that returns a set of existing objects (cf. *object preserving query* [21, 28]). This set can be interpreted as extent of a new class, which implements the behaviour of the query result. In most cases, this will be a subtype (specialization) or supertype (generalization) of the original object types. However, ODMG does not allow for object migration. The class membership of each object is determined at object creation time, and cannot be changed later on. Consequently, as soon as we want to add a new method to an object, which means nothing more than building a subtype, we need to create an independent class with individual instances.

Thus, whenever we want to add behaviour to an object or to restructure its properties, we need to create a new class with new instances. However, generation of new objects does not imply that each virtual class need to be fully instantiated. Surrogate objects can be created on demand. Furthermore, the creation of new classes is not a serious problem in the IRO–DB environment, where the virtual classes are established by the system administrator and are long-living. Admittedly, creating and instantiating new classes would not be a good approach for implementing short term user-defined views for the purpose of interactively querying the database.

Back references: Due to the fact that we use surrogate objects, we need to provide a means to navigate back to the original objects (cf. [3, 20, 34]). Unlike Bertino [3], who mentions this feature as a generic system function (*baseobject*), we implement dedicated *orig* relationships at the virtual classes, which contain references to the original objects and literals. This gives us more flexibility to define arbitrary derivations.

Identity and duplication problem: As we generate new objects for existing ones, we need to assure that subsequent accesses to the same virtual class always return the same surrogate object for a specific base object (*temporal object identity*). In other words, surrogate objects must persist during the whole transaction, and it must be avoided, that a second surrogate object is generated for a given base object. This can be done in three different ways:

- looking up the current extent before calling an object constructor
- implementing the object constructor in such a way that it returns any existing object instead of creating a new one [2]
- removing the duplicates shortly after their creation (cf. *DupEliminate* [30]).

In [14], we discuss these possibilities, but the final approach has not been fixed. The most simple solution of this problem, however, is to do without partial instantiation: When all objects are created in one step, then there are no duplicates.

Relationships and closedness: An additional fact that inhibits usage of simple queries for expressing views is the existence of relationships. Queries do not allow for propagation of attribute accesses. I.e., all attribute and relationship values must be given at object creation time. As a consequence, referenced objects must be created, before the referencing object can be generated. Such a nested object generation, however, needs sophisticated checks to avoid object duplication, and is nearly impossible for circular or bidirectional relationships, or for merging different relationships under specific consistency constraints. Furthermore, a full instantiation of an object with all its references may lead to a full instantiation of the whole database, because all objects that are transitively related to that object need to be created. Therefore, a two-level approach seems to be worthwhile: When an object is created, it is generated without any attribute value, or only with those that are explicitly listed. All other attributes and relationships are computed at access time.

3.3.2 View Specification

The above design choices lead to the following realization, where views are represented as virtual classes with partial instantiation and provision of back references. The specification of a virtual class consists of two parts: the interface specification and the mapping specification. The interface is specified in standard ODMG syntax, and the derivation and mapping information is given in a similar mapping definition block. Furthermore, named OQL queries are used to allow different merge operations for relationships. The mapping specification is a real extension of ODL. Although it would be possible to represent mapping information in the form of application classes, these specifications define the behaviour of some class and should thus be part of the language.

Interface Specification: Interface specification of virtual classes is done with the standard ODMG interface declaration syntax. Virtual class interfaces cannot be distinguished from ordinary ODMG class interfaces.

```
interface clsname {
    extent          extname;
    keys            keyatt [ ,keyatt ... ];
    attribute       attType  attname; ...
    relationship    relType  pathname inverse class::invpath; ...
};
```

Mapping Specification: In addition to the interface definition each class needs information about how to determine the extent and how to map the attributes onto the local ones. This mapping information is given in a separate block, which looks in general as follows:

```
mapping [ imported ] clsname {
  origin     typename    orig1; ...
  def_ext    extname     as select clsname(orig1:i1, ...)
                         from ... in ...
                         where ...;
  def_att    attname     as query; ...
  def_rel    pathname    as [ element( )
                         select otherclsname(orig1:i1, ...)
                         from ... in ...
                         where ... [ ) ];
};
```

The keyword **mapping** marks the block as a mapping definition for the virtual class *clsname*. A subsequent **imported** is only given for imported classes, to distinguish them from derived classes and to flag the external access.

The **origin** clauses define a set of private attributes that store the back-references to those objects, from which an instance of this class has been derived. In the case of an imported class, there is exactly one **origin** definition, which is a reference to an external class. A derived class, on the other hand, can be derived from more than one base class and may thus have several **origin** definitions. In most cases, each *orign* contains again a simple reference to the corresponding object of one base class. However, if an instance of the derived class corresponds to more than one object or to attribute values of a base class, some *orign* may be set-valued or contain additional values. In general, all contributions from one base class make up one **origin** entry.

The *extent derivation clause* starting with **def_ext** defines a query that provides full instantiation of the virtual class. It always consists of a constructor call for the class itself, with a list of *origs* as arguments. For import definitions, this constructor is called once for each instance of the local extent. In the case of derived classes, the **from** and **where** clauses may contain arbitrary OQL expressions to describe a correct merge of the base classes.

After the extent definition, a list of **def_att** lines defines the mapping for each attribute of the class. These declarative derivations are specified as OQL expressions that traverse to the corresponding attributes of the base objects. They are given for further maintenance of the derived classes and for a possible set-oriented optimization of attribute accesses inside of the query translator. In parallel, all derivations are coded into the appropriate *get_value* and *set_value* methods that allow for the usual object-based access to attributes.

The final relationship definitions (**def_rel**) are equivalent to the **def_att** clauses. The only difference is that it is necessary to call a constructor of the referenced class to provide for closedness of the schema. While traversal path derivation is very simple for imported classes, there must be a lot of consistency checking, when different relationships or the classes they connect are merged. Therefore, relationships between derived classes are expressed as separate, named OQL queries, which use a merging rule to compute a consistent set of object pairs (**define** relname **as select** ... **from** ... **where** ...;). The traversal path definitions are then represented as selections from that subquery.

These are all specifications that are necessary to describe federated schemata. Although we presented only a textual specification of class derivation, the integrator will normally work with a graphical tool (*Integrator's Workbench*), which will automatically generate this code. A more detailed discussion and a description of the object managers can be found in [14].

3.3.3 Example

Due to space limitations we give only a simple example, which is taken from the IRO–DB application domain. Assume a company that produces some kind of parts. While all production divisions work with a relational database (CIMDB), stock and trade management is handled with a hierarchical database (SYSDB). Currently these databases exchange data via file transfer. To overcome this unsatisfactory solution an integrated schema shall be developed that allows to access both databases from a common interface.

To overcome structural heterogeneity, either database gets a Local Database Adapter, which defines an export schema in ODMG format. Both databases export parts and production schedules, where parts have an identifier, a due date for the production, and a description. Each schedule consists of a quantity and of a due date for that quantity. But while SYSDB models schedules as objects, they are only value pairs that belong to parts in CIMDB. Furthermore, both system use a different naming. The export schemata are shown in Figure 3 and Figure 4.

In the next step of the integration, for each external schema an import schema is created. Each import class has the same name and the same attributes as its corresponding external class, except that the class name and extent name are prefixed with "*C_*" for CIMDB classes, and with "*S_*" for SYSDB classes. For example, the import class *C_PRT* propagates all accesses to its attributes to the corresponding base object of the remote class *CIMDB::PRT*. The corresponding specifications can be found in [14].

Now, we have both schemata available at the global node and can start integration by detecting corresponding schema parts. There is a one–to–one correspondence between the instances of *PART* and *PRT*. Their identification numbers (*part_id, prt_id*), the due dates (*due_date, prt_ddt*), and the description strings (*description, prt_dsc*) correspond as well. However, there is no counterpart for CIMDB's type flag (*prt_tpflg*), and schedules are modeled once as objects and once as literals. The structure of the SYSDB schema shall be the basis for the integrated schema. Therefore, the interfaces for the integrated classes are:

interface *Part* {
    extent   *parts*;

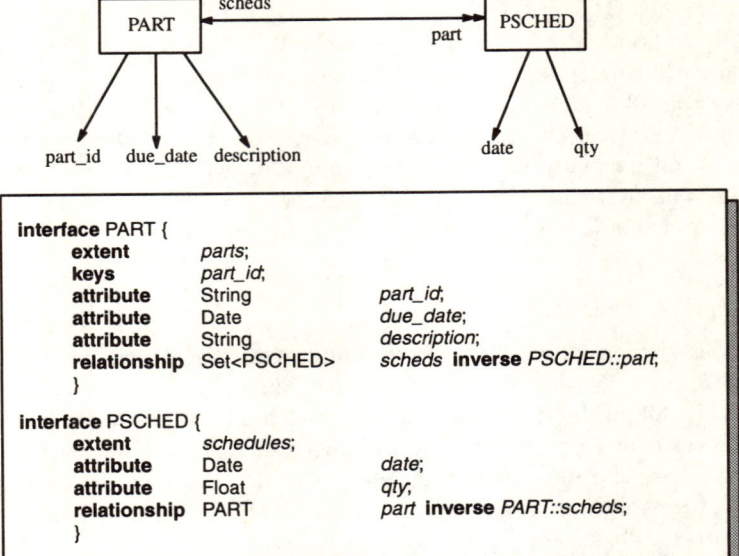

Figure 3: The export schema of SYSDB

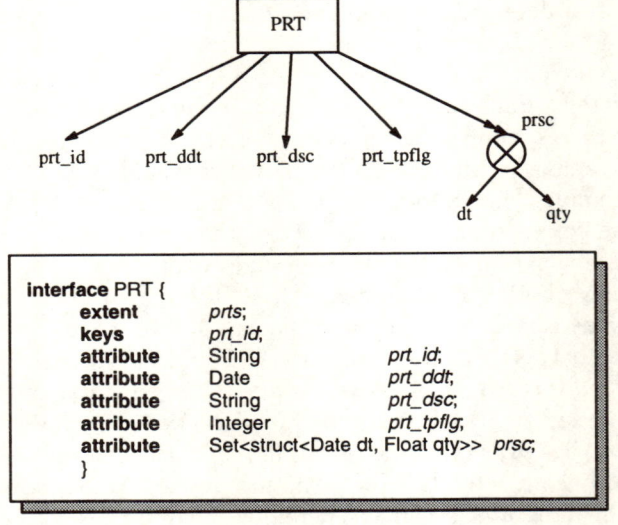

Figure 4: The export schema of CIMDB

```
    keys            part_id;
    attribute       String          part_id;
    attribute       Date            due_date;
    attribute       String          description;
    attribute       Integer         type_flag;
    relationship    Set<PSched>     scheds inverse PSched::part;
};

interface PSched {
    extent          pscheds;
    attribute       Date            date;
    attribute       Float           qty;
    relationship    Part            part inverse Part::scheds;
};
```

On this basis, the mappings are specified as follows:

```
mapping Part {
    origin      S_PART          sorig;
    origin      C_PRT           corig;
    def_ext     parts           as select Part(sorig: s_inst, corig: c_inst)
                                    from s_inst in s_parts, c_inst in c_prts
                                    where s_inst.part_id = c_inst.prt_id;
    def_att     part_id         as self.corig.prt_id or self.sorig.part_id;
    def_att     due_date        as self.corig.prt_ddt or self.sorig.upd_date;
    def_att     description     as self.corig.prt_dsc or self.sorig.description;
    def_att     type_flag       as self.corig.prt_tpflg;
    def_rel     scheds          as select r.psched
                                    from r in Part_PSched
                                    where r.part = self;
};

mapping PSched {
    origin      S_PSCHED                                               sorig;
    origin      struct<C_PRT part, Date dt, Float qty>  corig;
    def_ext     pscheds         as select PSched(sorig: sinst,
                                            corig: struct(part: cprt, dt: cval.dt,
                                                          qty: cval.qty))
                                    from sinst in s_schedules,
                                         cprt in c_prts, cval in cprt.prsc
                                    where sinst.part.part_id = cprt.prt_id
                                    and sinst.qty = cval.qty
                                    and sinst.date = cval.dt;
    def_att     date            as self.corig.dt or self.sorig.date;
    def_att     qty             as self.corig.qty or self.sorig.qty;
    def_rel     part            as element(
                                    select r.part
```

```
            from r in Part_PSched
            where r.psched = self);
};
```

define *S_Part_PSched* **as**
  select **distinct** struct(part: p, psched: s)
  from p **in** parts, s **in** pscheds
  where (p.sorig != **nil**) **and** (s.sorig != **nil**) **and** (p.sorig = s.sorig.part);

define *C_Part_PSched* **as**
  select **distinct** struct(part: p, psched: s)
  from p **in** parts, s **in** pscheds
  where (p.corig != **nil**) **and** (s.corig != **nil**) **and** (p.corig = s.corig.part);

define *Part_PSched* **as**
  select **distinct** rel
  from rel **in** (S_Part_PSched **union** C_Part_PSched)
  where **not exists** rel2 **in** (S_Part_PSched **union** C_Part_PSched) :
    (rel != rel2) **and** (rel.psched = rel2.psched);

The origins and the extent derivation clause of class *Part* define a simple 1-to-1 unification of part objects that agree on the part identifier. The special **or** operator evaluates from left to right and returns the first non-**nil** value. This is necessary to be able to handle incomplete and inconsistent information. For example, if the *prt_ddt* of the *corig* object is undefined, or if *corig* itself is **nil**, which, of course, could only happen if we use an outer join instead of a natural join, the *due_date* value is taken from the *sorig* base object. However, if *corig.prt_ddt* exists, it overrides any value from sorig. The derivation of *type_flag* does not need an **or**, because it will always come from CIMDB. Likewise, it is necessary to make the access-operator (. or →) safe with respect to **nil**-values. As it is impossible to catch an exception inside of an OQL query, any navigation through a **nil** object should return **nil**.

The *corig* part of *PSched* is an example for literal objectification. The tuple consisting of a *C_PRT*, a quantity and its due date, corresponds to one *S_PSCHED* object, when both values and the related part object correspond.

The relationship between the derived classes is defined as a separate OQL query, to be able to check the cardinality of the result (1:n). To ease the specification, the two auxiliary queries *S_Part_PSched* and *C_Part_PSched* describe the contributions from each single database.

4 Data Dictionary for Federated Schemata

In order to work with virtual classes, it is necessary to store the meta information of these classes in a data dictionary at the Interoperable Layer. In addition to the standard information that is defined in ODL, we need to represent all the mapping information, which is given in the mapping clauses we introduced in the previous chapter.

The standard ODL information for ODMG databases is specified in interface definitions, like the one given in Subsection 2.2. For each interface the Data Dictionary must contain the following components:

- an *interface name*

- a list of *supertypes*

- an optional *extent*, which includes both the *extent name*, and a reference to the extent itself, i.e. the set of instances

- an optional list of *keys*, each consisting of a single property or of a list of properties

- a list of *attributes*, each having a *name* and a *domain*

- a list of *traversal* paths with a *name*, a *domain*, which is always an interface or a collection of interfaces, and an optional reference to the *inverse traversal path*

- a list of *operations*, each with a *name* and a *signature*

Additional information, which is not related to single interfaces, must also be stored:

- a *Schema* groups a set of interfaces

- a *Database* is an instantiation of a schema on a specific site

- a *Relationship* groups every two inverse traversal paths

- distinguished *get_value* and *set_value* operations may be defined for each attribute to implement a special access behaviour

Although the whole mapping information can be compiled into *get_extent*, *get_value*, and *set_value* functions, maintenance of the integrated schema makes it necessary to represent explicitly as much of this mapping information as possible. Furthermore, this declarative information can be used for query optimization, because it allows to replace method calls by the derivation expression. According to the previous chapter, such a mapping clause contains:

- a flag *imported*, distinguishing derived from imported classes

- a list of *origins*, establishing the unidirectional links to the corresponding base classes. Each origin is represented as a private attribute, which is hidden from the user, but accessible for the Query Translator.

- a flag *is_private*, to mark an attribute as private (eg an origin)

- the *kind* of an interface, which may be *external, imported, derived*, or *standard* (cf. Figure 2)

- *derivation expressions* for attributes, traversal paths, relationships and extents, in the form of queries

The structure of the complete Data Dictionary that is capable of storing all the enumerated information, is shown in OMT notation in Figure 5. The implementation of the Data Dictionary is based on the C++ binding of the corresponding ODL definitions. In addition, a dedicated base class provides general procedures for importing new databases, compiling ODL descriptions, and so on.

The complete specification of the whole Data Dictionary, including all interfaces, the interactions with other modules, and further discussions, is given in the IRO–DB document [4].

Comparison with ODMG and CORBA

Unfortunately, there is no real Data Dictionary in the current version of the ODMG standard. [6] contains some interface definitions distributed over the whole book, and [23] presents a *Simplified Meta Model* in a graphical representation. However, even this information is incomplete and contradictory. Some types are defined on either source, the interfaces are not explained, and it seems, that both mix up the instance level and the descriptor level at many places.

Nevertheless, we tried to stick as closely as possible to this partial Data Dictionary proposal and based our work on the schema in [23]. Some renamings make the Data Dictionary more compatible with the CORBA standard and clarify the meaning of the classes (we are working on descriptors, not on instances of the application). Overall grouping into schemata and databases, and an explicit domain representation have been added. The properties and methods of a type are now stored in two different relationships. The implementation-specific types *class* and *object* have been removed, and for simplicity, we did not yet introduce representations of constants, exceptions, named datatypes, and method signatures to the Data Dictionary, although they will be part of ODMG.

The CORBA standard [19], on the other hand, provides a rather low level repository for interface specifications. A more or less untyped containment relationship is established between the single interface constituents, and there is only very little additional information for each descriptor class.

Compared to that approach, we took some of the classes, provided typed relationships and delayed some classes for a later phase of the project. Paths and relationships have been added, and our domain representation differs from CORBA's typecodes.

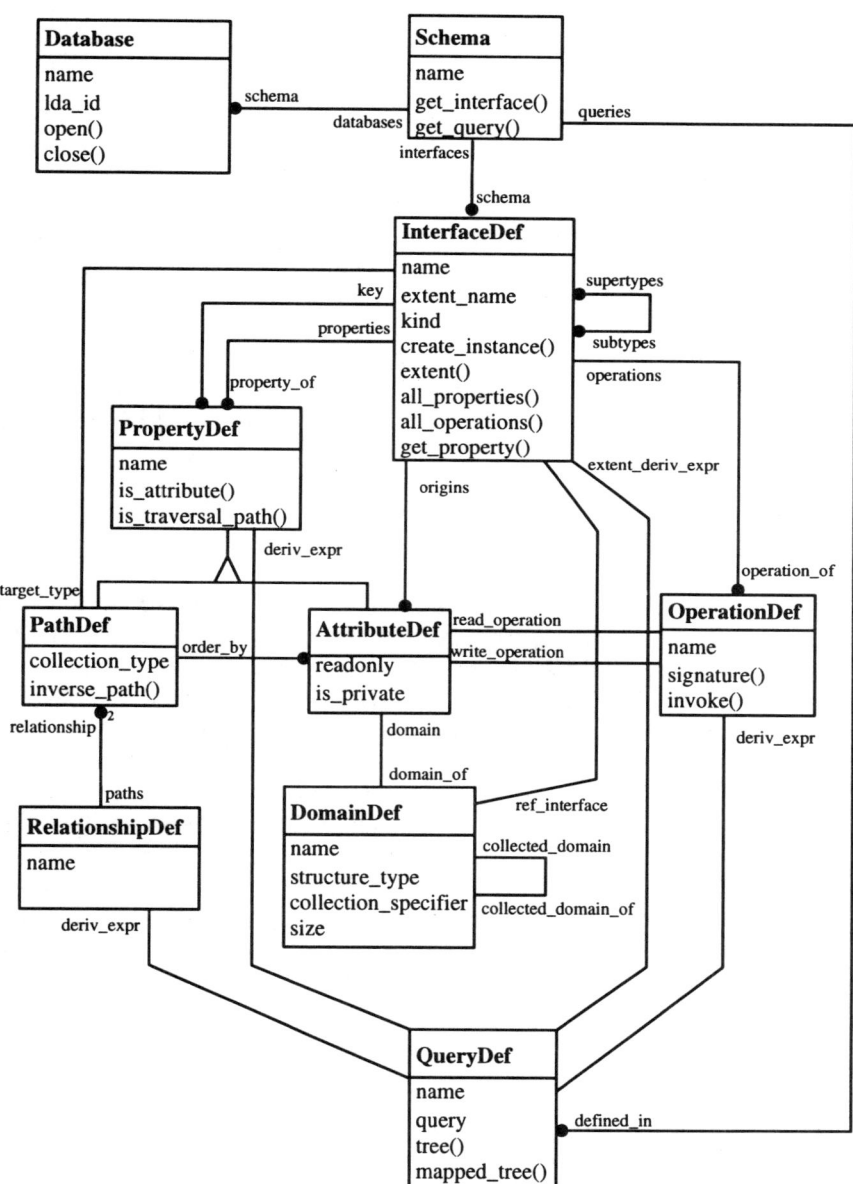

Figure 5: The Interoperable Data Dictionary

5 Conclusions and Future Work

We presented an approach for modelling federated schemata in ODMG. In contrast to other object-oriented database management systems, ODMG is very restrictive with respect to run-time modifications of existing objects. Both the lack of object migration and the additional demands from the IRO–DB project, which are the access to external objects, the unification of objects, and the object creation from data, made it necessary to define virtual classes, which are instantiated on demand during query evaluation. A separate mapping definition clause provides a powerful means to express all kinds of derivations in a simple and declarative way. Only the specification of relationships is more complicated, due to the complex consistency rules for relationship integration. Furthermore, we presented a Data Dictionary to keep the schema information.

An additional shortcoming of the missing object migration is the fact that surrogate objects must be created in the most specific class. Whenever we integrate subclass hierarchies, an access to an incomplete extent of a superclass must very carefully detect, where new objects have to be created. Although this can be solved by providing elaborated extent derivation clauses, it has to be investigated, whether there is also a generic way of handling this problem. In this situation it would be a benefit, if ODMG provided at least restricted migration.

A real problem with respect to schema integration is the lack of nullvalues in ODMG. As we discovered in the meantime, it is not even planned to introduce this notion into ODMG. Therefore, the mentioned **or** operator will not be implemented either. The derivation and integration of methods has been delayed and will be tackled in a future phase of the project.

In addition to pure integration, virtual classes can also be used as an overall framework to exchange data between local databases. As the local databases considered in IRO–DB are autonomous, they cannot be modified in such a way that a local update automatically triggers an update of shared data in another database [12]. Contrarily, global applications have to guarantee that consistency is achieved within certain time frames [33]. Such a control can for example be realized by periodically retrieving shared data into a view object, and then updating now explicitly related original objects appropriately.

References

[1] Serge Abiteboul. Virtuality in Object-Oriented Databases. Preliminary report, I.N.R.I.A. France, 1990.

[2] Serge Abiteboul and Anthony Bonner. Objects and Views. In *Proceedings of the ACM SIGMOD Conference on Management of Data (Denver, June 1991)*, volume 20(2), pages 238–247. ACM Press, 1991.

[3] Elisa Bertino. A View Mechanism for Object-Oriented Databases. In *Proc. of the Int. Conf. on Extending Database Technology EDBT'92 (Vienna,*

Austria, March 1992), volume 580 of *Lecture Notes in Computer Science*, pages 136–151. Springer, 1992.

[4] Ralph Busse, Georges Attali, Peter Fankhauser. Design Document for Data Dictionary (D4–3/1). Tech. Rep. IRO/SPEC/GMD/D4–3.1-V1.3/RB940722, ESPRIT–III Programme, IRO–DB Project P8629, 1994.

[5] Kwang June Byeon and Dennis McLeod. Towards the Unification of Views and Versions for Object Databases. In *Object Technologies for Advanced Software, First JSSST International Symposium (Kanazawa, Japan, November 1993)*, volume 742 of *Lecture Notes in Computer Science*, pages 220–236. Springer, 1993.

[6] Rick G. G. Cattell, editor. *The Object Database Standard: ODMG–93*. Morgan Kaufmann, San Mateo, California, 1993.

[7] Qiming Chen and Ming-Chien Shan. Abstract View Objects for Multiple OODB Integration. In *Object Technologies for Advanced Software, First JSSST Internat. Symposium (Kanazawa, Japan, Nov. 1993)*, volume 742 of *Lecture Notes in Computer Science*, pages 237–250. Springer, 1993.

[8] Jan Chomicki and Witold Litwin. Declarative Definition of Object-Oriented Multidatabase Mappings. In M. Tamer Özsu, Umeshwar Dayal, and Patrick Valduriez, editors, *Distributed Object Management*, pages 307–325. Morgan Kaufmann, San Mateo, California, 1992.

[9] Umeshwar Dayal. Queries and Views in an Object-Oriented Data Model. In *Proceedings of the 2nd International Workshop on DBPL*, 1989.

[10] Michael Dobrovnik and Johann Eder. Adding View Support to ODMG–93. In *Proc. of the Int. Workshop on Advances in Databases and Information Systems ADBIS'94 (Moscow, Russia, May 1994)*. Russian Academy of Sciences, 1994.

[11] Cássio Souza dos Santos, Serge Abiteboul, and Claude Delobel. Virtual Schemas and Bases. In *Advances in Database Technology – Proceedings of the 4th International Conference on Extending Database Technology EDBT'94 (Cambridge, UK, March 1994)*, volume 779 of *Lecture Notes in Computer Science*, pages 81–94. Springer, 1994.

[12] F. Eliassen and R. Karlsen. Interoperability and Object Identity. *SIGMOD RECORD*, 20(4):25–29, 1991.

[13] Peter Fankhauser. *Explorative Unification for Semantic Database Interoperability*. PhD thesis draft, Technical University of Vienna, Austria, September 1994.

[14] Peter Fankhauser, Ralph Busse, Gerald Huck. IOM Design Specification Document (D4–2/1). Tech. Rep. IRO/SPEC/GMD/D4–2.1–V1.5/0805, ESPRIT–III Programme, IRO–DB Project P8629, 1994.

[15] Peter Fankhauser, Martin Kracker, and Erich J. Neuhold. Semantic vs. Structural Resemblance of Classes. *Special SIGMOD RECORD Issue on Semantic Issues in Multidatabase Systems*, 20(4), December 1991.

[16] Peter Fankhauser and Erich J. Neuhold. Knowledge Based Integration of Heterogeneous Databases. In *IFIP Workshop DS-5 Semantics of Interoperable Databases (Lorne, Australia, November 1992)*, 1992.

[17] Georges Gardarin, Sofiane Gannouni, Beatrice Finance, Peter Fankhauser, Wolfgang Klas, Dominique Pastre, Régis Legoff, Antonis Ramfos. IRO-DB: A Distributed System Federating Object and Relational Databases. In O. Bukhres and A. K. Elmagarmid, editors, *Object Oriented Multidatabase Systems*. Prentice Hall, Sep. 1994. To appear.

[18] D. Georgakopoulos, Marek Rusinkiewicz, and Amit P. Sheth. On Serializability of Multidatabase Transactions Through Forced Local Conflicts. In *Proceedings of the 7th International Conference on Data Engineering (Kobe, Japan, April 1991)*, pages 314–323. IEEE Computer Society Press, Los Alamitos, California, 1991.

[19] Object Management Group. The Common Object Request Broker: Architecture and Specification. Technical Report OMG Document Number 91.12.1, OMG, December 1991.

[20] Sandra Heiler and Stanley Zdonik. Object Views: Extending the Vision. In *Proceedings of the 6th International Conference on Data Engineering (Los Angeles, California, February 1990)*, pages 86–93. IEEE Computer Society Press, Los Alamitos, California, 1990.

[21] Andreas Heuer and Peter Sander. Preserving and Generating Objects in the LIVING IN A LATTICE Rule Language. In *Proc. of the 7th Int. Conf. on Data Engineering (Kobe, Japan, April 1991)*, pages 562–569. IEEE Computer Society Press, Los Alamitos, California, 1991.

[22] Wolfgang Klas, Peter Fankhauser, Peter Muth, Thomas C. Rakow, and Erich J. Neuhold. Database Integration using the Open Object-Oriented Database System VODAK. In Omran Bukhres and Ahmed K. Elmagarmid, editors, *Object Oriented Multidatabase Systems*. Prentice Hall, September 1994. To appear.

[23] Mary Loomis, Tom Atwood, Rick Cattell, Joshua Duhl, Guy Ferran, and Drew Wade. The ODMG Object Model. *Journal of Object-Oriented Programming*, pages 64–69, June 1993.

[24] Jean-Claude Mamou and Claudia Bauzer Medeiros. Interactive Manipulation of Object-Oriented Views. In *Proceedings of the 7th International Conference on Data Engineering (Kobe, Japan, April 1991)*, pages 60–69. IEEE Computer Society Press, Los Alamitos, California, 1991.

[25] Elke Rundensteiner. Multiview: A Methodology for Supporting Multiple Views in Object-Oriented Databases. In *Proceedings of the 18th International Conference on Very Large Data Bases (Vancouver, Canada, August 1992)*. Morgan Kaufmann, San Mateo, California, 1992.

[26] Hans-Jörg Schek and Mark H. Scholl. Evolution of Data Models. In A. Blaser, editor, *Database-Systems of the 90s, International Symposium, (Mueggelsee, Berlin, FRG, November 1990)*, volume 466 of *Lecture Notes in Computer Science*, pages 135–153. Springer, 1990.

[27] Marc H. Scholl, Christian Laasch, and Markus Tresch. Updatable views in object-oriented databases. In *Proceedings DOOD (Munich, December 1991)*, volume 566 of *Lecture Notes in Computer Science*. Springer, 1991.

[28] Marc H. Scholl and Hans-Jörg Schek. A Relational Object Model. In *Proceedings ICDT (Paris, December 1990)*, volume 470 of *Lecture Notes in Computer Science*. Springer, 1990.

[29] Marc H. Scholl, Hans-Jörg Schek, and Markus Tresch. Object Algebra and Views for Multi-Objectbases. In M. Tamer Özsu, Umeshwar Dayal, and Patrick Valduriez, editors, *Distributed Object Management*, pages 336–359. Morgan Kaufmann, San Mateo, California, 1992.

[30] Gail M. Shaw and Stanley B. Zdonik. A Query Algebra for Object-Oriented Databases. In *Proceedings of the 6th International Conference on Data Engineering (Los Angeles, California, February 1990)*. IEEE Computer Society Press, Los Alamitos, California, 1990.

[31] Amit P. Sheth and James A. Larson. Federated Database Systems for Managing Distributed, Heterogeneous, and Autonomous Databases. *ACM Computing Surveys*, 22(3):183–236, 1990.

[32] Katsumi Tanaka, Masatoshi Yoshikawa, and Kozo Ishihara. Schema Virtualization in Object-Oriented Databases. In *Proceedings of the 4th IEEE International Conference on Data Engineering (Los Angeles, California, February 1988)*, pages 23–30. IEEE Computer Society Press, Los Alamitos, California, 1988.

[33] D. Woelk, W. Shen, M. Huhns, and P. Cannata. Model driven enterprise information management in Carnot. Technical Report Carnot–130–92, MCC, 1992.

[34] Suk I. Yoo and Hai Jin Chang. An Object-Oriented Query Model Supporting Views. In *Object Technologies for Advanced Software, First JSSST International Symposium (Kanazawa, Japan, November 1993)*, volume 742 of *Lecture Notes in Computer Science*, pages 251–263. Springer, 1993.

ADDS Transaction Management System *

Yuri Breitbart
Department of Computer Science
University of Kentucky
Lexington, KY 40506, USA

Abstract

ADDS (Amoco Distributed Database Management System) is a multi-database system that allows users to retrieve and manipulate data from heterogeneous database sources located in distributed heterogeneous hardware and software environments. This paper describes *ADDS* transaction management system, including system recovery procedures. The system guarantees both a consistent database retrieval and update in the heterogeneous distributed database environment. The prototype of the system was implemented and tested in the research environment of Amoco Production Company.

1 Introduction

Enormous investments made by industry in various database applications and essential heterogeneity of user data processing envoronment effectively precludes redesign of *pre-existing* applications and therefore requires a heterogeneous database management system that preserves user independence and autonomy and at the same time allows users to take advantage of varous data sources located either at different company locations or even outside of the company.

ADDS is a software system that provides a uniform interface to various pre-existing heterogeneous databases. Databases that contain related information are described as an integrated database (called *composite database*) using the ADDS data definition language. The integrated database permits users to manipulate data simultaneously from several databases using the ADDS query and data manipulation languages without knowing the specifics of the underlying DBMSs. The *ADDS* project initiated in the middle of 1980's had the following goals [BT84, Kim94]:

---

*This material is based in part upon work supported by NSF under grant IRI-92121301.

1. Provide an SQL compatible, easy to use query and data manipulation languages as a part of the ADDS user interface. Users of the system should not be concerned either with data location or with specifics of any local DBMS that contains the required data.

2. The design of the system should guarantee an easy expandability. That means that an incorporation of any new DBMS and/or file manager should not cause major redesign of the system.

3. Autonomy of individual systems that are integrated by *ADDS* should be preserved. We consider two basic types of autonomy: design and execution autonomies. The design autonomy requires that no changes should be made to individual systems in order to accomodate *ADDS*. The execution autonomy requires that preexisting users applications should remain operational without making any changes to them. Furthermore, an ADDS transaction can be aborted by local DBMS at any time, including the time that the transaction is in the process of committing its results.

4. Ensure global and local consistency of the integrated data sources in the presence of failures.

5. Minimize the ADDS system response time as well as the overhead incurred.

The ADDS approach is to provide tools for a logical integration of the data needed by an application into one logical database, called *composite database (CDB)*. Such integration creates the illusion of a single database system, and hides from users the intricacies of different DBMSs and access methods. It shields users from a need to know either the location, or internal structure of local DBMS data, or details of local systems in accessing the local data. ADDS guarantees a consistent and efficient, as well as a "quick and dirty", access to the data. ADDS users are provided with a relational interface to integrated data sources and presented with a relational view of the data.

ADDS is capable of integrating relational, network and hierarchical databases. The system has an extensive Data Definition Language that allows users to define their integrated application and mapping between logical (addressable in ADDS) and physical data that is represented by these logical data. ADDS uses a relational data model to represent a logical view of a composite database from the users viewpoint. User is presented with a set of relations defined on a set of attributes.

Users program operating on a composite database use SQL language statements to perform operations that are further propogated to the level of local DBMSs. The ADDS system software eventually translates SQL statements into languages of native DBMSs. The information required to resolve various data conflicts is stored in the ADDS data directory. The ADDS directory also contains information about composite database schemas that describe uniform views of the various preexisting databases that are components of the composite database, an equivalent description of the local databases in terms of the ADDS data model, and various users' views of the composite database.

ADDS users are provided with options to select different levels of consistency for their transactions. For example, users that are interested only in data retrieval and that are willing to accept in some cases inconsistent data may require only serializability of local schedules, whereas users that want to update data in different data sources and concerned with mutual consistency of replicated data may require a global serializability of any combination of local and global transactions.

We assume that failures may occur at any time during transaction processing. The *ADDS* transaction processing algorithms are resilient to the main type of failures in the ADDS environment: site failures. A site failure means that no data can be either retrieved or updated by ADDS at a local site. There are two main reasons for such failures.

1. A local DBMS failed at some site. In this case every database source under that DBMS is not accessible. This, in turn, means that every ADDS logical relation that describes a physical data source under the failed DBMS is also not accessible. After a DBMS recovery, a local database consistency is assured by the local DBMS software. Global database consistency is assured by the ADDS recovery manager.

2. An ADDS local access module failed. The local DBMS treat this failure as a transaction abort at the local site. In this case, ADDS is responsible for the restoration of the local database to the consistent state from its viewpoint after the ADDS local access module is restored.

If failures occur while a global transaction is active, then no specific recovery actions on the part of ADDS are required since local DBMSs assure global database consistency by undoing the transaction at each local site. Hence, the recovery manager is responsible for a transaction recovery only in case when a failure occurred during the execution of a transaction's commit operation.

In order to ensure the atomicity of global transactions, the two-phase commit protocol [BHG87] is used. When ADDS encounters the commit operation of the transaction, it sends to each local site that was involved in this execution of a *prepare-to-commit* message. Each site receiving the message determines if it can commit the transaction. If it can commit, it forces all the log records for the transaction to stable storage and notifies ADDS whether it is ready to commit. However, the local site's DBMS is not aware that the transaction is in prepared state and thus can abort it. It may lead to the situation that the transaction will be committed at one site and aborted at another one. Thus the major task of the ADDS recovery manager is to guarantee that in such cases the transaction atomicity still can be guaranteed.

The ADDS system was designed and developed primarily in an IBM operating environment. Users access the system from either VM or MVS operating environments. The current version of ADDS, however, allows users to access data from UNIX workstations and PCs that use the DOS operating system. ADDS proved to be useful especially for engineering and scientific applications that need both business oriented data located on mainframes and scientific data located either on workstations or supercomputer platforms.

The problems of heterogeneous database management systems were extensively addressed in the literature [SL90, BGS92]. The first designed and implemented multidatabase system prototype was Multibase [LR82]. Multibase provides a uniform integrated interface for retrieving data from pre-existing heterogeneous, distributed databases. It uses a global schema to create an integrated view of the data. Multibase uses a functional data model and functional language DAPLEX [Ship81] to generate a global data model and to retrieve data from the integrated data sources, respectively. Multibase is strictly a retrieval system without any transaction management features. Several additional prototype systems are described in [TTC+90]. To the best of our knowledge we are not aware of any multidatabase system with transaction management facilities that guarantee global database consistency. The ADDS overview is given in [Kim94]. In this paper we describe the ADDS Transaction mManagement System.

The remainder of the paper is organized as follows. The next Section describes the ADDS notion of data item and transaction. In Section 3 we provide a general overview of the ADDS system. In Section 4 we describe the ADDS Transaction Manager, Sections 5 and 6 describe ADDS Scheduler and Recovery Manager algorithms. Section 7 concludes the paper.

2 ADDS Data Items and Transactions

In this Section we discuss ADDS notion of data item and transaction. We assume that each local DBMS uses the strict 2PL protocol [BHG87] and global transactions are being executed at local site together with local transactions.

2.1 ADDS Data Item Notion

A notion of a data item plays a crucial role in the ADDS transaction management design. As we stated above, ADDS does not contain any data. It rather accesses data at local sites. Thus, the ADDS data item notion relates to physical data items stored at local sites. However, these items must be accessible by user interface of the local site. For example, if an IMS database DB is available to the ADDS users, then DB is considered the ADDS data item. Hence, we assume that ADDS data item is a physical database source integrated by ADDS and that is accessible by ADDS user interface.

If, however, the local data source DB is a part of some view for some IMS application, and this view is integrated by ADDS, then the view becomes an ADDS data item and DB itself is not the ADDS data item.

Therefore, each data item in ADDS is fully characterized by the physical database name as it is known to the local DBMS, the site name, where the database is located, the name of DBMS system that manages the database, and the DBMS specific information that uniquely identifies the database within the local DBMS. For example, in the SQL/DS environment, a SQL relation considered as an ADDS data item, is uniquely identified by the SQL database name where the relation is defined. In the IMS environment, on the other hand, an MVS partition name where an IMS physical or logical database resides, uniquely identifies an ADDS data item.

A set of ADDS data items is defined in the ADDS directory. Each data item in ADDS is assigned a unique data item identification by the ADDS system at the time that the data item is defined by the ADDS system administrator. Every data item in ADDS can be either updateable by ADDS transactions or can be updated only outside of the ADDS system, by local transactions. In the latter case, such data item is called locally updateable, while in the former - globally updateable. No ADDS data item can be both locally and globally updateable. For example, the ADDS data item that has originated from the physical database at a local site may or may not be globally updateable (depending on the ADDS database administrator decision). On the other hand, the ADDS data item that has originated from the logical view of some physical data item at a local site cannot ne globally updateable.

2.2 ADDS Transaction Notion

ADDS global transactions (i.e. transactions that are executed under the ADDS system control) results from the execution of a user program written in a high level programming language (e.g., C, or PASCAL) that contains embedded ADDS commands to retrieve and/or manipulate data from various data sources.

ADDS transactions consist of the operations *begin, read, write, commit, abort, open, and close,* Operations *readwrite* correspond to the ADDS any retrieval and update statements, respectively. Compiling of an ADDS retrieval statement from the ADDS program generates one or more read commands for the ADDS transaction. On the other hand, compiling of an ADDS update statement from the program always generates a single write statement in the ADDS transaction.

Upon begin operation, the transaction manager assigns an identifier to the transaction, records its timestamp and type (i.e. whether the transaction is read-only or it is an update transaction). Upon open operation, the transction manager checks whether the program is authorized to acces the CDB referred in the program. Only a single CDB per transaction may be opened at the time. Upon close operation the transaction manager is notified that another CDB can be opened, if required. Commit and abort operation are generated either as a result of the users request or or as operations submitted by the transaction manager of ADDS. Their implementation as well as implementation of read and write operations is discussed in the subsequent sections.

3 Transaction Manager Algorithm

The objective of the ADDS system is to ensure a consistency of all local data sources executing global transactions at local sites in the presence of local transactions at these sites (i.e. transactions that are executing outside of the ADDS system control). This should be achieved under the following assumptions:

1. The ADDS system is not aware of local transactions It is not provided with any local DBMS control information (such as wait-for-graph, local DBMS transaction log, local schedule, etc.). Therefore, ADDS operating in the absence of such information makes the most pessimistic assumptions regarding coordination of global transaction at local sites. In other words, it must to the certain degree, assume Murphy's law: if something may go wrong, it will go wrong.

2. No changes can be made to the local DBMS software. Consequently, without any changes, a local DBMS is not able to distinguish between global and local transactions which are active at local site. Furthermore, a local DBMS at one site is not able to communicate directly with local DBMSs at other sites to synchronize an execution of a global transaction that is executing at several sites.

3. Each local DBMS uses the strict two phase locking protocol (S2PL) (i.e. locks are released only after a transaction aborts or commits) [BHG87]. A local lock is required to execute a transaction operation at the local site. A local DBMS should allocate a local lock (read or write, depending on the operation). If a lock cannot be granted, then the DBMS either blocks the transaction, or aborts it if blocking causes a local deadlock. If a local DBMS discovers a local deadlock, this information is not made available to the ADDS. If a local DBMS chooses to abort a global transaction, then a server reports to the recovery manager that it was aborted by the local DBMS (see discussion below). Since each local DBMS uses the S2PL protocol, a local serializability is assured. The local DBMS ensures a freedom from a a local deadlock. Global deadlocks, however, may occur.

4. ADDS system distinguishes between the two types of locks for the same data item: global and local. Global locks are allocated by the ADDS scheduler to indicate that there is a global transaction that will need a local lock for the data item at some site. Actual locks are local and allocated at the local level by the local DBMS. Global locks cannot actually prevent a local transaction from obtaining or keeping a local lock. On the other hand, if a global transaction is given an exclusive global lock on a data item, then no other global transaction can obtain either global or local lock on the same data item.

5. The transaction manager never submits the transaction's operation to the scheduler until it receives a response that the previous operation of the same transaction has obtained required local locks to perform the operation.

6. The ADDS data items may be replicated at different sites.

7. For each update transaction (i.e., a transaction that is declared by the user as such), an ADDS server allocated to the transaction at the local site will not be deallocated until the transaction has been committed or aborted. It should be noted, however, that we do not propose for retrieval transactions to keep servers until the transaction is committed or aborted. Because of that, it is possible that the user may run into inconsistent data retrieval. We believe that an inconsistent retrieval may be tolerated by the user at his/her choice, but the inconsistent update may cause problems to other users and consequently is not allowed.

8. Each local DBMS is capable to commit or abort any transaction running at the local site as well as to recover from local system failures. However, local DBMS's may not coordinate their commit, abort, and recover actions. The ADDS transaction management performs these tasks.

During a transaction processing in ADDS, a transaction can be in one of the following global states: active, aborted, committed, blocked, and ready. A transaction is active, if an operation begin has been processed by the transaction manager, but neither commit nor abort has been processed. A transaction is aborted, if an abort has been processed on behalf of the transaction at at least one local site at which the transaction has a server. A transaction is blocked, if it has requested a global data lock but it did not receive the lock and the transaction is waiting to receive the lock. A transaction is ready, if the transaction manager processed every operation of the transaction, each transaction server reported a completion of all transaction operations that the server was processing and each server log is written to a stable storage. Finally, a transaction is committed, if a commit message is sent to at least one site at which the transaction was executing.

4 Scheduler Algorithm

In this section we outline the scheduler algorithm. The scheduler uses the two phase locking mechanism to acquire and release global locks. It assures a serializability of the schedule at the global level. We distinguish between global *read* and *write* locks. A global transaction that needs to read data requests only a global *read* lock. A global *read* lock can be shared by several global transactions. A global transaction that needs to write a global data item requests a global *write* lock. No two transactions can share a global *write* lock. If a global transaction keeps a global *read* (*write*) lock on a data item, then no global *write* (*read*) lock on the same data item can be granted to any other transaction. The scheduler maintains a *global lock table* for the set of global data items.

The scheduler's *global lock table* is, in fact, a record that a global transaction needs a local lock to work with the data item. As such, if two global transactions request conflicting global locks (locks are conflicting, if they are requested by two different transactions on the same data item and one of the requested locks is a *write* lock) the scheduler will not let one of the transactions proceed because it knows that the two transactions will cause a conflict at the local site.

The scheduler does not release a transaction's global locks until the transaction aborts or successfully commits. In this regard the scheduler uses strict two-phase locking protocol [BHG87]. This leads to a peculiar situation for a global transaction that successfully commits at one site and fails to commit at the other one. The local locks that the transaction keeps at both sites are released by local DBMSs at these sites. On the other hand, the scheduler does not release global locks allocated to the transaction until the recovery manager successfully commits the transaction after redoing it at the failed site.

The transaction manager submits transaction operations to the scheduler. If a submitted operation is an abort, then it is unconditionally passed to the recovery system. Any other transaction operation may be delayed to assure global database consistency. If the scheduler receives a *read* (*write*) operation, it tries to set a global *read* (*write*) lock for the data item. If the lock cannot be granted (because of a conflicting lock kept by some other global transaction), it uses a wait-die scheme to decide whether the global transaction should wait or it should be aborted (i.e. if a transaction requesting a global lock on a data item has a smaller timestamp than any transaction holding a lock on the data item, then it is allowed to wait, otherwise it aborts the transaction). If a global transaction is allowed to wait for a global lock, then the transaction state becomes *blocked* and the transaction is placed on the *blocked* queue. In addition to that the transaction is placed on a *global wait for graph*. A global wait for graph is defined as a graph $G = (N, E)$, where E is a set of transactions and E is a set of edges defined as follows: $< T_i, T_j >$ belongs to E if and only if there is a data item such that T_j has a global lock on it and T_i has requested a conflicting global lock on it. The transaction becomes *executing* again only after it can obtain global locks that the transaction was waiting for. The wait-die scheme ensures that global transactions on the *blocked* queue cannot enter a deadlock.

To schedule a commit operation, the scheduler uses two basic data structures: *transaction graph* and *wait − for − commit list*.

A *transaction graph* $TG = (TS, E)$ is a bipartite graph whose set of nodes TS consists of a set of global transactions and a set of local sites. Edges from E may connect only transaction nodes with site nodes. An edge $<T, S>$ belongs to E if and only if the transaction T was active at site S and the scheduler scheduled a commit for T.

A waitforcommit list $(WFCL)$ consists of global transactions that cannot yet be scheduled to execute a commit operation. For each transaction T_i on the list, the list contains a set of transactions $T_i, ..., T_i$ whose commit operation should be completed or aborted before the commit of T_i can be scheduled. A transaction on the list, however, need not necessarily wait for the completion of every transaction in the set of transactions it waits for. It may be ready to be scheduled for a commit operation after some of transactions from the set successfully commit (and in some cases, a successful commit of only one transaction from the set would be sufficient to schedule the transaction's commit!).

The scheduler uses the following algorithm to schedule a commit operation. The input consists of a transaction identification T_i and a set of sites SS at which the transaction is active.

1. If adding new edges between T_i and each site from SS causes a loop in the transaction graph, then T_i's commit operation is not scheduled. T_i is placed on the $WFCL$. Transactions from loops, that are generated by adding T_i to the transaction graph, are added to the set of transactions that T_i should wait for.

2. Otherwise, the scheduler adds new edges between T_i and every site from SS to the transaction graph, schedules T_i's commit, and sends the commit to the recovery manager.

5 Recovery Manager Algorithm

In this section we describe the four recovery manager (recovery manager) procedures for executing the *read/write*, abort, commit and *restart* operations.

RW (T_i, x, v, S_j) - this procedure is used to execute either *read* or *write* operations by global transaction T_i on global data item x, located at site S_j. The value of the data item x to be read or written to is v.

Abort (T_i, SS) - this procedure is used to abort transaction T_i at each site from SS where it was performing its operations.

Commit (T_i, SS) - this procedure is used to install the results of T_i permanently in the global database at sites from SS, where the transaction was performing its operations.

Restart - this procedure is used to restore a consistent global database state after a failure has occured.

The first four operations are passed to the recovery manager from the the scheduler. The last one is initiated by the recovery manager after the ADDS recovers after a system failure. The data structures used by the recovery manager procedures are as follows:

1. A *global wait − for − graph* ($GWFG$), also used by the scheduler;

2. A *wait − for − commit list* ($WFCL$), also used by the scheduler;

3. A *global database log* described in the section 3; and

4. A *potential conflict graph* (PCG) [BREI89a].

After T_i has received local locks to proceed with the operation at S_j, the transaction is waiting either for data or for the message from the local DBMS reporting the result of the operation. In the multidatabase environment, each *read/write* operation may require a relatively long time to execute. During that time the recovery manager should be informed whether the transaction is working at site S_j or is waiting for required local locks. If it is waiting for local locks, it may be involved in a deadlock. In the latter case, the recovery manager should take actions to break a possible deadlock. However, we do not want the recovery manager to interrupt the transaction's operation just because it takes too long to execute. That decision should be left to the user submitting the transaction. By requesting local locks first, the recovery manager ensures that it will not interrupt a transaction that has received local locks. The recovery manager will interpret a long wait for local locks as a possible deadlock situation. In the latter case, it calls the *Abort* procedure to break a potential deadlock.

The RW procedure does not work with the global log. However, the server performing the *write* operation on behalf of the global transaction records all changes into a server log. The server log becomes a part of the global log during the *restart* operation of the recovery manager. The global log contains at this point only one record about transaction T_i, the record indicating that the transaction is active. This record is placed on the global log after the transaction manager has processed the transaction's *begin* statement.

At the time that the abort message is sent to each site at which the transaction is active, the transaction could be active or it could have started the commit operation. If the transaction is active, then the global log contains only one record pertaining to the transaction (the record that is placed in the log after processing the *begin* statement). If, however, the transaction has started a commit operation, it can have several records on the global log, depending on what stage of the commit operation the abort is called.

Transaction abort may also occur when global transaction T_i is aborted by the local DBMS at some local site from the SS. In such a case, the recovery manager, after the receiving the message that the transaction is aborted at the local site, calls the *Abort* procedure to complete an abort operation at every other site at which the transaction is active. Upon completion of the abort operation, the recovery manager checks the GWFG and $WFCL$ to determine whether any transaction can either be given global locks released by the aborted transaction or can start the commit operation.

The commit process uses the two-phase commit protocol [BHG87]. At the first stage, the recovery manager sends a ready message to each server that is involved in transaction execution. Each server, upon receiving the ready message, copies the contents of the server log into stable storage and responds with the ready message to the recovery manager. If a server fails to copy the server's log successfully, then it will not respond to the recovery manager. In any event, if, at this stage, at least one of the servers fails to respond, the recovery manager aborts the transaction (step 3 of the procedure).

The second stage of the commit procedure starts with the recovery manager sending a commit message to every transaction's server and records it in the global log. Starting from this point, the recovery manager guarantees that the changes that have been made by the transaction will be permanently installed in the global database, regardless of any system, transaction, server, communication, and site failures.

At step 6 of the procedure, we describe the actions of the recovery manager in cases in which the *commit complete* message does not reach the recovery manager during the *timeout* period. The fact that the message did not arrive indicates that either the server or the site failed, or a communication failure occured preventing messages from a server to the recovery manager. In either of these events, the recovery manager attempts to restart the server until it succeeds after either site or communication is restored. The recovery manager at this point is assured that the server's log has been copied into stable storage and all information required to restore the local database values are recorded and can not be destroyed by any system failure. If the recovery manager restarts the transaction at a site, it changes its status at the site to waiting, since, at this time, the recovery manager initiates a new (from the viewpoint of the local DBMS) transaction. This transaction (again, from the local DBMS viewpoint) needs to write into some local data items and, therefore, needs to obtain local *write* locks.

The restarted transaction's local lock requests may create a deadlock situation with other global transactions either active or being restarted at the same time. Thus the algorithm combines the potential conflict graph, the global wait-for-graph and the wait-for-commit list to detect and break a potential global deadlock, if any should occur. In the next section we prove that the algorithm always finds and breaks global deadlock. However, a restarted transaction can never be aborted if a deadlock has occured (or may occur!), since the recovery manager has already guaranteed that the new data value will be installed in the database.

The server restart process is idempotent. If the restarted server fails, then it can be again restarted without creating an inconsistent global database state. Eventually, the restarted server will be able to complete the restart process, and only then will the data that has been locked at the global level be unlocked for access by other global transactions.

Regardless of how many servers have failed during the transaction commit operation, the scheduler guarantees global database consistency. Let us consider the case that during commit, transaction T_i has failed at sites $S_j1, ..., S_jr$. In this case, the recovery manager restarts T_i at these sites. However, for each site $S_i1, ..., S_jr$, the recovery manager will restart the transaction with a new timestamp. This allows the recovery manager to consider each restarted transaction at the local site as a new global transaction. On the other hand, the recovery manager also has a record connecting all restarted transsactions related to the failed global transaction. This trick permits us to maintain a main restriction of the mode, namely, each global transaction may not be in the waiting state at more than one local site.

The *Restart* process is part of the recovery process after an ADDS system failure. The main purpose of the *Restart* process is to complete a commit for all global transactions that the recovery manager has guaranteed will be committed.

The *Restart* process works with both the global and server logs. At the first pass of the log, it eliminates from the global log records of all global transactions that were either active or in process of abort, or that started the commit operation but the commit message was not sent to any of the transaction executing sites. The recovery manager should not be concerned with undoing any global transaction that has not reached a decision to commit before the failure The undo process for such transactions will be performed by the local DBMS systems. At the second pass of the global log, the *Restart* process will redo any committed transaction or such transaction that a decision to commit has reached at least one of its sites before the failure.

6 Conclusions

We have discussed here the ADDS transaction management mechanism that guarantees global database consistency and atomicity. The system discussed here assumes that each local database is using the strict two-phase locking protocol. The ADDS transaction management mechanism uses global locks and commit graph to guarantee both global database consistency and atomicity of global transactions. It also uses a forward recovery approach by redoing global transactions that failed to commit at any local site.

ADDS has been tested with a variety of *live* users applications and has gained wide acceptance by the user community within Amoco. The ADDS transaction management system was implemented at Amoco Production Company Research Center and was tested in a prototype mode. The test proved a viability of the approach but also has uncovered some weaknesses of the approach. The main weakness of the approach is a high coarseness of ADDS data items. It leads to a reduced global transaction throughput in the ADDS environment. It appears, however, that the high throughput is not the major requirement for update transactions in a multidatabase environment. The main requirement is to maintain a mutual consistency of semantically related company data. In that respect ADDS proved to be a valuable tool.

References

[BHG87]   P. A. Bernstein, V. Hadzilacos, and N. Goodman. *Concurrency Control and Recovery in Database Systems*. Addison-Wesley, Reading, MA, 1987.

[BGS92]   Y. Breitbart, H. Garcia-Molina, A. Silberschatz, Overview of Multidatabase Transaction Management, VLDB Journal 1(2), 1992.

[BLS91]   Y. Breitbart, W. Litwin, A. Silberschatz. Deadlock Problems in a Multidatabase Environment. In *Digest of Papers COMPCON, Spring 91*. San Francisco, CA, pp 145-151, February 1991.

[BST90]   Y. Breitbart, A. Silberschatz, and G. R. Thompson. Reliable transaction management in a multidatabase system. In *Proceedings of ACM-SIGMOD 1990 International Conference on Management of Data, Atlantic City, New Jersey*, pages 215–224, 1990.

[BT84]   Y. Breitbart, L. Tieman. ADDS - Heterogeneous Distributed Database System. In Distributed Data Sharing Systems, F. Schreiber, W. Litwin (eds), North Holland, 1984, pp.7-24

[GPZ85]   V. Gligor, R. Popescu-Zeletin, "Concurrency Control Issues in Distributed Heter ogeneous Database Management Systems." Distributed Data Sharing Systems. Eds. F. Schreiber and W. Litwin. North-Holland, 1985, 43-56.

[Kim94] Won Kim. Modern Database Management (Object Oriented & Multidatabase Technologies) Addison-Wesley, 1994.

[LR82] T. Landers, R. Rosenberg. An Overview of Multibase. In *Distributed Databases, H. J. Schneider (ed.)*. North-Holland Publishing Co., 1982.

[RSL78] D. Rosenkrantz, R. Stearns, P. Lewis, System Level Concurrency Control for Distributed Database Systems, ACM Transactions on Database Systems 3(2), 1978.

[Ship81] D. Shipman. The Functional Data Model and the Data Language DAPLEX. ACM Transaction on Database Systems, 6:1, 1981.

[SL90] A. Sheth, J. A. Larson. Federated Databases: Attributes and Integration. ACM Computing Surveys, 22:3, 1990.

[TTC+90] G. Thomas, G. Thompson, C. W. Chung, E. Barkmeyer, F. Carter, M. Templeton, S. Fox, B. Hartman. Heterogeneous Distributed Database Systems for Production Use. ACM Computing Surveys, 22:3, 1990.

[VW92] J. Veijalainen and A. Wolski. Prepare and Commit Certification for Decentralized Transaction Management in Rigorous Heterogeneous Multidatabases. In *Proceedings of the 8th International Conference on Data Engineering* Phoenix, AZ 1992.

Persistent Object Systems and Interoperability: Linguistic and Architectural Requirements

Kazimierz Subieta

Institute of Computer Science, Polish Academy of Sciences
Warszawa, Poland

Abstract

An important aspect of currently developed persistent object systems is support for interoperability with other systems. A central issue in supporting interoperability is achieving type compatibility. We argue that abstraction is also a key interoperability issue. The level of abstraction depends on such features as modularity, encapsulation, orthogonality, minimality, clean and precise semantics, universality, extensibility, type safety and genericity, and others. In the paper we discuss these concepts and some architectures of gateways.

1 Introduction

The term *interoperability* refers to the ability of independently developed systems to operate with each other. In the database domain interoperability is recently of special importance. The communication cost in computer networks is rapidly decreased, data storages are cheaper, databases become larger, and their content covers more and more important aspects of humans' life; thus demands of database clients concerning convenient access to various databases are growing. On the other hand, database applications are created for various hardware platforms and operating systems, with different physical data organizations, conceptual data models, query languages (QLs), programming languages (PLs), database management systems, utilities, and so on. For many organizations investment in a database system is very large. New systems and programming interfaces constantly appearing on the market are in contradiction with this investment. Thus one of the challenges concerns *legacy applications* — adopting by novel systems databases organized and processed according to obsolete technologies.

Interoperability of persistent object systems (POS) has many features that are common to another long-lived topic, known in software engineering under the name "software reuse" [17]. Software reuse concerns adopting programs or pieces of program code for new purposes, e.g., by inspecting and modifying a source, or dynamic binding of library procedures, classes, etc. Interoperability addresses the dynamic aspect of software reuse, amplified by the requirement concerning standardization of interfaces. Standardization becomes a key issue if programming objects (data, types, classes, methods, procedures, modules, etc.) created and maintained under some system are to be directly used by a foreign system.

Fast progress in computer technologies causes that both software reuse and interoperability have still failed to become common software practice. Obsolete standards, languages, technical solutions, software design methods are hardly accepted and taken into account by proponents of novel scientific and technological ideas. There is also no standards and agreement concerning basic properties of future database systems; compare e.g. [2] and [32].

Growth of computer networks and distributed databases causes that a key aspect of newly developed systems is their support for interaction with other systems. In [35], presenting votes of professionals concerning "hot" database topics, legacy applications are on the third position from the top. Currently it is very hard to promote in the commercial world a system which does not conform to popular industry standards and beliefs aiming interoperability. It is often said that the meaning of these problems is growing: "all systems in the future will be distributed, connected, complex" [27]. This is a novel psychological, technical and intellectual challenge for system developers. Trying to develop the "best" features of their artifacts they must also think how these features correspond to paralelly developed systems, how they are open for modifications, extensions and connections with other systems, and how they could meet properties and demands of systems that will be developed in the future.

Various factors contributing to interoperability of POS can be vaguely grupped into *semantic interoperability* and *operational interoperability* [24]. Semantic interoperability concerns mappings between different data models or building a common (global) super-model. Recent results in the conceptual data modelling, view and schema integration, heterogeneous databases (e.g. [31, 36, 19, 16, 4]), and query processing in heterogeneous distributed databases resulted in substantial understanding of the first issue.

Operational interoperability concerns stored data, query/programming languages acting on these data, performance issues, and internal or external interfaces. In contrast to semantic interoperability the problem of operational interoperability is still in the infant phase. Current research in the area of heterogeneous databases takes into account simple retrieval queries [12, 18, 31] or particular query operators such as join [10]. Real database applications, however, require features of universal PLs. Various database models, hardware platforms and architectures, data formats, access languages and protocols, error messages, system catalogs, and achieving proper computational universality, reliability and performance make the general approach to the problem to be a terrible challenge.

Achieving good quality of operational interoperability is a prerequisite for methods aiming semantic interoperability; hence some ideas concerning semantic interoperability may appear to be unrealistic for lack of operational interoperability. Currently, however, operational interoperability depends on clever implementation tricks rather than on the systematic approach [23]. For systems being currently on the market the realistic possibility is the case-to-case approach relying on building gateways from a system to another system, which (with some luck) can work with proper reliability, performance and pragmatic universality. There are various examples: Ingres contains gateways to other SQL servers (e.g. DB2 and SQL/DS) and non-SQL databases (e.g. created under IMS) [7]; GemStone [8] has a SQL-based gateway to Sybase, Ingres, Oracle and Informix; Oracle makes possible to access foreign databases made under DB2, SQL/DS, Lotus 1-2-3 and dBase; Sybase's SQL gateways support most of the leading relational database engines, including DB2, Oracle, Ingres and Informix; etc. Our experience concerns implementation of a fully transparent gateway from the database programming language DBPL (extended Modula-2) [29] to SQL servers [22, 23].

Many complementary industrial and scientific developments aim the interoperabilty challenge; we note the following:

- Increase the level of program reuse. A progress in this respect was made by establishing a common link format, regardless of high-level programming languages. IBM's System Object Model (SOM) and Distributed SOM creates a new standard - a binary-level, link format, allowing for dynamic linking without re-compiling other components, regardless of hardware and software environment [27]. Approaches to establish standards for Remote Procedure Calls (RPC) aim interoperability in distributed systems.

- Open/distributed transaction management and processing, [26, 5].

- Open architectures of persistent object systems, language neutral specification of programming objects (data, objects, types, procedures, modules, etc.) [3, 26, 5].

- Modularization and encapsulation, with separation of specification and implementaion. The old software engineering principle received recently a new atention in the context of object-oriented databases [2, 37].

- Standardization of languages and interfaces. Standardization has either positive and negative aspects: too late standardization leads to chaos, too early standardization fixes immature artifacts and brakes the progress. As an example, there are extreme opinions concerning the SQL standard: e.g. [32] postulates the "intergalactic" meaning of SQL in the future, and [11, 33, 7] consider the standard as immature and incomplete. Despite doubts, if systems to be connected preserve some (even incomplete) standard, interoperability is much easier. The ultimate goal of design efforts aiming interoperability is standardization supporting full portability of data and software.

- Preserving principles of data and program conceptual abstraction. Various research efforts [3, 7, 17, 30, 38] aim reducing from programmer's views and interfaces secondary or technical details and shifting programmer interfaces to the conceptual level.

Our basic thesis, which we would like to promote, concerns the meaning of abstraction issues in the development of interoperable programs. Abstraction means clean vision of system's languages and architecture, hence it is central for standardization and for further ability of a developed system to interoperate with other systems. The level of abstraction depends on general features: modularity, encapsulation, orthogonality, minimality, clean and precise semantics, universality, extensibility, type safety together with genericity, and others.

The paper is organized as follows. In Section 2 we present some classical views on interoperability. In Section 3 we discuss abstraction aspects which may contribute to interoperability, and in Section 4 we present some architectures of gateways.

2 Classical Interoperability: ADT and RPC

In software engineering a central issue in supporting interoperability is achieving *type compatibility* so that data objects or procedures used in one program can be shared by another program, that may be written in another language [38]. To avoid bindings to the data representation level, interoperability should be shifted to a more abstract (specification) level, where data are seen via abstract data type (ADT) operations.

While this view is true for classical PLs data types, we argue that it is simplified for POS. Several aspects disturb to handle database objects by the ADT approach. These are the following.

- *Autonomy of the foreign system.* Persistent object systems have various strategies concerned access rights, which cannot be shared. Direct access to data violates this autonomy.

- *Concurrent access, transaction processing and recovery.* Logging, locking and recovery are the subject of subtle algorithms having internal states, which cannot be accessed and disturbed from outside.

- *Performance.* Systems are tuned by various performance enhancements, for example, indices and query optimizers, which can be handled from outside with difficulties. Query optimizers are implemented for a particular user interface, thus to employ the optimizer, one must use this interface.

- *Irrelevance of the ADT approach to bulk data.* For bulk data types the ADT approach fails, since it must fix access methods (for example, through operators such as *first*, *next* and *end-of*), or — in terms of input-output semantics — the numer of required operators is infinite. (For this reason bulk types are served by QLs.)

Thus we argue that interoperability with another POS must involve data interfaces, i.e., object manager routines or an access language. While some type compatibility between systems to be connected remains a basic factor, it is usually impossible to separate this factor from data manipulation aspects.

Operational interoperability is assumed in the technology called remote procedure calls (RPC). RPC concerns calling procedures that are outside the address space of a given program. Several RPC systems are proposed, in particular Sun Microsystems' Open Network Computing (ONC), Distributed Computing Environment (DCE) developed by the Open Software Foundation (OSF), ANSAware, Courier RPC of Xerox, and other [6]. However, the programming interface assumed in RPC (usually C functions) is limited. The complexity of data and control in POS (bulk types, complex objects, classes, QLs, transactions, active rules, etc.) much axceeds the complexity assumed in classical PLs, such as C; see the discussion in [14]. A step beyond RPC are distributed object-based systems as extensions of PLs like C++, Smalltalk, Trellis, or Eiffel. This approach aims at providing support for object interaction (identifying, locating, and accessing objects) in a heterogeneous distributed environment. Distributed object-based systems require further standardization effort, which must concern not only procedure calls, but also data formats, naming and binding, access languages, query results, and so on.

Taking into account both data structures and programming interfaces we argue that rising the abstraction level is of primary importance for interoperability, since it allows for reducing the number and complexity of concepts which need to be understood and handled by programmers implementing interoperable software.

In the database domain much attention is devoted to abstraction. This is expressed in commonly used terms such as "data independence", "semantic data models", "conceptual schema", "declarative QL", etc. Practice of commercial database systems, however, is far from the ideal. The well-known impedance mismatch problem can be considered as an example of violating abstraction principles by introducing low-level mechanisms, such as cursors, host variables, description and communication areas, very specific rules of updating, and irregular rules concerning syntax and semantics. In practice, rising the abstraction level for DBPLs is a difficult task. The next section shows some aspects of basic abstraction principles.

3 Abstraction: The Key to Interoperability

The general aspects influencing interoperabiltiy include encapsulation, modularity, orthogonality, minimality, clean and precise semantics, universality, extensibility, type safety and genericity, and others. We discuss them in the following.

3.1 Encapsulation and Modularity

Encapsulation is an old principle of software engineering (proposed by D. Parnas in 1972). Currently it is considered in three contexts: modules, ADTs, and classes. For all three cases encapsulation means isolation of the programmer from implementation details of some programming objects. Abstracting from implementation details supports both interoperability and program reuse.

Modules, ADTs and classes have different encapsulation properties. Typically, modules (e.g. Modula-2) cannot export/import views (restrictions) over bulk complex data; this may present a disadvantage for database systems. Similarly, objects in object-oriented approaches do not export their attributes; this (apparently) leaves no room for QLs. We argue that for POS both concepts have to be improved.

Modularity supports interoperability in three ways: (1) due to encapsulation, complexity of the module's interface is reduced; (2) clean specification of dependencies between modules clarifies a view how a particular module could be interfaced to other systems; (3) separation of module's interface and implementation supports locality of changes thus simplifies modifications aiming cooperation with other systems.

3.2 Orthogonality

Orthogonality means freedom in combining system's or language's features. Orthogonality may concern data, QLs, and PLs. In the data dimension orthogonality implies freedom in combination of type constructors, in particular, the possibility to nest bulk data. It also implies the possibility to combine classical data types with types required by multi-media applications (BLOBs), such as text, graphics and sound. Many current approaches assume orthogonality of types and persistence. Also, many approaches assume the possibilty of combination of static data with interpreted objects, such as views, procedures, constraints, active rules, and access restrictions. For query/programming languages orthogonality implies free combination of language constructs, and avoiding highly specialized constructs, big syntactic and semantic patterns, irregular treatment, and large context dependencies.

Orthogonality supports interoperability, since free combination of data types increases the possibility to match another database format, and free combination of query/programming constructs simplifies automatic generation of queries/programs. Orthogonality reduces the number of exceptional or additional rules and constraints, thus simplifies programming interfaces and reduces the size of manuals.

3.3 Minimality

The Ockham's razor (as few concepts as possible) is a good principle in the development of system features, interfaces, and query/programming languages. Minimality requires careful analysis of introduced concepts and features in order to discover redundancies and possibilities of generalization. A progress in this respect has been made by developers of relational database systems, which are based on canonical data representation and unified access languages abstracting from access details. The relational model, however, does not deal with more sophisticated database objects, such as database procedures, rules, forms, system classes, etc. This caused growth of specialized features in commercial RDBMS.

Minimality is compromised by bottom-up evolution and eclecticism: *ad hoc* adding and mixing various ideas and solutions. Most of all this is caused by the temptation to extend system functionalities in response to lack of sufficient universality, new demands, new technologies, or conformity with recent buzzwords and beliefs. Eclecticism is striking in commercial RDBMS: SQL-based databases are mixed with object-oriented concepts (objects, classes, methods), classical programming concepts (variables, arrays, pointers, etc.), and navigational data access via cursors *a la* CODASYL DML. For example, in Ingres/Windows 4GL [15] dynamic arrays have all properties of relations, but cannot be queried by SQL — they are served by other constructs. Obviously, the resulting programming interface violates the Ockham's principle.

Absence of redundant features obviously simplifies the development of interoperable software.

3.4 Clean and precise semantics

We understand "semantics" as a mapping between language's constructs and other formal objects. Interoperability most of all depends on the formal, "machine" meaning. However, mathematical specification of semantics is almost always unfeasible and unpractical, since in non-trivial cases it leads to the explosion of mathematical formulas, which cannot be handled manually and cannot be easily understood by designers and programmers. Moreover, formality does not mean precision, since formal models usually neglect various language features, sometimes of vital importance. Perhaps the best example is the relational algebra, which is enough formal, but not enough precise to deal with many features implemented in query languages (duplicates, ordering, updating, etc.).

By clean and precise semantics we understand a reasonable description of language's features in a natural language, with some aid of general computer terminology, notions related to particular hardware or software platforms, and mathematical concepts. Our experience with commercial systems has shown that lack of clean and precise semantics of system interfaces and languages makes interoperability problems especially hard and frustrating. Programming of interoperable software requires iterative experiments in order to explain system features. Since usually it is impossible to test all cases, the resulting software may not be sufficiently reliable and universal.

3.5 Universality

The concept of universality is frequently misunderstood. We note the "relational completeness", which is essentially an ill-motivated element of the relational doctrine. Some authors (e.g. [2]) postulate computational universality, which is defined as the power of the Turing machine: easy to achieve through integrating procedural features. The real problem is different: it concerns the *pragmatic universality*, which denotes reasonable possibilities in serving data structures, system features, and computer resources.

Pragmatic universality of data structures means a rich type system which includes classical atomic types, long fields (BLOBs) related to multi-media, interpreted objects (views, functions, procedures, virtual attributes, types, constraints, active rules), and type constructors (tuples, records, relations, sets, bags, sequences, arrays, ADTs, classes, variants, null values, etc.) Modern typing systems assume the possibility of orthogonal combination of type constructors and orthogonality of types and persistence [1]. In POS data repositories (classes, modules, files, etc.) and relationships between them (inheritance, import/export) become properties of data structures and may imply specific language options.

Sometimes types of objects are additionally qualified by access restrictions (for example, access to object attributes inside and outside methods in O_2 [25]), by special syntax of access expressions (see Ingres/Windows 4GL [15]), or by special treatment of distinguished attributes (primary keys in DBPL [29]). In different languages values of some types can or cannot be used in expressions, used as parameters, or returned by functions. Properties of data structures can also be qualified as static (compile time) or dynamic (run time). The dynamic case implies many untypical possibilities: creating, deleting, inserting, copying, modifying, changing data name, etc.

Pragmatic universality is supported by programming abstractions, such as procedures, functions, types, ADTs, modules and classes. Usually programmers expect that procedures and functions may have parameters, can be recursive, and can update data objects via their parameters and via side effects. Some programming features can be upgraded to the first-class citizenship (e.g. types and data names) and can be stored in a database (e.g., views, rules, database procedures). To increase genericity, PLs introduce higher-order functions, polymorphism, macro-definitions and linguistic reflection.

The presented list of features is not complete, but it shows the spectrum of design choices. A consequence of rich possibilities concerning data structures is growth of the number of programming options required to serve them.

To achieve better potential for interoperability some authors propose to reduce the number of options. The power is achieved by orthogonality; see the "RISC" model [20] or "lean languages and models" [30] based on a relatively small kernel of orthogonal functionalities. The "add-on" philosophy [21], which assumes building new features (e.g. QLs, transaction processing) on the top of basic fuctionalities, aims the similar goal.

Developing a more universal system increases a chance to cover and adopt features of another system. However, if data structures and programming features of two systems are incompatible, interoperation will lose parts of functionalities of both systems. Highly specialized system features disturb its modifiability and adaptability to novel demands.

3.6 Extensibility

Several scientific and commerical effors aim extensibility of POS. Usually, their life is long, thus demands to extend or modify their data structures and processes are highly probable [1]. The commercial product literature uses the term *open system* as "open for extensions" or "open for interoperation". This means possibilities to modify or build system's add-ons on the top of its standard functionalities. Usually POS clients have limited possibilities in this respect e.g., to modify a data model (schema evolution) or to modify a QL. Extendible systems supply the clients in reasonable capabilities allowing him to taylor functionalities to their own needs. Several research efforts aim this goal, in particular DASDBS [28] and Exodus [9] are (to some extend) neutral to data models, and Postgres [34] makes possible to define new ADTs. Schema evolution issues are discussed in [1, 3, 16, 32].

3.7 Type safety and genericity

Strong and static typing is a well-understood and commonly accepted technique contributing to interoperability. The main motivations for it is enforcing constraints on data objects local to a single program, and detecting program errors as early as possible. Evolution of typing systems in PLs has resulted in other effects: clarification of the data structure concepts, clean semantics of program constructs and interaction between program modules, clear view on data and programming abstractions, and supporting human-oriented data views. In POS it is necessary to identify, interpret, store, retrieve and manipulate objects that outlive a single program execution and may exist independently of the application that created them. This implies the demand for language-independent mechanisms for typing shared, persistent objects.

Modern typing systems based on structural type equivalence, full orthogonality of type constructors, orthogonality of types and persistence, and various forms of polymorphism supports either modularity, orthogonality, minimality, universality, and clean semantics, thus in many ways support interoperability.

3.8 Other factors contributing to interoperability

Higher abstraction level is supported by various features of POS, in particular:

- QLs, programming through macroscopic operations, seamless integration of a QL with imperative constructs. Currently the SQL standard supports interoperability between relational database management systems. Despite many attempts to adopt SQL for object-oriented databases, achieving simplicity, universality and clean semantics within this paradigm is difficult. We believe that a new QL standard should be developed for advanced database models.

- Avoiding big context dependencies in programming (searching in extensive program code or documentation text during preparation of programs).

- Avoiding side effects of programming constructs or features not covered by the basic language philosophy or a mathematical ideology. The execution model of logic programs, duplicates and updating in relational query languages, operations on a state in functional languages are examples of violating this principle.

- Smooth, clean and consistent treatment of exceptional cases in the programming, such as null values, variants, exceptions, run-time errors, user breaks, etc.

- Clean semantics, and rules of design and use of interpreted elements stored in a database, such as views, active rules, constraints, derived data, database procedures.

- Standardization of system dictionaries and catalogs, standardization of interfaces to them [7], minimal, consistent and standardized system of error messages.

- Object-orientation. Objects encapsulated into the method layer can be considered as units of interoperation in open distributed systems [37]. In many cases, however, methods are insufficient as the interface to objects [13]. Thus the notion of encapsulation should be extended to cover export of some object attributes and invariant of classes such as constraints and active rules.

4 Architectures of Gateways

Complexity of a gateway depends on the following contradictory factors:

- **Discrepancies** between data models and interfaces of systems A and B to be connected.

- **Transparency**: how many concepts from the foreign system B are involved into the programmer's interface of the system A. (The ideal is full transparency: there is no concept of the foreign system the programmer should be aware of.)

- **Universality**: how many capabilities of the system B can be potentially utilized by the programmer from the system A; how many capabilities of the system A can be used to make applications which process data organized under the system B.

- **Performance**: the overhead due to processing via the gateway.

- *Other factors*, in particular: reliability, concurrency and transaction processing, authorization, access and utilization of meta-data.

Some architectures of gateways are listed below.

A package of procedures organizing access to foreign database files. As we have already noted, the method has disadvantages. In particular, indices, catalogs, query optimizers, etc. are very difficult to utilize. Since this approach violates the autonomy of the foreign system, it can be used in special cases only.

Virtual, transparent mapping of a foreign database files into a view of a target database system. For updating, such a mapping is usually difficult to implement. The approach shares disadvantages of the previous approach. An advantage is transparency of the gateway for the programmers.

Package of procedures calling object manager routines. Some systems (Oracle, O_2) support data/object manager procedures for external use. The advantage concerns a possibility of utilization of all features of the foreign system. A disadvantages concerns cryptic notation of procedure calls, and semantics dependent on a large context.

Precompiler of database manipulation statements embedded in a host PL. The method introduces a little overhead over the previous method, but it avoids cryptic notation and large context dependencies. Mixing two different languages, however, suffers from impedance mismatch.

Direct mapping of a targed language into a language specific for foreign system. This approach is conceptually the most straightforward. Since databases must be updated and processed, and the processing can involve sophisticated options, the mapping may be difficult or impossible [22].

Mapping references to foreign databases from the target POS into calls of object manager routines of the foreign system, Figure 1. The mapping can be accomplished during compilation or run time. Advantages: fully transparent interface, possibility to implement strong static type checking, and possibility to employ all features of the foreign system that are maintained by its object manager. The approach is difficult to implement, since it requires some compatibility of data views of both systems (including compatibility for updating) and sufficiently generic routines of the foreign system. This approach was used during the implementation of the gateway from DBPL to INGRES [22, 23].

Our experience has shown that implementing a transparent gateway on the top of an existing system is very difficult because systems are usually designed

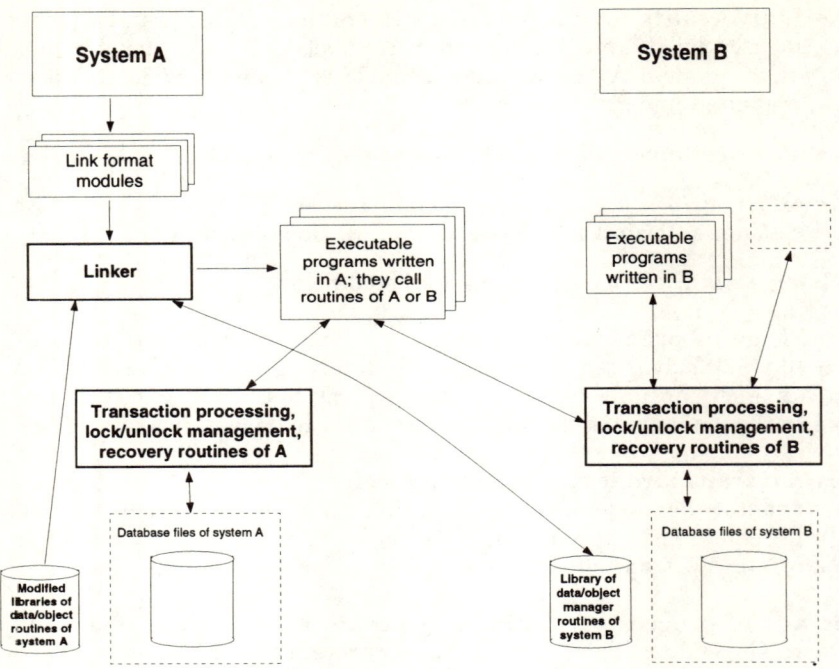

Figure 1: Architecture for mapping references to foreign databases into calls of foreign routines

without assumptions concerning such extensions. Thus, novel systems aiming interoperability should be build according to open architecture, in which external database objects and functionalities are not hard-wired into different architectural layers, interfaces and system features. An example of such architecture is presented in [3].

Conclusion

Analysis of aspects, architectures and scenarios of interoperation has led us to the thesis that rising the abstraction level for data and database interfaces is of primary importance for further interoperability potential. The abstraction is supported by general principles such as modularity, orthogonality, universality, minimality, clean and precise semantics, type safety and genericity. These ideas have proper treatment in database systems and DBPLs developed in the academic world; unfortunately, they seems to be underestimated in the commercial world. Thus we believe that good interoperability of future systems much depends on better understanding of practical problems in the academic world, and transfering ideas from the academic world to the commercial world.

References

[1] M. Atkinson. Questioning Persistent Types. Proc. 2nd DBPL Workshop, Gleneden Beach, Oregon, 1989

[2] M. Atkinson, F. Bancilhon, D. DeWitt, K. Dittrich, D. Maier, and S. Zdonik. The Object-Oriented Database System Manifesto. Proc. 1-st Intl. Conf. on Deductive and Object Oriented Databases, Kyoto, 1989, pp.40-57

[3] M.P. Atkinson. Persistent Foundations for Scalable Multi-paradigmal Systems. $FIDE_2$, ESPRIT BRA Project 6309, Technical Report Series, FIDE/92/51, 1992. (Proc. Intl. Workshop on Distributed Object Management, Edmonton, Canada, Aug.1992, Morgan Kaufmann, 1992)

[4] C. Batini, S. Ceri, S.B. Navathe. Conceptual Database Design, An Entity-Relationship Approach. Benjamin/Cummings 1992

[5] P.A. Bernstein, P.O. Gyllstrom, T. Wimberg. STDL - A Portable Language for Transaction Processing. Proc. 19th VLDB Conf., Dublin, Ireland, 1993, pp.218-229

[6] M. Bever, K. Geihs, L. Heuser, M. Mühlhäuser, A. Schill. Distributed Systems, OSF DCE and Beyond. Proc. Intl. DCE Workshop, Karlsruhe, Germany, Oct. 1993. Springer LNCS 731, 1993, pp.1-20

[7] M. Bishop, E. Wasiolek. The Big Picture. Ingres Release 6.0. Relational Technology Inc. 1/90, 1990.

[8] P. Butterworth, A. Otis, J. Stein. The GemStone Object Database Management System. Communications of the ACM, Vol.34, No.10, Oct.1991, pp.64-77

[9] M.J. Carey, D.J.DeWitt, S.L. Vandenberg. A Data Model and Query Language for EXODUS. Proc. ACM SIGMOD Conf., 1988, pp.413-423

[10] A. Chatterjee, A. Segev. Data Manipulation in Heterogeneous Databases. ACM SIGMOD Record, Vol.20, No.4, 1991, pp.64-68

[11] C.J. Date. Where SQL Falls Short. Datamation, May 1, 1987

[12] U. Dayal. Query Processing in a Multidatabase System. (In) Query Processing in Database Systems, Springer, New York 1985, pp.81-108

[13] U. Dayal. Queries and Views in an Object-Oriented Data Model. Proc. 2nd DBPL Workshop, Gleneden Beach, Oregon, 1989, pp.80-102

[14] J. Gray. Where Is Transaction Processing Headed? OTM Spectrum Reports, Vol.7, Report 2, May 1993, pp.14-19

[15] Application Editor User's Guide for INGRES/Windows 4GL for the UNIX and VMS Operating Systems. Language Reference Manual for INGRES/Windows 4GL for the UNIX and VMS Operating Systems. INGRES Release 6, Ingres Corporation, August 1990.

[16] W. Kent. The Breakdown of the Information Model in Multi-Database Systems. ACM SIGMOD Record, Vol.20, No.4, 1991, pp.10-15

[17] C.W. Krueger. Software Reuse. ACM Computing Surveys, Vol.24, No.2, 1992, pp.131-184

[18] W. Litwin, A. Abdellatif. Multidatabase Interoperability. IEEE Computing, Vol.19, No.12, Dec.1986, pp.10-18

[19] W. Litwin, L. Mark, N. Roussopoulos. Interoperability of Multiple Autonomous Databases. ACM Computing Surveys, Vol.22, No.3, 1990, pp.267-293

[20] F. Manola, S. Heiler An Approach to Interoperable Object Models. Unpublished Report, 1992

[21] F. Matthes, J.W. Schmidt. Bulk Types: Built-In or Add-On. Proc. 3rd Intl. Workshop on Database Programming Languages, Nafplion, Greece, Morgan Kaufmann, September 1991

[22] F. Matthes, A. Rudloff, J.W. Schmidt, K. Subieta. A Gateway from a DBPL to INGRES: Modula-2, DBPL, SQL+C, INGRES. $FIDE_2$, ESPRIT BRA PROJECT 6309 Technical Report Series FIDE/92/54, 1992

[23] F. Matthes, A. Rudloff, J.W. Schmidt, K. Subieta. A Gateway from DBPL to Ingres. Proc. 1st Intl. Conf. on Applications of Databases, Vadstena, Sweden, 1994

[24] M.-A. Neimat, M.-C. Shan. Database Research at HP Labs. ACM SIGMOD Record, Vol.20, No.4, 1991, pp.92-97

[25] The O_2 User Manual, Version 4.1. O_2 Technology, Versailles, France, October 1992

[26] OTM Spectrum Reports. Open Transaction Management - Strategies for multi-platform environments in 1990s., Vol.7, Reports 1-3, (Available from Spectrum Reports, Inc., PO Box 301368, Escondido, CA 92030, USA)

[27] Objects and Transactions to Come Together? OTM Spectrum Reports, Vol.7, Report 3, August 1993, pp.15-20

[28] H.-J. Schek, H.-B. Paul, M.H. Scholl, G. Weikum. The DASDBS Project: Objectives, Experiences, and Future Prospects. IEEE Transactions on Knowledge and Data Enginering, Vol.2, No.1, 1990, pp.25-43

[29] J.W. Schmidt, F Matthes. The Database Programming Language DBPL, Rationale and Report. FIDE, ESPRIT BRA Project 3070, Technical Report Series, FIDE/92/46, 1992

[30] J.W. Schmidt, F Matthes. Lean Languages and Models: Towards an Interoperable Kernel for Persistent Object Systems. Proc. IEEE Intl. Workshop on Research Issues in Data Engineering RIDE '93 Vienna, Austria, April 19-20, 1993

[31] A.P. Sheth, J.A. Larson. Federated Database Systems for Managing Distributed, Heterogeneous, and Autonomous Databases. ACM Computing Surveys, Vol.22, No.3, 1990, pp.183-236

[32] M. Stonebraker, L.A. Rowe, B. Lindsay, J. Gray, M. Carey, M. Brodie, P. Bernstein, D. Beech. Third-Generation Data Base System Manifesto. ACM SIGMOD Record, Vol.19, No.3, 1990, pp.31-44

[33] M. Stonebraker. Future Trends in Database Systems. IEEE Transactions on Knowledge and Data Engineering, Vol.1, No.1, March 1989, pp.33-44

[34] M. Stonebraker, L.A. Rowe, and M. Hirohama. The Implementation of POSTGRES. IEEE Transactions on Knowledge and Data Engineering, Vol.2, No.1, 1990, pp.125-142

[35] M. Stonebraker, R. Agraval, U. Dayal, E.J. Neuhold, A. Reuter. DBMS Research at a Crossroad: the Vienna Update. Proc. 19th Intl. Conf. on Very Large Data Bases, Dublin, Ireland, August 1993, pp.688-692

[36] G. Thomas, G.R.Thompson, C.-W. Chung, E. Barkmeyer, F. Carter, M. Templeton, S. Fox, B. Hartman. Heterogeneous Distributed Database Systems for Production Use. ACM Computing Surveys, Vol.22, No.3, 1990, pp.237-266

[37] J. Tibbets, B. Bernstein. Objects and transactions. OTM Spectrum Reports, Vol.7, Report 3, August 1993, pp.21-26

[38] J.C. Wilden, A.L. Wolf, W.R. Rosenblatt, P.L. Tarr. Specification-Level Interoperability. Communications of the ACM, Vol.34, No.5, May 1991, pp.72-87

Applications and Interfaces

CSCW – PARADIGM OF MODERN APPLIED INFORMATICS AND PROBLEM OF EAST-WEST RELATIONSHIPS

Serg S. Azarov   Anatoly A. Stogny

Institute of Applied Informatics
23-b, Krasnoarmeiskaya street,
252004, Kiev-4, Ukraine
Phone: (044) 228-26-97, Fax: (044) 228-27-97,
email: azarov@asinfor.kiev.ua

Abstract

The main goal of the paper is to define Computer Support for Cooperative Works (CSCW) and include next steps:
 –to identify types of activities in an Organizational Control Information Systems (OCIS) and space-time interaction forms of activities which can be characterized as Collaboration and Cooperation;
 –to define and describe Collaboration and Cooperation in an OCIS by an OCIS Conceptual Model.
 On this base we would like to show ways of possible decisions for future relationships can appear between the eastern and western Computer Society. The paage limitation makes us to show our reasoning very brifly.

Introduction

All of us may agree that computing problems and operational problems are very different things. We would like to show that however there are very many connections among Organization Systems problems, DBMS, Open System and CSCW and all of these kinds of things are revolving around Coordination. The page limitation makes us to show our reasoning very briefly that is why we can only state that at the present time Organization Systems find it's incarnations in different forms [1-6]: OCS–Organizational Computing Systems; CIS–Cooperative Information Systems; ICIS–Intelligent Cooperative Information Systems; Groupware. We think that this Organization System variety can be present by a generalized notion–OCIS or Organizational Control and Information Systems. We think also that this Organization System variety can be explain as follows. Ten years ago we could state two paradigms of these R&D:
 –the A-paradigm (from Apparatus) which include a software and a hardware vision of the R&D problems;

–the S-paradigm (from System) which is based on multidisciplinary visions of the R&D problems.

The A-paradigm can be present by two paths – Automation of Work Place (AWP) and Automation of Communication. The first includes Languages, DBMS, Word-processing, Spreadsheets or Integrated Packages, Graphics, Expert Systems and Hypertext Systems. The second one include now E-mail, LAN, Client-server, Groupware.

The S-paradigm can be present by three paths: System Analysis, System Design and Consulting. System Analysis is represented now by Structured Analysis, Business Games, Simulation and OCIS Conceptual Modelling [7]. System Design finds it's incarnation in CASE and Integrated Computer Aided System Engineering (I-CASE) [8]. A very business-oriented way of System Design is called as the Consulting.

Concepts of Open System and CSCW are known already many years but activate itself influences after a second part of 80th only. We have to agree that this is a process connected with spontaneous modifications of Organizational Systems. For the Open System concept we can say that it spawns an activity in a de facto standard movement appealed to a soft and hardware market. An appearance of CSCW paradigm problem of Organization System R&D can be explain by next facts:

–the CSCW is a real way to an explanation of distributed computing in OCIS;

–a distributed computing is more developed in DBMS and communication technologies areas;

–all of that preconditions spawn a deep difference between Theory and Practice.

Really the CSCW and the Open System concepts initially reflect to Organization and Technologic aspects correspondingly:

–the CSCW as a concept depends on self-organizational processes and gives to modern Data Base theory an organizational basis (a Data Base Theory there can be considers as effective informational realization of relationships within OCIS);

–the CSCW appeals to S-paradigm but do not exhausts it;

–the Open Systems as a concept depends on self-organizational processes of OCIS internetworking and gives to modern Data Base theory a standard communicational basis (a Data Base Theory there can be considers as effective informational realization of relationships among many OCIS);

–the problem of an openness for applied systems is remained including standards and multi-media open system standards that is why the Open Systems appeal to A-paradigm but do not exhaust it.

An idea of synthesis of these paradigms and concepts is soaring in air. This situation and an idea of synthesis demand a developing of clear definitions for all used notions and first of all for basic notions Collaboration and Cooperation. That is why the stepped goals of our paper are:

–to identify types of activities and it's forms of space-time interactions which characterize Collaboration and Cooperation;

–to define and describe Collaboration and Cooperation in an OCIS by an OCIS Conceptual Model;

–to define Computer Support for Cooperative Works (CSCW).

Taking in consideration that all of that have spawned a difference between Theory and Practice we would like to show in the second part of the paper different ways of a penetration of the CSCW to mentalities of the west and east man and, therefor, to show the way of the our collaboration.

1 CSCW – Paradigm of Modern Applied Informatics

1.1 Premises of conceptual modelling

As we just say above the Coordination is represented in A- and S- paradigms in different ways but if the synthesis of A- and S- paradigms is possible than because the CSCW and the Open System concepts are incarnations of A- and S- paradigm there are all basses to suppose that CSCW will be in future the leading synthetic paradigm of Computer Science.

Unfortunately now for that the CSCW has no enough properties of a synthesizing system. In fact if developers declare that its applied systems are built as a cooperative system then they sooner or later come to all principles and tasks of Open System on a technological level. From other side if the CSCW considers a computer supports a main cornerstone then a modern progress of CSCW will be connected with a progress in open IT only but will not have enough successes that are connected with the human factor in OCIS–namely interface, organizational, social, etc.

That is why we can consider now the CSCW (in the organizational aspect) as a historical development of an office automation approach on the transition to all forms of Cooperative System Approach [7]. However of course can be CAD/CAM/CAE and other interpretation of CSCW. This transition is characterized by a phenomenon that when a software environment is built by the CSCW R&D we must do not only copy or modify an organizational and functional structures of a source system by mapping to computer networks but consider co-understanding, co-disign, co-developing, co-decision making and co-solving phenomena on the whole co-actions within such structures. The essences of the phenomena consist in that they promote to a self-organizing of a OCIS. The studding of an essence of all this forms of co-actions promotes to a strict understanding of a CSCW. An illustration of an office automation origin of CSCW is a fact that the software incarnation of CSCW now is a Groupware, that is, a software environment of an OCIS. However we can state that a Groupware exists now rather as meetingware (email, teleconference, communicational environment) then a management of information flows, plans and schedules [6-8].

We think that the Groupware via S-paradigm can be wider–it must:

–be a superstructure under a communicational environment of distributed Data Bases (DB) or Expert Systems (ES);

–serve as a environment for decision support systems in distributed groupeworks;

–serve as a practice base of a transition to a distributed data processing with human Collaborational and Cooperational properties (for example–like a client-server concept).

In a social aspect the Groupware can not be dictated (foisted) to an OCIS as a groupedware or snoopware. For a real joint of a Collaboration Works phenomenon in an OCIS it needs to be done an effect (consequence) of a motivation of all employees and subsystems. Moreover a need with such environment appears if:

–organizational and communicational structures in an innovation process keep its balance;

–users easy recognize in a software environment innovation the traits of familiar to him an operational and an informational system of communications.

We can suppress that a source goal of organization will play an important role in a motivation and consolidation for such works. For example–needs in Groupware can take place in OCIS like hotels, hospitals, banks and CAD/CAM firms where an operational and informational situation is distributed among executors but has the iniform and clear expression goal: an optimal using of resources. After that the Groupware as a concept assumes a character and traits rather of an invariant functional software environment model then of a conglomeration of a set of particular control functions set only. For this task first of all we will decide the question of the definition of Collaboration and Cooperation.

A consideration of premises will carry out in turn: definition of an Intelligent Information Processor as a OCIS basic element; considering of levels of interactions in OCIS; show a group behavior specific in OCIS.

1.2 Basic definitions

Thus we can consider a Collaboration and a Cooperation. What does it mean generally? For the answer we introduce a new notion an Intelligent Information Processor (IIP) as a couple Man-Computer:

$$IIP = \{\{\{Operations\}, \{Information\ Objects\}, IT = \{SW/HW\}\}.\}$$

Here the first set of components relate to Man and describe his logical operational and informational environment. The second set relates to technological executive environment that is realized by means of Information and Communication Technologies (ICT) in a very wide sense. The set {Operations} have a structure {<Goal, Action>} and {Information Objects} is considered as nature-language and/or formal types of representations of information that is run by an operational processing. Now we can to describe Collaboration and Cooperation:

–Collaboration–propose a potential space-time interaction of different IIPs on the base of a common perception of problems that are interprets as a partial

coincidence of IIP components;
  –Cooperation–propose an actual space-time interaction of different IIPs on the base of a fixed coincident of a defined intersection of IIP components.

In another word–to express a collaboration mean to answer on the questions: what is IIPs doing, why and how, what is the difference and coincidence between what, how and why for many IIPs. By analogy, to express a cooperation mean to fix a collaboration as stated above and then to define relations, degrees and forms of interactions and interfluence of difference IIPs when we answer on this what, how and why.

1.3 OCIS: forms of interactions

In our understanding of a CSCW we result from a definition that types of activities (what, how and why) are formal and informal control functions that are invariant relatively groupworks. Space-time interactions for s of these types of activities demand of a specification of operational and informational environment and conditions of communication. In order to show a correctness of such assumption we will pick out informational and operational forms of interact ones in OCIS. The effectiveness of OCIS depends on a degree of a computerization of these forms for providing Collaboration and Cooperation. An Informational form changed in the ways:
  –to make more effective information service of collaborated IIPs and IIP-groups, for example, transition to different forms of Tools IS: DBs, Full Text DBs (FTDB), Deductive DBs (DDB), KBs, Expert Systems (ES), Hypertext Systems;
  –to increase a meaningfulness of information for caring out of control operations and problem solving, for example, transition to a multi-media and hyper-media systems.

An operational form takes it starting from a problem of a data and knowledge integration, procedural representations of actions (by rules) and joint actions of System Analysts and DB Administrator. It concentrates its attention on an expediention to consider many aspects of automation and communication not for an information guaranteeing only but for getting the results in forms of operations and functions. The meaning of an operational form have increased with a transmission of accents from workplace problems to group interactions problems (joint decision making, development and implement of control functions), because a completeness of an operation or functions on a defined workplace start a begin or have influence on of another operation on another workplace.

1.4 OCIS: levels of interactions

We pick out now fore levels of interactions in computerized Organizational Systems: document-circulation (turnover); verbalize-informational; nonverbal informational; problem solving or decision making.

First level of interactions is a document-circulation one that is connected with roles. A bearer of a role is an IIP in a OCIS formal hierarchy where every IIP is connected with several IIPs and fixes the right of access to data from document-circulation. The document-circulation is mapped to adequacy scheme and subschema of DB, FTDB, DDB, multi-media and hyper-media systems. Collaboration and Cooperation on the level are reduced to a registering of actions with DB/KB/documentation, to a fixation of different IIP operation intersection and to description of priorities, clinches and conflict solving rules. There are some problems of the level: synchronization of different role {Operations}, fixation of {Information Objects} and rules of an actualization. However {Information Objects} having nature of data, knowledge or documents have not a shade of individual role features.

Second level. A cause of a consideration of this level consists in that information from a human factor point of view can not be reduced by IIP definitions to {Information Objects} only. The level inserts into every role and in a document-circulation an individual (personal) context. This level of human factor of informational interactions has a signal character and has an important influence on a forming of conditions for Collaboration and Cooperation in OCIS and on states of information flows in OCIS. The level can be displayed in several kinds: verbal-informational interactions, i.e., an interchange of information objects with denotation nature (for instance, jargon or stock phrases which are accepted in small groups); nonverbal-informational interactions, i.e., interchange of information objects with connotation nature (jests, mimics, sounds). These sublevels of interactions are not represented in a document-circulation but must be represent in a Conceptual Model of OCIS. That is why we need to interpret IIPs just not as a role only but as a person. R&D of this level is very important. If a computerization of a OCIS is carried out in ways of a team-structure and a mobile-office then there is a danger to lose a traditional verbal- and nonverbal information. Such a losing is influence on a quality or forms of a control. The representations of a personal context allow to register effects of influence by small groups and to build an adequate data processing, problem solving or decision making. Collaboration and Cooperation on this level demand to insert a connotation to system interface as special pictograms for modeling of a verbal- and a nonverbal-informational level of interactions and comes to multi-media document-circulation problem.

Third level of interactions reflects OCIS social aspect and is interested from OCIS self-organization point of view. The point is that in every OCIS appear spontaneously a system of mutual obligations that is an announces of evident and hidden form of ethics. Real Collaboration and Cooperation in OCIS are impossible without such forms of decency. This system of mutual obligations namely predefines the forms of nonverbal-informational interactions and is a guarantee of OCIS stability. The insertion of new objects into an OCIS structure has an important influence on an individual filling of friendly in OCIS. This level is not formalized now and is in a sphere of psychological and sociology studding (at last as a regisration of phenomena). Second and third levels in CSCW are not developed practically but must be insert to Conceptual Model of OCIS and be modeled in multi-media environment (for instance, by color, sound or pictograms).

Fourth level of interaction in OCIS is connected with a problem solving or decision making processes and can be partly formalized. Standardized and unstandardized classes of solutions are picked out In a problem solving or decision making areas in OCIS. The standardized solutions appear when typical situations take place and are connection with a fixed set of alternatives. This class of solutions can be formalized for instance by decision tables, and-or trees, ES. The automatization of the class depends on a privet and group experience, fullness of information, standard goals and functions of the OCIS. However there is a class of nonstandardized solutions when atypical situations in a OCIS take place (a plan or graphics deflection, system modifications, new works, etc.). An engine of this solution is not defined generally and it has many attributes of heuristics. Collaboration and Cooperation on this level are defined by many factors including consult information, information quality demands, conditions of system of mutual obligations, personal qualities of decision makers. From premises shown above followed that the CSCW as a system of artifacts, paradigms, communication and information technologies is intended to provide of an informational, operational and communicational coordination and a service for Groupware in given applied system independently from its types and forms. A next widening of an IIP structure must include an integration of formal-structural and informal-structural aspects, operational and documentation aspects, verbal-informational and nonverbal-informational aspects and an aspect that take into consideration properties of IIPs as a person. That is why it is necessary also to specify the notion of actions and co-actions.

2 On Conceptual Modelling

At a glimpse it is impossible to describe all and different actions in a different OCIS when these actions are related to different levels of interactions in OCIS and which different decision makers understand in different way. It is imaging for us that we can formulate an adequacy definition of Collaboration and Cooperation on a base of an OCIS Conceptual Model only. On a base of a OCIS Conceptual Modelling it is possible to describe a typology of basic processes in n OCIS. For this aim OCIS Conceptual Model must provide representations of all forms and levels of interactions in an OCIS as a system of interacted IIPs. In this way IIPs as elements must be represented in a form of metadata with number, symbol and lexicographical interpretations and causal OCIS relationships.

2.1 Basic frame

Such IIP and OCIS interpretation appeal to a notion representation like a frame representation and semantic network. The structure of frame will consider as follows:

{Name of Frame {<<Name of Slot ><Value of Slot>>}}.

Fore basic frames will specify and represent all IIP elements describing behavior IIP in OCIS. These frames reflect levels of interactions in OCIS were picking out above, formally structure (operational and documental) and informally structure (verb l-informational and nonverbal-informational interactions):

{ ROLE { 1.<Person><frame-copy PERSON pointer>;
2.<Relations><frame-copies ROLE pointer list>;
3.<Actions><list of action's names> }}.

{ ACTION { 1.<Action Names><description of context>;
2.<Aim><criterion or value>;
3.<Data><list of data names>;
4.<Alternatives><list of actions>;
5.<Choice rule><description of preferences>;
6.<Source><frame-copy ROLE pointer>;
7.<Executor><frame copy ROLE pointer>;
8.<Recipient><frame-copy ROLE pointer>;
9.<Resources><criterion or value>;
10.<Consequence><criterion or value> }}.

{ DOCUMENT { 1. <Standard><identifier>;
2.<Structure><logical, lay-out>;
3.<Data><list of data names>;
4.<Source><frame-copy ROLE pointer>;
5.<Executor><frame-copy ROLE pointer>;
6.<Recipient><frame-copy ROLE pointer>;
7.<Bearer><form of document representation> }}.

{ PERSON { 1. <Identifier><data>;
2.<Motives><list of nonformal aims>;
3.<Priorities of motives><velues>;
4.<Stimulus><list of nonformal influence to person>;
5.<Priority of stimulus><values>;
6.<Factors><list and values>;
7.<Relations><frame-copies PERSON pointer list>;
8.<Role><poiter to frame-copies ROLE>;
9.<External estimation><values> }}.

It necessary to say that such forms of representation have a form of metadescriptions. On the base we can uncover all slots of the frames in data structures, documents, operations and ICT in an IIP sense. Note an analogy between formal and informal a OCIS structure that can be valued by the frame representation:

FORMAL STRUCTURE   INFORMAL STRUCTURE
Formal Goals,   Motives,
Organization,   Small groups, Mutual Obligations System,

Roles,   Persons

　　　　　　　　{Information Objects}:

Data/Knowledge,   Stimulus,
Documents,   Verbal- and Nonverbal- information,
Alternatives,   Priority,
Actions,   Behavior

Hence it follows that CSCW must take into consideration all nuances for representing an adequacy software interface and processing environment. The frames allow us to begin of the OCIS Conceptual Modelling. Every methodology considers two aspects of modelling: a static and a dynamic structure. In this connection a static structure of system is represented in a OCIS Conceptual Model as follows:

–a main structural element IIP is represented by the set of basic frames;

–frames ROLE represent a formal-structural relationships in an OCIS and formal OCIS structure is represented by a tree-graph in the nodes of which are IIPs;

–frames PERSON represent informal-structural relationships in an OCIS and informal relationships (verbal-informational and nonverbal informational levels of interactions) are represented by a graph in the nodes of which are frames PERSON;

–a general OCIS structure as a set of IIPs form by laying an informal relationships on a formal structure;

–an OCIS Conceptual Model OCIS is represented by a frame semantic network in a base of which lay a coupled graph of a OCIS structure.

A dynamic is represented in CM OCIS as follows:

–operational and informational aspects of OCIS is uncovered by attaching to the static OCIS structure the exemplars of frames DOCUMENT and ACTION for an every given role;

–a workplace is represented as a frame structure reflecting to the data relationships (frame exemplars ACTION), document relationships (frame exemplars DOCUMENT), role and person relationships (one frame exemplar ROLE and PERSON).

Hereby an OCIS Conceptual Model is represent by a semantic frame network on a base of oriented graph of an OCIS structure. There are frame exemplars of ROLE in a node of it corresponded to control functions (relationships of frames ROLE and ACTION). An influence of a human factor is accounted in interrelationships of corresponding frame exemplars ROLE and PERSON.

So the OCIS Conceptual Model provides a metadescription of an OCIS. On the metadescription are specified a variety of forms of Collaboration and Cooperation in an operational and informational structure of OCIS. From the OCIS Conceptual Model follow a full specified program of a realization and supporting of a groupwork. The forms of a groupwork are communication planing, a transaction-oriented Groupware and infological methods of an expression of OCIS interaction levels: 1) description of OCIS (objectivization); 2) goals, roles, operations and communicational channels among IIPs (operationality); 3) documents texts and data are used by roles in OCIS (creation of operation-information relationships); 4) relationships among all elements of documents, texts, data, knowledge and functional elements (preconditions for using of hypertext). An OCIS Conceptual Model gets the source material for specification of the operational and informational conditions: the automated operations for frames ACTION (email-messages, transactions, operations for document making and processing, control operations, operations of role state analysis, etc.); the information for operations above-mentioned (attributes, values, relations, structures of DB/KB); communications (traffic of data flows, hardware and forms of organizational interconnections).

2.2 Typology

Let us consider the typologies of actions, informational flows and of communications in a context of an OCIS Conceptual Model.

The nation of action is full defined by frame ACTION. For creation a typology of action accounting problem solving consider a subset of frame ACTION of slots and will represent this subset as follows:

$D = <(I,L),R,A,C,DMP>$ (*),

where: D–decision; I–source information, i.e., conditions in a form of data or knowledge; L–a set of goals; R–a structured subject area, i.e., formalized data an/or knowledge representation; A–admitted alternatives of D in a sense of L; C–decision selection rules; DMP–Decision Making Person.

The couple (I,L) called a precondition of an action and generalized next intuition procedural forms of interactions in OCIS: problem, situation, task and operation. Let us postulate generalization principles for the procedural forms, show relationships among them and get a definition of a decision for the procedural forms. As far as by a frame ACTION definitions forming of decision depend on subset $<(I,L),R,A,C,DMP = ROLE$ and/or $PERSON>$, then a procedural form variety can be define by a detailing of subset of slots from this frame.

A TASK we will call a couple <Conditions :: = Data/Knowledge, Aims> or with a frame ACTION notation–<I–are known, L–are known>, where I–a subset of conditions which are understood as a semantic organization of data or knowledge, L–a set of goals.

An OPERATION we will call full defined an ACTION without alternatives, that is: <i–are known, l–are known>, where i belong to I, and l belong to L.

A SITUATION is a TASK like a view <I–are known, L–are unknown>.

A PROBLEM is a TASK like a view <I–are unknown, L–are known>. To understand what do you want means to find attributes from couple <I–are unknown, L–are unknown>. Problem Solving means defining of the task family Z, a set of inputs I (data) and mapping C: Z->L on a set of outputs (goals). Sometimes it is possible to get a construct describing of the mapping by algorithms. In a real life problem it is necessary that solved tasks were defined and algorithms are not necessary because DMPs can use any unclassified heuristics. Hence a solving decision invariant to a procedural form will consider as a couple <D, C>, then:

TASK SOLVING is denoted (represented) by defining of a mapping $C:D->D$ and $D:I->L$.

SITUATION SOLVING is denoted (represent) by defining of L and than are reduced to TASK SOLVING.

PROBLEM SOLVING intends structurization of a problem; the result of such structurization is picking out of task or situation prototypes (like a classification or an expert evaluation). The succession of steps are: first step is defining of a task c ass Z, second one is picking out a set of data I for Z, next one is fixing a set of situations; next one is defying a set of goals L; at last—reeducating problem to task solving. Hereby the problem solving process is connected with a construct describing of a task class Z or with selecting alternative actions on a set D. This selection is defined by preferences C partially defined like fuzzy set preferences. Decisions are solved according several preferences are complex one. For picking out of collaboration and cooperation acts will distinguish actions on own actions belonged to given role or to given roles and inductive actions performed in defined time or when other actions from other level and belonged to other roles are completed.

Informal relationships are modeled by person connections, priorities of information flow processing and by redefining of preference relationships on a set D. All these things have fixed in frames ACTION and PERSON.

Lets fix a common view on forms of space-time communications: Face-to-Face (Same Times and Same Place), Synchronous Distributed Interaction (Same Times and Different Place), Asynchronous Interaction (Different Times and Same Place), Asynchronous Distributed Interaction (Different Times and Different Place). Collaboration and Cooperation are growing just on a background of these forms of space communications.

Now we will test expressed possibilities of frames on a description of an informational flows typology in an OCIS. All information flows in an OCIS according its formal structure can be separated on descending (from top to bottom), ascending (from bottom to top) and horizontal (consult).

Descending flows have a imperative nature and contain as typical component (according to frame ACTION): a1–work instructions (frame ACTION, slots 1,3,6,7,8); a2–information about relations among actions (frame ACTION); a3–structure (frame ACTION slots 1,2,7); a4–motives and factors (frame PERSON, slots 2-5). Inclusion slots <alternatives>, <choice rule> and <consequence> to work instructions means predominance of administrative principles in OCIS controlling. Besides that presence or absence these slots in work instructions are distinguished a standard level of problem solving from unstandard one accordingly.

Ascending flows have nature of reporting for centralized OCIS and consult nature for decentralizes OCIS and contains as typical components: b1–information about executed actions or tasks (frame ACTION, slots 2,9,10);

b2–information about structure and signification of data flows (frame DOCUMENT frame ACTION, slots 7,9,10); b3–role state data (all of slots from frames ROLE, ACTION, PERSON); b4–data about control level problems (any combinations of the open model of OCIS); b5–information about control principles (frame ACTION, slots <actions>, <source>, <executor>, <recipient>, <resources>, <choice rule>, <resources>, <consequence>, from PERSON slots value>, from frame <ROLE><identifier>).

Horizontal flows are form in conditions of tend to decentralization and contain consult, reference and work information on next questions: c1–task states (slots <actions> and <data>); c2–task solving methods (frame ACTION, slots <alternative >, <choice rule>, <resources>, <consequence>; c3–plans (slots <actions>, <resources>); c4–nonformal relationships (frame PERSON).

The operational and informational determinism of an OCIS and control flows allow us to specify preconditions for Collaboration and Cooperation:

–every ROLE of a level is described by its own subset of actions or decisions by sense of (*); the intersections of different roles are not necessary empty

–it is important to pick out levels of a standardized control;

–the correcting of these components and fixing a system of preferences is an important goal of modelling;

–in an OCIS some level's roles have a set of preferences relationships on a set of alternatives (may be in a sense of fuzzy set);

–in a set of <actions> of frame ROLE is important to distinguish own operations and inductive operations.

The uncovering of slots and its realization in forms of data structure–(for example - an additional attributes organizing in a forms of flags or semaphores which signal operational interrelations) is an infological aspect of modelling, simulation or product rules which can be realizing according an OCIS Frame Conceptual Model. We can model PCs in an OCIS as components by putting into operation according interpretations of frame slots. For instance, a frame ROLE can consider as an automated workplace (AWP) having a soft- and hardware. Its slot <action> can consider as a et of automated actions (text editing and processing, spreadsheet processing, emailing, personal DB, document processing technology, work instructions etc). By analogy we can consider <relationships> as an indication to a formal belonging of given AWP to given LAN and channels. We can also create a subslot <gateway software> with a list of a service has been given by WANs, standards, protocols, etc.

3 Problem of East-West Relationships

In consequence of the notion defying above we can state a wide spectrum of the OCIS R&D area. All of the Collaboration and Cooperation phenomena spawn the discords between Theory and Practice not only among eastern scientists but (that is more important) among scientists from East and West Science Communities. There are several points of these discords such as:

  1. Eastern scientists have only knowledge about investigations (on the

whole) and in any way prefer the S-paradigm point of view on this problem. ¿From other side eastern developers have only knowledge about market products and in any way depend on an A-paradigm of this problem because the investigations have not been put on the modern IT are not accessible for our users. We may interpret the MIS-branch researches Centralized OCIS oriented on S-paradigm (for example by Glushkov principles) and make ITs help by automatization up-down. An Office Automation branch researches Decentralized OCIS oriented on A-paradigm and makes ITs help by automatization down-up. The rich eastern MIS experiences are lost on the whole (for instance Glushkon's principals of the MIS building that were based on a paradigm synthesis). A synthesis of these branches is possible by a OCIS Conceptual Modelling and Prototyping.

2. The western scientists have knowledge about investigations and market products.

3. Western Science Community has relationships with many Programs (for instance–ESPRIT, COPERNICUS) where it can revise the old visions and form new visions and form a new one. Because now we can see a dependence eastern developer from a western market only it is imaging for us to open for they an access to such Program. That is why our opinion is based on a point of view that in a modern OCIS the S-paradigm and A-paradigm can be jointed because a computer and a human being must be consider as a united element (as was be described above). An A-paradigm (computers) defines a tactic of innovation in an OCIS while the S-paradigm (human factor) defines a future form of existence of an OCIS. As far as the S-paradigm is constantly changed under an influence of an A-paradigm (a market of computer environment) it defines a strategy of innovation in an OCIS and the demands to the developed OCIS software and communicational environment.

How we can evaluate the profit and ways of such participation? For decision this problem we offer to your attention the Scheme of Experimental OCIS Rationalization. The Scheme joints many concepts and describes many ways of obligatory R&D. The main sense of the Scheme of Experimental OCIS Rationalization is to organize the motivated path: OCIS problem–System Approach Structure–OCIS Conceptual Modeling-Prototyping. On this way we can use such approach:

INFOLOGICAL MODELLING including (for different goals and tasks) Design of Workplace DB or Design of Simulation DB or Design of KB for ES or Multi-media or Hyper-media System Design. Of course, when we need we can move from simple the Design of Workplace DB to complex the Hyper-media System Design.

PASSIVE EXPERIMENT including (for different goals and tasks) Workplace or LAN Monitoring, Testing of Person, Demoprototype Development and Development of Groupware. By analogy we can use all of the components or move from simple to complex.

NATURAL EXPERIMENT including Computer Education, Gaming and Development of Innovation strategy. This approach is very important for OCIS (legacy system) and practically is not known for eastern OCIS developers.

ACTIVE EXPERIMENT including Simulation, Groupware Simulation, Developing of Schemes of Problem Solving. By Scheme of Experimental OCIS Rationalization we can move along the approaches or combine some components from any approaches. The Scheme of Experimental OCIS Rationalization can organize the advance to Open System and CSCW. Ideally the Scheme of Experimental OCIS Rationalization may be developed as an Expert-simulation Rapid Application Development System on the base of I-CASE. Western investigators can fix the more important points on the Scheme and profitable ways for investigations to eastern researchers. Of course this Scheme is not final and may be corrected get one's bearings the independent judgments. However we cane use the Program for forming a common view on a building our relationships at least for classifying the R&D.

4 Conclusion

1. There are all basics for supporting that a CSCW will be in nearest future a most popular paradigm of Computer Science but now it has not enough system properties.

2. The system properties of CSCW depend on results of researchers of Collaboration and Cooperation phenomena that cane be examined from the level of interaction point of view mentioned above.

3. There are many distinguishes between Eastern and Western OCIS and user's points of view and it creates many new interesting problems for general theory of DBMS.

4. System properties can be researched via joint EastWest Projects separating an A-paradigm and a S-paradigm parts of Collaboration and Cooperation phenomena.

5. The Scheme of Experimental OCIS Rationalization can play a main role in separating the parts between eastern and western R&D.

6. The Scheme of Experimental OCIS Rationalization can show ways of possible decisions for relationships that can be between the Open System and the Selforganizations.

References

[1] Holt A. W. Coordination Technology: Fulfilling CSCW's Potential
Coordination Technology Inc. - 1988, - 16 p.

[2] J. Grudin. CSCW Introduction
Communications. - 1991., Vol.34, -N12. - P. 30-35.

[3] M.L. Brodie, S. Ceri. On Intelligent and Cooprative Information Systems: A Workshop Summary
IJIOCIS, - N1,2. September 1992. - P. 1-35.

[4] Dyson E. Groupware: a framework
Release 1.0.-N6.-1988.- 10 p.

[5] M.L. Brodie. The Promise of Distributed Computering, The Challenges of Legacy Systems
Academy of Science, Russia and NPO Gorsistemotechnika, Ukraine. August 1992. - 35 p.

[6] M.P. Papazoglou, S.C. Laufmann, T.K. Sellis. An Organizational Framework for Cooperating Intelligent Systems
IJICIS, - Vol.1, - N1. - P.169-202.

[7] Serg S. Azarov. About the One Approach to Development of the Term Knowledge Problem in "Office Automation Control Systems and Computers", Kiev. Academy of Science. -1991. N7. - P.18-22.

[8] Martin J. Rapid Application Development. N.Y. -1990. - 226 p.

Model Based User Interface Constructor with Consistency Checking

Kouba Z., Lažanský J., Mařík Vl., Štěpánková O., Vlček T.

Czech Technical University
Technická 2
CZ - 166 27 Prague, Czech Republic

The aim of this paper is to introduce the progress made by the authors in the development of a methodology for modelling the dependencies among data entries in a dialog box and design of a software tool supporting the user interface programming. An object oriented dialog box model and an event driven user interface architecture are analysed. The principal features of the user interface constructor consisting of a graphical user interface model editor and source code generator are introduced. The formal analysis of dependence among dialog entries [3] is utilised
*

1. Introduction

As contrast to well developed data modelling theory (relational algebra, object-oriented data models, ...) the attempts of formal user interface modelling are rare [3,4]. The experience says that the quality of the user interface is one of the most important conditions for success of the particular software application. User interface programming as a part of software developer's activities represents very complicated and tedious work. Those are reasons for development of means which would support the process of user interface design and programming.

Many commercially available programming environments equipped with an interactive user interface design facility already exist. These facilities usually make it possible to design the geometric layout of the data entries on the screen and to specify the validity conditions for particular data entries (e.g. FoxPro's Screen Builder). However, they do not usually take into account the mutual dependencies of several entries. In more complicated user interfaces, the mutual dependencies among entries represent the most difficult part of the programmer's work. Our aim is to describe these mutual dependencies by a model or, more precisely, to design a

---

* This research has been supported by the EU-PECO Project No. 9645 *Eurosat* and the Austrian government project No. GZ 45.339/2-IV/6a/94 *The Open Architecture of Knowledge-Based Systems*.

formalism capable to express mutual dependencies among entries of a general user interface dialog.

The model specifies also events which can arise in the course of the interactive entering data into the dialog box by the user.

Having such a model and the model based user interface constructor the user will interactively define code snippets (chunks of code) for handling particular events to achieve the required behaviour of the user interface. In the course of code generation these code snippets will be bind by the MBUIC into resulting source code.

2. Motivation

Fig. 1 represents schematically an example dialog box of a hypothetical information system on telecommunication lines. The dialog consist of a push button *ACCEPT* and five dialog entries *Line Ident, Transmission Means, Quality* and *Transmission Speed*.

The *Line Ident* entry identifies uniquely the particular telecommunication line. The other entries define the parameters of the line. These four lines are mutually dependent in the sense that not all combinations of their values are allowed.

Let the *Type* entry can have one of the values **RP** (line for transmission of radio programme) or **DP** (data transmission). The *Transmission Means* entry can be either **TF** (telephone equipment) or **TG** (telegraph equipment). The *Quality* entry can have the value of **T**, **A** or **Q** and defines the width of the frequency band. The meaning of the *Transmission Speed* entry is clear.

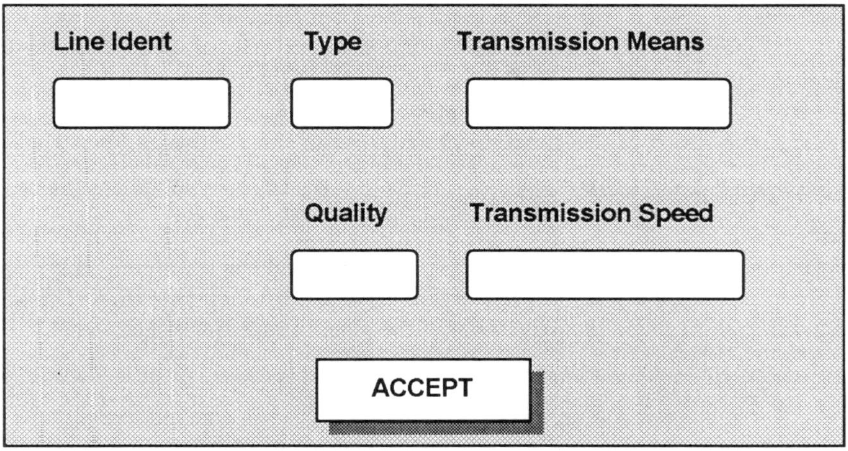

Fig. 1

The possible combination of values is introduced in the following table. The notice **disabled** means that the given entry must be disabled for the given combination of values.

TYPE	TRANSMISSION MEANS	QUALITY	TRANSMISSION SPEED
RP	TF	T, A, Q	disabled
DP	TF	disabled	1200, 2400, 4800, 9600, 19200
DP	TG	disabled	50, 100, 200

The program handling the dialog must ensure:
- the user is not enabled to fulfil incorrect combination of values of mutually dependent entries
- in case that some of the entries (e.g. *Transmission speed*) is realised as a popup, list etc. (i.e. it offers appropriate set of values for a choice), it must react on the change of another dependent entry (e.g. *Transmission means*) by resetting the set of offered values.

To ensure such a behaviour of the dialog the programmer should implement appropriate programming constructions which are repeated with minor modifications many times in the whole application. This fact motivated the authors to analyse a general behaviour of a user interface with the aim to develop a tool supporting easy and comfortable design and maintenance of the user interfaces.

At the very beginning the authors tried to utilise the well known methods of structured analysis. The analysis of the problem has shown that the classical means of the structural analysis like De Marco's Data Flow Diagrams are not suitable for the purposes of the user interface modelling because even for simple screen dialogs the models are too complex due to its generality. It is the reason why a new, more specialised, modelling methodology is needed.

3. Formal analysis

This section provides the formal analysis of the dependencies among the dialog entries in an user interface and the problems of consistence checking. The stuff introduced in this section is an overview of the recent results published in [3].

3.1. The Dialog

Under the term *dialog* we will understand a collection of data items. Each item represents a variable (of simple or structured type) of our computational process. We will call the item the (dialog) *entry*.

The variable corresponding to an entry can be of various types, it can be an integer or real number, a string or a structured type. Nevertheless, the domain of its values is always defined. In the case of a structured type one value of an entry is considered to be a tuple of simple type values.

3.2. Dependent entries

The formalism used in this section is very similar to that of relational database theory [1,2]. The main difference is the terminology (entry corresponds to attribute, etc.).

Let us denote e_1 some entry of a dialog and let the symbol Dom(e_1) denote the domain of all possible values of the entry (or variable represented by the entry) e_1.

Let the symbol Val(e_1) denote a particular value of the entry e_1. It means Val(e_1) $\in$ Dom(e_1).

Let $e_1, e_2, \ldots, e_n$ be some entries of a considered application. The symbol Dom($e_1, e_2, \ldots, e_n$) denotes a relation specifying all allowed tuples

$$<\text{Val}(e_1), \text{Val}(e_2), \ldots, \text{Val}(e_n)> \in \text{Dom}(e_1) \times \text{Dom}(e_2) \times \ldots \times \text{Dom}(e_n).$$

The entries $e_1, \ldots, e_n$ are **mutually independent** iff

$$\text{Dom}(e_1, e_2, \ldots, e_n) = \text{Dom}(e_1) \times \text{Dom}(e_2) \times \ldots \times \text{Dom}(e_n).$$

An important property of this notion is that it is downward closed w.r. to subsets. In other words if all the entries from a set $E = \{e_1, \ldots, e_n\}$ are mutually independent, then all the entries of any subset $E_1 \subset E$ are mutually independent, too.

The reverse statement does not hold. Consider the following negative example: Let $<x, y, z>$ be triplet of real number entries, let us define

$$\text{Dom}(<x, y, z>) = \{<x, y, z> ; (x = 0) \vee (y = 0) \vee (z = 0)\}.$$

Obviously,

$$\text{Dom}(x) \times \text{Dom}(y) \times \text{Dom}(z) = \mathcal{R} \times \mathcal{R} \times \mathcal{R}.$$

$$\text{Dom}(<x, y, z>) \neq \text{Dom}(x) \times \text{Dom}(y) \times \text{Dom}(z),$$

where $\mathcal{R}$ denotes set of all reals.

However, there holds under the specified conditions

$$\text{Dom}(x,y) = \text{Dom}(y,z) = \text{Dom}(x,z) = \mathcal{R} \times \mathcal{R}.$$

More generally, suppose the entries from a set $E = \{e_1, e_2, \ldots, e_n\}$ are not mutually independent. Nevertheless, there can be a subset $E_1 \subset E$ such that all entries from the set E_1 are mutually independent.

3.3. Data dependencies from the user's point of view

We have mentioned the notion of entry dependencies. It seems to be useful to make a remark on dealing with dependencies from a user's point of view.

Let us take into account that the user can fill in the entries sequentially. He can not change more than one entry at once. The problem of data consistency (given by the dependencies) arises here.

The dependence definition through relation (i.e. subset of a Cartesian product of sets) specifies constraints posted on the final values of entries, which appear in the dependence. This definition is static in some sense. It does not describe how to transit from one point to another, i.e. the feasible sequence of entering the data. The following analysis illustrates the problem in more detail.

Let us have two dependent entries e_1 and e_2.

There are several ways how to solve the dependence of both entries, some of them being introduced here:

Postponed consistency check

The user can fill in both entries freely but the change of their values will be accepted after the global check has been done.

The global check tries to verify that $Val(e_1, e_2) \in Dom(e_1, e_2)$. If the check is not successful, the user is informed about inconsistency and the data change will be refused (we do not consider details of refusing the change here).

The postponed consistency check is simple to implement but its disadvantage is that until the consistency check (invoked e.g. by pressing a "push button") the inconsistent values of variables may exist.

Immediate consistency check

The other possibility of implementation of an entry dependence is to ensure consistent contents of both entries at every moment.

Let the user change the value of the entry e_1 and let the entries e_1, e_2 be dependent. After filling in (or changing) the entry e_1, the conditional domain of the entry e_2 denoted as $Dom(e_2 \mid e_1 = Val(e_1))$ is evaluated.
If the current value $Val(e_2)$ belongs to the conditional domain

$$Dom(e_2 \mid e_1 = Val(e_1)),$$

both the entries are consistent. In the opposite case the value of e_2 will be automatically changed to a default value $Val(e_2) = V_{def,2}(Val(e_1))$ ensuring

$$Val(e_2) \in Dom(e_2 \mid e_1 = Val(e_1)).$$

The mechanism of immediate consistency check should work in both directions.

If we change the value of e_2 so that $Val(e_2)$ does not belong to $Dom(e_2 \mid e_1 = Val(e_1))$, the mechanism evaluates $Dom(e_1 \mid e_2 = Val(e_2))$ and it automatically changes the value of e_1 to satisfy the requirement $Val(e_1) \in Dom(e_1 \mid e_2 = Val(e_2))$. This approach can be generalised to multidimensional dependence, too.

4. OO - Model

The behaviour of the user interface in its nature is the event driven one. The change of the entry's value invokes an event in the dialog which has to be processed and may issue into the change in other dependent entry/entries. This mechanism of events generating and processing can be understood as message transfer among entries. From this abstraction it is very close to the object oriented model.

This section analyses such an object oriented model of the user interface dialog behaviour. It is assumed that the user designs the interface in a graphical representation having a specialised tool at his disposal. The figure Fig. 1 introduces schematically representation of a model.

The *Model editor* deals with two types of graphical objects representing the interface model elements. The rectangular ones represent the dialog entry objects and define the behaviour of the particular entries of the dialog - e.g. the way of entering the data, the format and transformation function for displaying the data, etc. The circle object is linked with one or more rectangular ones and represents the dependence of corresponding dialog entries. The number of entry objects connected with dependence object denotes the arity of the dependence. In general a dependence object is responsible for the consistency checks introduced above. It evaluates the domain of an entry in the condition given by the values of the remaining entries taking part in the dependence.

The user describes the interface entries and their relationships using these two basic graphical objects. The user has at disposal two hierarchies of classes for implementation of the interface model elements - one hierarchy of dialog entry

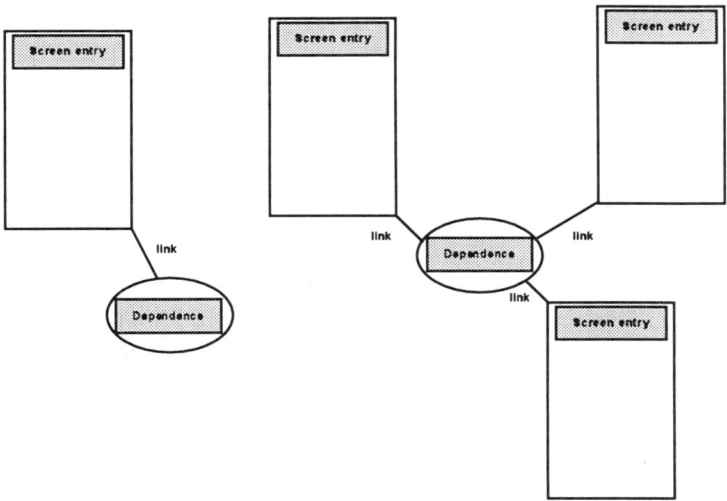

Fig. 1

objects and the other one for dependence objects. The roots of both hierarchies are the abstract classes providing the general behaviour. From abstract class Entry the classes for each typical dialog entry like editable field, check box, list etc. are derived. From abstract class Dependence the classes providing the realisation of the various types of dependencies are derived.

It is expected that the user - the designer of the interface - will choose the appropriate class from the corresponding hierarchy. When necessary he derives a new class by overriding and/or adding new methods. He will define the methods in the target programming language. The methods represent code snippets which will be assembled by the interface code generator into the interface source code.

Note: This approach enables the process of the model definition to be of object oriented nature even if the target programming language has no object oriented features.

Internally the user interface program will have the structure shown by Fig. 2:

The Entry object has at least the following instance variables:

- Next - the pointer to the next object in the bi-directional list of dialog entry objects
- Previous - the pointer to the previous object in the bi-directional list of dialog entry objects
- Data store - the pointer to the buffer storing the entries' value
- Enabled - variable describing the current state of the entry, i.e. enabled/disabled, visible/invisible, etc.
- Dependence - the pointer to the particular Dependence object or to the Dialog manager in the case of the dialog entry (usually push button terminating the

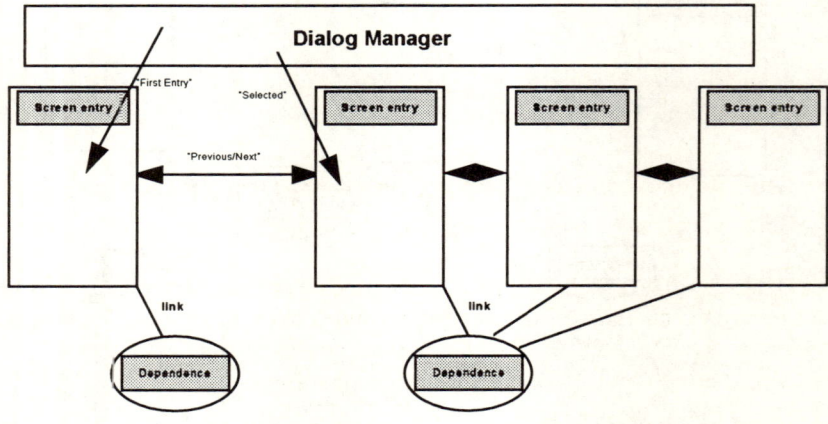

Fig. 2

dialog) invoking the postponed consistence check.

The Entry object should respond the following messages:
- Select - sets the entry to the "selected" state
- Unselect - sets the entry to the "unselected" state
- Enable - sets the variable Enabled and calls the Display method.
- Display - displays the object in appropriate manner according to its state.
- Transform - transforms the internal representation of the displayed entry into the required form and vice versa, e.g. the string of digits into the number, etc.

From the dependence checking point of view each Entry object responds three important methods:
- When - this method performs the necessary activities when the user attempts to select the given dialog entry. According to the result the selection of the entry is either enabled or disabled.
- Valid - this method performs the necessary activities when the user attempts to leave the selected dialog entry. The main task of this method is to ensure the consistency. This is done by asking corresponding object referred by the instance variable Dependence to perform the consistency check.

The instance variables and methods introduced above are the basic ones, which the abstract class Entry introduces. The derived classes supporting the dialog entries like *List*, *Combo Box* etc. can have further ones.

Each particular Dependence object provides the services for its related dialog entries. For each object there is a method for consistency checking.

The Dependence object should respond the messages:
- Check - consistency checking

For such objects like lists, pop-ups, combo boxes (i.e. entries which offer a discrete set of values for the choice) the Dependence object evaluates the conditional domain for particular related entries:
- GetFirstValue - provides the first member of the conditional domain.
- GetNextValue - provides the next member of the conditional domain.

The Dialog Manager is responsible for the global control of the dialog. It receives the external events (keyboard, mouse, etc.) and convert them to the messages sent to appropriate entry objects. The Dialog manager has two instance variables of special meaning:
- First - the pointer to the first object in the bi-directional list of dialog entry objects

- Selected - the pointer to the currently selected object. Immediately after the dialog activation the 'Selected' is set to the value of 'First'.

Its methods are:
- Activate - performs the necessary actions before displaying/activating the dialog.
- Deactivate - by analogy - performs deactivation of the dialog.
- Check - performs postponed consistency check by sending the Check message to all Entry objects involved in the list referred by the instance variable First.
- ChangeSelection - attempts to deselect currently selected dialog entry and select the desired one in the following way:
  1. sends the Valid message to the currently selected object. If failed, stops.
  2. sends the When message to the desired object. If failed, stops.
  3. sends the Unselect and Display messages to the currently selected object.
  4. sends the Select and Display messages to the new one.
- NextEntry / PreviousEntry - invokes the ChangeSelection method for the Entry object referred by Next / Previous instance variables of the currently selected Entry object.

5. Conclusion

The concepts of event driven programming and object oriented programming can form a unified and elegant programming style.

The concept of data consistency checks is in agreement with the event driven programming approach. The immediate consistency check may be implemented as a method of the object representing the entry. After entering new data, this method informs other entries about the change by sending a specific event. The dependent entries react to this event by changing their conditional domain and by testing their actual values. Any discovered inconsistency may result in a new event.

The complete design of the dialog in a user interface consists of four stages:
1. The design of the dialog geometrical layout
2. The specification of the dependencies among dialog entries
3. Definition of the supporting code snippets (methods of the entry objects)
4. Target source code generation

The only stage two is independent on graphical environment and programming environment. This is the reason why it is necessary to develop both the library of various dialog entry objects making a bridge between the MBUIC and the given graphical and programming environment and the target code generator. Actually the authors are working on implementation of MBUIC for the MS-Windows and Borland Object Vision environment.

6. References

[1] Alagić S.: Object-Oriented Database Programming, Springer Verlag, New York, 1988

[2] Gardarin G., Valduriez P.: Relational Databases and Knowledge Bases, Addison-Wesley, 1989

[3] Kouba Z., Lažanský J., Mařík Vl., Štěpánková O., Vlček T.: Model Based User Interface Constructor for CIM. In: Knowledge Based Hybrid Systems, IFIP Transactions, Elsevier Science Publishers B.V., North-Holland, Amsterdam, 1993

[4] Pree W.: Object-Oriented Versus Conventional Construction of User Interface Prototyping Tools, VWG™, Wien, 1992

Author Index

Alagić, S. 125
Apers, P.M.G. 183
Atzeni, P. 346
Azarov, S.S. 411
Basarab, I.A. 221
Beeri, C. 159
Breitbart, Y. 380
Busse, R. 356
Ceri, S. 3
Chaban, I. 232
Croft, W.B. 194
Dogac, A. 77
Eder, J. 109
Engels, G. 303
Evrendilek, C. 77
Fankhauser, P. 356
Formica, A. 48
Frank, H. 109
Fuhr, N. 206
Gubsky, B.V. 221
Gustas, R. 275
Haav, H.-M. 147
Kalinichenko, L. 232, 331
Kappel, G. 289
Koc, K. 77
Kouba, Z. 426
Kuznetsov, S.D. 138
Lausen, G. 17
Lažanský, J. 426
Liebhart, W. 109
Löhr, P. 303
Ludäscher, B. 17
Manthey, R. 3
Mařík, V. 426
Matthes, F. 90, 159
Missikoff, M. 48
Neuhold, E.J. 356

Nikitchenko, N.S. 221
Red'ko, V.N. 221
Rudloff, A. 90
Rykowski, J. 249
Schmidt, J.W. 90, 159
Schrefl, M. 289
Štěpánková, O. 426
Stogny, A.A. 411
Subieta, K. 159, 394
Terenzi, R. 48
Thalheim, B. 263
Torlone, R. 346
Tsalenko, M. Sh. 33
Vlček, T. 426
Wieczerzycki, W. 249
Wolfengagen, V.E. 61
Zadorozhny, V. 232
Zamulin, A.V. 315

Published in 1990-92

AI and Cognitive Science '89, Dublin City University, Eire, 14-15 September 1989
Alan F. Smeaton and Gabriel McDermott (Eds)

Specification and Verification of Concurrent Systems, University of Stirling, Scotland, 6-8 July 1988
C. Rattray (Ed.)

Semantics for Concurrency, Proceedings of the International BCS-FACS Workshop, Sponsored by Logic for IT (S.E.R.C.), University of Leicester, UK, 23-25 July 1990
M. Z. Kwiatkowska, M. W. Shields and R. M. Thomas (Eds)

Functional Programming, Glasgow 1989
Proceedings of the 1989 Glasgow Workshop, Fraserburgh, Scotland, 21-23 August 1989
Kei Davis and John Hughes (Eds)

Persistent Object Systems, Proceedings of the Third International Workshop, Newcastle, Australia, 10-13 January 1989
John Rosenberg and David Koch (Eds)

Z User Workshop, Oxford 1989, Proceedings of the Fourth Annual Z User Meeting, Oxford, 15 December 1989
J. E. Nicholls (Ed.)

Formal Methods for Trustworthy Computer Systems (FM89), Halifax, Canada, 23-27 July 1989
Dan Craigen (Editor) and Karen Summerskill (Assistant Editor)

Security and Persistence, Proceedings of the International Workshop on Computer Architectures to Support Security and Persistence of Information, Bremen, West Germany, 8-11 May 1990
John Rosenberg and J. Leslie Keedy (Eds)

Women into Computing: Selected Papers 1988-1990
Gillian Lovegrove and Barbara Segal (Eds)

3rd Refinement Workshop (organised by BCS-FACS, and sponsored by IBM UK Laboratories, Hursley Park and the Programming Research Group, University of Oxford), Hursley Park, 9-11 January 1990
Carroll Morgan and J. C. P. Woodcock (Eds)

Designing Correct Circuits, Workshop jointly organised by the Universities of Oxford and Glasgow, Oxford, 26-28 September 1990
Geraint Jones and Mary Sheeran (Eds)

Functional Programming, Glasgow 1990
Proceedings of the 1990 Glasgow Workshop on Functional Programming, Ullapool, Scotland, 13-15 August 1990
Simon L. Peyton Jones, Graham Hutton and Carsten Kehler Holst (Eds)

4th Refinement Workshop, Proceedings of the 4th Refinement Workshop, organised by BCS-FACS, Cambridge, 9-11 January 1991
Joseph M. Morris and Roger C. Shaw (Eds)

AI and Cognitive Science '90, University of Ulster at Jordanstown, 20-21 September 1990
Michael F. McTear and Norman Creaney (Eds)

Software Re-use, Utrecht 1989, Proceedings of the Software Re-use Workshop, Utrecht, The Netherlands, 23-24 November 1989
Liesbeth Dusink and Patrick Hall (Eds)

Z User Workshop, 1990, Proceedings of the Fifth Annual Z User Meeting, Oxford, 17-18 December 1990
J.E. Nicholls (Ed.)

IV Higher Order Workshop, Banff 1990
Proceedings of the IV Higher Order Workshop, Banff, Alberta, Canada, 10-14 September 1990
Graham Birtwistle (Ed.)

ALPUK91, Proceedings of the 3rd UK Annual Conference on Logic Programming, Edinburgh, 10-12 April 1991
Geraint A.Wiggins, Chris Mellish and Tim Duncan (Eds)

Specifications of Database Systems
International Workshop on Specifications of Database Systems, Glasgow, 3-5 July 1991
David J. Harper and Moira C. Norrie (Eds)

7th UK Computer and Telecommunications Performance Engineering Workshop
Edinburgh, 22-23 July 1991
J. Hillston, P.J.B. King and R.J. Pooley (Eds)

Logic Program Synthesis and Transformation
Proceedings of LOPSTR 91, International Workshop on Logic Program Synthesis and Transformation, University of Manchester, 4-5 July 1991
T.P. Clement and K.-K. Lau (Eds)

Declarative Programming, Sasbachwalden 1991
PHOENIX Seminar and Workshop on Declarative Programming, Sasbachwalden, Black Forest, Germany, 18-22 November 1991
John Darlington and Roland Dietrich (Eds)

Building Interactive Systems: Architectures and Tools
Philip Gray and Roger Took (Eds)

Functional Programming, Glasgow 1991
Proceedings of the 1991 Glasgow Workshop on Functional Programming, Portree, Isle of Skye, 12–14 August 1991
Rogardt Heldal, Carsten Kehler Holst and Philip Wadler (Eds)

Object Orientation in Z
Susan Stepney, Rosalind Barden and David Cooper (Eds)

Code Generation – Concepts, Tools, Techniques
Proceedings of the International Workshop on Code Generation, Dagstuhl, Germany, 20–24 May 1991
Robert Giegerich and Susan L. Graham (Eds)

Z User Workshop, York 1991, Proceedings of the Sixth Annual Z User Meeting, York, 16–17 December 1991
J.E. Nicholls (Ed.)

Formal Aspects of Measurement
Proceedings of the BCS-FACS Workshop on Formal Aspects of Measurement, South Bank University, London, 5 May 1991
Tim Denvir, Ros Herman and R.W. Whitty (Eds)

AI and Cognitive Science '91 University College, Cork, 19–20 September 1991
Humphrey Sorensen (Ed.)

5th Refinement Workshop, Proceedings of the 5th Refinement Workshop, organised by BCS-FACS, London, 8–10 January 1992
Cliff B. Jones, Roger C. Shaw and Tim Denvir (Eds)

Algebraic Methodology and Software Technology (AMAST'91)
Proceedings of the Second International Conference on Algebraic Methodology and Software Technology, Iowa City, USA, 22–25 May 1991
M. Nivat, C. Rattray, T. Rus and G. Scollo (Eds)

ALPUK92, Proceedings of the 4th UK Conference on Logic Programming, London, 30 March–1 April 1992
Krysia Broda (Ed.)

Logic Program Synthesis and Transformation
Proceedings of LOPSTR 92, International Workshop on Logic Program Synthesis and Transformation, University of Manchester, 2–3 July 1992
Kung-Kiu Lau and Tim Clement (Eds)

NAPAW 92, Proceedings of the First North American Process Algebra Workshop, Stony Brook, New York, USA, 28 August 1992
S. Purushothaman and Amy Zwarico (Eds)

First International Workshop on Larch
Proceedings of the First International Workshop on Larch, Dedham, Massachusetts, USA, 13–15 July 1992
Ursula Martin and Jeannette M. Wing (Eds)

Persistent Object Systems
Proceedings of the Fifth International Workshop on Persistent Object Systems, San Miniato (Pisa), Italy, 1–4 September 1992
Antonio Albano and Ron Morrison (Eds)

Formal Methods in Databases and Software Engineering, Proceedings of the Workshop on Formal Methods in Databases and Software Engineering, Montreal, Canada, 15–16 May 1992
V.S. Alagar, Laks V.S. Lakshmanan and F. Sadri (Eds)

Modelling Database Dynamics
Selected Papers from the Fourth International Workshop on Foundations of Models and Languages for Data and Objects, Volkse, Germany, 19–22 October 1992
Udo W. Lipeck and Bernhard Thalheim (Eds)

14th Information Retrieval Colloquium
Proceedings of the BCS 14th Information Retrieval Colloquium, University of Lancaster, 13–14 April 1992
Tony McEnery and Chris Paice (Eds)

Functional Programming, Glasgow 1992
Proceedings of the 1992 Glasgow Workshop on Functional Programming, Ayr, Scotland, 6–8 July 1992
John Launchbury and Patrick Sansom (Eds)

Z User Workshop, London 1992
Proceedings of the Seventh Annual Z User Meeting, London, 14–15 December 1992
J.P. Bowen and J.E. Nicholls (Eds)

Interfaces to Database Systems (IDS92)
Proceedings of the First International Workshop on Interfaces to Database Systems, Glasgow, 1–3 July 1992
Richard Cooper (Ed.)

AI and Cognitive Science '92
University of Limerick, 10–11 September 1992
Kevin Ryan and Richard F.E. Sutcliffe (Eds)

Theory and Formal Methods 1993
Proceedings of the First Imperial College Department of Computing Workshop on Theory and Formal Methods, Isle of Thorns Conference Centre, Chelwood Gate, Sussex, UK, 29–31 March 1993
Geoffrey Burn, Simon Gay and Mark Ryan (Eds)